T0210855

Communications in Computer and Information Science   1266

Commenced Publication in 2007
Founding and Former Series Editors:
Simone Diniz Junqueira Barbosa, Phoebe Chen, Alfredo Cuzzocrea,
Xiaoyong Du, Orhun Kara, Igor Kotenko, Ting Liu, Krishna M. Sivalingam,
Dominik Ślęzak, Takashi Washio, Xiaokang Yang, and Junsong Yuan

More information about this series at http://www.springer.com/series/7899

Martin Shepperd · Fernando Brito e Abreu ·
Alberto Rodrigues da Silva ·
Ricardo Pérez-Castillo (Eds.)

Quality of Information and Communications Technology

13th International Conference, QUATIC 2020
Faro, Portugal, September 9–11, 2020
Proceedings

 Springer

Editors
Martin Shepperd (iD)
Brunel University
London, UK

Fernando Brito e Abreu (iD)
Lisbon University Institute
Lisbon, Portugal

Alberto Rodrigues da Silva (iD)
University of Lisbon
Lisbon, Portugal

Ricardo Pérez-Castillo (iD)
University of Castilla-La Mancha
Talavera de la Reina, Spain

ISSN 1865-0929   ISSN 1865-0937 (electronic)
Communications in Computer and Information Science
ISBN 978-3-030-58792-5   ISBN 978-3-030-58793-2 (eBook)
https://doi.org/10.1007/978-3-030-58793-2

This Springer imprint is published by the registered company Springer Nature Switzerland AG
The registered company address is: Gewerbestrasse 11, 6330 Cham, Switzerland

Preface

The International Conference on the Quality of Information and Communications Technology (QUATIC) serves as a forum for disseminating advanced methods, techniques, and tools in support of quality approaches to ICT engineering and management. Practitioners and researchers are encouraged to exchange ideas and approaches on how to adopt a quality culture in ICT process and product improvement and to provide practical studies in varying contexts.

QUATIC 2020 was led by Martin Shepperd (Brunel University London, UK) and Fernando Brito e Abreu (University Institute of Lisbon, Portugal) as program chairs. The organizing chair of this 13th edition of QUATIC was Alberto Rodrigues da Silva (University of Lisbon, Portugal) and was locally organized by the University of Algarve, Portugal, with Paula Ventura Martins and Marielba Zacarias. QUATIC 2020 was planned to be held on September 9–11, 2020, in Faro, Algarve, Portugal. Unfortunately, due to the effects of the COVID-19 pandemic, QUATIC 2020 was conducted as a fully online conference.

This volume is a collection of high-quality peer-reviewed research papers received from all over the world. QUATIC 2020 attracted a good number of submissions from different areas spanning over several thematic tracks, proposed in the call for papers, in various cutting-edge technologies of specialized focus, organized and chaired by eminent experts of each field. The following eight of those thematic tracks correspond, on a one-to-one basis, to QUATIC 2020 sessions:

- Quality Aspects in Machine Learning, AI and Data Analytics (Leandro Minku, UBir, UK)
- Evidence-Based Software Quality Engineering (Tracy Hall, LU, UK)
- Human and Artificial Intelligences for Software Evolution (Nicolas Anquetil, Inria, University of Lille1, France)
- Process Modeling, Improvement and Assessment (Karol Frühauf, Infogem AG, Switzerland)
- Software Quality Education and Training (Claudia Werner, UFRJ, Brazil)
- Quality Aspects in Quantum Computing (Manuel Serrano, UCLM, Spain)
- Safety, Security and Privacy (Ana Rosa Cavalli, IPPs, Télécom SudParis, France)
- ICT Verification and Validation (Antonia Bertolino, ISTI-CNR, Italy)

Three additional thematic tracks were proposed in the call for papers, but due to the lesser number of submissions and the exigent review process, they had to be merged in a joint session named RE, MDD and Agile. The original tracks were:

- ICT Requirements Engineering (Luis Olsina, UNLPam, Argentina)
- Agile Methods (Kai Petersen, FUAS, Germany, and Blekinge Institute of Technology, Sweden)
- Model-Driven Methods (Manuel Wimmer, JKU Linz, Austria)

Technical Papers Summary

The Technical Program Committee of QUATIC 2020 was made up of 153 international academic and industrial domain experts, from organizations in 29 different countries on 5 continents. Based on a rigorous peer-review process by the Technical Program Committee members along with external experts as reviewers, the best quality papers were identified for presentation and publication.

The review was carried out in a double-blind process with a minimum of three reviews per submission. Submitted papers came from more than 20 countries and accepted papers originated in organizations from Spain (8), Italy (6), France (5), Portugal (4), Brazil, Germany, the UK (3), among others. Out of the submission pool of 81 papers, 27 (33.3%) were accepted as full papers for inclusion in the proceedings and 12 (14.8%) as short papers.

Invited Talks

QUATIC 2020 was fortunate to have three invited talks presented by outstanding keynote speakers. The first keynote was by Tom Mens at the University of Mons, Belgium, where he has directed the Software Engineering Lab for over 15 years. He co-edited two Springer books *Software Evolution* and *Evolving Software Systems,* and published numerous highly-cited software engineering articles in peer-reviewed international software engineering conferences and journals. His talk was titled: "Is my software ecosystem healthy? It depends!"

The second keynote speaker was Letizia Jaccheri from the Department of Computer Science of the Norwegian University of Science and Technology, Norway, where she was the head of the department from 2013 to 2017. Besides having published numerous highly-cited software engineering articles in peer-reviewed international software engineering conferences and journals, she is an ACM Distinguished Speaker. Her talk was titled: "From software through art to social entrepreneurship."

The third talk was given co-jointly by João Paulo Carvalho and João Nunes from Quidgest SA, a very active voice from the Portuguese IT industry. João Paulo Carvalho is Founder and Senior Partner of Quidgest, and João Nunes is a technology enthusiast, business savvy problem-solver, and white-hat hacker. Quidgest is a global technology company, headquartered in Lisbon, Portugal. With over 30 years of experience, Quidgest has been a pioneer and a leader in the modeling and automatic generation of software, with two main resources: the Genio platform and an R&D team exclusively dedicated to the development of new features and technologies. Their talk was titled: "Built-In Quality in Software Development Automation with Models and Artificial Intelligence."

SEDES Doctoral Symposium

In addition, there was a co-located doctoral student symposium, chaired by Vasco Amaral (Universidade Nova de Lisboa, Portugal), with proceedings published as a standalone volume of the CEUR Workshop Proceedings series. CEUR-WS.org is a free open-access publication service operated by Aachen University, Germany. We are particularly pleased to support this event, as the doctoral students represent much of the future for our community.

September 2020   Martin Shepperd
                                              Fernando Brito e Abreu
                                           Alberto Rodrigues da Silva
                                              Ricardo Pérez-Castillo

Acknowledgments

As proceedings editors, we wish to thank all the people and organizations that directly or indirectly supported this event. Thanks to the thematic track and PhD symposium chairs and all other members of the Scientific Committee for their many contributions and reviews that guarantee the overall quality of the QUATIC 2020 conference.

Thanks to our colleagues from the University of Algarve for all the organizational details required for hosting the conference, despite the fact that the constraints and difficulties associated with the pandemic obliged us to do it fully online. Thanks to our colleagues that participate at different levels in the organization of the conference. Thanks to the QUATIC's Steering Committee members for their guidance and support throughout the whole process.

Also, a special thanks to all the organizations involved in this conference, including promoters (IPQ and CS03), supporters (University of Algarve, Brunel University, ISCTE-IUL, IST-UL, UCLM, FCT-UNL, FE-UP, University of Minho, CNR, and University of Coimbra), sponsors (ACM, Quidgest, and ATOS), and partners (NEEI/ UALG and APQ).

Finally, but not least, special thanks to all the authors and participants at the conference. Without their efforts, there would be no conference or proceedings. Thank you for contributing to the critical mass of researchers who keep this conference alive for what we expect to be many years to come.

Organization

Program Committee Chairs

Martin Shepperd   Brunel University London, UK
Fernando Brito e Abreu   Instituto Universitário de Lisboa, Portugal

Thematic Track Chairs

ICT Verification and Validation

Antonia Bertolino   National Research Council (CNR), Italy

Process Modeling, Improvement and Assessment

Karol Frühauf   NFOGEM AG, Switzerland

Human and Artificial Intelligences for Software Evolution

Nicolas Anquetil   Inria, University of Lille 1, France

Evidence-Based Software Quality Engineering

Tracy Hall   Lancaster University, UK

Safety, Security and Privacy

Ana Cavalli   Institut Polytechnique De Paris, Télécom SudParis, France

Quality Aspects in Quantum Computing

Manuel Serrano   Universidad de Castilla-La-Mancha, Spain

Quality Aspects in Machine Learning, AI and Data Analytics

Leandro Minku   University of Birmingham, UK

Software Quality Education and Training

Claudia Werner   Universidade Federal do Rio de Janeiro, Brazil

Requirements Engineering, Model-Driven and Agile Development[1]

Luis Olsina	Universidad Nacional de La Pampa, Argentina
Manuel Wimmer	Johannes Kepler University Linz, Austria
Kai Petersen	Blekinge Institute of Technology, Sweden

PhD Symposium (SEDES)[2]

Vasco Amaral	Universidade Nova de Lisboa, Portugal

Program Committee Members

Abdelhak-Djamel Seriai	University of Montpellier, France
Agnieszka Jakóbik	Cracow University of Technology, Poland
Alberto Silva	Universidade de Lisboa, Portugal
Alejandro Maté	University of Alicante, Spain
Alessandra Bagnato	Softeam, France
Alexandros Chatzigeorgiou	University of Macedonia, Greece
Ambrosio Toval	Universidad de Murcia, Spain
Ana Respício	Universidade de Lisboa, Portugal
Ana Paiva	University of Porto, Portugal
Ana Regina Rocha	COPPE/UFRJ, Brazil
Andrea Janes	Free University of Bozen-Bolzano, Italy
Andreas Ulrich	Siemens AG, Germany
Andreas Nehfort	Nehfort IT-Consulting KG, Austria
Andreas Wortmann	RWTH Aachen University, Germany
Andres Diaz-Pace	UNICEN University, Argentina
Antonino Sabetta	SAP Labs, Germany
Antonio Cicchetti	Mälardalen University, Sweden
Antonio Vallecillo	Universidad de Málaga, Spain
Apostolos Ampatzoglou	University of Macedonia, Greece
Ayşe Tosun	Istanbul Technical University (ITU), Turkey
Bartosz Walter	Poznań University of Technology, Poland
Beatriz Marín	Universidad Diego Portales, Chile
Benoit Combemale	University of Toulouse, Inria, France
Breno Miranda	Università di Pisa, Brazil
Christelle Urtado	Ecole des Mines d'Alès, France
Christopher Fuhrman	École de Technologie Supérieure, Canada
Chun Wai Chiu	University of Birmingham, UK
Claudia Raibulet	University of Milano-Bicocca, Italy
Daniel Strüber	Radboud University, The Netherlands
Denis Silveira	Universidade Federal de Pernambunco, Brazil
Diego Perez-Palacin	Linnaeus University, Spain

---

[1] Merge of three proposed tracks (in the CFP), due to the number of accepted submissions.
[2] SEDES has separate proceedings, published as a CEUR volume.

Edgardo Montes de Oca   Montimage, France
Eduardo Figueiredo   Federal University of Minas Gerais, Brazil
Eduardo Spinosa   Federal University of Paraná, Brazil
Elena-María   Universidad de Castilla-La-Mancha, Spain
  Navarro-Martínez
Emilia Mendes   Blekinge Institute of Technology, Sweden
Emilio Insfran   Universitat Politècnica de València, Spain
Emily Navarro   University of California, Irvine, USA
Erkuden Rios Velasco   Tecnalia, Spain
Eugene Syriani   University of Montreal, Canada
Fabio Calefato   University of Bari, Mexico
Fabio Palomba   University of Salerno, Italy
Fatiha Zaidi   Université Paris-Sud XI, France
Fayola Peters   West Virginia University, USA
Ferdinand Gramsamer   INFOGEM AG, Switzerland
Flavio Oquendo   Université Bretagne-Sud (UBS), France
Francesca Lonetti   CNR-ISTI, Italy
Francisco Gortázar   Universidad Rey Juan Carlos, Spain
Frank Phillipson   TNO, The Netherlands
Frédéric Cuppens   Polytechnique Montreal, Canada
Gabriel García-Mireles   Universidad de Sonora, Mexico
Gerhard Fessler   Fessler Sprenger und Partner GmbH, Switzerland
Geylani Kardas   Ege University, Turkey
Gordana Rakic   University of Novi Sad, Serbia
Gregory Kapfhammer   Allegheny College, USA
Grischa Liebel   Reykjavik University, Iceland
Guido Peterssen Nodarse   Alhambra-Eidos, Spain
Guillermo Hernandez   aQuantum, Spain
Gul Calikli   The Open University, UK
Gustavo Rossi   LIFIA, UNLP, Argentina
Hector Menendez   Middlesex University London, UK
Honghui Du   University of Leicester, UK
Ignacio Rodríguez de   Universidad de Castilla-La-Mancha, Spain
  Guzmán
Ioannis Parissis   Université Grenoble Alpes, France
Ioannis Stamelos   Aristotle University of Thessaloniki, Greece
Isabel Sofia Sousa Brito   Instituto Politécnico de Beja, Portugal
Ivano Malavolta   Vrije Universiteit Amsterdam, The Netherlands
Jaejoon Lee   University of East Anglia, UK
Javier Troya   University of Seville, Spain
Jean Petric   Lancaster University, UK
Jefferson Seide Molléri   Simula Metropolitan Center for Digital Engineering,
       Norway
Jesús Morán   University of Oviedo, Spain
João Gama   University of Porto, Portugal
João Araújo   Universidade NOVA de Lisboa, Portugal

João Pascoal Faria	University of Porto, INESC TEC, Portugal
Joaquin Garcia-Alfaro	Institut Polytechnique De Paris, Télécom SudParis, France
Johnny Marques	Instituto Tecnológico de Aeronáutica (ITA), Brazil
Jordi Tura	Max-Planck-Institut für Quantenoptik, Germany
Jorge Casillas	University of Granada, Spain
Jose Luis de la Vara	Universidad de Castilla-La-Mancha, Spain
José Luis Hevia	Alhambra-Eidos, Spain
Jose Manuel Molina Lopez	Universidad Carlos III de Madrid, Spain
Juan De Lara	Universidad Autonoma de Madrid, Spain
Juan Manuel Murillo	Universidad de Extremadura, Spain
Juan Manuel Vara	Universidad Rey Juan Carlos, Spain
Juan Pablo Carvallo	Universidad del Azuay, Ecuador
Kathia Marcal de Oliveira	LAMIH, CNRS, UMR 8201, France
Ken Power	Independent Consultant, Ireland
Lavazza Luigi	Università degli Studi dell'Insubria, Italy
Lech Madeyski	Wroclaw University of Science and Technology, Poland
Lerina Aversano	Università degli Studi del Sannio, Italy
Lidia Lopez	Universitat Politècnica de Catalunya, Spain
Loli Burgueño	Open University of Catalonia, Spain
Luiz Marcio Cysneiros	York University, Canada
M.J. Escalona	University of Seville, Spain
Macario Polo	Universidad de Castilla-La-Mancha, Spain
Man Zhang	Kristiania University College, Norway
Marcello Thiry	Univali, Brazil
Marcos Didonet Del Fabro	Universidade Federal do Paraná, Brazil
Maria Lencastre	Universidade de Pernambuco, Brazil
Mario Piattini	Universidad de Castilla-La-Mancha, Spain
Michael Felderer	University of Innsbruck, Austria
Miguel Goulão	Universidade NOVA de Lisboa, Portugal
Miguel Ehécatl Morales Trujillo	University of Canterbury, New Zealand
Moises Rodríguez	AQCLab, Spain
Nathan Baddoo	University of Hertfordshire, UK
Nelly Condori-Fernández	Universidade da Coruña, Spain
Nemitari Ajienka	Nottingham Trent University, UK
Nora Cuppens	Polytechnique Montreal, Canada
Oscar Pastor Lopez	Universitat Politècnica de València, Spain
Patricia Mcquaid	California Polytechnic State University, USA
Patrizio Pelliccione	Chalmers University of Technology, Sweden
Pedro Guerreiro	Universidade do Algarve, Portugal
Rachel Harrison	Oxford Brookes University, UK
Rafael Capilla-Sevilla	Universidad Rey Juan Carlos, Spain
Ralf Kneuper	IUBH Internationale Hochschule, Germany
Ricardo Perez-Castillo	Universidad de Castilla-La-Mancha, Spain

Robert Clarisó	Open University of Catalonia, Spain
Roberto Pietrantuono	University of Naples Federico II, Italy
Sandro Morasca	Università degli Studi dell'Insubria, Italy
Shuo Wang	University of Birmingham, UK
Sigrid Eldh	Ericsson AB, Sweden
Stefan Klikovits	National Institute of Informatics, Japan
Stephen MacDonell	University of Otago, New Zealand
Steve Counsell	Brunel University, UK
Sven Casteleyn	Universitat Jaume I, Spain
Sylvia Ilieva	Sofia University, Bulgaria
Timo Kehrer	Humboldt-Universität zu Berlin, Germany
Toacy Oliveira	COPPE/UFRJ, Brazil
Vahid Garousi	Queen's University Belfast, UK
Valentina Casola	University of Napoli Federico II, Italy
Valter Camargo	Federal University of São Carlos, Brazil
Vânia Neves	Universidade Federal Fluminense, Brazil
Wissam Mallouli	Montimage, France
Xiaofeng Wang	Free University of Bozen-Bolzano, Italy
Yania Crespo	University of Valladolid, Spain

Organizing Committee

General Chair

Alberto Silva	Universidade de Lisboa, Portugal

Local Co-chairs

Paula Ventura Martins	Universidade do Algarve, Portugal
Marielba Zacarias	Universidade do Algarve, Portugal

Proceedings Chair

Ricardo Perez del Castillo	Universidad de Castilla-La-Mancha, Spain

Publicity Chair

Américo Rio	ISCTE-IUL and UNL, Portugal

Web Chair

José Pereira dos Reis	ISCTE-IUL, Portugal

Sponsors Chair

Margarida Madeira	Universidade do Algarve, Portugal

Industrial Day Co-chairs

Hugo Barros	CRIA, Universidade do Algarve, Portugal
Miguel Fernandes	Dengun and Algarve Tech Hub, Portugal

Additional Reviewers

Huu Nghia Nguyen
Sónia Teixeira
Rita Nogueira
Vinh Hoa La

Contributing Organizations

Promoters

Supporters

UNIVERSIDADE DE COIMBRA

Sponsors

Partners

Contents

Process Modeling, Improvement and Assessment

Software Quality Education and Training

Quality Aspects in Machine Learning, AI and Data Analytics

Perceived Quality of Artificial Intelligence in Smart Service Systems: A Structured Approach

Jens Neuhüttler[1]([✉]) [iD], Rudolf Fischer[1], Walter Ganz[1], and Florian Urmetzer[2]

[1] Fraunhofer IAO, Nobelstr. 12, 70569 Stuttgart, Germany
{Jens.Neuhuettler,Walter.Ganz}@iao.fraunhofer.de
[2] University of Cambridge, 17 Charles Babbage Road, Cambridge CB3 0FS, UK
ftu20@cam.ac

Abstract. Smart Service Systems are becoming increasingly important in almost all industries and areas of life. In order to make use of data from the Internet of Things for individualizing and automatizing service offerings, Artificial intelligence (AI) is a key technology. However, only little is known about how users and potential customers perceive quality of these AI-based Smart Services and how companies can develop them accordingly. To this end, our paper presents a framework concept for addressing quality of Smart Services systematically. The framework integrates known and novel quality aspects and thus supports a systematic and quality-focused development. In addition, our paper presents exemplary AI-relevant quality aspects in more detail. First of all, AI-based Smart Service Systems will be characterized in more detail and existing quality concepts will be presented in order to enable a holistic quality assessment.

Keywords: Smart services · Artificial intelligence · Quality

1 Introduction

The progressive developments in digitalization and, in particular, the increasing integration of physical objects with sensor technology and communication capability are changing the existing service systems in nearly all industries and areas of life [1]. The data collected on the Internet of Things permit comprehensive conclusions about the condition of the physical objects, their utilization and their application-specific context. This information provides the basis for offering individualized and sometimes automated smart services, which constitute individually configurable bundles of bundles of products, digital services and physically delivered services [2]. The development and provision of such service packages require an orchestration of physical objects, technologies, data, persons and organizations – thus smart services are understood as complex service systems [3]. Methods of artificial intelligence (AI) play a key role in tapping the potentials of individualization and automation within such systems [4]. For example, AI is used for autonomous extraction of the information required for individualization from

© Springer Nature Switzerland AG 2020
M. Shepperd et al. (Eds.): QUATIC 2020, CCIS 1266, pp. 3–16, 2020.
https://doi.org/10.1007/978-3-030-58793-2_1

a large pool of data, some of which are not structured at all, or for a more automated or even autonomous provision of smart services, for example, by the use of physical or digital robots [5].

Notwithstanding the undeniable opportunities, many enterprises face a number of challenges in the development of smart services [6]. Among other issues, the question arises of how smart service systems can be designed in such a way that the added value perceived by potential customers outweighs the risks involved, such as poor protection of sensitive data or loss of control [7]. The design of the AI elements plays a significant role in this regard as well: On the one hand, self-learning algorithms and autonomous systems can add value by way of individualized provision of services. On the other hand, the loss of personal relationships and the use of complex and therefore non-transparent algorithms have a negative impact on the risk perceived. Research on smart service systems and the use of artificial intelligence is still in its early stages in this regard and provides hardly any knowledge about the expectations of potential customers [8]. There is also a lack of suitable concepts, methods and tools to develop smart services systematically [9]. In this context, one of the key issues is to better understand the perception of quality by potential customers of smart services and thereby support business in the development of successful and accepted solutions [10]. Even though established concepts exist already regarding quality perceptions of individual elements of smart services (e.g. digital services), knowledge about the perceptions of data-based bundling or the use of AI methods and tools is scarce to date.

2   AI-Based Smart Service Systems

2.1   Characterization of Smart Service Systems

With a view to providing a systematic view of the quality of AI-based smart service systems, these are characterized first. Despite their increasing significance, a distinct definition of smart services has not yet evolved in the scientific literature. Nevertheless, it is possible to identify in the existing conceptual publications some common characteristics that are relevant for our article [3, 11]:

- Smart services are based on physical objects equipped with sensor technology and with networking capability, referred to as intelligent products [12], which collect status, utilization, and environment data [13].
- The provision of smart services is based on intensive utilization of data, where sensor data, user-generated data as well as data from external sources are used [14].
- The data available are collected on digital platforms, analysed and interpreted by algorithms and transformed to application-specific information [15].
- Based on the information acquired, smart services represent service packages customized to the specific context and individual needs of customers [2].
- Depending on the type of smart service, they can comprise digital and physically delivered service elements in varying proportions [16].

These characteristics of smart service systems are highly significant for the development of an integrative framework for quality assessment. The relationship between AI and smart service systems is described in more detail in the next section.

2.2 Artificial Intelligence in Smart Service Systems

The concept of artificial intelligence refers to IT solutions and methods completing tasks autonomously, where the underlying rules for processing are not explicitly predefined by humans [17]. The umbrella term of AI combines different concepts for model forming, various learning methods and algorithms [18]. The superiority of AI in comparison with conventional analytical methods stems from its capability to process and structure large amounts of data autonomously. Some of the main reasons for the growing significance of AI are, on the one hand, the existence of large amounts of data produced by the increase in physical product networking, which constitute an essential basis for the application of AI and, on the other hand, the decreasing cost of processing power required for data processing [4]. Machine learning methods are the technological core of AI. These algorithms extract information autonomously, recognize regular patterns in data, adaptively respond to a changing environment and predict future events. The typical domain of AI is wherever highly complex and very large volumes of data exist that are unmanageable for humans. Mastering this complexity generates value, for example, in form of new customer insights for an individual adaption [19].

The possibilities of gathering information by pattern recognition and the prediction of future events by the use of AI have a high impact on smart service systems since the use of these methods offers numerous opportunities: The development of new services, raising the degree of individualization or automatic performance of activities of service employees. At the same time, AI also changes the nature of the encounter and interaction between provider and user. The potential for individualization and automation of an AI-based service depends on the extent to which the algorithm supports the personnel or should intervene in the activities in a way which is transparent to the customer or may perform them completely autonomously with the customer [8]. The application of AI in smart service systems is illustrated in Fig. 1, using the well-known layer model.

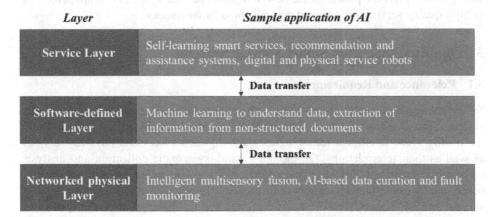

Layer	Sample application of AI
Service Layer	Self-learning smart services, recommendation and assistance systems, digital and physical service robots
	↑ Data transfer ↓
Software-defined Layer	Machine learning to understand data, extraction of information from non-structured documents
	↑ Data transfer ↓
Networked physical Layer	Intelligent multisensory fusion, AI-based data curation and fault monitoring

Fig. 1. Sample application of AI in smart service systems (Source: [2] and [4])

The model comprises three layers, where the networked physical layer is used as the basis for data acquisition. The next higher layer is a software-defined layer, where data processing occurs. The findings gathered from this layer are utilized at the service layer to develop and deliver individualized and to some extent, automated solutions. Tasks can be efficiently supported or even performed autonomously by AI applications at each of these layers. Sensing technology used for acquiring and transmitting the data may be susceptible to errors and, for example, produce spikes or fail completely for certain periods. The loss of data quality thereby incurred can be compensated by AI by detecting implausible or missing values and replacing these by estimated values. Frequently this often involves not only individual sensors but entire infrastructures and wide networks of devices, the collective data of which need to be arranged in an intelligent way. Moreover, usually data from outside sources are used for contextualization and also require curation. At the software-defined layer, information and findings are extracted from the data and the advantages of machine-based learning methods can unfold here. Once the model calculations have revealed regular patterns and which characteristics are interrelated when certain events occur, the personnel at the service layer can be supported in their work by AI systems or it is even possible to develop self-learning and autonomously acting smart services (e.g. chatbots). In this way, AI knowledge can be used to extract knowledge about situations, personal habits and preferences of customers to produce an individual adaptation which improves the resulting quality of the solution.

However, this involves some challenges. On the one hand, the technology must be capable of reading different formats of unstructured data, process and analyse large amounts of these in real time, solve problems autonomously and improve itself continuously. On the other hand, the design of AI-based smart service systems accepted by users involves a number of questions: How and on which basis are decisions made? Do users want to interact with a machine at all and do they want to know that their contact is a chatbot and not a person? How can such interaction be designed in an empathetic way? How much decision-making power is automated? How deep should AI intervene in the personal actions of personnel and customers? The following chapters aim at providing initial reference points for the design of smart service systems that are perceived as high-quality service systems and thus accepted by customers.

3 Quality Aspects for Smart Service Systems

3.1 Relevance and Requirements

Safeguarding a high quality is one of the core issues in the development of smart service systems. The challenge is, on the one hand, to include different service elements into the quality view: intelligent technologies, data, digital services and physical services as well as their interrelations. On the other hand, systematic collection and analysis of possibly sensitive personal or operational data involves new risks and insecurities perceived, for example, with regard to data security, the ethics of algorithms or perceived surveillance by sensors [7]. These factors influence the perception of the quality of smart services on the part of the users and for this reason, the conceptualization of perceptions of quality is a core subject of research [10]. The identification of useful quality categories and the criteria to be used for evaluation may support solution providers in their endeavour to meet customers' needs better, create added value and thus establish services successfully in the market. Quality categories and criteria can be used in this context as some kind of development guideline to reduce uncertainties and be applied in different phases of smart service development. For example, quality categories can be used to identify and analyse the requirements of potential customers in a structured way. Specifically in early phases of development of complex service systems, users often find it difficult to express expectations and needs precisely and comprehensively without having predefined categories at hand. Furthermore, the categories and criteria may already be used at an early stage in iterative test cycles to evaluate concepts and prototypes with users and thereby prevent undesirable developments [20]. However, to offer added value to service providers, a quality view should meet some requirements resulting from the characteristics outlined in the characterization of smart service systems [21]:

- It should include all smart service elements perceived by customers.
- A concept should permit an assessment of different design variants of smart services, ranging from entirely digital ones to data-based interactions between people.
- It should be compatible with other models and methods in smart service engineering.
- Specific characteristics of AI-based Smart Services should be considered.

The following section gives a brief overview of existing concepts of perceived quality in the individual areas of smart service systems.

3.2 Existing Quality Concepts in the Context of Smart Service Systems

For simple products, objective criteria such as, for example, durability or consumption of resources are suitable for a quality assessment from the perspectives of provider and user. However, since smart service systems are complex solutions, users in particular lack the technical knowledge to make an objective assessment. Moreover, many service elements of smart service systems have a high degree of intangibility (e.g. digital process activities, algorithms and data), which makes an objective assessment even more difficult. Objective quality criteria are therefore substituted by the subjective construct of service quality. This describes the ability of a provider to produce the quality of a primarily intangible service that requires the participation of the user in accordance with the user's expectations at a certain level of requirements [22]. Hence, the quality of the smart service system should attain a specific performance level, which in turn is defined from the perspective of the users. With a view to making perceived quality measurable, numerous constructs have evolved in science, which permit assessment on the part of users by means of quality categories and criteria [23].

Probably the most widely used quality model for services provided by persons is the SERVQUAL model of [23]. The model comprises five different quality dimensions (tangibles, reliability, responsiveness, assurance and empathy) that are used by customers to evaluate service quality. There are also other models and approaches in scientific literature, which make service quality measurable either in other industries or with other or specific focuses of research. Numerous different quality models also exist for digital services offered on the Internet. For example, [24] have transferred the SERVQUAL model to digital services and highlighted the categories of efficiency, system availability, fulfillment and privacy as generally applicable quality criteria in the E-S-QUAL model.

In addition to monolithic quality models, there are also approaches that consider the quality assessment of combined smart service elements [25]. E.g. [26] address hybrid service packages with a combination of the quality dimensions from SERVQUAL and E-S-QUAL, [27] combine dimensions from SERVQUAL and Technology-Acceptance-Model (TAM) for quality assessment of product/service systems. However, there is no model known to the authors that address all elements of a smart service.

Furthermore, there is no distinct and specific model for the perceived quality assessment of AI-based services to date. Nevertheless there are indeed related publications addressing the design of AI applications, which therefore fit the objective mentioned in previous section. For example, with regard to the acceptance of AI, one of the questions is how to design the interaction between users and machines in a meaningful way that is compatible with human needs. This implies that major ethical and social issues about the use of artificial intelligence get into focus in addition to the technological development. However, with regard to such discussions it should be noted that social compatibility is not determined directly by technology but rather how it is used in the first instance. It is necessary to find and define an appropriate framework for this. For quality assurance of AI-based decisions, there are already some principles available which can be used in designing the framework of use. In the first place, it is important to establish transparency and traceability. This is true for both the calculations and the decisions taken on this basis. As a consequence of the complexity of the processes, traceability is ensured only to a limited extent, however, efforts should be made to achieve it as far as possible. Moreover, such decisions and their formation have to be documented. This is the only way how information can be given about the parameters used for the decision, which in turn generates transparency. In addition, the consequences of the use of AI have to be revisable if certain decisions should be obviously wrong and human intervention and correction becomes necessary. One criterion associated with this addresses the users' wish to remain the final decision-making instance in case of doubt. This is true at least until the outcome quality of AI reaches a level which is generally accepted by the stakeholders involved [28]. The framework for explaining the acceptance of AI in customer contact situations proposed by [8] is a key contribution to the identification of quality aspects of AI-based smart service systems. In this context, the self-service technology model according to [29] serves as a basis involving various influence factors regarding the open-mindedness towards and long-term adoption of new technologies. On this basis, [8] supplement another three factors for the acceptance of AI applications: Security concerns, trust, and perceived discomfort. The first two factors appear to be intuitively plausible as prerequisites for the acceptance of AI applications. Customers recognize the added value of AI-based services such as, for example, speed or convenience, and want to benefit from these. However, this requires sharing personal information which is basically worth to be protected. This loss in privacy requires advance trust in the service provider; otherwise the advantages of AI-based applications cannot be utilized. The aspect of perceived discomfort requires a more detailed explanation: this relates to any suggestions of the algorithm which ignore social norms and may therefore cause discomfort. In summary, the use of AI enables the customer to utilize individually tailored services, save time and generate more comfort. However, these advantages involve the risk of severe failures of service delivery, loss of control and curtailment of privacy.

3.3 Assessment of Existing Approaches

The approaches identified in literature provide a suitable basis for a concept of quality perceptions in smart service systems and initial reference points for relevant quality categories and criteria. However, none of the approaches identified includes all service elements of a smart service system or allows a comparative view of different design variants. Those approaches which address more than one service element usually combine existing quality models, however, are not conceived for the specific characteristics of AI-based smart service systems or address only partial aspects of perceived quality. Moreover, the quality models are not geared to the systematic development of integrated service packages and therefore their structures are not mutually compatible. For this reason, the next chapter of the present article proposes an integrative conceptual framework which incorporates the existing quality categories and criteria but also supplements these with additional aspects and, hence, accommodates the specific character of AI-based smart service systems.

4 Integrative Conceptual Framework for Quality Assessment of AI-Based Smart Service Systems

4.1 Structure of the Integrative Conceptual Framework

The integrative conceptual framework, which was first introduced by [30], is structured as a matrix and comprises 12 design fields of smart service systems. They can be evaluated using the predefined quality categories and criteria (cf. Fig. 2). Structuring the horizontal axis was done using the design dimensions of resource, process and outcome to achieve compatibility with existing tools and models of smart service engineering [31]. Structuring along these dimensions is also frequently applied in current service research, for example, for smart service system structuring or assessing the effects of digitalization [32]. The resources dimension comprises resources required for the smart service system, i.e. technical infrastructures, products, algorithms, technologies and competencies of individuals. The process dimension describes the delivery of the smart service as a sequence of activities of the stakeholders of the ecosystem and is characterized by interactions between people (customer and provider), information systems (e.g. digital services) and physical objects (e.g. intelligent technologies and sensors). The outcome dimension addresses the perception of the usefulness of the various service elements as well as the overall solution from the customer perspective. Evaluating the various dimensions enables developers to obtain more precise information about potential causes of negative perceptions of quality and address these more specifically in subsequent development cycles. A negative overall perception may be attributable either to the delivery process or to the resources employed; the related measures for improvement derived therefrom differ accordingly.

The vertical axis of the integrative conceptual framework comprises the perceivable elements of an AI-based smart service system: Technology and data, digital services

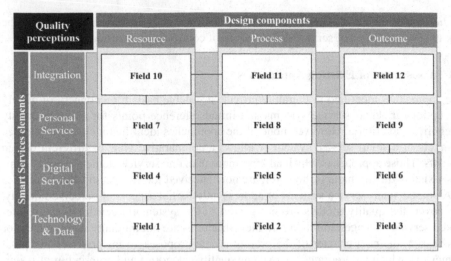

Fig. 2. Conceptual framework for quality assessment of smart service systems (Source: [30])

and services delivered physically. These are derived from the layer model of smart service systems (cf. Fig. 1) and were adjusted to the perspective of users and the elements perceivable to them. The "Technology and data" service element comprises the basis of data acquisition and transmission, i.e. physical objects with networking capability, which collect status, usage and context data. While field 1 of the conceptual framework considers the fundamental equipment as well as aesthetic aspects of the intelligent technologies, field 2 addresses the perceived quality of the technologies in the delivery process. Among other items, this also involves AI techniques which make it possible to integrate and pre-condition the various sensor data. Field 3 holds quality categories which make it possible to evaluate the data basis acquired by means of the intelligent technologies from the user's perspective. The data basis produced is used as a structure factor in the "Digital services" service element together with ready-made content and algorithms created by the provider (field 4). These are translated into different forms of added value in a digital process, utilizing also other information, user activities or networked objects (field 5). New insights about the current condition or the usage process emerge (e.g. of a physical object, of one's own body, of public infrastructures). They already constitute per se an added value of the digital service within the smart service system and are evaluated in field 6. Furthermore, however, it is also possible to create digital value-added services from the data basis generated such as, automated forward-looking route planning or other personalized recommendation systems. Aspects like the design of standardized interfaces, real-time data availability as well as the development of transparent algorithms are key success factors of AI-based service systems. In addition, working out privacy and security concepts for the data, part of which are highly sensitive, plays a key role in the design of digital services. Frequently there is some conflict between the necessary anonymization of the data and the creation of appropriate added value by the individualization of data [33]. Moreover, the use of AI techniques leads to new and automated forms of interaction in the digital process. In addition to digital services, services delivered physically will continue to play a key role in AI-based service systems also in the future [16]. In this context, two different forms can be distinguished. On the one hand, these are personal services, the resources of which are the capacities and competencies of personnel as well as physical infrastructures of the provider (field 8). On the other hand, services delivered physically may also be provided by automated or autonomously acting systems made available by the provider as a structure. Both forms are characterized by an interactive process between providing and requesting units which requires physical activities (field 8). A parcel delivery service is an example of the two forms. Parcel delivery may be performed by a person using suitable equipment (vehicle, digital assistant, etc.) or by an autonomously acting service robot (e.g. a vehicle or a drone). The perceived benefit of the solution or the physical intervention is addressed in field 9 of the conceptual framework. In the short and medium term, the processes of services provided by persons will particularly comprise activities for solving complex tasks that require creative, intuitive or empathetic abilities of personnel or physical interventions on persons themselves or in their close personal environment [34]. On the other hand, repetitive knowledge-based routine tasks will increasingly be provided with the aid of AI-based digital services and are therefore addressed in the fields 4 to 6.

Distinguishing between the perceptions of quality of digital and personal services makes it possible for enterprises to apply the same conceptual framework within the smart service system for the development of various types of service offerings and take their specific characteristics into account: From digital information services (e.g. data visualization) through digital value-added services (e.g. digital parking lot booking) to digitally supported and physically delivered services (e.g. demand-driven waste collection). The "Integration" service element was added to the conceptual framework as another core element because synchronization of the above described service elements and safeguarding a constant quality level across all service types and activities between the various parties involved should be regarded as essential drivers for the development of high-quality smart service systems [35]. In addition to the integration of structure factors (field 10), particularly the integration of digital and physical process elements (field 11) and the perception of the overall benefit of the smart service system (field 12) are key items to be assessed.

4.2 Quality Aspects for AI-Based Smart Service Systems

The preceding section presented the structure of the integrative conceptual framework that is used for structuring categories and criteria for the quality assessment of smart service systems. In addition to numerous well-known criteria, also some data-specific and AI-specific quality criteria were identified and included in the conceptual framework from the expert interviews and a follow-up search in literature. Table 1 shows a selection of these criteria along the 12 fields of the integrative conceptual framework that can be utilized together with other categories and criteria for the assessment of the perceived quality of AI-based smart service systems.

Table 1. Summary of sample quality criteria with relevance for AI

No.	Description of quality field	Exemplary quality aspect with regard to AI or data
1	Perception of the intelligent technologies used for data acquisition as well as external data sources	• Appropriateness of sensor measurement intervals for use case • Perceived relation between required data and promised value • Selection of external data sources for the application • Perceived surveillance or discomfort using smart technologies • Transparency and understandability of a privacy concept
2	Perceived quality of the use of intelligent technologies (e.g. wearables) and data curation	• Convenience of the use of smart technology in customer journey • Intuitive and low-error operation of technology • Perceived control over data acquisition process • Trustworthiness of technology • Intrusiveness in personal space and domains
3	Perception of the data basis generated and the contribution of the technologies and data to the overall benefit	• Reliability of connectivity and data transfer • Trouble-free data transmission to back-end • Up-to-dateness, precision and completeness of the data • Perceived credibility of the results • Relevance of the data for use case • Realization of innovation potentials due to use of data
4	Perception of the predefined content of digital applications and algorithms used	• Up-to-dateness, transparency of the analysis methods used • Perceived barriers for integrating user-generated data • Compatibility of interfaces with application environment • Protection of the system against unauthorized access
5	Perception of the interactive usage process of the digital service adapted to individual requirements	• Intuitive use of digital tools (e.g. for data analysis) • Naturalness of AI-based interaction forms (e.g. chatbots or voice control) • Quick & adaptive system interaction • Adaptability of digital processes to real-time data • Ex-post documentation of automated activities
6	Perception of the data visualization and the benefit created from value-added services	• Perceived support by digital assistants • Constant degree of fulfillment of the service • Added value from use of information • Clarity of data visualization • Reduction of complexity for users • Perceived increase in process efficiency
7	Perception of the personnel required for delivery, the equipment used and the physical environment	• Credibility and relevance of personnel competencies in handling AI applications • Up-to-dateness and capability of personnel equipment • Safety precautions when using physical service robots • Functional scope of physical service robots
8	Perception of the interactive process, where persons or physical objects are brought in by provider and user	• Unobstructed access to (real-time) data of users by personnel • Transparent and plausible course of action of the personnel • Short-term and quick adaptation to customer's wishes and real-time data • Contentment despite AI-based extension of personnel skills and knowledge

(continued)

Table 1. (*continued*)

No.	Description of quality field	Exemplary quality aspect with regard to AI or data
9	Perception service result and contribution to the overall benefit and to the personal relationship	• More efficient delivery with the support of digital assistants and physical service robots • No deterioration of social interactions by digital support • Familiarity because of personal interaction
10	Perception of the integrative quality of the resources used and the stakeholders of the ecosystem	• Balanced involvement of physical, digital and personal components and functions • Trustworthiness of the stakeholders involved in the ecosystem • Absence of dependence on individual partners or technologies
11	Perception of the integrative quality and allocation of tasks among the stakeholders	• Coordinated process logic between digital and personal services • Reasonable assignment of activities among users, providers and technical systems • Clear role and task description for user activities
12	Perceived overall benefit of the smart service system	• Improved match of solution with the individual customer issue • Higher emotional and social added value by the use of AI • Enabling of service-oriented business model variants (e.g. subscription)

The sample list of quality criteria with relevance for AI shows already that numerous different aspects need to be considered for the assessment of smart service systems. Depending on the design of the smart service system, not all of the criteria in the conceptual framework are of interest, because either the service elements do not play a role or the prototype defined at the development level cannot yet be evaluated with respect to the criteria. A useful application in the development of smart services occurs, for example, in the testing phase. For an assessment of a specific smart service prototype in a specific phase of development, the quality categories and criteria included in the integrative conceptual framework need to be selected individually for the specific test groups addressed.

5 Summary and Outlook

The article presents an integrative framework for the quality assessment of smart service systems which includes quality aspects of existing approaches and methods. Moreover, specific quality criteria were supplemented which address the use of artificial intelligence in smart service systems. Arranged in 12 design fields, the conceptual framework is structured in such a way that either all service elements perceived by customers or only those parts that are relevant for development can be explored. In this way, our research contributes to the current discussion about an increasingly collaborative and interdisciplinary development of smart service systems [6] and the distributed value creation on smart service platforms [33]. The integrative conceptual framework can be used, for example, by enterprises to extend quality assessment to service elements provided by third parties (e.g. AI tools), structure quality-related requirements or assess integration activities as a key element of smart service systems. Structuring along the service dimensions of structure, process and outcome additionally permits a technical-logical compatibility with existing methods and tools of service engineering.

The large number of quality categories and criteria identified for the assessment of a smart service system suggests that the conceptual framework is not a suitable measuring instrument for customer surveys like SERVQUAL. Rather, the conceptual framework is addressed to organizations that want to consider relevant quality aspects in the system-atic development of AI-based smart service systems and test their fulfillment. Which categories and criteria from the conceptual framework are actually relevant depends on the service elements to be integrated, the development phase and the maturity of proto-types of service elements created. Deliberate focusing on quality perceptions in smart service systems and considering various forms of interaction (human-to-human, human-to-machine and machine-to-machine) makes it possible that the integrative conceptual framework gives a first impression of new methods and approaches that attempt to merge a humanistic and technology-centric service paradigm [36]. Even though the influence of intelligent technologies and data on service delivery is continuously increasing, the subjective perception of potential users and personnel in the development of high-quality smart service systems should continue to play a key role.

However, apart from the potential outlined it is necessary to highlight some limi-tations of the integrative conceptual framework. To some extent, the quality categories and criteria were adopted from empirically validated quality models and some were sup-plemented based on expert interviews and workshops. Even though the assessment of smart service systems using the conceptual framework has already proven to be highly useful in several projects in practice, a large-scale validation of the interaction among the criteria and/or categories does not yet exist. It is true that a generally applicable valida-tion can hardly be realized because of the application-specific selection of design fields, categories and criteria and this should be taken into account when utilizing the con-ceptual framework in practice. Furthermore, particularly the AI-specific quality criteria should be regularly reviewed and adapted because of the rapidly progressing technolog-ical options. With regard to the significance and weighting of the individual assessment categories, it is also necessary to consider potential differences between applications, industries addressed and the relevant culture area [37]. For evaluating the significance of different elements and criteria, decision techniques, such as the Analytical Hierarchy Process (AHP) could be applied.

References

1. Bruhn, M., Hadwich, K.: Dienstleistungen 4.0 – Erscheinungsformen, Transformation-sprozesse und Managementimplikationen. In: Bruhn, M., Hadwich, K. (eds.) Forum Dien-stleistungsmanagement: Dienstleistungen 4.0, vol. 1, pp. 1–39. Springer, Wiesbaden (2017). https://doi.org/10.1007/978-3-658-17550-4_1
2. Bullinger, H.-J., Ganz, W., Neuhüttler, J.: Smart Services – Chancen und Herausforderun-gen digitalisierter Dienstleistungssysteme für Unternehmen. In: Bruhn, M., Hadwich, K. (eds.) Forum Dienstleistungsmanagement: Dienstleistungen 4.0, vol. 1, pp. 97–120. Springer, Wiesbaden (2017). https://doi.org/10.1007/978-3-658-17550-4_4

3. Lim, C., Maglio, P.P.: Clarifying the concept of smart service system. In: Maglio, P.P., Kieliszewski, C.A., Spohrer, J.C., Lyons, K., Patrício, L., Sawatani, Y. (eds.) Handbook of Service Science. SSRISE, vol. 2, pp. 349–376. Springer, Cham (2019). https://doi.org/10.1007/978-3-319-98512-1_16

4. Wahlster, W.: Künstliche Intelligenz als Treiber der zweiten Digitalisierungswelle, IM + IO, vol. 2 (2017)

5. Wirtz, J., et al.: Brave new world - service robots in the frontline. J. Serv. Manag. 29(5), 907–931 (2018)

6. Anke, J., Meyer, K., Alt, R., Holze, J., Kahlert, E.: Lernen aus Anwendung: Transfer-orientierte Entwicklung von Methoden für das Smart Service Engineering. In: Meyer, K., Klingner, S., Zinke, C. (eds.) Service Engineering, pp. 91–107. Springer, Wiesbaden (2018). https://doi.org/10.1007/978-3-658-20905-6_7

7. Wünderlich, N.V., et al.: "Futurizing" smart service - implications for service researchers and managers. J. Serv. Manag. 29(6), 442–447 (2015)

8. Ostrom, A.L., Fotheringham, D., Bitner, M.J.: Customer acceptance of AI in service encounters: understanding antecedents and consequences. In: Maglio, P.P., Kieliszewski, C.A., Spohrer, J.C., Lyons, K., Patrício, L., Sawatani, Y. (eds.) Handbook of Service Science. SSRISE, vol. 2, pp. 77–103. Springer, Cham (2019). https://doi.org/10.1007/978-3-319-985 12-1_5

9. Meiren, T., Neuhüttler, J.: Smart Services im Maschinenbau - Systematische Entwicklung digital unterstützter Dienstleistungen. wt-online 7(8), 555–557 (2019)

10. Maglio, P.P., Lim, C.H.: Innovation and big data in smart service systems. J. Innov. Manag. 4(1), 11–21 (2016)

11. Beverungen, D., Müller, O., Matzner, M., Mendling, J., vom Brocke, J.: Conceptualizing smart service systems. Electron. Mark. 29(1), 7–18 (2017). https://doi.org/10.1007/s12525-017-0270-5

12. Allmendinger, G., Lombreglia, R.: Four strategies for the age of smart services. Harvard Bus. Rev. 83(10), 131–145 (2005)

13. Porter, M.E., Heppelmann, J.E.: How smart, connected products are transforming competition. Harvard Bus. Rev. 92(11), 64–88 (2014)

14. Lim, C., Kim, M.-J., Kim, K.-H., Kim, H.-J., Maglio, P.P.: Using data to advance service: managerial issues and theoretical implications from action research. J. Serv. Theory Pract. 28(1), 99–128 (2018)

15. Stich, V., Hoffmann, J., Heimes, P.: Software-definierte Plattformen - Eigenschaften, Integrationsanforderungen und Praxiserfahrungen in produzierenden Unternehmen. HMD – Prax Wi.-Inf. 55(1), 25–43 (2018)

16. Wünderlich, N.V., von Wangenheim, F., Bitner, M.J.: High tech and high touch: a framework for understanding user attitudes and behaviors related to smart interactive services. J. Serv. Res. 16(1), 3–20 (2012)

17. Tombeil, A.-S., Kremer, D., Neuhüttler, J., Dukino, C., Ganz, W.: Potenziale von Künstlicher Intelligenz in der Dienstleistungsarbeit. In: Bruhn, M., Hadwich, K. (eds.) Forum Dienstleistungsmanagement: Automatisierung und Personalisierung von Dienstleistungen, pp. 135–154. Springer, Wiesbaden (2020). https://doi.org/10.1007/978-3-658-30168-2_5

18. Kreutzer, R.T., Sirrenberg, M.: Künstliche Intelligenz verstehen - Grundlagen – Use-Cases – unternehmenseigene KI-Journey. Springer, Wiesbaden (2019). https://doi.org/10.1007/978-3-658-25561-9

19. McColl-Kennedy, J.R., Zaki, M., Lemon, K.N., Urmetzer, F., Neely, A.: Gaining customer experience insights that matter. J. Serv. Res. 22(1), 8–26 (2019)

20. Spath, D., Ganz, W., Meiren, T.: Dienstleistungen in der digitalen Gesellschaft - Chancen und Herausforderungen der Digitalisierung für Lösungsanbieter. In: Boes, A. (ed.) Dienstleistungen in der digitalen Gesellschaft, pp. 25–34. Campus, Frankfurt Main (2014)

21. Neuhüttler, J., Woyke, I., Ganz, W., Spath, D.: An approach for a quality-based test of industrial smart service concepts. In: Ahram, T.Z. (ed.) AHFE 2018. AISC, vol. 787, pp. 171–182. Springer, Cham (2019). https://doi.org/10.1007/978-3-319-94229-2_17

22. Bruhn, M.: Qualitätsmanagement für Dienstleistungen - Grundlagen – Konzepte – Methoden. Springer Gabler, Berlin (2016)

23. Parasuraman, A., Zeithaml, V.A., Berry, L.L.: SERVQUAL: a multiple-item scale for measuring consumer perceptions of service quality. J. Retail. **64**(1), 12–40 (1988)

24. Parasuraman, A., Zeithaml, V.A., Malhotra, A.: E-S-QUAL - a multiple-item scale for assessing electronic service quality. J. Serv. Res. **7**(5), 1–21 (2005)

25. Neuhuettler, J., Ganz, W., Liu, J.: An integrated approach for measuring and managing quality of smart senior care services. In: Ahram, T.Z., Karwowski, W. (eds.) Advances in The Human Side of Service Engineering. AISC, vol. 494, pp. 309–318. Springer, Cham (2017). https://doi.org/10.1007/978-3-319-41947-3_29

26. Wang, T., Yeh, R., Yen, D.C., Nugroho, C.A.: Electronic and in-person service quality of hybrid services. Serv. Ind. J. **36**(13–14), 638–657 (2016)

27. Böhm, M., Sczudlek, A., Knebel, U., Leimeister, J.M., Krcmar, H.: Qualitätsmanagement bei hybriden Produkten: Ein Ansatz zur Messung der Leistungsqualität hybrider Produkte. In: Leimeister, J.M., Krcmar, H., Halle, M., Möslein, K. (eds.) Hybride Wertschöpfung in der Gesundheitsförderung. Innovation - Dienstleistung - IT, pp. 155–172. Eul Verlag, Lohmar (2010)

28. Weber, M., Burchardt, A.: Künstliche Intelligenz. https://www.dfki.de. Accessed 29 Aug 2019

29. Meuter, M.L., Bitner, M.J., Ostrom, A.L., Brown, S.W.: Choosing among alternative service delivery modes - an investigation of customer trial of self-service technologies. J. Market. **69**(2), 61–83 (2005)

30. Neuhüttler, J., Ganz, W., Spath, D.: An integrative quality framework for developing industrial smart services. Serv. Sci. **11**(3), 157–171 (2019)

31. Bullinger, H.-J., Fähnrich, K.-P., Meiren, T.: Service engineering - methodical development of new service products. Int. J. Prod. Econ. **85**(3), 275–287 (2003)

32. Falter, M., Bürkin, B., Hadwich, K.: Ausprägungen der Digitalisierung im Arbeitsumfeld und deren Auswirkungen auf das Mitarbeiterwohlbefinden. In: Arnold, C., Knödler, H. (eds.) Die informatisierte Service-Ökonomie - Veränderungen im privaten und öffentlichen Sektor, pp. 65–92. Springer, Wiesbaden (2018). https://doi.org/10.1007/978-3-658-21528-6_4

33. Moser, B., Jussen, P., Rösner, C.: Smart-Service-Plattformen - Gestaltungsempfehlungen am Beispiel der digitalisierten Landwirtschaft. In: Stich, V., Schumann, J.H., Beverungen, D., Gudergan, G., Jussen, P. (eds.) Digitale Dienstleistungsinnovationen - Smart Services agil und kundenorientiert entwickeln, pp. 601–624. Springer, Berlin (2019). https://doi.org/10.1007/978-3-662-59517-6_29

34. Huang, M.-H., Rust, R.T.: Artificial intelligence in service. J. Serv. Res. **21**(2), 155–172 (2018)

35. Geigenmüller, A., Leischnig, A.: Zur Relevanz von Allianzmanagementfähigkeit bei kooperativen Dienstleistungen. In: Bruhn, M., Hadwich, K. (eds.) Forum Dienstleistungsmanagement: Kooperative Dienstleistungen - Spannungsfelder zwischen Service Cooperation und Service Coopetition. FD, pp. 57–69. Springer, Wiesbaden (2019). https://doi.org/10.1007/978-3-658-26389-8_3

36. Keating, B.W., McColl-Kennedy, J.R., Solnet, D.: Theorizing beyond the horizon - service research in 2050. J Serv. Man. **29**(5), 766–775 (2018)

37. Zhang, W., Neuhüttler, J., Chen, M., Ganz, W.: Smart services conditions and preferences – an analysis of chinese and german manufacturing markets. In: Ahram, T.Z. (ed.) AHFE 2018. AISC, vol. 787, pp. 183–194. Springer, Cham (2019). https://doi.org/10.1007/978-3-319-94229-2_18

Towards Guidelines for Assessing Qualities of Machine Learning Systems

Julien Siebert[1]([✉]), Lisa Joeckel[1], Jens Heidrich[1], Koji Nakamichi[2], Kyoko Ohashi[2], Isao Namba[2], Rieko Yamamoto[2], and Mikio Aoyama[3]

[1] Fraunhofer IESE, Kaiserslautern, Germany
{julien.siebert,lisa.joeckel,jens.heidrich}@iese.fraunhofer.de
[2] Fujitsu Laboratories Ltd., Kawasaki, Japan
{nakamichi,ohashi.kyoko,namba,r.yamamoto}@fujitsu.com
[3] Nanzan University, Nagoya, Japan
mikio.aoyama@nifty.com

Abstract. Nowadays, systems containing components based on machine learning (ML) methods are becoming more widespread. In order to ensure the intended behavior of a software system, there are standards that define necessary quality aspects of the system and its components (such as ISO/IEC 25010). Due to the different nature of ML, we have to adjust quality aspects or add additional ones (such as trustworthiness) and be very precise about which aspect is really relevant for which object of interest (such as completeness of training data), and how to objectively assess adherence to quality requirements. In this article, we present the construction of a quality model (i.e., evaluation objects, quality aspects, and metrics) for an ML system based on an industrial use case. This quality model enables practitioners to specify and assess quality requirements for such kinds of ML systems objectively. In the future, we want to learn how the term quality differs between different types of ML systems and come up with general guidelines for specifying and assessing qualities of ML systems.

Keywords: Machine learning · Software quality · Quality evaluation

1 Introduction

The digital transformation enables digital products and services that are based on data or on models derived from data. The construction of these models for algorithmic decision-making is increasingly based on artificial intelligence (AI) methods, which enable innovative solutions such as automated driving or predictive maintenance. Our research focuses on ML systems, i.e., software-intensive systems containing one or more components that use models built with ML methods. The functionality of these components is not defined by the programmer in the classical way, but is learned from data. Developing and operating ML systems raises new challenges in comparison to "classical" software engineering [1, 2]. First, the behavior is fundamentally different from traditional software: The relationship between the input and the outcome of the model is only defined

© Springer Nature Switzerland AG 2020
M. Shepperd et al. (Eds.): QUATIC 2020, CCIS 1266, pp. 17–31, 2020.
https://doi.org/10.1007/978-3-030-58793-2_2

for a subset of the data, which leads to uncertainty in model outcomes for previously unseen data. Second, common development principles from software engineering, such as encapsulation and modularity, have to be rethought, e.g., neural networks cannot simply be cut into smaller sub-nets and reused as modules. Third, the development and integration of ML components is a multi-disciplinary approach: It requires knowledge about the application domain, knowledge about how to construct ML models, and finally, knowledge about software engineering. Fourth, quality assurance, and specifically testing, works differently than in traditional software. This is because ML targets problems where the expected solution is inherently difficult to formalize [3].

In order to ensure the intended quality of a software system, there are standards that define necessary quality aspects of the system and its components. For instance, ISO/IEC 25010 [4] defines quality models for software and systems; i.e., a hierarchy of quality aspects of interest and how to quantify and assess them. Due to the different nature of ML, these quality models cannot be applied directly as they are. Some have to be adjusted in their definition (e.g., reusability of ML systems) and some need to be added (e.g., trustworthiness). We also have to be very precise about which quality aspect is relevant for which part of the overall system. For instance, in an ML system, the algorithms executing the model play a far less significant role than the data used for training and testing. For developing meaningful quality models, it is necessary to understand the application context of the use case and what kind of ML method is used.

In this article, we present the construction of a concrete quality model for an ML system based on an industrial use case. In this paper, we will first discuss related work and summarize the gaps that we would like to close with our contribution. Second, we will define the different views one can take on an ML system and relevant measurement objects, which will have to be evaluated for a specific use case and application context. Third, we will describe our general methodological approach for quality modeling of ML systems based on an industrial use case. This includes specifically the quality model containing all relevant quality aspects and concrete metrics for each measurement object of interest. This quality model enables practitioners to specify and assess quality requirements for such kinds of ML systems. Fourth, we will discuss the usefulness of the identified quality aspects based on an evaluation together with experts from industry. Last, we will present major lessons learned and give an outlook on future research, where we want to find out how the term quality differs between different types of ML systems (e.g., based on the ML method used or the way the ML component is integrated into the overall system). This will helps us come up with more general guidelines for specifying and assessing qualities of ML systems.

2 Related Work

To build a quality model, it is first necessary to define quality attributes. In the literature, some quite generic quality models for software and systems, such as ISO/IEC 25010 [4] or ISO/IEC 8000 [5], can be found. These standards propose different quality attribute definitions grouped into several categories with a decomposition structure (e.g., Product quality is decomposed into eight attributes, such as Functional Suitability, which is decomposed into sub-attributes, such as Functional Correctness). With the advance and the widespread adoption of ML methods, new and more specific quality proposals have emerged (such as the EU Ethics Guidelines for Trustworthy AI [6], the German DIN SPEC 92001 [7], or the Japanese QA4AI consortium [8]) as well as certification guidelines [9, 10].

Some of the new quality attributes are rather generic, so they cover not only ML but also other AI disciplines. These include:

- **Transparency and accountability** (e.g., reproducibility, interpretability and explainability, auditability, minimization, and reporting of negative impact)
- **Diversity, non-discrimination, fairness**, as well as **societal and environmental well-being** (e.g., avoidance of unfair bias, accessibility and universal design, stakeholder participation, sustainability, and environmental friendliness)
- **Security, safety, data protection** (e.g., respect for privacy, quality and integrity of data, access to data, and ability to cope with erroneous, noisy, unknown, and adversarial input data)
- **Technical robustness, reliability, dependability** (e.g., correctness of output, estimation of model uncertainty, robustness against harmful inputs, errors, or unexpected situations)
- **Human agency and oversight, legal and ethical aspects** (e.g., possibility of human agency and human oversight, respect for fundamental rights)

Some quality attributes are more specific to interactive and embodied AI (like assistants or robots), such as intelligent behavior and personality [8, 11, 12]. The quality attributes are applied to measurement objects. These objects can represent processes, products, impacted users, or external objects.

It is not uncommon to describe the system under study in terms of different views and measurement objects and to group the different quality attributes under these views/objects. For example, in [3], the authors define a set of quality attributes, such as correctness (i.e., goodness of fit), robustness, efficiency, etc. They also relate these quality attributes to different views/objects: data, learning program, and framework (e.g., Weka, TensorFlow). In [13], the authors distinguish between three main quality aspects, namely service quality, product quality, and platform quality. They also describe different views/objects on the system: the training dataset, the neural network, the hyper parameters, "the inference in vivo" (corresponding to the decision outputted by the ML component at runtime) and the machine learning platform. DIN-SPEC 92001 also provides a description in terms of views/objects: data, model, platform, and environment. As a last example, the authors in [8] provide five main quality aspects related to views/objects, namely data integrity, model robustness, system quality, process agility, and customer expectation, including a total of 49 quality sub-attributes.

In the literature, we see that a consensus exists around what quality aspects need to be measured. However, the naming of the quality attributes and the naming of the measurement objects (or the views) has not yet stabilized.

The same conclusion can be reached for quality attributes related to the process. Process models related to data analysis methods (such as knowledge engineering, data mining, ML, etc.) have been around for decades [14, 15]. In the last years, more case studies and literature reviews have been conducted to assess the challenges perceived by developers of ML components, as well as their processes and best practices [1, 3, 16, 17]. We see that there is a consensus on the definition of tasks, roles, and how the process should be organized for developing and operating ML components. However, it is less clear how the ML process impacts quality. Implementing quality improvement actions requires a good understanding of the process: which steps are performed, which people/roles are involved, which measurement objects are affected, etc.

We also see that, because the field of ML is large, the importance of certain quality attributes and metrics for quantifying them depend on the concrete context and use case and have to be addressed in different tasks of the process model used. For instance, the availability of a ground truth is one important factor (see Fig. 1): (a) If the full ground truth exists (as in the case of reinforcement learning, for example), then test oracles exist. Consequently, the quality mainly depends on the test oracle itself, and the quality can be safely measured using the available ground truth. (b) If only a partial ground truth exists (as in the case of semi-supervised or supervised learning), data quality and its representativeness have to be analyzed carefully. (c) If no ground truth exists (as in the case of unsupervised learning), the assumptions made by the learning algorithms and those made during the model evaluation play a significant role with respect to quality. The type of ML tasks that is performed (such as regression, classification, clustering, outlier detection, dimensionality reduction, etc.) also has an impact on the quality assessment. Each type of task is accompanied by corresponding quality metrics. For example, for classification tasks, the goodness of fit can be measured by accuracy, precision, recall, f-score, etc. [18], but for clustering, other measures are needed [19]. The metrics chosen will depend on the use case. For example, in the case of binary classification tasks, the cost of a false-positive may not be the same as the cost of a false-negative. Some metrics might not be compatible with one another, as is the case, for example, for fairness measures [20, 21].

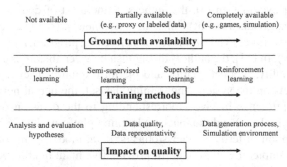

Fig. 1. The availability of ground truth data (labels) has a direct impact on the analysis or training methods used as well as on the definition of quality metrics and their assessment.

The literature provides a solid basis of relevant quality attributes, measurement objects, process models, etc. However, we see different gaps that have not been addressed so far: (1) There is a lack of unique and clear definitions of views on ML systems (e.g., what is the definition of a platform view in [7], or should hyper-parameters be included as a separate view). (2) Existing quality models are often too abstract to be of value for practitioners (e.g., in terms of proposed metrics) and require guidelines for tailoring to be applicable [22]. (3) The combination of and the relationship between quality attributes and related metrics have not been sufficiently investigated yet, and it is not clear whether they can be satisfied altogether. (4) Comprehensive development guidelines for quality-aware ML systems, which would bring together the different ML quality models, processes, and views, are largely missing or not made explicit.

In the remainder of this article, we will contribute mainly to closing the first two gaps. However, our overall research goal is aimed at coming up with comprehensive development guidelines for quality-aware ML systems.

3   Views on ML Systems

Many factors can influence the quality of a software system (code, hardware, development process, usage scenarios, etc.). In our approach, we tried to systematically identify groups of factors belonging together. We propose different "views" that would be helpful in categorizing quality attributes and corresponding quality metrics together with the objects to be measured. These views are: model view, data view, system view, infrastructure view, and environment view (see Fig. 2 for an illustrative overview). Note that a given quality model may or may not use all the views, as the relevant ones are selected according to the use case.

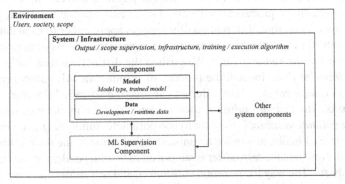

Fig. 2. Overview of the different views on the software system and measurement objects that influence the system's quality.

Model View. The model view is concerned with quality aspects belonging to what is called *a model* in machine learning. The model is the part that is trained on data in order to perform a given task (e.g., a classification, regression, dimensionality reduction, etc.). Note that an ML component normally does not contain only a single model but may be composed of several models, usually organized in a directed acyclic graph (also called a pipeline) [17]. The specificity of an ML component is the way it is built. We have to distinguish between the development phase (where the training and the evaluation of the pipeline is done) and the operation phase (where the artifacts created in the previous phase are deployed and used in production, i.e., at runtime), because these two phases may be implemented with different technologies (e.g., R/Python for learning, Web/Java on the application side) or have different quality demands (e.g., using a large quantity of data, operating under short latency, etc.).

In the model view, we have made a distinction between what we call a *model type* (e.g., decision trees, neural networks, etc.) and a *trained model* (e.g., a specific instance of a neural network trained on a specific dataset using a specific *training algorithm*). Again, the goal of this distinction is to separate quality aspects related to a specific object instance from those related to the object type. For example, the *appropriateness* of a given model applies to a *model type* (like the family of decision trees), whereas the *goodness of fit* applies to a specific trained instance. Note that we also separate the model from its *training algorithm* (i.e., the algorithm that takes *training data* and a *model type* as input and outputs a *trained model*) and its *execution algorithm* (i.e., the algorithm that takes *runtime data* and a *trained model* as input and outputs a decision, for instance a classification of inputted *runtime data*). The argumentation is that the training and execution algorithms are pieces of "classical" software whose quality aspects can be described and measured using existing standards.

Data View. The data view is concerned with the quality aspects related to the data. The term data here describes the data that is used as input for a model. We further distinguish between the *development data*, i.e., data used during the development phase to train the ML component, and *runtime data*, i.e., the dataset used during the operation phase. The distinction is made because these can be different physical objects, stored in different databases, potentially preprocessed or accessed differently during the development and operation phases. Therefore, different quality aspects apply either to each dataset separately or to both (for example, by comparing the representativeness of the *development data* with regard to the *runtime data*). We pushed the distinction even further concerning the *development data*. Indeed, the process of training an ML component requires splitting the *development data* into different subsets: the so-called training, validation, and test subsets. The *training subset* is used to determine the model parameters during training. The *validation subset* is used for hyper-parameter tuning (e.g., maximum depth of a decision tree). Finally, to provide an unbiased evaluation of the *trained model*, a *test subset* is used. Note that the *test subset* is supposed to be independent of the training and validation subsets. The way the *training, validation,* and *test subsets* are chosen have an impact on the quality of the evaluation of the trained model.

System View. First, an ML component is usually organized in a pipeline of tasks. Developing such a pipeline is by nature experimental. A given pipeline may be trained several times with different model types, training algorithms, or datasets. The way these subcomponents are connected have an impact on quality (see, for example, the problem of data leakage [23]). Second, the ML component is part of a larger system, i.e., it consumes data from one or several sources and interacts with other ML or non-ML components. Since, a decision outputted by an ML component is always subject to uncertainty, and since wrong decisions might impact the system's overall quality, considering the flow of information from the system input through all components to the system output is important in order to understand the impact of the ML components' quality on the overall system behavior. Typical quality aspects related to the system view include, among others, data dependencies and feedback loops [2]. In our use case, the output of the ML component is monitored in order to detect and correct wrong decisions. This monitoring also has its own quality aspects that may be relevant for the use case at stake (e.g., monitoring effectiveness and efficiency).

Infrastructure View. What we call the infrastructure view is closely related to the system view. However, the view is here more focused on the quality aspects related to how the system is concretely implemented (e.g., hardware, training libraries). We decided to separate both views in order to highlight some specificities of ML components. For example, the efficiency of the *training* and *execution algorithms* is a quality attribute that belongs to this view. The same applies to the suitability of the infrastructure either for training or for executing ML components. For example, current trained deep learning models used for natural language processing are several gigabytes in size, and require several days (or weeks) of training on dedicated hardware machines (GPU clusters). The trained model cannot be executed on embedded devices due to computational and storage limitations.

Environment View. The *environment* consists of elements that (1) are external to the system under consideration, and (2) interact either directly or indirectly with the system. This includes the users. For ML systems, several environmental aspects may have a direct influence on the quality. These are, for example, aspects causing quality deficits in the data. This is strongly related to the notion of concept drift. Since an ML component is built for and tested in a given context of use (or target application scope), its quality will decrease when this context changes [24]. A self-adapting ML component dependent on the environment also raises further quality-related challenges (see, for example, the problems faced by the Microsoft chatbot Tay). Viceversa, an ML component can also have an impact on its environment, e.g., in terms of resource usage or societal discrimination [6].

4 Quality Modeling for ML Systems

Many aspects can influence the quality of a software component using ML and deriving a quality model for a specific use case may not be trivial. In this section, we will illustrate the approach we used to derive a quality model. The use case and the resulting quality model will be presented as well.

Our approach can be summarized as follows. We started by defining the relevant use case. This is usually done through interviews with the appropriate stakeholders. During these interviews, we made it clear what type of problem the ML component was supposed to solve (e.g., classification), what the intended application scope was (i.e., in which context the ML component should be used, what could change and how often), and whether some ground truth is available. We then used the views defined in the previous section to select pertinent measurement objects for the use case. From that point on, we selected quality attributes of interest and derived corresponding metrics (see Fig. 3).

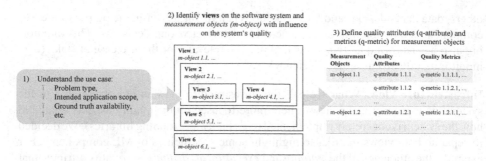

Fig. 3. Overview of the approach used to derive a specific quality model.

The industrial use case was as follows. Fujitsu's Accounting Center receives purchase order requests (POR) in digital form that need to be categorized for further treatment. This task was traditionally done by human operators and is now performed by an ML component. This component is trained with labeled examples of POR that used to be categorized in the past by human operators. The goal of the ML system is to reduce operating cost at an acceptable level of classification accuracy (comparable to humans). During the interviews, some quality issues were mentioned. First, the development and operation of ML components are complex and associated with high cost and risks. Several areas of expertise come into play when developing and operating an ML system. This may lead to potential communication and coordination problems. Furthermore, if wrong classifications do occur, finding the root cause of such a failure is not trivial. In order to deal with this, a monitoring system was implemented in conjunction with a correction engine based on expert rules. The ML component was re-trained when too many categorization failures were detected. This use case illustrates some of the quality issues encountered while developing and operating software systems using ML components.

Table 1 presents the quality model we derived for the use case described above. For each view on the ML system, we defined a set of relevant quality attributes and corresponding measurement objects. For each attribute, we either give examples of concrete metrics for objectively evaluating the quality, or, if this is not possible, define examples for items one would have to check in order to address the respective quality. The quality model was designed to be specific enough to address the described use case appropriately (including supervision- and classification-related quality attributes), but also contains generic elements to allow it to be applied to other (similar) use cases (such as most attributes related to data and model).

How these measures could be aggregated in order to get an overall evaluation of the ML system and how to define quality improvement strategies for the use case are issues beyond the scope of this article.

5   Discussion

In this article, we first proposed a categorization of quality attributes as well as measurement objects in the form of different views/objects. This classification is the result

Table 1. Overview of the derived quality model

View	Measurement object	Quality attribute	Example quality metrics and checklists
Model	Model type	**Appropriateness:** Degree to which the *model type* is appropriate for the current task (e.g., classification, etc.) and can deal with the current data type (e.g., numerical, categorical)	Prerequisites for model type
	Trained model	**Development correctness (Goodness of Fit):** Ability of the model to perform the current task measured on the development dataset	Precision, Recall, F-score, etc. for training
		Runtime correctness (Goodness of Fit): Same as above measured on the runtime dataset	Precision, Recall, F-score, etc. at runtime
		Relevance (Bias-Variance tradeoff): Degree to which the model achieves a good bias-variance trade-off (neither underfitting nor overfitting the data)	Variance of cross-validation goodness of fit
		Robustness: Ability of the model to handle noise or data with missing values and still make correct predictions	Equalized Loss of Accuracy (ELA)
		Stability: Degree to which a trained model generates repeatable results when it is trained on different subsets of the training dataset	Leave-one-out cross-validation stability.
		Fairness: Ability of the model to output fair decisions	Equalized odds
		Interpretability: Degree to which the trained model can be interpreted by humans	Complexity metrics (e.g., no. of parameters, depth)
		Resource utilization: Resources used by the model when it is already trained	Required storage space

(*continued*)

Table 1. (*continued*)

View	Measurement object	Quality attribute	Example quality metrics and checklists
Data	Development data	**Representativeness:** Degree to which the data is representative of the statistical population	Statistical tests (e.g., two-sample t-test, etc.)
		Correctness: Degree to which the data is free from errors	Outlier detection metrics (e.g., Z-score).
		Completeness: Degree to which the data is free from missing values	No. of missing values
		Currentness: Degree to which the data is up to date w.r.t. the current task	Age of data
		Intra-Consistency: Consistency of the data within a dataset, e.g., the data does not contradict itself or the formatting is consistent	Value ranges, word counts
		Train/Test Independence: Degree to which the *training* and *test subsets* are independent of one another	Statistical tests (e.g., two-sample t-test, etc.)
		Balancedness: Degree to which all classes (labels) are equally represented in the dataset	Ratio of classes
		Absence of Bias: Degree to which the data is free from bias against a given group	Ratios of groups
	Development and runtime data	**Inter-Consistency:** Consistency between different datasets, e.g., formatting, sampling methods used	Value ranges, crosswise outlier detection metrics
Environment	Training process	**Environmental Impact:** Degree to which the training process impacts the environment.	Energy consumption.
	Society	**Social Impact:** Degree to which the ML component impacts society	Impact on employees

(*continued*)

Table 1. (*continued*)

View	Measurement object	Quality attribute	Example quality metrics and checklists
	Scope	**Scope Compliance:** Degree to which the application of the ML component respects its intended scope of use	Value ranges, novelty detection metrics
System	Output supervision	**Effectiveness:** Degree to which the output supervision algorithm detects false outcomes of the ML component	False positive/negative detection rate
		Supervision Overhead/Efficiency: Resources used for monitoring a given ML component	Time, memory used, etc.
	Scope supervision	**Effectiveness:** Degree to which the scope supervision algorithm detects context changes	No. of out-of-scope cases
		Supervision Overhead/Efficiency: Resources used for monitoring the application scope	Time memory used, etc.
	Other non-ML components	Here we refer to the relevant subset of the quality attributes of the standard ISO/IEC 25010, which are not listed here for space reasons	
Infrastructure	Infrastructure	**Infrastructure Suitability:** Degree to which the infrastructure matches the ML component needs (e.g., in terms of hardware type, computation capability, bandwidth, memory, etc.)	Computational and storage capabilities
	Training algorithm	**Training Efficiency:** Resources used for training a given model	Time, memory used, etc.
	Execution algorithm	**Execution Efficiency:** Resources used for executing a given trained model	Time, memory used, etc.

of a literature-based review, discussions with industrial partners, and our own experience in ML component development. To scientifically assess and consolidate a useful and systematic grouping of quality attributes for ML systems (as well as measurement objects), several iterations will be necessary (e.g., case study, systematic literature review, mapping study).

We also derived a quality model specifically tailored for a given use case. The definition and relevance of the quality attributes were first discussed internally in a workshop with experts. Later, three case studies with a focus on requirements engineering for ML systems were conducted by Fujitsu Laboratories [25]. In this paper, the authors present the overall requirements engineering process, but do not go into the details of the quality model presented. The performed case studies confirmed that the quality attributes identified were valid and meaningful for ML developers, especially in the context of requirements specification.

In terms of limitations, we see three main aspects:

1. We did not address process-related aspects yet, i.e., what qualities have to be assured in which activity and handled by which role. We believe that the proposed views/objects can help to establish a mapping between roles (e.g., Data Scientist, Data Engineer, etc.) and quality attributes or metrics. For example, Data Scientists are usually in charge of building models, and are in direct line when it comes to measuring the impact of data quality on the models' outcomes. However, Data Engineers are the ones that can usually implement new data quality improvement actions. Architects with a good understanding of ML will be needed in order to solve problems on the system level.

2. The identified views may be incomplete and currently focus more on the later stages of CRISP-DM, missing the stages of Business Understanding (i.e., ML requirements) and Data Understanding, and their related measurement objects. For example, Data Understanding is by nature rather experimental and the artifacts produced at this stage usually consist of a set of decisions (e.g., which data preparation algorithm to choose) and may be accompanied by code snippets or visualizations (e.g., notebooks, reports). An open question is whether the views should be augmented with new measurement objects (such as specific ML requirements documents, experiment reports or notebooks, etc.) or whether another classification direction based upon processes is needed.

3. Finally, our viewpoint for defining the quality model was more from the data science perspective. Integration with classical software/system engineering qualities (such as those defined by ISO/IEC 25010) is missing. There is as yet no consensus on the naming of ML-related quality attributes. Furthermore, whereas some of the proposed attributes can be easily classified under existing ISO/IEC 25010 ones (e.g., the model's Goodness of Fit could potentially belong to Functional Correctness), others may be more difficult to classify (such as Scope Compliance). Whether the ISO/IEC 25010 is the right framework for ML components is still an open issue.

6 Lessons Learned and Conclusions

This article presented how we constructed a concrete quality model for an ML system based on an industrial use case. We are completely aware that the model we developed is quite specific to the case and that other use cases may require different quality aspects and, in consequence, different metrics. However, we would like to share an excerpt from the lessons we learned from following the described methodological approach. Even though some of these are known from other fields, we nonetheless think it is worth mentioning them in the context of developing ML systems:

1. Context and use case must be clear. As pointed out before, there are many application fields and potential ML-based solutions available. It is very important to be as clear as possible about the general application context. ML models should never ever be used just for the sake of being fancy, but always because there is the profound assumption that they will add concrete value for the application context. The quality aspects that are important mainly depend on this.
2. Iterative approach: The ML model, its application context, and its use case have to be adjusted over time and some initial assumptions will turn out to be false. Therefore, it is important to follow an iterative approach when developing the ML system and to be able to quickly identify dead ends and take different paths. Having a clear picture of what quality aspects are important and how to quantify them is crucial for this, as it allows us to immediately see whether we can fulfill them with our solution path.
3. Multidisciplinary work: As we stated at the beginning of this article, different kinds of knowledge must come together for developing quality-aware ML systems. For instance, a data scientist knows how to measure the fairness or stability of the trained model, a software/system engineer knows how to assure the quality of the overall system, and a domain expert knows whether the ML system really solves the problem better than a traditional software system.
4. The devil is in the details: We learned that it is easy to talk about abstract generic quality aspects, such as those defined by ISO/IEC 25010, on a high level. To define meaningful quality aspects, we had to break them down into concrete qualities of measurement objects and define how to operationalize these aspects with metrics.
5. Quality-aware process/guidelines: Even though there are defined processes for ML model building (such as CRISP-DM) and for software engineering (such as rich and agile processes) with elaborate practices for improvement (such as DevOps approaches), an integrated process is missing, nor do guidelines exist on how to bring everything together with a clear focus on the quality of ML systems.

Regarding future work, we first plan to perform more case studies to empirically validate the different quality aspects in more detail, specifically their relevance for practitioners and how to deal with them in different process stages. Second, we want to apply this method to other ML problems (like regression, or unsupervised problems) and learn about the impact on the quality model. Third, we intend to package our insights into development guidelines for quality-aware ML systems.

References

1. Wan, Z., Xia, X., Lo, D., Murphy, G.C.: How does machine learning change software development practices? IEEE Trans. Softw. Eng. 1 (2019)

2. Sculley, D., et al.: Hidden technical debt in machine learning systems. In: Proceedings of the 28th International Conference on Neural Information Processing Systems, pp. 2503–2511 (2015)
3. Zhang, J.M., Harman, M., Ma, L., Liu, Y.: Machine learning testing: survey, landscapes and horizons. IEEE Trans. Softw. Eng. 1 (2020)
4. ISO/IEC 25010:2011: Systems and software engineering—Systems and software Quality Requirements and Evaluation (SQuaRE)—System and software quality models
5. ISO/TS 8000:2011: Data Quality
6. High-Level Expert Group on Artificial Intelligence: Ethics Guidelines for Trustworthy AI. European Commission (2019)
7. DIN SPEC 92001-01: Künstliche Intelligenz - Life Cycle Prozesse und Qualitätsanforderungen. Teil 1: Qualitäts-Meta-Modell. Beuth Verlag GmbH, Berlin
8. Hamada, K., Ishikawa, F., Masuda, S., Matsuya, M., Ujita, Y.: Guidelines for quality assurance of machine learning-based artificial intelligence. In: SEKE2020: the 32nd International Conference on Software Engineering & Knowledge Engineering, pp. 335–341 (2020)
9. Trustworthy Use of Artificial Intelligence. Priorities from a Philosophical, Ethical, Legal, and Technological Viewpoint as a Basis for Certification of Artificial Intelligence. Fraunhofer Institute for Intelligent Analysis and Information Systems IAIS Schloss Birlinghoven (2019)
10. From Principles to Practice. An interdisciplinary framework to operationalise AI ethics. VDE, Bertelsmann Stiftung (2020)
11. Marselis, R., Shaukat, H., Gansel, T.: Testing of Artificial Intelligence. Sogeti, Paris (2017)
12. Marselis, R., Shaukat, H.: Machine Intelligence Quality Characteristics. How to Measure the Quality of Artificial Intelligence and Robotics. Sogeti, Paris (2018)
13. Nakajima, S.: Quality assurance of machine learning software. In: 2018 IEEE 7th Global Conference on Consumer Electronics (GCCE), 9–12 October 2018, pp. 601–604. IEEE, Piscataway (2018)
14. Mariscal, G., Marbán, Ó., Fernández, C.: A survey of data mining and knowledge discovery process models and methodologies. Knowl. Eng. Rev. 25, 137–166 (2010)
15. Martinez-Plumed, F., et al.: CRISP-DM twenty years later: from data mining processes to data science trajectories. IEEE Trans. Knowl. Data Eng. 1 (2020)
16. Lwakatare, L.E., Raj, A., Bosch, J., Olsson, H.H., Crnkovic, I.: A taxonomy of software engineering challenges for machine learning systems: an empirical investigation. In: Kruchten, P., Fraser, S., Coallier, F. (eds.) XP 2019. LNBIP, vol. 355, pp. 227–243. Springer, Cham (2019). https://doi.org/10.1007/978-3-030-19034-7_14
17. Amershi, S., et al.: Software engineering for machine learning: a case study. In: 2019 IEEE/ACM 41st International Conference on Software Engineering: Software Engineering in Practice (ICSE-SEIP), pp. 291–300 (2019)
18. Hossin, M., Sulaiman, M.N.: A review on evaluation metrics for data classification evaluations. IJDKP 5, 1–11 (2015)
19. Emmons, S., Kobourov, S., Gallant, M., Börner, K.: Analysis of network clustering algorithms and cluster quality metrics at scale. PLoS ONE 11, e0159161 (2016)
20. Barocas, S., Boyd, D.: Engaging the ethics of data science in practice. Commun. ACM 60, 23–25 (2017)
21. Kleinberg, J., Mullainathan, S., Raghavan, M.: Inherent Trade-Offs in the Fair Determination of Risk Scores. arXiv.org (2016)
22. Wagner, S., et al.: Operationalised product quality models and assessment: the Quamoco approach. Inf. Softw. Technol. 62, 101–123 (2015)
23. Kaufman, S., Rosset, S., Perlich, C.: Leakage in data mining. In: Apte, C., Ghosh, J., Smyth, P. (eds.) Proceedings of the 17th ACM SIGKDD International Conference on Knowledge Discovery and Data Mining, San Diego, Ca, USA, 21–24 August 2011, p. 556. ACM, New York (2011)

24. Kläs, M., Vollmer, A.M.: Uncertainty in machine learning applications: a practice-driven classification of uncertainty. In: Gallina, B., Skavhaug, A., Schoitsch, E., Bitsch, F. (eds.) SAFECOMP 2018. LNCS, vol. 11094, pp. 431–438. Springer, Cham (2018). https://doi.org/10.1007/978-3-319-99229-7_36
25. Nakamichi, K., et al.: Requirements-driven method to determine quality characteristics and measurements for machine learning software and its evaluation. In: 28th IEEE International Requirements Engineering Conference (RE'20)

Data Cleaning: A Case Study with OpenRefine and Trifacta Wrangler

Dessislava Petrova-Antonova$^{(\boxtimes)}$ and Rumyana Tancheva

GATE Institute, Sofia University "St. Kl. Ohridski", Sofia, Bulgaria
d.petrova@fmi.uni-sofia.bg, rumy.tancheva@gmail.com

Abstract. Data cleaning is the most time-consuming activity in data science projects aimed at delivery high-quality datasets to provide accuracy of the corresponding trained models. Due to variability of the data types and formats, data origin and acquisition, different data quality problems arise leading to development of variety cleaning techniques and tools. This paper provides a mapping between nature, scope and dimension of data quality problems and a comparative analysis of widely used tools dealing with those problems. The existing data cleaning techniques serve as a basis for comparing the cleaning capabilities of the tools. Furthermore, a cases study addressing the presented data quality problems and cleaning techniques is presented utilizing one of the commonly used software products OpenRefine and Trifacta Wrangler. Although the application of the similar data cleaning techniques on the same dataset, the results show that the performance of the tools is different.

Keywords: Data cleaning · Data quality · Data cleaning techniques and tools

1 Introduction

According to IDC, the collective sum of the world's data will grow to a 175ZB by 2025, [1]. The management and analysis of such unprecedented amount of data is a key success factor to exploit benefits of it. It has estimated that up to 80% of the effort of data scientists is spent on preparing the data for the analytics, where data cleaning constitutes up to 60% [2], which is often neglected. Since data acquisition methods often cause problems such as out-of-range values, missing values and impossible data combinations, analyzing data without cleaning produces inaccurate and undesirable results. Data cleaning is one of the most critical steps in AI projects, removing data violations and providing data quality.

This paper provides an insight into data anomalies. The current software tools and platforms for data cleaning are analyzed based on the supported data preparation methods, including data cleaning. The main research question is how effective are currently available tools in preparation of the data for analytics. In order to answer it, two software tools are selected from the analyzed ones to complete a particular scenario.

The rest of the paper is structured as follows. Section 2 outlines data quality problems and presents a comparison analysis of the most commonly used data cleaning tools. Section 3 describes a case study by using the software tools OpenRefine and Trifacta

© Springer Nature Switzerland AG 2020
M. Shepperd et al. (Eds.): QUATIC 2020, CCIS 1266, pp. 32–40, 2020.
https://doi.org/10.1007/978-3-030-58793-2_3

Wrangler to show a practical application of data cleaning techniques. Section 4 discusses the obtained results. Finally, Sect. 5 summarizes the paper.

2 Data Quality and Cleaning

Producing high quality datasets require data problems to be identified and cleaned using different data cleaning techniques. Although there are different taxonomies and methodologies of data anomalies [3–6], to the best of our knowledge a command accepted definition does not exists. This is due to the diversity of data quality violations data types, formats and domains. Thus, a lot of methods for detection of data quality problems are proposed, but neither of them fit in all situations. The dimension of data quality is a feature of the data that can be used to assess the quality of data. The state-of-the-art literature includes various definitions of data quality dimensions [7, 8] such as Consistency, Completeness, Uniqueness, Accuracy, Validity and Timeless. Regarding the scope, the data quality problems occur in cell values, column headers, rows or in cell values and column headers at the same time [9]. In order to speed-up the process of data preparation

Table 1. Data preparation and cleaning tools.

Data cleaning techniques	Clean & match	Rapid miner	TIBCO clarity	Data ladder	OpenRefine	Trifacta	DataCleaner
Data profiling	●	●	●	●	●	●	●
Missing values	●	●	●	●	●	●	●
Fuzzy matching	●	●	●	●	●	●	●
Outliers	○	●	●	○	●	●	●
Spelling variations	●	○	○	○	●	●	●
Email address validation	●	○	●	○	○	●	●
Data standardization	●	○	●	●	○	●	●
Phone number validation	○	○	●	○	●	●	●
Data aggregation	○	●	●	○	○	●	●
Clustering	○	●	● (cells)	○	●	○	○
Data enrichment	○	●	○	●	●	●	○
De-duplication	●	●	●	●	●	●	●
Language	N/A	R, Groovy	GREL	N/A	GREL	Wrangler	JavaScript

and cleaning, an automation is needed. One of the most commonly used tools are Win-Pure Clean & Match, RapidMiner, TIBCO Clarity, Data Ladder, OpenRefine, Trifacta and Data Cleaner, which comparison is shown in Table 1.

The tools differ in supported data formats, techniques for data filtering, enrichment, clustering, etc. For example, WinPure Clean & Match and Data Ladder adopt the fuzzy matching technique to match keying errors and transpositions and reading errors or to visually score matches, assign weights, and group non-exact matches. The fuzzy logic is also used by Data Cleaner to customize cleansing rules and compose them into several scenarios. TIBCO Clarity and Openefine supports the General Refine Expression Language (GREL) for data manipulation, including transformation and normalization, while RapidMiner and Trifacta are based on Groovy and Wrangler languages respectively. Data Ladder and Trifacta implement advanced functionality for data enrichment, ensuring that the new data is also cleaned.

3   Case Study

This section presents a case study showing the application of the existing data cleaning techniques on a sample dataset using OpenRefine and Trifacta tools. A sample dataset including information about scientific journals is downloaded [10]. The dataset contains 11 377 rows with information for scholarship journals. The journals are described in 5 columns: ISSN, journal_name, pub_name, is_hybrid, category and url.

3.1   Data Cleaning with OpenRefine

This section presents the implementation of data cleaning with OpenRefine.

Cleaning of Structural Errors. The cleaning of structural errors is started with the ISSN column by removing leading and trailing whitespaces as well as the consecutive whitespaces. Next, the data format of the values of the ISSN column is checked. 1 row is found, where the values of the ISSN and "journal_name" columns are switched. In addition, an ASCII table is used to check the ISSNs for invalid characters. During the cleaning of the "journal_name" column, clusters of similar string values are identified and for each one the right journal title is selected based on the title corresponding to the ISSN in web. The fast and simple clustering method is "Fingerprint", shown in Fig. 1.

"N-Gram Fingerprint" is an alternative method of "Fingerprint". The only difference is that it uses n-grams instead of tokens. The "N-Gram Fingerprint" method doesn't have advantages over the "Fingerprint" method, when big values for n-grams are used. When 1-grams and 2-grams are used the method finds clusters that the previous method cannot discover. The "Phonetic Fingerprint" is a method that transforms tokens into the way they are pronounced. It is appliable when there are errors caused by people misunderstanding or bad spelling.

Some of the cells of the "journal_name" column store multiple values, namely the journal title and additional information related to the open access of the journal or journal URL. A new column "Comments" are created to store the additional information, which is not part of the journal title. The data in the "pub_name", "category" and "url" columns are processed in a similar way. The results are presented in Table 2.

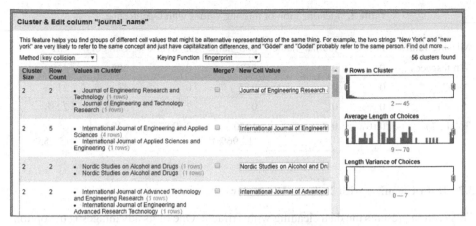

Fig. 1. Application of the "Fingerprint" method with OpenRefine.

Table 2. Processed fields with OpenRefine.

Clustering method	journal_name	pub_name	Category	Url
"n-gram fingerprint"	22	207	132	4
"fingerprint"	21	2	0	0
"phonetic fingerprint"	3	22	0	0
Total number of processed fields	46	231	132	4

Duplicate Rows Removal. The searching for duplicate rows is performed on the ISSN column of the dataset by using the Duplicates facet command of OpenRefine. 3 duplicate ISSNs are found. The rows with ISSN "0001-527X" and those with ISSNs "0024-4937" are identical and 1 row from each pair id removed. The information of the second pair of rows with ISSN "0004-1254" matches only by the ISSN, which indicates data inconsistency. The ISSN value is corrected by manual checking in the web.

Outliers Removal. The allowed values for the column "is_hybrid" can be either 0 or 1 and any other value is interpreted as outlier. In order to identify whether the journal is with open or closed access, a manual search in the web is performed.

Identification of Missing Values. In order to identify missing values, all cells containing "nan", "NULL" or whitespaces are found (see Table 3).

The "pub_name" column contains 1470 missing values, which is 12.96% from the total number of records. Thus, it is not recommended to delete them, because a lot of data will be lost. The missing values are filled with a string value "missing" to indicate that the corresponding cells does not contain valuable information.

Table 3. Identification of missing values with OpenRefine.

Missing values	Issn	journal_name	pub_name	is_hybrid	Category	Url
Whitespaces	0	0	553	0	205	4289
"nan"	0	0	917	0	42	21
"NULL"	0	0	0	2	5856	2238
Total (%)	0 (0%)	0 (0%)	1470 (12.96%)	2 (0.02%)	6103 (53.65%)	6548 (57.55%)

3.2 Data Cleaning with Trifacta Wrangler

This section presents the data cleaning with Trifacta. One of its advantages is the option to record the applied data processing steps as a "Recipe" procedure. This allows for application the same procedure to different datasets with similar problems.

Cleaning of Structural Errors. Since Trifacta enables the same operation to be applied to multiple columns, the leading and trailing whitespaces and quotes are quickly removed from all columns, except the "is_hybrid" column. Next, the values in the ISSN column are processed. There is 1 record, which ISSN exceeds the maximum allowed length (9 characters). The values of the ISSN and "journal_name" columns are switched for that record. In order to check the exact format of the values in the ISSN column a regular expression is defined using the Wrangler language. Additional column, called "ISSN1" is created, where all valued that match the regular expression are copied and the rest are represented with whitespaces. The records with the last character of the ISSN written with a lowercase "x" are found and corrected. The values in the "journal_name" column are unified by using the "N-Gram Fingerprint" method. In addition, "Fingerprint" and "Pronunciation" methods are applied to achieve more precise results. The "Pronunciation" method identifies clusters based on the language pronunciation using the "Double Metaphone"algorithm. The results are summarized in Table 4.

Table 4. Processed fields with Trifacta Wragler.

Clustering method	journal_name	pub_name	Category	Url
"n-gram fingerprint"	21	206	132	4
"fingerprint"	21	5	0	0
"phonetic fingerprint"	1	8	0	0
Total number of processed fields	43	219	132	4

The "journal_name" column has cells with additional to the journal title information, which should be moved to a separate column. All values, which length is between 91 and 119 characters are kept in their initial state. The remain values are manually processed and redundant information is moved to a new "Comments" column.

Duplicate Rows Removal. Trifacta gives a quick overview for the current status of a given column. Figure 2 shows a summary for the ISSN column. The duplicated records with ISSN 0001-527X and 0024-4937 are deleted. The records with ISSN 0004-1254 have different values in the "journal_name" column. After checking, it was found that the ISSN of the Journal "Arquivos De Neuro-Psiquiatria" is wrong. Unfortunately, Trifacta does not provide an easy way for modification of single values. Its functionality is oriented towards modification of multiple fields that meet a given criterion.

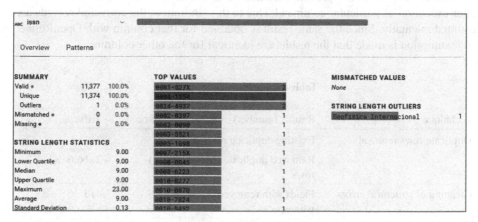

Fig. 2. ISSN summary report by Trifacta Wrangler.

Outliers Removal. Trifacta Wrangler found only one outlier for the "is_hybrid" column with value 2. Based on the experiment with OpenRefine, this value is changed to 1.

Identification of Missing Values. The missing values are those represented with "nan", "NULL" or whitespaces. Unfortunately, Trifacta identifies only the whitespaces and marks them with "NULL". Therefore, additional operations are applied in order to be identified all missing values, including those represented with "nan" and "NULL". A summary of the identified missing values is presented in Table 5. Again, the missing values are filled with a string value "missing" for the purpose of analysis.

Table 5. Identification of missing values with Trifacta Wrangler.

Missing values	Issn	journal_name	pub_name	is_hybrid	Category	Url
Whitespaces	0	0	553	0	205	4289
"nan"	0	0	917	0	42	21
"NULL"	0	0	0	2	5856	2238
Total (%)	0 (0%)	0 (0%)	1470 (12.96%)	2 (0.02%)	6103 (53.65%)	6548 (57.55%)

4 Result Analysis

Although the same data cleaning techniques are applied, the performance of each tool is different (see Table 6) and each one has different advantages and disadvantages (see Table 7). Trifacta does not catch all duplicate rows, since it does not allow editing of single field, if there are several fields suitable for processing. The result obtained by the Trifacta for number of fields with removed whitespaces is based on an assumption, because the tool does not provide information about the number of changed records after execution of particular command. Due to this limitation, the corrected records are counted manually. Since the same result is obtained for that column with OpenRefine, an assumption is made that the results are identical for the other columns.

Table 6. Summary of results.

Technique	Results (number)	OpenRefine	Trifacta
Duplicate rows removal	Existing duplicate rows	3	3
	Removed duplicate rows	3 (100%)	2 (66.66%)
Cleaning of structural errors	Fields with removed whitespaces	413	413
	Fields with incorrect format	6	6
	Fields with corrected format	6 (100%)	6 (100%)
Clustering of text facets	Unified fields	413	98
Outliers	Existing outliers	1	1
	Removed outliers	1 (100%)	1 (100%)
Missing values	Existing missing values	14123	14123
	Identified missing values	14123 (100%)	14123 (100%)

There is also a difference in the results for the number of unified fields. This is due to the differences in the implementation of "Fingerprint" and "N-Gram Fingerprint" methods. The tools use different techniques to split the strings into tokens. OpenRefine clears the punctuation and control characters first, and then the strings are split into sections using blank spaces. Trifacta uses empty spaces or punctuation and control characters as delimiters, which are not removed in advance. This leads to differences in the proposed groups for unification, although both tools use the same methods. For example, the group, including "Parkinson's Disease" and "Parkinsons Disease", is not treated in the same way. OpenRefine detects it based on the "Fingerprint" method, while Trifacta detects it only if the "Pronunciation" method is applied. The differences in the results are also

Table 7. Tools' advantages and disadvantages.

	Advantages	Disadvantages
OpenRefine	(1) Easy modification of a single field; (2) The field is not necessary to satisfy a given criterion to be changed; (3) Multiple records processing; (4) Statistics on the number of records processed with a given operation	(1) Doesn't support processing of large datasets
Trifacta	(1) Record the applied data processing steps as a "Recipe" procedure; (2) Non-blocking processing of large datasets; (3) Supports easier to use functions; (4) Different method for filling the missing values	(1) Single field cannot be modified; (2) Allows only modification of multiple fields that meet a given criterion; (3) Missing information for the number of records processed with a given operation

due to the third method of clustering. Trifacta uses the "Double Metaphone" method, while OpenRefine uses the "Phonetic Fingerprint" method ("Metaphone 3" and "Co-longe Phonetic"). The application of the "Metaphone 3" method is thought to increase the accuracy of results from 89% to 98% in comparison to the "Double Metaphone" method for the most common English words [11]. The number of removed outliers and missing values are the same for both tools.

5 Conclusions

Data preparation and especially data cleaning is the most time and effort consuming task of the most data science projects. This leads to development of a broad range of data cleaning techniques and tools that handle variety data quality problems. This paper outlines data quality problems providing a mapping between its nature, scope and dimension. The most commonly used tools and platforms for data cleaning are studied and compared according to the supported data cleaning techniques. In order to provide more deep understanding of data quality issues, a sample case study is performed using two different data cleaning tools, namely OpenRefine and Trifacta Wrangler. The results show that the performance of the tools is different although the application of the similar data cleaning techniques on the same dataset.

Acknowledgements. This research work has been supported by GATE project, funded by the Horizon 2020 WIDESPREAD-2018-2020 TEAMING Phase 2 programme under grant agreement no. 857155 and Big4Smart and ITDGate projects, funded by the Bulgarian National Science fund, under agreement no. DN12/9 and agreement no. DN 02/11.

References

1. Reinsel, D., Gantz, J., Rydning, J.: The Digitization of the World. IDC White Paper (2018)
2. CrowdFlower, Data Science, Report (2016). https://visit.figure-eight.com/rs/416-ZBE-142/images/CrowdFlower_DataScienceReport_2016.pdf. Accessed 17 Mar 2020
3. Sebestyen, G., Hangan, A., Czako, Z., Kovacs, G.: A taxonomy and platform for anomaly detection. In: International Conference on Automation, Quality and Testing, Robotics, pp. 1–6 (2018)
4. Batini, C., Barone, D., Mastrella, M., Maurino, A., Ruffini, C.: A framework and a methodology for data quality assessment and monitoring. In: International Conference on Information Quality, pp. 333–346 (2007)
5. Kim, W., Choi, B., Kim, S., Lee, D.: A taxonomy of dirty data. Data Min. Knowl. Disc. **7**, 81–99 (2003)
6. Josko, J.M.B., Oikawa, M.K., Ferreira, J.E.: A formal taxonomy to improve data defect description. In: Gao, H., Kim, J., Sakurai, Y. (eds.) DASFAA 2016. LNCS, vol. 9645, pp. 307–320. Springer, Cham (2016). https://doi.org/10.1007/978-3-319-32055-7_25
7. Sidi, F., Panahy, P.H.S., Affendey, L.S., Jabar, M., Ibrahim, H., Mustapha, A.: Data quality: a survey of data quality dimensions. In: International Conference on Information Retrieval & Knowledge Management. IEEE (2012)
8. Laranjeiro, N., Soydemir, S.N., Bernardino, J.: A survey on data quality: classifying poor data. In: 21st Pacific Rim International Symposium on Dependable Computing (PRDC), IEEE (2015)
9. Sukhobok, D., Nikolov, N., Roman, D.: Tabular data anomaly patterns. In: International Conference on Big Data Innovations and Applications (Innovate-Data), IEEE (2017)
10. https://github.com/FlourishOA/Data. Accessed 03 Feb 2020
11. Chan, K., Vasardani, M., Winter, S.: Getting lost in cities: spatial patterns of phonetically confusing street names. Trans. GIS **19**(4), 535–562 (2014)

NSP Dataset and Offline Signature Verification

Dmitry V. Bakhteev[1]([✉]) [iD] and Roman Sudarikov[2] [iD]

[1] Department of Criminalistics,
Ural State Law University, Yekaterinburg, Russian Federation
ae@crimlib.info
[2] Institute of Formal and Applied Linguistics,
Charles University, Prague, Czech Republic
sudarikov@ufal.mff.cuni.cz

Abstract. Offline signature verification is a challenging task for both computer science and forensics. Skilled forgeries often cannot be recognized by humans, which leads to the need to develop automated forged signatures recognition methods, which in turn requires the creation of different datasets for training models, which include the NSP – the first dataset with Cyrillic offline signatures, including genuine signatures with their skilled and simple forgeries. The process of collecting data for this dataset is described in detail. In the process of collecting samples we reformulated the forensic classification of signatures by criterion of their structure and forgery vulnerability. Gathered database was evaluated using a Siamese neural network model and the results are compared with the same model trained on CEDAR dataset.

Keywords: Offline signature verification · Signature forensics · Siamese neural networks

1 Introduction

In the history of mankind, dozens of different methods of remote identification of person have been created, introduced and lost. Handwritten signatures turned out to be the most stable and suitable for use as props for documents used in economic and law enforcement activities, mainly due to their comparative ease of execution and non-invasive methods of receipt. In forensics, the signature carries an identification and diagnostic value. Identification allows to establish a specific performer of signature, determine whether it is genuine or forged. Two objects are always involved in the identification process, the authenticity of one of which is always precisely known. Diagnostics of the signature allows to establish the characteristics of its performer: both their identity and some personality traits.

Forgeries from the point of view of the method of their performing can be divided into three types: auto-forgery, simple and skilled forgeries. In the case of auto-forgery, the performer is the owner of the signature, the purpose of such

© Springer Nature Switzerland AG 2020
M. Shepperd et al. (Eds.): QUATIC 2020, CCIS 1266, pp. 41–49, 2020.
https://doi.org/10.1007/978-3-030-58793-2_4

an action is the alleged future refusal to recognize the document as properly signed. In the case of simple forgeries within the framework of this study, we understand forgeries, for the creation of which forger had knowledge about the signer's name and examples of his handwritten signatures. We do not recognize as such signatures made without an images of the signer's signature [3]. Of course, in cases of law enforcement, such cases do occur, but their resolving is not a big problem due to the low similarity between existing genuine documents and forged ones. Skilled forgeries are performed not only in the presence of examples of genuine signatures, but also with the help of special skills of the forger.

Whole signature verification field can be divided into two main categories by acquisition type: online and offline verification. Online signature verification deals with analysis of the signatures while they are captured using a digitizing device and takes into the account sequence of the strokes over time, pen position, pen pressure, etc. Offline verification on the other hand acquires the signature after the process is finished, most commonly in a form of a digital image.

The practical scope of combining forensic methods with the possibilities of offline signature recognition expands the possibilities of identification processes in civil, commercial and law enforcement activities and expands communication between academic disciplines and practice.

The outline of the paper is the following: Sect. 2 is devoted to the review of related works in the field of signature verification, Sect. 3 describes the process of collecting NSP dataset and processing done around it. Section 4 discusses some of the forensic discoveries made during the dataset collection, and Sect. 5 details the assessment experiments carried out using collected dataset. Finally, Sect. 6 concludes the paper with future work.

2   Related Works

Most of the recent advancements in the field of offline signature verification including the researches of Deep Learning methods are described by [3]. The work reviewed both most commonly used datasets (CEDAR [4], MCYT [5] and GPDS [8]) and different approaches to offline signature verification, starting from classic Machine Learning algorithms such as Support Vector Machines (SVM) and Hidden Markov Models, followed by Deep Neural Networks and classifiers ensembles. Here it is also appropriate to mention two different types of verification models, which are *writer-independent* and *writer-dependent*. As it is clear from the names, the former models can be applied to any signature verification task, independently of whether or not they saw the subject's signatures in the training set. The latter models though need to be exposed to the subject's signatures during the training.

There are also different approaches in feature extraction and Convolutional Neural Networks (CNN) composition, as presented by [1] and [7]. The former introduced SigNet – convolutional Siamese neural network, which learns writer independent features and shows good performance on cross domain datasets. The latter showed performance improvements by combining CNN feature extraction with SVM writer-independent classifier.

As it was mentioned previously currently there are several benchmark datasets in the field of signature verification: CEDAR [4], MCYT[5], GPDS [8] and BHSig260 [6]. Characteristics of NSP dataset in comparison with some other existing datasets are presented in Table 1.

Table 1. Comparison of offline signature datasets

	Handwriting system	Signers	Signatures (genuine/forged)
NSP	Cyrillic	224	40 562 (12 596/28 056)
CEDAR	Latin	55	2640 (1320/1320)
MCYT	Latin	330	16 500 (8250/8250)
GPDS-960	Latin	960	51 849 (23 049/28 800)
BHSig260	Bangla, Hindi	260	14 040 (6240/7800)

3   NSP Dataset Collection

The NSP handwritten signature dataset contains 56 genuine signatures and from 112 to 224 corresponding forgeries for one signer. The genuine signatures were taken from signers in two-sheets form, each including 28 boxes for signatures and fields for some information about signer (name, age, dominant hand). Such a quantity is explained by the fact that, in order to obtain reliable knowledge about the degree of variational changes in the signature of one person, it is necessary to consistently receive at least 50 signatures according to the methods of production of handwriting examinations. In the end of this process, most signers lose focus, their hand gets tired, then control over the accuracy of movements decreases and the signature becomes more automatic, so we receive an almost full space of possible signatures variations. Smaller amounts of signatures may not give reliable results.

Table 2. Distribution of the NSP signature dataset.

	Signers	Avg age	Right-/Left-handedness	Genuine	Forgeries (skilled/simple)
Male	100	28	76/6	5 600	12 383 (6 212/6 171)
Female	123	29	92/6	6 940	15 561 (7 784/7 777)
Total	224	29	168/12	12 596	28 056 (14 052/14 004)

It should be noted that the signatures of the residents of the Russian Federation are usually Cyrillic (with rare exceptions), which distinguishes the NSP dataset from those described earlier in Sect. 2.

Fig. 1. Left signature (genuine) has a vertical stroke (marked), while the left one (unskilled forgery) lacks it.

Fig. 2. Example of signature, crossing both signature line and vertical lines of the box.

Forgeries were made in both skilled and unskilled (simple) forms. Skilled forgeries were done by group of 12 people, each of them with an experience either in artistry or forensic examination of handwritten documents. Our hypothesis was that such skills will allow forger to make an almost exact copy of given signature, either on the basis of its graphical appearance – in case of artists, or by understanding forensic features of signature – for forensic experts. Unskilled (simple) forgeries were done by people with no experience in handwriting examination and/or signature forgery, so forgers often lost sight of one or another characteristic of the forged signature (see example on Fig. 1).

Every forger (in both skilled and unskilled situations) was provided by two sheets of genuine signatures, so they knew name of signer, his age, so they have an ability to transcript questioned symbols in a signature correctly. Signatures of left-handed signers were forged only by left-handed forgers; then both left-handed and right-handed forgers were involved in making forgeries for right-handed signatures. Forgers independently chose which exact signatures they would copy. This decision was made as a simulation of the situation of a real document forgery when it is not known exactly which signatures are used as a sample for forgery.

Forgeries were also done on the forms of 28 boxes, so the resulting set of signatures for one person contains 2 sheets of genuine signatures and from 4 to 8 sheets with forgeries. Forgeries were prepared without the use of special technical means, such as use of a plotter, transfer paper, wet copying, source of background lighting, etc.

After that, the resulting sheets with genuine signatures and forgeries were scanned at a resolution of 600 DPI; the digital images were divided into separate images with one signature per image. Individual images of signatures were obtained by automatically cutting the image of the sheet along the lines of the form and then manually trimming each signature to the borders of the rectangle at the extreme points of the signature. If the signature strokes cross the line of the box, such signature was left in the dataset. Additionally, in forms with later samples, we used imitation of the signature line in the bottom four rows of the form. Accordingly, both horizontal and vertical lines can be found on the obtained images (see an example in Fig. 2). In any case, offline signature verification technologies are practice-oriented, and signatures in practice are usually

Fig. 3. Examples of signatures of type 1, containing several letters.

Fig. 4. Examples of signatures of type 2, containing some of the first letters of the last name of the signer with possible initials.

combined with other details of the document, like seals' imprints and lines of the form of the document.

Statistical data about the composition of NSP dataset are summarized in Table 2. Some signers did not provide information about themselves, this explains the inconsistencies in the Table 2.

The whole process of gathering genuine signatures was accomplished under the supervision of a project team member. Forgers (both categories) were given instructions, and the results of their work were carefully checked. All participants in the experiment were instructed on the rules for working with personal data, the corresponding confirmation was taken from them.

4 Types of Signatures

According to the design and composition of signatures of residents of the Russian Federation such signatures can be conditionally differentiated into four types:

1. Signatures based on the performance of several letters (usually from 1 to 3), which have low readability and low resistance to forgery methods (Fig. 3).
2. Signatures containing some initials and the first few letters of the surname, most characters are readable. This archetype is dominant in Russia, because it combines the speed of execution and the overall complexity sufficient to counter simple forgery methods, expressed in a significant number of private features displayed in the signature. Usually such signatures are stretched horizontally (Fig. 4).
3. Signatures, which are the spelling of a last name (often together with the name and patronymic) without complicating or simplifying elements, the usual handwriting for the performer (Fig. 5). Those signatures are usually not well defended against forgery due to their slower pace of performance, while other types of signatures are performed with an increased pace compared to regular writing of the signer.
4. Signatures-drawings of complex design, consisting of conditional elements that do not form letters and having mainly superscript-subscript elegant,

Fig. 5. Examples of signatures of type 3, containing full last name of the signer.

Fig. 6. Examples of letterless signatures of type 4.

Table 3. Experiment datasets

	Signers	Genuine (per signer)	Forgeries (per Genuine)	Total pairs
CEDAR				
Train	40	24	24	34 080
Validation	10	24	24	8 520
Test	5	24	24	4 260
NSP				
Train	138	56	30	444 360
Validation	40	56	30	128 800
Test	10	56	30	32 200

elaborate strokes of a complex structure. They are complex systems of multidirectional movements overlapping each other, movements of a complicated structure, usually with continuous connectivity. Their resistance to forging methods varies (Fig. 6).

5   Experiments

To demonstrate the relative complexity of the dataset, it was decided to take one of the best performing models, namely convolutional Siamese neural network model [1] and show it's performance on NSP dataset as well as CEDAR [4] dataset.

For the experiments, we have separated NSP dataset described above into 3 parts: training, validation and test. Distribution was the following - 138 signers used in the training, 40 – in validation and 10 in test. Signers were assigned randomly at the beginning of each experiment run, to provide more consistent and reliable results. For each signer we have used 56 genuine signatures and for each genuine signature we have picked 30 forgeries at random to have a balanced number of genuine-genuine and genuine-forged samples.

An experiment was carried out using CEDAR [4] dataset, to serve as a reference point for the used model. For CEDAR dataset we have used 40 signers for training, 10 for validation and 5 for test. For each signer we have used all 24 available genuine signatures and 24 available forgeries

Final setup for experiments on both NSP and CEDAR datasets is shown in Table 3. For both experiments, signature samples were resized to 220 × 155 pixels to normalize signature sizes and keep the input vector space reasonably small.

Models setup followed [1] approach with similar layer configuration with implementation done using Keras framework with Tensorflow as backend. To show that trained model is comparable with the results in [1], it was evaluated first on CEDAR [4] dataset and then on NSP dataset.

Both experiments were following the same evaluation steps. The best epoch was selected based on contrastive loss function [2] value on the validation set. The output of a model is a distance metric, which doesn't directly predicts the class of images, but rather the distance between them. Thus a threshold is needed to be determined to decide if the input images belong to the same class or not, i.e. if both signatures are genuine or one is forged. In the experiments the same validation set was used to estimate the best threshold to map output distance value to binary classes. This estimated threshold was then used to translate the output of the model on the test set samples into the binary classes.

Table 4. Experiment results

Dataset	FAR	FRR	Accuracy
CEDAR	8.33	0.00	94.37
NSP (9-runs mean)	17.80 ± 2.22	20.56 ± 2.60	80.87 ± 1.39

5.1   Experiment Results

The results for both NSP and CEDAR datasets are presented in the Table 4, with the following metrics: False Rejection Rate (FRR), False Acceptance Rate (FAR) and accuracy. FRR is computed as a ratio of false negative samples divided by the total number of positive samples. FAR is computed as a ratio of false positive samples divided by the total number of negative samples. Accuracy is computed as a ratio between a sum of all true positive and true negative predicted pairs and a sum of all number of pairs examined.

For CEDAR experiment, FRR is the same as in the results by [1], but FAR and accuracy differ, which can be attributed to the way loss function threshold is estimated in current experiment, since validation set is specifically used to estimate the threshold value for output separation. Table 5 shows resulting confusion matrix with the exact numbers. The results show that the model performs on a comparable level to the similar works.

Table 5. CEDAR confusion matrix

		True	
		Genuine	Forged
Predicted	Genuine	1 380	240
	Forged	0	2 640

Table 6. NSP confusion matrix

		True	
		Genuine	Forged
Predicted	Genuine	12 995	3 496
	Forged	2 405	13 304

NSP experiment was run nine times and the mean results with 95% confidence interval were reported in the Table 4. For NSP experiment, the results are lower than CEDAR ones, which could be attributed to higher complexity and diversity of the signatures in NSP dataset. Confusion matrix presented in Table 6 shows the results for one of the experiment runs just to give an idea of the predictions distribution.

6   Conclusion/Discussion

Siamese neural network model showed promising results as well as left the room for potential improvements.

In out future work on the models we are planning to evaluate different model architectures on NSP dataset as well as work more on cross-dataset experiments where models would be trained on NSP dataset and then tested on GPDS and MCYT datasets to see how well the model can generalize features which could be transferred between different script.

The collection of signature samples for the dataset is not completed (and, hopefully, will not be), several hundred new signatures are included in it weekly, which allows increasing both the size and variety of data.

Acknowledgements. The reported study was funded by RFBR according to the research project № 18-29-16001.

References

1. Dey, S., Dutta, A., Toledo, J.I., Ghosh, S.K., Lladós, J., Pal, U.: Signet: convolutional siamese network for writer independent offline signature verification. arXiv preprint arXiv:1707.02131 (2017)
2. Hadsell, R., Chopra, S., LeCun, Y.: Dimensionality reduction by learning an invariant mapping. In: 2006 IEEE Computer Society Conference on Computer Vision and Pattern Recognition (CVPR 2006), vol. 2, pp. 1735–1742. IEEE (2006)
3. Hafemann, L.G., Sabourin, R., Oliveira, L.S.: Offline handwritten signature verification–literature review. In: 2017 Seventh International Conference on Image Processing Theory, Tools and Applications (IPTA), pp. 1–8. IEEE (2017)
4. Kalera, M.K., Srihari, S., Xu, A.: Offline signature verification and identification using distance statistics. Int. J. Pattern Recogn. Artif. Intell. **18**(07), 1339–1360 (2004)

5. Ortega-Garcia, J., et al.: MCYT baseline corpus: a bimodal biometric database. IEE Proc.-Vision Image Signal Process. **150**(6), 395–401 (2003)
6. Pal, S., Alaei, A., Pal, U., Blumenstein, M.: Performance of an off-line signature verification method based on texture features on a large indic-script signature dataset. In: 2016 12th IAPR Workshop on Document Analysis Systems (DAS), pp. 72–77 (2016)
7. Souza, V.L., Oliveira, A.L., Sabourin, R.: A writer-independent approach for offline signature verification using deep convolutional neural networks features. In: 2018 7th Brazilian Conference on Intelligent Systems (BRACIS), pp. 212–217. IEEE (2018)
8. Vargas, F., Ferrer, M., Travieso, C., Alonso, J.: Off-line handwritten signature GPDS-960 corpus. In: Ninth International Conference on Document Analysis and Recognition (ICDAR 2007), vol. 2, pp. 764–768. IEEE (2007)

Evidence-Based Software Quality Engineering

Applying Machine Learning in Technical Debt Management: Future Opportunities and Challenges

Angeliki-Agathi Tsintzira, Elvira-Maria Arvanitou[✉], Apostolos Ampatzoglou, and Alexander Chatzigeorgiou

Department of Applied Informatics, University of Macedonia, Thessaloniki, Greece
angeliki.agathi.tsintzira@gmail.com,
{e.arvanitou,a.ampatzoglou}@uom.edu.gr, achat@uom.gr

Abstract. Technical Debt Management (TDM) is a fast-growing field that in the last years has attracted the attention of both academia and industry. TDM is a complex process, in the sense that it relies on multiple and heterogeneous data sources (e.g., source code, feature requests, bugs, developers' activity, etc.), which cannot be straightforwardly synthesized; leading the community to using mostly qualitative empirical methods. However, empirical studies that involve expert judgement are inherently biased, compared to automated or semi-automated approaches. To overcome this limitation, the broader (not TDM) software engineering community has started to employ machine learning (ML) technologies. Our goal is to investigate the opportunity of applying ML technologies for TDM, through a Systematic Literature Review (SLR) on the application of ML to software engineering problems (since ML applications on TDM are limited). Thus, we have performed a broader scope study, i.e., on machine learning for software engineering, and then synthesize the results so as to achieve our high-level goal (i.e., possible application of ML in TDM). Therefore, we have conducted a literature review, by browsing the research corpus published in five high-quality SE journals, with the goal of cataloging: (a) the software engineering practices in which ML is used; (b) the machine learning technologies that are used for solving them; and (c) the intersection of the two: developing a problem-solution mapping. The results are useful to both academics and industry, since the former can identify possible gaps, and interesting future research directions, whereas the latter can obtain benefits by adopting ML technologies.

Keywords: Machine learning · Software quality · Literature review · Technical Debt · Technical Debt Management

1 Introduction

Software quality is a multidisciplinary topic, in the sense that quality is about: (a) how well software meets users' needs, (b) how well software conforms to its specifications from the developers' point of view, (c) how well inherent, structural characteristics of

© Springer Nature Switzerland AG 2020
M. Shepperd et al. (Eds.): QUATIC 2020, CCIS 1266, pp. 53–67, 2020.
https://doi.org/10.1007/978-3-030-58793-2_5

the software are achieved from the product point of view, and (d) how much the end-user is willing to pay for it from the value point of view [20]. In recent years, the structural view of software quality is discussed through a metaphor, termed Technical Debt (TD), which valuates poor software quality and the incurred maintainability problems [21]. Technical Debt Management (TDM) refers to all activities that can be performed for guaranteeing the efficient handling of TD, e.g., identifying, measuring, prioritizing, repaying, etc. A significant portion of TDM research is nowadays performed through qualitative empirical studies. However, inherently qualitative studies are subject to bias, in the sense that they heavily rely on expert judgement.

To alleviate such subjectivity, in traditional software quality research, researchers are nowadays exploiting the large amount of data that are available through software repositories. Such data enable researchers to perform large-scale quantitative studies, and adopt modern techniques, such as machine learning to effectively carry out a specific task without relying on explicit instructions or rules. For example, supervised machine learning techniques have been used to build models that can predict the number of defects in software systems. Based on the aforementioned applicability of ML technologies, we believe that there is an opportunity to apply ML in technical debt management. Nevertheless, to the best of our knowledge in the current TDM state-of-the-art there are limited studies that propose the use of ML explicitly for TDM (e.g., [6, 26]). Despite the fact that for some constituents of TD, e.g., code smell detection or change proneness assessment, some unsupervised or supervised ML approaches have been applied (e.g., [10]) these studies do not focus on the financial perspective of TD (e.g., economics of code smells, refactorings, changes), but only on the technical view of the phenomenon.

The goal of this study is to investigate how ML can be applied for TDM, by studying existing literature. Since, the state-of-the-art lacks a substantial amount of studies, we conducted a broader secondary study, i.e., on how machine learning approaches have been used in software engineering (SE) practices, by conducting a systematic literature review (SLR). Next, we interpret these findings in the context of TDM. We note that the nature of this study is exploratory, in the sense that it aims at providing a panorama of the intersection of the two fields (ML and SE), without going into details. For instance, we do not aim to provide trend analysis, or explore the benefits obtained by the use of ML (this would require an explanatory research setting). The reasons for this decision is the fact that ML and SE are quite broad and a single study would not be able to cover both goals: therefore we believe that an exploratory study is first required so as to setup the research scene. Thus, the main outcome of this study is the provision of:

c1: The current *status* of research on combining ML and software engineering. In particular, we investigate which software engineering practices are approached through ML technologies.

c2: The *opportunities* of applying ML in TDM. To achieve this goal, we map software engineering practices, in which ML has already been applied, to TDM activities and concepts.

c3: The *challenges* for the adoption of ML in TDM research.

Section 2 presents related work (i.e., secondary studies on ML and SE) and background concepts of TDM. Next, Sect. 3 provides the literature review protocol, whereas,

Sect. 4 presents the results of the study. Section 5 discusses the status, opportunities and challenges of applying ML to TDM research, whereas Sect. 6 displays threats to validity. Finally, Sect. 7 concludes the paper, and provides the implications to researchers and software development industry.

2 Related Work and Background Information

Related Work. In the literature we have been able to identify only one secondary study that summarizes the use of machine learning in software engineering. In particular, Zhang et al. [28] have surveyed the literature to identify the most commonly used ML technologies that have been applied in software engineering, and provide some guidelines on how to perform ML in software engineering. The main differences of this study compared to ours are: (a) we use a more systematic approach for obtaining and analyzing studies—i.e., a survey instead of a SLR; and (b) that our study is mapping the obtained results in the context of TDM. In addition to that, we have identified secondary studies that focus on specific software engineering practices, and underline the importance of using ML technologies. More specifically, Sharma and Spinellis [25] and Azeem et al. [5] performed secondary studies on code smell detection technologies and acknowledged that many modern approaches employ machine learning algorithms. In a similar context Heckman et al. [11] performed a SLR on approaches for providing bad design alerts, through static analysis. Finally, various studies that de-livered overviews of cost/effort estimation approaches emphasize the popularity of ML technologies for providing more accurate estimates [13, 24, 27].

Background Information. The TD metaphor relies on two concepts borrowed from economics: namely principal and interest. TD principal refers to the effort required to eliminate all inefficiencies that are identified in the current version of the software [2]. Whereas, TD interest refers to the extra maintenance effort required to modify the software, due to the presence of debt. For example, when an artifact needs to be maintained for the introduction of a new feature, additional effort needs to be spent in resolving it, due to inferior design quality [7]. Another concept related to TDM is interest probability. In TD literature, instability (i.e., the susceptibility of an artifact to change) is considered as a proxy of interest probability. In particular, artifacts of high instability are more probable to accumulate interest, since it manifests only during maintenance activities [4]. According to Li et al. [22], TDM can be decomposed to eight activities, synthesized as follows to four categories: (a) Visualizing TD—TD representation, communication that reflect the way that TD can be presented among stakeholders, and monitoring which follows the evolution of TD; (b) Quantifying TD—TD identification (i.e., finding which artifacts suffer from TD) and measurement (i.e., mapping the extent of the problem to some numerical value); (c) Prioritizing TD—The process of TD prioritization ranks identified TD items, according to certain predefined rules to support deciding which TD items should be repaid first and which TD items can be tolerated until later releases; and (d) Reducing TD—To reduce TD, two activities can be performed, namely TD prevention and TD repayment.

3 Study Design

This section presents the design of the systematic literature review. A protocol is a predetermined plan that describes research questions and how the study will be conducted. In the next sub-sections, we present the decisions taken in each study design phase [19].

Research Objectives and Research Questions. The goal of this study can be described as follows: *"Analyze* existing software engineering literature *for the purpose of* understanding the application of machine learning technologies for solving software engineering practices, *with respect to*: (a) the targeted software engineering practices; (b) the proposed machine learning solutions; and (c) the mapping between them". To systematically explore the aforementioned goal, our study is built around three RQs:

RQ_1: Which SE problems are solved with machine learning technologies?

$RQ_{1.1}$: Which SE practices are targeted by ML approaches?
$RQ_{1.2}$: Which quality attributes are benefited by the ML technologies?

RQ_2: Which machine learning technologies have been used for approaching software engineering problems?

$RQ_{2.1}$: Which are the most common learning styles (i.e., unsupervised, supervised, or semi-supervised) used in SE?
$RQ_{2.2}$: Which are the most common ML algorithms used in SE?

RQ_3: What is the mapping between SE problems and ML solutions?

Software engineering is a mature science field, which, however, strives for new solutions to its well-known problems. With the rise of artificial intelligence and the increment of the volume of data produced during software development, many researchers have tried to investigate how artificial intelligence (specifically machine learning) can aid in improving analysis and predictions problems. On the one hand, RQ1 tries to catalogue the software engineering practices that are approached through machine learning, placing special emphasis on the practices that are attempted to be improved and the targeted quality attributes (QA) of interest. On the other hand, RQ2 investigates machine learning technologies that aim at satisfactorily solving software engineering problems, compared to more traditional approaches. Special emphasis is placed on machine learning algorithms, learning styles, challenges, and success indicators. Finally, RQ3 attempts to synthesize the findings of the previous research questions with the goal of mapping solutions to practices in which machine learning is used.

Search Process. The search procedure aims at the identification of candidate primary studies. The search plan involved automated search into five top-quality publication venues. Narrowing the search space of the primary studies to specific top-quality venues is acknowledged as a well-known practice [19] for broad studies, in the sense that it guarantees the quality and relevance of primary studies [1]. Venue selection was based on the process applied by Karanatsiou et al. [15], in the well-known series of bibliometric studies for top-scholars and institutes in software engineering, being published for more than two decades by JSS. The venue selection process is based on four criteria: (a) venues *classified* as "Computer Software" by the Australian Research Council; (b) *evaluation* higher than or equal to level "B" in the same schema; (c) on average *more* than 1 *citation per month* per published article; and (d) *general-scope journals*, not restricted to phases or activities. Next, based on the above, we retained the top-5 journals (excluding magazines). In particular, we searched the articles identified in *Information and Software Technology, IEEE Transactions on Software Engineering, ACM Transactions on Software Engineering and Methodology, Journal of Systems and Software*, and *Empirical Software Engineering*. In particular, in Fig. 1 we present an overview of the process along with the number of studies at each step. Finally, we retrieved 90 primary studies. The oldest publication is from 1995 and the newsiest from 2019: 82% of the publications are from 2010 and on.

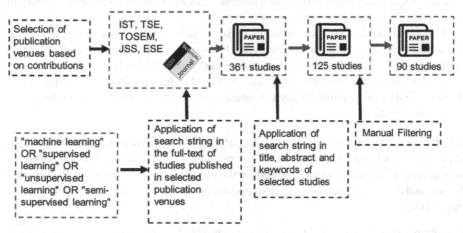

Fig. 1. Overview of search process

Since all publication venues are strictly on the software engineering field, the search string needed to be focused only on ML technologies. As keywords for the search string we have chosen to use simple and generic terms, which may yield as many meaningful results as possible without any bias or preference to a certain machine learning method or technique. Thus, apart from the term "machine learning" per se, we used the most common learning styles, i.e., "supervised", "unsupervised", and "semi-supervised" learning [3]. The search string has been applied to the abstract and title of the manuscripts of all selected venues, without any time constraints. The search has been conducted automatically through the DLs of each venue. The final search string was:

"machine learning" OR "supervised learning" OR "unsupervised learning" OR "semi-supervised learning"

Articles Filtering Phase. The papers that were selected as candidate primary studies in the review should be relevant to applications of machine learning in software engineering. In line with Dybå and Dingsøyr [8], an important element of the systematic mapping planning is to define the Inclusion Criteria (IC) and Exclusion Criteria (EC). A primary study is included if it satisfies one or more ICs, and it is excluded if it satisfies one or more ECs. The inclusion criteria of our systematic mapping are: *IC1*: The study applies one or more ML technologies to a SE practice; and *IC2*: The study defines one or more ways to evaluate quality with ML. The exclusion criteria of our systematic mapping are: *EC1*: Study is an editorial, keynote, opinion, tutorial, workshop summary report, poster, or panel; *EC2*: Study's full text is not available; and *EC3*: Study mentions ML only in introduction or related work section.

The identified articles went through these inclusion/exclusion criteria, by taking into account the full text of the articles. Article inclusion and exclusion was performed independently from the first and second author, and conflicts have been resolved through discussion among the first three authors. During this process 24 conflicts have been identified and resolved either through an unanimous inclusion or exclusion of the article under consideration.

Quality Assessment. We omitted the step of quality assessment for two reasons: (a) since all papers have been obtained from top-quality venues in software engineering, their quality is (to some extent) ensured by the rigorous review process of the selected venues; and (b) we have set no research questions on the quality of research in the domain under study.

Data Collection. During the data collection phase, we collected data on a set of variables that describe each primary study. Similarly to article inclusion/exclusion, the data collection process, has also been handled independently by the first author and the second author. If both reviewers assigned the same value to one variable, this value would be assigned to the variable without further discussion. Conflicts have been resolved at two levels, first the two authors discussed internally, if no consensus was reached, then the discussion was extended to the third author. First level conflicts have been found in 18 studies, whereas second level conflicts were resolved in 6 studies. For every study, we have extracted the following data: [*V1*] Year; [*V2*] Title; [*V3*] Publication Venue; [*V4*] SE practice (e.g., cost estimation, refactoring); [*V5*] Targeted QA (business [17] or product qualities [14]); [*V6*] Learning Styles (i.e., un-, semi-, or supervised); [*V7*] ML Algorithm; [*V8*] Challenges (challenges of applying ML to SE data); and [*V9*] Evaluation Metrics (for ML).

Data Analysis. From the aforementioned variables [V1], [V2] and [V3] have been used for documentation purposes only. The analysis strategy for the research questions is as follows: to answer RQ_1 and RQ_2, we provide frequencies on variables [V4]–[V5] and

[V6]-[V9], respectively. To answer RQ3, we perform crosstabulation of the same variables. We note that due to a lack of quantitative data, no hypothesis testing or statistical analysis has been conducted.

4 Results

In this section we present the results of data analysis, organized by RQ. We note that the synthesized view of the results (i.e., the transfer of the obtained results in TDM context) is provided in Sect. 5.

Table 1. Software engineering problems approached with ML

SE practice	#	SE problems
Defect management	21	Fault proneness prediction and prioritization, Defect prediction, Fault localization
Cost/Effort estimation	17	Development cost/effort estimation, Software maintenance effort prediction, Maintenance type classification
Design-time QAs	14	Change proneness prediction, User interface design, Software product and process quality assessment, Code smells, Patterns and tactics detection, API instability detection, Refactoring of test suites, Refactoring recommendations
Project management	12	Bug report and change requests assignment recommendations and prioritization, classification of software bugs, Commit log recommendations, Code review prioritization, Configuration management recommendation, Development activity detection, Software upgrades recommendation
Security	11	Malware, Malicious Code and Intrusion Classification/Detection, Fault Injection Detection, Software Vulnerabilities Detection
Requirements engineering	9	Functional requirements recommendations, Non-functional requirements detection, Requirements prioritization, Requirements assessment, Software SPL configurations detection, Application domain classification
Run-time QAs	3	Performance Prediction, Energy Efficiency Recommendations
Reuse	2	API usage recommendation, Code examples prioritization for reuse
Program comprehension	2	Trace recovery, Reverse engineering

Software Engineering Applications. In Table 1 we present the frequency of software engineering practices that are approached with ML. Through the analysis, we have identified 9 high-level (HL) software engineering practices. For each HL practice, we present their frequency, and SE problems which are solved through ML. By acknowledging the inherent relationship of TDM to maintainability, in Table 2, we provide an overview of the QAs that are targeted in each application of ML. From the obtained results we can observe that: (a) maintainability and its sub-characteristics (namely: testability, reusability, modifiability and analyzability) are a common target for ML technologies—i.e., ML technologies are relevant to TDM; and (b) business quality attributes are also targeted by ML—rendering them relevant to TDM, in the sense that optimizing business QAs is a main root for the accumulation of TD [18].

Table 2. Targeted quality attributes

HL QA	Freq.	Low Level QA
Maintainability	29	Testability, Reusability, Modifiability, Analyzability
Functional suitability	24	Functional correctness
Security	12	–
Business goals	10	Improve market position, Reduce cost of development
Performance efficiency	5	Resource utilization
Usability	1	–
Reliability	1	–

Machine Learning Technologies. To solve the aforementioned problems a variety of ML algorithms and learning styles have been used. The dominant learning style is supervised learning algorithms (89%), followed by unsupervised (6%) and semi-supervised learning (5%). In Table 3 we present the most frequently used algorithms (i.e., used in more than 10 studies). Apart from the algorithm name and the frequency of its appearance, we also provide the generic category in which it can be classified. We note in cases when the authors have not specified a concrete algorithm (e.g., neural networks) the term Generic has been used as the ML algorithm. To evaluate an ML solution there are many performance measures. Performance measures are typically specialized to the class of the problem: e.g., classification, regression, clustering etc. For problems with discrete output such as classification/clustering, researchers use metrics that compare the actual with the predicted values such as precision, recall, etc. For problems with continuous output, such as regression they prefer metrics that capture error rate of predictions—e.g., MMRE, pred(0.25), etc.

Mapping of SE practices to ML Approaches. As a next step, having presented the results originating from each discipline independently; we present a classification schema, in which we map the most common HL software engineering practices to the ML algorithms that have been used for solving them (see Fig. 2). To investigate if a

Table 3. Machine learning algorithms

ML algorithm	Freq.	Generic category
Bayesian networks	35	Probabilistic analysis
ID3, C4.5, CART	33	Decision trees
SVM	31	Kernel methods
Neural networks	18	Biologically-inspired computation
Random forest	15	Ensemble learner
Ripper	14	Rule system
Regression	13	Statistical analysis
K-Means	13	Clustering
KNN	12	Nearest neighbor

relation between specific ML algorithms and software engineering practices exists, we have performed a chi-square test. The results suggested that the two variables are associated (alpha < 0.01). Therefore, according to the findings of the SLR, specific algorithms appear to be more appropriate for specific practices and vice-versa.

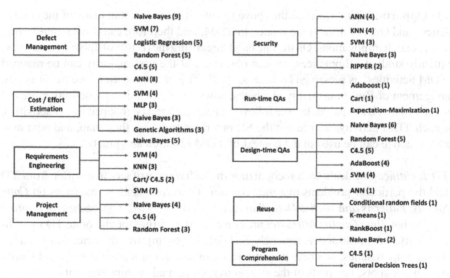

Fig. 2. Mapping of ML to software engineering practices

5   TDM Through Machine Learning

In this section we discuss the main findings of this work, i.e., the current status of research on using ML for SE problems, the identified opportunities for the TD community, and the challenges that might exist when applying ML in TDM research.

Current Status. We have observed that machine learning technologies have been applied to resolve multiple and quite diverse research problems; however, some of them appear to be prevalent. In particular, we observed that *defect management, cost/effort estimation, management of design-time quality attributes, recommendations for efficient project management*, and *detection of security threats* are the most common SE practices that have been investigated. We note that as management we refer to cases that we predict (future state), assess, classify, or detect a phenomenon of interest. In terms of quality attributes, the most relevant ones appeared to be the improvement of *maintainability* and *functional suitability* (i.e., correctness), followed by security and business quality attributes. In terms of ML algorithms, we suggest that Bayesian Networks, various Decision Trees, and SVM are the most frequently used ones. Finally, we identified that *Neural Network Analysis* appears to be fitting for *Cost/Effort Estimation* practices, *Bayesian Networks* for *Defect* and *Project Management* practices, and *Random Forrest* algorithms appear to be appropriate for *Managing Design-Time QAs*. On the other hand, *Clustering* and *Decision Trees* appear to be equally fitting for various SE practices.

TDM Opportunities. Based on the above results, it is evident that many of the studied practices and QAs of interest are related to TDM, and therefore can drive to interesting future research implications. On the one hand, regarding the results of Table 1 on the most frequently studied SE practices, we can observe that the vast majority can be mapped to TDM activities, as presented by Li et al. [22]. The only exceptions are Security and Management of Run-time quality attributes, whose inefficiencies, by definition are not categorized as TD. In particular, the following practices can be mapped to TD activities. For each TDM activity, we present the SE practices to which they map, and next how the SE practice can be used in the context of TDM research and practice.

- *TD Identification* deals with recognizing the software artifacts that suffer from TD and the particular problems that they contain. Therefore, studies that focus on **Code Smells, Patterns and Tactics Detection** (e.g., [9]) through ML approaches for *Improving Design-Time Quality Attributes* are considered as fitting for elaborate TD Identification. Based on the above, researchers should try to improve the detection accuracy of such approaches, whereas practitioners can use accompanying tools to identify design hot-spots, i.e., parts of the system that yield quality improvements.
- *TD Quantification*: Monetization is a key concept in the TD metaphor: to perform TDM, both principal and interest need to be quantified in some currency form. To this end, **Cost/Effort Estimation** methods (e.g., [10, 23]) are highly relevant. However, in these studies, the authors do not discuss the findings in the context of TD quantification. On the one hand, researchers are encouraged to introduce cost or effort estimation approaches (e.g., based on past data) to predict the cost of applying refactoring (i.e., related to *TD principal quantification*) or to predict the cost of future maintenance

effort (i.e., related to *TD interest quantification*). On the other hand, practitioners can use existing (or novel) such approaches, for getting monetary estimations of their TD, to improve the communication of poor software quality cost to higher non-technical management.

- *TD Prioritization*: In the literature, three ways of TD prioritization have been proposed, i.e., based on principal, interest, and interest probability. In that sense, studies that focus on **Change-** [16] and **Fault-proneness** [29] **assessment** are relevant to TD prioritization, since these concepts are closely related to *interest probability*: changes and faults lead to maintenance activities that can accumulate interest. Based on this, researchers can introduce algorithms that predict which software modules are more prone to changes and faults; providing practitioners with tool support for identifying modules that need special attention in their TDM. Finally, regarding cases in which a monetization of TD interest is not of primary importance for prioritization, ranking in terms of maintainability (i.e., a proxy of interest) is a satisfactory compromise of accuracy and ease of use. Therefore, any method that is used for assessing or characterizing the levels of QAs (e.g., maintainability [12]) can be useful for prioritization based on interest.

- *TD Repayment/Prevention*: Regarding TD repayment, currently there are various approaches that propose the **identification of refactoring opportunities**, or the **ordering** with which such **refactorings** shall be performed. Additionally, the adoption of **reuse strategies**, as well as the **creation** of **traces** along artifacts are expected to be beneficial for preventing the accumulation of new TD principal. Based on the above, on the one hand, researchers are expected to propose ML-based refactoring identification strategies by optimizing TD principal and interest minimization; allowing practitioners to perform more informed TD repayment. On the other hand, researchers are encouraged to first explore the relation between specific practices (e.g., traceability and reuse) to TD prevention, and if the relation is positive to provide mechanisms to practitioners for applying them into their system.

On the other hand, by considering the targeted quality attributes (see Table 2), we can also identify some connection to TDM. First, since the most frequently targeted quality attribute is maintainability, we can easily assume that all technologies used to improve maintainability are relevant to TD (see Sect. 2). Additionally, in many studies ML approaches are used to apply practices that aid in terms of the improvement of the market position of the product, or to reduce the development costs (e.g., by shrinking product time-to-market). In general, the satisfaction of business goals is roots of accumulating TD principal, e.g., bring the product to the market faster. Additionally, the improvement of the market position of a product can be considered as a by-product of TDM, especially in cases when combined through TD prioritization.

Challenges in Applying ML to TDM. As part of the analysis, we have identified specific challenges in applying ML to TDM practices. Among the most important ones we acknowledge the following. First, there is a need of a substantial pre-processing in the used datasets, so as to eliminate cases of imbalanced datasets, handling of duplicate values, multicollinearity of predictor variables, etc. Additionally, specifically in TDM it is expected to face many difficulties in creating a solid dataset, since the methods for quantifying TD are highly diverse and no state-of-practice techniques exist. Furthermore, for supervised learning algorithms labelling of training data (e.g. software modules) can be challenging as no universal approach for measuring TD exists. In contrast to other fields (e.g., cost estimation) there is a lack of benchmarks that can be used for training and testing of algorithms (e.g., COCOMO or ISBSG). Furthermore, a common challenge in applying ML in software engineering is the curse of dimensionality, in which the researcher shall limit the variables that shall be fed into the model. This challenge is also highly relevant to TDM, in the sense that TD is a multi-dimensional concept, whose assessment requires the consideration of multiple aspects (e.g., code smell, improper architectural decisions, etc.) but also people's habits and employed processes. Therefore, since the application of ML approaches requires a small subset of input variables to obtain a time-efficient, accurate, and noiseless model, it is of paramount importance to effectively perform data reduction.

6 Threats to Validity

In this section, we present the threats to validity that have been identified and mitigated as part of the study design. The threats are organized based on the guidelines for identifying, mitigating, and reporting threats to validity for secondary studies in software engineering proposed by Ampatzoglou et al. [1].

Study Selection Validity. To guarantee that all studies relevant to the topic have been identified, we systematically developed a search string, based on the types of existing machine learning approaches. However, it is possible that we have missed studies that mention in the title specific ML methods, such as deep learning, neutral networks, etc. To guarantee the relevance to software engineering, we have selected five journals that publish only SE articles. The full-texts of all articles were available through the used Digital Library, and were all written in English. Since our goal was to target high quality research only, we have excluded grey literature. To adequately filter articles, we have predefined a list of inclusion/exclusion criteria, which were discussed among others and piloted, with random screening, and authors voting.

Data Validity. Although we have limited our search to five publication venues, we have retrieved 90 papers for inclusion in the study and data collection, which constitutes our sample size as large enough for analysis. The selection of variables has been based on the set of research questions, and therefore is adequate for answering them. Although our results come from only five venues, we believe that there is no publication bias, since the articles in the top journals come from various communities. The quality of the primary studies is guaranteed by the quality of selected venues. To avoid data extraction bias, more than one author has been involved in the process: one has double-checked the results of the other, and agreement rates have been captured. In case of disagreement, open discussions have been performed.

Research Validity. To increase the reliability and replicability of the study, we involved more than one researcher to all steps of the process, and all data have been made available. Finally, we ensured that the correct research method has been used, i.e., an SLR since a synthesis was required to achieve the high-level goal. However, we acknowledge that the lack of direct related work has not allowed comparison of results; however, the experience of the authors on TDM research allowed interpretation of results, increasing generalisability.

7 Discussion/Conclusions

This study investigates how machine learning (ML) technologies can be applied in Technical Debt Management (TDM): to the best of our knowledge, there is no Systematic Literature Review study that focuses on how ML is applied to TDM. To achieve this goal, we have performed a broad literature review, i.e., on how ML technologies have been applied to solve SE practices in general. The results of the analysis suggest that: (a) the most common SE practices that have been approached through ML technologies are defect management and cost/effort estimation; (b) the target of these technologies is to improve both product (e.g., maintainability) and business (e.g., reduce development time) qualities; and (c) that some ML technologies better map to specific SE practices; however, others are so widespread that can be applicable to various cases.

The results of the study can provide multiple implications to researchers and software development industries. Regarding software development industries, the relevance of ML in resolving software engineering practices can highlight the potential benefits of hiring personnel (e.g., data scientists) that are dedicated in data analysis and interpretation. The outputs of the provided analysis can be proved useful in many aspects of the development, as presented in Table 2. Additionally, software practitioners are encouraged to incorporate into their daily processes tools (or research prototypes) that are based on ML, and make use of the provided recommendations, or assessments (e.g., predictions, detections, etc.). On the other hand, we suggest TDM researchers to start exploring the possibility of applying machine learning technologies in their research endeavours. More specifically, we prompt them to migrate solutions from traditional SE practices (e.g., cost estimation, smell detection, etc.) to the context of technical debt management, since they are considered as very relevant. Additionally, the existence of various and non-trivial challenges in the adoption of ML in TDM research, strengthens the aforementioned argumentation, in the sense that high-quality research outcomes shall be produced to resolve them.

Acknowledgements. Work reported in this paper has received funding from the European Union's Horizon 2020 research and innovation programme under grant agreement No 871177 (project: SmartCLIDE).

References

1. Ampatzoglou, A., Bibi, S., Avgeriou, P., Verbeek, M., Chatzigeorgiou, A.: Identifying, categorizing and mitigating threats to validity in software engineering secondary studies. Inf. Softw. Technol. **106**(2), 201–230 (2019)

2. Ampatzoglou, Ar., Ampatzoglou, Ap., Chatzigeorgiou, A., Avgeriou, P.: The financial aspect of managing technical debt: a systematic literature review. Inf. Soft. Technol. **64**(8), 52–73 (2015)

3. Aroussi, S., Mellouk, A.: Survey on machine learning-based QoE-QoS correlation models. In: International Conference on Computing, Management and Telecommunications (ComManTel'), Da Nang, Vietnam, 27–29 April 2014

4. Arvanitou, E.M., Ampatzoglou, A., Chatzigeorgiou, A., Avgeriou, P.: Introducing a ripple effect measure: a theoretical and empirical validation. In: International Symposium on Empirical Software Engineering and Measurement (ESEM 2015). IEEE, China, October 2015

5. Azeem, M.I., Palomba, F., Shi, L., Wang, Q.: Machine learning techniques for code smell detection: a systematic literature review and meta-analysis. Inf. Softw. Technol. **108**(4), 115–138 (2019)

6. Codabux, Z., Williams, B.J.: Technical debt prioritization using predictive analytics. In: 38th International Conference on Software Engineering Companion (ICSE 2016). ACM (2016)

7. Chatzigeorgiou, A., Ampatzoglou, Ap., Ampatzoglou, Ar., Amanatidis, T.: Estimating the breaking point for technical debt. In: 7th International Workshop on Managing Technical Debt (MTD 2015), 2 October 2015, pp. 53–56. IEEE, Germany (2015)

8. Dybå, T., Dingsøyr, T.: Empirical studies of agile software development: a systematic review. Inf. Softw. Technol. **50**(9–10), 833–859 (2008)

9. Arcelli Fontana, F., Mäntylä, M.V., Zanoni, M., Marino, A.: Comparing and experimenting machine learning techniques for code smell detection. Empir. Softw. Eng. **21**(3), 1143–1191 (2015). https://doi.org/10.1007/s10664-015-9378-4

10. Hamill, M., Goseva-Popstojanova, K.: Analyzing and predicting effort associated with finding and fixing software faults. Inf. Softw. Technol. **87**(7), 1–18 (2017)

11. Heckman, S., Williams, L.: A systematic literature review of actionable alert identification techniques for automated static code analysis. Inf. Softw. Technol. **53**(4), 363–387 (2011)

12. Herbold, S., Grabowski, J., Waack, S.: Calculation and optimisation of thresholds for sets of software metrics. Empir. Softw. Eng. **16**(6), 812–841 (2011). https://doi.org/10.1007/s10 664-011-9162-z

13. Idri, A., Hosni, M., Abran, A.: Systematic literature review of ensemble effort estimation. J. Syst. Softw. **118**(8), 151–175 (2016)

14. ISO/IEC 25010:2011, Systems and software engineering—Systems and software Quality Requirements and Evaluation (SQuaRE)—System and software quality models, Geneva, Switzerland (2011)

15. Karanatsiou, D., Li, Y., Arvanitou, E.M., Misirlis, N., Wong, W.E.: A bibliometric assessment of software engineering scholars and institutions (2010–2017). J. Syst. Softw. **147**(1), 246–261 (2019)

16. Kaur, L., Mishra, A.: Cognitive complexity as a quantifier of version to version Java-based source code change: an empirical probe. Inf. Softw. Technol. **102** (2019)

17. Kazman, R., Bass, L.: Categorizing Business Goals for Software Architectures. CMU/SEI-2005-TR-021 (2005)

18. Kazman, R., et al.: A case study in locating the architectural roots of technical debt. In: 37th International Conference on Software Engineering, 16–24 May 2015. IEEE, Florence (2015)

19. Kitchenham, B., Brereton, O.P., Budgen, D., Turner, M., Bailey, J., Linkman, S.: Systematic literature reviews in software engineering – a systematic literature review. Inf. Softw. Technol. **51**(1), 7–15 (2009)

20. Kitchenham, B., Pfleeger, S.L.: Software quality: the elusive target. IEEE Softw. **13**(1), 12–21 (1996)

21. Kruchten, P., Nord, R.L., Ozkaya, I.: Technical debt: from metaphor to theory and practice. IEEE Softw. **29**(6), 18–21 (2006)

22. Li, Z., Avgeriou, P., Liang, P.: A systematic mapping study on technical debt and its management. J. Syst. Softw. **101**(3), 193–220 (2015)
23. Mair, C., et al.: An investigation of machine learning based prediction systems. J. Syst. Softw. **53**(1), 23–29 (2000)
24. Myrtveit, I., Stensrud, E., Shepperd, M.: Reliability and validity in comparative studies of software prediction models. IEEE Trans. Softw. Eng. **31**(5), 380–391 (2005)
25. Sharma, T., Spinellis, D.: A survey on software smells. J. Syst. Softw. **138**(4), 158–173 (2018)
26. Skourletopoulos, G., Mavromoustakis, C., Bahsoon, R., Masotrakis, G., Pallis, E.: Predicting and quantifying the technical debt in cloud software engineering. In: 19th International Workshop on Computer-Aided Modeling and Design of Communication Links and Networks (CAMAD). IEEE Computer Society (2014)
27. Wen, J., Li, S., Lin, Z., Hu, Y., Huang, C.: Systematic literature review of machine learning based software development effort estimation models. Inf. Softw. Technol. **54**(1), 41–59 (2012)
28. Zhang, D., Tsai, J.J.P.: Machine learning and software engineering. In: 14th IEEE International Conference on Tools with Artificial Intelligence (ICTAI 2002), 4–6 November 2002 (2002)
29. Zhou, Y., Leung, H.: Empirical analysis of object-oriented design metrics for predicting high and low severity faults. Trans. Softw. Eng. **32**(10), 771–789 (2006)

On the Temporality of Introducing Code Technical Debt

Georgios Digkas[1,2](✉)[iD], Apostolos Ampatzoglou[2][iD],
Alexander Chatzigeorgiou[2][iD], and Paris Avgeriou[1][iD]

[1] Institute of Mathematics and Computer Science, University of Groningen,
Groningen, Netherlands
g.digkas@rug.nl, paris@cs.rug.nl
[2] Department of Applied Informatics, University of Macedonia,
Thessaloniki, Greece
{a.ampatzoglou,achat}@uom.edu.gr

Abstract. Code Technical Debt (TD) is intentionally or unintentionally created when developers introduce inefficiencies in the codebase. This can be attributed to various reasons such as heavy work-load, tight delivery schedule, unawareness of good practices, etc. To shed light into the context that leads to technical debt accumulation, in this paper we investigate: (a) the temporality of code technical debt introduction in new methods, i.e., whether the introduction of technical debt is stable across the lifespan of the project, or if its evolution presents spikes; and (b) the relation of technical debt introduction and the development team's workload in a given period. To answer these questions, we perform a case study on twenty-seven Apache projects, and inspect the number of Technical Debt Items introduced in 6-month sliding temporal windows. The results of the study suggest that: (a) overall, the number of Technical Debt Items introduced through new code is a stable metric, although it presents some spikes; and (b) the number of commits performed is not strongly correlated to the number of introduced Technical Debt Items.

Keywords: Technical debt temporality · Case study · New code debt · Metrics fluctuation

1 Introduction

Technical debt (TD) at the code level refers to inefficiencies introduced in the source code of an application during the implementation or the maintenance phase [1]. These inefficiencies manifest themselves as violations of coding standards, complex and hard to understand code, code duplicates, etc. [2]. According to Alves et al. [3] code TD is the most studied type of technical debt, and based on Ampatzoglou et al. [4] it is one of the most important in industry.

There has been significant work on how code TD evolves and how it accumulates over time. However, existing studies have looked at TD evolution as a whole, without distinguishing between technical debt that is added as new code,

© Springer Nature Switzerland AG 2020
M. Shepperd et al. (Eds.): QUATIC 2020, CCIS 1266, pp. 68–82, 2020.
https://doi.org/10.1007/978-3-030-58793-2_6

and technical debt that is added or modified in existing code. In this paper, we focus only on the introduction of new code TD, i.e. TD inserted in the system in the form of new Technical Debt Items (TDIs). More specifically we study new methods (our scope is object-oriented systems) that contain TD and we look at the introduction of this type of new TD as a temporal phenomenon.

Focusing on TD that is introduced by new code, as opposed to TD that is introduced by modifying existing code, can provide a unique insight. Specifically, the new TDIs introduced by new methods at each commit (either new methods in existing classes or new methods in entirely new classes) reflect more accurately the type of problems and the timepoint at which they are introduced. In other words, new methods are more representative of the developers' practices and knowledge level, compared to method modifications whose type and timeliness is often dictated by the need to fix a bug or to extend an already existing functionality. Thus, we study the temporality of TD through a clearer source.

In particular, we explore: (*1*) if the number of introduced TDIs is uniformly spread across evolution, or whether there are time windows in which more TDIs are inserted; and (*2*) if the number of TDIs that is introduced along evolution is related to the activity (intensity of commits) of developers in different time windows. Projects could exhibit either a stability in the introduction of code TDIs across evolution or experience fluctuations with isolated or repeating spikes of introduced code TDIs. In the former case one could assume that accumulation of TD is most probably due to factors that are constantly present in the entire lifetime of the project, such as employees' skills, used methodologies, tools, management practices, etc. In the latter case, one could postulate that the insertion of new code TDIs is a highly temporal phenomenon depending on volatile factors such as feature requests, changing schedules, pressure to fix bugs, etc.

To achieve this goal, we explore the evolution of twenty-seven projects by the Apache Software Foundation (ASF), and we track the number of new TDIs inserted in each commit. Next, we create a 6-month sliding window, and we calculate the cumulative number of inserted TDIs for each window, as well as the number of commits in the same time period. To answer the first question, we use a metric property (termed SMF—see Sect. 3.2) that is able to assess metrics fluctuation along time and characterize them as either stable or sensitive. To answer the second question we correlate the number of commits for each window to the number of inserted TDIs. The reporting and interpretation of the results is performed at the project level.

The rest of the paper is organized as follows: in Sect. 2 we present related work and in Sect. 3 background information important for understanding the study. In Sect. 4, we present the design of the case study, while Sect. 5 elaborates on the results. Section 6 interprets the results and provides implications for researchers and practitioners. Finally, in Sect. 7 we present threats to validity and in Sect. 8, we conclude the paper.

2   Related Work

Many studies have explored the evolution of code quality, and the reasons for its degradation. Since this paper focuses on the introduction of TD over time, we organize this sub-section into causes of TD introduction and TD evolution.

Causes of Technical Debt Introduction: Tufano et al. [5] studied the evolution of code smells with the goal of understanding when and why code smells are introduced and observed the life cycle of five code smells. The results indicate that: (a) in the majority of the cases code smells are introduced with the creation of the corresponding classes or files; (b) while projects evolve, "smelly" code artifacts tend to become more problematic; (c) new code smells are introduced when software engineers implement new features or when they extend the functionality of the existing ones; (d) the developers who introduce new code smells, are the ones who work under pressure and not necessarily the newcomers; and (e) the majority of the smells are not removed during the project's evolution and few of them are removed as a direct consequence of refactoring operations.

According to Kazman et al. [6] who conducted a case study on the roots of architecture debt, Architectural Technical Debt (ATD) is extremely common and probably the most important type of TD because it consumes the largest percentage of maintenance effort. Their findings suggest that architectural debt is extremely easy to introduce: programmers typically want to introduce new features or fix bugs; however, by changing the code they often undermine the architectural structure leading to the accumulation of ATD.

Martini et al. [7] conducted a case study on five software companies to understand the causes that introduce ATD. Large software companies try to deliver as fast as possible in order to satisfy their customers' needs, usually taking shortcuts, thereby introducing ATD. If the debt is not paid-off, it starts to accumulate and this makes feature development more difficult.

Evolution of Technical Debt: Although TD is a multifaceted concept, one of the key constituents of code TD is the presence of code smells. One of the first studies that investigate the evolution of code smells was conducted by Olbrich et al. [8]. They investigated the evolution of two code smells, God Class and Shotgun Surgery, on two OSS projects. The results show that along software development, there are phases where the number of code smells can either increase or decrease and those phases are not affected by the size of the systems. Chatzigeorgiou and Manakos [9] have investigated the evolution of the Long Method, Feature Envy, State Checking, and God Class smells in two open-source software projects. The results suggested that as projects evolve the number of smells tends to increase. Another interesting finding is that a significant percentage of smells was not due to software ageing, since some smells were present right from the first version of the code in which they reside. Peters and Zaidman [10] studied the lifespan of the God Class, Feature Envy, Data Class, Message Chain Class, and Long Parameter List smells. The analysis of eight open-source software projects, confirmed that the number of smells increases, as projects evolve.

Digkas et al. [11] tracked the evolution of TD in sixty-six open-source Java projects by the ASF, over a period of 5 years. In order to detect issues that incur TD, they relied on SonarQube. The results show that on the one hand, there is a significant increasing trend on the size, complexity, number of TDIs, and the total TD over time, which seems to confirm the software aging phenomenon. But on the other hand, when TD is normalized over the non-commented lines of code, an evident decreasing trend over time is present for many of the projects. This could possibly be attributed to: (a) developers that perform refactoring activities and fix some of the open TDIs; or (b) developers that introduce better quality code in each commit (compared to the project's existing code base).

> *Despite the fact that code TD introduction has been widely explored, we lack evidence on: (a) the way in which TD is introduced, i.e. whether there is stable increase, or large fluctuations exist, and (b) if such fluctuations coincide with large-scale changes in the codebase.*

3   Background Information

In this section we present information that is necessary for understanding the paper.

3.1   Identifying New TD Items Along Evolution

To analyze software systems and measure TD throughout their evolution, we have used SonarQube 7.9.2 LTS. SQ relies on a set of rules which are checked by static source code analysis; every time a piece of code breaks one of those coding or design rules, a Technical Debt Issue is raised. SQ estimates the effort (in minutes) required to eliminate the identified TDIs. This effort is obtained by assigning a time estimate for fixing each type of problem and by multiplying the number of all TDIs of that type with that estimate.

Considering that software systems evolve through a number of revisions and that in each revision several types of changes may occur simultaneously, we look at the three major types of code changes: the introduction of new code, the deletion and the modification of existing code. In this paper we work at the method level, that is, we aggregate all TDIs reported by SQ for individual lines to the method in which they belong. The reason for this decision is that monitoring changes at the instruction level would be more complex and less accurate considering that several types of changes can simultaneously occur in some statements (e.g., modification and introduction of new code). Furthermore, tracking changes at the instruction level is challenging, as one would have to map each instruction (in a particular revision) to the corresponding instruction in the previous revision. This process is complicated by the insertion of new statements, comments, blank lines, etc. Therefore, to be certain about the classification of changes, we monitor changes at the method level.

At each revision a class can be added, deleted, modified, renamed or remain unchanged. The same applies for the methods. As explained above, we only focus on the introduced TDIs in the newly inserted methods. A new method can be added either in an existing class or upon the creation of a new class. To distinguish the newly inserted methods for each commit from the deleted, modified, renamed, and unchanged ones, we rely on the Gumtree Spoon AST Diff tool [12]. For each revision, first, we detect all changes that occurred in the corresponding commit at the file-level, i.e. we identify the added, modified, renamed, and deleted files. Then, we exclude the deleted files which do not exist anymore in the examined commit. For the added files/classes, we consider all methods as new code; in other words we consider them as newly inserted methods in new classes. For the modified and renamed files we compare their AST with the AST in the previous revision (using the Gumtree Spoon tool). By this comparison we identify the newly inserted methods in existing classes.

After identifying which methods have been inserted into the project (in the commit under study) and their span (starting/ending line in the file), we can further identify TDIs. For this step we analyze the project using SQ. Then, we retrieve all the TDIs (via SQ's API) and keep only the ones that can be mapped to the newly inserted methods. This is performed by matching the line in which each TDI is reported by SQ with the method containing that line.

3.2   Fluctuation of Software Metrics

Software Metrics Fluctuation (SMF) is a property of metrics, defined as *"the degree to which a metric score changes from one version of the system to the other"* [13]. Using SMF, metrics can be characterized as **sensitive** (changes induce high variation on the metric score) or **stable** (changes induce low variation). To capture the SMF property of a metric, that property should:

- Take into account the order of measurements in a metric time series. This is the main characteristic that a fluctuation property should hold, in the sense that it should quantify the extent to which a score changes between two subsequent time points.
- Yield values that can be intuitively interpreted, especially for border cases. Therefore, if a score does not change at all, its fluctuation should be evaluated to zero. Any other change pattern should result in a non-zero fluctuation value. Finally, the highest value should be obtained for time series that constantly change and fluctuate between the two ends of their range, for every pair of successive versions of the software.

To assess SMF, in this paper, we use a measure proposed by Arvanitou et al. [13], namely `mf`. The measure is defined as: *"the average deviation from zero of the difference ratios between every pair of successive versions"*, as shown below.

$$mf = \sqrt{\frac{\sum_{i=2}^{n} \left(\frac{score_i - score_{i-1}}{score_{i-1}} \right)^2}{n-1}} \tag{1}$$

In the study that introduced SMF [13], the authors also explored various alternatives (such as coefficient of variance, and auto-correlation-of-lag-one), which however, were not able to capture the aforementioned properties of SMF.

4   Case Study Design

In this section, we present the design of the case study which was based on the linear-analytic structure as described by Runeson et al. [14].

4.1   Research Questions

As already mentioned in the Introduction Section, we ask two research questions.

RQ$_1$: *Does the number of introduced technical debt items by new code fluctuate along evolution?*

The answer to this research question will unveil if in different time periods, different amounts of TD are introduced. The answer reflects the main goal of this study, i.e., to investigate the temporality of the TD phenomenon. Specifically, this answer will enable us to characterize TDIs introduction as either stable, or sensitive to temporal influence. In addition, we will study any possible spikes in the evolution on new code TD, which might be indicators of "extra-ordinary" events along evolution. The frequency and the timing (early, middle, or late in the project) of such spikes will also be explored and reported.

RQ$_2$: *Does the amount of introduced technical debt items by new code, correlate to the activity of developers?*

To increase the confidence in the results of the previous research question, we study a potentially important confounding factor for this empirical setup: developers' activity. Considering that we are not analyzing at the individual commit level, but over periods of time, there is a non-negligible chance that in these periods the developers' activity (number of commits) is not stable; therefore, spikes in new code TDIs could be due to more intense programming activity in the corresponding periods.

4.2   Cases and Units of Analysis

This study is characterized as a multiple, embedded case study [14], in which the cases are open-source software (OSS) projects, while the units of analysis are the source code commits (per project) over different time periods. Specifically, for each project, we analyse the amount of code TDIs added over 6-month time periods across the project history (see Sect. 4.3 for more details). The reason for selecting to perform this study on OSS systems is the vast amount of data that is available in terms of revisions and classes. The long history that is available for each project enables researchers to observe overall trends in the evolution of their quality. To retrieve data from only high-quality projects that evolve over a period of time, we looked into ASF projects and investigated the projects presented in Table 1. The selection of projects was based on the following criteria:

– The software is actively maintained. To ensure this, we sorted projects based on the date of their last commit.

Table 1. Selected Projects

Project	Classes	NCLOC	Analyzed revisions	Project	Classes	NCLOC	Analyzed revisions
Atlas	932	87637	1454	Knox	1083	51429	1033
Beam	3757	176663	2780	Kylin	1658	128531	3205
Calcite	2606	186633	1448	Metron	1433	72579	548
Cayenne	2615	164170	2116	MyFaces	1843	174158	1211
Commons IO	132	10500	1059	NiFi	4256	371031	1490
CXF	4111	353085	5079	oozie	1082	97597	587
DeltaSpike	951	46182	513	OpenWebBeans	561	44299	1583
Drill	4655	316552	1316	PDFBox	1279	136916	3758
Dubbo	943	61865	728	Pulsar	1837	147182	1503
Flink	5632	341149	5329	SIS	1948	181588	828
Flume	790	51897	789	Storm	3958	243574	738
Giraph	1414	72972	668	TinkerPop	1698	95652	5178
Jackrabbit	2883	273574	4260	Zeppelin	1209	89193	1562
jclouds	5687	227459	4323				

- The software is written in Java and uses Maven as a build tool. This ensures that the project can be built and allows the retrieval of the project's language version from the corresponding pom.xml file.
- The software contains more than 100 classes to ensure the inclusion of systems with a substantial size, functionality and complexity.
- The software has more than 1000 commits. We have included this criterion for similar reasons to the previous criterion and to be able to observe trends in the evolution of their quality. Moreover, this number of revisions provides an adequate set of repeated measures as input to the statistical analysis.

4.3   Data Collection

To build the dataset for our analysis, we relied on the process described in Section 3.1. In particular, for each project, we have been able to build a dataset containing: (a) the commit SHA; (b) the commit timestamp; and (c) the number of introduced TDIs by the new code of this commit. Next, starting from the first commit timestamp, we created a 6-month time-window that slides monthly, along the evolution of the project. Based on these time-windows, we have created our units of analysis, as shown in Fig. 1. For example, by considering a project that spans across 22 months (M1-M22), we are able to create 16 units of analysis.

For each period captured by the time-window, we summed the number of TDIs that were introduced in all commits included in the timeframe. Therefore, the final dataset consists of three variables: $[V_1]$ time-window (in months/year); $[V_2]$ number of commits in the time-window; and $[V_3]$ number of TDIs introduced by new code in the time-window. A replication package is available online[1].

---

[1] https://drive.google.com/drive/folders/1oF51ZPlXSiIL-mM-W2kHs7vi63Ij5n8P.

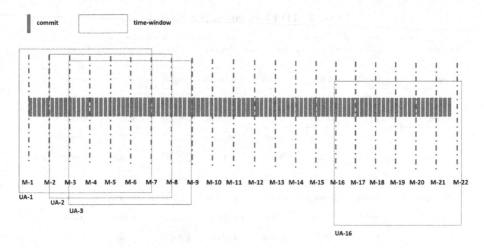

Fig. 1. Demarcating Units of Analysis (sliding temporal windows)

4.4 Data Analysis

Data analysis was performed on the aforementioned raw dataset. To answer RQ_1, for each project, we first assess fluctuation by calculating SMF and basic descriptive statistics of the dependent variable [V_3]. Next, to visualize extreme projects (the most stable and most sensitive), we use a line chart representing the evolution of TDIs introduced by new code. By inspecting the line chart, we highlight spikes in the introduction of TDIs, and discuss, if they seemed more concentrated in the beginning, middle, or end of the project. To answer RQ_2, we performed Pearson correlation analyses, and for extreme cases we visualize the relation through scatterplots, and present the co-evolution of number of commits and the number of TDIs in a single line chart.

5 Results

5.1 Fluctuation Analysis (RQ1)

In Table 2, we observe the results of the fluctuation analysis for the number of TDIs introduced by new code, in the 27 cases of the study, based on the value of the SMF metric. We can observe that for 16 out of 27 projects the number of TDIs introduced by new code can be considered as stable, whereas in the rest 11 projects as sensitive (dark and light grey cell shading in column SMF respectively).

To provide a visual insight on the discussed fluctuations, in Fig. 2, we present the evolution of one extremely stable project, namely `Metron`, and a sensitive one, namely `SIS`. We note that even for the most "stable" projects, some spikes still exist; however, the spikes are small in height. A visual analysis of fluctuations in all projects (figures are available in the online material) revealed that

Table 2. TD Fluctuation per Project

Project	SMF	Corr. Coef.	Sig. Level	Spk	Project	SMF	Corr. Coef.	Sig. Level	Spk
Atlas	0.538	0.500	0.000	1	Knox	0.301	0.361	0.002	2
Beam	0.509	0.502	0.002	3	Kylin	0.343	0.598	0.000	3
Calcite	11.902	0.150	0.195		Metron	0.162	0.551	0.002	0
Cayenne	1.019	0.584	0.000		MyFaces	2.992	0.355	0.000	
Commons IO	1.344	0.661	0.000		NiFi	0.024	0.302	0.073	1
CXF	0.762	0.363	0.000	3	oozie	0.451	0.198	0.075	1
DeltaSpike	1.396	0.791	0.000		jclouds	0.467	0.890	0.000	1
Drill	0.335	0.519	0.001	1	PDFBox	3.505	−0.066	0.493	
Dubbo	1.900	0.929	0.000		Pulsar	0.456	0.768	0.000	1
Flink	4.080	0.353	0.001		SIS	9.558	0.482	0.000	
Flume	0.340	0.922	0.000	1	Storm	0.389	0.071	0.611	2
Giraph	1.174	0.463	0.000		TinkerPop	0.156	0.802	0.000	1
Jackrabbit	1.639	0.453	0.000		Zeppelin	0.320	0.161	0.220	2
OpenWebBeans	0.492	0.436	0.000	1					

Spk = Spikes

fluctuations of TD are distributed across the entire project lifetime. This observation is a first indication that these spikes might be irrelevant to the time period that they appeared, questioning a relation between TD introduction and project maturity. Nevertheless, this finding needs further investigation.

5.2   Correlation Analysis: Fluctuation vs. Activity (RQ2)

To investigate if the fluctuation of the number of TDIs that is inserted by new code is due to some temporal phenomenon that occurs in the given time period, we need to exclude the most obvious confounding factor, i.e., developers' activity.

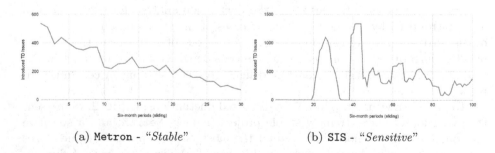

(a) Metron - "*Stable*"   (b) SIS - "*Sensitive*"

Fig. 2. Indicative project evolution

One of the first tentative interpretations on the existence of high spikes as those presented in Fig. 2(b), would be that in the corresponding time windows, lots of code has been committed. To explore the existence of this confounding factor, in Table 2 we highlight with light-gray cell shading (in column Corr. Coef.) the cases in which the correlation is strong (>0.7 [15]) and at the same time statistically significant (p<0.001). The findings suggest that only in 22% of the projects this correlation is strong. So only in these cases, the commit activity could explain the fluctuations in the number of TDIs that is added by new code. To visualize this result, we present the scatter plot and the evolution of both variables in a single line chart, in Figs. 3a–b for Dubbo (the project with the highest correlation), and in Figs. 4a–b for PDFBox (the project with the lowest correlation). In the scatter plots, each dot represents a 6-month period, mapping the values of the two variables for which we seek correlation. For strong correlations, dots are expected to concentrate around the central diagonal.

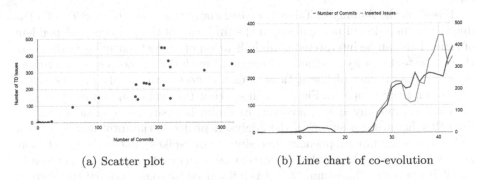

(a) Scatter plot   (b) Line chart of co-evolution

Fig. 3. Correlation analysis for Dubbo: fluctuation related to developers' activity

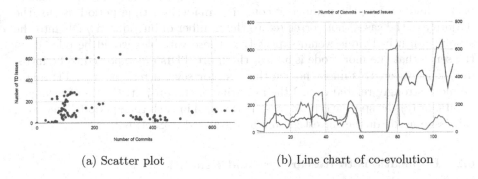

(a) Scatter plot   (b) Line chart of co-evolution

Fig. 4. Correlation analysis for PDFBox: fluctuation NOT related to developers' activity

6   Discussion

6.1   Interpretation of Results

The high-level goal of this study was to investigate if the introduction of TDIs (by adding new code) is a temporal phenomenon, that diverges over time. Based on the findings, some temporality can be claimed only for a number of projects. In particular, based on the fluctuation of TDIs due to the introduction of new code (see Sect. 5.1), we can classify the projects in three categories through visual inspection of the evolution graphs: (a) stable projects without any temporality— i.e., negligible fluctuations (0–1 spike, 10 projects); (b) stable projects that are not sensitive, but some "extra-ordinary" spikes occur (>1 spikes, 6 projects); and (c) sensitive projects (many spikes, 11 projects). The number of spikes of each project is reported in Table 2 (column 'Spk'); note that we only provide the number of spikes for the stable projects, since sensitive projects have multiple ones.

   Based on the findings of Table 2, we can claim that the introduction of TDIs due to the insertion of new code is, in the majority of the projects, independent of time. This can be interpreted as an indication of project maturity, in the sense that consistent quality is achieved throughout evolution. However, even for these projects, the absence of fluctuations does not necessarily imply the absence of any trend. For example, in Fig.2 we can see that the evolution of project Metron does not exhibit any spikes; however, its trend is clearly a decreasing one. On the other hand, for a subset of the analyzed projects, the introduction of new code TDIs is a temporal phenomenon, since many spikes exist in their evolution. For these projects, the number of introduced TDIs in each period is not stable, and it is reasonable to assume that it is influenced by some external parameters. This observation renders important the study of potential external factors that drive the accumulation of TDIs along the evolution of a software project.

   The second research question that we have explored led to a rather unexpected finding: i.e., the number of commits, made in a time period, is (for the majority of the cases) not correlated to the number of introduced TDIs into the system. Intuitively, one would expect that these variables would be related, in the sense that the more code is added, the more TDIs are expected to be introduced. However, this might not be the case for several reasons, i.e., TD might be more strongly related to: (a) the maturity of the project; (b) the developers' habits; or (c) the specific type of tasks performed in each time period. Therefore, this issue needs further investigation, as discussed in Sect. 6.2.

6.2   Implications to Researchers and Practitioners

Based on the results we are able to provide some first implications to both researchers and practitioners. Regarding **researchers**, we can claim that the accumulation of new code TDIs reflects (at least to some extent) the characteristics of the development process: by being stable in most cases, the introduction of new code TD is probably less related to external factors, and primarily dependent on the capabilities of the team. However, for a non-negligible number of projects, timing seems to be an important factor for studying the accumulation of technical debt: TDIs do not seem to be uniformly introduced along evolution, but rather behave as a temporal phenomenon, with multiple and (in some cases) large fluctuations. Therefore, we propose that researchers:

- For stable projects, investigate further the relation between the constant rate of introduction of new code TDIs with the practices followed by the developers. It would also be valuable to compare stable projects, but with different trends (increasing vs. decreasing), with respect to their key properties.
- For sensitive projects, perform explanatory studies to unveil the reasons for which spikes occur in the evolution of the introduced TD. Such studies could identify possible reasons (e.g., changes in the programming team, changes in used libraries or frameworks, impact of business goals) that lead teams/projects with a rather stable accumulation of TD, to perform worse under certain circumstances.
- Based on the output of the above, researchers should work on more accurate TD prevention methodologies that will attack the heart of the problem, based on the particular conditions of each project. For example, a project that is expected to undergo staff turnover, or will face tight deadlines, should calibrate its quality gates to ensure TD does not grow beyond thresholds.

Regarding *practitioners*, we suggest the following implications:

- We encourage them to perform fluctuation analysis and investigate the reasons for the existence of high or frequent peaks in the evolution of introduced TDIs. Understanding the consequences of their way of working in certain periods (which might lead to excessive accumulation of TD) can prove beneficial for process improvement purposes and quality control.
- We advise them to classify their project in the categories mentioned in Sect. 6.1. If their project is sensitive or if the observed trend is a steadily increasing one, then they need to perform a root cause analysis regarding the parameters that affect the accumulation of new code TD. Some of them may be mitigated, for example moving certain developers to different teams, or reprioritizing the backlog to include more refactoring.

7 Threats to Validity

In this section, we discuss threats to the validity of the study, including threats to construct, external validity and reliability. The study does not aim at establishing cause-and-effect relations; thus it is not concerned with internal validity.

Construct Validity reflects how far the examined phenomenon is connected to the intended objectives. The main threat is related to the accuracy by which TD can be captured by static analysis tools such as SQ. Rule violations reported as TDIs are only one manifestation of actual code and design inefficiencies. Furthermore, it is known that such tools are not capable of identifying architectural problems or other types of TD such as requirements, test or build debt. In addition, we consider only TD that can be mapped to methods, thus ignoring changes which might occur at the level of files. However, while SQ is by far not perfect in identifying TD, other static analysis tools suffer from similar limitations.

Another construct validity threat is related to the use of the number of commits as a surrogate of the workload that has been carried out by the project participants. Since in open-source projects, voluntary contribution is interleaved with the rest of the developers' activities, we acknowledge that a 'busy' or 'relaxed' period in terms of commits, does not necessarily reflect the actual work conditions of the developers. Moreover, commits differ in the amount of work that they carry: some commits might be accompanied by many changes in several files while other are related to only a few changes. Further research is required to derive the actual workload of developers committing to an OSS project.

Reliability reflects whether the study has been conducted and reported in a way that others can replicate it and reach the same results. To mitigate this threat, the study protocol is explicitly described listing all data collection and analysis steps. The only subjective data interpretation concerns the identification of spikes (which however is of secondary importance); therefore, to a large extent, researcher bias has been avoided. A replication package (see footnote 1) is available with all available data to allow for an independent replication of the investigation.

External Validity examines the applicability of the findings in other settings, e.g., other software projects, other programming languages and possibly other TD tools. We have focused only on Java Apache projects that use Maven as a build tool. This limits the ability to generalize the findings to other projects. The fact that the study focuses on 27 projects of the ASF, which are highly active and popular among software developers partially mitigates threats to generalization. Nevertheless, replication studies on the effect of new code on the evolution of TD are needed to strengthen the validity of the derived conclusions.

8   Conclusions

Studying the phenomenon of introducing code TDIs is a research direction that is important for building tools aimed at preventing the accumulation of TD. In this study, we focus on code technical debt, and in particular, we explore the temporality of the TD introduction phenomenon. To this end, we explore if the introduction of TDIs changes in different time periods, and if these changes can be attributes to the developers' activity in the corresponding period. To explore these two questions, we have performed a case study on the complete evolution of twenty-seven projects from the ASF.

The results of the study suggested that for the majority of the projects the evolution on TD introduction is stable, i.e., there are not many (at maximum 2) high fluctuations in TDIs introduction, due to new code. However, a non-negligible part of projects (approx. 40%) present high and frequent fluctuations. This result suggest that TD introduction is only partially a temporal phenomenon, with more TD being introduced in some time periods. The additional exploration of the phenomenon led to the conclusion that the spikes in the evolution of TD introduction are not correlated with spikes in the development activity, suggesting that the number of commits in the examined period is not the main factor affecting the existence of 'excessive TD introduction.

Acknowledgement. Work reported in this paper has received funding from the European Union's Horizon 2020 research and innovation programme under grant agreement No 780572 (project SDK4ED) and under grant agreement No 801015 (project EXA2PRO).

References

1. Li, Z., Avgeriou, P., Liang, P.: A systematic mapping study on technical debt and its management. J. Syst. Soft. **101**, 193–220 (2015)
2. Letouzey, J.-L.: The SQALE method for evaluating technical debt. In: 2012 Third International Workshop on Managing Technical Debt (MTD), pp.31–36. IEEE (2012)
3. Alves, V., Niu, N., Alves, C., Valença, G.: Requirements engineering for software product lines: a systematic literature review. Inf. Soft. Technol. **52**(8), 806–820 (2010)
4. Ampatzoglou, A., et al.: The perception of technical debt in the embedded systems domain: an industrial case study. In: 2016 IEEE 8th International Workshop on Managing Technical Debt (MTD), pp. 9–16. IEEE (2016)
5. Tufano, M., et al.: When and why your code starts to smell bad (and whether the smells go away). IEEE Trans. Softw. Eng. **43**(11), 1063–1088 (2017)
6. Kazman, R., et al.: A case study in locating the architectural roots of technical debt. In: 2015 IEEE/ACM 37th IEEE International Conference on Software Engineering, vol. 2, pp. 179–188. IEEE (2015)
7. Martini, A., Bosch, J., Chaudron, M.: Investigating architectural technical debt accumulation and refactoring over time: a multiple-case study. Inf. Softw. Technol. **67**, 237–253 (2015)
8. Olbrich, S., Cruzes, D.S., Basili, V., Zazworka, N.: The evolution and impact of code smells: A case study of two open source systems. In: 2009 3rd International Symposium on Empirical Software Engineering and Measurement, pp. 390–400. IEEE (2009)
9. Chatzigeorgiou, A., Manakos, A.: Investigating the evolution of code smells in object-oriented systems. Innov. Syst. Softw. Eng. **10**(1), 3–18 (2013). https://doi.org/10.1007/s11334-013-0205-z
10. Peters, R., Zaidman, A.: Evaluating the lifespan of code smells using software repository mining. In: 2012 16th European Conference on Software Maintenance and Reengineering, pp. 411–416. IEEE (2012)
11. Digkas, G., Lungu, M., Chatzigeorgiou, A., Avgeriou, P.: The evolution of technical debt in the apache ecosystem. In: Lopes, A., de Lemos, R. (eds.) ECSA 2017. LNCS, vol. 10475, pp. 51–66. Springer, Cham (2017). https://doi.org/10.1007/978-3-319-65831-5_4

12. Falleri, J.-R., Morandat, F., Blanc, X., Martinez, M., Monperrus, M.: Fine-grained and accurate source code differencing. In: Proceedings of the 29th ACM/IEEE International Conference on Automated Software Engineering, pp. 313–324. ACM (2014)
13. Arvanitou, E.-M., Ampatzoglou, A., Chatzigeorgiou, A., Avgeriou, P.: Software metrics fluctuation: a property for assisting the metric selection process. Inf. Softw. Technol. **72**, 110–124 (2016)
14. Runeson, P., Host, M., Rainer, A., Regnell, B.: Case Study Research in Software Engineering: Guidelines and Examples. Wiley, Hoboken (2012)
15. Field, A.: Discovering Statistics Using IBM SPSS Statistics. Sage Publications Ltd. (2013)

Is Complexity of Re-test a Reason
Why Some Refactorings Are Buggy?
an Empirical Perspective

Steve Counsell[✉], Steve Swift, Mahir Arzoky, and Giuseppe Destefanis

Department of Computer Science, Brunel University, London, UK
steve.counsell@brunel.ac.uk

Abstract. In this short paper, we explore one simple, yet unexplored question about the relationship between refactoring and bugs. Is the complexity of re-testing code immediately after refactoring a reason why some refactorings are buggy? To facilitate our analysis, we use a set of over four thousand refactorings mined from three open-source systems and decomposed into the four test categories of van Deursen and Moonen. Preliminary results showed that, compared with non-buggy classes, buggy classes had been subjected to more refactorings where a large re-test commitment was required; extent of re-test may therefore be a significant factor in determining whether refactoring creates bugs. Our finding supports that of Bavota et al. - that more and better testing after certain refactoring practices could reduce the harm that refactorings cause.

1 Introduction

Since the 1990's and the seminal texts on refactoring were published by Opdyke [8] and Fowler et al. [5], refactoring has been the subject of hundreds of empirical studies and become a vital tool in the daily work of a developer. Refactoring can be defined as the process of: *"Changing a software system in such a way that it does not alter the external behavior of the code yet improves its internal structure"* [5]. Despite this multitude of prior studies, there are still a range unanswered research questions. One of these is the link between refactoring and bugs. So, does refactoring cause bugs and if it does, then which types of refactorings cause bugs the most often? Every refactoring requires the developer to re-test the affected code to ensure that program behaviour has been preserved. So, an equally relevant research question to ask is whether the extent of re-test required post-refactoring influences the level of bugs in a system. To assess the level of post-test necessary, we use a taxonomy developed by van Deursen and Moonen [9]. The taxonomy categorizes each of 72 refactorings according to how difficult it is to unit post-test and it thus indicates the level of effort required to ensure that the refactoring has been successfully applied. Results from our analysis showed a tendency for buggy classes to have a higher number of refactorings with extensive re-test (compared to non-buggy classes). This implies that

© Springer Nature Switzerland AG 2020
M. Shepperd et al. (Eds.): QUATIC 2020, CCIS 1266, pp. 83–90, 2020.
https://doi.org/10.1007/978-3-030-58793-2_7

if we do complex and lengthy refactorings, then we should take every step to ensure that program behaviour has been preserved. The remainder of the paper is organized as follows. In Sect. 2, we describe information on the systems studied and taxonomies/data. We then present results through an analysis of the three systems (Sect. 3), before discussing results in Sect. 4. Finally, we conclude and point to further work in Sect. 5.

2   Preliminaries

2.1   Taxonomy of van Deursen and Moonen

To assess the extent of unit, post-refactoring testing required for every refactoring, we use the taxonomy developed by van Deursen and Moonen (V&M) [9]. The purpose of the taxonomy is to allocate each of Fowler's 72 refactorings [5] to a category, depending on the complexity and extent of the post-test required after that refactoring had taken place. The taxonomy is motivated by V&M as follows: *"One of the dangers of refactoring is that a programmer unintentionally changes the systems' behavior. Ideally, it can be verified that this did not happen by checking that all the tests pass after refactoring. In practice however, there are refactorings that will invalidate tests (e.g., when a method is moved to another class and the test still expects it in the original class)"*. In short, the categories represent an increasingly complex post-refactoring test effort commitment on the part of the developer and the taxonomy reflects the fact that some refactorings restructure the code in such a way that unit tests can only pass after the refactoring once those tests have been modified. The four categories identified by V&M are as follows:

1. **Compatible**: Refactorings that do not change the original interface. In the compatible refactoring category, we can use existing tests to check the refactoring. One example is the Extract method refactoring [5], which takes a section of code from a method and forms a new method (or methods) with that code. However, since this refactoring creates at least one new method, we need to add tests that document and verify that the new method has actually preserved behaviour.
2. **Backwards compatible**: Refactorings that change the original interface and are inherently backwards compatible since they extend the interface. In the case of this set of refactorings, according to V&M, *"... the tests keep running via the original interface and will pass if the refactoring preserves tested behavior. Depending on the refactoring, we might need to add more tests covering the extensions"*. One example of this refactoring type is Consolidate Conditional Expression, which re-arranges a conditional statement into a simpler and less complex format. The conditions in the statement do not change and it *might* be possible to use the same test on the changed code.
3. **Make backwards compatible**: This applies to refactorings that change the original interface and can be made backwards compatible by adapting the old interface. For example, the Move method [5] refactoring physically

moves a method from one class to another class and can be made backwards compatible by adding a wrapper method to retain the old interface.
4. **Incompatible**: This applies to refactorings that change the original interface and are not backwards compatible because they may, for example, change the types of classes that are involved. This makes it difficult to wrap the changes. The refactoring destroys the original interface and, as such, all tests that rely on the old interface need to be adjusted.

In theory, Compatible refactorings require less post refactoring test effort than those in the Backwards compatible category, which in turn require less effort than refactoring in the Make backwards Compatible category etc. In line with this, we adopt the stance that Compatible refactorings are the most straightforward to re-test and Incompatible refactorings the most complex; this is essentially the message that V&M convey in their work.

2.2   Systems Analysed

Our analysis in this paper is facilitated by the earlier work of Bavota et al. [2]. In their analysis, they describe how some refactorings were more likely to induce a bug than others, using the set of Fowler's refactoring activities as the vehicle. Results indicated that, while some kinds of refactorings were not likely to be harmful, others tended to induce bugs frequently (i.e., were harmful). In their study, they used refactoring and bug data extracted from three open-source systems and made that data available. We use that same data in this paper to explore refactorings but from a purely re-test perspective. The systems studied were: Xerces, ApacheAnt and ArgoUML. Xerces is a Java XML parser, ApacheAnt a build tool and library primarily designed for Java applications and ArgoUML a UML modelling tool[1]. Table 1 shows summary statistics for the three systems including: the period of time over which the system was studied, the releases analysed, the number of releases and, finally, the number of classes. The summary statistics in Table 1 are reproduced from the paper by Bavota et al.

Table 1. Three systems studied (summary data)

System	Period	Analyzed	Rel.	No. classes
Xerces	Nov '99–Nov '10	1.0.4-2.9.1	33	181-776
ApacheAnt	Jan '00–Dec '10	1.2-1.8.2	17	87-1191
ArgoUML	Oct '02–Dec '11	0.12-0.34	13	777-1519

---

[1] http://ant.apache.org/, http://argouml.tigris.org/, http://xerces.apache.org/xerces-j/.

2.3 V&M Decomposition

Table 2 shows the number of refactorings across each system and the number of refactorings in each of V&M's categories; here, Comp. or comp denotes Compatible, b/comp. denotes Backwards compatible and Incomp. represents Incompatible. The refactorings were collected in the original study of Bavota et al. by the Ref-Finder tool [6] and we use exactly the same set of refactorings. In the Xerces system for example, there were 1528 refactorings in total; of that total, 668 were "Compatible", 218 "Backwards compatible", 510 "Make backwards compatible" and 132 "Incompatible".

Table 2. Categories of V&M across the three systems

System	Comp.	Backwards comp.	Make b/comp.	Incomp.	Total
Xer.	668	218	510	132	1528
Apac.	290	67	142	21	520
Argo.	788	194	837	194	2013
Total	**1746**	**479**	**1489**	**347**	**4061**

From Table 2, we also see that the Compatible category forms the largest number (1746) and that ArgoUML has the highest number of overall refactorings (2013) across the four categories. Significant numbers of Make backwards compatible refactorings can also be seen; Incompatible refactorings were relatively small in number (just 347 from 4061 (8.54%)). The numbers in the table thereby give a mixed picture in terms of a developer's propensity to choose refactorings with a less complex required post-refactoring test. It seems that they are as likely to undertake complex refactorings (with long re-test requirements) as they are simpler ones. The numbers of Incompatible refactorings are comparable with the numbers of Backwards compatible refactoring, even though the former represents the lengthiest post refactoring test required. Based on the evidence from Table 2, it appears that developers do not necessarily choose refactorings with a low post-refactoring test burden according to the taxonomy of V&M.

3 Data Analysis

3.1 Buggy Classes

To further our analysis, we looked at the type of refactorings in each system for classes where *at least* one bug had been recorded due to a refactoring and the V&M categories of those refactorings. Table 3 lists the name of the refactorings and, for each of the three systems abbreviated to Xer,. Apa., and Arg., the number of refactorings, total and the V&M category of that refactoring. In the Xerces system, there were 26 Add parameter refactorings made to classes with at least one bug and across all three systems there were 68 Add parameter refactorings in total. Add parameter falls into the "Make backwards compatible" category of refactoring. We note that for space in the paper (there were in excess of 35 types of refactoring), we have left out any refactoring where, across the three systems, there were less than ten refactorings of that type - we do include these in reported analyses, however. We have also abbreviated some refactorings in Table 3 for space purposes. In full and in the order of the table, these are: Consolidate conditional expression, Consolidate duplicate conditional fragments, Introduce explaining variable, Remove assignments to parameters, Replace method with method object, Replace nested conditional with guard clauses and Replace magic number with symbolic constant.

Table 3. V&M categories (buggy classes)

Refactoring	Xer.	Apa.	Arg.	Total	V& M category
Add parameter	26	10	32	68	Make b/comp.
Cons. cond. expression	11	5	3	19	Backwards comp.
Cons. dup. cond. frag.	16	11	13	40	Comp.
Extract method	11	11	19	41	Backwards comp.
Inline method	6	2	2	10	Incomp.
Intr. explaining variable	5	7	14	26	Comp.
Intr. null object	9	8	13	30	Comp.
Inline method	2	0	10	12	Comp.
Move field	11	3	63	77	Incomp.
Move method	7	8	40	55	Make b/comp.
Remove ass. parameters	8	4	9	21	Comp.
Remove control flag	3	5	11	19	Comp.
Remove parameter	24	7	31	62	Make b/comp.
Rename method	19	9	17	45	Make b/comp.
Rep. meth. w meth. o.	16	0	80	96	Comp.
Rep. nest. cond. w g.	12	0	8	20	Comp.
Rep. mag. no. w sym. c.	16	13	7	36	Comp

In terms of the totals and including 13 refactorings left out of the table for the Compatible category, there were 313 (43.84%) refactorings. For the Backwards compatible category and including 8 refactorings left out of the table, there were 68 refactorings in the category (9.52%). For the Make backwards compatible category and including 9 refactorings not in the table, there were 239 refactorings in that category (33.47%). Finally, for the Incompatible category, including 7 not in the table, there were 94 refactorings (13.17%). Overall, this means that 53.36% of all refactorings with at least one bug were drawn from the Compatible and Backwards compatible categories. Most notable from the data, however, is that 46.64% of refactorings in classes with at least one bug were in the Make backwards compatible and Incompatible categories (i.e., those requiring the most post-test effort).

3.2   Non-buggy Classes

Table 4 shows the corresponding data for classes where *no bug* was recorded. So, for the Xerces system, 581 refactorings had been applied to classes with no recorded bug in the Compatible category. Similarly, 115 refactorings in the Incompatible category had been applied to classes with no yet recorded bugs. It also shows the total in each category and the percent that those totals reflect of the total number of refactorings. For comparison, we also include the percent for the buggy refactorings from Table 3. For example, there were 1311 Compatible refactorings across the three systems and this represents 42.57% of the total. For the buggy total in Table reftbl3, the corresponding percent was 43.84.

Table 4. V&M categories (non-buggy classes)

System	Comp.	Backwards comp.	Make b/comp.	Incomp.
Xerces	581	196	434	115
ApacheAnt	242	51	108	16
ArgoUML	488	134	607	107
Total	**1311**	**381**	**1149**	**238**
% non-buggy	**42.58**	**12.37**	**37.32**	**7.73**
(% buggy)	**(43.84)**	**(9.52)**	**(33.47)**	**(13.17)**

The most notable feature of Table 4 is the contrast between the number of Make backwards compatible and Incompatible refactorings compared with the set of data from Table 3. From the set of non-buggy classes totalling 3079 refactorings, we see that the Compatible category accounted for 42.58% the Back compatible category accounted for 12.37%, the Make backwards compatible category 37.32% and the Incompatible category just 7.73%. In total therefore, 54.94% were drawn from the Compatible and Backwards compatible categories and 45.06% from the Make backwards compatible and Incompatible categories.

From this data, the percentages are similar across buggy and non-buggy classes for three of the four categories. It is the relatively larger number of Incompatible refactorings (13.17%) in buggy classes compared with non-buggy classes - the corresponding value in non-buggy was almost half. We posit that the cause of bugs in the buggy classes was due directly to the extra number of Incompatible buggy refactorings. In particular, we single out the Move field refactoring in the ArgoUML system with 66 individual instances of this refactoring. As its name suggests, this refactoring should be applied when: "*A method is used more in another class than in its own class"*. The solution is to move that method to the class where it is being used most. Move method is a refactoring whose key purpose is to reduce coupling, a feature of systems that is widely acknowledged (when in excess) as contributing to the code buggyness [1,3]. So, while the Move method may well solve one problem, it may cause others due to the re-test required and the bug potential as a result.

We carried out Chi-square test to determine statistical significance of buggyness and its influence on the different categories [4]. We used a $2 * 4$ contingency table, with buggy and non-buggy representing the two rows in the table and the four columns representing the categories of refactoring and totals. The contingency table is therefore an amalgamation of the results found in Tables 3 and 4, representing buggy and non-buggy sets of refactorings and the numbers of refactorings in each, respectively. The Chi-square analysis gave a p-value of 0.00001 (degrees of freedom $= 3$). This value is less than <0.01 and we therefore fail to accept the null hypothesis of independence between buggyness and refactoring category. The buggyness of a class *is* dependent on the category of refactoring.

4   Discussion

Our short paper precludes a full treatment of the literature in the area. However, our analysis is heavily informed by the work of Bavota et al. [2]. They explored the buggyness of Fowler's set of 72 refactorings. Their conclusion was that more accurate code inspection and testing activities needed to be in place to prevent refactorings causing harm to code and seeding bugs. Our analysis has shown the same rule applies, but that it may be the extent of post-refactoring test that may be a contributory factor to bugs. We would qualify this by saying that if you undertake refactorings in the Incompatible category according to V&M, then extra care and attention should be invested in the testing process to make sure it is done properly. The refactoring literature on trends and traits in refactorings and the closely linked topic of code smells is well-documented [5]; however, the issue of the damage that post-refactoring can do is still largely undocumented. In this paper, we take the first steps in that research direction.

We also need to consider the threats to the validity of our study. Firstly, we have only examined three systems, which is a small sample. There is no guarantee that, were we to study more systems, the same results would be found. Secondly, the taxonomy of V&M studied in this paper is theoretical only and, unlike the study of Bavota et al. [2], is not empirically-based. This could be criticised since it is an untried taxonomy "in the field". Thirdly, we have studied only open-source code; industrial code may show altogether different features. Fourthly, the message that this work has conveyed is that refactorings with high post-test may cause bug-related problems. But there may be multiple other factors to consider in the development process. For example, the experience of the developer, the age of the system or the refactoring strategy adopted by the organization. Finally, we cannot be sure of the proportion of automated refactorings used in this study *vis-a-vis* those carried out manually; we assume a manual approach to refactoring. However, there is empirical evidence suggesting that a high proportion of developers prefer manual refactoring anyway [7].

5   Conclusions and Future Work

In this paper, we explored a single research question related to refactoring. The question asked whether the harm that refactoring can do was related to the amount of re-test necessary after applying a refactoring. The taxonomy of van Deursen and Moonen was used to support our analysis and this placed every refactoring into one of four categories in ascending difficulty of testing. Preliminary results showed that, compared with non-buggy classes, buggy classes had been subjected to more refactorings where a large re-test commitment was required. This implies that refactorings causing bugs may be simply down to the test load and human errors that may arise from that; for larger, more complex refactorings there is more room for human error than for smaller, less complex ones. Future work will focus on experiments with industrial developers to see if refactorings with low post requirements are, experimentally, more likely to induce a bug. This will take the form of a replication of Bavota's study. Finally, it would be interesting to extend our study to other open-source systems and to multiple application domains.

References

1. Basili, V., Briand, L., Melo, W.: A validation of object-oriented design metrics as quality indicators. IEEE Trans. Soft. Eng. **22**(10), 751–761 (1996)
2. Bavota, G., De Carluccio, B., De Lucia, A., Di Penta, M., Oliveto, R., Strollo, O.: When does a refactoring induce bugs? An empirical study. In: 12th IEEE Conference on Source Code Analysis and Manipulation, SCAM 2012, Italy, 2012, pp. 104–113 (2012)
3. Briand, L., Devanbu, P., Melo, W.: An investigation into coupling measures for C++. In: International Conference on Software Engineering, vol. 12 (1999)
4. Field, A.: Discovering Statistics Using IBM SPSS Statistics, 4th edn. Sage Publications Ltd., Thousand Oaks (2013)
5. Fowler, M.: Refactoring: Improving the Design of Existing Code. Addison-Wesley Longman Publishing Co. Inc., Boston (1999)
6. Kim, M., Gee, M., Loh, A., Rachatasumrit, N.: Ref-finder: a refactoring reconstruction tool based on logic query templates, pp. 371–372 (January 2010)
7. Negara, S., Chen, N., Vakilian, M., Johnson, R.E., Dig, D.: A comparative study of manual and automated refactorings. In: Castagna, G. (ed.) ECOOP 2013. LNCS, vol. 7920, pp. 552–576. Springer, Heidelberg (2013). https://doi.org/10.1007/978-3-642-39038-8_23
8. Opdyke, W.: Refactoring: a program restructuring aid in designing object-oriented application frameworks. Ph.D. thesis, Univ. of Illinois (1992)
9. van Deursen, A., Moonen, L.: The video store revisited - thoughts on refactoring and testing. In: Proceedings - XP 2002, Sardinia, Italy (2002)

Human and Artificial Intelligences
for Software Evolution

Suggesting Descriptive Method Names: An Exploratory Study of Two Machine Learning Approaches

Oleksandr Zaitsev[1,2]([✉]), Stephane Ducasse[1], Alexandre Bergel[3], and Mathieu Eveillard[2]

[1] Inria, Univ. Lille, CNRS, Centrale Lille, UMR 9189 - CRIStAL, Lille, France
{oleksandr.zaitsev,stephane.ducasse}@inria.fr
[2] Arolla, Paris, France
mathieu.eveillard@arolla.fr
[3] ISCLab, Department of Computer Science (DCC), University of Chile, Santiago, Chile
abergel@dcc.uchile.cl

Abstract. Programming is a form of communication between the person who is writing code and the one reading it. Nevertheless, very often developers neglect readability, and even well-written code becomes less understandable as software evolves. Together with the growing complexity of software systems, this creates an increasing need for automated tools for improving the readability of source code. In this work, we focus on method names and study how a descriptive name can be automatically generated from a method's body. We experiment with two approaches from the field of text summarization: One based on TF-IDF and the other on deep recurrent neural network. We collect a dataset of methods from 50 real world projects. We evaluate our approaches by comparing the generated names to the actual ones and report the result using Precision and Recall metrics. For TF-IDF, we get results as good as 28% precision and 45% recall; and for deep neural network, 46% precision and 32% recall.

Keywords: Software evolution · Machine learning · Method names

1 Introduction

The approach to programming has significantly changed in the past few decades. Instructions written by programmers are not solely meant for a computer to execute. Source code must be read by humans in many critical situations (e.g., bug fixing, maintenance) [15]. Developers spend most of their time reading the source code. According to Kent Beck and Robert Martin [6,18], the ratio of time spent reading versus writing is well over 10 to 1. Making source code easier to read decreases the cost of software development and maintenance. In practice, the

© Springer Nature Switzerland AG 2020
M. Shepperd et al. (Eds.): QUATIC 2020, CCIS 1266, pp. 93–106, 2020.
https://doi.org/10.1007/978-3-030-58793-2_8

readability of source code is often overlooked. Despite understanding the importance of clean code, developers choose poor names for their entities, create long functions and God classes (a well known code smell), fail to write documentation comments [9,16]. But even good development ethics can not ensure that the system remains clean and comprehensive over time. Software evolves [8], code gets refactored and modified, which often changes the purpose of variables, functions, and classes, as well as the relations between them. Good identifier names will degrade over time, bad ones will become even more misleading. Improving and updating identifier names is one of the key aspects of maintaining an evolving software system. This is a complicated task that requires a profound understanding of the entire system at all times. In the context of large software systems that continue growing in size and complexity [17], such understanding is virtually impossible without the assistance of automated tools. We need tools that will support developers in maintaining the consistency and understandability of the codebase. In this paper, we focus on the quality of method names and study how a descriptive name can be generated from a method's body. We approach this problem as a problem of text summarization and explore two approaches: one based on TF-IDF [19] and the other one using a deep recurrent neural network [23]. These methods were chosen because the first one is a most widely used *extractive approach*, meaning that it generates the summary by extracting the words from the text it is given; and the second one is a state of the art *abstractive approach*, meaning that it can produce words that were not present in the original text. In our case, the summary to generate is the method name, and the original text is the method body. We collected a dataset of 132,046 methods from 50 of real world projects. We cleaned and tokenized this code and used it to train the two models to suggest descriptive names for methods. We evaluate the approaches by comparing method names proposed by our models to the actual names of these methods. Those actual names were given by the programmers so they can be considered the ground truth. After training the models on 70% of methods and evaluating their suggestions on other 20% of methods, we achieved 28% precision, 45% recall with TF-IDF model and 46% precision, 32% recall with a deep learning model. The contribution of this paper are: (i) we argue that programming languages syntax and conventions influence the preprocessing of source code and names, and we propose a methodology for the Pharo programming language; and (ii) we give and compare first results for two text summarization approaches, one abstractive and one extractive.

The rest of this paper is structured as follow: In Sect. 2 we present the two machine learning models that we considered. In Sect. 3, we describe the collection, tokenization and filtering of source code and method names. Then, in Sect. 4 we present the experiment setup used to test the two approaches. We present and discuss the results in Sect. 5. We close the paper with discussion of related work, Sect. 6 and the conclusion 7.

2   Two Approaches for Text Summarization

Source code written by programmers has statistical properties similar to the natural languages such as English or Chinese. In fact, code is even more repetitive and predictable than natural languages [12]. Which means natural language processing approaches should be applicable to it. In this context, method names can be seen as summaries of their method bodies in the same way as title is a summary of an article. Therefore, the problem of generating method names can be seen as a problem of summarizing the source code in method's body with a couple of English words. We will just extract all identifiers in a method body, then we split them into words either by CamelCase or on underscores. That way, a method body becomes a document that we want to summarize. This preparation step is described in Sect. 3. Text summarization is divided into extractive approaches and abstractive ones. We selected one approach from each for our experiment: extractive is done with TF-IDF combined with an n-gram language model; abstractive is done with an attention based sequence to sequence neural network.

2.1   Extractive Model: TF-IDF with N-Grams

This approach is based on two steps: first extract the important words with TF-IDF, and then order them with n-gram language model. TF-IDF stands for *Term Frequency-Inverse Document Frequency*, a measure of word importance that works by determining the relative frequency of a word in a specific document compared to the inverse proportion of that word over the entire corpus of documents [19]. Intuitively, this means that the high TF-IDF scores will be assigned to words that are frequent in a given document and rare in all other ones. It allows one to find the most representative words (keywords) in a document and therefore can be used to summarize the given document. TF-IDF score is low for words that frequently occur in the language—such as "and", "the", etc. for English—and high for words that are frequent only in a given document. The word scores are also used to decide how many words there will be in the summary, the naive solution being to fix a threshold score above which words will make up the summary. However, to get a human readable summary of a document, the keywords also need to be ordered in a "natural" way. For this we use the *n-gram language model*, a probabilistic model that learns the probability distribution of n-grams (sequences of n words) which can be used to compute the joint probability of any given sequence of words. For summarization, a simple solution consists in generating all possible permutations of the keywords extracted by TF-IDF, and then find the most likely one. TF-IDF, as used in Information Retrieval, is trained and applied on the same data. To use it on previously unseen data (summarizing new documents) it must be slightly adapted. IDF is computed on the initial dataset, that can be called training dataset. This allows to compute a measure of "surpriseness" of each word within the domain of the training dataset. Then TF is computed on a, possibly new, document to be summarized. This can raise a problem if the new document contains words never appearing in the training dataset. In this case, IDF would be a division by 0. A simple solution is to remove such new words. To avoid a similar problem with n-gram model, words that do not appear both in documents and summaries are removed. If they appeared in the documents but not the summaries, they could be extracted by TF-IDF, but not ordered by the n-gram model.

2.2   Abstractive Model: Sequence to Sequence Neural Network

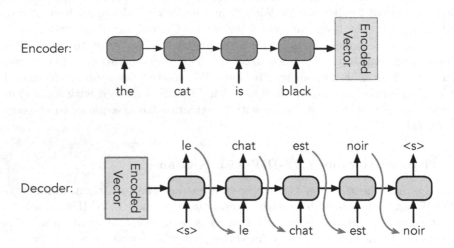

Fig. 1. Using sequence to sequence recurrent neural network to translate an English sentence *"the cat is black"* to a French sentence *"le chat est noir"*. *Encoder* takes a sequence of English words as input and encodes it with a fixed sized vector of numbers. *Decoder* takes this vector as input and produces the sequence of French words. (Color figure online)

Recently [21] argued that abstractive summarization could be seen as a translation problem from text to summary. Automated text translation is a very prolific research domain. Among the numerous approaches, we wanted one that made as little assumption as possible on the problem to solve. We chose a neural network approach that maps an input sequence (the document) to an output sequence (the summary) and is commonly used for neural machine translation. It can also be applied to the summarization problem additional knowledge about the nature of the sequences other than the list of words they are made of. Specifically, we use a *sequence to sequence recurrent neural network with GRU cells and attention-based decoder* [7,13,23]. The fact that the neural network is *recurrent* allows one to have an input sequence of any length. In Fig. 1, it means that each cell (green or yellow boxes) is actually the same in the network that links to itself. The figure itself shows an hypothetical unrolled network where each word is processed by one cell. The *Sequence to sequence* neural network (aka encoder decoder neural network) means that we join two recurrent neural networks, where the first learns to encode the input sequence into a fixed sized vector (see Figure) and the second learns to decode that vector into an output sequence. Notice that this encoded vector is actually the (hidden) state of the cell at the end of the input sequence. In the encoder, the output of the cell (vertical arrow) is ignored, thus not represented in the Figure. In the decoder, the output is plugged back as the input for the next step. The decoder generates the output sequence word by word including the special "end of sequence" word (<s> in the Figure). This way, the decoder decides by itself the length of the output sequence. The fact that both are recurrent neural networks, means that the size of the input and output sequences can be decorrelated which is important for the purpose of summarization. Finally such networks tend to give more importance to the latest words and possibly forget the first ones. This is an issue for us because, if on average, English sentences have around 20 words, in our experiments, the average size of methods exceeds 130 words [26]. The common approach to fight against this problem is the *attention mechanism* (not illustrated in the Figure) that ensures that the position of a word in the input sequence does not affect the output. It takes the form of an additional layer that decides independently what attention to give to each input word.

In Fig. 1, we give two examples of the process, on top, of the translation from English to French, and on bottom, of the translation of a tokenized source code sentence into a tokenized method name.

3 Applying the Learning Models to Source Code

In this section, we first give some specificities of the Pharo language that influence how we applied the model. Then we describe how to prepare the methods to train and apply the models described in the previous section.

Each method translates into two sequences of words:

- The words extracted by splitting all identifiers in the method's body. This will form a "document" that the models must summarize.
- The words extracted by splitting the method's name. This will be used to train the models on body summarization.

3.1 Pharo Language Specificities

As stated in the Introduction, the language syntax and conventions have an impact on how we can apply the model. Pharo[1] has a number of specificities that illustrate this point:

1. Variables are not statically typed, a model could learn from the information about the types of variables, but it is not available in Pharo.

---

[1] pharo.org/.

2. Pharo has in-place argument in method names. Unlike C like language where arguments are grouped in parentheses at the end of a function call, in Pharo, arguments are inserted between the parts of a method name. This way, for example, the Java statement " bob.send(email,emma);" translates to " bob send: email to: emma." in Pharo. The consequences are that method names are longer, their vocabulary larger and they must be split at the right place to introduce the parameters. Longer names are not a problem *per se*, this is part of the model training process to learn the right length for a name. Splitting names at the correct place to introduce parameter is out of the scope of this paper. We generate method names as a list of words without the colons.

3. Because of the in-place arguments, method names in Pharo contain many stop words such as *on, with, and, to*, etc. Method names in languages like Java, Python, or C contain mostly nouns, verbs, and adjectives that are highly representative of method's purpose, for example, print (string , stream) or add(element, array). Method names in Pharo use stop words to separate and describe those arguments, for example, print : string on: stream or add: element to: array. It can be harder for extractive model to generate stop words because they do not necessarily appear in source code, and will most likely be discarded as too generic. We will explore the issue of stop words in Sect. 5.1.

4. Programming conventions dictate that methods should be very short in Pharo. In our experiment, the median length was three lines of code (mean around six) [26]. This means that documents are short with few words which may influence the models.

5. Some meta information about the methods is specified by calling certain methods from the body of the given method. For example an abstract method is a method that calls self subclassResponsibility . This obviously affects the model because the body of an abstract method has no relation with its name.

3.2 Data Preparation: Extracting Words from Source Code

To extract words from the methods body we: (1) only keep the identifiers in the method's body; (2) split the identifiers into alphabetic words; (3) convert words to lowercase. Only keeping identifiers means that we remove comments, symbols, numbers, strings, and characters. Note that in Pharo, true, false , and nil are not reserved words but variable containing predefined objects. As such we keep them as identifiers. Local variable declarations (see below, |n|) and block arguments (see below, :char) are also ignored. Because there is no type associated to them and they, normally, appear elsewhere in the source code, they bring very little information. After splitting the identifiers, we may end up with numbers that were part of the identifier, these are discarded as they are not alphabetical words (we also ignore the underscores and/or colons that were parts of the identifiers). So for example, the following hypothetical method body that computes the length of a string[2]:

```
"Computes the length of aString"
| n |
n := 1.
self do: [:char | n := n + 1].
↑ n
```

will result in the "document": *"n self do n n n"*. This is a perfect example of the issue that short methods raise. It is impossible to abstract a correct name for this method from the sequence of words we extract. Fortunately, many methods are more informative. Method names are decomposed in the same way. For example, the name printOn: delimiter : last : becomes: *"print on delimiter last"*

3.3   Data Preparation: Filtering the Dataset

Furthermore, to apply the model, some methods need to be discarded:

- Methods with names from which no words could be extracted. Overloaded operators (*e.g.* +) or strangely named methods (*e.g.* _42) would produce no words at the tokenization step described in Sect. 3.2;
- Methods with empty body after preparation. Similarly, some very short methods, for example returning only a constant, or empty hooks, would have an empty body after preparation;
- Fully duplicated methods, with same name and implementation, are reduced to only one instance so as not to bias the model. Note that duplicated method names with different bodies (*e.g.* toString in Java) are kept;
- Too long methods, more than 500 words in the body, are rejected for practical reasons. Training the model with such methods becomes too long to be practical. This problem comes from the attention mechanism (see Sect. 2.2) that requires to know the maximum input length and becomes very slow because of that, even for the shorter methods;
- Getters and setters are very easy to generate (most IDEs can actually do it), yet probabilistic models could fail on them. Therefore it seems better to leave them out of the scope of a method name generation model;
- Test methods name can also be easily generated, but this is done from a completely different source of information, usually the name of a method or class that is being tested, not their own body. Test method naming also follows different conventions that would require a specific model to learn;
- We said that abstract methods in Pharo were implemented with only a call to subclassResponsibility. It makes sense to remove them from the training set as it is impossible to learn anything from their body and this would just introduce noise in the model. The same goes for methods consisting of the

---

[2] The actual meaning of the code is not important, but, double quotes delimit comments, pipes delimit local variables declaration, square brackets delimit lambda functions, and caret is a return.

sole call to shouldNotImplement call, that allows to "remove" an unwanted inherited method.
- Methods whose body would consist only of the words super, self [3], true, false, nil are also filtered out. Such bodies only add noise and are akin to empty bodies.

3.4 Finetuning the Models

Training the probabilistic models involves hyperparameter tuning. This is done by training them on a (large) subset of the dataset and validating them on a disjoint (smaller) subset. By fine tuning the parameters, one tries to achieve the best possible results. Assuming the dataset used is large and representative enough, this needs to be done only once for a given programming language. For training set, we used 70% of the whole dataset, and for validating, we used another 10%. The remaining 20% were required for the study and comparison of the two models and will be discussed in the next section. The Extractive model (TF-IDF), unlike the abstractive one, cannot automatically decide how many words it should generate. Therefore we used the following heuristics: We keep only those words with TF-IDF score above a certain threshold. There is a lower and upper boundaries on the number of words that can be kept. If no words pass the threshold, we keep the one with the highest TF-IDF score. If too many words pass the threshold, we keep only the highest TF-IDF scores. The TF-IDF threshold was fixed to the one that gave the best F1 score (see Sect. 4.1) on the validation dataset. The value is 2.5 for Pharo. The upper bound value was set to 5 words, so that the n-gram model would not take too much time to find the most meaningful order of those words. For the Abstractive model (Sequence to Sequence Neural Network) one needs to tune parameters such as the size of the hidden state vector, the learning rate, and the teacher forcing ratio[4]. These parameters were selected to give the highest F1 score on the validation dataset. The quality measures are discussed in Sect. 4.1). For Pharo, we recommend to set hidden state vector = 256; learning rate = 0.01; and teacher forcing ratio = 0.5.

4   Experiment Setup

To compare the two models, we set up an experiment on some real world Pharo projects. We shuffled and split our data into three non-intersecting subsets. The first two were already presented in the previous section: training set (70%) and validation set (10%). For comparing the models, we also need a third independent set—test set (20%)—it is used to evaluate the final trained model on data not seen during the training itself so that the training and parameter tunning are not biased towards the test.

---

[3] this.
[4] The probability that during training the word generated by the model is substituted by the word from a real name. It is used to make the training smoother.

4.1 Quality Metrics

A given method name can be considered good by one developer and bad by another. In this study, we adopt a simplified approach for automatic evaluation which assumes that most methods in our dataset are well named, and therefore can be used as ground truth to evaluate our models. The actual name is called *reference name*, the ones generated by the models are the *candidate names*. We report four different metrics of similarity between candidate and reference names: *exact match, average precision, average recall*, and *average F1 score. Exact match score* is the simplest and the strictest metric. It is the percentage of candidate names that match exactly the reference names. This is our only metric that takes into account the order of words. Exact match score is easy to interpret, but very restrictive. Candidate name that is similar to the reference but does not match it exactly, will receive the score of 0, as if it was completely different. We used precision, recall, and their derived metric F1. These three metrics consider every name as a set of words. *Precision* counts the percentage of words from the candidate name that also appear in a reference name. *Recall* counts the percentage of words from the reference name that also appear in a candidate name. *F1 Score* is the harmonic mean[5] of precision and recall [22]. We compute these three metrics for each method and report the average of those values.

4.2 Random Baseline

Because of the limited vocabulary [26] and the fact that source code is highly repetitive [12], we can get good results just by selecting the words randomly. Therefore we will also compare our models to a random model as a baseline: The *random extractive model* generates name for a given method by selecting K random words from its source code. A random abstractive model, selecting K random words from all method names in our training set, would make little sense as it would have close to 0% chance of finding the right word (in our dataset, there are 8,211 words [26]). We set K equal to 3, which is the average number of words in the method names from out training set.

5 Results

In this section, we present and discuss the results of our experiment evaluation. We experimented on 50 projects selected from Pharo ecosystem. The list of projects, some information about them, and how they were selected, is available in our technical report [26]. We collected 132,046 methods out of which we kept 92,127 (61%) after the filtering process described in Sect. 3. The three datasets described in Sect. 4 have: 64,488 methods in the training set; 9,212 methods in the validation set; and 18,425 methods in the test set. Table 1 contains several examples of method names that were generated by our abstractive model.

---

[5] Harmonic mean is more intuitive than the arithmetic mean when computing a mean of ratios.

Table 1. Examples of method names generated with the abstractive model. The first column contains the source code of a method which was used as input, the second column contains the real method name which was unknown to the model, and the third column contains the generated name.

Source code	Real name	Generated name
self assert : self newNode isComment.	testIsComment	testIsComment
r := aColor red . g := aColor green . b := aColor blue .	color	color
aVisitor visitDraggableInteraction : self with: args	acceptWith	accept
aPackage isPackage ifFalse : [^ self]. self addElement: aPackage in: self packages.	addPackage	addPackage

5.1 Evaluation Results

We present the results of the experiment in Table 2. As could be expected, the random model gives bad results for exact match (0%). Its results for precision (20%), recall (26%), and F1 score (21%) are not so bad. This is caused by the small vocabulary.

Table 2. Evaluation results calculated on the test set for three models: the *random model* that selects three random words from source code, *extractive model* based on TF-IDF and n-gram model, and the *abstractive model* based on a sequence to sequence deep neural network.

Model	Exact match	Precision	Recall	F1 score
Random	0%	20%	26%	21%
Extractive	2%	28%	45%	33%
Abstractive	11%	46%	32%	36%

The extractive model shows an improvement over these results, with 2% exact match, precision of 28%, recall of 45%, and F1 score of 33%. The extractive model cannot propose new words that did not appear in the method body, this should reflect on a low recall which is not the case. Many methods in Pharo call another one with a similar name (to add a default parameter for example) which could be an explanation here. Further studies are needed to better understand this issue. The abstractive model has the best results, with 11% exact match, precision of 46%, recall of 32%, and F1 score of 36%. The high exact match is surprising and may be as good as what a human would achieve. Additionally, in Fig. 2, we plot the intermediary results of the abstractive model, one data point every 1,000 iterations. The scores are evaluated against the validation set, not the test set. This is what we used to finetune the parameters of the model. For comparison, we also draw the performance of the extractive model (dashed lines) evaluated on the validation set. F1 scores of the extractive and abstractive models are almost the same. However, extractive model performs worse based on the exact match score. We can try to explain this by the presence of many stop words (e.g. with, on, to) in the names of Pharo methods (see Sect. 3.1). One might argue that a language like Java, that usually does not exhibit such stop words in method names, could have better score here. To validate this hypothesis, we have identified 127 generic words such as *on, with, and,* etc. that

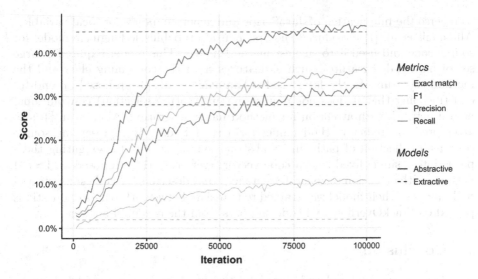

Fig. 2. Training of the abstractive model (measurements were taken once every 1000 iterations). The dashed lines are the scores achieved by the extractive model

are considered stop words in English[6]. We removed every occurrence of those words in the method names of training, validation, and test sets. Then we rerun the experiments and evaluated our three models on the new data to observe the effect that stop words have on the generation of method names. Against our hypothesis, the exact match of the extractive model was not affected by removing the stop words, it remained 2%. As for the abstractive model, its exact match score increased by 2% giving us 13% of exactly matched method names. The changes of precision, recall, and F1 score for random, extractive, and abstractive models are inconclusive and seem to be purely mechanical.

6 Related Work

Following the work of Gabel et al. [10] who performed the first study of the uniqueness of code and found that source code is highly repetitive, Hindle et al. [11,12] explored the predictability of code, and claimed that source code is even more repetitive and predictable than natural languages. They claimed that this predictability allows us to model code with statistical language models, proposed the notion of software naturalness and pioneered the applications of natural language processing (NLP) to the source code. Deep learning proved to be very effective in modelling source code—in recent years, deep learning models for source code found many applications for code completion [2,20,24]. Bavi et al. [5] used auto-encoder network together with a recurrent neural network

---

[6] The complete list of stop words that we used in this study can be found here: https:// gist.github.com/olekscode/125804150f2a559a171bf695c0a3f809.

to reverse the minification of JavaScript and generate names for local variables. Allamanis et al. [1] introduced the first neural probabilistic language model for source code and used it to suggest method names. This model required a large set of hard-coded features, such as features from the containing class and the method signature. In the later study, Allamanis et al. [3] proposed an end-to-end (meaning that it does not require manual feature selection) convolutional neural network with attention for method name generation. Alon et al. [4] also attempted to predict method names form their bodies by representing source code as a collection of paths in its abstract syntax tree and aggregating these paths into a single fixed-length code vector. Iyer et al. [14] proposed an LSTM network with attention to generate sentences that describe C# code snippets and SQL queries. Their model was trained to translate between the titles of questions posted on StackOverflow and code snippets from the accepted answers.

7   Conclusion

In this work, we explored and compared two machine learning models for text summarization when applied to the problem of generating descriptive method names from method bodies and thus improving the readability of source code. The first model is based on TF-IDF and n-gram language model, it performs the extractive text summarization by selecting important words from the source code of a method and putting them into a meaningful order. Second model is an attention-based sequence to sequence neural network which performs an abstractive summarization—it can generate method names from words that have never appeared in source code. After applying and evaluating our models on the dataset of methods collected from 50 real-life projects written in Pharo, we have reported the average precision score of 28% for extractive and 46% for abstractive models, as well as the average recall of 45% for extractive and 32% for abstractive model. 11% of method names generated by our abstractive model for methods from an independent test set are exactly the same as the real names given to those methods by developers.

Threats to Validity. The method names generated with our abstractive approach are only as good as the names on which the model was trained. The project that we have included into our dataset were handpicked by experts as the ones that follow good coding practices. However, we did not manually validate each one of the 64,488 method names in the training set, so this can be a threat to validity. A similar threat is the validity of evaluation. We have considered the real method names from our dataset as ground truth and used them to evaluate the generated names. Such approach is based on the assumption that the original names are good. In the follow-up study, we plan to perform a manual qualitative evaluation of the generated names.

Future Work. The evaluation technique could be enhanced by supporting the four automatic metrics of exact match, precision, recall, and F1 score with a human evaluation performed on a small subset of methods. For example, a model that generates a name, "on" for a method whose real name is "printOn:", will be awarded with 100% precision and 50% recall. Alternatively, if the real method name is "sumOfIntegers", a reasonably good name such as "addAllIntegerNumbers" will be scored with 0 by all metrics. Those cases would be easily spotted by a human evaluator. The same experiment should be tried with other programming languages as we saw that Pharo methods are typically small (a few lines of code) which limits the vocabulary available for both approaches. This can have good or adverse consequences on the results. In this work, we removed code comments and string literals because our study was focused on generating method names by summarizing source code. However, as we discussed in Sect. 3.2, many methods are very short and do not contain enough valuable information in their source code to generate a meaningful method name. A good extension for our study would be to utilize the natural language method descriptions provided in code comments. As it was mentioned in Sect. 1 where we discussed the motivation, the automatic suggestion of method names can be used to improve the readability of source code, which eventually would improve bug fixing and feature request incorporation times. We plan to target this problem through a controlled experiment or a longitudinal case study in the follow-up journal paper. Another interesting follow-up study would be to do cross project (or cross domain) training. In this paper, we trained on all projects (domains) mixed but it seems reasonable to assume that different projects would have different naming convention and vocabulary. Again, this could impact the results.

Acknowledgements. This work is based on the Master's thesis of Oleksandr Zaitsev defended at the Ukrainian Catholic University [25]. Oleksandr would like to thank the University of Chile, Inria Lille, Pharo Association, and Arolla for financial support. Alexandre Bergel thanks the financial sponsor of Lam Research and project FONDECYT Regular 1200067.

References

1. Allamanis, M., Barr, E.T., Bird, C., Sutton, C.: Suggesting accurate method and class names. In: Proceedings of the 2015 10th Joint Meeting on Foundations of Software Engineering, pp. 38–49. ACM (2015)
2. Allamanis, M., Barr, E.T., Devanbu, P., Sutton, C.: A survey of machine learning for big code and naturalness. ACM Comput. Surv. (CSUR) **51**(4), 81 (2018)
3. Allamanis, M., Peng, H., Sutton, C.: A convolutional attention network for extreme summarization of source code. In: International Conference on Machine Learning, pp. 2091–2100 (2016)
4. Alon, U., Zilberstein, M., Levy, O., Yahav, E.: code2vec: learning distributed representations of code. arXiv preprint arXiv:1803.09473 (2018)
5. Bavishi, R., Pradel, M., Sen, K.: Context2name: a deep learning-based approach to infer natural variable names from usage contexts. arXiv preprint arXiv:1809.05193 (2018)
6. Beck, K.: Test Driven Development: By Example. Addison-Wesley Longman (2002)

7. Cho, K., Van Merriënboer, B., Bahdanau, D., Bengio, Y.: On the properties of neural machine translation: encoder-decoder approaches. arXiv preprint arXiv:1409.1259 (2014)
8. Demeyer, S., Ducasse, S., Nierstrasz, O.: Object-Oriented Reengineering Patterns. Morgan Kaufmann, Burlington (2002)
9. Fowler, M., Beck, K., Brant, J., Opdyke, W., Roberts, D.: Refactoring: Improving the Design of Existing Code. Addison Wesley, Boston (1999)
10. Gabel, M., Su, Z.: A study of the uniqueness of source code. In: Proceedings of the Eighteenth ACM SIGSOFT International Symposium on Foundations of Software Engineering, pp. 147–156. ACM (2010)
11. Hindle, A., Barr, E.T., Gabel, M., Su, Z., Devanbu, P.: On the naturalness of software. Commun. ACM $59(5)$, 122–131 (2016)
12. Hindle, A., Barr, E.T., Su, Z., Gabel, M., Devanbu, P.: On the naturalness of software. In: 2012 34th International Conference on Software Engineering (ICSE), pp. 837–847. IEEE (2012)
13. Hochreiter, S., Schmidhuber, J.: Long short-term memory. Neural Comput. $9(8)$, 1735–1780 (1997)
14. Iyer, S., Konstas, I., Cheung, A., Zettlemoyer, L.: Summarizing source code using a neural attention model. In: Proceedings of the 54th Annual Meeting of the Association for Computational Linguistics (Volume 1: Long Papers), vol. 1, pp. 2073–2083 (2016)
15. Knuth, D.E.: Literate programming. Comput. J. $27(2)$, 97–111 (1984)
16. Koenig, A.: Patterns and antipatterns. J. Object-Oriented Program. $8(1)$, 46–48 (1995)
17. Lehman, M., Belady, L.: Program Evolution: Processes of Software Change. London Academic Press, London (1985). ftp://ftp.umh.ac.be/pub/ftp_infofs/1985/ProgramEvolution.pdf
18. Martin, R.C.: Clean Code: A Handbook of Agile Software Craftsmanship. Pearson Education, London (2009)
19. Ramos, J.: Using TF-IDF to determine word relevance in document queries. In: Proceedings of the First Instructional Conference on Machine Learning, vol. 242, pp. 133–142 (2003)
20. Raychev, V., Vechev, M., Yahav, E.: Code completion with statistical language models. In: ACM SIGPLAN Notices, vol. 49, pp. 419–428. ACM (2014)
21. Rush, A.M., Harvard, S., Chopra, S., Weston, J.: A neural attention model for sentence summarization. In: Proceedings of the 2015 Conference on Empirical Methods in Natural Language Processing, ACLWeb (2017)
22. Sasaki, Y., et al.: The truth of the F-measure. Teach Tutor Mater $1(5)$, 1–5 (2007)
23. Sutskever, I., Vinyals, O., Le, Q.V.: Sequence to sequence learning with neural networks. In: Advances in Neural Information Processing Systems, pp. 3104–3112 (2014)
24. White, M., Vendome, C., Linares-Vásquez, M., Poshyvanyk, D.: Toward deep learning software repositories. In: Proceedings of the 12th Working Conference on Mining Software Repositories, pp. 334–345. IEEE Press (2015)
25. Zaitsev, O.: Aspects of software naturalness through the generation of identifier names. Master's thesis, Ukrainian Catholic University, Faculty of Applied Sciences, Department of Computer Sciences, Lviv, Ukraine (January 2019). http://er.ucu.edu.ua/handle/1/1338. under sup. of Stéphane Ducasse and Alexandre Bergel
26. Zaitsev, O., Ducasse, S., Anquetil, N.: Characterizing pharo code: a technical report. Technical report, Inria Lille Nord Europe - Laboratoire CRIStAL - Université de Lille; Arolla (January 2020). https://hal.inria.fr/hal-02440055

Challenges for Layout Validation: Lessons Learned

Santiago Bragagnolo[1,2(✉)], Benoît Verhaeghe[1,2], Abderrahmane Seriai[1], Mustapha Derras[1], and Anne Etien[2]

[1] Berger-Levrault, Montpellier, France
{santiago.bragagnolo,benoit.verhaeghe,
abderrahmane.seriai,mustapha.derras}@berger-levrault.com
[2] Université de Lille, CNRS, Inria, Centrale Lille, UMR 9189 – CRIStAL,
Lille, France
{santiago.bragagnolo,benoit.verhaeghe,anne.etien}@inria.fr

Abstract. Companies are migrating their software systems. The migration process contemplates many steps, UI migration is one of them. To validate the UI migration, most existing approaches rely on visual structure (DOM) comparison. However, in previous work, we experimented such validation and reported that it is not sufficient to ensure a result that is equivalent or even identical to the visual structure of the interface to be migrated. Indeed, two similar DOM may be rendered completely differently. So, we decide to focus on the layout migration validation. We propose a first visual comparison approach for migrated layout validation and experiment it on an industrial case. Hence, from this first experiment and already existing studies on image comparison field, we highlight challenges for layout comparison. For each challenge, we propose possible solutions, and we detail the three main features we need to create a good layout validation approach.

Keywords: GUI migration · Challenges · Comparison · Validation

1 Introduction

With the fast evolution of programming languages and frameworks, companies tend to update their software more and more. This evolution may imply the migration of their application GUI [15]. To ensure the proper software operation after the update, one needs to validate and ensure the correct the migration of GUI. Whereas manual validation is always possible, it is tedious, error-prone, time-consuming, and is expensive for the companies. So we look for automatic validation approaches.

While approaches base their validation on DOM[1] comparison [4], few discute the validation of the rendered UI. The visual aspect of an application is mostly neglected, although it is essential for the end-user of the application [11], and thus

---

[1] Document Object Model.

© Springer Nature Switzerland AG 2020
M. Shepperd et al. (Eds.): QUATIC 2020, CCIS 1266, pp. 107–119, 2020.
https://doi.org/10.1007/978-3-030-58793-2_9

to the acceptance of the new software. Since the software may also be accepted or rejected by its look and feel, we consider that UI validation is extremely important for the success of the migration.

A migration process has one of two different objectives in relation to the migration of the UI: such process is rather **visually constant**, or **layout constant**. In the case where a migration process is visually constant, it aims to produce a migrated version with identical UI, from the layout of the widgets, to the look and feel of the widgets. In the other hand, when the migration process is layout constant, it aims to produce an enriched migrated version with the same layout, but possibly visually different widgets. In both cases, the validation of the migrated layout is a first step to the UI validation.

Inspired by other research fields [3,13,14], we propose an approach to compare the layout of migrated applications with the original layouts. We experimented with this approach on a real industrial migration project. From this experience, we report a list of challenges for layout validation and provide some solutions.

In the further sections, we discuss the need for validation in general and particularly about layout validation (Sect. 2). We present the different existing approaches to tackle down this problematics (Sect. 3), to explain the position of our solution. We draft our validation process (Sect. 4), and give place to the core of this article, the report of challenges (Sect. 5), where we describe each of the problematics we found on the development of our method. We identify the features that can help to solve those challenges (Sect. 6), and after a conclusion, we present the middle term goals of our work (Sect. 7).

2   UI Validation

Our work takes place in collaboration with Berger-Levrault[2], a major IT company selling Web applications developed in GWT. Unfortunately, GWT is no longer maintained and the last update was made in 2015. As a consequence, Berger-Levrault decided to migrate its applications to Angular 6. This migration is crucial since Berger-Levrault has more than 8 applications in GWT each including more than 500 web pages.

In preceding work [15], we proposed an approach to migrate the front-end of applications. We implemented this approach to migrate the GWT applications of Berger-Levrault to Angular. Once the migration is performed, we need to validate that the applications are correctly migrated.

Migration and validation are part of the same process. Once the validation is done, the results are going to be used for enhancing the migration and fixing errors. This new migration has to be validated once again, triggering a new process of migration. This loop recurs again until the process of migration is finished. In this context, manual validation for each iteration of the migration process is expensive in terms of money and time. Hence, we propose to rely on automatic validation.

---

[2] https://www.berger-levrault.com.

In this section we present the main migration validation approach we tried from the literature and detail why it is not sufficient (Sect. 2.1). Then we detail what is a layout validation (Sect. 2.2).

2.1   Current Migration Validation Approach

In the experimentations of validation of UI we started trying to use the common means proposed by the literature. [5,7] and [11] defined metrics to verify the success of the migration process. They checked that all the widgets and attributes are detected by their tools. Each widget and attribute must be identified and reachable, which means the entity type must be discovered, migrated, and present in the target applications. Each widget should also belong to the right container and its attributes created with the right value.

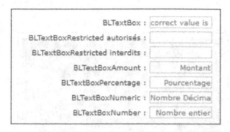

(b) Angular migration

(a) GWT original

Fig. 1. Migration of a page without considering the layout

We experimented with the above validation on the case of Berger-Levrault. Despite that, it reported good results according to the proposed metrics, the origin and generated UIs were completely different. Figure 1 presents the migration of one web page of a Berger-Levrault application. On the left-hand side (Fig. 1a), it shows the original page, and on the right-hand side (Fig. 1b) the page after the migration.

The traditional DOM proposes a tree as containing structure, where we can have elements composed by other elements, defining a strong relation of containment and scoping. Like this we can define a document with header, body and footer. Each of these parts can hold internal divisions, sections as well as widgets and components, recursively contained. Comparing DOM expecting to have a direct implication on the page rendering is the first solution. Two pages (the original and the migrated ones) may have equivalent DOM and thus plainly satisfy the proposed metrics. However, the migrated UI (Fig. 1b) and the original version (Fig. 1a) do not have much in common to the human eye.

Comparing DOM might be a good starting point to compare pages but it is, now-a-days, certainly not sufficient. In modern applications, the layout and style are managed orthogonally to the DOM composition. Thus, these approaches are not suitable for validating modern applications.

This is why we propose to add another dimension to the validation of the UI migration: the layout.

2.2   Layout Validation

From Merriam&Webster dictionary[3] a Layout is *the plan or design or arrangement of something laid out.*

From this definition, we consider that the layout is the position of the UI elements the one against the others. In a UI, we have two main kinds of components. Those that contain other components, for defining groups of components, and those that are contained. The components containing others, such as field set, card, panels, etc., are responsible for defining the main disposition of the contained elements in the page. For this reason we call those UI elements: "structural layout elements".

(a) Page

(b) Page's structural layout elements

Fig. 2. A layout example

In Fig. 2, we present the relationship between the UI and its layout. Figure 2a shows the page as interpreted by the browser. And, in Fig. 2b we highlighted the structural layout elements of the showed content. By highlighting these structural layout elements we are thus revealing the layout. The empty layout boxes belong to adds that have been silenced by the usage of ad-blocking plugins.

As we pointed out previously in Sect. 1, the migration may be required to be visually constant or layout constant. To validate that the migrated UI complies with the UI expectations we must take into account at least the layout.

---

[3] https://www.merriam-webster.com/dictionary/layout.

3   State of the Art

To compare the rendered UI after performing a migration, several solutions can be considered regarding the approaches existing in the literature. First, in Sect. 3.1, we expose existing validation approaches used to compare the visual aspect of two software systems. Second, in Sect. 3.2, we present approaches from other research fields that are related to image comparisons and which we think we can use in our domain.

3.1   Applications Comparison

Moran et al. [9] compared the UI of android applications. They proposed an approach to detect GUI changes in evolving mobile applications (e.g., between two versions of the same application). Their approach has two main concerns: mapping the screens between the applications version (i.e., which previous screen corresponds to which actual screen), and detecting the GUI changes. For the change detection, they rely on a pixel by pixel comparison of the screenshots of the previous and current applications.

Sánchez Ramón et al. [12] proposed an approach to infer a hierarchical layout from a UI with hardcoded widgets positions. To retrieve this layout, they use the closeness metric between two widgets. This metric allows them to compute the visual proximity of two elements in a UI. By grouping widgets together, they create the new layout definition.

Cao et al. [3] migrated web archives from HTML4 to HTML5. To validate the migration they proposed to segment the original and the migrated pages in blocks using the DOM. Then, they took screenshots of the original and migrated applications with blocks and computed the differences between the two pages.

Sanoja and Gançarski [13] proposed a segmentation method for web page analysis. Their method consists on dividing a web page into blocks. To retrieve the blocks, CSS and HTML provide them the position of all widgets on the web page, and they use background space to separate two blocks. For example, if there is no space between two elements, they are considered in the same block.

Alpuente and Romero [1] proposed UI comparison based on DOM analysis. Since the observation that two different DOM may render the same UI, they proposed to infer the visual structure (i.e., tree) of a web application from its DOM. To do so, they classified the HTML tags into four categories, the group, the row, the col, and the text. Then, they translated the HTML DOM using their terminology, and they compressed the new UI tree. The compression corresponds to a simplification of the new tree, for example, by grouping two groups together. They considered two different pages having the same visual tree as visually similar.

The authors proposed different ways to represents layouts, infer them, and compare them. Some approaches rely on DOM information and DOM comparison while others rely on screenshot comparison. Except [9] and [1], comparison approaches use blocks as a way to simplify the comparison problem and focus on the layout aspect. The blocks were created from DOM information.

3.2   Images Comparison

Another strategy to compare images is to take inspiration from the work on image retrieval. This field is focused on determining if an image is similar to or contains another one.

Van Beusekom et al. [14] proposed an approach to retrieve images based on their layouts. To do so, they extracted from each image its layout. The structural layout elements are represented by blocks. Then, to compute the distance between two images, the authors compute the distance between the layouts, and so between the blocks. To improve their result, they also match each block of an image with the other block of the compared image.

Finally, the image comparison approaches [6,10] are used to identify image similarity. This approach allows one to compare two images and find if an image is present in the other. It can be used to determine if two images are originally identical even after distortion or rotation, or to determine if part of an image is present in another one.

The proposed approaches might be used to compare two screenshots. However, since those approaches have been designed to retrieve an image inside another it is different from our problem. So, further work must be done to verify if their results are relevant in our context.

4   First Sketch of Solution

To validate the migration of the layout, *i.e.*, the identical positioning of UI elements the ones against the others, we proposed and implemented an approach[4].

Our approach aims to highlight the structural layout elements. It is inspired by the definition of blocks proposed by Sanoja and Gançarski [13], Cao et al. [3] and Van Beusekom et al. [14] The approach is divided into five steps.

First step: detecting pages to validate. The first step concerns the original and the target applications. For each of them, this step consists in detecting all the pages for which we have to validate the migration. By detection, we mean being able to reach given pages if the list is known or crawling the full application in the opposite case. Reaching a page is rather trivial, in traditional web development approaches; by precising the related URL. However, it becomes complex, for example in modern single page applications (from now on, SPA)[5], where different components are accessed not by using URL, but by applying specific flows of user interactions, *e.g.,*click, double click, hover, etc. The output of this step is a list of pages of the source application to validate, the way to access them, their corresponding pages in the migrated application as well as the way to access these latter. There are different techniques of crawling and discovery that suit this case. In the context

---

[4] https://github.com/badetitou/Pasino.
[5] A Single page application is a web application or website that interacts with the web browser by dynamically rewriting the current web page.

of Berger-Levrault, we rely on the migration tool that provides us this information gathered during the process of migration.

The four next steps are iteratively repeated for each couple of pages (one of the source application and its corresponding one in the migrated application). We describe the next step for a couple of source and migrated pages.

Second step: browsing original and migrated pages. The two pages are browsed by using a browser (*i.e.*, Firefox, Chrome, Edge, Safari, etc.). The same issues are faced concerning SPA applications what is the case for Berger-Levrault applications. In that cases, we use Selenium[6] to navigate through pages by simulating user interactions and access to the page to analyze.

Third step: creating blocks. Each browsed page must be prepared and normalized for further comparisons, *i.e.*, the size of the pages must be the same before taking screenshots to ease future image comparison. In this step, we choose and extract the elements to compare. Since we are validating layouts, we must emphasize the structural layout elements with their inner structural layout elements. Since we are not validating the look of the components, such as buttons, labels, text boxes, etc., we must underemphasize or silence the content for ignoring the comparison of these details. Concretely, we *create blocks* corresponding to each of the structural layout elements. In the context of Berger-Levrault, we apply a new CSS on the pages. The CSS converts all fieldset widgets into blocks with transparency. Thus, we can look at blocks composition.

Fourth step: taking screenshot. Our approach relies on a visual validation. Consequently, after creating the blocks, we take snapshot of the result as a visual mean of comparison. So we get an image with only structural layout elements.

Fifth step: comparing. We compare, pixel by pixel, the screenshots of the source application and the ones of the migrated application.

We applied our tool on the migration project of Berger-Levrault from GWT to Angular. Figure 3 shows the screenshots created by our approach using blocks. On the left-hand side, it shows the original page screenshot and its corresponding screenshot after applying the creation of blocks. On the right-hand side, it shows the equivalent screenshots for the migrated page.

Although it looks visually equivalent, and there are no differences between the two, the distance between the blocks and the size of the blocks are slightly different. Figure 4 shows the difference pixel by pixel of the blocks screenshots. Red pixels represent positions where there are differences between the source and the migrated pages. Even though there are few perceptual differences between the two images, the comparison of the blocks reports 9% of the exported image incorrectly migrated.

This 9% may look like a small number. In our context, this is not true. Indeed, Fig. 5 shows pixel by pixel comparison, between the original page and

---

[6] https://www.selenium.dev/.

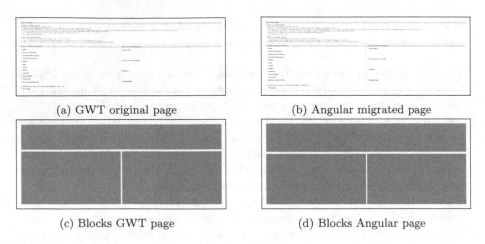

(a) GWT original page   (b) Angular migrated page

(c) Blocks GWT page   (d) Blocks Angular page

Fig. 3. Apply approach on GWT to Angular migration

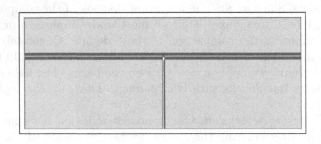

Fig. 4. *Diff* between pages (Color figure online)

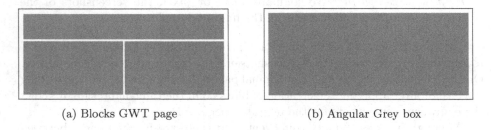

(a) Blocks GWT page   (b) Angular Grey box

Fig. 5. Difference in between original and a full grey block

a full grey block of the same size. As can be seen in Fig. 6, following the same strategy to measure the difference between the two screenshots, it was reported 5% of the image bad exported. So, our strategy reports that a full grey block layout is better than the one created from a real migration. But, it is completely false. Thus, it confirms that we need a smarter way to validate layout migration.

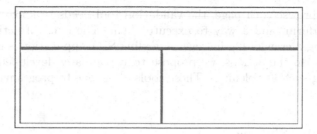

Fig. 6. *Diff* between original and a full grey block

5   Challenges of Layout Validation

From our experiment and the state of the art, we identified several challenges for the layout validation. Those challenges have to be considered for future layout validation tools. We identified 6 challenges: structural layout elements (Sect. 5.1), Ajax-based architecture (Sect. 5.2), successive shifting (Sect. 5.3), dynamic content (Sect. 5.4), interactive widget (Sect. 5.5), and overlap (Sect. 5.6).

5.1   Structural Layout Elements

Problem: One major problem is how to identify the structural layout elements in a page. In our experiment, we considered that fieldsets are the structural layout elements of all pages. However, layout also exists in pages where the DOM does not contain any fieldsets. So, one challenge is to define how the layout is expressed.

Solution: We identified two ways to solve this problem. One is to rely on DOM and CSS information. For each source language, we need to manually define what are the structural elements. For example, it can be CSS classes in modern web applications; or table nesting in legacy systems, as GWT. The other solution is to extract the structural layout by analyzing the screenshots [13].

5.2   Ajax-Based Architecture

Problem: One requirement to validate the UI migration is to be able to browse each couple of source and migrated UI pages. One can think, for a web application, of using URL of each page as a reference. However, recent web applications are developed using the Ajax framework. Ajax allows developers to modify the UI of a page without properly navigating, *e.g.,* changing the URL. It is the case of SPA promoted by recent UI frameworks: Angular, React, etc. So to browse a page, a tool can not simply get the URL content but need to perform actions on the UI.

Solution: To browse each page, the validation tool needs to know the suite of actions to perform, and a way to execute them. The suite of actions can be extracted using a crawler [2], however, crawling SPA application is complex [8]. Then, to perform the actions, we propose to use already developed tools used in GUI testing such as Selenium. Those tools allow one to programs interaction with a UI.

5.3   Successive Shifting

Problem: As identified by [13], the shifting of one block (because it is rendered with an incorrect size or position) may cause shifting of other blocks. Moreover, a slight error repeated on each block (for example each block is larger by only a few pixels) may create important differences in a screenshot but impact only slightly the layout.

Solution: Instead of comparing an image pixel by pixel or block position by block position, one can compare the position of blocks relative to visually near blocks. Thus, the validation approach will report minimal differences and not completely different pages. This comparison is more complex because it requires block identification, *i.e.,* recognizing the same blocks in source and migrated applications.

5.4   Dynamic Content

Problem: Some widgets, such as a table, can display information coming from an external server. If the received data changed, or if the component does not receive the data, the widget does not fill the same space in the original and migrated UI. While missing data does not impact the layout definition (in terms of relationships), it impacts the pixel to pixel comparison.

Solution: We found two ways to solve this problem. One is to identify the blocks in the original and migrated UI, then to compute the relationship between blocks. If the relationships are the same in the original and migrated UI, then the UI have the same layout. The other is to empty out the dynamic components applying some javascript routines, and thus do not consider data but still the default size of the component.

5.5   Interactive Widget

Problem: Some widgets are interactive. It is the case of the expandable panel, a panel that can be *opened* or *closed* by the user. The state of such components does not impact the layout but can change the size of the blocks. Thus, in block to block or pixel to pixel comparison, the validation tool reports bad migration whereas for example, states are not the same, by default in both applications.

Solution: One solution is to collect the state of the widgets in the original application, and then to set the state of the widgets in the migrated application before taking the screenshot. To set the states, one can use a tool such as Selenium.

5.6 Overlap

Problem: User interfaces are composed of multiple structural layout elements, *i.e.,* panel, fieldset, card. Proposed approaches, like ours, validate the layout migration by comparing layout composing blocks. Such approaches must consider that some layout elements overlap other layout elements. So, the z-index, *i.e.,* defining which widget is rendered on top of which one, must be extracted to validate correctly the interface.

Solution: One solution to handle the overlap is to use transparency when displaying the blocks. This solves the problem of a block inside another, but it does not provide much information about which block is on top of which one. One could use the DOM structure and CSS to extract this missing information.

6 Validation Helping Feature

Additionally to the identified challenges, we propose three important next features for validation approach that would help solving the challenges: block identification (Sect. 6.1), traceability (Section 6.2), and comparing the relationship between elements (Sect. 6.3).

6.1 Block Identification

Currently, our approach is based on the comparison pixel by pixel of two screenshots. Those screenshots are divided into blocks, but those blocks are not considered during the comparison. However, identifying the block in the screenshot would enable one to perform more precise analyses. For example, one can count the number of blocks or compare the pixels of a source block with the rest of the migrated UI.

At the same time, such a feature will ease the traceability feature (see next subsection) and allows one to compute blocks relationship, which is the main concept of what layouts are.

6.2 Traceability

The traceability is the ability to identify blocks couple, *i.e.,* which block in the source application corresponds to which one in the migrated application. We identified two ways to trace blocks: by analyzing the source code of the UI, or by comparing blocks position between source and migrated UI.

For the source code, one can use DOM information to retrieve the block couples. Indeed, DOM elements may have a unique id that can be migrated and so used to retrieve the block. One can also think of using XPath to retrieve the same element in the UI.

In case the source code of the migrated or the source application does not contain enough information, and if it is not editable, one can rely on comparing blocks position if the block identification (see preceding section) is enabled. Indeed, if the blocks are identified, one can recreate part of the blocks couples by comparing the position of blocks in the source and migrated application. Two blocks with approximately the same position in the source and migrated applications are likely to represent the same UI element.

Having the traceability will allow more precise analyses. Instead of comparing the UI of source application with the migrated one, one will be able to perform the analysis block by block.

6.3   Block Relationship

The block identification should enable the block relationship analysis. Instead of comparing pixel by pixel or block by block, the approach can compare the relationships between the blocks. Indeed, relationships are what define layout.

To do so, we need to extract from source and migrated screenshots the relationship between blocks, and compare them. Such an extraction might be difficult because of the preceding identified challenges. However, dealing with block relationship would be the final step in layout migration validation.

7   Conclusion and Future Work

From a previous experiment, we identified the lack of approach to test the layout of migrated GUI. Moreover, many validation techniques proposed in the literature are getting obsolete with modern frameworks and architectures. In this paper, we explored the state of the art and proposed a new simple approach based on other research fields. Thus, we identified future challenges in layout migration validation.

Finally, we proposed three main future work projects we will study: the block identification in an image, the traceability between source and migrated GUI, and the relationship between the blocks.

References

1. Alpuente, M., Romero, D.: A visual technique for web pages comparison. Electron. Notes Theor. Comput. Sci. **235**, 3–18 (2009)
2. Amalfitano, D., Fasolino, A.R., Tramontana, P.: A GUI crawling-based technique for android mobile application testing. In: 2011 IEEE Fourth International Conference on Software Testing, Verification and Validation Workshops, pp. 252–261. IEEE (2011). ISBN 978-1-4577-0019-4. https://doi.org/10.1109/ICSTW.2011.77. http://ieeexplore.ieee.org/document/5954416/

3. Cao, J., Mao, B., Luo, J.: A segmentation method for web page analysis using shrinking and dividing. Int. J. Parallel Emergent Distrib. Syst. **25**(2), 93–104 (2010)
4. Hayakawa, T., Hasegawa, S., Yoshika, S., Hikita, T.: Maintaining web applications by translating among different RIA technologies. GSTF J. Comput. **2**(1), 250–256 (2012)
5. Joorabchi, M.E., Mesbah, A.: Reverse engineering iOS mobile applications. In: 2012 19th Working Conference on Reverse Engineering, pp. 177–186. IEEE (2012). ISBN 978-0-7695-4891-3, 978-1-4673-4536-1. https://doi.org/10.1109/WCRE.2012.27. http://ieeexplore.ieee.org/document/6385113/
6. Karami, E., Prasad, S., Shehata, M.: Image matching using sift, surf, brief and orb: performance comparison for distorted images. arXiv preprint arXiv:1710.02726 (2017)
7. Memon, A., Banerjee, I., Nagarajan, A.: GUI ripping: reverse engineering of graphical user interfaces for testing. In: Proceedings of the IEEE Working Conference on Reverse Engineering (WCRE 2003), pp. 260–269. IEEE Computer Society Press, Los Alamitos, November 2003
8. Mesbah, A., van Deursen, A., Lenselink, S.: Crawling ajax-based web applications through dynamic analysis of user interface state changes. ACM Trans. Web **6**(1), 1–30 (2012). ISSN 15591131. https://doi.org/10.1145/2109205.2109208. http://dl.acm.org/citation.cfm?doid=2109205.2109208
9. Moran, K., Watson, C., Hoskins, J., Purnell, G., Poshyvanyk, D.: Detecting and summarizing GUI changes in evolving mobile apps. arXiv:1807.09440 [cs], July 2018
10. Morel, J.M., Yu, G.: ASIFT: a new framework for fully affine invariant image comparison. SIAM J. Imaging Sci. **2**(2), 438–469 (2009)
11. Sánchez Ramón, O., Sánchez Cuadrado, J., García Molina, J.: Model-driven reverse engineering of legacy graphical user interfaces. Autom. Softw. Eng. **21**(2), 147–186 (2014). ISSN 0928-8910, 1573-7535. https://doi.org/10.1007/s10515-013-0130-2
12. Sánchez Ramón, Ó., Sánchez Cuadrado, J., García Molina, J., Vanderdonckt, J.: A layout inference algorithm for graphical user interfaces. Inf. Softw. Technol. **70**, 155–175 (2016)
13. Sanoja, A., Gançarski, S.: Migrating web archives from HTML4 to HTML5: a block-based approach and its evaluation. In: Kirikova, M., Nørvåg, K., Papadopoulos, G.A. (eds.) ADBIS 2017. LNCS, vol. 10509, pp. 375–393. Springer, Cham (2017). https://doi.org/10.1007/978-3-319-66917-5_25. ISBN 978-3-319-66917-5
14. Van Beusekom, J., Keysers, D., Shafait, F., Breuel, T.M.: Distance measures for layout-based document image retrieval. In: Second International Conference on Document Image Analysis for Libraries (DIAL 2006). IEEE (2006)
15. Verhaeghe, B., et al.: GUI migration using MDE from GWT to angular 6: an industrial case. In: 2019 IEEE 26th International Conference on Software Analysis, Evolution and Reengineering (SANER), Hangzhou, China (2019). https://hal.inria.fr/hal-02019015

Towards Automated Taxonomy Generation for Grouping App Reviews: A Preliminary Empirical Study

Saurabh Malgaonkar[✉], Sherlock A. Licorish, and Bastin Tony Roy Savarimuthu

Department of Information Science, University of Otago, Dunedin, New Zealand
{saurabh.malgaonkar,sherlock.licorish,
tony.savarimuthu}@otago.ac.nz

Abstract. App reviews often reflect end-users' requests, issues or suggestions for supporting app maintenance and evolution. Hence, researchers have evaluated several classification approaches for identifying and classifying such app reviews. However, these classification approaches are driven by manually derived taxonomies. This is a limitation given the burden of human involvement, numerous app reviews and dependency on the availability of domain knowledge to perform classification. In this pilot study, we develop and evaluate a novel approach towards the automatic generation of a dynamic taxonomy that groups related app reviews. Our approach uses natural language processing, feature engineering and word sense disambiguation to automatically generate the taxonomy. We validated the proposed approach with app reviews extracted from the popular My Tracks app, where outcomes revealed a 72% match with a manual taxonomy generated from domain knowledge provided by humans. Our approach shows promise for rapidly supporting software maintenance and evolution.

Keywords: App reviews · Natural language processing · Contextual semantic similarity · Taxonomy · Classification

1 Introduction

Informative reviews expressed in natural language pertaining to apps contain valuable information reflecting requests for app features, specific issues (encountered bugs) related to the app or suggestions for improvements [21]. App developers are thus always on the lookout for efficient methods to classify and analyse such app reviews to convert them into actionable knowledge [21]. This knowledge contributes significantly towards software maintenance and evolution [17]. In the past, researchers have employed classification approaches as one of the methods to obtain actionable knowledge from app reviews [17]. Such classification approaches group together app reviews having common characteristics into specific categories based on a taxonomy derived manually from domain knowledge. This domain knowledge is made available by domain experts (humans) [17], which is burdensome, especially when there are numerous app reviews. In this study, we

© Springer Nature Switzerland AG 2020
M. Shepperd et al. (Eds.): QUATIC 2020, CCIS 1266, pp. 120–134, 2020.
https://doi.org/10.1007/978-3-030-58793-2_10

address the above-mentioned challenges by proposing and evaluating a novel classification approach which groups app reviews based on an *automatically generated taxonomy*. The automatic generation of the taxonomy is inspired by multiple knowledge domains such as natural language processing, feature engineering and word sense disambiguation based on contextual semantic similarity [11]. In the development of our novel approach we first extract informative reviews from a vast pool of app reviews using an automated rule-based filtering approach [6]. Next, we utilise natural language processing to perform necessary text pre-processing operations [1], and later tag the nouns as app features that are being reported, and the associated adjectives and verbs as the descriptors explaining the complaints about issues or requests/suggestion pertaining to those app features [13, 16]. These are modelled as the basis for representing the categories of the taxonomy. Finally, the categories of the taxonomy are used for grouping the informative reviews, which are then evaluated. To the best of our knowledge, our proposed classification approach offers a unique contribution to the app reviews mining and software maintenance domains. Our prime contributions are: (1) an approach for automatic generation of app reviews taxonomies, (2) empirical evidence pointing to the effectiveness of our approach, and (3) a set of recommendations for how the approach should be used.

The following two research questions motivated our enquiry:

RQ1. How can an approach be developed to automatically generate a taxonomy to classify app reviews into groups?
RQ2. How will the automated taxonomy compare to one developed manually?

We review related work in Sect. 2, evaluate multiple domains in view of combining various methods to answer RQ1 in Sect. 3, and further evaluate these methods in Sect. 4. Section 5 provides our results to answer RQ2. We discuss outcomes and their implications in Sect. 6, and consider threats to validity in Sect. 7. Section 8 presents concluding remarks and future work.

2 Research Gaps and Related Studies

A review of the literature reveals that all classification approaches for grouping app reviews are driven by domain knowledge made available manually by experts. For instance, Maalej et al. [17] manually created four specific categories to classify app reviews using basic keyword lookup grouping mechanism, Naïve Bayes, Decision Tress or Maximum Entropy. Panichella et al. [22] have created a taxonomy to classify app reviews using the J48 machine learning method. Ciurumelea et al. [7] have used a taxonomy comprising of five set of customised categories to classify app reviews using the Gradient Boosted Trees classifier. In the study, a set of random app reviews are manually labelled into categories by a domain expert. Later, the performance of a set of classifiers such as Naïve Bayes, SVM and logistic regression were evaluated towards the automation of the classification task. Di Sorbo et al. [8] have developed a more fine-grained taxonomy where app developers are required to manually check each grouped app review for context subsequently. Such studies raise the question '*What if under certain circumstances the domain knowledge required for classification is unavailable?*'.

Furthermore, the need to manually analyse app reviews seems to be unavoidable in most of the previously generated solutions. For instance, Maalej et al. [17] group app reviews into one of four categories: 'bug reports', 'feature requests', 'user experience', and 'ratings'. Of note here is that the taxonomy does not identify specific details (e.g., which feature is buggy), thus requiring app developers to analyse each app review for the necessary information after classification is performed. This challenge remains for the other taxonomies reviewed above as well. A critical evaluation of the abovementioned studies and others is presented here[1]. Here it is observed that there is no universal manually derived taxonomy made available for classifying app reviews, so that the classification process could be independent of the availability of domain knowledge. Another major drawback of manually created taxonomies which use knowledge from domain experts is the necessity to update the taxonomy as the software product evolves. To address such drawbacks, we were motivated to develop and evaluate an automated taxonomy generation approach for classifying app reviews.

3   Automatically Generating Taxonomy (RQ1)

In this section we explore the concepts and methods that lead to the design of an automated taxonomy from a corpus of app reviews.

3.1   Feature Engineering

The identification of product features is a crucial step during any product engineering (or re-engineering) process [4]. However, feature identification could be challenging due to variations in the way product reviews are specified, and thus domain knowledge becomes necessary. With the possession of domain knowledge, features may be identified by analysing the grammar structure of product reviews, where identifiers may be evident [13, 16]. To date, researchers have used parts of speech (POS) tagging for this purpose [13, 16]. Thus, we take inspiration from this approach for developing our taxonomy. We assume that nouns mentioned in app reviews are app features, and adjectives and verbs are issues, suggestions or requests related to the particular app feature [13, 16]. For example, consider the app review, "*GPS* (noun - app feature) is *inaccurate* (adjective - issue) and has to be *improved* (verb - request/suggestion)" [13, 16]. In the example, *GPS* is the app feature, *inaccurate* depicts the issue associated with the app feature, and *improved* reflects the request pertaining to the app feature [13, 16]. These patterns may form the core of a potential taxonomy generated through feature engineering, as depicted in Fig. 1, where an example is illustrated. Such a taxonomy would aid towards the grouping of similar app reviews. We next consider our investigation of suitable semantic similarity methods.

3.2   Semantic Similarity Methods

Corpus-based methods are often used to determine the semantic similarity between words [20]. These methods operate on the principle of word sense disambiguation by

---

[1] https://tinyurl.com/wy8tc39.

examining word pairs and their context of use [20]. Word pairs are awarded a score given the strength of their association [20]. Such analyses may take multiple forms: (1) similarity measures based on features, (2) similarity measures based on graphical edges, (3) similarity measures based on information theory, or (4) similarity measures based on knowledge distribution [25]. These methods use dictionaries which provide formal descriptions of the words that can be compared for semantic similarity purposes (e.g., medical knowledge on genes).

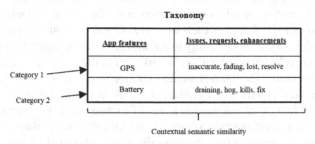

Fig. 1. An example of a generated taxonomy through feature engineering

Therefore, these knowledge sources (dictionaries) need to be created before computing necessary semantic measures [20]. Thus, the major disadvantage of semantic similarity methods that use dictionaries is that they are entirely dependent on the existence of domain knowledge. There may also be variations in the way words are used in different contexts by humans [20], which poses a challenge. This challenge lies at the heart of our proposal to automatically generate taxonomy from app reviews. We contend that the need to involve domain experts required for previously proposed taxonomies is problematic. In fact, even if such curated knowledge were available, differences in the way words are used by software users would pose a challenge. For example, the meaning of the word 'draining' in a dictionary is 'making a particular liquid run out of a particular space'. However, in terms of app reviews, 'draining' is associated with the consumption of a device's battery power. That said, given the nature of app reviews, most often, the words that are in close proximity of each other are often contextually similar [17]. This is because, app reviews often contain semantically similar words in close vicinity of each other [26]. For instance, consider the app review: '*not possible to accurately track time and distance*'. This app review indicates that the particular app is not able to accurately track time and distance. Of note here is that 'accurately', 'track', 'time', and 'distance' are in close proximity to each other, potentially indicating their contextual semantic similarities. This pattern is repeated for many app reviews, suggesting that in vector space representation of words (from app reviews), semantically similar words in terms of their contextual application are often close to each other, while the extraneous words are distant [26]. This forms the basis for the generation of our taxonomy which identifies the verbs and adjectives that are semantically closer to a particular noun based on their context of usage. Hence, we investigated three methods (COALS, PPMI and GloVe) that measure semantic similarities between words, and evaluated these methods in view of selecting the best performing one for our taxonomy generation. We selected these methods because they have been evaluated against other methods showing superior performance [5, 23, 24].

3.2.1 COALS

Correlated Occurrence Analogue to Lexical Semantic (COALS) is a word vector distance proximity method that addresses the drawbacks of its predecessor Hyperspace Analogue to Language (HAL) and the well-known method Latent Semantic Analysis (LSA) [24]. Initially, COALS creates a word-word co-occurrence matrix from the text corpus, using a ramped window of size four. For each word $w1$, COALS counts the number of times every other word $w2$ occurs in proximity to $w1$, and stores the weighted count of the total occurrences of the relevant word pairs ($w1$ with $w2$) in the respective cell of the word-word ($w1 - w2$) matrix. The ramped window of size four is responsible for generating the appropriate word counts. For instance, if $w2$ occurs adjacent to $w1$, the window assigns a count of four, if $w2$ is separated from $w1$ by one word, the window generates a count of three, and so forth, down to a count of one for a distance of three words. Finally, the word-word co-occurrence matrix portrays the weighted sum of all occurrences of $w2$ in proximity to $w1$. In the next stage, the Pearson's correlation coefficient is calculated between the weighted vector counts of the occurrence of words $w1$ and $w2$. This, in general, provides further insights into the vicinity of $w2$ with $w1$. Furthermore, with this context in the background, COALS converts all the negative correlation values in the matrix to zero, and computes the square roots of the positive ones. The square root operation further normalizes the matrix, thus making COALS unbiased towards larger positive values. The positive values of the matrix correspond to the word-word pairs that convey a substantial amount of information. Finally, the semantic similarity score S of word pair ($w1$ and $w2$) is calculated using the data present in the normalized matrix. Since COALS operates only on positive values, the correlation distance measure is known to provide accurate results than the cosine measure, as correlations tend to be subtler than cosines [24].

3.2.2 PPMI

Pointwise Mutual Information (PMI) calculates the degree of co-occurrence between two words ($w1$ and $w2$), as defined by PMI $(w1, w2) = \log_2 (p(w1, w2)/(p(w1) * p(w2)))$ [5]. This formula, in general, considers the probability of co-occurrence of two words given their joint distribution (occurring together), and their individual distribution (separate individual counts). However, the PPMI determines the co-occurrence of two words by considering only the positive PMI values, and the formula is stated as PPMI $(w1, w2) = \max(\log_2 (p(w1, w2)/(p(w1)* p(w2))), 0)$ [5]. Both methods create the word-word occurrence matrix to utilise the counts of the particular word-word pair along with the individual counts of each word present in that pair. PPMI first prepares the word-word co-occurrence matrix. Then, the PPMI formula is applied on each word-word pair entry in the matrix, i.e., PPMI is computed on the word-word co-occurrence matrix. Finally, cosine distance is used to determine the semantic similarity score of any word pair ($w1$ and $w2$).

3.2.3 GloVe

Global Vectors for Word Representation (GloVe) is a global logarithmic based bilinear regression method that inherits the strengths of the co-occurrence matrix and the application of context window [23]. Initially, it generates a word-word co-occurrence matrix that stores the count of the number of times a particular word $(w1)$ occurs in the context of another word $(w2)$. Furthermore, this method considers only the nonzero counts generated in the word-word co-occurrence matrix for further processing. After the generation of the word-word co-occurrence matrix, the method provides insights on the semantics of words from the perspective of the word-word co-occurrence matrix using probabilistic operations and highlights the contextual similarity between the words through the resulting vectors. For each word in the matrix, the method creates a function $f\left(Vw1, \ Vw2, \tilde{V}w\right)$ by calculating the probability of word $(w1)$ that appears in the context of the other word $(w2)$ with reference (context) to another word (w). The V in the function indicates the particular word vector and $\tilde{V}$ is the representation of the vector space of the contextual word w, which is used to determine the degree of contextual semantic similarity between $w1$ and $w2$. The relationship between the words $w1$ and $w2$ is determined by processing the ratio of the words' co-occurrence probabilities with reference to a contextual word w. The authors use a weighted least squares (WLS) regression approach to deal with fewer counts of word-word pairs occurring in the matrix, thus preventing any bias and avoiding noisy information. Finally, the method returns the semantic similarity score S of word pair $(w1$ and $w2)$.

3.3 Pareto Distribution Law

Irrespective of the best performing method being shortlisted for generating the necessary taxonomy for grouping informative reviews, we still face the challenge of determining the number of relevant categories for the taxonomy. The question is, *do we model all individual nouns (app features) and their associated adjectives and verbs (requests, issues or suggestions) as categories?* We address this challenge with the assistance of Pareto distribution law which provides the 80–20 rule that states that 80% of the contribution towards a cause is given by 20% of its specific participating entities [12]. The application of this law is common in the software engineering field. For instance, Archak et al. [2] have applied the law to identify 20% of the crucial product features that had an impact on 80% of sales. We take inspiration from this study and utilise the Pareto distribution law to shortlist entries (noun-adjectives/verbs) to generate our taxonomy in which we identify 20% of the categories reflecting 80% of the app features along with their associated issues, requests or suggestions. All other app features are then grouped in a neutral "Others" category. It is to be noted that the particular app feature in the taxonomy represents the name of the particular group.

3.4 Keyword Lookup Grouping Mechanism

After finalising the suitable semantic similarity method and determining the number of categories based on the Pareto distribution law, we utilise the keyword lookup (string matching) grouping mechanism to group informative reviews into relevant groups [17].

An informative review from the corpus gets categorised into a particular group if a word from the informative review matches with any word of a particular group present in the taxonomy (app features, issues, suggestions, or requests). That said, as noted above, if any informative review does not get categorised in any group, it is grouped in the 'Others' group to prevent the loss of information.

4 Experimental Setup and Evaluation

This section provides details regarding the procedures employed to drive our experiment and validate the primary outcomes of this study. First, we provide a brief introduction to the dataset that was used for experimentation purpose (Sect. 4.1). We then provide details on the text pre-processing operations that were performed (Sect. 4.2). Thereafter, we provide details regarding the three methods (COALS, PPMI, and GloVe) that were used to generate the required entries (noun-adjectives/verbs) and evaluations of the subsequent outcomes (Sect. 4.3). We next provide details of evaluations setup for our automatically generated taxonomy (Sects. 4.4). Our experiments were conducted using Python[2].

4.1 Dataset

In order to demonstrate and evaluate our approach to automatically generate taxonomies for grouping informative reviews we utilise the My Tracks[3] dataset which consist of 4,440 app reviews. My Tracks Android app assists its end-users to automatically or manually set and track feasible routes for their outdoor activities such as jogging, walking, skiing, biking, and so on. The app also allows end-users to check statistics of their activities in terms of the distance travelled, speed, ground elevation levels or calories burned. Further, this app allows end-users to save summary statistics on their computer, or share the same data with other similar apps, thus exhibiting a wide spectrum of functionalities to make it highly eligible for evaluation purpose. In addition, the My Tracks dataset was selected in this study as we have previously provided software maintenance insights for the developers of this app, and thus this software (app) provides a good baseline for evaluating our preliminary outcomes in this study. We extracted 1,628 informative app reviews using the automated filtering approach mentioned in [6]. Using this approach, 35% of the app reviews were manually labelled as either informative (app feature requests, issues, suggestions for improvements) or non-informative (useless content, e.g., baseless criticisms or praises). Thereafter, Expectation Maximization of Multinomial Naïve Bayes is used to predict the labels of the remaining 65% of the app reviews [6].

4.2 Text Pre-processing

Initially, we performed the basic text pre-processing operations on the extracted informative reviews such as removal of special characters, punctuations, whitespaces and numbers. Thereafter, we converted the pre-processed informative reviews into lower

---

[2] https://www.python.org/.
[3] https://tinyurl.com/w4azwge.

characters, eliminate stop-words and perform lemmatization [1]. That said, the initial task of the experiment is to identify nouns, adjectives, and verbs from the pre-processed informative reviews (refer to Sects. 3.1 and 3.2 for examples). To achieve this outcome, we use the average perceptron POS tagger as it outperforms the other types of POS taggers and is known to scale across domains [10]. After tagging the necessary nouns, adjectives, and verbs in the pre-processed informative reviews, we provide the tagged informative reviews (e.g., GPS – NOUN, inaccurate – ADJECTIVE, drain – VERB) as input to each of the semantic similarity methods (COALS, PPMI, and GloVe) for their evaluation. We provide details regarding this process next.

4.3 Evaluation of COALS, PPMI and GloVe

The objective of the evaluation process is to shortlist the best performing semantic similarity method based on its accuracy in determining the contextual semantic similarity between nouns and adjectives or verbs occurring in informative reviews. Initially the semantic scores generated by the methods (COALS, PPMI, and GloVe) for each word pair are compared with those assigned manually by the three authors, and later through Pearson correlation analysis, the accuracy of the method is determined [18]. The higher the degree of correlation between the authors' scores, and those generated by the particular method for each word pair, the greater is the accuracy of the method. To accomplish the objective of assigning the semantic scores to each word pair using a compatible range, we map the semantic similarity numerical scale (0–1) onto the interval scale (Low-Medium-High) in conforming to convention [3]. Thus, we map the 10 numerical semantic scores produced by COALS, PPMI, and GloVe (0, 0.1, 0.2, 0.3, 0.4, 0.5, 0.6, 0.7, 0.8, 0.9, 1) onto 3 interval scales (Low, Medium, and High) using the class interval method [3]. Based on the computed class interval scale range, we map numerical scales in range 0–0.3 as the *Low* interval scale, numerical scales in the range 0.4–0.6 as the *Medium* interval scale, and finally numerical scales in the range 0.7–1.0 as the *High* interval scale. Table 1 illustrates the rationale behind the assignment of semantic scores with the support of relevant entries as an example.

We use the guidelines in Table 1 to evaluate the results generated by the COALS, PPMI, and GloVe methods. Each method generated results that consisted of several entries wherein each entry represents a noun and the adjectives and verbs semantically similar to the particular noun. For example, consider that 'phone' is returned as a noun, and COALS identified a semantically similar verb as 'scrolling' (0.9 - High), with other adjectives and verbs having varying scores. The average semantic score is then computed for entries associated with the 'phone' noun. These outcomes are then evaluated against manually assigned pairs, where Fleiss's Kappa statistics are then computed to assess reliability [9].

4.4 Evaluation of Generated Taxonomy

We validate the automatically generated taxonomy using a qualitative content analysis approach [19]. For this process, initially the first noun entry from the automatically generated taxonomy is selected. We then check for the presence of the noun in the pool of informative reviews. Next, we manually analyse each informative review to determine

Table 1. Protocol for manual assignment of semantic scores

Range and label	Justification for the semantic score assignment	Word pair and example
0–0.3 low	Word pair entries falling in this range represent a low semantic score, as there is an irrational relationship observed between the word pair. Such word pairs lack word sense disambiguation	"I got it on my '**phone**' and tried it but '**imy**' was like half a mile but said 2000 ft, please fix"
0.4–0.6 medium	Word pair entries falling in this range reflect a moderate level of contextual semantic similarity. The relationship between the word pair is rational	"I did a 3-mile straight line flat '**trip**' which my tracks recorded as a completely '**jagged**' 4.6-mile distance..."
0.7–1.0 high	There is a firm agreement with the semantic similarity between the word pair entries falling in this interval range. This is supported by previous evidence of the features' defect	"'**battery**' '**drain**' 9000, I never launched this app and it was 'draining' my 'battery'."

the set of adjectives and verbs that are associated with the noun in question. After every informative review is analysed, we extend the list of adjectives and verbs (in the reviews) that are relevant to the noun under scrutiny. Finally, the list of manually finalised adjectives and verbs pertaining to the specific noun entry are compared against those present in the automatically generated taxonomy, to compute accuracy. Accuracy indicates the percentage of adjectives and verbs that are common to both the automatically generated taxonomy and manual taxonomy (i.e., final list of manually finalised adjectives and verbs pertaining to the noun entries). The entire process is repeated for all the noun entries present in the automatically generated taxonomy until no noun entry is left for evaluation. An overall average accuracy percentage is then computed, reflecting the overall accuracy of the automatically generated taxonomy. Finally, we repeat the reliability checks for the manual analysis as explained in Sect. 4.3.

5 Results and Generated Taxonomy Validity (RQ2)

In this section, we compare the outcomes of the automated taxonomy against a manually developed taxonomy for a unique case (My Tracks). These outcomes provide context for answering RQ2, and also provide triangulations for RQ1.

5.1 COALS, PPMI and GloVe

We ran COALS, PPMI and GloVe individually on the My Tracks corpus of pre-processed informative reviews to identify adjectives and verbs that are semantically similar to relevant nouns. Each method generated results that highlighted entries indicating nouns, and their respective associated semantically similar adjectives and verbs. The result generated by each method consisted of 2,095 entries (i.e., 2095 app features and their associated issues, requests or suggestions). In ensuring reliable outcomes, the G*Power tool[4] was used for sampling an appropriate number of records for manual analysis, where it was recommended that 325 entries comprised a representative sample (95% confidence level, 5% error). These checks helped us to determine the accuracy of the three methods (COALS, PPMI, and GloVe), and support the validation process (refer to Sect. 4.3). First, we record the semantic scores generated by COALS, PPMI, and GloVe for each noun-adjective and noun-verb pair. Next, the three authors independently assigned a semantic score in the range of 0 to 1 (Low-Medium-High) based on the defined numerical interval scale for each noun-verb, or noun-adjective word pair (refer to Table 1). Later, we checked the entries present in the COALS, PPMI, and GloVe results, and assessed these against the manual scores that were assigned (comparing averages). Finally, we run the Pearson's correlation test to check the accuracy of PPMI, GloVe, and COALS against the manually assigned score, where results showed that the semantic scores generated by GloVe and COALS positively correlated with those assigned manually ($r = 0.54$ and $r = 0.62$ respectively). This indicates a substantial level of agreement between the automated and manual process [18]. However, a negative correlation was observed for PPMI ($r = -0.21$), indicating significant disagreement between the scores generated by PPMI and the manual analysis. COALS recorded the highest degree of convergence between the automated and manual analysis.

Formal reliability assessments done between the three authors for each of the 325 entries (total: 975 entries) using the Fleiss's Kappa coefficient returned 0.67, which is interpreted as substantial agreement between coders [9]. Hence, based on these outcomes, we shortlisted COALS for automatic taxonomy generation. We next applied the Pareto distribution law on the results generated by COALS to identify the necessary entries (categories) required for grouping informative reviews. This returned 199 entries that depicted respective nouns along with their associated adjectives and verbs (as categories). A subset of this outcome is visualised in Fig. 2 as an undirected graph, where ten prominent nouns (app features) and their adjectives or verbs (issues, requests or suggestions) are depicted. For example, it is shows that the 'stats' (statistics) of the workout and the 'map' selected for the workout are 'unreadable' to the end-user.

5.2 Generated Taxonomy Validity

We evaluated the accuracy of the automatically generated taxonomy by analysing the 199 entries as mentioned in Sect. 4.4. The overall accuracy was found to be 72%, which indicates a substantial match between the manual taxonomy generated by domain experts and the automatically generated taxonomy [15]. In addition, with regards to the reliability assessment pertaining to assignment of manual semantic scores, there was general agreement observed as all authors were able to manually develop the taxonomy from the informative reviews. When we validated the informative reviews grouping results generated by the keyword lookup grouping mechanism (refer to Sect. 3.4) the accuracy was 98.3%. The slight imperfection was due to misspelled words.

---

[4] https://tinyurl.com/y4ny72jy.

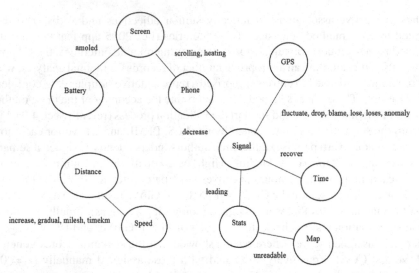

Fig. 2. Partial taxonomy showing interdependencies among app features and associated issues/requests/suggestions

6   Discussion and Implications

RQ1. How can an approach be developed to automatically generate a taxonomy to classify app reviews into groups? **The findings reported in this study show that it is possible to develop an approach that automatically generates a taxonomy to classify app reviews into groups.** This approach is able to directly extract app features-issues/requests/suggestions from a corpus of app reviews, without requiring human involvement. This has implication for effective software evolution and maintenance where limited software developers are available to manually analyse numerous software product reviews. While text mining involving POS is popular and has been used previously, the level of human participation that is involved with labelling app reviews in support of manually generating taxonomies could be a challenge [17]. **Feature engineering approaches assisted in building a suitable taxonomy framework for grouping similar app reviews, thereby solving a significant problem that is evident for manually generated taxonomies.** Our primary objective was to determine the issues/requests/suggestions (verbs/adjectives) that were semantically similar to app features (nouns) for which we evaluated COALS, PPMI, and GloVe, with COALS outperforming the other methods. Here we see that probabilistic methods (PPMI and GloVe) performed less favourably than the word vector distance approximation method (COALS). While our primary goal was not to investigate the performance of these methods that are used for measuring semantic similarity, the differences in outcomes noted may be due to the way COALS directly operates on the distances of vector data belonging to respective word pairs. This is held to be notable in determining word relations based on the principle of word sense disambiguation [11]. This is in contrast to PPMI which tends to be biased towards infrequent word pairs, and GloVe which operates on word embeddings. Further scrutiny of these methods would benefit future research on automatic taxonomy generation. **The application of a reliable contextual semantic similarity method addresses another drawback that is observed for manually generated taxonomies** - *the appropriate data for the categories of a taxonomy* [17]. Human-generated taxonomies provide a limited number of categories, and thus, classification approaches often provide a holistic view of grouped app reviews which is unsuitable if there are numerous app reviews. This issue is addressed in our approach, however, a new problem created relates to the automatic generation of a taxonomy that is large. **The application of the Pareto distribution law seems useful in determining the prominent categories as the Pareto distribution law appropriately prioritises the most significant categories while still retaining an "Others" category** [12]. The fundamental string matching then provides a near perfect approach for assigning informative reviews to created groups [17], in completing the automatically generated taxonomy which software engineering research focused on app store mining may learn from.

RQ2. How will the automated taxonomy compare to one developed manually? Our automatically generated taxonomy compared favourably to the one that was developed manually. **We observed 72% overlap in the two taxonomies, suggesting that the appropriate combination of concepts and methods from multiple domains provided an intuitive solution that closely aligned with human thinking.** This is noteworthy in that our investigation is preliminary, and the semantic similarity methods (e.g., COALS) have not been refined and tuned for optimization (including the threshold settings), which are known to lead to improvements [27]. In addition, it is to be noted that we utilised the best performing automated app reviews filtering approach to extract informative reviews. However, this approach is not 100% accurate based on the reported F-measure of 0.89 for the app reviews of My Tracks. Hence, there may be non-informative reviews in our sample, which could possibly compromise the accuracy of the automatically generated taxonomy. To this end, the outcomes reported in this work are conservative. That said, other research studies have benefited from optimization improvements. For example, COALS was integrated with SVD and subjected to specific SVD parameters (careful tuning) to generate optimal data required towards named entity recognition through means of latent semantics [14]. **We believe that the wider evaluated taxonomy that was created for app developers provides an explicit view of the prominent app features and their associated issues, requests or suggestions expressed in the app reviews.** Thus, app developers may directly generate taxonomies from app reviews without the need for classification to identify issues, requests or suggestions pertaining to app features, reducing the manually demanding tasks. **Additionally, such a taxonomy indirectly represents prioritised app features along with their associated requests, issues or suggestions requiring immediate remedial action,** as the groups (nouns) are modelled in descending order of prominence [16]. In fact, the partial taxonomy presented reveals that the app features share some common set of issues, requests or suggestions. This finding could be crucial to app developers, **as it would significantly assist them in discovering dependencies among the app features that could be important in identifying the impact of one app feature on another or the common characteristics (related issues, requests, suggestions) that are shared among app features** [16]. Aspects of the software architecture may also be detected from this visualization (e.g., speed and distance modules are related). Furthermore, based on the observed hierarchical dependencies among app features, resolving certain issues, requests or suggestions associated with specific app features will reduce the burden of defects on other related app features. Beyond these unintended benefits, our proposed approach requires limited human involvement and automatically extracts a wide spread of categories organically. In addition, our empirical evaluations revealed satisfactory outcomes when our approach is assessed against one that is manually derived, albeit we have used a single case study. Thus, we believe that our automated taxonomy generation approach may be useful for the software engineering practitioner community.

7   Threats to Validity

Internal Validity: Coming out of the text pre-processing and POS tagging pipeline, it was not feasible to evaluate the nouns, adjectives and verbs that do not reflect app features, issues, suggestions or requests, or those that were misclassified due to the overhead involved with manual evaluations. In addition, investigations done using manual analysis are always criticized for subjectivity. *External Validity*: We have used a single dataset in this study, which may affect the generalizability of this study. *Construct Validity*: The Pareto distribution law returned 199 entries (categories) for the taxonomy, which may seem excessive. That said, our manual evaluation confirmed that these entries were largely relevant. We have worked to remove this threat by performing rigorous reliability assessments where concrete agreements were observed.

8   Conclusion and Future Work

Previous work has attempted to address the challenge of classifying and analysing app reviews in support of software evolution and maintenance. Typically, the developed classification approaches group together app reviews having common characteristics into specific categories based on a taxonomy which is derived manually from domain knowledge. However, such domain knowledge may not be readily available, and when app reviews increase in number, scalability challenges are encountered for manually derived taxonomies. We addressed these limitations in this study, and developed a novel approach for automatically generating a taxonomy to group app reviews, without the need for the availability of domain knowledge from domain experts. Based on empirical evaluations reported in this study, the outcome of our approach compares favourably to one that was manually generated, and thus seems useful for grouping app reviews. We intend to validate our approach using a larger sample of apps in future work and investigate various optimization methods for improving the performance of our approach. Beyond app reviews, the feasibility of this proposed approach can also be investigated on issue and request trackers (e.g., Jira).

References

1. Aggarwal, C., Zhai, C.: Mining Text Data. Springer, Boston (2012). https://doi.org/10.1007/978-1-4614-3223-4

2. Archak, N., Ghose, A., Ipeirotis, P.G.: Show me the money! Deriving the pricing power of product features by mining consumer reviews. In: Proceedings of the 13th SIGKDD, pp. 56–65. ACM (2007)
3. Boehm, B., Port, D.: Educating software engineering students to manage risk. In: Proceedings of the 23rd ICSE, pp. 591–600. IEEE Computer Society (2001)
4. Boutkova, E.: Experience with variability management in requirement specifications. In: 15th SPLC, pp. 303–312. IEEE (2011)
5. Bullinaria, J.A., Levy, J.P.: Extracting semantic representations from word co-occurrence statistics: a computational study. Behav. Res. Methods **39**, 510–526 (2007). https://doi.org/10.3758/BF03193020
6. Chen, N., Lin, J., Hoi, S.C.H., et al.: AR-miner: mining informative reviews for developers from mobile app marketplace. In: Proceedings of the 36th ICSE, pp. 767–778. ACM, Hyderabad (2014)
7. Ciurumelea, A., Panichella, S., Gall, H.C.: Automated user reviews analyser. In: ICSE, pp. 317–318 (2018)
8. Di Sorbo, A., Panichella, S., Alexandru, C.V., et al.: What would users change in my app? Summarizing app reviews for recommending software changes. In: Proceedings of the 24th SIGSOFT, pp. 499–510. ACM (2016)
9. Fleiss, J.L., Cohen, J.: The equivalence of weighted kappa and the intraclass correlation coefficient as measures of reliability. Educ. Psychol. Measur. **33**, 613–619 (1973)
10. Hajič, J., Raab, J., Spousta, M.: Semi-supervised training for the averaged perceptron POS tagger. In: Proceedings of the 12th ACL, pp. 763–771. Association for Computational Linguistics (2009)
11. Karov, Y., Edelman, S.: Similarity-based word sense disambiguation. Comput. Linguist. **24**, 41–59 (1998)
12. Kiremire, A.R.: The application of the pareto principle in software engineering, 13 January (2011)
13. Ko, Y., Park, S., Seo, J.: Web-based requirements elicitation supporting system using requirements categorization. In: Proceedings of the 12th SEKE 2000, Chicago, USA, pp. 344–351 (2000)
14. Konkol, M., Brychcín, T., Konopík, M.: Latent semantics in named entity recognition. Expert Syst. Appl. **42**, 3470–3479 (2015)
15. Kropp, R.P., Stoker, H.W., Bashaw, W.: The validation of the taxonomy of educational objectives. J. Exp. Educ. **34**, 69–76 (1966)
16. Licorish, S.A., Savarimuthu, B.T.R., Keertipati, S.: Attributes that predict which features to fix: lessons for app store mining. In: Proceedings of the 21st EASE, pp. 108–117. ACM, Karlskrona (2017)
17. Maalej, W., Kurtanović, Z., Nabil, H., Stanik, C.: On the automatic classification of app reviews. Requirements Eng. **21**(3), 311–331 (2016). https://doi.org/10.1007/s00766-016-0251-9
18. Martinez-Gil, J.: An overview of textual semantic similarity measures based on web intelligence. Artif. Intell. Rev. **42**(4), 935–943 (2012). https://doi.org/10.1007/s10462-012-9349-8
19. Mayring, P.: Qualitative content analysis. A Companion Qual. Res. **1**, 159–176 (2004)
20. Mihalcea, R., Corley, C., Strapparava, C.: Corpus-based and knowledge-based measures of text semantic similarity. In: AAAI, pp. 775–780 (2006)
21. Pagano, D., Maalej, W.: User feedback in the appstore: an empirical study. In: 2013 21st Requirements Engineering, pp. 125–134. IEEE (2013)
22. Panichella, S., Di Sorbo, A., Guzman, E., et al.: ARdoc: app reviews development oriented classifier. In: Proceedings of the 24th SIGSOFT, pp. 1023–1027. ACM (2016)

23. Pennington, J., Socher, R., Manning, C.: GloVe: global vectors for word representation. In: Proceedings of the EMNLP, pp. 1532–1543 (2014)
24. Rohde, D.L., Gonnerman, L.M., Plaut, D.C.: An improved model of semantic similarity based on lexical co-occurrence. Commun. ACM **8**, 116 (2006)
25. Sánchez, D., Batet, M., Isern, D.: Ontology-based information content computation. Knowl.-Based Syst. **24**, 297–303 (2011)
26. Snijders, R., Dalpiaz, F., Hosseini, M., et al.: Crowd-centric requirements engineering. In: UCC, pp. 614–615 (2014)
27. Zhang, M., Palade, V., Wang, Y., et al.: Word representation with salient features. IEEE Access **7**, 30157–30173 (2019)

Zones of Pain: Visualising the Relationship Between Software Architecture and Defects

Jean Petrić(✉), Tracy Hall(✉), and David Bowes(✉)

Lancaster University, Lancaster, UK
{j.petric,tracy.hall,d.h.bowes}@lancaster.ac.uk

Abstract. Substantial development time is devoted to software maintenance and testing. As development resources are usually finite, there is a risk that some components receive insufficient effort for thorough testing. Architectural complexity (e.g. tight coupling) can make effective testing particularly challenging. Software components with high architectural complexity are more likely be defect–prone. The aim of this study is to investigate the relationship between established architectural attributes and defect–proneness. We used the architectural attributes: abstractness, instability and distance to measure the architectural complexity of software components. We investigated the ability of these attributes to discriminate between defective and non-defective components on four open source systems. We visualised defect–proneness by plotting architectural complexity and defectiveness using Martin's 'Zones of Pain'. Our results show that architecture has an inconsistent impact on defect– proneness. Some architecturally complex components seem immune to defects in some projects. In other projects architecturally complex components significantly suffer from defects. Where architectural complexity does increase defect–proneness the impact is strong. We recommend practitioners monitor the architectural complexity of their software components over time by visualising potential defect–proneness using Martin's Zones of Pain.

Keywords: Software defects · Software architecture · Software evolution

1 Introduction

We aim to investigate the effect of architecture on defect–proneness. We build on previous work which looked at the relationship between some aspects of architecture and defects. Elish et al. compared the ability of three metric suites, which capture various static features of code, to predict pre– and post–defects [8]. Elish et al. demonstrated that Martin's suite of metrics [14] significantly outperformed the other two metric suites analysed. Jaafar et al. examined the impact of

© Springer Nature Switzerland AG 2020
M. Shepperd et al. (Eds.): QUATIC 2020, CCIS 1266, pp. 135–143, 2020.
https://doi.org/10.1007/978-3-030-58793-2_11

design patterns on defect–proneness and reported that components with anti–patterns are more defect–prone than others [12]. Jaafar et al. further demonstrated that components with anti–patterns are also those most involved in structural changes. However, it remains unclear if a complex architecture increases the likelihood of defect–proneness. To the best of our knowledge, no study has investigated the impact of architectural complexity on defect–proneness.

We used three metrics from Martin's [14] suite of metrics to measure the architectural complexity of software components. These are *abstractness*, *instability* and *distance from the main sequence* (short, *distance*). *Abstractness* (A) is defined as the ratio of interfaces and abstract classes in a component to the total number of classes in the component. *Instability* (I) is defined as the ratio between outward dependencies of a component and the total number of dependencies entering the component. Finally, *distance* (D) is defined as the absolute value of A and I which represent the distance from the main sequence in the '*tension plot*' (i.e. Fig. 1). We also used Martin's notions of the "zone of pain" and "zone of uselessness", collectively called the "zone of exclusion", to categorise components by their architectural complexity. We investigated whether defect–proneness is more likely to occur in the zone of exclusion. We further investigated the likelihood of defect–proneness for components in the zone of exclusion compared to other components.

We set out to answer to research questions: **RQ1.** *What is the effect of architectural attributes on the defect-proneness of software components for the investigated open source systems?*; **RQ2.** *What is the proportion of defective components in the zone of exclusion for the investigated open source systems?* Our contributions are three–fold. Firstly, we show that architectural complexity is a promising indicator of defect–proneness. Architectural complexity may give complementary information with the addition of other metrics to defect prediction models. Secondly, we show that the relationship between architectural complexity and defect–proneness is not simple. Future studies are needed to understand which factors affect the relationship between architecture and defect–proneness. Thirdly, we provide all tools and data to the community for future analysis and replication.

The rest of this paper is structured as follows. The next section discusses the background to this work which is followed by a detailed methodology section. Section 4 then presents and discusses the results. Section 5 outlines related work, followed by the conclusions in Sect. 5.

2   Background

Many code design approaches to building reusable, maintainable and testable software have been proposed over the years. For example, Gamma et al. [9] documented over 20 reusable solutions for object–oriented systems, whilst Jaafar et al. conducted an empirical study to investigate the impact of design patterns on software maintenance and defectiveness [12]. Other work has focused on investigating problematic coding approaches that may hamper reusability, maintainability and testability. For example, Khomh et al. showed that classes containing anti–patterns are more frequently changed and more defect–prone than others in almost all releases of the four systems they analysed [13]. Hall et al. demonstrated that some code smells have a small but significantly nega- tive effect on software defects [10]. Bavota et al. demonstrated that test smells impede the maintainability of software tests [6].

Many static code metrics have been used as a means to assess their impact on defect–proneness. For example, the CK suite [7], the MOOD suite [1], and Martin's suite [14] are amongst frequently used ones. Elish et al. showed that prediction models based on Martin's suite of metrics performed best amongst the three suites [8]. Almugrin et al. modified Martin's suite based on the concept of responsibility [3] and later showed that the modified suite yielded high corre- lation with respect to maintainability and testability [4]. In this study we focus on the architectural attributes of software. We use three architectural attributes defined by Martin [14] to explore their relationship with defect–proneness of software components.

3   Methodology

3.1   Architectural Metrics

Equations 1 depict *abstractness* (A), *instability* (I) and *distance from the main sequence* (D), respectively. In A, N_a is the number of abstract classes and inter- faces in the component, whilst N_c is the number of concrete classes in the com- ponent. A is in the range of 0 and 1, where $A = 0$ indicates the component contains no abstract classes or interfaces. On the other hand, $A = 1$ indicates that the component contains nothing but abstract classes or interfaces. In I, Fan_{in} represents the number of inward, whilst Fan_{out} the number of outward dependencies. I value also spans from 0 to 1, where 0 indicates maximally sta- ble component and 1 maximally unstable component. Finally, D calculates the euclidean distance from the main sequence. D also ranges between 0 and 1, where 0 indicates that the component is on the main sequence, whilst 1 indicates that the component is as far away from the main sequence as possible. When $D \approx 1$ the component is inside the zone of exclusion, either in the ZoP or ZoU. Figure 1 shows the relationship between the three metrics. We anticipate that compo- nents on and close to the MS should be less affected by defects compared to components in the ZoE. We use *tension plots* to visualise defective components across different snapshots of software evolution.

$$A = \frac{N_a}{N_c} \qquad I = \frac{Fan_{out}}{Fan_{out} + Fan_{in}} \qquad D = |A + I - 1| \qquad (1)$$

3.2   Experiment

We used four open source projects shown in Table 1. All projects come from the *apache* community. We selected these projects because they use similar devel- opment standards which reduces issues that arise from analysing different open

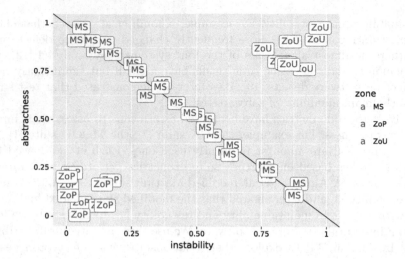

Fig. 1. The *tension plot* showing the relationship between A, I and D. Extreme values of A and I are driving components towards the zones of exclusion (also called, 'zones of pain').

source projects. In addition, these projects generally belong to the same domain, i.e. Java libraries, are of reasonable size and widely used in the community. Table 1 summarises the chosen projects. The *# defects* and *# analysed commits* columns are the total numbers of defective files and commits, respectively, throughout the project's history. The last two columns represent the average numbers of packages and classes for all analysed commits (these are the numbers per commit across the software history).

We collected two sets of data. The first set of data is a collection of defects for each project in Table 1. We used the SZZ algorithm to extract defective files for each commit throughout the project's history [15]. The second set of data contains the architectural metrics (A, I and D) for each of the four projects. Due to the lack of existing static metric tools that work on the latest Java versions, we developed *JavaMetrics*[1] to collect A, I and D metrics. For each project, we collected the metrics against all *git* commits. Finally, we amalgamated the information from the first and second set of data to get a list of metrics for all defective and non-defective components throughout each project's history. We also cleaned the datasets which scripts are available online[2].

To answer RQ1 we investigated whether complex components are likely to be more defective compared to their simpler counterparts. To reduce the bias we compared only components of similar size. We removed non–defective components which are 30% smaller or bigger than the defective components. Larger thresholds would include more components but would also defeat the purpose of comparing similar sizes. Smaller thresholds leave few components to compare.

---

[1] https://github.com/lancsunise/JavaMetrics.
[2] https://github.com/lancsunise/quatic20_replication.

Table 1. Open source projects used in this paper

Project	# defects	# analysed commits	# avg. package	# avg. class
hadoop-common	1617	10509	428	8362
camel	10501	44609	2081	14681
derby	5130	8269	230	2790
hive	11122	14377	621	12703

30% threshold resulted in the right balance for further statistical analysis. To answer RQ2 we used an approach similar to *binary testedness* previously reported by Ahmed et al. [2] and Bach et al. [5]. *Binary testedness* separates source code in two (binary) groups. In its original form, one binary group is code covered with tests whilst another group is code with no associated tests. It is then possible, for a given snapshot, to count the occurrences of defective components for covered and uncovered code. If fewer defects end up in the covered compared to the uncovered group, we establish that testing is effective. Note that defects should initially be extracted via some form of defect prediction, rather than exposed by tests (i.e. tests would not be able to uncover any defects in uncovered code). We undertook a similar experiment to validate whether some architectural attributes lead to more defect–prone components. We defined Eq. 2 to calculate the defect–proneness of components with $D \approx 0$ and $D \approx 1$. We used three thresholds, 0.2, 0.4 and 0.6 to calculate the ratios defined in Eq. 2.

$$R_{D\approx0} = \frac{N_{d0}}{N_{d0} + N_{nd0}}, R_{D\approx1} = \frac{N_{d1}}{N_{d1} + N_{nd1}} \tag{2}$$

Each equation represents the ratio of defective components over the total number of components for a particular region of the *tension plot*. $R_{D\approx0}$ are components similar to the green components, whilst $R_{D\approx1}$ are components similar to the red components in Fig. 1. N_d and N_{nd} are the counts of defective and non–defective components for the specific region of the *tension plot*, respectively.

4   Results and Analysis

Our RQ1 investigates whether architecturally complex components are likely to be more defect–prone compared to architecturally simpler components. If architecturally complex components were more defective on average, we would expect them to be farther away from the *MS*. To test the hypothesis whether defective components tend to have a greater *distance*, we used a one–sided non–parametric Mann–Whitney U test. We used the Mann–Whitney U test because of different numbers of instances between defective and non–defective components. For all projects except *derby* the $p-values$ were at least $5.596E-3$ or lower confirming that there is a statistical significance to conclude that architecturally complex components are more likely to be defective than their simpler counterparts.

Given that there is a significant difference between *distance* and defectiveness in most cases, we investigated the magnitude of this difference. To estimate the magnitude we used the ratios defined in Eq. 2 for three different thresholds: 0.2, 0.4 and 0.6. These thresholds represent the maximum "shift" from the *MS* that divides the *tension plot* into two groups, as previously explained in Sect. 3.2. The expectation is to see $R_{D\approx 1} > R_{D\approx 0}$ for the thresholds approaching closer to 1. In other words, defectiveness of components increase as they are approaching closer to the *ZoE*. By calculating $\frac{R_{D\approx 1}}{R_{D\approx 0}}$ it is possible to estimate the magnitude (scale) of the difference between the two groups. Table 2 reports these details.

Table 2. Ratios of defective and non-defective components based on the distance from the Main Sequence

Project	Shift	rdef	rnondef	Scale	p–val
hadoop-common	0.2	0.129 (±0.129)	0.105 (±0.199)	1.223	0.266
hadoop-common	0.4	0.208 (±0.233)	0.140 (±0.206)	1.492	0.303
hadoop-common	0.6	0.405 (±0.45)	0.074 (±0.13)	5.449	0.102
derby	0.2	0.036 (±0.115)	0.103 (±0.119)	0.345	1.000
derby	0.4	0.022 (±0.078)	0.075 (±0.074)	0.288	1.000
derby	0.6	0.018 (±0.107)	0.054 (±0.035)	0.33	1.000
camel	0.2	0.060 (±0.099)	0.021 (±0.061)	2.838	0.000
camel	0.4	0.070 (±0.139)	0.028 (±0.078)	2.529	1.000
camel	0.6	0.119 (±0.315)	0.047 (±0.084)	2.54	1.000
hive	0.2	0.082 (±0.152)	0.083 (±0.157)	0.987	0.839
hive	0.4	0.033 (±0.129)	0.088 (±0.094)	0.373	1.000
hive	0.6	0.020 (±0.088)	0.030 (±0.02)	0.657	1.000

Table 2 presents the ratios and scale of the two groups of components for all four projects and the different thresholds. The first column is the project name, *shift* corresponds to the distance from the *MS*, *rdef* and *rnondef* are $R_{D\approx 1}$ and $R_{D\approx 0}$, respectively. The *scale* represents the magnitude $\frac{R_{D\approx 1}}{R_{D\approx 0}}$. *scale* > 1 means that architecturally complex components are indeed more likely to be defect–prone, whilst *scale* < 0 shows the opposite. In addition, *scale* = 2 shows that there are two times more defective components in the *ZoE* than around the *MS*. Finally, *p-val* shows whether the differences between $R_{D\approx 1}$ and $R_{D\approx 0}$ are significant. From Table 2, for *camel*, the scale is close to 3 for all the thresholds which indicates that an architecturally complex component is almost 3 times more likely to be defect–prone. On the other hand, *derby* shows very similar results with the scale close to 0.3 indicating that simpler components are 3 times more likely to be defect–prone. Figure 2 is an example of using the *tension plot* for a real–world project. The figure shows the arrangement of defective and non–defective components for 11 commits of *hadoop-common*. Each subplot in

Fig. 2 represents the state of defective and non–defective components for one *git* commit. Figure 2 clearly shows that for four commits, *0d5ed9*, *382ec9*, *46a7e0* and *f3a5d1* the most architecturally complex components are defective.

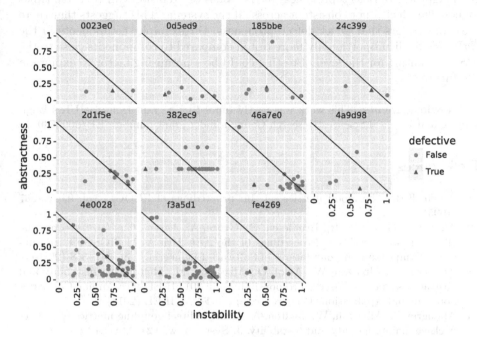

Fig. 2. Abstractness vs Instability for the top defective *hadoop-common* snapshots

5   Conclusions

Our findings suggest that architectural complexity of a component, as defined by Martin [14], does not always increase its likelihood to be defect–prone. There could be multiple reasons why this is the case. One reason is that complex components in some projects are more thoroughly tested compared to complex components in other projects. We suspect this to be unlikely in our analysis, given that we used the projects from the same community which follows the same protocol. Another, more likely reason, could be the difference in responsibilities of components in the *ZoE* compared to components close to the *MS*. As other studies have shown, practitioners spend more time maintaining and testing complex components (e.g. [3,11]), which may leave more opportunity for defects to slip unnoticed in simpler components.

Overall, our analysis showed that for three out of the four considered systems architectural complexity has a strong relationship with defects. A strategic refactoring of components in the zones of exclusion by introducing abstraction is likely to reduce architectural complexity of components and decrease overall defect–proneness of the system. Visualisation techniques, such as the tension plot, as well as the Martin metrics can be an effective way for practitioners to determine which components require more attention. However, even though the magnitude of defect–proneness in the zones of exclusion can be three times higher, the effect is not consistent across all the systems. This suggests that there are more factors that affect defect–proneness. For example, components in the *ZoE* may be disproportionally more tested compared to components close to the *MS*. Accounting for the level of testing could be a promising factor to explore in the future.

Acknowledgements. This work was partly funded by a grant from the UK's Engineering and Physical Sciences Research Council under grant number: EP/S005730/1.

References

1. Abreu, F.B.: The mood metrics set. In: proceedings of ECOOP, vol. 95, p. 267 (1995)
2. Ahmed, I., Gopinath, R., Brindescu, C., Groce, A., Jensen, C.: Can testedness be effectively measured? In: Proceedings of the 2016 24th ACM SIGSOFT International Symposium on Foundations of Software Engineering, pp. 547–558 (2016)
3. Almugrin, S., Albattah, W., Alaql, O., Alzahrani, M., Melton, A.: Instability and abstractness metrics based on responsibility. In: 2014 IEEE 38th Annual Computer Software and Applications Conference, pp. 364–373. IEEE (2014)
4. Almugrin, S., Albattah, W., Melton, A.: Using indirect coupling metrics to predict package maintainability and testability. J. Syst. Softw. **121**, 298–310 (2016)
5. Bach, T., Andrzejak, A., Pannemans, R., Lo, D.: The impact of coverage on bug density in a large industrial software project. In: Empirical Software Engineering and Measurement (ESEM), pp. 307–313. IEEE (2017)
6. Bavota, G., Qusef, A., Oliveto, R., De Lucia, A., Binkley, D.: Are test smells really harmful? An empirical study. Empirical Softw. Eng. **20**(4), 1052–1094 (2015)
7. Chidamber, S.R., Kemerer, C.F.: A metrics suite for object oriented design. IEEE Trans. Softw. Eng. **20**(6), 476–493 (1994)
8. Elish, M.O., Al-Yafei, A.H., Al-Mulhem, M.: Empirical comparison of three metrics suites for fault prediction in packages of object-oriented systems: A case study of eclipse. Adv. Eng. Softw. **42**(10), 852–859 (2011)
9. Gamma, E.: Design Patterns: Elements of Reusable Object-oriented Software. Pearson Education, India (1995)
10. Hall, T., Zhang, M., Bowes, D., Sun, Y.: Some code smells have a significant but small effect on faults. ACM Trans. Softw. Eng. Methodol. (TOSEM) **23**(4), 1–39 (2014)
11. Izurieta, C., Bieman, J.M.: Testing consequences of grime buildup in object oriented design patterns. In: 2008 1st International Conference on Software Testing, Verification, and Validation, pp. 171–179 (2008)
12. Jaafar, F., Guéhéneuc, Y.-G., Hamel, S., Khomh, F., Zulkernine, M.: Evaluating the impact of design pattern and anti-pattern dependencies on changes and faults. Empirical Softw. Eng. **21**(3), 896–931 (2015). https://doi.org/10.1007/s10664-015-9361-0

13. Khomh, F., Di Penta, M., Guéhéneuc, Y.G., Antoniol, G.: An exploratory study of the impact of antipatterns on class change-and fault-proneness. Empirical Softw. Eng. **17**(3), 243–275 (2012)
14. Martin, R.C.: Agile Software Development: Principles, Patterns, and Practices. Prentice Hall, Upper Saddle River (2003)
15. Śliwerski, J., Zimmermann, T., Zeller, A.: When do changes induce fixes? In: Proceedings of the 2005 International Workshop on Mining Software Repositories, MSR 2005, pp. 1–5. ACM, New York (2005)

An Empirical Study on the Persistence of SpotBugs Issues in Open-Source Software Evolution

Luigi Lavazza[✉][ID], Davide Tosi[ID], and Sandro Morasca[ID]

Università degli Studi dell'Insubria, Varese, Italy
{luigi.lavazza,davide.tosi,sandro.morasca}@uninsubria.it

Abstract. *Background.* Static analyzers can be useful to software developers in detecting and locating code issues and, in addition, classifying their nature. The main problem of static analyzers, however, is that they may signal too many false alarms. *Objective.* In this paper, we investigate whether code issues that are detected by SpotBugs persist in software code, or if they get removed. We chose SpotBugs because it is one of the best-known and most used static analyzers. *Method.* We carried out an empirical study on five open-source Java programs and took into account two versions of each of them, to check whether the issues signaled by SpotBugs on the older version had been removed by the time the newer version was released. A total of 1,006 issues were signaled by SpotBugs. *Results.* Our results show that about half of the issues signaled disappeared between the two versions, but the correction rate was uneven across projects. Issues about the correctness of software code were more likely to be no longer present in the newer version than other types of warnings. *Conclusions.* Further investigations are required, to understand why some projects appear more active than others in correcting SpotBugs issues, and why very few high-severity warnings were observed in the analyzed code. Nonetheless, the fact that about half of the issues flagged by SpotBugs were removed indicates that the tool is effective in detecting incorrect or otherwise problematic code.

Keywords: Static analyzers · Bugs · Bug persistence · SpotBugs · Bad code patterns

1 Introduction

To reduce Quality Assurance (QA) times and costs, a number of techniques have been devised and a number of tools have been built to automate QA activities.

Specifically, defect detectors based on static code analysis can help improve software quality and decrease QA times and costs, because of several reasons:

- Analysis is very quick and is practically free of charge. For instance, SpotBugs is open-source code and it can be installed very easily. The only configuration needed to analyze a project is the indication of which folders contain the

© Springer Nature Switzerland AG 2020
M. Shepperd et al. (Eds.): QUATIC 2020, CCIS 1266, pp. 144–151, 2020.
https://doi.org/10.1007/978-3-030-58793-2_12

target code. Analysis is quite fast: for instance, we analyzed 1097 classes from `log4j` with SpotBugs with a recent laptop PC in about 30 s.
- The issues found are of types that are difficult to find via testing. Moreover, testing can detect a failure, but usually it does not provide indications about the kind of defect that caused the failure and its location. On the contrary, most of the warnings issued by the static analyzers point to very specific types of defect and locations in the code.
- Even though static analyzers issue warnings that are sometimes false alarms, manually inspecting the code flagged as possibly defective by static analyzers is generally easy. In this sense, static analyzers can be seen as a way to guide manual inspections.
- Warnings are classified in defect types. This allows developers to compile catalogs of frequent defect types and identify and adopt techniques to avoid such types of defects.

However, tools based on static analysis identify code patterns that are usually—but not always—associated with problematic code. As a result, most tools provide warnings concerning possible defects, i.e., it is not certain that a warning actually corresponds to defective code. This is a typical characteristic of these tools, which can reduce their appeal to software developers, who may get frustrated by the high degree of uncertainty about the warnings and the possibly excessive rate of false alarms, which leads to spending a good deal of time and effort on inspecting code that turns out to be correct. This may totally defeat the purpose of using defect detectors, by further delaying product delivery and increasing costs. In practice, using SpotBugs or similar tools is useful if the number of false positives is reasonably small.

Therefore, practitioners are mostly interested in the effectiveness of static analyzers, i.e., they need to know how many actual defects can be found, of what types, if these defects are worth any correction effort, etc.

In this paper, we focus on SpotBugs (formerly known as FindBugs [6]), which is a very popular tool for defect detection via static code analysis. Specifically, we investigate whether the issues found by SpotBugs on a small set of open-source products are actually relevant in practice. To this end, we analyzed two versions of each of these products. We then evaluated how many issues that were reported by SpotBugs in the first release no longer appeared in the second release. We interpret that the disappearance of an issue is generally due to a voluntary action of improving the code. The code may have been changed for other reasons, but the fact that an issue disappears is typically an indication that it was worth modifying the code in a way that got rid of the issue.

2 SpotBugs

SpotBugs [3] is a static analysis tool that looks for bugs in Java source code. The tool is free software, distributed under the GNU Lesser General Public License. SpotBugs inherits all of the features of its predecessor FindBugs [1,6] and adds new analyses to check more than 400 bug patterns. SpotBugs checks for bug patterns such as null pointer dereferencing, infinite recursive loops, bad uses of the Java libraries and deadlocks. SpotBugs is available as an Eclipse plugin or as a standalone program and can be downloaded from [3].

In SpotBugs, bug patterns are classified by means of several variables, such as: the type of violation, its category, the rank of the bug, and the confidence of the discovery process.

Ten categories are identified [2], such as "Bad Practice" (i.e., violations of recommended and essential coding practice, like hash code and equals problems, cloneable idiom, dropped exceptions, Serializable problems, and misuse of finalize), "Correctness" (i.e., probable bug - an apparent coding mistake resulting in code that was probably not what the developer intended), or "Multithreaded correctness" (i.e., code flaw issues having to do with threads, locks, and volatiles). The complete list of bug descriptions can be found in [2].

The rank of each warning concerns the severity of the potential bug, and spans from 1 (most severe) to 20 (least severe). Four rank levels are also defined: "scariest" ($1 \leq rank \leq 4$), "scary" ($5 \leq rank \leq 9$), "worrying" ($10 \leq rank \leq 14$), "of concern" ($15 \leq rank \leq 20$).

Moreover, a "confidence" (named "priority" in early releases) is associated to each warning: high confidence (1), normal confidence (2) and low confidence (3), to highlight the quality of the detection process.

3   The Empirical Study

There are in principle several ways to address the objectives described in the Introduction. We decided to base our evaluations on objective—though possibly indirect—observations.

We considered that, if an issue was observed in a given release and disappeared in a following release, developers had deemed it useful to remove the issue. We are not interested in understanding if the issue was removed in the context of an activity specifically aimed at removing the issue or in the context of an activity having another purpose. Rewriting the code in a way that solves a potential problem is proof that modifying the problematic code was preferable. We are also not interested in understanding if the removed issue was connected to a defect that could cause failures or if it was just a piece of poorly written code, which could possibly cause maintenance problems in the future.

Accordingly, we selected a few open-source programs and analyzed two versions of each program. The sets of SpotBugs warnings concerning the two releases were compared, to identify issues that were present in the earlier release and had been removed in the following release.

Since we are interested in deriving evidence that is practically useful to developers, we selected a set of open-source software products that are used in real-life projects. These programs were used in a proprietary web portal that had been previously analyzed by one of the authors.

Data about the analyzed open-source programs are summarized in Table 1.

Table 1. The analyzed programs.

Program	Initial version			Final version		
	Release	Date	#classes	Release	Date	#classes
hibernate-search	5.8.0	Sept 2017	951	5.11.5	Feb 2020	962 (+1%)
jcaptcha	1.0-RC6	May 2007	310	1.0	Feb 2009	270 (−13%)
log4j	2.12.1	Aug 2019	1097	2.13.1	Feb 2020	1112 (+1%)
openSymphony	2.2.1	July 2003	60	2.2.2	Jan 2004	51 (−15%)
pdfbox	1.8.16	Oct 2018	710	2.0.14	Feb 2019	846 (+19%)

The rightmost column gives also the percentage variation in the number of classes between the two versions of the same product. The most relevant variation occurs for pdfbox, in which the newer version contained 19% more classes than the older one. The first four projects in Table 1 have the same number of version and only change the specific release, so they may not have introduced substantial modifications in their functionalities.

SpotBugs classifies warnings by rank (i.e., severity) and confidence. Therefore, it can be expected that the issues with the highest rank and confidence are the ones that are most frequently corrected.

However, out of over one thousand total warnings, only 2 belong to the "scariest" level (of these, none was corrected), and 17 belong to the "scary" level (of these, only 8 were corrected). Of 54 "worrying" warnings, 35 were corrected, and of the remaining 933 "of concern" warnings, 442 were corrected.

As for confidence, Figure 1 shows the distribution of corrected issues by confidence. It can be observed that the percentage of corrected issues increases with confidence. This behavior is consistent with the definition of confidence: we can expect that a greater fraction of the low-confidence warnings are false positives, hence a smaller fraction of low-confidence warnings is corrected. Nonetheless, it can also be noted that the differences are quite small: this phenomenon is possibly due to SpotBugs not being very accurate in evaluating the level of confidence to be assigned to warnings.

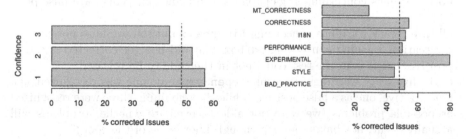

Fig. 1. Percentage of corrected issues by warning confidence (left), and percentage of corrected issues by warning type (right). The dashed line indicates the mean.

SpotBugs also classifies warnings by category. It is thus interesting to check whether some issue categories receive greater attentions from developers. Figure 1 shows that most categories get around 50% corrections; exceptions are "experimental" issues, with over 80% corrections, and multithreaded correctness ("MT_correctness") issues, with around 30% corrections. According to SpotBugs documentation, experimental issues are those concerning not fully vetted bug patterns: the fact that so many get cleared seems to indicate that these patterns actually detect some type of undesirable situation, hence SpotBugs developers should promote these bugs to a consolidated category.

Another observation concerning the corrected issues is that different open-source projects appear to behave differently with respect to correcting SpotBugs issues. Table 2 shows that while log4j and hibernate-search corrected less than 10% of SpotBugs issues, the other projects corrected many more issues, with pdfbox correcting 90% of the reported issues.

The differences noted among products persist if the rank level is also considered, as shown in Table 2.

Table 2. Corrected issues by software product and rank level.

Product	Corrected - issued				
	Scariest	Scary	Worrying	of concern	Total
pdfbox-1.8.16	0 1	6 6	23 23	313 350	342 380
jcaptcha-1.0-RC6	0 0	2 2	8 9	62 167	72 178
log4j-2.12.1	0 1	0 1	3 14	13 235	16 251
hibernate-search-5.8.0	0 0	0 3	1 7	9 98	10 108
openSymphony-2.2.1	0 0	0 5	0 1	45 83	45 89

Eleven warnings at the "scariest" and "scary" levels were not treated. This is somewhat surprising, since we expect that most serious issues receive the most attention and are therefore removed. To better understand these cases, we manually investigated the concerned code. Manual inspections revealed that:

– both warnings concerning log4j (one scariest and one scary) are false positives;
– all three scary warnings concerning hibernate-search are false positives;
– the scariest warning concerning pdfbox that did not get corrected is a true positive, but it is in the test code, not in the code to be released;
– of the five scary warnings concerning openSymphony, one was recognized as a true positive, one as a false positive, while the remaining three were recognized as possible problems (we were not able to evaluate whether problems will actually occur, not having a deep enough knowledge of the code).

In conclusion, the majority of scary and scariest warnings turned out to be false positives.

4   Discussion

The following observations can be made, based on the results of the empirical study.

- Overall, 485 issues—out of 1006 warnings—disappeared. This seems to indicate that about half of SpotBugs warnings concerned code that was worth revising.
- Some projects corrected many issues, while others did not. This is a phenomenon worth pointing out, even though our analysis does not provide any explanation for this.
- SpotBugs produced few high-level rank warnings. This fact supports the hypothesis that SpotBugs's ranking is correct and the considered open-source software projects put great attention in preventing the occurrence of most serious issues in released code. However, given the very small number of highest-level rank warnings, we can hardly evaluate their corrections, because the data set is too small for a thorough statistical analysis. In addition, most warnings at the highest ranks turned out to be false positives, which seem to provide more evidence for the high quality of the considered projects.
- Higher confidence warnings are corrected more frequently than lower confidence ones. This fact indicates that lower-confidence warnings include more false positives than higher-confidence warnings.
- Warnings of type "correctness" were corrected more frequently than all other types, except for "experimental" warnings. This fact seems to indicate that the warnings concerning correctness, which are likely the most interesting ones for developers, include more true positives, therefore they are definitely worth considering.

In conclusion, our analysis indicates that the usage of static analyzers can help developers detect weak points and defects in their code. Overall, about half the warnings concern code that needs to be modified, or at least can benefit from being modified. It is also worth noting that the warnings provided by SpotBugs indicate very specific types of problems and also indicate where the problem is located in the code. Therefore, developers know where to look and what to look for: this makes manual verification of warnings fairly straightforward. Accordingly, the fact that half of the manual verification results in finding no real problem does not involve wasting much effort. On the contrary, the verification activities that highlight real issues drive correction actions that are generally straightforward.

5   Related Work

A great deal of effort has been dedicated to understanding the accuracy of static analysis tools. Rahman et al. [8] compared the defect prediction capabilities of FindBugs, PMD and Jlint against statistical defect prediction based on historical data. Vetrò et al. [12,13] evaluated the accuracy of FindBugs by inspecting manually the source code highlighted by FindBugs as buggy code. Ayewah et al. evaluated the issues found by FindBugs in production software developed by Sun and Google [4], while Vestola applied FindBugs to Valuatum's system to understand the proportion of real bugs and false positives [11]. Tomassi considered 320 real Java bugs from the BugSwarm dataset to determine which of these bugs are actually detected by SpotBugs [10]. Jingyue et al. evaluated five open-source static analysis IDE plugins to compare how many categories of software vulnerabilities the plugins can detect, and how accurate they are [7]. All these papers focus on the accuracy of static analysis tools without investigating any deeper on how much software developers take into account the identified potential bugs. On the contrary, in this paper we take into consideration what happens after bug detection, based on the idea that practically relevant issues are more likely to be treated.

Some research has focused on understanding corrective maintenance activities to evaluate bug survival time. For instance, Canfora et al. [5] found correlations between the bug classification/severity with high (low) survival times as the change to fix the code could be more (less) obvious to be performed, or the bug might manifest itself only under certain conditions.

Other studies focus on the characterization of bugs in different releases of the same software product. For instance, the authors of a recent paper [9] analyzed 37 Java projects and concluded that post-release bugs are different from pre-release bugs because they are more complex to fix (requiring developers to modify several source code files), and because they involve code additions.

In [14], Zhou et al. focus specifically on differences in bugs and bug-fixing processes between desktop and smartphone software. They analyzed 444,129 bug reports in 88 open source projects on Desktop, Android, and iOS systems to discover similarities and differences in the bug processing. They find that iOS bugs were fixed three times faster compared to Android and Desktop systems.

The studies [5,9,14] used more detailed information than we did. Collecting and analyzing richer information is among our future objectives.

6   Conclusions

Tools that detect possibly problematic code patterns based on static code analysis can be very beneficial for software quality assurance.

In this paper, we focused on SpotBugs [3], which is a very popular tool for defect detection via static code analysis. Specifically, we investigated whether the issues found by SpotBugs are actually relevant in practice. To this end, we analyzed two versions of five open-source software products via SpotBugs. We consider that issues that were reported by SpotBugs in the first release and no longer appeared in the second release were actually worth correction.

By analyzing the corrected issues we found that: 1) about half the warnings issued by SpotBugs concern issues that were corrected; 2) more than 60% of the warnings concerning correctness are corrected; 3) the number of correct issues increases with the warning confidence.

Overall, SpotBugs seems to provide valuable indications concerning code that needs corrections.

There are some interesting facts that we could not investigate in this paper and will be the subject of future work. We shall investigate why different open-source projects seem to address SpotBugs issues to very different extents. We shall also try to understand which corrections were addressed on purpose, e.g., for correcting the bug correctly associated to the warning, and which ones were performed in the context of broad refactoring activities or while maintaining the code for other reasons, not directly connected with the warning. Finally, we would like to understand why the likelihood of correction seems largely independent of issue severity or confidence. Possibly we shall try to get some answers directly from developers, rather than infer them via data analysis.

Acknowledgments. This work has been partially supported by the "Fondo di ricerca d'Ateneo" of the Università degli Studi dell'Insubria.

References

1. FindBugs website (2020). http://findbugs.sourceforge.net/
2. SpotBugs documentation website (2020). https://spotbugs.readthedocs.io/en/latest/
3. SpotBugs website (2020). https://spotbugs.github.io/
4. Ayewah, N., Pugh, W., Morgenthaler, J.D., Penix, J., Zhou, Y.: Evaluating static analysis defect warnings on production software (2007)
5. Canfora, G., Ceccarelli, M., Cerulo, L., Di Penta, M.: How Long Does a Bug Survive? An Empirical Study. In: 2011 18th Working Conference on Reverse Engineering, pp. 191–200 (2011)
6. Hovemeyer, D., Pugh, W.: Finding bugs is easy. ACM SIGPLAN Not. **39**(12), 92–106 (2004)
7. Li, J., Beba, S., Karlsen, M.M.: Evaluation of open-source IDE plugins for detecting security vulnerabilities. In: EASE, pp. 200–209. ACM (2019)
8. Rahman, F., Khatri, S., Barr, E.T., Devanbu, P.: Comparing static bug finders and statistical prediction. In: International Conference on Software Engineering, pp. 424–434 (2014)
9. Rwemalika, R., Kintis, M., Papadakis, M., Le Traon, Y., Lorrach, P.: An industrial study on the differences between pre-release and post-release bugs. In: IEEE International Conference on Software Maintenance and Evolution (ICSME), pp. 92–102 (2019)
10. Tomassi, D.A.: Bugs in the wild: examining the effectiveness of static analyzers at finding real-world bugs. In: ESEC/FSE 2018, pp. 980–982. ACM (2018)
11. Vestola, M.: Evaluating and enhancing FindBugs to detect bugs from mature software; case study in valuatum (2012)
12. Vetrò, A., Morisio, M., Torchiano, M.: An empirical validation of FindBugs issues related to defects. In: EASE, pp. 144–153. IET (2011)
13. Vetrò, A., Torchiano, M., Morisio, M.: Assessing the precision of FindBugs by mining Java projects developed at a university. In: 7th Mining Software Repositories, pp. 110–113. IEEE (2010)
14. Zhou, B., Neamtiu, I., Gupta, R.: A cross-platform analysis of bugs and bug-fixing in open source projects: desktop vs. Android vs. IOS. In: 19th EASE. ACM (2015)

Process Modeling, Improvement
and Assessment

Applying Continual Service Improvement Practices to Study Quality of Healthcare Information System Services: A Case Study

Sanna Heikkinen[1], Marko Jäntti[2(✉)], and Kaija Saranto[2]

[1] Istekki Oy, P.O Box 2000, 70601 Kuopio, Finland
sanna.heikkinen@istekki.fi
[2] University of Eastern Finland, P.O Box 1627, 70211 Kuopio, Finland
{marko.jantti,kaija.saranto}@uef.fi

Abstract. Continual Service Improvement (CSI) plays a critical role in increasing the quality of IT services leading to better customer satisfaction. However, a key challenge in service management is that service provider organizations do not identify CSI activities although they carry out improvements task on daily basis. An ad hoc approach to CSI may result in delays in improvement projects, poor transparency of improvements tasks and lack of focus in service improvement. The research problem of this study is: how to manage service-related improvements with ISO/IEC 20000 compliant CSI model. The main contribution of this paper is to study how service-related improvements are managed. By using case study methodology, we shall describe how CSI can be applied to healthcare information system services. Case study results are analyzed through a Socio-Technical System (STS) view. Our results show that service improvements can be managed with an ERP system including CSI records, workflows and status monitoring of CSI. Additionally, applying CSI to healthcare information systems requires a new set of skills from service managers covering service management, healthcare and medical device regulation. Finally, we show that multiactor network may cause challenges to CSI such as coordinating multiple vendors, stakeholders and customer representatives.

Keywords: Continual Service Improvement · Service quality · IT service management

1 Introduction

Continual Service Improvement (CSI) [7] is a service lifecycle phase that is responsible for improving the quality of IT services and underlying products,

Supported by Digiteknologian TKI-ympäristö project A74338 (ERDF, Regional Council of Pohjois-Savo).

M. Shepperd et al. (Eds.): QUATIC 2020, CCIS 1266, pp. 155–168, 2020.
https://doi.org/10.1007/978-3-030-58793-2_13

components, processes and practices. CSI (Continual Improvement in IT Infrastructure Library Edition 4 [2]) may initiate and manage improvements regarding continuity management, risk management, availability management, capacity management, as well as service operations of the service provider. Interoperability and security of IT services play a crucial role especially in healthcare sector where IT-related incidents (especially software incidents) or poorly managed technical changes can cause service downtime or prevent access to healthcare systems. Technical failures may cause risks to patient safety.

Previous studies on IT service management (ITSM) have mainly focused on success factors of IT service management [24], challenges in service operation processes [15] or other IT service management areas than continual improvement such as implementation of preventive service systems [3], measurement of IT service management [9] and implementing ITIL with Lean methods [20].

However, their findings can be used to deploy continual improvement in a more systematic way. Deployment of CSI should take into account factors that are crucial to any ITSM initiative [12] such as senior management involvement, competence and training, information and communication to staff and stakeholders, and culture.

In Finland, it is mandatory for healthcare organizations to have procedures on how staff can participate on quality management and patient safety improvement actions. Medical Devices Act (629/2010) [19] maintains and promotes the safety of instruments and equipment in healthcare as well as their use. For example, staff can participate on quality assurance by reporting potential threaths or incidents to the HaiPro patient safety violations systems [22].

In order to perform change and technological transformation, IT service providers need to play an active role in developing digital solutions that integrate with healthcare processes and systems. For example, nowadays in Finland electronic patient records (EPRs) and filmless picture archiving and communications systems (PACS) are source of important patient information covering 100% of both primary and specialized care [6]. This information system needs to be updated and continually improved to deploy new features through a large number of IT service providers and suppliers.

IT service providers and healthcare organizations need to improve their own operations (internal improvement) in order to create, deliver and support healthcare services and deal with the growing number of legal requirements and medical regulations. Related to ISO/IEC 20000 service management standard [13], the organization shall have procedures to monitor changes in legal, regulatory, and vendor requirements. The study of Varsha and Ganesh [1] revealed that using appropriate quality management standards the quality of delivered service was improved.

While many IT service provider organizations are aware of the need of continual improvement, they often struggle with improvement actions (e.g., clear service roadmap or service improvement plans, schedules, monitoring) due to lack of a process to manage improvements [11]. Additionally, one of the challenges is that organizations are not able to measure the maturity of continual improvement although there are service management maturity frameworks and standards (for example, ISO/IEC TS 33074:2020 [14]) available.

However, improvements or innovations in healthcare need engagement of multiple stakeholders. IT service providers manage effective and efficient service delivery and they need to be able to rapidly respond to the requirements of the customers and service requests and feedback from service users. Healthcare professionals represent the business perspective and participate in defining the requirements for services.

In this paper, the goal is to study how IT service providers utilize continual service improvement in their operations and services they offer. The focus is on service improvement practices of a Finnish IT service provider company. The results of this study can be used by service managers, business managers, and any other service employees to improve service delivery in a multiactor network and the ability of the company to respond to rapid cyclical developments. The results can be applied for understanding the social and technical aspects of managing improvements related to IT services.

The remainder of the paper is organized as follows. Section 2 describes the research methods. Section 3 presents the results of the study. Section 4 provides an analysis, and conclusions are given in Sect. 5.

2   Research Methods

This study aimed at answering the following research problem: How to manage service-related improvements with ISO 20000 compliant CSI model? In this study, we used a case study method with single organization to answer the research problem. The research problem was divided into three research questions:

– How service-related improvements are managed in Enterprise Resource Planning (ERP) software?
– How CSI model can be applied to IT services on the healthcare domain?
– How CSI is operated in a multiactor network?

This study focused on continual service improvement methods in the context of IT service management. By using case study methodology, we shall present how CSI can be utilized by IT service provider in the healthcare IT services. The case study can be defined as "an empirical inquiry that investigates a contemporary phenomenon within its real-life context" [25]. The real life context refers to daily service management of an IT service provider organization (see Fig. 1).

In this study, we focused on exploring the CSI activities of IT service provider in a healthcare domain. CSI in our case involves measurement of services and service processes, identification of improvement ideas through measurement and management of improvement actions [11]. Results are presented through Socio-Technical System (STS) view. STS focussed at the phenomenological level, identifying the types of socio-technical interactions that occur when humans use IT

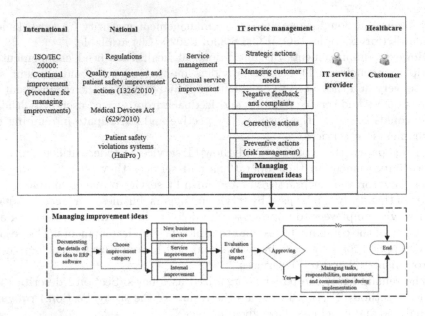

Fig. 1. The context of the case study.

in health settings [8]. As a theoretical framework of the study we used service science, information technology (IT) service management, Continual Service Improvement (CSI), quality management (preventive actions, corrective actions), ISO/IEC 20000 service management standard (improvement management), as well as healthcare laws and regulations (e.g. HaiPro).

2.1   Case Organization

The case organization Alfa has over 600 employees and provides information, communication and medical technology services to its customers in Finland. Alfa also operates in a service integrator role for social and healthcare organizations and municipalities. The case organization was selected because the main author of this paper was working for the case organization, thus having an easy access to data. Additionally, we considered the case as a representative case of a typical IT service provider organization because its service operations and processes are compliant with standards (ISO/IEC 20000, ISO 9001) and it delivers IT services to customers in healthcare domain by using a core ITSM system (ERP in this paper). This study can be considered as exploratory case study with service improvement aspects [21].

2.2   Data Collection Methods

Data for this study was collected by using multiple sources of evidence from the case organization Alfa during the year 2019. The data was captured by the first author while the second author participated in supervising and documenting the case study, and third author provided additional insights regarding the socio-technical system and healthcare information systems.

- Documentation: case documentation such as quality handbook, ITSM process descriptions, ITMS process charts, standards: ISO 9001 and ISO/IEC 20000, monthly steering board info, intranet information letters)
- Archival records: improvement records in the ERP software
- Interviews/discussions: CSI process owner, quality manager, quality specialist, group managers, ITSM tool specialist, process managers in Service Management Office (SMO)
- Participative observation: observations on CSI, participation in SMO meeting, participation in a business steering group meeting
- Validation interviews (number of staff): ERP software main user (1), Security manager (1), Information management specialist (1), Software architect (1), Directors (4), HR Development Manager (1), Executive Assistant (1), Development manager (3)
- Semi-structured theme interviews: two service managers of social and healthcare information system services
- Direct observations: Listening and making notes from conversations during training sessions (ITIL 4)

2.3   Data Analysis Methods

The research problem of this research is to describe how to manage service-related improvements with ISO/IEC 20000 compliant CSI model. According to socio-technical theory [17], an organization consists of two interdependent systems [18]. First, it includes a social system including the people and organizational structures. Second, it involves a technical system including tasks and processes as well as technologies and tools that people use to produce goods or services to their customers.

The findings of the study were analysed by using within case analysis technique and taking into account four aspects involved in the Socio-Technical System (STS). Adopting the Socio-Technical System enables viewing the service improvement practices as a wider and more sustainable perspective than just as a single process area of IT service management. We shall describe four viewpoints and present how to keep the continual improvement momentum going on in the context of an IT service organization. In this study, the results shall be analyzed through socio-technical components [5] in a way similar to the study of Blomberg, Cater-Steel and Soar [4].

3   Results

The results of this study are presented in this paper according to three research questions. These research questions are used to answer the main research problem of this study: How to manage service-related improvements with ISO 20000 compliant CSI model?

3.1 How Service-Related Improvements Are Managed in Enterprise Resource Planning (ERP) Software?

In case Alfa, ERP software (service management system) has been developed to support effective way of work and management of customer needs (lead), projects, invoices, and support request (ticket) in a one master data tool.

Discussion with the continual improvement process owner revealed the need to collect and manage employee's improvement ideas related to new business service innovations, IT services or internal practices via ERP software. The author of this paper designed the workflow to the ERP software based on the ISO/IEC 20000 standard requirements concerning management of improvement ideas (see Fig. 1).

The process of managing improvement ideas guides employees to operate with improvement records always in the same way. This type of model supports and increases quality to the management process and encourages employees to think how ideas would benefit the services of the organization.

The ERP software (deployed in 2018) enables designing particular forms of ticket workflows and tasks to processes. The author designed a form where service-related ideas can be documented in a basic web form. This supports a structured and informative form of Continual Improvement record. The employees see this valuable because it forces to document basic information on improvements (description, benefits, quality aspects).

During the study, we identified a challenge in the information quality of improvement records. Ideas may be received like a post it notes with incomplete information. Improvement records can be directed to a right group or people for evaluation by using automation. The improvement record can be used to replace case organization's other forms such as financial expenditure form and minimize the number of emails related to processing and content of ideas. This provides the employees better opportunities to learn and remember only one tool where they can document ideas. The improvement record includes the following functionalities:

- Categorization and subcategorization of the improvement idea: enables effective routing of improvement idea to a right team or a person
  - Improvement of current service ticket type (shall be assigned to quality management group)
  - Internal improvement idea (shall be assigned to area manager, for example, improvement ideas related to corporate security shall be assigned to security manager, human resources-related improvement ideas to the HR Development Manager)
  - New business opportunity (shall be assigned to Business Development group)
- Reminders: After two weeks of documenting the idea, the reviewer will receive an automatic reminder of the pending evaluation. The evaluation must be done within 21 days. This is seen important because it forces to conduct a review and make either a Go or a No Go decision.

- Evaluation of the improvement idea: Each idea is evaluated by using multiple factors, such as expected business benefits, business impact, leading to measurable results, time required for implementation, required resources, impact to customer, summary of evaluation, decision of implementation.
- Communication of decision: Information on the decision (not implemented/implemented) shall be delivered automatically to the person who submitted the idea and the support person who performed the evaluation
- Status monitoring: The status (new, waiting evaluation, on handling, closed) of the development idea changes automatically (new, pending evaluation, implementation, etc.)

The tool provides employees a channel to represent ideas related to new business service innovation, a service or an internal practice and increases the visibility of ideas to employees. This enables employees to make a conversation of ideas and support the progress. During the study, we observed the need is to ensure that there is clear role to evaluate ideas, keep the implementation work going on, and active dialog between participants.

There is a large number of potential ideas but in relation to benefits (cost, effective, resources, risks) there is need to make selection. It is important to review ideas by using the same attributes and aspects to ensure the equality of ideas.

During the study, we captured comments (participative observation, interviews) that indicated the need to communicate improvement ideas to employees and ensure that the processes are in place to support smooth management of improvements. This includes identification of new ideas and allocating them to the right people who can make the evaluation, motivated employees to design the solution and work with implementation, as well as communicating the benefits that are achieved.

The observations and interviews revealed the need of a ticket, because a customer may suggest, for example, ideas related to internal practices and at the moment it is not clear for employees how to manage this type of ideas. Customer feedback and ideas should be brought under case organization's processing and someone should take action on them. One of the interviewees commented that it is good that there is a tool to support the management practice, but there is also need for employees that perform the implementation of improvements in addition to their normal work.

3.2 How CSI Model Can Be Applied to IT Services on the Healthcare Domain

How Service is Measured? In case organization, quality manuals describe measurement and metrics on service and customer satisfaction (e.g. customer surveys, customer feedback, project meetings, project feedback). The researchers observed that measurement of the service benefits and impact is a challenging task to perform. There should be common criteria and methods on how service benefits can be evaluated. This type of analysis could show how IT service brings broader benefits to customer and this data can be used by sales staff to increase service sales. For example, regarding the robotics service there are viewpoints such as cost quality aspects (patient safety, data transfer), and employee experience (less manual checks and data copy and paste between systems).

What Type of Knowhow Is Required in a Service Manager Role? IT service organization need different roles and skills on work. For example, one important skill type for service managers are interaction skills, because they manage the performance of provided service by working together with the customer, organization's experts and suppliers. Interviews revealed also need for customer relationship management, service pricing, performance of maintenance, contract management, procurement, contract management, service reporting to organization management and to customers, continual improvement of the operational services.

For service delivery, service managers need to have knowhow on ITSM practices such as incident management, change and project management, continuity and availability management, and service level management. Additionally, they need to have tools for monitoring the service management. Service managers reported that they have business intelligence (BI) tools to monitor the profitability of the service. They can use the tool to identify and analyse the costs of the service and service profitability. In the future, the service managers would need to increase skills at service design, Medical Device Regulation related to healthcare systems and service improvement perspectives in Finland, and benchmark to competitors.

How Service Managers Perform Service Improvement? According to interviews, in IT and healthcare domains there is no other alternative than continual improvement. Healthcare legislation and regulative frameworks result in continuous stream of changes to the requirements due to government's social and healthcare reform. Additionally, customers' growing need for digitalization requires that IT service providers pay attention to improve services and service management. In our case organization, continual improvement is performed in many levels, roles, cycles and actions.

The researchers observed that continual service improvement is important in case organization from value creation perspective. The case organization's goal is to add value to customers and do things for the customers by supporting their operations in a way that the customer can focus on their own business and the service provider organization will take care of the IT service improvement and IT-related problems.

The service manager of case Alfa commented in interviews that service improvement requires IT service management processes that are running smoothly and there should be time to develop those processes that supports the IT service delivery.

Which Roles Participate in Decision Making of Service Related Improvements? While improving the service there might be different roles that participate in the design and decision making. It depends on the scope of improvement activity. In the case organization, participating roles included business manager, specialists and service managers.

Depending on the value of investment and other factors described earlier in this paper decision-making authorization is defined and limits for purchases are set. The service manager gathers information from various sources to make the business decision to move forward. We observed that it has been a little unclear who will decide the bigger and smaller improvement thing.

Sometimes the implementation of development ideas may involve investments that are seen to result in sufficient benefits through the calculations and whether it is worthwhile to continue the implementation. From the company's management perspective, it would be better if ideas should be refined and not directly presented as raw ideas in strategic decision-making.

In case organization, the business development team evaluates and filters new business ideas which are recorded in the ERP system. If there is only one person to decide, then there is a risk of not recognizing the potential.

How Service Review Meetings Are Organized? According to the case Alfa's quality manual, 2–4 service meetings are organized annually. Service managers reported that meetings include overall service situation such as service development needs, service functionality in production, customer satisfaction, potential cost increase needs, and from the quality point of view, the number of service requests from the ERP tool.

Participation depends on the meeting subject and could include customer's information management persons (e.g. responsible and accountable persons, system administrators and executives). Service meetings are case-by-case, which allows to choose the best customer relationship management model when there is really no one-size-fits-all model.

3.3 How CSI Is Operated in Multiactor Network?

Which Actors and Stakeholders Are Related to the Service? The case organization utilizes suppliers to provide the service. The suppliers are social and healthcare system and equipment providers. Additionally, service-related actors are the case organization's business units and the production groups (e.g., network, database, integrations), customer representatives and other authorities such as the Finnish Institute for Health and Welfare (THL), Digital and Population Data Services Agency, the Ministry of Social Affairs and Health, and the Social Insurance Institution of Finland (KELA). Existing ICT communication tools (e.g. Skype, Teams) enable cooperation with suppliers and customers.

How Improvements Are Implemented in Multiactor Network and Which Challenges Has Been Identified? According to the interviewee, service improvement requires a good cooperation with suppliers and support from organization's management. To make things progress there is need to identify right channels for ideas and contact persons to communicate with regarding the idea. The case organization has recognized that service development in multiactor network is a complex and time-consuming process. The most demanding step is the co-ordination if there are multiple vendors, other stakeholders and the customer involved in the development.

Service improvement begins with identification of a customer's needs, planning, kickoff and review of suppliers' offers. When the solution to a customer need is known internally and externally, then the offer from the case organization will be introduced to the customer. The scope of improvement affects the delivery model where large implementations can be managed as projects and smaller implementations can be managed as service requests. One of the interviewees commented that it is good if a service manager would be involved in the improvement because he/she can ensure that the business perspective is taken into account.

To provide service via a multiactor model, the goal is to integrate the services of internal and external service providers into a seamless service chain. Certain challenges have been identified in delivering the service in terms of information flow and managing information on the supplier's operating practices. Additionally, one of the interviewees pointed out challenges related to service support times. The case organization needs to take into account all supplier contracts to define service support times and service levels.

What Types of Expectations Customers Have Regarding the Service?
The operating environment of service is becoming more diverse and customers expect that the case organization is able to provide customers with solutions holistically through a wide catalogue of services. The expectations are related to meeting the agreed service level requirements, for example, response times should match customers' requirements and service times for operations should follow defined service levels. Additionally, staff needs to be aware what is happening in the service environment, have readiness to improve the provided service, and to collaborate and engage stakeholders. Customers also expect that the case organization monitors the operating environment and provides added value, not only from a perspective of a single service, but holistically from a wider business perspective.

4 Analysis

Table 1 shows the analysis of results according to two elements of social view. Data source has been described by using abbreviations: IN = Validation interviews and theme interviews, DI = Discussions, DO = Documentation, PO = Partic. observation, DOB = Direct observation, PA = Physical artefacts. Other abbreviations: CSI = Continual Service Improvement.

A within-case analysis technique [10] was applied to analyze the data from the case organization. The focus was in the continual service improvement. This requires skilled service staff, appropriate organizational structure, defined processes and effective tools to support service delivery. Next, we shall present the analysis by using the components of the Socio-Technical System as patterns (categories).

People: The IT service provider needs competent staff to lead the service improvement implementation and smooth service delivery to the customer. Utilizing staff throughout the organization to identify unnecessary job bottlenecks increases job satisfaction. When new business service innovation, IT service, or internal practice is recognized by staff and customer, employees are encouraged to make a conversation about the recorded ideas and process the ideas together.

The customer expectation is that the case organization can provide added value, not only from a perspective of a single service, but holistically from a wider business perspective. The service provider needs to be aware of what is happening in the service environment and take proactive actions, have readiness to improve the provided service, and to collaborate and engage various stakeholder groups.

Table 1. Summary of key findings according to 4 views in the Socio-Technical System

STS	Findings (source)	Implication to CSI
People	Interaction and cooperation skills IN	Ensure that CSI skills exist
	Creativity & innovation to improve services DI, IN	Foster innovation skills
	The tool provides a channel to present	Utilize the full org. potential
	ideas related to service innovation DI, IN	in CSI
	Be aware of changes in service environment IN	Know the service environment
	Have readiness to improve provided service IN	
	Collaborate and engage stakeholders IN	Plan engagement
Structure	Various roles participate in design, decision	Set clear roles and responsibilities
	making, and implementing improvements. IN	to support smooth CSI.
	Communicate improvements to employees IN	Create visibility to CSI
	Measurement of the service benefits and	Emphasize managem. of benefits
	impact from value creation perspective. IN	
Process	Meetings with customers and	Organize service meetings
	suppliers related to service delivery. IN, DO	to improve service delivery
	Planning the future roadmap helps to gather	Use roadmaps to show
	and implement service improvements. IN, DO	direction for improvement
	Managing improvement ideas process ensures	Define a process for
	unified processing of ideas. IN, DO, PO, DI	managing improvements
	Common methods and criteria needed to	Evaluation of improvements
	evaluate service improvement targets. IN, AR,	requires clear criteria
	DO	
Technology	ERP should enable managing service	Design a system supporting
	tasks and support effective work. DO, PO, IN	service lifecycle management
	ERP should produce monitoring data DO, PO, IN	
	Design a workflow where ideas can be	Use standardized
	captured in a common form; helps creating	procedures and workflows
	an informative impr. record. DO, PO, IN	in ITSM tools

Structure: In order to provide service via a multiactor model, the case organization aims at integrating the services of internal and external service providers into a seamless service chain. To improve service, there is need to ensure that there are clear roles to evaluate ideas, motivated employees to design the solution, keeping the implementation work going on, active dialog between participants, and effective communication on the benefits that have been achieved.

If there is a service roadmap or a service improvement plan (SIP), it would help to prioritizing the improvement ideas. Additionally, SIP could help staff to be proactive and manage the workload effectively. ISO/IEC 20000 standard requires that IT service providers measure services and implemented improvements and take necessary actions if targets are not achieved. The case organization could pay more attention to identification of benefits (e.g, patient safety, increased employee experience), impact and goal-orientation while defining metrics.

Process: IT service provider collects service improvements during meetings with customers and suppliers. Meetings include overall service situation such as service development needs, service functionality in production, customer satisfaction, potential cost increase needs, and from the quality point of view, the number of support tickets from the ERP tool. Workflows in the ERP tool support and increase quality to the management of processes in the same way. There is a large number of ITSM process frameworks available for improvement purposes [16].

The ERP system supports a structured and informative form of Continual Improvement record. The employees see this valuable because it forces to document basic information on improvements (description, benefits, quality aspects). A well-known and familiar management process for improvements encourages employees to think how ideas would benefit the services and customers. Additionally, there should be common methods and criteria on how service improvement targets can be evaluated.

Technology: The ERP system should enable managing service lifecycle processes and workflows within the case organization. This supports identifying and analyzing the costs of the service and issues related to the effectiveness of the service profitability.

Our results support the findings of previous studies in CSI by emphasizing the need for systematic management of continual improvement actions for services [11]. However, this study did not deal with CSI based on maturity models [23] but instead applied a Socio-Technical Theory model in order to establish foundation for continual improvement practices.

5   Conclusions

This study aimed at answering the research problem: how to manage service-related improvements with ISO/IEC 20000 compliant CSI model. The main contribution of this paper was to present a case study focusing on studying continual service improvement practices of an IT service provider organization. The study consisted of three research questions. Regarding the first research question (How service-related improvements are managed?), we observed that the ERP system plays a central role in continual service improvement of the case organization. The ERP system includes CSI records, workflows, priorization and categorization of improvement ideas, communication of decision and status monitoring of continual improvement records.

The second research question (How CSI model can be applied to IT services on the healthcare domain?) focused on studying CSI in the context of healthcare information system services. Our findings indicate that continual improvement can be seen as a mandatory process area for healthcare information system services because they need to respond to the changes in healthcare legislation, regulative frameworks and customers' changing needs. We observed that service managers need not only service management skills but also skills and knowhow on Medical Device Regulation related to healthcare systems. Additionally, service managers need information on customers' strategies, improvement roadmaps and actual service performance as well as solutions that help customers holistically.

Our findings from the third research question (How CSI is operated in a multiactor network?) revealed that service development in a multiactor network is a complex and time-consuming process. One of the major challenges is how to coordinate multiple vendors, stakeholders and customer representatives involved in the improvement. The multiactor model of service provision aims at integrating the services of internal and external service providers into a seamless service chain.

The following limitations are related to this case study: First, our study included only one case organization with limited number of interviewees and qualitative data. It would be interesting to conduct a study that compares CSI procedures of multiple organizations and utilizes both qualitative and quantitative data. Second, the selection of interviewees can also be seen as a limitation. Interviews could have included customer representatives to provide richer insights to CSI. Third, case study as a research method does not allow us to generalize research findings to other organizations. However, we are able to extend the theory of service management through our results. We aimed at improving the validity of the study by using multiple data sources and two interviewees validating and reviewing the case study. Reliability was improved by utilizing case study datastore and maintaining the chain of evidence.

References

1. Agarwal, V., Ganesh, L.: Implementing quality healthcare strategies for improving service delivery at private hospitals in India. J. Health Manag. **19**(1), 159–169 (2017)
2. Axelos: ITIL Foundation ITIL 4 Edition. The Stationary Office, UK (2020)
3. Barkai, O., Harison, E.: Preventive service management: towards pro-active improvement of service quality. Rev. Bus. Inf. Syst. **15**, 19–30 (2011)
4. Blumberg, M., Cater-Steel, A., Rajaeian, M., Soar, J.: Effective organisational change to achieve successful ITIL implementation: lessons learned from a multiple case study of large Australian firms. J. Enterp. Inf. Manag. 496–516 (2019)
5. Bostrom, R.P., Heinen, J.S.: MIS problems and failures: a socio-technical perspective. part I: the causes. MIS Q. **1**(3), 17–32 (1977)
6. Braithwaite, J., Mannion, R., Matsuyama, Y.: Health Systems Improvement Across the Globe: Success Stories From 60 Countries. CRC Press (2018)
7. Office, C.: ITIL Continual Service Improvement. The Stationary Office, UK (2011)

8. Coiera, E.: Putting the technical back into socio-technical systems research. Int. J. Med. Inf. **76**(1), 98–103 (2007)
9. Cronholm, S., Salomonson, N.: Measures that matters: service quality in it service management. Int. J. Qual. Serv. Sci. **6**, 60–75 (2014)
10. Eisenhardt, K.: Building theories from case study research. Acad. Manag. Rev. **14**, 532–550 (1989)
11. Heikkinen, S., Jäntti, M.: Studying continual service improvement and monitoring the quality of ITSM. In: Piattini, M., Rupino da Cunha, P., García Rodríguez de Guzmán, I., Pérez-Castillo, R. (eds.) QUATIC 2019. CCIS, vol. 1010, pp. 193–206. Springer, Cham (2019). https://doi.org/10.1007/978-3-030-29238-6_14
12. Iden, J., Eikebrokk, T.: Implementing it service management: a systematic literature review. Int. J. Inf. Manag. **33**, 512–523 (2013)
13. ISO/IEC 20000:1: Information technology - Service management - Part 1: Service management system requirements. Finnish Standard Association (2018)
14. ISO/IEC TS 33074:2020: Information technology – Process assessment – Process capability assessment model for service management. ISO Copyright Office (2020)
15. Jäntti, M., Cater-Steel, A.: Proactive management of it operations to improve it services. J. Inf. Syst. Technol. Manag.: JISTEM **14**(2), 191–218 (2017)
16. Jäntti, M., Hotti, V.: Defining the relationships between it service management and it service governance. Inf. Technol. Manag. **17**(2), 141–150 (2016)
17. Leavitt, H.J.: Applied organization change in industry: structural, technical and human approaches. In: New Perspectives in Organization Research, pp. 55–71 (1964)
18. Lyytinen, K., Mathiassen, L., Ropponen, J.: Attention shaping and software risk - a categorical analysis of four classical risk management approaches. Inf. Syst. Res. **9**, 233–255 (1998)
19. Ministry of Social Affairs and Health: Medical devices act (1482/2019) (2019)
20. Obwegeser, N., Nielsen, D.T., Spandet, N.M.: Continual process improvement for ITIL service operations: a lean perspective. Inf. Syst. Manag. **36**(2), 141–167 (2019)
21. Runeson, P., Höst, M.: Guidelines for conducting and reporting case study research in software engineering. Empirical Softw. Eng. **14**(2), 131–164 (2009)
22. Ruuhilehto, K., Kaila, M., Keistinen, T., Kinnunen, M., Vuorenkoski, L., Wallenius, J.: Haipro-what was learned from patient safety incidents in Finnish health care units in 2007 to 2009? Duodecim Med. J. **127**, 1033–1040 (2011)
23. Shrestha, A., Cater-Steel, A., Toleman, M.: Virtualising process assessments to facilitate continual service improvement in it service management. In: Australasian Conference on Information Systems, pp. 1–14. Association for Information Systems, AIS, Asia and the Pacific (2015)
24. Tan, W.G., Cater-Steel, A., Toleman, M.: Implementing it service management: a case study focussing on critical success factors. J. Comput. Inf. Syst. **50**(2), 1–12 (2009)
25. Yin, R.: Case Study Research: Design and Methods, 5th edn. SAGE (2014)

A Personal Opinion Survey on Process Compliance Checking in the Safety Context

Julieth Patricia Castellanos Ardila[✉] and Barbara Gallina

IDT, Mälardalen University, Västerås, Sweden
{julieth.castellanos,barbara.gallina}@mdh.se

Abstract. Manually checking the compliance of process plans against the requirements of applicable standards is a common practice in the safety-critical context. We hypothesize that automating this task could be of interest. To test our hypothesis, we conducted a personal opinion survey among practitioners who participate in safety-related process compliance checking. In this paper, we present the results of this survey. Practitioners indicated the methods used and their challenges, as well as their interest in a novel method that could permit them to move from manual to automated practices via compliance checking.

Keywords: (Automated) compliance checking · Process plan · Safety-critical · Current practices · Challenges · Personal opinion survey

1 Introduction

Safety standards usually include requirements that prescribe the planning of tasks, and the resources required and produced, e.g., personnel, work products, and tools. Nair et al. [13], reports 9 essential process plans required in safety assessment, i.e., Safety Management, Communication, Risk Management, Configuration Management, Development, Verification and Validation, Modification Procedures, Operation Procedures, and Staff Competence. Manually checking the compliance of such plans against the requirements of applicable standards is a common practice. The checklists used can be obtained by listing the requirements of the standard, or listing personal or organizational practices [15]. A process compliance checklist, which has been accurately filled-in, requires a proper evaluation of the satisfaction of the requirements. Thus, missed requirements are highlighted, providing hints to improve the process.

Process compliance checking could be overwhelming due to the sheer volume and complexity of the knowledge included in the standards. Thus, we hypothesize that automating this task could be of interest. To test our hypothesis, we conducted a personal opinion survey [12] among practitioners who participate in safety-related process compliance checking. In this paper, we present the results

© Springer Nature Switzerland AG 2020
M. Shepperd et al. (Eds.): QUATIC 2020, CCIS 1266, pp. 169–183, 2020.
https://doi.org/10.1007/978-3-030-58793-2_14

of this survey. In particular, practitioners indicated the methods used and their challenges, as well as their interest in a novel method that could permit them to move from manual to automated process compliance checking. These results contribute to systematizing the knowledge about process compliance checking and finding methods and tools for facilitating this practice.

The rest of the paper is organized as follows. In Sect. 2, we present essential background. In Sect. 3, we present the research method used to conduct the survey. In Sect. 4, we present the survey results. In Sect. 5, we discuss our findings. In Sect. 6, we examine related work. Finally, in Sect. 7, we conclude our work and present future work.

2   Background

This section presents essential background.

2.1   Facilitating Automated Process Compliance Checking

In the context of the European project AMASS (Architecture-driven, Multi-concern and Seamless Assurance and Certification of Cyber-Physical Systems)[1], we proposed a process-centered planning-time method for safety-related process compliance checking [4,5]. The method requires users to create artifacts in a SPEM 2.0 (Systems & Software Process Engineering Metamodel)[2] reference implementation supported with Eclipse Process Framework (EPF) Composer[3] (see Fig. 1), as follows. (1) Method content, which are elements that are part of a process, i.e., roles, tasks, work products, and guidance. (2) A knowledge base of compliance information based on the formalization of standard requirements in Formal Contract Logic (FCL) [10]. FCL is a defeasible deontic logic, i.e., it supports the modeling of norms representing obligations and permissions in a normative context that can be defeated by evolving knowledge. In FCL, a rule has the form: r: $a_1, ..., a_n \Rightarrow c$, where r is the rule identifier, $a_1, ..., a_n$ are the propositions that represent the conditions of the applicability of the norm, and c is the concluding proposition that contains normative effects. For this, SPEM 2.0 guidance elements are customized as requirements, FCL rules, and compliance effects (which correspond to the propositions of the rules). (3) Compliance effects are annotated in the process tasks. As compliance effects describe the concrete actions prescribed by the standard requirements, users need to evaluate each task action and define its effects in the overall process compliance to make the annotation. For example, the task *Start software Unit Design Process* indicates that the process is performed and has two inputs. Thus, the annotated compliance effects are *addressSwUnitDesignProcess*, *ProvideSwArchitecturalDesign* and *ProvideSwSafetyRequirements*. (4-a) A sequential representation of the process plan, as well as its dynamic representation (4-b), are created by using the compliance

---

[1] https://www.amass-ecsel.eu/.
[2] https://www.omg.org/spec/SPEM/About-SPEM/.
[3] https://www.eclipse.org/epf/.

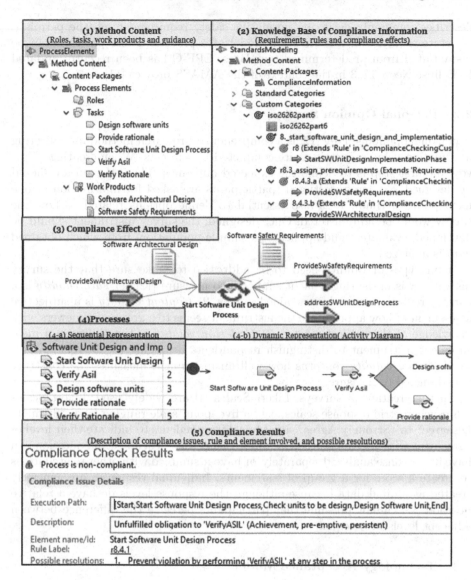

Fig. 1. Method for facilitating automated process compliance checking.

annotated tasks. The dynamic representation is used to automatically generate a compliance state representation of the process, which permits automatic compliance analysis with the compliance checker Regorous[4]. Regorous provides (5) compliance checking results, i.e., description of compliance issues, rules and elements involved, and possible resolutions. For facilitating FCL formalization, the concept of Safety Compliance Pattern (SCP) [3,6] has been defined. An SCP

---

[4] https://research.csiro.au/data61/regorous/.

describes commonly occurring normative safety requirements on the permissible state sequence of a finite state model of a process. These patterns can be instantiated from predetermined templates. EPF-C has been recently updated to Eclipse Neon 4.6.3 in the context of the AMASS project [11].

2.2 Personal Opinion Surveys

A personal opinion survey [12] is a comprehensive research method for collecting information using a questionnaire completed by subjects. When creating a survey, the first step is to define the expected outcomes. Then, the survey should be designed, e.g., cross-sectional (participants are asked for information at one fixed point in time). It is also essential to define options related to how the survey would be administered. Once designed, the survey instrument should be developed, evaluated, and applied to a sample population, from which obtained data is analyzed.

Four types of validity need to be addressed to make sure that the survey instrument is measuring what it supposes to measure [12]. 1) *Face validity* is a cursory review of items by untrained judges. 2) *Content validity* is a subjective assessment of how appropriate the instrument seems to a group of reviewers with knowledge of the subject matter. 3) *Criterion validity* is the ability of a measurement instrument to distinguish respondents belonging to different groups. 4) *Construct validity* concerns how well an instrument measures the construct it is designed to measure.

In the creation of surveys, Likert Scales [1] are widely used. Likert Scales are psychometric response scales, e.g., a five–point scale ranging from "Strongly Disagree" to "Strongly Agree," used to ask respondents to indicate their level of agreement with a given statement. On a Likert scale, each specific question can have its response analyzed separately, or have it summed with other related items to create a score for a group of statements. Individual responses are generally treated as ordinal data because although the response levels do have a relative position, we cannot presume that participants perceive the difference between adjacent levels to be equal.

2.3 Technology Acceptance Model

The Technology Acceptance Model (TAM) [7] provides general determinants of computer acceptance. TAM is capable of explaining user behavior across a broad range of end-user computing technologies and user populations, while at the same time being theoretically justified. TAM focuses on three main facets of user acceptance. The first is the degree to which a person believes that using a particular method will be free of effort (Perceived Usability). The second is related to a person's subjective probability that using a particular system would enhance his/her job (Perceived Usefulness). The third is the extent to which a person intends to use a particular system (Intention to Use).

3 Research Method

In this section, we present the details regarding the creation of a personal opinion survey. We followed the guidelines recalled in Sects. 2.2 and 2.3.

3.1 Research Questions

In this survey, we aim at gathering information about current industrial practices and challenges in process compliance checking, as well as the acceptance level of the method for automated compliance checking (recalled in Sect. 2.1). Within this scope, we formulate the research questions presented below.

- RQ1: How do practitioners currently perform process compliance checking?
- RQ2: What are the challenges that practitioners face when performing process compliance checking?
- RQ3: What is the level of acceptance of practitioners regarding a novel method for facilitating automated compliance checking?

3.2 Survey Design

We designed a cross-sectional web-based personal opinion survey, whose goal is to collect data relevant to answer the research questions presented in Sect. 3.1. The target population is practitioners involved in process compliance checking in the safety-related context. The final survey[5], which starts with a short introduction to the purpose of the study, is composed of 21 questions, which are organized into four parts.

1. **Demographics.** Questions 1–7 aim at gathering the background characteristics of the practitioners.
2. **Current practices.** Questions 8–14 aim at gathering information about practitioners' experiences in compliance checking.
3. **Challenges.** Questions 15 and 16 aim at inquiring about the challenges appearing in process compliance checking. In question 15, practitioners rate the importance of 7 possible challenges by using a five-point Likert scale ranging from Unimportant to Very Important. Question 16 is an open question in which practitioners can write further challenges.
4. **Automated process compliance checking.** First, practitioners read information about the method for facilitating automated compliance checking recalled in Sect. 2.1. Then, we present the questions 17–21 as a series of claims from which we seek practitioners' degree of acceptance regarding the user acceptance aspects described in the TAM model (see Sect. 2.3), i.e., the method usefulness, usability, and user's intention to use it. To collect the answers, we use a five-point Likert Scale ranging from Strongly Agree to Strongly Disagree.

---

[5] https://www.dropbox.com/s/efcab84me7kxpj8/FinalSurvey.pdf?dl=0.

We were interested in the practitioners' overall experience. Thus, where possible, the practitioners were allowed to select more than one option to indicate their experience regarding several practices. Practitioners were also given the possibility to mention additional options or answer "Don't know" if this was the case. We consider that completing the survey would take between 20–25 min.

3.3 Instrument Evaluation and Data Collection

The first author created a set of initial questions. The second author helped to structure and design the survey by providing comments for cleaning ambiguity and a more in-depth analysis that led to the formulation of further questions. Then, we distributed the survey to a selected group of safety experts during the Scandinavian Conference on System & Software Safety[6]. One expert provided valuable comments that were used to improve the survey. The final evaluation was performed by both authors, improving textual explanations and questions.

The data was collected from January 22th to February 28th of 2020. The survey was distributed via personal e-mail invitations. The selection of the practitioners included industrial experts (on purpose, we discarded research institutions) that participate in European projects related to certification and self-assessment. We also extracted industrial-related practitioners from conferences, symposiums, and workshops related to safety assurance. In total, we obtained 15 valid responses from which 8 were received after the initial invitation letter, and 7 were received after a reminder e-mail.

3.4 Subject Characteristics and Data Analysis

The valid answers were obtained from practitioners mostly working in the consultatory branch (see Fig. 2a and Fig. 2g) which have experience demonstrating process compliance checking in 13 countries (see Fig. 2b), predominantly Europe. The practitioners have experience in 9 safety-related domains (see Fig. 2c) and 13 standards (see Fig. 2d), where automotive is the most represented. The major interest of the practitioners, which shows higher levels of expertise (see Fig. 2f) in process compliance checking, is to get the compliance certification and improve processes (see Fig. 2g). The analysis of our survey was adjusted with the information provided in the "Others" option.

3.5 Survey Validity

The four types of validity of the survey instrument (recalled in Sect. 2.2) were addressed as follows. To avoid *face validity*, we perform a careful review of our survey instrument in several stages and with experts in the field of safety certification. *Content validity* was assured by doing a careful literature review on the topic and validating as well with experts. Regarding *criterion validity*, we assure that the practitioners' background was related to the type of expertise we

---

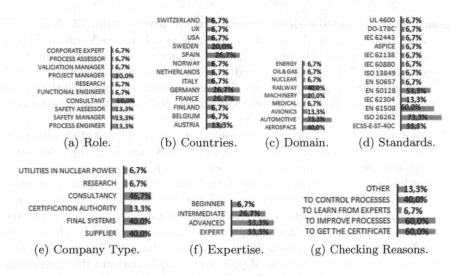

(a) Role.   (b) Countries.   (c) Domain.   (d) Standards.

(e) Company Type.   (f) Expertise.   (g) Checking Reasons.

Fig. 2. Demographic results.

were looking by making a careful selection process. For reducing the *construct validity*, we allow the practitioners to include the "Others" option. Thus, the threat of providing an incomplete list of options is minimized. Additionally, to avoid evaluation apprehension, we guaranteed confidentiality and anonymity of the responses.

4   Survey Results

In this section, we present the results of the survey by answering the research questions presented in Sect. 3.1.

4.1   Current Practices (RQ1)

Figure 3a shows the 9 process plans (recalled in the introductory part) provided as alternatives in the questionnaire in the vertical axis, and the percentage of

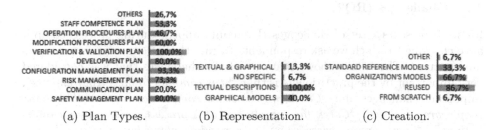

(a) Plan Types.   (b) Representation.   (c) Creation.

Fig. 3. Information regarding processes.

respondents, who selected each type in the horizontal axis. Figure 3a shows that practitioners have performed compliance checking mostly on the Verification and Validation, Configuration Management, Safety Management, Development, Risk Management, and Modification Procedure Plans. The remaining plans listed were less considered as part of the practitioners' compliance checking duties. In the "Others" option, practitioners mentioned the Software Quality Assurance, Safety Assessment, Documentation, and Cybersecurity Plans.

Current practices indicate that processes are mostly represented with only text, but graphical representations are also relevant (see Fig. 3b). Moreover, process plan reuse is a common practice (see Fig. 3c).

Regarding checklist preparation, we found that the three alternatives given in the questionnaire are almost equally used (see Fig. 4a). The practice of compliance checking is done in different ways. Most commonly, practitioners take every requirement and check it against the information provided by the process specification (see Fig. 4b). Practitioners also base the compliance assessment on other practices, such as the use of points of compliance, and the assessment of strengths and weaknesses of the findings. It is common that practitioners use software tools for performing compliance management tasks (see Fig. 4c). Rational doors, Microsoft suite (e.g., Word, Excel, and MS project), opencert, verification studio, engineering studio, stages (for modeling processes) were the tools mentioned by practitioners in the survey.

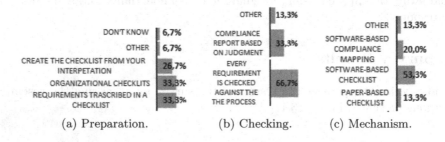

(a) Preparation.   (b) Checking.   (c) Mechanism.

Fig. 4. Information regarding compliance checking.

4.2 Challenges (RQ2)

Figure 5 presents a set of challenges that could appear during process compliance checking to which we ask respondents to rate them from very important to unimportant. The results shows that one of the challenges that was considered very important by the practitioners is that *"it is common to miss requirements"*. Important challenges are: *"Check process-based compliance requires that many people are involved"*, *"Check the compliance of a process requires many interactions"*, *"Check process-based compliance requires many hours of work"*, and *"It isn't easy to determine the kind of information that should be provided as*

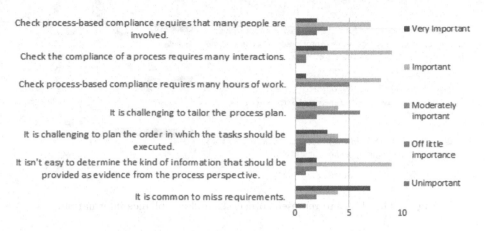

Fig. 5. Challenges in process compliance checking.

evidence from the process perspective." The practitioners considered the other challenges moderately important. The practitioners also have the option to list their challenges to which they answer that *"Sometimes there is no access to the evidence"*, *"Sometimes the safety assessor could have different interpretations"*, and *"It is difficult to check the user acceptance of the defined processes."*

4.3 Automatic Process Compliance Checking (RQ3)

This part of the survey gathered data regarding the user acceptance level of the method for facilitating automated process compliance checking (recalled in Sect. 2.1). Initial evaluation is performed on FCL, which is the logic used to formalize the requirements prescribed by the standards. Practitioners somewhat agree that the formalization of standard requirements could be facilitated with FCL since it provides the compliance concepts and there are safety compliance patterns to instantiate (see Fig. 6). Practitioners also somewhat agree that FCL

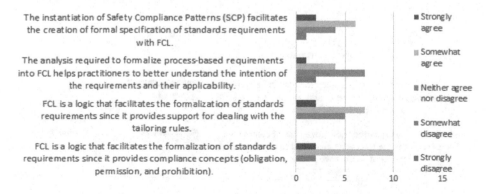

Fig. 6. The ability to formalize requirements with FCL.

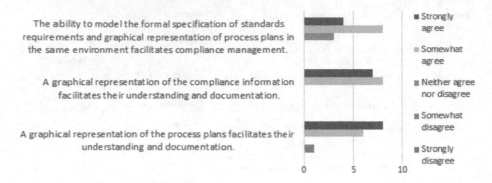

Fig. 7. The ability to represent processes and compliance information.

can be used to support the creation of the tailoring rules. However, most of the practitioners are neutral whether the analysis required to formalize process requirements could help them to understand their intention.

Regarding the ability of the method to represent processes and compliance information (see Fig. 7) we found that the majority of the practitioners somewhat agree with the statements regarding the provision of graphical representations. In particular, graphical representation of the compliance information, as well as process plans, facilitate their understanding and documentation. Similarly, the majority of the practitioners somewhat agree that this aspect also would facilitate compliance management.

Then, we focused on the ability of the method to perform automated compliance checking (see Fig. 8). As the figure depicts, the ability to perform automated compliance checking is seen by the majority of the practitioners as favorable. In particular, practitioners somewhat agree that the iterative application of automated compliance checking can help them to reach process plans with compliant states. Moreover, the majority of the practitioners strongly agree that modifying a compliant process plan to define a new process reduces the work that needs to be done. Finally, traceability could be facilitated with a hierarchically

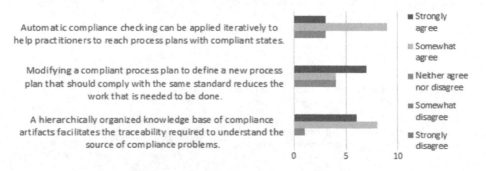

Fig. 8. The ability to perform automated compliance checking.

organized knowledge-based of compliance artifacts. Such an organization helps to understand the source of compliance problems.

Figure 9 shows the results regarding the perceived usability aspect of the method. Practitioners do not strongly agree or strongly disagree with any of the questionnaire's options. However, there are two statements that practitioners somewhat agree: it is easy to 1) trace uncompliant situations and 1) graphically model process elements.

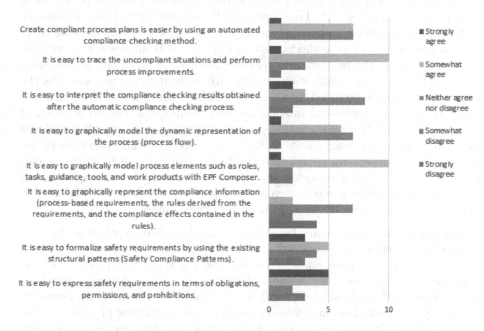

Fig. 9. Perceived usability aspect of the method.

Finally, one question was asked to the practitioners about their intention to use the method. As Fig. 10 depicts 67% of the practitioners indicated that they would use the method for facilitating automated compliance checking if it were made available. In contrast, 13% of the practitioners do not know, and 20% would not do it.

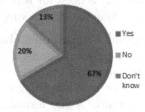

Fig. 10. Intention to use.

5 Discussion

In this section, based upon the result of the survey, we discuss our findings.

Current Practices: Given the characteristics of the subjects, presented in Sect. 3.4, we consider our sample to be representative of the European safety-critical context. For this kind of population, process compliance checking is not only the way towards a safety certificate but also a mechanism for process improvement (see Fig. 2g). Their current practices include the checking of a variety of process plans (see Fig. 3a). Additional plan types respect to the ones described in the introductory part were considered necessary in the safety-critical context, i.e., Software Quality Assurance Plan, Safety Assessment Plan, Documentation Plan, and Cybersecurity Plan (see Sect. 4.1). Thus, it seems that compliance management from the process perspective is a growing area. Practitioners also create process plans mostly by reusing previous processes or their elements (see Fig. 3c). This aspect indicates that support for reusability is significant in process compliance management. We also could see that there are different ways to create checklists (see Fig. 4a). It is interesting to see that most of the time, the practitioners receive the checklist from the organization (which is based on the organization's experience in the domain) or transcribe the actual requirements provided by the standard direct into a checklist. In those cases, there is not additional intellectual work included in the preparation of the checklist, and the provision of a general, widely accepted checklist could be useful for minimizing such initial work. Finally, most of the practitioners use software tools to perform compliance checking to support their activities (see Fig. 4c). Thus, it is not expected that the introduction of more sophisticated software tools would generate extreme distortions in their daily job. However, it would be good to revise the ways to introduce them smoothly.

Challenges: Practitioners are faced with several challenges when performing compliance checking, as presented in Sect. 4.2. In general, practitioners consider that compliance checking is prone-to-error. For them, it is possible to miss requirements. Moreover, they consider that it is not easy to determine the kind of information that should be provided as evidence (or there is no access to evidence), and that there are different possible interpretations provided by the assessors. In addition, practitioners consider that compliance checking is time-consuming since it requires many hours of work and several iterations. Finally, many people in the organization are needed making it also resource-consuming. Thus, there is a need for solutions that provide more confidence and efficiency in process compliance checking.

Automated Compliance checking: User acceptance is a major for any technological endeavor. In general, as we presented in Sect. 4.3, there are advantages regarding automated process compliance checking. In particular, as depicted in Fig. 6, there is a good degree of acceptance for the characteristics provided by FCL, which is the formal approach used for requirements representation. However, there is some hesitation regarding its usage, as expected with formal methods. In particular, practitioners do not see how the analysis required to formalize process requirements would help them to understand their intention. For this reason, it is necessary to explain further the formalization part of the method by providing more guidance and examples. As presented in Fig. 7 and Fig. 8, the ability to represent processes and compliance information graphically and the ability to automatically check compliance also have a good degree of acceptance. Thus, the method has high acceptability potential, and its graphical representations are considered the strongest advantage. Finally, as presented in Fig. 9, two aspects regarding the method are considered easy to use, i.e., graphically represent process models and trace uncompliant situations. However, we need to provide mechanisms for improving the tool usability in terms of compliance information representation, which appears to be not easy to use by practitioners. In addition, we need to improve the representation of checking results. For facilitating these aspects, we can provide more specific graphical representations of the compliance artifacts and, after backpropagating the results of Regorous into EPF Composer, present them in a suitable user interface that provides detailed explanations. Finally, practitioners show a willingness to use the method, which could be helpful for evolving from the current manual practices to automated practices via compliance checking.

6 Related Work

Nair et al. [15] performed in-depth interviews with 7 safety-related practitioners, which show the importance of checklists in safety assessment. In [14], a personal opinion survey was applied to 53 experts to study safety evidence management practices. Our survey also analyzed the use of the process plans analyzed in [14], and found that additional process-related plans are required in safety assessment. In [2], the authors present the results of interviews with practitioners regarding change impact analysis, which is essential during safety assessment. De la Vara et al. [8] surveyed safety evidence, particularly the circumstances under which it is created, the tool support used, and the challenges faced. In contrast to the works previously mentioned [2,8,14,15] our focus is to investigate the currently used methods and its challenging aspects in process compliance checking, as well as the practitioner's interest in novel methods for facilitating the automation of this task. The work conducted by Diebold and Scherr [9] reports industrial practices regarding the use of software process descriptions. In particular, the survey shows that companies use different process representations, i.e., graphical, table-based, or structured text notations. It also shows that the use of formal models and their advantages are highly desirable by practitioners. Our study differs from [9] in that we also include aspects regarding the use of formal descriptions of processes for compliance checking.

7 Conclusions and Future Work

In this paper, we presented the results of a personal opinion survey conducted among practitioners who participate in process compliance checking in the safety-critical context. The practitioners indicated that they mostly represent process plans and standard requirements by using software-based tools. Thus, software-based compliance checking aids are not new for them. However, practitioners consider that process compliance checking is prone-to-error; e.g., missing requirements is a common problem. Process compliance checking also requires many hours of work and several people. Finally, the practitioners show a favorable position regarding automated process compliance checking based on SPEM 2.0-like artifacts. They also indicated usability aspects regarding the formalization of requirements that we need to revisit and improve.

Future work will include more empirical research with the use of interviews and observations to see, for instance, how practitioners carry out their compliance checking in real settings. In addition, the usability aspects will be revisited, in order to provide more guidance and improve the representation of compliance artifacts and checking results. Finally, the tool support will be concretized to facilitate evaluations in terms of efficiency through industrial case studies.

References

1. Bertram, D.: Likert Scales Are the Meaning of Life. CPSC 681-Topic Report (2006). http://poincare.matf.bg.ac.rs/~kristina/topic-dane-likert.pdf
2. Borg, M., de la Vara, J.L., Wnuk, K.: Practitioners' perspectives on change impact analysis for safety-critical software – a preliminary analysis. In: Skavhaug, A., Guiochet, J., Schoitsch, E., Bitsch, F. (eds.) SAFECOMP 2016. LNCS, vol. 9923, pp. 346–358. Springer, Cham (2016). https://doi.org/10.1007/978-3-319-45480-1_28
3. Castellanos Ardila, J.P., Gallina, B.: Formal contract logic based patterns for facilitating compliance checking against ISO 26262. In: 1st Workshop on Technologies for Regulatory Compliance, pp. 65–72 (2017)
4. Castellanos Ardila, J.P., Gallina, B., Ul Muram, F.: Enabling compliance checking against safety standards from SPEM 2.0 Process Models. In: Euromicro Conference on Software Engineering and Advanced Applications, pp. 45–49 (2018)
5. Castellanos Ardila, J.P., Gallina, B., Ul Muram, F.: Transforming SPEM 2.0-compatible process models into models checkable for compliance. In: Stamelos, I., O'Connor, R.V., Rout, T., Dorling, A. (eds.) SPICE 2018. CCIS, vol. 918, pp. 233–247. Springer, Cham (2018). https://doi.org/10.1007/978-3-030-00623-5_16
6. Castellanos Ardila, J., Gallina, B., Governatori, G.: Lessons learned while formalizing ISO 26262 for compliance checking. In: 2nd Workshop on Technologies for Regulatory Compliance, pp. 1–12 (2018)
7. Davis, F.: A technology acceptance model for empirically testing new end-user information systems: theory and results. Massachusetts Institute of Technology (1985)
8. De La Vara, J., Borg, M., Wnuk, K., Moonen, L.: An industrial survey of safety evidence change impact analysis practice. IEEE Trans. Softw. Eng. 42(12), 1095–1117 (2016)
9. Diebold, P., Scherr, S.: Software process models vs descriptions: what do practitioners use and need? J. Softw.: Evol. Process 29(11), 1–13 (2017)
10. Governatori, G.: Representing business contracts in RuleML. Int. J. Coop. Inf. Syst. 14(02n03), 181–216 (2005)
11. Javed, M., Gallina, B.: Get EPF Composer back to the future: a trip from Galileo to Photon after 11 years. In: EclipseCon (2018)
12. Kitchenham, B., Pfleeger, S.: Personal opinion surveys. In: Shull, F., Singer, J., Sjøberg, D.I.K. (eds.) Guide to Advanced Empirical Software Engineering, pp. 63–92. Springer, London (2008). https://doi.org/10.1007/978-1-84800-044-5_3
13. Nair, S., De La Vara, J., Sabetzadeh, M., Briand, L.: An extended systematic literature review on provision of evidence for safety certification. Inf. Softw. Technol. 56(7), 689–717 (2014)

14. Nair, S., De La Vara, J., Sabetzadeh, M., Falessi, D.: Evidence management for compliance of critical systems with safety standards: a survey on the state of practice. Inf. Softw. Technol. **60**, 1–15 (2015)
15. Nair, S., Kelly, T., Jørgensen, M.: A report on the state-of-the-practice of safety evidence assessment. Technical report (2014)

Systematic Literature Review of DevOps Models

Monika Gasparaite⬤, Kristina Naudziunaite⬤, and Saulius Ragaisis[(✉)]⬤

Institute of Computer Science, Vilnius University, Vilnius, Lithuania
monika.gasparaite@gmail.com, kr.naudziunaite@gmail.com,
saulius.ragaisis@mif.vu.lt

Abstract. DevOps can be defined as a set of practices that enables development and operations teams to collaborate in order to produce reliable and high-quality products. Even though DevOps is still a new phenomenon, DevOps practices can be successfully applied in numerous companies. However, it remains unclear what DevOps models currently exist. In this paper, the availability of DevOps models is analyzed by means of a systematic literature review. 24 papers with DevOps models were found and 4 papers were selected as relevant.

Keywords: Systematic literature review · DevOps · Maturity models · DevOps process areas

1 Introduction

Currently, Agile is one of the most popular and widely used methodologies due to its ability to manage projects with ever-changing requirements. However, while Agile practices simplify communication with stakeholders, especially between the development team and customer, communication with the operations team is often ignored. As a result, more and more companies are adopting DevOps practices allowing them to bridge the gap between development and operations. These practices could be adapted in companies, but it is still difficult to assess the process improvement as there are no acknowledged DevOps maturity models. The goal of these models is to assess the current maturity level and identify the measures for process improvement. Of course, there are some well-known and widely used general process assessment models such as CMMI. However, existing studies [1] indicate that these models are not suitable for the assessment of DevOps process. Therefore, it becomes important to determine the existing variety of DevOps models. A systematic literature review is conducted in order to achieve this goal.

2 Related Work and Research Methodology

No systematic literature reviews describing DevOps models have been found. However, a study has been found [2], which overviews several DevOps maturity models and compares them with each other. All described DevOps models [3–9] have been found in this systematic literature review as well. In addition, there exist a few literature reviews

© Springer Nature Switzerland AG 2020
M. Shepperd et al. (Eds.): QUATIC 2020, CCIS 1266, pp. 184–198, 2020.
https://doi.org/10.1007/978-3-030-58793-2_15

[10–12] that analyze characteristics and definition of DevOps. A small number of existing researches shows that the situation of DevOps models must be investigated.

This study was carried out following B. Kitchenham and S. Charters guidelines for performing systematic literature reviews in software engineering [13] because:

- It has been specifically developed for the field of software engineering.
- Guidelines are well-known and widely used, for instance [10–12, 14–16].

Figure 1 presents the adapted method for performing a systematic literature review. All steps of this method are examined further.

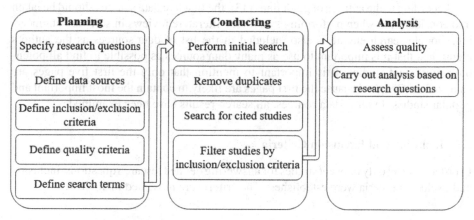

Fig. 1. Systematic literature review process

3 Planning

3.1 Research Questions

The definition of research questions is the most important part of planning a systematic literature review as all research steps rely on them. Literature search, filtering, and analysis are performed in such a way that the research questions could be answered. For these reasons, questions need to be clear and specific [13]. In order to achieve the goal of this study, the following research questions were defined:

- RQ1: What DevOps models exist?
- RQ2: Which process areas of DevOps are emphasized by models?
- RQ3: Are found DevOps models suitable for practical use?
- RQ4: Does the comparison of DevOps models exist? If yes, how the comparison has been performed?

A comparison of different models reveals more valuable information about them. Consequently, questions related to the comparison of DevOps models are included as well.

3.2 Data Sources

The literature search was performed on six databases and search engines:

- IEEE Xplore Digital Library,
- ACM Digital Library,
- Google Scholar,
- Science Direct,
- Springer Link, and
- Google.

According to the authors of guidelines [13], the first five data sources should be taken into consideration when performing systematic literature reviews in software engineering. Google search engine is also included in the list of data sources as the authors mentioned that it is important to use as many data sources as possible to find all potentially important studies. It is important to mention that only the first five pages are analyzed on Google, because the first pages are likely to contain the most important and popular studies. In other data sources, all search results have been examined.

3.3 Inclusion and Exclusion Criteria

In order to select only relevant studies for answering defined research questions, inclusion and exclusion criteria were established. The criteria are presented in Table 1.

Table 1. Inclusion and exclusion criteria

No.	Criteria name	Inclusion criteria	Exclusion criteria
1.	Year	Papers published since 2009	Papers published before 2009
2.	Language	English	Non-English
3.	Availability	Full text is available	Full text is unavailable
4.	Content	DevOps model is provided	DevOps model is not provided

Defined criteria were selected for the following reasons:

- The concept of DevOps was first officially mentioned at DevOpsDays conference in 2009. Accordingly, it was decided to exclude studies older than 2009.
- English language was selected due to its common use in the scientific environment [17].
- Sources that are only partially available are not included. Such sources are not suitable for further analysis.
- Only papers that describe DevOps models are suitable since the goal of this review is to find all relevant DevOps models. It is important to note that a study, which provides a DevOps model developed by other authors, is excluded from further analysis by

the content criterion. The aim of this is to discover only the primary studies. It is also possible that the same authors present the DevOps model in several studies (for example, in the final master thesis and the scientific paper based on it). In this case, the largest and most recent study is selected. Other studies are treated as duplicates.

3.4 Quality Criteria

In addition to inclusion and exclusion criteria, quality criteria are used to assess the quality of the studies that were selected according to the inclusion criteria. The following quality criteria were defined:

- Does the DevOps model contain non-graphical content?
- Is the DevOps model based on other scientific papers?
- Is the DevOps model referred by other scientific papers?
- Are the elements of the DevOps model justified?

These quality criteria were selected due to several reasons:

- One of the goals of this review is to select the most detailed DevOps models. Therefore, papers without textual explanations are not appropriate.
- Paper that refers to other scientific papers is more likely to be relevant and suitable for further investigation. The same goes for the models that are referred by other papers.
- The validity of the model components (process areas, requirements, maturity levels) increases the probability of non-bias.

Each question has two possible answers: yes and no. The positive answer is rated 1, while the negative answer is rated 0. Thus, the study will be rated on a scale from 0 to 4. Papers with a score of 3 or 4 will be considered suitable for further investigation.

3.5 Search Terms

The following search string has been selected and adjusted to address defined research questions:

DevOps AND ("maturity model" OR "capability model" OR "process reference model" OR "process model" OR "process assessment model").

In some cases, the search string has been customized to suit some specific requirements of the digital databases. For example, if the database does not support logical operators, they are removed, and several search terms have been applied.

4 Conducting the Review

Study selection is a multistage process. The following steps were taken:

- Performing initial search.
- Removing duplicate studies.

- Manually performing search in references of studies found by the initial search. The aim is to find more studies, which provide DevOps models.
- Filtering studies considering the inclusion/exclusion criteria. If the study does not meet at least one of the inclusion criteria, the other criteria are no longer checked, and the study is excluded. The inclusion/exclusion criteria are checked in the order presented in Table 1.

The results of the conducted search are summarized in Fig. 2.

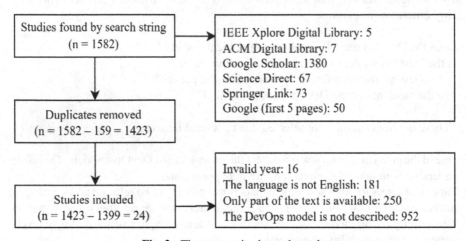

Fig. 2. The summarized search results

Mendeley was used to organize and analyze the studies. It helped to group the papers by data sources and identify duplicates.

Table 2 provides the detailed results of selected studies grouped by data sources. The table shows how many studies were filtered according to each inclusion/exclusion criterion.

A total of 1582 studies were found. After excluding 159 duplicates, a total of 1423 unique studies were obtained. After filtering studies by inclusion/exclusion criteria it was found that only 24 studies were suitable for quality analysis.

Most of the studies selected for quality analysis were found in Google Scholar and Google search engines. SpringerLink database found only one study, which satisfied inclusion criteria.

Most of the studies were excluded due to content criterion – the absence of DevOps model. Studies have not met content criterion because of the following reasons:

- Described DevOps model is developed by other authors.
- Another model (e.g. Agile) is described, while the word DevOps is mentioned somewhere in the study.
- The word DevOps is mentioned in literature references – the study is not related to DevOps at all.

Table 2. Search results

Nr.	Data source	In total	Excluded by criterion				Included studies
			Year	Language	Availability	Content	
1.	IEEE Xplore	5	0	0	0	5	0
2.	ACM Digital Library	7	0	0	0	7	0
3.	Google Scholar	1380	16	183	261	912	8
4.	Science Direct	67	0	0	7	60	0
5.	SpringerLink	73	0	7	0	65	1
6.	Google	50	0	0	1	30	19
In total (not unique):		1582	16	190	269	1079	28
In total (unique):		1423	16	181	250	952	24

Table 3 provides references of the selected studies. This table shows only the search engines and databases in which at least one study was selected by inclusion criteria. The following types of studies are provided:

Table 3. References of studies describing DevOps models

Search engine	Selected studies	Cited studies	Unique studies
Google Scholar	[3, 4, 6, 7, 9, 18–20]	[3–9, 29, 31, 32]	[3–9, 18–34]
SpringerLink	[21]	–	
Google	[4–6, 8, 9, 21–34]	–	

- Studies found by search string and met the inclusion criteria.
- Studies cited in selected studies and met the inclusion criteria.
- Unique studies obtained from selected and cited studies.

All studies found among the cited ones were also found by the initial search. This greatly increases the likelihood that the search string has been defined correctly.

There are two types of cited studies – research papers and articles published on the Internet. All these research papers were found using the same data source as the studies in which citations were found. All cited online articles were found in the first five pages of Google in the primary search.

5 Analysis

5.1 Quality Assessment

Each study is rated based on the quality criteria defined. Table 4 presents the results of the quality assessment.

Table 4. Results of quality assessment

No.	Study	Not only graphical content presented	Based on scientific papers	Referred by other scientific papers	Model components are justified	Final score
1.	[9]	Yes	Yes	Yes	Yes	4
2.	[7]	Yes	Yes	Yes	No	3
3.	[4]	Yes	Yes	Yes	No	3
4.	[19]	Yes	Yes	No	Yes	3
5.	[3]	Yes	No	Yes	No	2
6.	[6]	Yes	No	Yes	No	2
7.	[5]	Yes	No	Yes	No	2
8.	[31]	Yes	No	Yes	No	2
9.	[18]	No	Yes	No	No	1
10.	[23]	Yes	No	No	No	1
11.	[8]	No	No	Yes	No	1
12.	[21]	No	Yes	No	No	1
13.	[25]	Yes	No	No	No	1
14.	[26]	Yes	No	No	No	1
15.	[28]	No	No	Yes	No	1
16.	[29]	No	No	Yes	No	1
17.	[30]	Yes	No	No	No	1
18.	[32]	No	No	Yes	No	1
19.	[34]	Yes	No	No	No	1
20.	[20]	No	Yes	No	No	1
21.	[22]	No	No	No	No	0
22.	[24]	No	No	No	No	0
23.	[27]	No	No	No	No	0
24.	[33]	No	No	No	No	0

According to the chosen selection rule, only papers with scores 3 and 4 are selected as the most relevant papers. They are presented in Table 5.

Table 5. Papers selected by quality criteria

Study	Authors	Title	Type
[9]	Rico de Feijter, Rob van Vliet, Erik Jagroep, Sietse Overbeek, and Sjaak Brinkkemper	Towards the adoption of DevOps in software product organizations: A maturity model approach	Technical report
[7]	Ineta Bucena, Marite Kirikova	Simplifying the DevOps Adoption Process	Conference paper
[4]	Samer I. Mohamed	DevOps shiSting soStware engineering strategy-value based perspective	Journal paper
[19]	Jeroen M. Radstaak	Developing a DevOps maturity model: A validated model to evaluate the maturity of DevOps in organizations	Master thesis

The model presented in [9] is the largest and most comprehensive model found. It is a non-traditional model because of focus area representation, which allows an unlimited number of maturity and capability levels as well as different evaluation intervals for each focus area [35]. For simplicity, it will be referred as Focus Area model. The model describes sixteen focus areas that are logically grouped into three perspectives: (1) culture and communication, (2) product, process, and quality, and (3) foundation.

Bucena-Kirikova model [7] is created to guide small enterprises in DevOps adoption process. This model is based on the old SW-CMM approach and has the same five maturity levels. The model defines four enterprise areas that are assigned to all maturity levels. The model also has a non-assessment part: for each enterprise area corresponding DevOps practices are proposed together with recommended tools. These model elements facilitate DevOps implementation.

Mohamed model [4] is based on the current CMMI approach but all four dimensions defined in the model are assigned to all five maturity levels. Mohamed model provides detailed descriptions of each maturity level for each dimension, but the general concepts of maturity levels are not provided.

Radstaak model [19] is based on CMMI also but the representation of the model is continuous. This model is primarily dedicated to (South)East-Asia region. The model defines five capability levels and eighteen capabilities to assess. It is unclear why the author uses the term "capability" instead of "process area". Although the author has chosen continuous representation of the model, he calls the model "maturity model". In general, this model provides a lot of DevOps ideas, but incorrect use of terms raises doubts about the quality of the model.

All four models have their own terms (focus area, enterprise area, dimension, capability) for the term "process area" which is used in CMMI. From now on, the standard term "process area" will be used to discuss all models. More details about the models are provided answering the research questions.

5.2 Answers to Research Questions

RQ1: What DevOps Models Exist? According to the defined inclusion/exclusion criteria, 24 papers were found. They are presented in Table 6. All models, except [9] and [19], are models of staged representation. The numbers of maturity/capability levels and process areas are quite different in DevOps models.

Table 6. Papers found by inclusion/exclusion criteria

No.	Study	Representation	Maturity/capability levels	Process areas
1.	[9]	**Focus area**	**11**	**16**
2.	[7]	**Staged**	**5**	**4**
3.	[4]	**Staged**	**5**	**4**
4.	[19]	**Continuous**	**5**	**18**
5.	[3]	Staged	4	4
6.	[6]	Staged	5	3
7.	[5]	Staged	5	3
8.	[31]	Staged	4	4
9.	[18]	Staged	5	Explicitly not defined
10.	[23]	Staged	5	Explicitly not defined
11.	[8]	Staged	4	7
12.	[21]	Staged	3	Explicitly not defined
13.	[25]	Staged	3	Explicitly not defined
14.	[26]	Staged	4	Explicitly not defined
15.	[28]	Staged	5	5
16.	[29]	Staged	5	4
17.	[30]	Staged	4	7
18.	[32]	Staged	4	4
19.	[34]	Staged	5	7
20.	[20]	Staged	5	Only general characteristics
21.	[22]	Staged	4	Explicitly not defined
22.	[24]	Staged	5	3
23.	[27]	Staged	5	Explicitly not defined
24.	[33]	Staged	5	Explicitly not defined

RQ2: Which Process Areas of DevOps are Emphasized by Models? The highlight of process areas has been examined only in the most relevant DevOps models that satisfied quality criteria – Focus Area [9], Bucena-Kirikova [7], Mohamed [4], and Radstaak [19] models.

Culture. Culture is understood as a frequent communication and collaboration between teams of different disciplines. Culture is an important aspect of all four models. Mohamed model defines communication/collaboration process area, Bucena-Kirikova – people and culture process areas, Focus Area – culture process area, which includes communication, knowledge sharing, trust and respect, team organization, release alignment categories. Radstaak model has two separate process area groups, one dedicated for culture and another for communication & collaboration. Although these process area groups are separate in the model, we assume that we can combine them for summarizing DevOps characteristics. Need to mention that the culture process area group in Radstaak model includes team structure, process improvement, and feedback cycle while communication & collaboration process area group includes communication & coordination and collaboration process areas. Interestingly, all DevOps models define culture-related process areas while classic models such as CMMI do not have them.

Automation. All four models emphasize the importance of automation. Automation is desired for system build, testing, deployment. Radstaak model also defines automation of processes such as environments (test, staging, production, etc.) management, generation of documentation & configurations, and delivery process.

Measurement. All four models define the need to collect metrics. Radstaak model defines communication, collaboration, automation, quality (improvement performance) metrics. Bucena-Kirikova model provides metrics related to the quality of collaboration, Focus Area – code quality and production environment metrics, Mohamed – automation, governance, communication, and quality metrics.

Optimization. All four models emphasize optimization activities, but none of the models explicitly specify it as a separate process area.

Monitoring. All four models highlight monitoring. Bucena-Kirikova model defines core, integrated monitoring, Focus Area – code quality, culture of collaboration, development & operations processes, incident, root cause monitoring, Mohamed – defect monitoring, Radstaak – requirements, incidents, quality, resources, software, and build monitoring.

Release. All models except Mohamed have direct requirements for software release, but only Focus Area model explicitly specifies this process area.

Testing. Three models [7, 9, 19] focus on testing. Focus Area model specifies testing types such as unit, regression, and acceptance testing. Radstaak also refers to testing techniques such as systematic, requirements-based, integrated testing. Bucena-Kirikova model not only outlines testing types but also provides possible testing tools, such as Cucumber or Selenium.

Deployment. Focus Area, Bucena-Kirikova, and Radstaak models define deployment-related actions. All these models represent one of the most important DevOps activities - continuous deployment.

Quality. Quality characteristics are defined in these models: Mohamed model explicitly specifies the quality process area, Radstaak indicates the quality assurance of the overall process, Focus Area model gives the biggest attention to the quality in comparison with other models. This model includes activities such as software code reviews, pair programming, and automatic code quality monitoring.

Process. This area defines the main characteristics of the overall process. Three models highlight this area. Bucena-Kirikova model characterizes not only the overall process but also the individual processes as software delivery, development, testing, project management, and deployment processes. In Focus Area model there is a group of separate process areas which is named "Product, process, and quality". Radstaak model has a process improvement process area.

Infrastructure. Infrastructure includes the management of environments. It is defined by Focus Area, Bucena-Kirikova, and Radstaak models.

Configuration Management. This process area is highlighted by Focus Area, Bucena-Kirikova, and Radstaak models.

Incident Management. This process area is highlighted by Focus Area, Bucena-Kirikova, and Radstaak models.

Documentation. Radstaak model emphasizes the importance of having accessible and up-to-date documentation. Documentation is also mentioned in Focus Area and Bucena-Kirikova models.

Planning. Planning activities are defined by Bucena-Kirikova model only.

Governance. Governance is related to the control of various process areas, describing how well they work together. It is defined by the Mohamed model only.

RQ3: Are Found Devops Models Suitable For Practical Use? Suitability for practical use is investigated only for DevOps models selected by quality criteria – Focus Area [9], Bucena-Kirikova [7], Mohamed [4], and Radstaak [19] models. Three necessary characteristics of the model to be applied in practice must be considered - the completeness of the model, the clarity of model requirements, and the clarity of the assessment method.

In Focus Area model requirements are formulated in a clear and precise manner. Examples of possible requirement implementation are given which helps better understand the presented requirements. There are clearly defined requirements for each maturity level, so the reached maturity level is clear. The model has been validated by applying it to 7 different cases. Data for the assessment was collected by setting out self-assessments with 45 questions, but details for interpreting the answers are not given. Therefore, the assessment process is not clear enough. Although there is a doubt if the assessment could be done by persons other than the authors, it is highly likely that the model can be successfully applied in practice.

While Bucena-Kirikova model is not as large and detailed as Focus Area model, it also touches many aspects of software development, from programming to project management. Although many of the model's requirements are clearly formulated there are some unpopular terms that make the model a bit more difficult to understand. Also, there are some incorrect requirements (e.g. requirement for the second maturity level of process area PR2 defines Scrum development, whereas the requirement for the higher maturity level is Agile development) and some requirements arranged in an illogical order (e.g. requirement for the fifth maturity level of process area PR1 is development process integrated with Six sigma, whereas all other requirements in the PR1 are about the delivery process). The model does not explicitly state how the requirement must be assessed (e.g. does the requirement must be fully implemented or not). However, the proposed maturity model has been tested in a national branch of an international company with an internal IT development team. Therefore, it can be argued that the model can be successfully applied in other companies by the model authors. With the paper [7] alone, it is impossible to put the model into practice.

Although most requirements in Mohamed model are formulated explicitly, some requirements lack clarity as it is not clear how the requirement can be enforced (different interpretations of the requirement are possible). The assessment process is not mentioned at all. For these reasons, the model can be applied in practice only as guidelines for adopting DevOps in the company.

Most of the requirements in Radstaak model appear to be sufficiently understood from the title of requirements, but only a small amount of the requirements is explained more broadly. Therefore, different interpretations of requirements are possible. Also, there is a section on how to apply this model in a company. The DevOps model has been validated by applying it to 8 different projects. However, the model does not explicitly state how the requirements must be assessed. Although validation of the model shows that the model is applicable in practice, the source describing this model [19] does not provide all steps required for full practical use.

In general, it can be argued that Focus Area and Bucena-Kirikova models can be successfully applied in practice by anyone if authors of the models would document the adopted assessment methods in academic publications.

RQ4: Does the Comparison of DevOps Models Exist? If yes, how the Comparison has been Performed? A conducted systematic literature review indicates that no formal comparison of DevOps models has been made so far. Only comparisons at a very superficial level are presented discussing process areas similarities, for example, [2, 36].

6 Limitations

Although this systematic literature review was conducted in a disciplined manner, potential limitations must be acknowledged. There is a potential risk of missing relevant literature since all papers written in other languages than English were excluded. However, we have reasonable grounds to believe this risk is rather low because English language is the most popular language in the academic field. Another possible limitation is selection bias. To reduce this threat, the review was conducted and validated by two independent researchers. Another area of concern is that this paper covers publications that were published before the end of 2019. As a result, the results of this research can quickly become outdated since the number of new DevOps models is increasing constantly.

7 Conclusions

This paper presents a systematic literature review of DevOps maturity/capability models found in the six most popular databases and search engines. The systematic review was performed by two authors independently in May 2019 and in October 2019. We found 24 DevOps models and 4 of them were considered suitable for further investigation according to quality assessment. DevOps process areas highlighted by all 4 models were culture, automation, measurement, optimization, monitoring, and release. Although 2 models were complete enough and requirements were sufficiently clear, none of the models' authors have documented the adopted assessment method in an academic publication which makes unclear how to fully use the models in practice. Therefore, we believe that the practical usability of those 2 models is possible but would be problematic for persons other than the authors. Finally, a conducted systematic literature review indicated that no formal DevOps models comparison has been made. The systematic review results will serve as a knowledge base about DevOps maturity/capability models existing in academic literature. Future research would benefit from a comparison of models in order to find whether the understanding of DevOps implementation is similar in the models.

References

1. Rong, G., Zhang, H., Shao, D.: CMMI guided process improvement for DevOps projects: an exploratory case study. In: Proceedings of the International Conference on Software and Systems Process, pp. 76–85. ACM (2016)
2. Zarour, M.I., Alhammad, N., Alenezi, M., Alsarayrah, K.: A research on DevOps maturity models (2019)
3. IBM Developer. https://developer.ibm.com/articles/d-adoption-paths/. Accessed 15 Oct 2019
4. Mohamed, S.I.: Devops shifting software engineering strategy value-based perspective. Int. J. Comput. Eng. 17(2), 51–57 (2015)
5. Menzel, G., Macaulay, A. https://www.capgemini.com/de-de/wp-content/uploads/sites/5/2016/03/devops-the-future-of-application-lifecycle-automation.pdf. Accessed 15 Oct 2019
6. Inbar, S., et al.: DevOps and OpsDev: how maturity model works (2013). http://h30499.www3.hp.com/t5/Business-Service-Management-BAC/DevOps-and-OpsDev-How-Maturity-Model-Works/bap/6042901. Accessed 15 Oct 2019
7. Bucena, I., Kirikova, M.: Simplifying the DevOps adoption process. In: Joint Proceedings of the BIR 2017 pre-BIR Forum, Workshops and Doctoral Consortium Co-located with 16th International Conference on Perspectives in Business Informatics Research (BIR 2017), Copenhagen, Denmark (2017)
8. Eficode.   https://www.eficode.com/hubfs/documents/Eficode-English-Devops-Guide.pdf?hsLang=en. Accessed 15 Oct 2019
9. de Feijter, R., van Vliet, R., Jagroep, E., Overbeek, S., Brinkkemper, S.: Towards the adoption of DevOps in software product organizations: a maturity model approach. Technical report, Utrecht University (2017)
10. Erich, F., Amrit, C., Daneva, M.: Report: DevOps literature review. https://www.researchgate.net/publication/267330992_Report_DevOps_Literature_Review
11. Jabbari, R., bin Ali, N., Petersen, K., Tanveer, B.: What is DevOps? A systematic mapping study on definitions and practices. In: Proceedings of the Scientific Workshop Proceedings of XP2016, p. 12. ACM (2016)

12. Sánchez-Gordón, M., Colomo-Palacios, R.: Characterizing DevOps culture: a systematic literature review. In: Stamelos, I., O'Connor, R.V., Rout, T., Dorling, A. (eds.) SPICE 2018. CCIS, vol. 918, pp. 3–15. Springer, Cham (2018). https://doi.org/10.1007/978-3-030-006 23-5_1
13. Kitchenham, B., Charters, S.: Guidelines for performing systematic literature reviews in software engineering. Keele University and Durham University Joint Report (2007)
14. Calderón, A., Trinidad, M., Ruiz, M., O'Connor, R.V.: Teaching software processes and standards: a review of serious games approaches. In: Stamelos, I., O'Connor, R.V., Rout, T., Dorling, A. (eds.) SPICE 2018. CCIS, vol. 918, pp. 154–166. Springer, Cham (2018). https://doi.org/10.1007/978-3-030-00623-5_11
15. Fernández Del Carpio, A., Angarita, L.B.: Techniques based on data science for software processes: a systematic literature review. In: Stamelos, I., O'Connor, R.V., Rout, T., Dorling, A. (eds.) SPICE 2018. CCIS, vol. 918, pp. 16–30. Springer, Cham (2018). https://doi.org/10.1007/978-3-030-00623-5_2
16. Trinidad, M., Calderón, A., Ruiz, M.: A systematic literature review on the gamification monitoring phase: how SPI standards can contribute to gamification maturity. In: Stamelos, I., O'Connor, R.V., Rout, T., Dorling, A. (eds.) SPICE 2018. CCIS, vol. 918, pp. 31–44. Springer, Cham (2018). https://doi.org/10.1007/978-3-030-00623-5_3
17. Kaplan, R.: The Dominance of English as a Language of Science: Effects on Other Languages and Language Communities, pp. 3–26 (2001)
18. Abdelkebir, S., Maleh, Y., Belaissaoui, M.: An agile framework for ITS management in organizations: a case study based on DevOps. In: Proceedings of the 2nd International Conference on Computing and Wireless Communication Systems, p. 67. ACM, Larache (2017)
19. Radstaak, J.M.: Developing a DevOps maturity model: a validated model to evaluate the maturity of DevOps in organizations. Master thesis, University of Twente (2019)
20. Zage, D., Zage, W.: Components of a modern quality approach to software development. Final Report, Ball State University (2015)
21. Hemon, A., Lyonnet, B., Rowe, F., Fitzgerald, B.: Conceptualizing the transition from agile to DevOps: a maturity model for a smarter is function. In: Elbanna, A., Dwivedi, Y.K., Bunker, D., Wastell, D. (eds.) TDIT 2018. IAICT, vol. 533, pp. 209–223. Springer, Cham (2019). https://doi.org/10.1007/978-3-030-04315-5_15
22. Bluemeric. http://blog.bluemeric.com/devops-maturity-model/. Accessed 15 Oct 2019
23. The CloudBees: Assessing DevOps maturity using a quadrant model. White paper (2016)
24. Micro Focus. https://www.microfocus.com/media/data-sheet/devops_solution_discovery_ workshop_ds.pdf. Accessed 15 Oct 2019
25. Jeremiah, J. https://gitlab.com/gitlab-com/www-gitlab-com/issues/2095. Accessed 15 Oct 2019
26. Kavis, M. https://www.forbes.com/sites/mikekavis/2017/11/17/the-four-stages-of-devops-maturity/#6879baca2f62. Accessed 15 Oct 2019
27. Kumar, A. https://vitalflux.com/devops-maturity-model-telstra-devops-implementation/. Accessed 15 Oct 2019
28. Mendes, N. https://atlassianblog.wpengine.com/wp-content/uploads/xM_Atlassian_Dev Ops_Survey_Web_Final.pdf. Accessed 15 Oct 2019
29. Parks, J. https://solinea.com/blog/solinea-devops-maturity-model. Accessed 15 Oct 2019
30. Plutora. https://www.plutora.com/devops-at-scale/maturity-level. Accessed 15 Oct 2019
31. Poelwijk, S.: https://blog.leaseweb.com/2016/05/30/maturity-model-devops-teams/. Accessed 15 Oct 2019
32. Schneider, C.: Security DevOps-staying secure in agile projects. In: OWASP App-Sec Europe (2015)
33. Techtown. http://techtowntraining.com/resources/tools-resources/devops-maturity-model-quiz. Accessed 15 Oct 2019

34. Verstraete, C.: https://cloudsourceblog.com/2016/11/15/. Accessed 15 Oct 2019
35. Koomen, T., Pol, M.: Improvement of the test process using TPI (1998). https://itq.ch/pdf/tpi/tpi_uk.PDF. Accessed 17 Apr 2020
36. Seppä-Lassila, T.: An assessment of DevOps maturity in a software project. Master thesis, University of Turku (2017)

Measuring the Maturity of BizDevOps

Eduardo Sanjurjo[1], Oscar Pedreira[1]([✉]), Felix García[2], and Mario Piattini[2]

[1] Universidade da Coruña, Centro de Investigación CITIC, 15071 Elviña, A Coruña, Spain
{eduardo.sanjurjo.royo,oscar.pedreira}@udc.es
[2] Information Technologies and Systems Institute (ITSI), Universidad de Castilla-La Mancha, Paseo de la Universidad 4, 13071 Ciudad Real, Spain
{Felix.Garcia,Mario.Piattini}@uclm.es

Abstract. DevOps has emerged as an effective approach to the interaction between development and operations. This approach has been extended to the interaction with business functions, generating the term BizDevOps. Although many proposals and tools support BizDevOps from a technical viewpoint, there has been no significant progress in management aspects, such as the evaluation of practices and processes involved in the area. In this article, we propose a maturity model for BizDevOps, based on relevant international standards, and apply this model to a software company, which demonstrates its applicability.

Keywords: Maturity model · DevOps · BizDevOps

1 Introduction

Agility and flexibility in IT operations is a necessity for companies to quickly meet customer demands, market conditions, competitive pressures, or legal changes. This implies, among other aspects, shortening the time from a request to the release of the software update that fulfils that request. For this reason, the software development units and the operations units must be effectively integrated. However, in many companies, this integration is weak. The DevOps paradigm is based on lean and agile principles and assumes that software development and system operations must continuously collaborate to deliver software that meets the organization's requirements quickly [1, 2]. The term continuous software engineering is closely linked to DevOps and assumes that the software development process can continuously release new versions of the software that can be deployed in production [3].

Different works also propose integrating business functions and needs into the software development process [4, 5]. The reason is that many organizations consider software development as an integral part of their vision and strategy. However, addressing only the technical aspects may be insufficient and result in a lack of alignment between people, processes, businesses, and technology to ensure that business priorities are maintained throughout the DevOps flow. Therefore, the business teams must be integrated with the DevOps teams. BizDevOps is defined in [5] as the "integration of experts in the domain with DevOps teams". In this article, we will use the term BizDevOps, which includes and expands the term DevOps.

© Springer Nature Switzerland AG 2020
M. Shepperd et al. (Eds.): QUATIC 2020, CCIS 1266, pp. 199–210, 2020.
https://doi.org/10.1007/978-3-030-58793-2_16

Despite the importance of implementing BizDevOps in companies, there are no standard methods and processes [6] nor standard practices [7] to guide that implementation. In this work, we address the development of a maturity reference model for BizDevOps, which can guide an implementation of BizDevOps based on compliance with good practices currently included in standards of the IT sector.

The rest of this paper is structured as follows: Sect. 2 summarizes related work. In Sect. 3 we present MMBDO, a maturity model for BizDevOps. In Sect. 4 we present a case study on the application of MMBDO in a software development company. Finally, Sect. 5 presents the conclusions and lines for future work.

2 Related Work

Faced with a traditional approach, in which the areas of development and systems work separately and collaborate through inefficient interaction mechanisms, the DevOps philosophy assumes a continuous and natural integration between these two areas. The objective of DevOps is the delivery and deployment of new software releases to be automatic, direct, and, in most cases, immediate, as well as ensuring that intermediate versions of the software are as stable as possible.

Currently, the most technical aspects of the DevOps approach may be the most popular, with a strong focus on concepts such as continuous integration, testing, and continuous analysis of software and automatic application deployment. However, DevOps must include management elements, especially in large and complex organizations. Fitzgerald and Stol [4] coined the term *continuous software engineering*, which extends the concept of continuous integration to the entire software life cycle and business aspects, structuring it in three phases: strategy and business planning, development, and operations. Thus, within the strategy and planning category, they contemplate activities such as planning and continuous budgeting, in the development phase they add activities such as continuous compliance, continuous security, or continuous evolution, and in the operations phase, activities such as real-time continuous monitoring [4].

Process reference models typically guide the implementation of management systems and continuous improvement in software engineering. A process reference model includes a set of good practices, grouped into process areas in the context of an activity or set of activities. In general, this set of good practices is defined in the form of process requirements, expected results, and suggestions on how to achieve those requirements and results. Reference process models can be used in conjunction with assessment models to establish an assessment and certification framework. Within this framework, the processes of an organization can be assessed for compliance. Also, these assessments may be the first step for process improvement.

Over the years, many process models have emerged in the context of information and communication technologies (ICT). In software development, the most used processes are included in CMMI [8] and ISO 12207/MMIS [9, 10], which present a set of good practices in different process areas of software development. A characteristic of these models is that the assessment of the process requirements is structured on capability levels for each process area, and organization maturity models, depending on the level of capability the organization reaches in the different process areas. In the field of information security, the family of ISO 27000 standards [11] proposes a set of processes for the management of information security and the many controls associated with this activity. ISO 20000 [12] and ITIL play a similar role in the field of quality management of ICT services. Although these models are the most widespread in the industry, other process models have been proposed from academic and professional sources over the last years, addressing other activity areas or specific contexts. For example, the COMPETISOFT project defined a reference process model [13] for software development in SMEs.

Process models are used in organizations to perform process assessments that set the basis for compliance certification and process improvement. For example, [10] details how AENOR (a Spanish standardization and certification body) uses the family of ISO 33000 standards [14] for the assessment of software development processes.

Somehow, some of the main practices of DevOps are included in the "traditional" process models. For example, software testing appears in CMMI and ISO 12207, although the process models do not refer that requirements of these areas have to be met in a specific way. In this paper, we present the first version of a specific maturity model for BizDevOps (MMBDO), which will be the basis for a complete framework for the evaluation of capability levels and maturity of BizDevOps practices. MMBDO is based on the MMIS maturity model, described in [10]. MMBDO includes the processes included in MMIS, adapts some of them to the needs of BizDevOps and adds new processes, specific to BizDevOps. Although standards such as ISO 12207/MMIS can be seen as aligned with traditional software development approaches (predictive or "waterfall") and DevOps is mainly an agile approach, we consider it is correct to base MMBDO on MMIS, which is based on ISO 12207, since ISO 12207 indicates in its 2017 version: *"This document does not prescribe any particular life cycle model. Instead, it defines a set of processes, termed life cycle processes, which can be used in the definition of the system's life cycle [...]–These life cycle models can incorporate agile techniques and methods"*.

The evaluation of DevOps processes has already been addressed. For example, Mohamed [15] proposes a maturity model based on five levels, which coincide with those of CMMI (Initial, Managed, Defined, Quantitatively Managed, Optimizing). The proposal of [15] is structured in the dimensions of communication, automation, governance, and quality management. Meanwhile, Sahid et al. [16] propose an ITSM agility maturity model based on DevOps, with the same five levels proposed in [15]. The most complete DevOps competency model currently is proposed by de Feitjer et al. [17] and is structured in three perspectives: culture and collaboration, product, process and quality; and fundamentals. Based on this competency model, [17] proposes a capability model with nine levels (from 0 to 8), for each one of the focus areas, framed in the dimensions of the competence model.

After analysing the existing reference process models for ICT and the relevant bibliography, we observed that there are proposals for DevOps maturity, mainly based on the five levels described in CMMI, but there is no approach based on one, or several, existing international standards, neither in DevOps nor in BizDevOps, which is the objective of this article. From the result of this preliminary analysis, we carried out a systematic review to have an insight into the coverage level of each of the processes we consider relevant for BizDevOps in the literature.

3 A Maturity Model for BizDevOps

In this section, we present the first version of the Maturity Reference Model for BizDevOps (MMBDO). This model is based on widely recognized international IT standards and considers both business and technical related process areas. More specifically, MMBDO considers the following existing process models:

- The family of ISO/IEC 33000 standards [14] for the evaluation of process capability and organizational maturity, a proven reference in terms of quality evaluation in software development processes.
- The ISO/IEC/IEEE 12207:2017 [9] standard for software development lifecycle management.
- The family of ISO/IEC 20000 [12] standards for ICT service management.
- The family of ISO/IEC 27000 [11] standards for information security management.
- The Software Engineering Maturity Model Version 2.0 (MMIS V.2) developed by AENOR in [10].

A first version of MMBDO was defined based on MMIS V.2, and processed derived from the best practices detected in the literature were incorporated. Also, we have incorporated the corresponding maturity levels into the new model processes, based on expert judgment. Table 1 shows the processes comprised in the first version of MMBDO. The first three columns show the process area, the process number in MMIS (*New* for those not included in MMIS), and the process number in MMBDO. Columns labeled 1 to 5 show the maturity levels. The last column shows the relation of the process with MMIS: I (included from MMIS), M (modified from MMIS), N (New), and NI (not included). MMBDO uses the process area groups of ISO 12207 to guarantee its conformity with them.

In Table 1 we also show that the model maintains the same process groups (Agreement, Organizational, Technical Management, and Technical) of ISO 12207, to guarantee its conformity with them.

All processes are adopted from [4], except "Transition", "Continuous validation", and "Operation". The processes "Project Planning", "Continuous Monitoring", "Continuous Business Planning", "Continuous Integration" and "Continuous Validation", are a modification or extension of processes from MMIS V.2 (Project planning, Measurement, Business or mission analysis, Integration, and Validation, respectively). The "Transition" and "Operation" processes are adopted from ISO 12207, although they do not appear in MMIS. Therefore, MMBDO has eleven updated processes or additional regarding the MMIS V.2 model to give specific coverage to BizDevOps. The MMBDO model consists of twenty-seven processes: the twenty-one included in the MMIS V.2 model (of which five have been updated), plus six new processes. In the MMBDO model, we keep the sixteen processes unchanged at their same level of maturity as in MMIS, and we have included the maturity levels of the new or updated processes.

Table 2 shows the description of the new or updated processes included in the model regarding the sources considered:

Table 1. MMBDO: BizDevOps maturity reference process model

Process area	MMIS	MMBDO	Processes	1	2	3	4	5	E
Agreement	6.1.1		Acquisition						NI
	6.1.2		Supply		X				I
Organizational	6.2.1		Life cycle model management		X				I
	6.2.2		Infrastructure Management			X			I
	6.2.3		Project Portfolio Management				X		I
	6.2.4		Human resources management			X			I
	6.2.5		Quality management						NI
	6.2.6		Knowledge management					X	I
Technical management	6.3.1	1	Project planning	X					M
	6.3.2		Evaluation and control of projects		X				I
	6.3.3		Decision management			X			I
	6.3.4		Risk management			X			I
	6.3.5		Configuration management		X				I
	6.3.6		Information management						NI
	6.3.7	2	Continuous Monitoring			X			M
	6.3.8		Quality assurance		X				I
	New	3	Continuous Improvement				X		N
	6.4.1	4	Continuous Business Planning					X	M
Technical	6.4.2		Definition of stakeholder needs and requirements		X				I
	6.4.3		Definition of system/software requirements			X			I
	6.4.4		Architecture Definition			X			I
	6.4.5		Design definition						NI
	6.4.6		System definition						NI
	6.4.7		Implementation	X					I
	6.4.8	5	Continuous Integration			X			M
	New	6	Continuous Delivery		X				N
	New	7	Continuous Deployment			X			N
	6.4.9		Verification			X			I
	6.4.10	8	Transition		X				N
	6.4.11	9	Continuous Validation				X		M
	6.4.12	10	Operation		X				N
	6.4.13		Maintenance						NI
	New	11	Continuous Security (SecOps)			X			N
	6.4.14		Retirement						NI

Table 2. Description of MMBDO processes

Process	Description
Project planning (Technical management)	The purpose of the Project Planning process is to produce and coordinate effective and workable plans *Source*: Adopted from [4]. Extension of the "Project Planning (6.3.1)" process, from the ISO/IEC 12207 standard
Continuous monitoring (Technical management)	As the historical boundary between design-time and runtime research in software engineering is blurring, in the context of continuous execution of cloud services, runtime behaviours of all kinds must be monitored to allow for early detection of service quality problems, such as performance degradation and also compliance with service level agreements (SLA) *Source*: Adopted from [4]. Extension of the "Measurement (6.3.7)" process, from the ISO/IEC 12207 standard
Continuous improvement (Technical management)	The organization must have incorporated processes that identify areas for improvement while the organization matures and learns from the processes it has adopted. Many businesses have process improvement teams that work on process improvement based on observations and lessons learned, others allow the teams that adopt the processes to self-evaluate, and determine their process improvement paths. Regardless of the method used, the objective is to facilitate continuous improvement *Source*: Adopted from [4]
Continuous business Planning (Technical)	It is a holistic effort that involves multiple stakeholders, from Business teams to Software Development teams, in which the plans are dynamic and open artefacts that evolve in response to changes in the business environment and, therefore, involve a closer integration between planning and execution *Source*: Adopted from [4]. Extension of the "Business or mission analysis (6.4.1)" process, from the ISO/IEC 12207 standard
Continuous Integration (Technical)	A process (generally automatic activation) consisting of interconnected steps, such as compiling code, running unit and acceptance tests, validating code coverage, verifying compliance with standard coding and building deployment packages *Source*: Adopted from [4]. Extension of the "Integration (6.4.8)" process, from the ISO/IEC 12207 standard
Continuous Delivery (Technical)	Continuous delivery is the practice of continuously implementing good software compilations automatically in some environments, but not necessarily to real users *Source*: Adopted from [4]

(continued)

Table 2. (*continued*)

Process	Description
Continuous deployment (Technical)	Continuous deployment involves continuous delivery and is the practice of ensuring that the software is continuously ready for launch and implementation to real customer *Source*: Adopted from [4]
Transition (Technical)	The purpose of the transition process is to establish a capacity for a system to provide services specified by the requirements of those interested in the operating environment. This process moves the system in an orderly and planned manner to the operational state, so that the system is functional, operational, and compatible with other operational systems *Source*: Coming from ISO/IEC 12.207 (not included in MMIS)
Continuous validation (Technical)	The purpose of this process is to provide objective evidence that the system, when used, meets the business or mission objectives and stakeholder requirements, achieving its intended use in its intended operational environment The objective of validating a system or system element is to be able to rely on its ability to achieve the intended mission or use under specific operating conditions. The validation is ratified by the stakeholders. This process provides the necessary information so that the identified anomalies can be resolved by the appropriate technical process where the anomaly was created *Source*: Extension of the "Validation (6.4.11)" process, from the ISO/IEC 12207 standard.
Operation (Technical)	The purpose of the Operation process is to use the system to deliver its services This process establishes requirements and assigns personnel to operate the system, and monitors services and system performance. To maintain services, identify and analyse operational anomalies concerning agreements, stakeholder requirements, and organizational restrictions *Source*: Coming from ISO/IEC 12207 (not included in MMIS)
Continuous security (Technical)	Continuous security involves transforming security, evolving from being treated as another non-functional requirement, to being a key concern in all phases of the development life cycle and even after deployment, backed by a smart and lightweight approach to identifying vulnerabilities of security *Source*: Adopted from [4]

4   A Case Study on Assessing the Maturity of BizDevOps

In this section, we present a case study on the application of MMBDO to assess the BizDevOps processes in a real company. We have applied the case-study method, following the guidelines of Runeson [18], and the template for case studies presented in [19]. The remaining of this section describes the company in which we carried out the case study, the interview procedure, and the interview results and lessons learned.

4.1 Background

The case study has been carried out at a software development and consultancy company (in the rest of the document, we will refer to it as SwDevCompany). SwDevCompany is a Spanish company that provides a wide range of software products and advanced services with high added value. SwDevCompany offers its clients a portfolio of products, along with tailor-made developments, in a balanced and diversified way. The company works for clients from different activity sectors (such as banking, government, industry, telecommunications, etc.), sizes, and countries.

The strength of the commercial offer of SwDevCompany is based on its position as one of the leading digital transformation companies in Spain. SwDevCompany also adds a differential methodology, an expanded portfolio of business solutions, a delivery and support model aimed at generating impact, and a flexible organization based on multidisciplinary teams, made up of specialists with very specific profiles.

Regarding its DevOps processes, SwDevCompany has a business unit dedicated to implementing a DevOps framework. The DevOps team is composed of four DevOps engineers exclusively dedicated to the DevOps project, and 26 architects from the different projects that make use of the DevOps framework. The project architects are in charge of implementing the DevOps framework in their projects.

4.2 Design

According to the approach presented in [20], this current case study is a holistic individual case, because we have focused on the single case of SwDevCompany. The object of study is the MMBDO Maturity Model presented in the previous section.

The main purpose of the case study is to validate MMBDO from the information obtained in its application in a real environment and from the feedback received by the experts that participated in its application. Table 3 shows the research questions of the case study. The main research question is if MMBDO is a feasible model for assessing the maturity of BizDevOps processes. This main research question is detailed into two more specific questions about the completeness of the processes included in MMBDO and its usefulness as a process improvement tool in BizDevOps environments.

4.3 Field Procedure and Data Collection

The field procedure was directly determined by the new processes identified in MMBDO. The SwDevCompany DevOps team was interviewed according to our research questions. The data collected in the interviews with the head of the DevOps team were stored in documents, and the results obtained were reflected in this document.

Table 3. Research questions of the case study

Research questions	
MRQ	Is MMBDO feasible for assessing the maturity of an organization regarding its BizDevOps processes?
SRQ1	Is MMDBO adequate regarding its processes? That is, is there any process that should be included/excluded in/from MMDBO?
SRQ2	Is MMDBO adequate regarding its usefulness for continuous improvement of BizDevOps processes?

4.4 Intervention

This subsection summarizes the most relevant information that can be extracted from the application of MMBDO to SwDevCompany and the interview with the DevOps team of SwDevCompany, concerning the adequateness and completeness of the MMBDO's processes and its usefulness for process improvement in a BizDevOps context. To carry out the evaluation, we took into account the desired results, tasks, and work products for each of the processes, and compared them with the results, tasks and work products currently carried out by the company SwDevCompany. It is important to highlight that we have focused, for the evaluation, on the new processes and the updated processes on the MMIS model. The interviewer team consisted of two consultants, with years of experience in the implementation and evaluation of software project management systems and information security based on international standards.

Application of MMBDO
Regarding the application of MMBDO in SwDevCompany, we could conclude that:

- SwDevCompany currently fully complies with the processes of "Project Planning", "Continuous monitoring" (using the Prometheus tool), "Continuous integration", and "Continuous Delivery" (that is MMBDO's processes 1, 2, 5 and 6).
- SwDevCompany currently complies partially with processes 3, 7, 8 and 10 of MMBDO, since they are yet implementing them: "Continuous improvement", "Continuous deployment", "Transition", and "Operation".
- SwDevCompany does not currently comply with the rest of the processes of MMBDO (4, 9 and 11), since, at this time, they are either not yet implemented, or in the very initial implementation steps: "Continuous Business Planning", "Continuous Validation", and "Continuous Security – SecOps". More specifically, the Transition process is defined by the company but has not been carried out for the moment in any of the projects that are in the DevOps field (it has not been necessary to take control of any project that was managed by another company, nor transfer control of any project to another company or different area).

We gathered specific information about how specific processes were implemented. For example, the DevOps team detailed the activities being carried out concerning process 2, "Continuous Improvement", are: frontend & backend unit testing coverage, static code analysis tools, automatic review of code bugs, different unit testing frameworks depending on the technology, integration testing framework, performance testing framework, console errors/warnings, code lint review.

Interview

After carrying out the interview, we concluded the DevOps team of SwDevCompany considered that the application of MMBDO is feasible to assess the maturity of an organization according to the BizDevOps processes. MMBDO provides a framework for evaluating the current situation and, according to the desired situation, provides a roadmap to get to the desired maturity level.

Table 4 shows the conclusions of the interview, regarding the case study questions:

Table 4. Answers to the research questions of the case study

Answers to the research questions	
MRQ	The DevOps team of SwDevCompany considered that MMBDO is feasible to assess the organization's maturity regarding its BizDevOps practices. MMBDO allows evaluating the current situation (as-is) and, according to the desired scenario (to-be), provides a roadmap for improvement
SRQ1	The DevOps team considered the processes included in MMBDO are adequate to assess BizDevOps processes. Regarding specific processes, they indicated that the "Software quality verification" activity could be highlighted. This activity is currently included in processes 3, "Continuous Improvement", and 5, "Continuous Integration", but we concluded that, due to its importance, this activity could be a process of the model itself On the other hand, we concluded that the scope of process 10, "Operation" may be revised to re-define it, because several of its activities are distributed among other processes of the model (e.g. 2, 5, 6, and 7)
SRQ2	The DevOps team indicated that, by having defined results, tasks, and work products for each process, MMBDO allows the company to compare its current and objective situations to improve its BizDevOps processes. Also, they considered that if this model is used by numerous companies of different sizes and sectors, the company may also benefit from the best practices of other companies (as long as they are incorporated into the model

4.5 Analysis of the Results and Lessons Learned from the Case Study

The case study confirms the adequateness of the processes indicated in the model. SwDevCompany currently implements four processes of the model and is implementing another four processes, while, for the rest of the processes of the model, they are not yet implemented, or are in the initial implementation process.

However, future work will include revising the software quality verification activity (currently included in processes 3 and 5), to verify the feasibility of this activity to be a process of the model itself. We also study the scope of process 10, "Operation", in deeper, because several of its activities are distributed among several of the other processes of the Model (e.g. 2, 5, 6, and 7).

The case study also validates the feasibility of applying MMBDO to measure the maturity of an organization regarding its BizDevOps processes. In this way, the model can serve the company both to assess its current situation regarding the BizDevOps processes and to help it improve this situation to achieve the next levels of maturity.

5 Conclusions

This paper presents MMBDO, a maturity assessment model for BizDevOps, based on internationally recognized ICT process standards. We have defined the model based on the result of a systematic review, and have taken as a basis the processes of the maturity model for the development of MMIS V.2 [10], completing it with eleven additional or modified processes specific to BizDevOps.

We have also presented the results of a case study in a Spanish software development and consultancy company, that allowed us to validate the adequateness of the maturity model MMBDO in a real scenario. The case study confirms the validity of the model, and its processes, although it also revealed information that may guide future work to refine the processes of the model.

Future work includes completing the model by defining the capability and maturity levels of these processes included in MMBDO and completing the validation of the model with a wider case study, by interviewing managers and employees of areas involved in BizDevOps activities in different organizations, of different sizes.

Acknowledgements. This work was supported by: BIZDEVOPS-Global (RTI2018-098309-B-C31 and RTI2018-098309-B-C32), MINECO y FEDER; Centros singulares de investigación de Galicia (ED431G/01), Grupo de Referencia Competitiva (ED431C 2017/58), and ConectaPEME GEMA (IN852A 2018/14), Xunta de Galicia y FEDER.

References

1. Waller, J., Ehmke, N.C., Hasselbring, W.: Including performance benchmarks into continuous integration to enable DevOps. ACM Softw. Eng. Notes **40**, 1–4 (2015)
2. Wettinger, J., Breitenbucher, U., Leymann, F.: Standards-based DevOps automation and integration using TOSCA. In: Proceedings of 7th International Conference on Utility and Cloud Computing, (UCC 2014), pp. 59–68. IEEE Press (2014)
3. Bosch, J.: Continuous Software Engineering. Springer, Dordrecht (2014). https://doi.org/10.1007/978-3-319-11283-1
4. Fitzgerald, B., Stol, K.J.: Continuous software engineering: a roadmap and agenda. J. Syst. Softw. **123**, 176–189 (2017)
5. Wiedemann, A., Wiesche, M., Gewald, H., Krcmar, H.: Implementing the planning process within DevOps teams to achieve continuous innovation. In: Proceedings of the 52nd Hawaii International Conference on System Sciences (2019)

6. Erich, F., Amrit, C., Daneva, M.: A mapping study on cooperation between information system development and operations. In: Jedlitschka, A., Kuvaja, P., Kuhrmann, M., Männistö, T., Münch, J., Raatikainen, M. (eds.) Product-Focused Software Process Improvement. PROFES 2014. LNCS, vol 8892, pp. 277–280. Springer, Cham (2014). https://doi.org/10.1007/978-3-319-13835-0_21

7. Lwakatare, L.E., Kuvaja, P., Oivo, M.: An exploratory study of DevOps extending the dimensions of DevOps with practices. In: Proceedings of 11th International Conference on Software Engineering Advances (ICSEA), pp. 91–99 (2016)

8. Chrissis, M.B., Konrad, M., Shrum, S.: CMMI for Development: Guidelines for Process Integration and Product Improvement. Addison-Wesley, Boston (2011)

9. ISO/IEC: ISO/IEC 12207:2017 Systems and software engineering – Software life cycle processes (2017)

10. Garzás, J., Pino, F.J., Piattini, M., Fernández, C.M.: A maturity model for the Spanish software industry based on ISO standards. Comput. Stand. Interfaces 35, 616–628 (2013)

11. ISO: ISO - ISO/IEC 27001 Information security management (2017)

12. ISO/IEC: ISO/IEC 20000-1:2011(E), Information Technology - Service Management Part 1: Service management system requirements (2011)

13. Oktaba, H., García, F., Piattini, M., Ruiz, F., Pino, F.J., Alquuicira, C.: Software process improvement: the competisoft project. IEEE Comput. 40, 21–28 (2007)

14. ISO/IEC: ISO/IEC 33001:2015 Information technology – Process assessment – Concepts and terminology (2015)

15. Mohamed, S.I.: DevOps shifting software engineering strategy value based perspective. IOSR J. Comput. Eng. 17, 2278–2661 (2015)

16. Sahid, A., Maleh, Y., Belaissaoui, M.: An agile framework for ITS management in organizations. A case study based on DevOps. In: Proceedings of International Conference on Computing and Wireless Communication System, pp. 1–8. ACM (2017)

17. Feijter, R., Vliet, R., Jagroep, E., Overbeek, S., Brinkkemper, S.: Towards the adoption of DevOps in software product organizations: a maturity model approach (2017)

18. Runeson, P., Host, M., Rainer, A., Regnell, B.: Case Study Research in Software Engineering - Guidelines and Examples. Wiley, Hoboken (2012)

19. Brereton, P., Kitchenham, B., Budgen, D., Li, Z.: Using a protocol template for case study planning. In: Proceedings of International Conference on Evaluation and Assessment in Software Engineering (EASE 2008), pp. 41–48. BCS (2008)

20. Yin, R.K.: Collecting Case Study Evidence. SAGE Publications, Thousand Oaks (2013)

Process Compliance Re-Certification Efficiency Enabled by EPF-C ∘ BVR-T: A Case Study

Barbara Gallina$^{(\boxtimes)}$ⓘ, Aleksandër Pulla, Antonela Bregu,
and Julieth Patricia Castellanos Ardila

IDT, Mälardalen University, Västerås, Sweden
{barbara.gallina,julieth.castellanos}@mdh.se,
{asa19008,abu19002}@student.mdh.se

Abstract. With today's ever increasing demands on process (re)certification, enabling (re)certification efficiency is paramount. Within the EU AMASS project, we delivered a tool-chain, called, in this paper, EPF-C ∘ BVR-T, obtained by the integration of EPF Composer (EPF-C) and BVR Tool (BVR-T). This tool-chain supports process engineers in the engineering and compliance demonstration activities as well as variability and change management. The compliance recertification efficiency enabled by the tool-chain has not been evaluated for changes triggered by different jurisdictions, which impose the release of new standards. Thus, to fill this gap, in this case study paper, we focus on the medical domain, precisely on the evolution of the ISO 14971 process for risk analysis and evaluation for medical devices. Based on a set of efficiency-related criteria, we evaluate the recertification efficiency enabled by the change management strategy implemented in the tool-chain.

Keywords: (Re)certification · Process compliance · ISO 14971

1 Introduction

With today's ever increasing demands on process (re)certification, enabling (re)certification efficiency is paramount. The AMASS project [18] has delivered the first de-facto platform for (re)certification [17]. This platform includes a tool-chain, called EPF-C ∘ BVR-T in this paper, obtained by integrating EPF Composer (EPF-C) and BVR Tool (BVR-T). EPF-C ∘ BVR-T supports process engineers in the engineering and compliance demonstration activities as well as variability and change management. The compliance recertification efficiency of the tool-chain has been illustrated and partially demonstrated in the space domain taking into consideration recertification needs in case of different types of changes, e.g. criticality level [4], concern (safety/security [6]). However, the

Partially funded by EU and VINNOVA via the ECSEL JU under grant agreement No. 692474, AMASS project.

ⓒ Springer Nature Switzerland AG 2020
M. Shepperd et al. (Eds.): QUATIC 2020, CCIS 1266, pp. 211–219, 2020.
https://doi.org/10.1007/978-3-030-58793-2_17

tool-chain has not been evaluated in the medical domain and never for handling the recertification effort needed in case of products crossing jurisdictions and thus having to comply with different versions of the same standard. As known, medical devices are governed by a broad range of national and international regulations and medical equipment certification standards. These regulatory requirements are complex and vary between regions, which can make it challenging to gain medical approval for products within a specific targeted market. An evident example is represented by the requirements, included within ISO 14971:2007 and its evolution (EN ISO 14971:2012, ISO 14971:2019), regarding the process for risk analysis and evaluation. When published, ISO 14971:2007 was internationally endorsed. Then, EN ISO 14971:2012 was released for the European market only as a version harmonised with a set of EU directives (90/385/EEC [3], 93/42/EEC [2], and 98/79/EC [16]). As a consequence of the new release, recertification was mandatory. Manufacturers of medical devices targeting an international market had to struggle to reconfigure their processes (i.e., provide new evidence) to get approval from the different regulatory bodies within the different jurisdictions within and outside EU. ISO 14971:2019 brought changes, making it internationally endorsed again. Given the challenging regulatory context in the medical domain and given the concrete need for a solution, in this paper, we present a reduced but meaningful portion of a case study focused on the ISO 14971-compliant process for risk analysis and evaluation. The interested reader may refer to [13] for the complete case study. During the execution of the case study, we use EPF-C ∘ BVR-T to engineer compliant processes as well as manage the variability and change in relation to the different versions of ISO 14971. Then, based on a set of efficiency-related criteria, we measure the re-certification efficiency, enabled by EPF-C ∘ BVR-T and we analyse the results.

The rest of the paper is organised as follows. In Sect. 2, we give an overview of EPF-C ∘ BVR-T for efficient process compliance management. In Sect. 3, we recall the fundamental information regarding the ISO 14971 and its evolution. In Sect. 4, we present the case study design and its execution. In Sect. 5, we present the analysis of the case study. In Sect. 6, we discuss related work. Finally, in Sect. 7, we draw our conclusion and sketch future work.

2   EPF-C ∘ BVR-T

EPF-C ∘ BVR-T [10] is a tool-chain, obtained by integrating EPF Composer (EPF-C), which was recently brought back to the future [11], and BVR Tool (BVR-T). EPF-C ∘ BVR-T supports efficient compliance management via reuse enabled by managing commonalities and variabilities, i.e., by implementing Safety-oriented Process Line Engineering (SoPLE) [5]. On the one hand, EPF-C (Eclipse Process Framework Composer)[1], which implements a metamodel that covers the major parts of SPEM 2.0 (Software & Systems Process Engineering Metamodel) [12], is used to model the base process and its related library. Essential elements are described in Table 1. A *role* represents who does a unit

---

[1] See https://www.eclipse.org/epf/.

of work, defined in a *task definition*. *Artifacts* and *deliverables* identify types of work products resulting from a task. *Guidelines, checklist*, and *practices* represent supplementary free-form documentation.

Table 1. Subset of Icons Used in SPEM 2.0/EPF Composer [12].

Role	Task Definition	Deliverable	Artifact	Practice	Checklist	Guidance
👤	⇨	✉	📄	⚜	☑	📊

On the other hand, BVR-T (Base Variability Resolution Tool)[2], which implements the BVR metamodel [7], is used to orthogonally model (VSpec model via VSpec editor), resolve (Resolution model via the Resolution editor) the variability at abstract level. Once a new configuration is solved, the binding between the abstract representation and the concrete representation (compliant to the EPF Composer's implemented metamodel) can be realised (Realization model via the Realization editor). More precisely, VSpec permits users to model the variability in a feature diagram-like fashion, embracing best practices of product line modelling and thus inheriting the efficiency of product line engineering best practices.

Table 2. VSpec

Element	Symbol
Choice	▭
Constraint	▱
Group	△

As Table 2 recalls, a choice represents a yes/no decision, a constraint, given in BCL (Basic Constraint Language), specifies restrictions on permissible resolution models, and a group dictates the number of choice resolutions, e.g., 1..1, which refers to *xor* in which one of the child features must be selected. For sake of clarity, we point out that Table 2 only recalls the BVR modelling elements used in this paper. Resolution permits users to make choices at variation points, where desired variants can be selected. Resolution also includes the possibility to validate the choices. Erroneous choices violating the cross-variation points constraints can be detected. Realization permits users to bind abstract resolutions with the concrete elements in the base model.

3   ISO 14971 and Its Evolution

ISO 14971 is the standard that was developed specifically for medical devices. It deals with processes for managing risks, primarily to the patient, but also to the operator, other persons, other equipment and the environment. This standard specifies a process through which the manufacturer of a medical device can identify hazards associated with a medical device, estimate and evaluate the risks associated with these hazards, control these risks, and monitor the effectiveness of the controls throughout the life cycle of the medical device. The content of ISO 14971 has been evolving over the years and different versions were published, incorporating consensus-based modifications and refinements. In this paper, we

---

[2] See https://github.com/SINTEF-9012/bvr.

limit our attention to ISO 14971:2007 [8], EN ISO 14971:2012 [1], and ISO 14971:2019 [9], and, more specifically, to the portion of the process that deals with risk analysis and evaluation.

Figure 1 depicts the portion of the process considered in this paper. On the right side of Fig. 1 two main differences are highlighted: 1) Risk Acceptability Principle, known as RAP, which stands for the principle that is followed for reducing risks related to medical devices, 2) Treatment of negligible risks. These differences emerge by conducting a comparative study of the different versions. Such differences are shown in detail in Table 3, where ALARP stands for *As Low As Reasonably Practicable*, while AFAP stands for *As Far As Possible*, which implies that all risks have to be reduced without there being room for economic considerations.

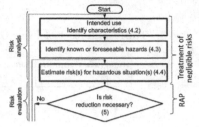

Fig. 1. Risk management

Table 3. Risk identification and evaluation differences among ISO 14971 versions

Standard	Treatment of negligible risks	Risk Acceptability Principle (RAP)
ISO 14971:2007	Discard negligible risks	ALARP (Demands risk reduction)
EN ISO 14971:2012	Take all risks (including negligible)	AFAP (Requires risk reduction)
ISO 14971:2019	Take all risks (including negligible)	ALARP/AFAP (Without affecting benefit-risk ratio)

The reader may refer to [13] for a complete analysis of ISO 14971 evolution focused on risk analysis and evaluation.

4   Case Study Design and Execution

In this section, we present the design and the execution of a reduced but meaningful portion of a case study, designed according to the guidelines given in [15].

4.1   Case Study Design: Objective and Selection

The objective of the case study is the evaluation of the cross-jurisdiction/cross version re-certification efficiency enabled by the change management strategy implemented in EPF-C ∘ BVR-T. With this goal in mind, we expect to answer the following question: is the cross-jurisdiction/cross-version recertification, enabled by EPF-C ∘ BVR-T, efficient? To evaluate the re-certification efficiency (i.e., the relationship between results achieved (recertification artefacts provision) and resources used (effort in terms of modelling time), as done in our previous work [4], we adopt and re-interpret in the context of process engineering a set of metrics, see Table 4. As Table 4 shows, Cp_i defines the set of process components for each process. The intersection of the common Cp_i(s) is equal to Size of Commonality (SoC). SoC is the input for the $PrRi$, which measures the extent of reusability of the common components for a specific process.

Table 4. Reuse metrics.

Size of Commonality (SoC)	Product-related Reusability (PrRi)
$SoC = \lvert \bigcap\limits_{i=i}^{n} Cp_i \rvert$	$PrRi = \frac{SoC}{\lvert Cp_i \rvert}$

As case study, we select the evolution of the ISO 14971 process for risk analysis and risk evaluation (recalled in Sect. 3).

4.2 Case Study Execution and Results

We model the process in EPF-C, and the VSpec and the Resolution in BVR-T. Figure 2 shows the modelling of process elements in EPF-C related to the three versions of the standard ISO 14971 (recalled in Sect. 3). For space reasons, in this paper, we only focus on the guidance part of each EPF-C plugin (highlighted in green). With a red square, we highlight the applicable RAP and treatment of negligible risk for each standard (recalled in Table 3).

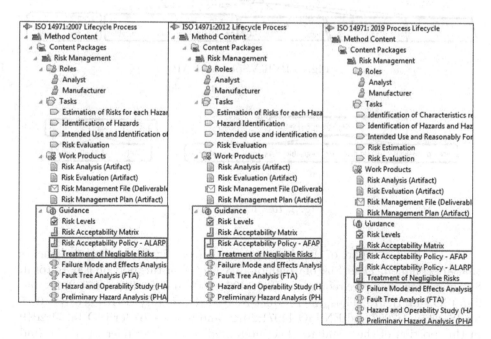

Fig. 2. EPF-C Plugins Targeting ISO14971:2007, ISO14971:2012 and ISO14971:2019

We model the variability for negligible risk in BVR VSpec (see Fig. 3). In particular, *Discard_negligible_risks* and *Take_negligible_risks_into_account* are defined in the VSpec as optional-multiplicity 1..1, implying that only one of them shall be applied, according to the constraints of the applicable standard. In a similar way, we model the variability associated with RAP (see Fig. 4). For the complete VSpec, embracing all the process elements considered in Fig. 2, the interested reader may refer to [13]. Once the variability is modelled, the resolution is performed. For example, if the process model must comply with EN ISO 14971:2012, we set true for the option *Take_negligible_risks_into_account* for the risk analysis (see Fig. 5a), while we set true for the option *AFAP* for the risk evaluation (see Fig. 5b).

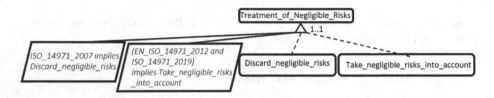

Fig. 3. BVR VSpec for the treatments of negligible risk

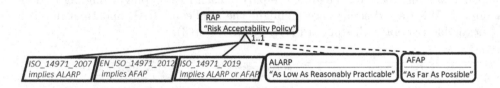

Fig. 4. BVR VSpec for RAP

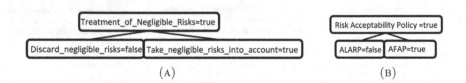

Fig. 5. Resolution models.

In the guidance part of the three standards (see Fig. 2), we find 6 elements that are common. Thus, Size of Commonality (SoC) for this portion is 6. In total, 8 guidance elements are required in ISO 14971:2007 and EN ISO 14971:2012, and 9 in ISO 14971:2019. Thus, the Product-related Reusability (PrRi) is $6/8 = 0.75$ for ISO 14971:2007 and EN ISO 14971:2012, and $6/9 = 0,67$ for ISO 14971:2019 in this portion of the standard. The interested reader may refer to [13] to find the complete measurement, which does not only focus on the guidance part.

5 Case Study Analysis

In this section, we analyse the results and answer the question presented in Sect. 4.1. The computation of SoC and PrRi shows a positive gain in terms of reusability. Thus, we can answer that the change management strategy, implemented in EPF-C ∘ BVR-T, is efficient when applied for handling changes related to cross-jurisdiction/cross version in the context of ISO 14971. As a consequence, this suggests that the provision of the new evidence, needed for recertification, can be obtained by reusing a significant amount of pre-existing evidence in terms of modelling artefacts. Thus, also the recertification is efficient.

6 Related Work

In the literature, other solutions have been proposed to increase efficiency via reuse, while engineering/assuring safety-critical systems and their processes, and case studies have been conducted to show their benefits. In the context of the OPENCOSS[3] project, for instance, a systematic approach for reusing safety certification artefacts was applied to a cross-domain (railway and avionics) case study [14] resulting into 50% of reuse. In contrast, our case study focuses on the medical domain and in the context of different jurisdictions. To the best of our knowledge, in the medical domain, our work represents a novelty and perhaps the seminal evidence to trigger the attention to the potential efficiency increase that could be gained by systematising and managing the variability that exists within the broad range of national and international regulations and medical equipment certification standards.

7 Conclusion and Future Work

In this paper, we conducted a case study-based evaluation of the process compliance recertification efficiency enabled by EPF-C ∘ BVR-T. Precisely, the ISO 14971 process for risk identification and evaluation for medical devices was in focus. EPF-C ∘ BVR-T was used to model the process evidence needed for certification, systematise reuse, and manage change (i.e., reconfigure to successfully re-certify). Based on a set of criteria, we evaluated the efficiency of the change management strategy, implemented in EPF-C ∘ BVR-T, and the results enabled us to draw conclusion on the recertification efficiency. Specifically, the case study showed that, via EPF-C ∘ BVR-T, efficient reconfiguration (i.e., efficient provision of artefacts needed for the recertification process) is possible. Thus, for instance, manufacturers targeting an international market can efficiently reconfigure and validate their processes to satisfy the requirements within/outside EU. This evaluation could represent the starting point for the adoption of the tool chain EPF-C ∘ BVR-T in the medical domain. In the future, we aim at

---

[3] Open Platform for EvolutioNary Certification of Safety-critical Systems- http://www.opencoss-project.eu/.

conducting a larger evaluation by considering the entire ISO 14971, as well as related standards (e.g., software process improvement, and security). In addition, in cooperation with industrial partners, we aim at evaluating EPF-C ○ BVR-T in realistic industrial settings, where processes are typically not derived by following the standard requirements by the book.

References

1. EN International Organization for Standardization (ISO) 14971:2012: Medical devices - Application of risk management to medical devices (ISO 14971:2007, Corrected version 2007–10-01), July 2012
2. The Council of the European Communities: Council Directive 93/42/EEC of 14 June 1993 concerning medical devices, June 1993
3. Council of the European Union: Council Directive 90/385/EEC of 20 June 1990 on the approximation of the laws of the Member States relating to active implantable medical devices, June 1990
4. Gallina, B., Iyer, S.: Towards quantitative evaluation of reuse within safety-oriented process lines. In: Larrucea, X., Santamaria, I., O'Connor, R.V., Messnarz, R. (eds.) EuroSPI 2018. CCIS, vol. 896, pp. 469–479. Springer, Cham (2018). https://doi.org/10.1007/978-3-319-97925-0_40
5. Gallina, B., Sljivo, I., Jaradat, O.: Towards a safety-oriented process line for enabling reuse in safety critical systems development and certification. In: 35th Annual IEEE Software Engineering Workshop, pp. 148–157 (2012). https://doi.org/10.1109/SEW.2012.22
6. Gallina, B.: Quantitative evaluation of tailoring within SPICE-compliant security-informed safety-oriented process lines. J. Softw.: Evol. Process - EuroSPI Special Issue **32**(3), 1–13 (2020). https://doi.org/10.1002/smr.2212
7. Haugen, Ø., Øgård, O.: BVR – better variability results. In: Amyot, D., Fonseca i Casas, P., Mussbacher, G. (eds.) SAM 2014. LNCS, vol. 8769, pp. 1–15. Springer, Cham (2014). https://doi.org/10.1007/978-3-319-11743-0_1
8. International Organization for Standardization (ISO) 14971:2007: Medical devices - Application of risk management to medical devices, March 2007
9. International Organization for Standardization (ISO) 14971:2019: Medical devices - Application of risk management to medical devices, December 2019
10. Javed, M., Gallina, B.: Safety-oriented process line engineering via seamless integration between EPF composer and BVR tool. In: 22nd International Systems and Software Product Line Conference. SPLC, vol. 2, pp. 23–28 (2018). https://doi.org/10.1145/3236405.3236406
11. Javed, M.A., Gallina, B.: Get EPF composer back to the future: a trip from Galileo to Photon after 11 years. In: EclipseCon, Toulouse, France, 13–14 June 2018 (2018)
12. OMG: Software & Systems Process Engineering Meta-Model Specification. Version 2.0. (2008)
13. Pulla, A., Bregu, A.: Evaluating the compliance re-certification efficiency enabled by the AMASS platform for medical devices. Master thesis, Mälardalen University, School of Innovation, Design and Engineering, Västerås, Sweden (2020). https://mdh.diva-portal.org/smash/get/diva2:1438427/FULLTEXT01.pdf
14. Ruiz, A., Juez, G., Espinoza, H., de la Vara, J.L., Larrucea, X.: Reuse of safety certification artefacts across standards and domains: a systematic approach. Reliab. Eng. Syst. Saf. **158**, 153–171 (2017). https://doi.org/10.1016/j.ress.2016.08.017

15. Runeson, P., Höst, M.: Guidelines for conducting and reporting case study research in software engineering. Empir. Softw. Eng. **14**(2), 131–164 (2009). https://doi.org/10.1007/s10664-008-9102-8
16. European Parliament & Council of the European Union: Directive 98/79/EC of the European Parliament and of the Council of 27 October 1998 on in vitro diagnostic medical devices, October 1998
17. de la Vara, J.L., Corredor, E.P., Lopez, A.R., Gallina, B.: The AMASS tool platform: an innovative solution for assurance and certification of cyber-physical systems. In: Joint Proceedings of REFSQ-2020 Workshops, Doctoral Symposium, Live Studies Track, and Poster Track co-located with the 26th International Conference on Requirements Engineering: Foundation for Software Quality (REFSQ), Pisa, Italy, 24 March 2020, vol. 2584. CEUR Workshop Proceedings (2020)
18. de la Vara, J.L., Parra, E., Ruiz, A., Gallina, B.: AMASS: a large-scale European project to improve the assurance and certification of cyber-physical systems. In: Franch, X., Männistö, T., Martínez-Fernández, S. (eds.) PROFES 2019. LNCS, vol. 11915, pp. 626–632. Springer, Cham (2019). https://doi.org/10.1007/978-3-030-35333-9_49

Software Quality Education and Training

Design of Secure Coding Challenges
for Cybersecurity Education
in the Industry

Tiago Gasiba[1,2](✉) [ID], Ulrike Lechner[2] [ID], Maria Pinto-Albuquerque[3] [ID],
and Alae Zouitni[4] [ID]

[1] Siemens AG, Munich, Germany
tiago.gasiba@siemens.com
[2] Universität der Bundeswehr München, Munich, Germany
ulrike.lechner@unibw.de
[3] Instituto Universitário de Lisboa (ISCTE-IUL), ISTAR-IUL, Lisboa, Portugal
maria.albuquerque@iscte-iul.pt
[4] Universität Passau, Passau, Germany
zouitni.alae@gmail.com

Abstract. According to a recent survey with more than 4000 software
developers, *"less than half of developers can spot security holes"*. As a
result, software products present a low-security quality expressed by vulnerabilities that can be exploited by cyber-criminals. This lack of quality and security is particularly dangerous if the software which contains
the vulnerabilities is deployed in critical infrastructures. Serious games,
and in particular, Capture-the-Flag (CTF) events, have shown promising results in improving secure coding awareness of software developers
in the industry. The challenges in the CTF event, to be useful, must be
adequately designed to address the target group. This paper presents
novel contributions by investigating which challenge types are adequate
to improve software developers' ability to write secure code in an industrial context. We propose 1) six challenge types usable in the industry
context, and 2) a structure for the CTF challenges. Our investigation also
presents results on 3) how to include hints and penalties into the cybersecurity challenges. We evaluated our work through a survey with security experts. While our results show that "traditional" challenge types
seem to be adequate, they also reveal a new class of challenges based on
code entry and interaction with an automated coach.

Keywords: Education · Teaching · Training · Secure coding ·
Industry · Cybersecurity · Capture-the-flag · Game analysis · Game
design · Cybersecurity challenge

1 Introduction

To improve the quality (ISO250xx [16]) of software in terms of security, several
standards such as IEC-62443-4-1 [15] and ISO 27001 [17] mandate the implementation of a secure software development lifecycle (S-SDLC). Additionally,

© Springer Nature Switzerland AG 2020
M. Shepperd et al. (Eds.): QUATIC 2020, CCIS 1266, pp. 223–237, 2020.
https://doi.org/10.1007/978-3-030-58793-2_18

in recognition of the importance of secure code and need to develop secure products [23,26], several companies have joined together and formed the SAFE-code [25] alliance to promote security best practices. Automatic tools such as Static Application Security Testing (SAST) [24] can be used to automate and aid in improving code quality. These tools scan the code basis for existing vulnerabilities, which must be fixed by software developers. However, previous research shows that this is not enough [22]: the reliability of such tools is still not good enough, and they cannot automatically fix the code - this is done by software developers who must also be trained in secure software development.

One of the methods currently being investigated and that is showing promising results are training methods based serious games of the type Capture-the-Flag (CTF). The concept of these kinds of games was originally developed in the pen-testing community. Several such games are continually being deployed around the world [7] nowadays by universities, companies, and even groups of individuals. However, most of the existing CTFs are not geared towards software developers in the industry. Gasiba et al. [10] have recently shown that, in order to raise awareness on secure coding in the industry, the game design must address the specific requirements of its target audience.

Typically CTFs can be categorized as follows: 1) *Attack-Only*, 2) *Attack-and-Defend* and 3) *Defend Only*. The participants of these CTFs are generally split into two categories: Red Team (attackers) and Blue Team (defenders). In *Attack-Only* Red team players try to exploit several systems to gain access and control. In *Attack-and-Defend* competitions, the Red team players attack systems that are being hardened and protected by blue team members. Finally, in *Defend Only* CTFs, the players answer questions on cybersecurity for points or configure and harden systems to be resilient to simulated attacks.

To address the needs of the industry and to better adapt to the players, Gasiba et al. [10] have proposed a defensive CTF approach and also outlined the requirements for the design of the defensive challenges. A proper design of challenge types based on these requirements is especially important in an industrial setting, as shown by an experiment by Barela et al. [3], where the type of the challenge (based on comics) was seen to be inadequate for CTFs in the industry.

Therefore, in this paper, we extend previous work by addressing the question of which types of defensive challenges are suitable for software developers. In particular, we are interested in the 1) structure of the said challenges and also on 2) which types of challenges can be used in a CTF-like competition to raise awareness of software developers in the industry. Our work is based on surveys administered through interviews with expert security trainers from the industry. The main contributions of this work are the following:

- design of defensive challenges for CTFs in the industry which aim at raising awareness on secure coding and secure coding guidelines
- definition of a challenge structure for industrial CTFs,
- definition of six different challenge types for industrial CTFs, and
- insight into different options on how to include hints and penalties in industrial CTFs.

We hope that this work can be used by designers of serious game and quality engineers as a guideline on how to design defensive challenges for CTFs aimed at raising awareness on secure coding on software developers in the industry.

In Sect. 2, we present previous work related to our research. Section 3 discusses our approach to the design of the defensive challenges. The results of our study are presented in Sect. 4. This section also presents a critical discussion on the obtained results, presents our main contribution to practical scenarios for possible games, and briefly discusses the threats to the validity of our findings. Finally, Sect. 5 summarizes our work and briefly discusses possible next steps.

2   Related Work

In [11], Graziotin et al. have shown that *happy developers are better coders*, i.e., produce higher quality code and software. Davis et al. in [8] show that CTF players experience fun during game play. Furthermore, Woody et al. [32] argue that *software vulnerabilities are quality defects*. Since fun and happiness are inter-related [30], these facts can be seen as a motivator to use Capture-the-Flag (CTF)-base serious games [9] to raise awareness [14] on the topic of secure coding for software developers in the industry, in order to improve code quality.

In [19] Mirkovic et al. introduced classroom CTF exercises as a form of cybersecurity education in academia. Their results show that the students that participated in this kind of event have enjoyed the training and have shown increased interest, attention, and focus towards cybersecurity topics. Additionally, in their study, Gonzalez et al. [13] shown similar results and state that cybersecurity training through serious games improves the students' education and skills, and has a positive impact on attracting students to cybersecurity field. They conclude that this kind of training can reduce the shortage of professionals in the field of cybersecurity. Several additional studies [2,4,8] also show the positive benefits of CTF in students' attention and performance.

However, using CTFs as a tool to raise cybersecurity awareness comes with different obstacles. In [10], Gasiba et al. elicit requirements for designing CTF challenges geared towards software developers in the industry and show that these CTF challenges should focus on the defensive perspective. Chung et al. [6] also evaluated different aspects related to CTFs and concluded two important issues related to CTFs: the challenge difficulty level and suitability the target audience.

In our work, we are interested in designing high-quality defensive CTF challenges for software developers in the industry that address the topic of secure coding guidelines [5] (SCG) and secure software development best practices [21] (SDBP). However, most of the currently existing work focuses on academia, where the target group is composed of current or future security experts, or pen-testers. Furthermore, most existing studies also focus on the offensive perspective and do not address the topic of SCG, and SDBP. As such, this study is driven by both the need to raise awareness on secure coding [1,20,33], and by the lack of design of defensive CTF challenge geared towards software developers in the industry. The research method used in this work is based on semi-structured interviews [31] and survey best practices as described by Grooves et al. [12] and Seaman et al. [28]. The design of the serious games is based on [9].

3   Approach to Challenge Design

In order to design defensive challenges for industrial CTFs, the authors have decided to focus on two different aspects: the challenge structure (CS) and the challenge type (CT). The content of the challenge (e.g. questions or example of software vulnerability), which are not the focus of the current work, can be derived from existing SCG [5] and SDBP [21]. The challenge structure reflects the mechanics of the challenge, i.e., how it is supposed to be deployed and how it should work. The challenge type specifies the different ways that the challenge can be presented to a participant. Figure 1 shows the steps that we have followed in our approach to design the defensive CTF challenges for an industrial context.

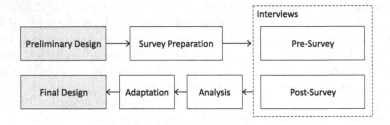

Fig. 1. Study approach

In the first step, we have created a preliminary design, containing a proposed CS and different CTs. For this, we conducted several informal discussions with one security expert. Additionally, based on our experience with past Capture-the-Flag events, we concluded the preliminary design of challenge structure and challenge types. In the next step, we created a two-phase survey [12,28]. The goal of the survey was to gather feedback and opinions, in a structured way, on the preliminary challenge structure and challenge types. It was used to facilitate the semi-structured interviews with several security experts. The interviews, carried out in the following step, were realized in face-to-face meetings. The meetings consisted of three parts: pre-survey, post-survey, and informal discussions. After the interviews, the collected feedback was transferred to digital form and was analyzed. The analysis step aims at understanding the joint agreement on the different suggested improvements by the security experts. The commonly suggested improvements were then used to adapt and change the preliminary design, which resulted in the final challenge design.

In the following sub-sections, we present details on the different phases of our approach. The results of the analysis, adaptation, and also the final challenge design will be presented in Sect. 4.

3.1 Preliminary Design

In the preliminary design, the authors conducted several informal discussions with a security expert which is also a trainer of secure coding in the industry. The security expert has more than 10 years of experience in the industry and has also knowledge and had previously participated in Capture-the-Flag events. Based on the experience of the security expert and also on the experience of the authors, preliminary design was derived.

3.2 Survey Preparation

In order to prepare for the interviews with security experts, a two-part survey [18] was developed by the authors. The developed survey underwent three reviews by three different cybersecurity experts: one holding a master of science in computer science and two holding a Ph.D. in IT security, whereby one is additionally a university lecturer in cybersecurity. The main goal of the pre-survey was to understand what types of challenges do experienced industry security experts find suitable for CTF-based awareness training. The post-survey' primary goal is to understand the level of agreement with the different preliminary challenges types. The pre-survey was conducted at the beginning of the meeting, before presenting the preliminary design. The post-survey was conducted after presenting the preliminary design. This split allowed the participants to think and reflect on their answers from the pre-survey and be prepared and more open-minded for the discussions on the post-survey. Splitting the survey into two parts was done in order to guarantee unbiased feedback collection from the security experts during the pre-survey. Both the pre-survey and post-survey asked the participants - *if they were to design a CTF challenge about secure coding for software developers in the industry, what kind of challenge structure and type would they use?*. The post-survey additionally asked questions on the preliminary design, in particular on *what would the participant change, add or remove to the presented preliminary design, what other challenge types would they additionally consider* and also on the expert opinion on *how to use penalties and hints in the challenges*. In total, the pre-survey consisted of 16 questions, of which 12 were multiple-choice, three were based on a Likert scale, and 1 was an open-ended question [29]. The post-survey consisted of 11 questions, whereby 5 were feedback questions based on a Likert scale, and 6 were open-ended questions.

3.3 Interviews

For the interview, the authors engaged 20 security experts with an average of 4 years of experience in the industry (minimum one year and maximum of 12 years). The experts were selected based on their experience, position, and background in the company - engaged in several consulting projects as a cybersecurity expert. A large part of the participants were also trainers themselves of different topics on cybersecurity. The selected participants were all familiar with CTF competitions. Half of the experts hold a Ph.D. degree in computer science or equivalent, and the remaining half holds a master of science in computer science or equivalent. The face-to-face interviews lasted for one hour and were carried out between the 1st of October 2019 and the 16th. During the interview, the first 20 min were dedicated to the pre-survey. Afterward, the preliminary design of CTF challenges was presented to the participants. The remaining 30 min were then spent on the post-survey, open-ended discussions and finished with 10 min of informal discussions on the results.

3.4   Analysis

In this stage, we gathered all the collected data from the pre-surveys, post-surveys, and informal discussions. The results using a Likert scale were analyzed using standard statistical methods. Due to its nature, the open-ended questions and the informal discussions need to be coded [28]. In order to guarantee the quality of this step, the transcripts were given to three security experts who were asked to perform the coding step manually. We have opted for a manual procedure rather than automated to ensure high quality, as automated coding has been previously shown not to achieve high accuracy [27]. The coding outcome of each expert was then collected and discussed together. Similarities and differences were then systematically addressed, and the final coding was derived by mutual agreement between the three experts.

3.5   Adaptation and Final Design

The last step consisted of using the feedback from the previous step to adapt and change the preliminary design accordingly. Only the proposed changes that were agreed by the majority of the participants (i.e., more than 2/3 after coding or 80% of participants) were considered for the final design. In Sect. 4, the final challenge design, including challenge structure and derived challenge types, will be presented in more detail.

4   Analysis and Results

In this section, we describe the results from the two-part survey interview, as outlined in the previous section. We present the final challenge structure and types, which take into consideration the feedback provided by all the security experts. Finally, we summarize the main contributions and briefly discuss the threat to the validity of our work.

4.1   Preliminary Design

As a result of the informal discussions with the security expert, the challenge structure was defined in two rounds: *round 1*: main challenge and *round 2*: presentation of secure coding guideline related to the challenge. No further details will be given for the initial design, as this was changed after the interview with the security experts, as shown in the next sub-sections. Section 4.4 details the final challenge structure. The derived initial challenge types were the following: Single Choice Question (CSQ), Multiple Choice Question (MCQ), Text Entry Challenge (TEC), Code Snippet Challenge (CSC), and Code Entry Challenge (CEC). Table 3 shows a summary of the challenge types. Further details are given in Sect. 4.5, together with the final design.

4.2   Pre-survey Results

Pre-survey results showed that the majority (55%) of the participants thought an adequate type of challenge would be of type *question and answer*, without specifying what they mean. Additionally, 85% answered that *some form of challenge involving coding* would be adequate, since the challenges should be based on SCG. However, some participants replied that *friendly hacking* exercises would also be a good exercise - this was discarded as these types of challenges are not defensive. One participant mentioned that an appropriate challenge would involve *fixing a problem on a vulnerable code snippet*.

Table 1. Coding results on hints and penalties

Question	Pre-survey results
When would you add the hints?	(30%) For all challenges
	(50%) For difficult challenges
	(20%) No opinion
How to design the hints?	(50%) Giving details on the answer
	(75%) Disclosing important concept
	(70%) Include an external reference
When would you add penalties?	(60%) Agree to introduce penalties
	(35%) Retrying the same challenge
	(65%) When using a hint
	(30%) Disagree to introduce penalties
	(30%) No opinion

Table 1 shows a summary of the agreement level of the participants towards questions asked during the pre-survey related the hints and penalties. The usage of hints was backed by 80% of the survey participants, for difficult challenges (50%) or all questions (30%). The hints should include details on how to solve the questions (50%) and point-out the secure coding concept behind the challenge (75%). The majority of the participants agreed that adding an external reference (e.g. link to an article on the web) is an appropriate way to design hints for challenges. Half of the participants agree that hints should disclose the essential concept behind the challenge, e.g., on which secure coding guideline the challenge is based. Only 75% of the participants agree that giving targeted hints (e.g., disclosing an important concept) is a good idea. During the informal discussions, several participants mentioned that the goal of the hints should be to make sure that the CTF players are learning secure coding concepts during the game. The hints should also be designed in order to lower player frustration and maximize the learn-effect. In particular, the types of hint should be precise and to the point, as industry players have a limited time to play the game.

In terms of penalty-points, 60% agreed to introduce them, 30% disagreed, and 10% had no opinion. The ones that agreed to introduce penalty points, 65% agreed that using hints should be penalized, and the remaining 35% agreed that retrying a challenge should be penalized. During the informal discussions, the survey participants mentioned that the intention to add penalties should be to motivate the player to find solutions by him/herself and not to rely on hints. Furthermore, the penalties should be small to lower the frustration level while maximizing the learning effect of the CTF players.

4.3   Post-survey Results

In the post-survey, the participants were shown all the derived challenge types and were asked to rate their agreement on the suitability for a CTF-like event with software developers in an industrial setting on a Likert scale. Table 2 shows the results of the post-survey for the five different challenge types. We use the standard mapping of the Likert scale as follows: from 1-*strongly disagree* to 5-*strongly agree*.

Table 2. Average agreement level

	SCQ	MCQ	TEC	CSC	CEC
Average	3.95	3.80	3.15	4.30	4.30
Std. deviation	0.76	1.00	1.04	1.26	0.92

The derived ranks of the preferred challenge types are the following (from highest agreement to lowest agreement): 1) Code-Entry-Challenge, 2) Code-Snippet Challenge, 3) Single-Choice Question, 4) Multiple-Choice Question and 5) Text-Entry Challenge. Although CSC and CEC have the same average agreement level, CSC has a higher standard deviation (i.e., higher uncertainty) than CEC; therefore, we have placed CEC in first place in the rank.

When the participants were asked about ideas for additional challenge types, 80% had *no new idea*, 15% answered yes, *they had an additional idea* and 5% had *no opinion*. The additional collected ideas were the following: a) *"something dynamic and fun"*, b) *"associating left and right lists"* (ASL) and c) *"modify code that has one vulnerability"*. The contribution (a) and (c) could not be mapped into an existing challenge type, nor could a new challenge type be discerned. However, (b) resulted in a new challenge type.

The participants were also asked what could be added to the existing challenges. The following additional points were collected with this question:

- Provide explanation at the end of the challenge, together with the flag
- Add explanations on multi-stage challenges
- Ask which coding guideline is not being followed in a code snippet
- Randomize the answers and randomize of the solutions
- Do not forget about the fun aspect when designing the challenge

These additional points were also used to improve the final challenge structure, as shown in the next sub-section.

4.4   Final Challenge Structure

The final challenge structure (CS) contains three phases consisting of four stages: *introduction* (phase 1), *challenge* and *logic* (phase 2) and *conclusion* (phase 3), as shown in Fig. 2. In the *introduction* stage (phase 1), a topic related to secure coding is introduced, which is helpful to solve and frame the challenge (e.g., secure coding guideline or previously related cybersecurity incident). This optional stage and can include a single-choice or multiple-choice question before proceeding to the next phase. In the second phase, the *challenge* stage contains the main CT according to a given challenge type, as presented in Sect. 4.5. In this stage, several hints can be given to the player depending on several factors, e.g., time taken by the player to solve the challenge or the previous number of attempts to solve the challenge. The *logic* stage is responsible for evaluating the solution to the challenge provided by the player and determining if it is correct (acceptable) or wrong (not acceptable). According to the analysis of the answer provided by the player, points or penalties might be awarded.

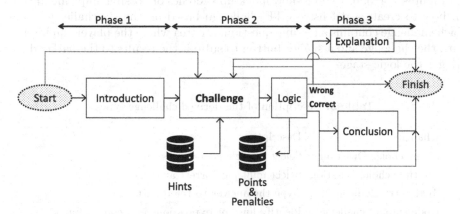

Fig. 2. Challenge structure

The third phase depends on the result of the logic stage. In case the player's answer was wrong, the following four options can occur: return to the challenge stage, give some explanation why the solution is wrong and return to the challenge stage, proceed to the finish or give an explanation why the solution is wrong and proceed to the finish. In case the player's solution was correct, the following two options can occur: give some concluding remarks (with an optional additional question) and then proceed to the finish or proceed to the finish. If a correct solution is achieved at the finish state, then a flag is presented to the player (according to the CTF rules). In the conclusion stage, additional useful information can be given to the player, e.g., an explanation of secure coding guidelines related to the challenge, the importance of the challenge in the industry context, for example, through lessons learned from past incidents or vulnerabilities.

4.5   Final Challenge Types

Table 3 shows the final six derived challenge types. In single-choice questions (SCQ), the participant is asked a question, and only one of the possible answers is the correct solution. In multiple-choice questions (MCQ), the correct solution must include more than one different answers. In text-entry questions (TEQ), the participant needs to type in the solution as text - this can be achieved, for example, by completing or writing a full sentence as the answer to the challenge. Code-snippet challenge (CSC) presents a piece of code to the participant and lets the participant select lines of code containing vulnerabilities or select changes to the code that would avoid vulnerabilities (i.e., respect SCG and SDBP). In code-entry challenges (CEC), the participant is given vulnerable code that needs to be changed or rewritten to eliminate the vulnerability by complying with SCG and SDBP. In associate left-right challenges, the participant needs to associate items in a list on the left to items in a list on the right.

Figures 3, 4, 5, 6, 7 and 8 show mock-up sketches of possible implementations on how to create a defensive CTF challenge based on the six challenge types. Each challenge contains a guiding question, an area where the player can interact with the challenge and a *submit* button to submit the results to the backend and trigger the logic stage.

Table 3. Description of the derived challenge types

Challenge type	Description
Single choice Question	Select a single correct answer
Multiple choice question	Select multiple correct answers
Text entry challenge	Type the answer to the question
Code snippet challenge	Identify lines or expressions in a code snippet
Code entry challenge	Write or adapt code to eliminate vulnerabilities
Associate left-right	Associate elements in left-list to those in right list

4.6   Observations

In this work, we designed defensive challenges for CTF events, which aim to raise secure coding awareness of software developers in the industry. Code-Entry Challenges were found to be among the most popular choice, while Text-Entry Questions among the least popular. Both the initial CS and the CT were updated as a result of the interviews with security experts. Interestingly, the informal discussions with the security experts did not result in CTs based on comics [3]. Another interesting observation is that all the security experts considered "simple" game types, i.e., no discussions took place on advanced challenge types based e.g., on Virtual Reality or Role-Playing-Games. This fact is likely related to the particular nature of the topic and deployment environment (industry). As such, challenge types that are more simple and traditional have been selected (e.g., Single-Choice Questions and Multiple-Choice Questions). One unexpected challenge type was the Code-Entry Challenge. Due to its complex nature, this type of challenge requires more investigation to understand how to create a challenge based on this type effectively.

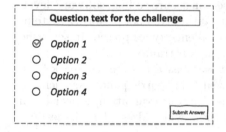

Fig. 3. Single-choice question

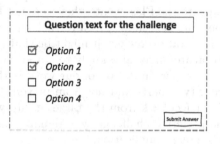

Fig. 4. Multiple-choice question

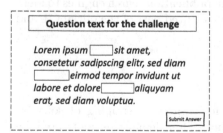

Fig. 5. Text-entry question

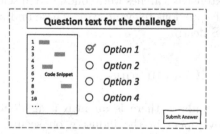

Fig. 6. Code-snippet question

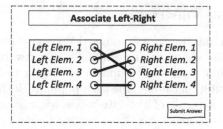

Fig. 7. Code-entry challenge   **Fig. 8.** Associate left-right

4.7   Threats to Validity

The work hereby presented is based on the knowledge and know-how obtained through interactive discussions and surveys from a group of 20 security experts from the industry. A possible threat to our conclusions is the limited number of participants and their company background.

Although the authors found previous work on defensive challenges for Capture-the-Flag events, they were not focused on secure coding, software developers, and the industry. Nevertheless, since the authors did not perform a systematic literature review, it might be that some challenge types present in scientific literature might also apply to our situation and constraints.

Another limitation of our work is that it was based only on feedback from security experts and not from players, i.e., real CTF participants. As such, no direct feedback from the target group was used in our evaluation, especially in the preferred challenge type ranking. The authors will address these issues in a subsequent publication.

Although the present work follows survey methodology and semi-structured interviews best practices, it lacks a systematic and academic approach. The reason for this is that the study was conducted in an industrial setting. However, extensive searches were conducted in scientific publication search engines to identify previous relevant work. These findings constituted part of the initial CT and CS design.

5   Conclusions

Nowadays, there is an increasing demand for awareness training of software developers in the industry on secure coding. This demand is motivated by requirements from quality standards and security standards. One promising new method to raise security awareness is the usage of Capture-the-Flag events. However, these events need to be specially designed in order to address the target audience and its requirements - software developers in the industry.

Recently the requirements that are needed for designing these games in an industrial setting have been investigated [10]. However, the authors of this previous work did not provide details on the challenge types but rather requirements on the overall game. The design of challenge types is not a trivial task, and poor quality challenges may result in inefficiencies (e.g., loss of productivity) that industrial companies are not willing to accept. Barela [3] et al. gives one such example, which has shown that challenge types based on comics, when deployed in CTF, might not be adequate for the event and its goals. Furthermore, the majority of the existing literature not only focuses on defensive challenges but also mostly addresses a target audience of security professionals, e.g., pen-testers.

In this work, we have addressed the design of defensive challenges for CTFs for the industry. We have derived a challenge structure and six different challenge types. Our work is based on semi-structured interviews with security experts and comprises a two-part survey and additional informal discussions. Our results show that security experts prefer *"traditional"* challenge types, based e.g., on Single-Choice and Multiple-Choice Questions. We have seen that the least preferred challenge type by security experts is the Text-Entry Challenges. Three additional challenge types have been discussed: Association Left-Right, Code-Entry Challenge, and Code-Snippet Challenge. The two latter types are well adapted to secure coding challenges since they use software code.

However, the unexpected new challenge type was the Code-Entry Challenge, where the player submits code to the backend, which decides if the challenge is correctly solved. A topic that needs additional investigation is the details on how to create such a challenge type. The results presented in this publication have been derived solely based on feedback from interviews with security experts. Further work is required to validate the derived challenge structure and challenge types in real CTF events in an industrial setting. In particular, the authors intend to give concrete examples of the implementation of the different derived challenge types in an upcoming publication. This further work will allow to refine further the challenge structure and challenge types based on the feedback from the CTF players themselves.

Acknowledgement. This work is financed by portuguese national funds through FCT - Fundação para a Ciência e Tecnologia, I.P., under the project FCT UIDB/04466/2020. Furthermore, the third author thanks the Instituto Universitário de Lisboa and ISTAR-IUL, for their support.

References

1. Acar, Y., Stransky, C., Wermke, D., Weir, C., Mazurek, M.L., Fahl, S.: Developers need support, too: a survey of security advice for software developers. In: 2017 IEEE Cybersecurity Development (SecDev), pp. 22–26. IEEE, September 2017
2. Aoyama, T., Nakano, T., Koshijima, I., Hashimoto, Y., Watanabe, K.: On the complexity of cybersecurity exercises proportional to preparedness. J. Disaster Res. **12**(5), 1081–1090 (2017)
3. Barela, J., Gasiba, E.T., Suppan, S., Berges, M., Beckers, K.: When interactive graphic storytelling fails. In: 2019 IEEE 27th International Requirements Engineering Conference Workshops (REW), pp. 164–169. IEEE, September 2019

4. Beuran, R., Chinen, K.I., Tan, Y., Shinoda, Y.: Towards effective cybersecurity education and training. Research report. School of Information Science, Graduate School of Advanced Science and Technology, Japan Advanced Institute of Science and Technology. IS-RR-2016, April 2016, pp. 1–16 (2016)
5. Carnegie Mellon University: SEI-CERT coding standards. https://wiki.sei.cmu.edu/confluence/display/seccode
6. Chung, K., Cohen, J.: Learning obstacles in the capture the flag model. In: 2014 USENIX Summit on Gaming, Games, and Gamification in Security Education (3GSE 2014). USENIX Association, San Diego (2014)
7. CTFtime team: CTFTime - all about CTF. https://ctftime.org
8. Davis, A., Leek, T., Zhivich, M., Gwinnup, K., Leonard, W.: The fun and future of CTF. In: 2014 USENIX Summit on Gaming, Games, and Gamification in Security Education (3GSE 2014). USENIX Association, San Diego (2014)
9. Dörner, R., Göbel, S., Effelsberg, W., Wiemeyer, J.: Serious Games: Foundations, Concepts and Practice, 1st edn. Springer, Cham (2016). https://doi.org/10.1007/978-3-319-40612-1
10. Gasiba, T., Beckers, K., Suppan, S., Rezabek, F.: On the requirements for serious games geared towards software developers in the industry. In: Damian, D.E., Perini, A., Lee, S. (eds.) 27th IEEE International Requirements Engineering Conference, RE 2019, Jeju Island, Korea (South), 23–27 September 2019. IEEE (2019)
11. Graziotin, D., Fagerholm, F., Wang, X., Abrahamsson, P.: What happens when software developers are (un)happy. J. Syst. Softw. **140**, 32–47 (2018)
12. Groves, R.M., Fowler, F., Couper, M., Lepkowski, J., Singer, E.: Survey Methodology, 2nd edn. Wiley, Hoboken (2009)
13. Gonzalez, H., Llamas, R., Ordaz, F.: Cybersecurity teaching through gamification: aligning training resources to our syllabus. Res. Comput. Sci. **146**, 35–43 (2017). https://doi.org/10.13053/rcs-146-1-4
14. Hänsch, N., Zinaida, B.: Specifying IT security awareness. In: 25th International Workshop on Database and Expert Systems Applications, Munich, Germany, pp. 326–330, September 2014
15. IEC 62443-4-1: Security for industrial automation and control systems - part 4-1: secure product development lifecycle requirements. Standard, International Electrotechnical Commission, January 2018
16. ISO: ISO 250xx Series. Standard, International Organization for Standardization, Geneva, CH (2005). http://iso25000.com/index.php/en/iso-25000-standards
17. ISO 27002: Information technology - security techniques - code of practice for information security controls. Standard, International Organization for Standardization, Geneva, CH, October 2013
18. Krosnick, J.A.: Questionnaire design. In: Vannette, D.L., Krosnick, J.A. (eds.) The Palgrave Handbook of Survey Research, pp. 439–455. Springer, Cham (2018). https://doi.org/10.1007/978-3-319-54395-6_53
19. Mirkovic, J., Peterson, P.: Class capture-the-flag exercises. In: 2014 USENIX Summit on Gaming, Games, and Gamification in Security Education (3GSE 2014) (2014)
20. Nance, K., Hay, B., Bishop, M.: Secure coding education: are we making progress? In: 16th Colloquium for Information Systems Security Education, pp. 83–88, June 2012
21. OWASP Top 10. https://www.owasp.org/images/7/72/OWASP_Top_10-2017_(en).pdf. Accessed June 2019

22. Oyetoyan, T.D., Milosheska, B., Grini, M., Soares Cruzes, D.: Myths and facts about static application security testing tools: an action research at telenor digital. In: Garbajosa, J., Wang, X., Aguiar, A. (eds.) XP 2018. LNBIP, vol. 314, pp. 86–103. Springer, Cham (2018). https://doi.org/10.1007/978-3-319-91602-6_6
23. Patel, S.: 2019 global developer report: DevSecOps finds security roadblocks divide teams, July 2020. https://about.gitlab.com/blog/2019/07/15/global-developer-report/. Accessed 15 July 2019
24. Rodriguez, M., Piattini, M., Ebert, C.: Software verification and validation technologies and tools. IEEE Softw. 36(2), 13–24 (2019)
25. SAFECode charter members: SAFECode - software assurance forum for excellence in code. https://safecode.org
26. Schneier, B.: Software developers and security, July 2020. https://www.schneier.com/blog/archives/2019/07/software_develo.html. Accessed 25 July 2019
27. Schonlau, M., Couper, M.: Semi-automated categorization of open-ended questions. Surv. Res. Methods 10(2), 143–152 (2016). https://ojs.ub.uni-konstanz.de/srm/article/view/6213
28. Seaman, C.: Qualitative methods in empirical studies of software engineering. IEEE Trans. Softw. Eng. 25(4), 557–572 (1999)
29. Smith, C.: Content analysis and narrative analysis. In: Handbook of Research Methods in Social and Personality Psychology, pp. 313–335 (2000)
30. Tews, M.J., Noe, R.A.: Does training have to be fun? A review and conceptual model of the role of fun in workplace training. Hum. Resour. Manag. Rev. 29(2), 226–238 (2019)
31. Whiting, L.: Semi-structured interviews: guidance for novice researchers. Nurs. Stand. 22, 35–40 (2008)
32. Woody, C., Ellison, R., Nichols, W.: Predicting cybersecurity using quality data. In: 2015 IEEE International Symposium on Technologies for Homeland Security (HST), pp. 1–5. IEEE (2015)
33. Yang, X.L., Lo, D., Xia, X., Wan, Z.Y., Sun, J.L.: What security questions do developers ask? A large-scale study of stack overflow posts. J. Comput. Sci. Technol. 31(5), 910–924 (2016)

Q-Scrum: A Framework for Quality in Safety-Critical Development

Johnny Cardoso Marques[✉][iD], Adilson Marques da Cunha[iD],
and Luiz Alberto Vieira Dias[iD]

Aeronautics Institute of Technology, São José dos Campos, São Paulo, Brazil
{johnny,cunha,vdias}@ita.br
http://www.comp.ita.br

Abstract. This paper describes an adapted Scrum framework applied to a successful academic experience, using Interdisciplinary Problem Based Learning (IPBL) to conceptualize, model, and develop safety-critical prototypes. It presents an adapted version of the Scrum agile method used to develop a safety-critical project, achieving compliance with software standards. It also reports the development of some academic projects using IPBL and involving students from four different courses yearly offered by the Aeronautics Institute of Technology. At the end of each year, a prototype was developed and presented by the students.

Keywords: Scrum · Safety-critical prototype · Quality · Agile · Compliance

1 Introduction

Many organizations have adopted Agile as a practice to deliver high-quality product releases with high value to the market [8,11]. While it is crucial to focus on the mechanics of Agile disciplines internally, it is also important to define what quality is, how customers view quality, and how it actually impacts customer satisfaction and loyalty in such a way that it brings additional business opportunities and enhances revenue [9]. Education involving agile development and software quality is desired.

This paper describes an adapted Scrum framework applied to a successful academic experience, using Interdisciplinary Problem Based Learning (IPBL) to conceptualize, model, and develop safety-critical prototypes. We have been applying our framework in projects developed, since 2013, at the Aeronautics Institute of Technology (*Instituto Tecnológico de Aeronáutica* - ITA).

Our projects involve undergraduate and graduate students from the following courses: CES-65 - Embedded Systems Project; CE-230 - Software Quality, Reliability, and Safety; CE-235 - Real-time Embedded Systems Project; and CE-237 - Advanced Topics on Software Testing. In summary, CES-65 and CE-235 courses tackle: the use of Software Engineering technologies, such as Integrated

M. Shepperd et al. (Eds.): QUATIC 2020, CCIS 1266, pp. 238–245, 2020.
https://doi.org/10.1007/978-3-030-58793-2_19

Computer-Aided Software Engineering Environment (I-CASE-E) tools; requirements specification, analysis, and design; and also the implementation of methods, tools, and techniques for real-time systems. The CE-230 course tackles: standards for software development; reviews, inspections, and audits; and also measurements and models of software reliability. Finally, the CE-237 tackles: innovations in the software testing process; agile testing; and also Test-Driven Development (TDD), and several types of black-box and white-box testing.

A safety-critical system is characterized by attributes such as functionality, reliability, safety, usability, effectiveness, interoperability, testability, maintainability, and portability. We offered to our students the opportunity to address all these attributes, using an Interdisciplinary Problem Based Learning (IPBL).

At the end of 17 weeks of the 2nd Semester of each year, a unique developed project prototype is presented by all students, as their final examinations, to Professors and also to some invited local Research and Development and Industrial community representatives. We use the IPBL as a student-centered pedagogy approach in which students learn about a subject through the experience of solving an open-ended problem, involving multiple disciplines. During their project execution, students conceptualize, model, and develop safety-critical prototypes within these 17 weeks.

Basically, our IPBL approach involves: just one **Problem Assigned** described in a Vision artifact; a minimum, necessary, and sufficient set of documentation artifact templates for three sprints development of **Needs**; and also an assigned mission accomplishment template artifact to be presented by all students, as part of their final examination and also to be delivered as a value prototype for the **Solution** of the problem previously assigned, as presented in Fig. 1.

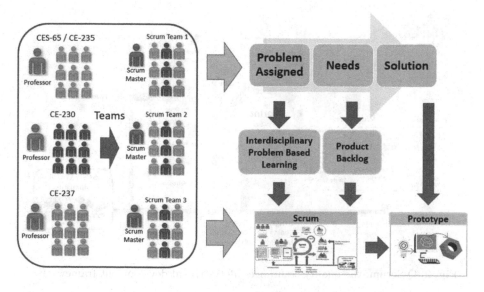

Fig. 1. The organization of Scrum Teams using Scrum to generate a prototype

2   Q-Scrum Framework

In the beginning of each Semester, Professors present the adapted version of Scrum named Q-Scrum and meaning Quality-Scrum, as a modified framework from the original Scrum proposed by Schwaber [10]. Other adaptations of Scrum are available [4,6]. This adaptation involves the organization using the same processes available in Software Standards (Requirements, Design, Modeling, Testing, Configuration Management, Quality Assurance, and Validation). By training students in our framework, we have been able to use the Scrum agile method, combine development with discipline, and achieve compliance with software standards.

Our prototype is divided into embedded system components. Each embedded system component is developed by different Scrum Teams (ST). Each ST is composed of 1 Student acting as Scrum Master (SM) and at most 8 Students acting as ST Members from the 4 different courses, as also presented in Fig. 1.

All students are assigned to develop User Stories. However, students from different courses have specific roles: the CES-65 and CE-235 students are assigned to design, model and implement solutions with the ANSYS Esterel SCADE [1]; the CE-230 students are assigned to conduct Walk-Throughs (WT) and Audits; and the CE-237 students are assigned to specify, create and execute Test Cases for User Stories.

At the beginning of each sprint, a Sprint Planning Meeting takes place. The Product Owner and the Scrum Team review the Product Backlog, discuss goals and the context of items. Each Scrum Team selects items from the Product Backlog to commit and complete by the end of each sprint. Figure 2 presents the Q-Scrum, as a Quality Assurance Safety-Critical Development Framework.

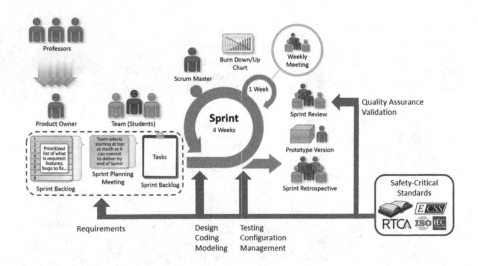

Fig. 2. Q-Scrum: the quality assurance safety-critical development framework

2.1 Sprints

The 17 weeks have 4 Sprints of 4 weeks plus 1 week for the Final Project Presentation. The Week 1 of each Sprint is dedicated to the Sprint Planning, for analyzing User Stories and creating their associated tasks. It is here, on the Week 1 that the Design and Modeling of each User Story also begins. The Week 2 continues with the Design and Modeling and, it is at the end of this week that Students perform the Walk-Through 1 (WT1). The Week 3 is dedicated to Tests and the Walk-Through 2 (WT2) is performed at its end. On the Week 4, the Sprint is finished and Students conduct Sprint Review, Retrospective, and Audit. They also deliver incremental new releases of Prototypes at the end of each Sprint. Figure 3 presents phases used during a typical sprint cycle of the Q-Scrum.

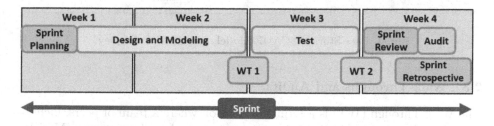

Fig. 3. A typical sprint cycle of the Q-Scrum and its phases.

2.2 User Stories and Model-Based Development

User Stories (US) are mapped from requirements, making it possible to estimate efforts to implement them, in a simple and direct way. Professors are the Product Owners (PO) and fulfill with students the Product Backlog artifact with System and Software Requirements that later on could be mapped to User Stories, following a specific format, adapted from [3]. User Stories contain behavioral descriptions or properties comprised of: (i) Performance aspects; (ii) Functionalities; (iii) External interfaces; and (iv) Limits, ranges, and data.

The Safety-Critical Application Development Environment (SCADE) from ANSYS is a Model-Based Systems Engineering (MBSE) environment dedicated to implement Safety-Critical Systems [1]. Previous works from the authors have explored the Model-Based Development in some aviation projects using SCADE [5,7]. The SCADE empowers users with a model-based development environment for critical embedded software. The SCADE Display empowers users with versatile graphics design and development environment for embedded Human Machine Interfaces (HMI), as presented in Fig. 4.

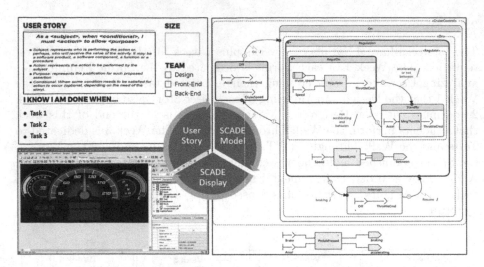

Fig. 4. User Stories, SCADE Model, and SCADE Display

2.3   Walk-Throughs and Audits

The Walk-Through (WT) is a formal evaluation where a team of peers, including the author, meets to examine work products such as User Stories, Models, or Tests. As presented in Fig. 5a, the Walk-Through 1 (WT1) focuses in the verification of User Stories and Models. It is executed at the end of Week 2. Professors request Scrum Teams to create their WT1 Checklists. Each WT1 checklist must achieve at least the following objectives: (i) Verify if User Stories are clear, testable, and non-ambiguous; (ii) Verify if Tasks are defined for each User Story; (iii) Ensure that all Tasks, when executed, accomplish User Stories; (iv) Ensure Models accomplish User Stories; and (v) Ensure that traceability between User Stories and Models is established and correct.

As presented in Fig. 5b, the Walk-Through 2 (WT2) focuses in the verification of Tests and is executed at the end of Week 3. Professors request Scrum Teams to create their WT2 checklists. Each WT2 checklist must achieve at least the following objectives: (i) Verify that Test Procedures were created and completely exercised each User Story; and (ii) Verify that Test Results are correct.

An Audit is a formal evaluation of processes and their outputs and evaluates consistency among work products. Audits are always conducted during the Week 4. Students must create an Audit checklist, to accomplish the following objectives: (i) Verify that Sprint Reviews are properly conducted; (ii) Identify and exercise some samples of the prototype, ensuring that User Stories, Models, and Tests are correct; (iii) Ensure Issues identified in WT1 and WT2 were corrected; (iv) Register additional Issues; and (v) Verify the compliance with applicable Software Standard.

Professors request Students to perform Audits, using the flowchart presented in Fig. 6. The CE-230 students collect artifacts (Step 1). The Audit is conducted

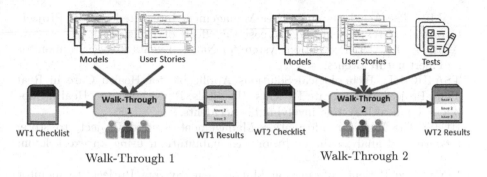

Fig. 5. Walk-Throughs (WT) of Q-Scrum

by using the created Audit Checklist (Step 2). Then, Issues are identified and requested for correction (Step 3). Finally, the CE-230 Students Confirm the Correction (Step 4).

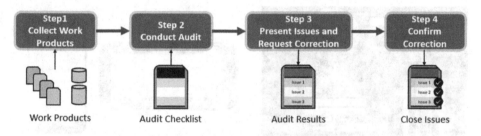

Fig. 6. Audit flow in a typical sprint cycle of the Q-Scrum

The IPBLs are always applied to safety-critical projects. Thus, Professors use applicable software standards for each environment: RTCA DO-178C (Aviation), ECSS-E-ST-40C (Space), and IEC 62304 (Medical).

3   Projects Using Q-SCRUM

Since 2013, we have been applying the IPBL and the Q-Scrum Agile in the development of 7 academic Safety-Critical Software prototypes (Fig. 7) involving the different environments of Aviation, Emergency, Medical, and Space in the following academic projects:

- ARTES: An Avionics Real-Time Embedded System Project, involving a Cockpit Display Systems (CDS) to control an Unmanned Aircraft Vehicle (UAV);
- BAMLIS: The Brazilian Academic Micro-satellite Launching Integrated System Project, involving an interdisciplinary academic project for spatial critical embedded system agile development [2];

- ACMIS: The Accidents and Crises Management Integrated System Project, to provide alert, prevent and decrease the effects of a crisis [12];
- APRES: The Alert Prevention System for Nature Events Project, to monitor and alert nature events;
- TSA4HC-RT: Technological Solutions Applicable for Health Care in Real Time Project, to integrate Patients, Hospitals, Physicians, and Health Suppliers in a health system involving big accidents;
- HIMS: The Hospital Information Management System Project, to store, retrieve, and analyze the evolution of rehabilitation, using an exoskeleton; and
- PIMS: The Patient Information Management System Project, to monitor wheelchair patients to perform daily activities.

Figure 7a presents an example of one Cockpit Display System (CDS) designed from the first academic project developed using the Q-Scrum (ARTES) and Fig. 7b presents examples of two Mobile CDS from the fourth academic project developed using the Q-Scrum (APRES).

CDS from ARTES Project

Mobile CDSs from APRES Project

Fig. 7. CDS examples

4   Conclusion

This paper described some successful experiences using Interdisciplinary Problem Based Learning (IPBL), to conceptualize, model, and develop safety-critical prototypes, using a Scrum framework adapted from Schwaber [10] and named Q-Scrum in the Brazilian Aeronautics Institute of Technology (*Instituto Tecnológico de Aeronáutica* - ITA).

On the past 7 years using the Q-Scrum academic framework, Professors were able to apply and get successful experiences with the Q-Scrum development and integration within 4 different courses, teaching how to apply quality assurance in safety-critical developments.

As a natural consequence of these academic in-classes experiments the following innovative approaches and contributions were accomplished:

- Application of agility, keeping the compliance with software standards;
- Use of Model-Based Development with the ANSYS Esterel SCADE;
- Creation of several checklists, supporting Walk-Throughs and audits;
- Cooperation in software quality education; and
- Use of multiple environments and standard driven-education.

Acknowledgements. The authors thank to: (i) the Aeronautics Institute of Technology (*Instituto Tecnológico de Aeronáutica* - ITA) for providing the motivation in R&D environment; and (ii) ANSYS Esterel for providing the SCADE to support these academic successful development experiences.

References

1. ANSYS: Embedded software. Electronic (2020). https://www.ansys.com/products/embedded-software
2. Goncalves, G.S., et al.: An interdisciplinary academic project for spatial critical embedded system agile development. In: 2015 IEEE/AIAA 34th Digital Avionics Systems Conference (DASC) (2015)
3. Leffingwell, D.: Agile Software Requirements, Lean Requirements Practices for Teams Programs and the Enterprise. Addison-Wesley, Boston (2011)
4. Marques, J., Cunha, A.: A reference method for airborne software requirements. In: 2013 IEEE/AIAA 32nd Digital Avionics Systems Conference (DASC) (2013)
5. Marques, J., da Cunha, A.M.: Tailoring traditional software life cycles to ensure compliance of rtca do-178c and do-331 with model-driven design. In: 2018 IEEE/AIAA 37th Digital Avionics Systems Conference (DASC) (2018)
6. Marques, J., Yelisetty, S.M.H., Cunha, A.M.D., Dias, L.A.V.: CARD-RM: a reference model for airborne software. In: 2013 10th International Conference on Information Technology: New Generations (2013)
7. Marques, J.C., Yelisetty, S.M.H., Dias, L.A.V., da Cunha, A.M.: Using model-based development as software low-level requirements to achieve airborne software certification. In: 2012 Ninth International Conference on Information Technology-New Generations (2012)
8. Merkow, M.: Secure, Resilient, and Agile Software Development. Auerbach Publications, Boca Raton (2019)
9. Nader-Rezvani, N.: An Executive's Guide to Software Quality in an Agile Organization: A Continuous Improvement Journey. Apress, New York (2018)
10. Schwaber, K.: Agile Project Management with Scrum. Microsoft Press, Redmond (2004)
11. Shah, S.H.: Quality Assurance in Agile Methodology. Grin Verlag, Munich (2018)
12. Siles, L.S., et al.: An integrated academic system prototype using accidents and crises management as PBL. In: Latifi, S. (ed.) Information Technology - New Generations. AISC, vol. 558, pp. 419–427. Springer, Cham (2018). https://doi.org/10.1007/978-3-319-54978-1_55

Quality Aspects in Quantum Computing

Reverse Engineering of Quantum Programs Toward KDM Models

Luis Jiménez-Navajas(✉) ⓘ, Ricardo Pérez-Castillo(✉) ⓘ, and Mario Piattini ⓘ

University of Castilla-La Mancha, 13071 Ciudad Real, Spain
{luis.jimeneznavajas,ricardo.pdelcastillo,
mario.piattini}@uclm.es

Abstract. The interest on quantum computing has grown dramatically due to its incomparable computation power and many promising applications. This new computing paradigm influences the way on how future information systems will be built. Legacy, classical systems cannot be simply replaced with quantum software by several reasons. First, legacy systems usually embed a lot of mission-critical knowledge over time, making its replacing too risky. Second, some business processes do not make sense to be supported through quantum computing because it supposes unnecessary expenses. This signifies that organizations need to adapt their classical information systems alongside new specific quantum applications, evolving toward hybrid information systems. Unfortunately, there are not specific methods for dealing with this challenge. We believe reengineering, and more specifically software modernization using model-driven engineering principles, could be useful for migrating classical systems toward hybrid ones. In particular, this paper presents a reverse engineering technique that analyses quantum software information from Q# code and generates more abstract models. These models are generated according to the Knowledge Discovery Metamodel (KDM) standard. The main implication is that through the usage of KDM the reengineering toward hybrid systems can be accomplished in an independent way regarding the specific quantum technology.

Keywords: Reengineering · Reverse engineering · Quantum computing · KDM · Q#

1 Introduction

In the history of software engineering, several methodologies, paradigms, frameworks and technologies have emerged, which changed the way of how software is developed. Nevertheless, the background of software programming has been almost the same, i.e., this is based in the Boolean algebra as one abstraction of the classical binary computers [1].

Quantum computing is a new computing paradigm with some new technology behind this. It applies phenomena of quantum physics to computing, such as superposition and entanglement. Furthermore, bits evolve into a new concept, the quantum bit or qubit.

© Springer Nature Switzerland AG 2020
M. Shepperd et al. (Eds.): QUATIC 2020, CCIS 1266, pp. 249–262, 2020.
https://doi.org/10.1007/978-3-030-58793-2_20

These changes allow us to get an exponential growth in computational power that are higher than the speed of the fastest supercomputer in the world.

As long as this new technology matures, organizations must face the modernization of their enterprise information systems, taking advantage of the benefits that quantum computing brings. This does not necessary mean to fully discard the classical information systems, because some of the supported business processes will not be probably supported through quantum computing. The same happens with the information systems that embedded a vast amount of mission-critical knowledge during their evolution. That knowledge is not present, probably, anywhere else. Thereby, the replacement of those legacy, classical information systems becomes too risky. As a consequence, we believe it is expected to find companies using classical-quantum information systems, which we have denominated hybrid information systems. These systems consist of a master classical system that make requests to quantum computers (typically in the cloud) to compute specific quantum algorithms. However, the evolution from classical systems into hybrid has not been treated before and there are no methods for dealing with this problem.

We propose a solution based on reengineering and more specifically on Architecture-Driven Modernization [2], which is the evolution of traditional reengineering that follows Model-Driven Engineering (MDE) approach. ADM advocates the usage of KDM [3] to accomplish such modernization. Software modernization can first analyse the software artefacts and their interrelationships in legacy systems, and it builds one or more representations of the legacy system according to KDM. The abstraction achieved through KDM ensures the interoperability between reverse engineering tools and other software modernization tools.

In particular, this paper focuses on the reverse engineering phase of the reengineering process. The main contribution is a reverse engineering technique to analyse quantum information (Q# code) and generates abstract models using KDM. For this solution, a quantum parser has first been built, which analyses the Q# files and constructs the corresponding abstract syntax tree (AST). Then, all the components and artefacts that have been recognized are mapped and represented into the KDM model. That is achieved through a KDM generator we have designed and built specifically for quantum code.

The main implication of this proposal is its contribution to the future and necessary reengineering of classical-quantum information systems, and the way on how the systems will evolve through years. Thereby, we believe the proposed reverse engineering technique, and particularly the whole reengineering process, will take a huge financial worth.

The remaining of the paper is structured as follows: Sect. 2 explains the state of art of quantum computing and reengineering. Then, Sect. 3 introduces Quantum Software Reengineering where the proposed technique is framed. After that, Sect. 4 details our proposal alongside its two main components, the Q# Parser and the KDM Generator. In Sect. 5 a supporting tool and some implementation details are provided. Finally, Sect. 6 draws the conclusion of this research.

2 State of the Art

2.1 Quantum Computing

Quantum computing started in the eighties when Paul Benioff proposed a quantum mechanical model of the Turing machine [4]. Some years later, the physicists Richard Feynman [5] and Yuri Manin [6] discovered the potential of how a quantum computer can simulate and process than a classical computer cannot. After a few years, the mathematician Peter Shor, developed an algorithm for quantum computers which factors integers, this means that by means of quantum computing, RSA-encrypted communications could be decrypted [7].

This new computing paradigm is the result of applying quantum mechanics to computing science. It changes the traditional bits, the smaller unit of information, with qubit. A qubit is usually represented with the electron spin or photons among other particles. A qubit is a multiple status quantum system (not only defined by zero and one as a classical bit) where there exist infinite possible values, as a sphere (see Fig. 1). This means that a qubit state might be zero and one at the same time. This phenomenon is known as superposition [8]. Superposition is the keystone of the exponential computational power; n qubits are represented by a superposition state vector in 2^n.

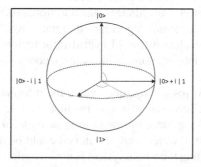

Fig. 1. Representation of a qubit based on the model of Felix Bloch [9].

The way of working with qubits it is through quantum circuits and quantum gates. Quantum circuits are collections of quantum gates interconnected by quantum wires [10], where qubit's states change consequently of those quantum gates, which, some of them, are internally composed of other quantum circuits but a lower level of abstraction and still using quantum mechanics phenomena; like classical logical gates where, for example, NAND gates are built internally with "AND" and "NOT" gates For example, the Hadamard gate is typically used for initializing the qubits, that is, force the qubit to have the same probabilities of being zero and one, in other terms, change the qubit's state into superposition. Other example of quantum gate is CNOT, which acts on two qubits making a comparison between them and changing the status of one qubit depending on the other's one.

Likewise happened in sixties with the space race, nowadays there is a similar race to get quantum supremacy. This race's goal is to demonstrate that quantum computing can solve a problem that a classical computer cannot [11]. Among many other, the head-to-head competitors of this race are IBM and Google. In fact, Google recently announced that has already achieved the quantum supremacy with a 54-qubit computer [12].

Together with the quantum computers, various quantum programming languages have been developed such as Q# or QASM among others. These programming languages include abstractions for building quantum gates and other quantum operations [13]. Most of these programming languages are open-source and can be used by anyone interested. On the one hand, having these open-source languages encourages the people to contribute on the global knowledge, developing algorithms and new theories. On the other hand, there are not guides of good practices to develop quantum code. There are not guidelines of how quality quantum software must be developed. To alleviate this problem the Talavera Manifesto for Quantum Software Engineering and Programming [14] proposes good practices for the correct development of quantum software.

2.2 Traditional Reengineering

In a near future, organizations will develop hybrid information systems that combines traditional information systems and quantum ones. The traditional will make all those processes and procedures that do not make sense to implement in quantum computing due to its complexity and price since these processed do not really take advantage of the huge computational power. Nevertheless, this traditional software might call to other operations implemented as quantum algorithms that run in remote quantum computers. Thus, to accomplish the evolution toward hybrid information systems, reengineering practices must be brought into the domain of quantum computing, which will deal with the mentioned challenges.

All the technology evolves among time and so the information systems. This evolution can have negative effects on those systems that were developed in the past, like degradation or aging, making those information systems *legacy* information systems, which means that the code in which were developed could be technologically obsolete [15]. Nevertheless, discarding the whole system is not an option if the target information systems must preserve business knowledge embedded in legacy ones. Reengineering allows the preservation of the business knowledge, making possible to carry out evolutionary maintenance of the legacy systems assuming low risks and low costs [16]. The three stages of reengineering process [17] are:

1. Reverse engineering: the system is analysed to identify its components and interrelationships and create representations of the system in another form or at a higher level of abstraction.
2. Restructuring: the transformation from one representation form to another at the same relative abstraction level, while preserving the subject system's external behaviour (functionality and semantics).
3. Forward engineering: the final stage consists of the renovation and reclamation, is the examination and alteration of a subject system to reconstitute it in a new form and the subsequent implementation of the form.

The overall reengineering task is presented as a "horseshoe" model [18], where the reengineering phase consists of the recovery of the architecture through source code artifacts. Then, in the restructuring phase, the generated architecture on the previous phase is reengineered to become the desired one, which can be modified to integrate new requirements. Finally, forward reengineering works on the instantiation of the new architecture.

The Architecture-driven Modernization (ADM) [19] consists of the use of tools that facilitate the analysis, refactoring and transformation of existing system towards a modernization for supporting new requirements, migration of systems or even their interoperability. To accomplish this, ADM makes use of reengineering and Model-driven engineering (MDE) [20], where software development's approach is done through defined abstract models.

3   Quantum Software Reengineering

The specific reverse engineering proposal presented in this paper is framed in a long-term research roadmap, a whole reengineering process for quantum software. We believe the quantum software reengineering is necessary to deal with today's and tomorrow's hybrid information systems.

We argue that reengineering and, in general, software modernization (its evolution adding an MDE approach) can be used to deal with challenges associated with hybrid information systems. Therefore, quantum software reengineering might be used in three complementary scenarios (see Fig. 2):

1. Migrate existing, isolated quantum algorithms and integrate them into the hybrid information systems.
2. Migrate classical legacy information systems toward hybrid architectures that support the integration of classical-quantum information systems.
3. Transform or add new business operations supported by quantum software that will be integrated into the target hybrid systems.

Figure 2 shows the overall quantum reengineering process. We propose a software modernization based on existing standards such as UML and KDM. The first stage is reverse engineering (which is the scope of this paper) and consist of analysing existing information systems artefacts such as the source code, database schemas, etc. It could analyse classical systems (scenario 1) plus quantum programs if these exist (scenario 2). The output of the reverse engineering phase is a set of KDM models that comprise a KDM repository. As we explained, this KDM repository represents, in a technology-agnostic way, all the different perspectives and concerns of the legacy information systems in a holistic way. In this way, previous knowledge and business rules might be preserved, and the impact of the integration of quantum programs is reduced. KDM is not specifically designed to work with qubits, which implies that KDM must be extended (through their ordinary extensions mechanisms) to support the representation of quantum software aspects.

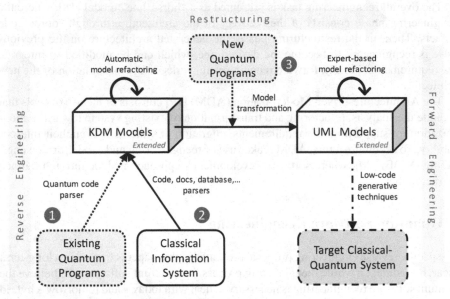

Fig. 2. Quantum reengineering process

The second stage is restructuring (see Fig. 2). KDM models are then (semi)automatically transformed into high-abstraction level models representing analysis and design aspects of the target hybrid systems. To achieve this, the metamodel employed in this case might be UML. Similar to the KDM extension, UML should be extended to support the new systems' analysis and design elements concerning quantum computing. In this point, software engineers can use this UML extension to manually model quantum aspects for new, target systems (scenario 3) which are integrated with the existing elements previously gathered by reverse engineering.

Finally, the forward engineering phase (see Fig. 2) consists of a set of techniques that are able to generate many parts of the source code for the target hybrid systems. Today, there exist many well-proven generators for different classical programming languages to produce code from UML models. However, there is no generators for quantum programming languages from high abstraction models. In our concern, this must be provided and integrated with other existing generative techniques. Both, restructuring and forward engineering are outside of the scope of this paper.

4   Reverse Engineering of Q# Programs

This section explains in detail the main contribution of this paper, the reverse engineering of quantum programs and, in particular, for Q# programming language. This proposal is framed in the reverse engineering stage of the overall quantum software reengineering process presented in previous section. This reverse engineering techniques is specifically focused on the scenario 1 (see Fig. 2).

There are several frameworks for developing quantum software which offer different options for the same purpose. Many of them allow to create quantum algorithms or programs without coding, i.e., in a graphical way, just with a quantum circuit composer, like IBM Quantum Experience [21], where you can use a real quantum computer for executing the quantum algorithms that you develop. For our purpose, all these are outside of the scope of this proposal, because no code is directly available. We need the source code for analysing the syntax and derive the AST.

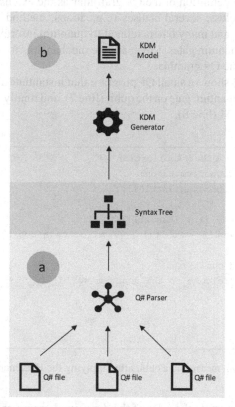

Fig. 3. Reverse engineering in Q# programming language.

Our proposed reverse engineering technique can be seen on Fig. 3 which is divided into two modules. First, a Q# parser takes and analyses Q# files. The parser considers a grammar for Q# to recognize Q# elements and build the respective AST. Second, KDM generator takes such ASTs to generate a common KDM model. It considers some mappings between Q# elements (as defined in AST) and KDM-compliant elements. This proposal could be extended with additional parser for other programming languages by changing the grammar-based rules of the parser. Same happens with the output of the proposal and if there is any interest of swapping into other metamodel rather than KDM, like for example UML, the code of the KDM Generator must be modified following the necessary rules.

4.1 Q# Parser

The Q# Parser is the one in charge of building the abstract syntax tree based on the Q# files that it receives. For achieving this it is necessary to define the grammar of the programming language under analysis. There are tools to build parser from grammars in an automatic manner. In this research the parser generator used is ANTLR [22], one of the most used in the industry.

It should be noticed that Q# was developed by considering C# as the syntax base. As a result, we started the definition of the Q# grammar as the extension of other existing C# grammar. Nevertheless, several clauses (e.g., loops, method definitions, etc.) are different regarding C#, and many others related to quantum information are genuine. In particular, the use of quantum gates, which are the mechanisms for working with qubits, need to be defined in the Q# grammar.

For example, Fig. 4 shows a small Q# program that instantiate a qubit (line 6), then it applies a Hadamard's quantum gate on the qubit (line 7), and finally the qubit is measured with the quantum gate M (line 8).

```
1  namespace Quantum.QSharpApplication1 {
2     open Microsoft.Quantum.Canon;
3     open Microsoft.Quantum.Intrinsic;
4
5     operation HelloQ () : (Result) {
6        using (var qubit = Qubit()){ // Allocate a qubit.
7           H(qubit);
8           let r = M(qubit);
9           Message("Welcome to the quantum world!");
10          return r;
11       }
12    }
13 }
```

Fig. 4. Q# program measuring a qubit after applying the Hadamard quantum gate.

Table 1 shows as example the rules of the developed grammar that are activated for the Q# program in Fig. 4. The whole grammar can be queried in the online material available at our GitHub repository. The definition of the whole parser must be staggered, where all the grammar of lowest level group for building higher levels until all the syntax is well defined. This way of defining all the syntax will set up the AST and following the examples of Table 1 and Fig. 4, the outgoing AST is presented in Fig. 5.

4.2 KDM Generator

The KDM Generator takes the AST generated from the Q# files and builds a KDM model. AST's nodes are considered by the KDM Generator and depending on the type of the node explored, the type of element on the KDM file is chosen and generated in the target model.

Table 1. Example of definition of quantum gates' lexicon and grammar.

LEXER
HADAMARD: 'H'; MEASURE: 'M';

PARSER
quantum_gates_one_op : HADAMARD I MEASURE ;
one_gate_op : quantum_gates_one_op OPEN_PARENS qubit_identifier CLOSE_PARENS ;
quantum_gate_op : one_gate_op I two_gate_op I three_gate_op ;

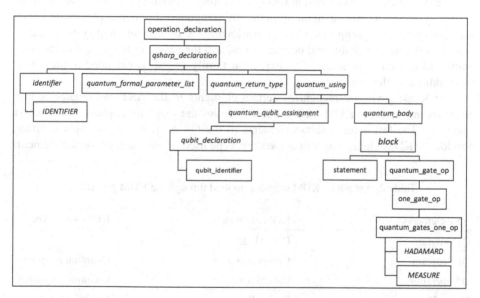

Fig. 5. Q# abstract syntax tree generated for the Q# code example.

All the AST elements which are important on the architecture of the program need to be specified on the KDM Generator, as well as the relations between those elements. The specification of those components on the outgoing KDM model, will be based on the KDM standard. Some elements in KDM are generic and are useful to represent elements for different programming languages. Hence, some elements must be annotated with specific stereotypes to provide specific semantic regarding quantum information.

KDM's approach do not define quantum entities, as quantum gates, variables which defined type are qubits or the way of how to measure them. As a result, we defined an extension family, the default extension mechanism provided by the KDM standard. All the components that exist in quantum programming language are thus represented in this extension family (see Fig. 6). The extension family groups a set of stereotypes that are then used in the ordinary elements provided by KDM.

```
<extensionFamily>
    <stereotype name="quantum programming language" />
    <stereotype name="quantum program" />
    <stereotype name="quantum operation" />
    <stereotype name="quantum gate" />
    <stereotype name="qubit" />
    <stereotype name="qubit measure" />
</extensionFamily>
```

Fig. 6. Extension family of KDM files for defining quantum entities.

The definition of this extension family will allow to extend previous classical information systems towards quantum programming languages by means of quantum software reengineering, going a step further to allowing the hybridization of systems, maintaining previous knowledge and business rules, and the reducing the impact of the integration of quantum programs. This extension family might be extended in the future with additional elements.

The KDM generator recognizes certain elements in the AST and creates certain elements in the target KDM model. Table 2 shows the mapping applied by the KDM generator. The left column shows elements in the Q# AST, while two right columns provide the KDM element as well as the stereotype used (if any) to annotate the element.

Table 2. Q# AST - KDM mapping applied through the KDM generator

AST elements	KDM element	KDM stereotype
Q# program	CodeModel	
Q# program	CompilationUnit	Quantum program
Q# operation	CallableUnit	Quantum operation
Qubit_Declaration	DefinedType	Qubit
Quantum_Gate	ActionElement	Quantum gate
Qubit_identifier (used as operand in a quantum_gate)	ActionRelation (type = Addresses)	
among AST elements appearing in a sequence	ActionRelation (type = Flow)	

Figure 7 shows the whole KDM model after applying the transformation depicted in Table 2 to the AST model (see Fig. 5) that was generated from the Q# code in Fig. 4. As we can see from line 3 to 10 of Fig. 7, the extension family is defined and the quantum elements of the code in Fig. 4 in lines 7 and 9 are located in lines 14 and 17 of the KDM file. In line 12, it is necessary to specify the program, in this case "Program.qs", which its stereotype points to "quantum program" in the extension family.

```
1   <?xml version="1.0" encoding="UTF-8"?>
2   <kdm:Segment xmlns:kdm="http://www.omg.org/spec/KDM/20160201/kdm"
    xmlns:action="http://www.omg.org/spec/KDM/20160201/action"
    xmlns:code="http://www.omg.org/spec/KDM/20160201/code"
    xmlns:xmi="http://www.omg.org/XMI"
    xmlns:xsi="http://www.w3.org/2001/XMLSchema-instance"
    xmi:version="2.0" name="Program_1587291045970.xml">
3       <extensionFamily xmi:id="id.0">
4           <stereotype xmi:id="id.1" name="quantum programming language"/>
5           <stereotype xmi:id="id.2" name="quantum program"/>
6           <stereotype xmi:id="id.3" name="quantum operation"/>
7           <stereotype xmi:id="id.4" name="quantum gate"/>
8           <stereotype xmi:id="id.5" name="qubit"/>
9           <stereotype xmi:id="id.6" name="qubit measure"/>
10      </extensionFamily>
11      <model xmi:id="id.7" xsi:type="code:CodeModel"
        name="Program_1587291045970.xml" action:action="code:Action">
12          <codeElement xsi:type="code:CompilationUnit" xmi:id="id.8"
            stereotype="id.2" name="Program.qs" >
13              <codeElement xsi:type="code:CallableUnit" xmi:id="id.9"
                name="HelloQ" stereotype="id.3" >
14                  <codeElement type="code:DefinedType" xmi:id="id.10"
                    name="qubit" stereotype="id.5">
15                      <codeElement type="code:ActionElement" name="Hadamard"
                        stereotype="id.4" xmi:id="id.11">
16                          <source language="Q#" snippet="H(q)" />
17                          <actionRelation xsi:type="action:Addresses"
                            from="id.11" to="id.10" />
18                          <actionRelation xsi:type="action:Flow"
                            from="id.11" to="id.12" />
19                      </codeElement>
20                      <codeElement type="code:ActionElement" name="Measure"
                        stereotype="id.4" xmi:id="id.12">
21                          <source language="Q#" snippet="M(q)" />
22                          <actionRelation xsi:type="action:Addresses"
                            from="id.12" to="id.10" />
23                      </codeElement>
24                  </codeElement>
25              </codeElement>
26          </codeElement>
27      </model>
28  </kdm:Segment>
```

Fig. 7. KDM file from code on Fig. 4

Develop a quantum program implies the use and declaration of qubits. Q# has an structure called "Operations" which are similar to conventional methods but only inside them you can work with qubits, as we can see in Fig. 4 from line 5 to 12, and in Fig. 7 it is defined in line 13 as a "Callable Unit". Then, the KDM's declaration of the qubit inside the operation is in line 14, with the type "Defined Type" due to it can be considered as a variable type, just like and integer or a string.

The element which better fits the definition of a quantum gate is the "Action Element", which defines a basic unit of behaviour. Those elements have the stereotype "quantum gate" (id 4 in line 7). Internally, the quantum gate definitions have the "source" element (lines 16 and 21) that store the code snippet of the quantum gate. Then, quantum gate entities collect some "Action Relation" entities tagged with the type 'Addresses' to reference qubits involved as operands in the quantum gate. In our example, it references a single qubit (lines 17 and 22) through the "from" and "to" attributes, that respectively contains references to the current quantum gate and to the qubit declaration. Additionally, the sequence flow in the program is modelled with "Action Relation" elements tagged as "Flow" and a pair of "from" and "to" attributes (check line 18).

One limitation of the KDM generator lies in the fact that it cannot recognize in which operation is the qubit used, but it does know where are declared. This is not a problem if the Q# attached files use just one operation, which is the most common scenario.

5   Supporting Tool

This section presents first some implementation details for the tool we have developed, which support the technique proposed.

As mentioned before, the proposal is divided into two main components, as shown in Fig. 3, where both have been developed with different tools but joined with the aim to getting closer into the hybridization of systems.

The Q# Parser (see Fig. 3 a) was developed with ANTLR, which is a powerful parser generator for reading, processing, executing or translating structured text or binary files [22]. This parser allows us to define the syntax of the programming languages for developing the AST. This syntax is divided into two sections (see Table 1), the "Lexer" where the lexicon and reserved words of the language are specified, and the "Parser", where the language's structures are described. Since Q# is based on C# and ANTLR has an open repository of defined languages, such as Java, C, C++, etc., instead of starting from scratch, we took one ANTLR's project for C# and adapted it to Q#, by defining the necessary key words, structures and modules.

The KDM Generator (see Fig. 3 b) was constructed with Java. It takes the AST explores all its nodes and children, and if it is a relevant component in the architecture of the file, it is saved into a matrix. Then, all those matrixes are explored and based on the definitions of the KDM model, all different types that can be saved are specified. If one of those matrixes contain quantum entities, like quantum gates or qubit declarations, a stereotype attribute is added to its KDM's representation. These stereotypes point to the extension family detailed on Sect. 4.2 and are necessary for the future extension of classical information systems towards the hybrid ones.

6   Conclusions and Future Work

The goal of this research is contributing to the reengineering of classical-quantum information systems. In particular, this paper has focused on the reverse engineering phase to be able to parser quantum code and generates KDM models. The proposed technique has been specifically developed for Q# code, but further grammar could be provided to extend this technique with parsers for other quantum programming language. Additionally, because of the usage of KDM, this technique ensures the independence from quantum technology. This is particularly important due to the maturity status of the quantum technology, i.e., with various new programming languages and development platforms appearing in parallel, as well as different quantum hardware architectures. Also, the outgoing KDM model, representing abstractions of classical-quantum information systems, can be used during the next phases of reengineering, i.e. restructuring and forward engineering.

The proposed technique is framed in a long-term research devoted to investigating how reengineering can help to migrate both classical and quantum information systems toward hybrid ones. We believe, the presented technique is a first step in this direction. Thus, the main implications of this work are that quantum software developers can abstract some quantum information together other information coming from classical systems and it can be integrated in a high-abstracted model. This is usefully, not only for the whole reengineering process, but also for the understanding the information systems' components and their relationships.

As we presented before, we have already detected some possible improvements, like the generation of KDM files from other quantum programming languages apart from Q#. Further parsers might be semi automatically generated through the development of grammars for additional quantum programming languages. As the future research lines, we expect to work in the following reengineering phases. First, we expect to develop a UML extension to represent analysis and design models of the target, hybrid information system. Then, some automatic model transformations between KDM and UML will be developed.

Acknowledgments. This research has been partially funded by the G3SOFT (SBPLY/17/180501/000150), and GEMA (SBPLY/17/180501/000293) projects funded by the 'Dirección General de Universidades, Investigación e Innovación – Consejería de Educación, Cultura y Deportes; Gobierno de Castilla-La Mancha'. This work is also part of the projects BIZDEVOPS-Global (RTI2018-098309-B-C31) and ECLIPSE (RTI2018-094283-B-C31) funded by Ministerio de Economía, Industria y Competitividad (MINECO) & Fondo Europeo de Desarrollo Regional (FEDER); and SMOQUIN (PID2019-104791RB-I00) funded by Spanish Ministry of Science and Innovation (MICINN).

References

1. Washburn, S.H.: Boolean algebra in electronic circuit design. Electr. Eng. **73**, 164 (2013). https://doi.org/10.1109/ee.1954.6439254

2. Pérez-Castillo, R., García Rodríguez de Guzmán, I., Piattini, M.: Architecture-driven modernization. Mod. Softw. Eng. Concepts Pract. Adv. Approaches, 75–103 (2010). https://doi.org/10.4018/978-1-60960-215-4.ch004
3. Pérez-Castillo, R., De Guzmán, I.G.R., Piattini, M.: Knowledge discovery metamodel-ISO/IEC 19506: a standard to modernize legacy systems. Comput. Stand. Interfaces **33**, 519–532 (2011). https://doi.org/10.1016/j.csi.2011.02.007
4. Benioff, P.: The computer as a physical system: a microscopic quantum mechanical Hamiltonian model of computers as represented by turing machines. J. Stat. Phys. **22**, 563–591 (1980). https://doi.org/10.1007/BF01011339
5. Feynman, R.P.: Simulating physics with computers. Int. J. Theor. Phys. **21**, 467–488 (1982). https://doi.org/10.1007/BF02650179
6. Manin, I.I.: Vychislimoe i nevychislimoe (1980)
7. Shor, P.W.: Polynomial-time algorithms for prime factorization and discrete logarithms on a quantum computer. SIAM J. Comput. **26**, 1484–1509 (1997). https://doi.org/10.1137/S0097539795293172
8. Schrödinger, E.: Die gegenwärtige Situation in der Quantenmechanik. Naturwissenschaften **23**, 807–812 (1935). https://doi.org/10.1007/BF01491891
9. Bloch, F.: Nuclear induction. Phys. Rev. **70**, 460–474 (1946). https://doi.org/10.1103/PhysRev.70.460
10. Marinescu, D.C.: Classical and quantum information (2012). https://doi.org/10.1016/C2009-0-64195-7
11. Preskill, J.: Quantum computing and the entanglement frontier, 1–18 (2012). http://arxiv.org/abs/1203.5813
12. Google's quantum blog (2019). https://www.blog.google/technology/ai/computing-takes-quantum-leap-forward/. Accessed 13 April 2020
13. Selinger, P.: A brief survey of quantum programming languages. In: Kameyama, Y., Stuckey, P.J. (eds.) FLOPS 2004. LNCS, vol. 2998, pp. 1–6. Springer, Heidelberg (2004). https://doi.org/10.1007/978-3-540-24754-8_1
14. Piattini, M., et al.: The Talavera manifesto for quantum software engineering and programming. In: CEUR Workshop Proceedings, vol. 2561, pp. 1–5 (2020)
15. William, M.: Ulrich, Legacy Systems: Transformation Strategies. Prentice Hall PTR, Upper Saddle River (2002)
16. De Lucia, A., Ferrucci, F., Tortora, G., Tucci, M.: Emerging methods, technologies, and process management in software engineering (2007). https://doi.org/10.1002/9780470238103
17. Chikofsky, E.J., Cross, J.H.: Reverse engineering and design recovery: a taxonomy. IEEE Softw. **7**, 13–17 (1990). https://doi.org/10.1109/52.43044
18. Kazman, R., Woods, S.G., Carriere, S.J.: Requirements for integrating software architecture and reengineering models: CORUM II. In: Reverse Engineering - Workshop Conference Proceedings, pp. 154–163 (1998). https://doi.org/10.1109/wcre.1998.723185
19. Ulrich, W.M., Newcomb, P.H.: Information systems transformation (2010). https://doi.org/10.1016/C2009-0-19987-7
20. Schmidt, D.C.: Model-Driven Engineering. Vanderbilt University Model-driven, Historia Santiago, vol. 39, pp. 2–9 (2006). http://www.computer.org/portal/site/computer/menuitem.e533b16739f5
21. IBM quantum experience homepage (2016). https://quantum-computing.ibm.com/. Accessed 23 April 2020
22. ANTLR homepage (n.d.). https://www.antlr.org/. Accessed 26 Mar 2020

Math and Physics Tools for Quality Quantum Programming

Ezequiel Murina[✉]

aQuantum, Madrid, Spain
ezequiel.murina@a-e.es

Abstract. We are in presence of a quantum computing revolution that will be critical for the dominant global position of nations in near future. Some quantum lab devices have been developed and important milestones have been reached, mainly in the branch of communications. In this scenario, it is urgent to educate people in quantum computing and technology, like it happens with disciplines such as science, technology, engineering, and mathematics promoted by government in order to instruct science-aware citizens. A solid knowledge base in math and physics is essential for a workforce able to develop high quality quantum technology. This work addresses the necessity of quantum literacy for the creation of a new workforce, proposing the basic math tools, and physics background for entering into the field of quantum programming. It also addresses a certification about Science Foundation for Quantum Programming, as a means for assuring the quality of quantum software professionals.

Keywords: Quantum literacy · Quantum programming · Quantum math-physics · Quantum certification

1 Introduction

1.1 Quantum Computing Race

Researchers predicted, before the Coronavirus crisis, that Quantum Technology will grow roughly 65 billion USD next two decades, reaching a global market worth of 300 billon USD by the year 2050 [1]. Nowadays, there are more than 40 companies working in projects related to quantum cybersecurity, algorithms, financial services, and communications [2].

China is the leading country in quantum communications, with a successful industrial application of quantum key distribution (QKD). Let us just mention the launch of a quantum satellite called *Micius*, in August 2016, and the three milestones reached: implementation of QKD from the satellite to the ground over a distance of up to 1200 km using the decoy state BB84 protocol; quantum teleportation of independent single-photon qubits from a ground observatory to a low-Earth-orbit satellite; and satellite-based distribution of entangled photon pairs to two locations separated by more than 1000 km on Earth [3].

M. Shepperd et al. (Eds.): QUATIC 2020, CCIS 1266, pp. 263–273, 2020.
https://doi.org/10.1007/978-3-030-58793-2_21

In February 2020, Trump's Administration destined 25 millon USD on what it calls a national "quantum internet", which consists of a network of machines designed to prevent the interception of digital communication [4]. The Kremlin, in turn, will inject up to 790 millon USD next 5 years into basic and applied quantum research at leading Russian laboratories with aims of creating a quantum computer [5].

Regarding to Europe, it is important to mention the advances in quantum hardware carried out by QuTech in the Netherlands. In February 2020, in collaboration with Intel, they resolved the issue of integrate qubits and their controlling electronic in the same chip [6]. This opens the possibility to the realization of large-scale quantum computers.

1.2   Quantum (il)Literacy. The State of Art

European Commission warns about the necessity of basic knowledge in quantum theory and quantum technology as a component of all engineer's education [7]. Furthermore, they emphasis that it is required to train not only "quantum engineers" but also a *quantum-aware* workforce by means of reinforcement of education, conferences, summer schools, student exchanges and international collaboration, among others.

In 2018, it started The Quantum Technologies Flagship Programme (QTflagship) which aims to place Europe at the forefront of what they called the second quantum revolution [7]. The first revolution began with the development of quantum physics and its impact in transistor and laser technology. Currently, a second revolution is unfolding with the advances in nanotechnology which allow a precise control of single quantum states and exploit properties like superposition and entanglement. The impact in technology is expected to be in four areas: quantum computation, quantum communication, quantum simulation and quantum sensing and metrology.

Some countries configured its owns programmes as ways to overcome quantum illiteracy and consolidate as the new "Sillicon Valley". The most relevant propositions are the UK National Quantum technologies programme, Netherlands Quantum Agenda for Quantum Technology [1] and the German programme called Quantum Technology Foundations and Applications [8]. Also the Talavera Manifesto, presented at QAN-SWER 2020, proposes some principles and commitments about the quantum software engineering and programming field, as well as some calls for action [9].

1.3   Forward a Quantum Literacy for Software Engineering: Math and Physics

Although currently there are several lab prototypes of quantum computing hardware, the technology is in constant progress and is not yet standardized. The same happens with the development of a software stack. Many high level quantum programming languages, quantum software development kits, quantum assembly languages, and quantum compilers have been developed. An exhaustive list may be found in reference [10]. It is not clear which of them will remain in near future and will depend on how the ongoing progress of quantum technology is taking place.

In this scenario, a standardized education is not available for future quantum engineers. But something is clear: quantum programming needs software engineers and programmers with a blend of specialized knowledge from math and physics. In that sense, it is critical to understand that the lack of this knowledge constitutes the handicap to overcome in order to go beyond being a quantum software literate and become an actual developer. Moreover, a solid base in math and physics will has a strong impact in quality of quantum software development.

Next sections describe the fundamentals of quantum physics and introduce minimal mathematical concepts relevant for starting to work in the field of quantum software engineering and programming. Section 5 presents Foundations of Quantum Science for Quantum Programming profile as a means for assuring the math and physics knowledge required for the quality of quantum professionals. Finally, the main conclusions are presented.

2   The Origin of Quantum Theory: A "Quantum"

The starting point of the fundamentals of quantum physics theory was in the beginning of 20th century, when Max Planck proposed a microscopic model which describes the black body electromagnetic spectrum. In simple words, he explained how materials change color with temperature. The model postulates that the energy exchange between molecules of a material and the surrounding electromagnetic radiation is not continuous but by means of discrete amounts, "quanta" ("quantum", in singular), afterward called photons. Moreover, photon energy is proportional to the frequency of the electromagnetic wave radiated or absorbed in the energy exchange process. The proportionality constant is known as Planck's constant. It quantifies the discretization of energy and somehow plays the role of a signature for identifying quantum effects in mathematical equations.

Eventually, the revolutionary idea of a "quantum" was confirmed by experiments and extended to other energy forms such as magnetic quantities (spin) or mechanical collective vibrations (phonons), among others. A formal definition can be formulated as follows: a quantum is the smallest amount of a physical quantity involved in an energy exchange between matter and radiation. This discretization of physical quantities imposed constraints on the behavior of classical systems and led to the origin of a quantum theory for studying them.

The development of a quantum theory found a driving force in the field of atomic physics, reaching a solid mathematical expression with Schrödinger's equation. In its origin, the equation intended to recover the "continuous" behavior of physical quantities by means of the introduction of another revolutionary concept, inspired in a previous proposal made by Louis de Broglie: the wave-particle duality. It consists in associating a wave to a particle (a matter wave) and describing its physics as a wave entity. Therefore, particles exhibit both particle and wave behaviors depending on the characteristic length scale of the system. Wave behavior turns relevant in atomic systems and smaller.

The description of particles as waves led to the Heisenberg principle, a consequence of Fourier analysis applied to matter waves. The principle establishes a limit to the precision in the determination of reciprocal physical quantities such as the same components of position and linear momentum.

3 Physics Fundamentals of Quantum Computing and Quantum Programming

3.1 Qubits

In classic computing, information is transmitted in binary units called bits that can adopt logic values of zero or one, representing a low or high electric voltage, respectively. In quantum computing, however, the units of information are call qubits and represent the quantum states of a system (the spin of an electron, for example). The main properties of qubits come from the wave behavior of the two-level system they represent in a logical layer: superposition and entanglement.

3.2 Superposition

The most general quantum state of a single qubit can be written as follows:

$$|\psi\rangle = \alpha|0\rangle + \beta|1\rangle; \tag{1}$$

being α, β complex numbers. Notation $|0\rangle$, $|1\rangle$ represents the states of a quantum particle that can access to only two different energy levels. The expression in Eq. (1) is called *superposition of states* due the qubit $|\psi\rangle$ is composed by a combination of state $|0\rangle$ in $\|\alpha^2\|$ proportion and state $|1\rangle$ in $\|\beta^2\|$ proportion.

The powerful of superposition is the infinity of possibilities it offers for mapping information and, even more important, the parallel access to this information. It allows pure states like $|0\rangle$ and $|1\rangle$, which are equivalent to bits with values of 0 and 1, respectively. But also are allowed all combinations of states given by different values of concentration $\|\alpha^2\|$ and $\|\beta^2\|$, inaccessible by classic information units like bits.

3.3 Entanglement

An entanglement state is a superposition of a pair of single qubits in a way that a strong correlation is created between them. This strong correlation consists in the deterministic nature of the state of one of the qubit once the other qubit is measured. An entanglement can be obtained by applying quantum gates on qubits, which allows a control of the interference of matter waves associated to each qubit in order to create the desired state. Next section will clarify this issue.

3.4 The Wave Function Collapse and the Inspection of a Quantum Variable

Quantum physics theory has an intrinsic stochastic nature. In general, one proceeds as follows: first, a matter wave is associated to a single massive nonrelativistic particle and, then, the time evolution of the matter wave is given by the solution of the Schrödinger's equation.

A matter wave contains all the information available about the particle it is associated to, and its modulus squared is interpreted as a probability distribution of location in the space. The physics information is recovering from the matter wave when measures are taken onto it. The measuring process affects the final quantum state of the matter wave measured. This is called the wave function collapse.

A quantum variable is a name that allocates the memory space, a set of qubits, where data will be stored. When a quantum variable is inspected, it has a stochastic nature in the sense that it is possible to recover different values with a given probability. Once one inspects its value, a quantum variable loses its stochastic nature and behaves as a "classic" variable. At low level, what it happens is that the wave function associated to the qubits collapses: in the measurement process (the inspection of the variable), the measuring device interacts with the qubits, the interaction changes the quantum state of the qubits and they adopt bit values of 0 or 1.

3.5 No-Copying Quantum Information

Information allocated in qubits in an unknown quantum state cannot be copied exactly. This is called the no-cloning theorem. For further discussion and a formal prove, see reference [11]. The term "exactly" means that only the orthogonal components of a qubit in a quantum superposition state can be copied.

Another issue to point out about the no-cloning theorem is that it relies on the use of the state of art quantum hardware devices that perform unitary transformation of the qubits. However, copying quantum information might be possible with the development of hardware devices able to perform non-unitary transformations.

3.6 Quantum Algorithms

The two main state of art quantum computing models are universal quantum computing and annealing quantum computing [12, 13]. The former will be describe in next paragraphs, the latter is based in mapping a computational problem onto an interaction model between qubits and is beyond the scope of this paper.

Quantum programming (QP) in the universal quantum computing model proceeds as follows: the sequence of instruction that composed an algorithm is decoding in a sequence of quantum logic gates (Q-gates) operating on qubits, in order to change its quantum states. In this context, the concept of logic circuit arises as a visualization diagram of the implementation of a quantum algorithm (Q-algorithm).

An example of a simple quantum circuit corresponding to the teleportation algorithm is shown in Fig. 1. It is related to moving quantum data between qubits using 3-qubits as inputs and considering as a single relevant output the final quantum state of one of them. From left to right, a CNOT gate acts on the first pairs of the 3-qubits, enumerated from top to bottom; then, a Hadamard gate H creates interference in the first qubits. Afterwards, measurements are taken on the first pair of 3-qubits. Finally, pure rotations over X and Z axis are applied depending on the information N and M received by a classic channel overflow. Note the low abstraction level of QP, very close to the computer architecture itself, dealing with combination of Q-gates to obtain an interesting result as an output of the Q-algorithm. There are neither loops nor shortcuts, just a serial sequence of transformation changing the qubit states in each step.

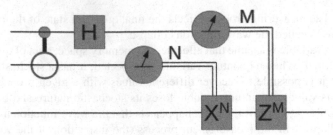

Fig. 1. Quantum circuit corresponding to the teleportation algorithm (Amended from reference [11]).

One of the main features of Q-gates is their reversibility, i.e., it is possible to recover and old quantum state from the new one applying the inverse transformation. This makes Q-gates have no analogue in classic logic gates, where many of them are not reversible.

3.7   Quantum Programming Language and the Execution of a Quantum Code

QP languages (Q-languages) implement a Q-algorithm at high level. In that sense, a new coding logic emerges due the quantum nature of qubits and how QP proceeds. They do not use logic structures for flow control such if-else, switch, for or while statements. Q-languages focus on the establishment of correlation among qubits (entanglements), creation of interference (apart from entangled states, others superposition states) and state projections (measurements).

Another feature of QP is the requirement of multiple times execution of the Q-algorithm once it is implemented by a high-level Q-language. On the one hand, inherent stochastic nature of qubits as a quantum device gives a probability distribution of occurrence to the possible outputs. The better sampling of this distribution, the more precision in the estimation of the mean value of outputs. On the other hand, there is noise coupled to the signal coming from operating with non-ideal Q-gates during the time coherence of qubits. In an ideal case, that is why a code have to be executed multiple times: good sampling of outputs and reduction of noise introduced by hardware. In non-ideal situations, other factors have to be taken into consideration, such as the interaction of qubits with the environment.

4   Math Tools for Quantum Programming

For becoming a quantum software engineer it is necessary to be fluently in linear algebra and understand the basic ideas of probability theory. Also, some knowledge in modular arithmetic (basically, mod 2) and complex numbers (addition, multiplication and Euler representation) is an advantage. At an advance level, Fourier analysis may be relevant.

Linear algebra introduces the notion of vector space and the tools required to deal with qubits and changes in its quantum states. The quantum state of a qubit is represented by a vector. A Q-gate action is mapping in a square matrix and its effect on a quantum state of a qubit emerges when a matrix-vector multiplication is carried out. Let us see an example. Given the quantum circuit shown in Fig. 1, assume the input for the first wire (from top to bottom) is a state like the following:

$$|\psi\rangle = \alpha(|0\rangle + |1\rangle) \tag{2}$$

being $\alpha = 1/\sqrt{(2)}$. Quantum state $\psi\rangle$ in expression (2) represents a superposition of qubits $0\rangle$ and $1\rangle$ in equal proportions. The vector representation is:

$$|0\rangle \Rightarrow \begin{bmatrix} 1 \\ 0 \end{bmatrix} \quad |1\rangle \Rightarrow \begin{bmatrix} 0 \\ 1 \end{bmatrix} \tag{3}$$

Suppose we proceed along the circuit. The first Q-gate (from left to right) is a CNOT gate. It does not affect the quantum state of $|\psi\rangle$ due this qubit is a control one in this case. The second Q-gate is a Hadamard gate, H. Its matrix representation is:

$$H \Rightarrow \alpha \begin{bmatrix} 1 & 1 \\ 1 & -1 \end{bmatrix} \tag{4}$$

Let us see the effect of the H application on $|\psi\rangle$:

$$H|\psi\rangle = \alpha(H|0\rangle + H|1\rangle) \tag{5}$$

and in matrix-vector representation:

$$H|0\rangle \Rightarrow \alpha \begin{bmatrix} 1 & 1 \\ 1 & -1 \end{bmatrix} \begin{bmatrix} 1 \\ 0 \end{bmatrix} = \alpha \begin{bmatrix} 1 \\ 1 \end{bmatrix} = \alpha \begin{bmatrix} 1 \\ 0 \end{bmatrix} + \alpha \begin{bmatrix} 0 \\ 1 \end{bmatrix} \tag{6}$$

$$H|0\rangle \Rightarrow \alpha(|0\rangle + |1\rangle)$$

In a similar way, one obtains:

$$H|1\rangle \Rightarrow \alpha(|0\rangle - |1\rangle) \tag{7}$$

From combination of expressions 5, 6, and 7 results:

$$H|\psi\rangle = |0\rangle \tag{8}$$

The physics background of these calculations is close related with interference of matter waves phenomenon. The effect of Hadamard gate is to create interference. When a quantum state is pure, i.e. when $\alpha = 0$ and $\beta = 1$, or vice verse, in Eq. (1), the state unfolds in equal proportions along the set of accessible quantum configuration. This homogeneous unfolding constitutes an isentropic thermodynamics trajectory. On can recover the initial state re-applying the Hadamard gate. This time, more interference is created and destroys the original one, as it is shown in previous example. Again, the process is isentropic and there is no energy dissipation considering and ideal case.

5 Foundations of Quantum Science for Quality Quantum Programming

5.1 Assuring the Quality of Quantum Professionals

To produce quality quantum software, as with classical software, engineers and programmers must have a set of scientific, technical and technological knowledge essential for developing the competences required to develop software.

In the case of the development of quantum software, knowledge of the fundamentals of quantum science is revealed as essential and, as has been shown before, knowledge of physics and mathematics is decisive. The level of maturity of the specific competences for the development of their tasks will depend on the degree of knowledge in these sciences. As we know, they are not the same competences required for an engineer as for a programmer, just as the competences required for a programmer are also different from those required for a software architect.

Given that we think that competencies play a determining role in the quality of quantum software development, as it happens with the quality of classic software, we consider that it is necessary to design a training model appropriate to the objective of developing these competences, which requires the appropriate combination of training with the completion of practices in a training model. In our opinion, this can be successfully achieved through a certification model specially designed for the development of quantum software that includes the competencies required for the different categories of the quantum workforce.

The purpose of certification of persons is to measure the competence of individuals. It is very important because it signifies an individual expertise and training to industry and organizations. Certification also helps industries to define and maintain standards. Confidence in the certification schemes for persons is achieved by means of a globally accepted process of assessment, and periodic re-assessments, of the competence of certified persons. So, certification assures the quality of quantum professionals.

In full coherence with all the aforementioned, in Piattini, Peterssen et al. [14], a ISO/IEC 17024-based certification schema with different categories to train and certify the needed quantum workforce is proposed. For this reason, we believe that it is very interesting to incorporate to this schema a category regarding a Foundations of Quantum Science for Quantum Programming.

Regarding competences, we propose a first level of definition using the European e-Competence Framework (e-CF) [15] which was established as "a tool to support mutual understanding and provide transparency of language through the articulation of competences required and deployed by ICT professionals (including both practitioners and managers)". The e-CF is structured from four dimensions:

- Dimension 1: 5 e-Competence areas, derived from the ICT business processes PLAN – BUILD – RUN – ENABLE – MANAGE
- Dimension 2: A set of reference e-Competences for each area, with a generic description for each competence. 40 competences identified in total provide the European generic reference definitions of the framework.

- Dimension 3: Proficiency levels of each e-Competence provide European reference level specifications on e-Competence levels e-1 to e-5.
- Dimension 4: Samples of knowledge and skills related to the e-Competences are indicated as optional framework components for inspiration.

At a second level of definition, specific knowledge is detailed.

5.2 Foundations of Quantum Science for Quantum Programming Profile

To efficiently train the workforce for quantum development, the competencies to be developed in the certifications for the different categories must be clearly defined. Otherwise, the greatest mistake would be made of not properly dimensioning the contents and practices to include in each one of them for the fulfillment of the objectives of each certification.

In almost two years of work that we have already dedicated to the research and development of Quantum Software Workforce, focused on the study of competencies and training for the workforce in Quantum Software Engineering and Programming, we have verified that, in general, all categories of the quantum workforce require, to varying degrees, the following minimum competencies to develop quality quantum software:

- Fundamental Physics
- Quantum Mechanics
- Mathematics
- Quantum Computers
- Quantum Algorithms
- Quantum Programming

Although we are currently working on defining the specific competencies for each of the categories we have identified in the quantum software development workforce, we have concluded that certified professionals at Foundations of Quantum Science for Quantum Programming will be able to tackle and tackle with quality the following tasks:

a) Develop quantum components and applications
b) Follow quantum development guidelines
c) Document quantum components and applications
d) Identify quantum software problems and repair
e) Perform regular maintenance on quantum software components
f) Write test program to assess quantum software quality
g) Communicate effectively with end users and customer management.

And so, the following general competences must be acquired:

e-CF Competences	Level
A.1. Application Design	1
B.1. Application Development	2
B.3. Testing	1
D.11. Needs Identification	2

Regarding knowledge, we group the specific concepts for this certification in three domains:

- Domain 1: Quantum Mathematics.
- Domain 2: Quantum Physics.
- Domain 3: Quantum Computer Realisation.

6 Conclusions

Quantum literacy is the starting point for safe transformations towards a quality and sustainable quantum industry. It should be a State policy in all modern countries, not only those interesting in accessing to a global dominant position next decades. In this work were discussing the first achievements in the area of quantum computing and some programmes for quantum research and education recently implemented. Also, they were presented the physics and math concepts in which quantum theory rely on.

The new software engineers need an interdisciplinary background with knowledge in math and physics that allow them to address the quantum challenges. Up to now there is not a standardized instruction to become a "Quantum Engineer". In this regard, we will offer the *Basic Science Foundations Certification for Quantum Software Engineers*. It will include an introductory course about quantum programming fundamental and also an intermediate-advanced course which gives a more detailed approach with the math and physics tools required in this field.

Acknowledgements. The author thanks professors Guido Peterssen and Mario Piattini for the very useful discussion about the topics presented in this paper.

References

1. TNO, QuTech, QuSoft, QT/e, NWO, h. L. Instituut, AMS-IX, S. Microsoft y m. EZK, National Agenda for Quantum Technology, TNO (2019)
2. W Contributors: List of companies involved in quantum computing or communication. Wikipedia. The Free Encyclopedia. https://en.wikipedia.org/wiki/List_of_companies_inv olved_in_quantum_computing_or_communication. Accessed 22 June 2020
3. Zhang, Q., Xu, F., Li, L., Liu, N.-L., Pan, J.-W.: Quantum information research in China. Quantum Sci. Technol. **4**, 040503 (2019)

4. Metz, C.: White House Earmarks New Money for A.I. and Quantum Computing. The New York Times. https://www.nytimes.com/2020/02/10/technology/white-house-earmarks-new-money-for-ai-and-quantum-computing.html. Accessed 22 June 2020
5. Schiermeier, Q.: Russia joins race to make quantum dreams a reality. Nature **577**, 14 (2020)
6. Patra, B., et al.: A scalable Cryo-CMOS 2-to-20 GHz digitally intensive controller for 4 × 32 frequency multiplexed spin qubits/transmons in 22 nm FinFET technology for quantum computers. In: 2020 IEEE International Solid- State Circuits Conference (ISSCC), Kunming, China (2020)
7. Riedel, M.F., Binosi, D., Thew, R., Calarco, T.: The European quantum technologies flagship programme. Quantum Sci. Technol. **2**, 030501 (2017)
8. Bayer, M., et al.: Quantum Technology Foundations and Applications. https://www.quantentechnologien.de/fileadmin/public/Redaktion/Dokumente/PDF/Publikationen/Qutega-QT-Grundlagen-und-Anwendungen-01-2017-C1.pdf. Accessed 22 June 2020
9. Piattini, M., et al.: The talavera manifesto. In: 1st International Workshop on the QuANtum SoftWare Engineering and pRogramming, Talavera de la Reina, Spain (2020)
10. W Contributors: Quantum programming. Wikipedia. The Free Encyclopedia. https://en.wikipedia.org/wiki/Quantum_programming. Accessed 22 June 2020
11. Nielsen, M.A., Chuang, I.L.: Quantum Computation and Quantum Information. Cambridge University Press (2000)
12. Silva, V.: Practical Quantum Computing for Developers: Programming Quantum Rigs in the Cloud Using Python, Quantum Assembly Language and IBM QExperience. Apress (2018)
13. Biswas, R., et al.: A NASA perspective on quantum computing: opportunities and challenges. Parallel Comput. **64**, 81–98 (2017)
14. Piattini, M., Petterssen, G., Pérez-Castillo, R., Hevia, J.L., Murina, E.: A certification schema for quantum software engineers (2020). Submitted to International Journal of Engineering Education
15. European Committee for Standardization (CEN): European-e-Competence-Framework-3.0 A common European Framework for ICT Professionals in all industry sectors. CEN. http://ecompetences.eu/wp-content/uploads/2014/02/European-e-Competence-Framework-3.0_CEN_CWA_16234-1_2014.pdf. Accessed 22 June 2020

Adapting COBIT for Quantum Computing Governance

Miguel Ángel Blanco$^{(\boxtimes)}$ and Mario Piattini

Alarcos Research Group, University of Castilla-La Mancha, Paseo de la Universidad, 4, 13071 Ciudad Real, Spain
miguelangel.blanco@gmail.com, Mario.Piattini@uclm.es

Abstract. Quantum computing is a new paradigm that uses the properties of quantum mechanics to achieve computers and technologies more powerful. Quantum Technology will solve some types of problems more efficiently than current technology. Every organization that wants to use all the power of quantum computing to be more competitive in its sector, must have a method that allows it to take advantage of all the value that this technology can provide. This article proposes the development of a framework for the Management and Governance of Quantum Computing based on COBIT.

Keywords: Governance · Management · Quantum computing

1 Introduction

Quantum computing is an emerging computing paradigm bases in some quantum phenomena [1], by which will be solved some types of problems more efficiently that current technology solves [2] and [3].

The particularity of the quantum computing and quantum technology is the use of the principles of quantum mechanics. These principles are used for development a new information theory based in the qubit concept that have the following characteristics [4]:

- **Quantum parallelism:** it is the capacity of the qubit to be in a superposition of states, being able to contain state information 0 and 1 at the same time.
- **Quantum entanglement:** it is the property by which two qubits are separated at any distance and the state of one of them is modified, the other is modified at the same time. In this situation the two qubits would form a quantum system.
- **Non-cloning theorem:** it is impossible to duplicate an unknown quantum state.

The main applications of the quantum technology are [5]:

- **Sensors.** Quantum sensors are very accurate because use the entanglement property for exceeding the quantum limit. Their applications are very varied such as metrology, scanner or navigation.

© Springer Nature Switzerland AG 2020
M. Shepperd et al. (Eds.): QUATIC 2020, CCIS 1266, pp. 274–283, 2020.
https://doi.org/10.1007/978-3-030-58793-2_22

- **Security and communications.** Quantum computing are capable to break efficiently the discrete logarithm using to create the security keys and the cryptosystems that uses them. For this reason, is necessary create a new discipline, the quantum cryptography with will help improve the transmission of information securely. One of the most important application of this technology will be the transmission of information through quantum channels.
- **Quantum simulation.** This technology will allow simulating the behavior of complex systems that is currently not possible with current computing. This field will enable develop new materials, drugs or predict the behavior of nature.

These applications will be developed thanks of the construction of quantum computers that will allow solve problems that are impossible solve with the actual technology.

Currently, it is very noteworthy to develop new classical algorithms using concepts or principles of quantum computing to improve applications of emerging technologies such as Blockchain, Artificial Intelligence, the Internet of Things and 5G. In the future it will be interesting, as indicated in [5] and [6], to consider and analyze how it may affect new applications and quantum computing in these emerging technologies:

- **Blockchain.** The application of this technology is carried out for the registration of transactions, immutable, decentralized, and consensual. Quantum technology will affect the Blockchain in these 4 situations: authentication, block mining, the reversibility of hash functions and the use of the internet and its protocols for communication between nodes.
- **Artificial intelligence.** There are a large number of studies where computation and quantum technology can have different applications in the use of artificial intelligence, such as solving problems that are very difficult to solve with current machine learning techniques, finding patterns and correlations in unstructured data sets that allow them to be classified or the analysis of data sets that may have intrinsic quantum type correlations.
- **Internet of things.** Internet of things consists of a network of electronic devices connected through the internet to solve many problems. Quantum technologies will impact this technology in the transmissions between the devices, requiring the creation of quantum telecommunications channels for the secure connection between them.
- **5G.** Will be necessary to develop the 5th generation of mobile communications, where greater speed and lower latency are achieved in the transmission of information. Many of the manufacturers of these networks are focusing their efforts and investments on making them resistant to quantum computing. Under this concept, the disciplines of cryptography and quantum security will be indispensable.

Quantum Technologies will be interesting analyze the impact of their results in multiple industrial sectors [7] and [8]:

- **Finance.** Some of the challenges in the finance sector to quantum technology are optimization of the asset price portfolio, risk analysis and fraud detection.

- **Insurance.** The potential applications in the insurance sector are the evaluation of financial instruments, options and guarantees in insurance products and measurement of operational risk.
- **Energy.** The two main challenges in the energy sector facing quantum technologies are optimizing current networks and predicting the appropriate use of energy.
- **Transport.** Traffic optimization is the most tangible application in this sector.
- **Logistics.** Optimization of operations related to optimizing the supply chain.
- **Automobile and aerospace.** The management and optimization of large fleets of cars or autonomous planes are the main challenges in this sector.
- **Chemist and pharmacist.** The simulation of molecules for the discovery of new compounds is the main application of Quantum Computing in these sectors.
- **Materials.** The simulation with quantum computing will be able to discover new materials to improve batteries, microcircuits or network architectures.

The companies whose business is one of the list will have to invest in quantum a new framework that help implement these technology and quantum computing in these companies [7]. Depending on the type of industrial sector, it is necessary to implement one type of quantum technology or another, the Table 1 shows this relationship.

Table 1. Relationship between sector and quantum technology

Sector	Computing	Communication	Simulation	Security	Sensors
Finance	X			X	
Insurance	X			X	
Energy	X	X	X	X	X
Transport	X	X			
Automobile	X	X	X	X	X
Aerospace	X	X	X	X	X
Logistics	X			X	
Chemist	X		X		
Pharmacist	X		X		
Materials	X		X		

Depending on the technology implemented by each company depending on the sector to which is belongs, it should focus on different government guidelines. The Table 2 shows the relationship between main governance guidelines and the quantum technologies.

The objective of this paper is proposed the changes to be made to COBIT 2019 to build a Governance and Management Framework for Quantum Computing and Technology.

The rest of the paper is organized as follows: Sect. 2 explains the most important elements of COBIT 2019 for the purpose of this study; Sect. 3 proposes the changes to be made on COBIT 2019 objectives to build the framework for Quantum Computing Governance; Sect. 4 presents the conclusions and the future work of this research.

Table 2. Relationship between quantum governance guidelines and quantum technology

Governance guideline	Computing	Communication and security	Simulation	Sensors
Development Management	X		X	
Testing Management	X		X	
Deliver Management	X			
Services Management	X	X	X	
Support Management	X	X	X	X
Security Management	X	X	X	X
Risks Management	X	X		X

2   COBIT 2019

COBIT 2019 [9] is a framework developed by ISACA (Information Systems Audit and Control Association), which has its origins in the control and audit of the IT area.

Nowadays COBIT 2019 is a framework focused on the Enterprise Governance of Information and Technology, aimed at the whole enterprise.

Enterprise Governance of Information and Technology is an integral part of corporate governance. It is exercised by the board that oversees the definition and implementation of processes, structures and relational mechanisms in the organization that enable both business and IT people to execute their responsibilities in support of business/IT alignment and the creation of business value from I&T–enabled business investments (see Fig. 1).

Fig. 1. The context of enterprise governance of information and technology

COBIT Framework cover two different disciplines, Governance and Management, that have the following characteristics:

- Governance ensures that

  - Stakeholder needs, conditions and options are evaluated to determine balanced, agreed-on enterprise objectives.
  - Direction is set through prioritization and decision making.
  - Performance and compliance are monitored against agreed-on direction and objectives.

• Management plans, builds, runs and monitors activities, in alignment with the direction set by governance body, to achieve the enterprise objectives and strategic.

These two disciplines groups 40 Governances Objectives that are the main components of COBIT, this set of Government Objectives is shown in Fig. 2.

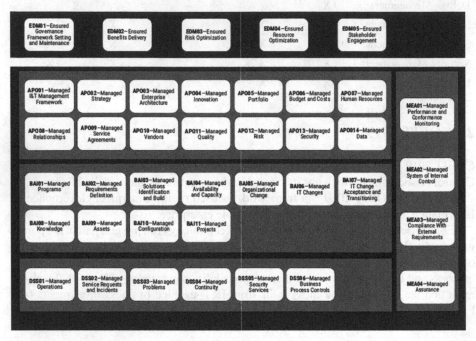

Fig. 2. COBIT core model

The main characteristics that has COBIT are the next:

• The Governance Framework is built based on 3 principles; is based on a conceptual model, should be open and flexible and should be aligned to relevant standards, framework and regulations.
• The Governance System build based on Governance Framework should based on six principles; provide Stakeholder value, is built from a number that work in a holistic way, should be dynamic in fact of the change in design factors that impact on Enterprise Governance of Information and Technology must be considered, distinguish between governance and management activities and structures, should be tailored to the enterprise's needs and should cover the enterprise end to end not only in IT function.
• COBIT Core Model groups a set of government objectives and these in turn are made up of a set of elements. These components are processes, organizational structures, policies and procedures, information flows, culture and behaviors, skills and infrastructure.

- Define design factors that should be use by the enterprise to build a best-fit governance system.
- The components are grouped by governance and management objectives that can be managed to the required capabilities levels.

Based on this COBIT structure, the next section will show a proposal for changes to be made to the COBIT Objectives for the development of a Framework for Quantum Technology Governance.

3   Toward a Framework for the Government of Quantum Technology

For developing the Framework for Quantum Technology Governance, we will begin by identifying the main components of COBIT to adapt, remove or add. These components are the Business Objectives that COBIT groups in 4 domains that are classified between the Government and Management disciplines:

- **Governance domains**

  - Evaluate, Direct and Monitor: Evaluates strategic options, directs senior management on the chosen strategic options and monitors the achievement of the strategy

- **Management domains**

  - Align, Plan and Organize: Addresses the overall organization, strategy and supporting activities for I&T.
  - Build, Acquire and Implement: Treats the definition, acquisition and implementation of I&T solutions and their integration in business processes.
  - Deliver, Service and Support: Addresses the operational delivery and support of I&T services, including security.
  - Monitor, Evaluate and Assess: Addresses performance monitoring and conformance of I&T with internal performance targets, internal control objectives and external requirements.

In the following sections, each one Business Objective is analyzed, and it is suggested what action must be carried out for each of them in for developing the Framework for Quantum Technology Governance. The different actions proposed are:

- Maintain: the objectives will be the same as in COBIT.
- Adapt: they will have to adapt to the needs for quantum computing management for the new Framework for Quantum Technology Governance.
- Remove: in this case the objectives do not have sense for the needs for quantum computing management and will be delete
- Include: in this case is necessary to include new Objectives in this domain to give consistency to the new context.

3.1 Adapting Objectives of Domain Evaluate, Direct and Monitor

The Domain Evaluate, Direct and Monitor (EDM) groups the following 5 objectives.

The Table 3 shows the actions to be carried out on each of the objectives of domain Evaluate, Direct and Monitor to develop the Framework for the Government of Quantum Technology and the features that are different between quantum computing and classical computing and affects to the business objective.

Table 3. Actions to be carried out in the Objectives of Domain EDM

Business objective	Action	Features
EDM01. Ensured Governance Framework Setting and Maintenance	Adapt	- External environment
EDM02. Ensured Benefits Delivery	Adapt	- Delivery benefit
EDM03. Ensured Risk Optimization	Adapt	- Risks
EDM04. Ensured Resource Optimization	Adapt	- Resources characteristics
EDM05. Ensured Stakeholder Engagement	Adapt	- Stakeholders needs
EDM06. Ensured the alignment between Governance Framework of Quantum Computing and Governance Framework of Classical Computing.	Include	- Coexistence between the classical and quantum paradigm in companies

3.2 Adapting Objectives of Domain Align, Plan and Organize

The Domain Align, Plan and Organize (APO) groups 14 Objectives:

The Table 4 shows the actions to be carried out on each of the objectives of domain Align, Plan and Organize to develop to develop the Framework for the Government of Quantum Technology and the features that are different between quantum computing and classical computing and affects to the business objective.

3.3 Domain Build, Acquire and Implement

The Domain Build, Acquire and Implement (BAI) groups 11 Objectives:

The Table 5 shows the actions to be carried out on each of these objectives

3.4 Domain Deliver, Service and Support

The Domain Deliver, Service and Support (DSS) groups 6 Objectives:

The Table 6 shows the actions to be carried out on each of the objectives of domain Deliver, Service and Support to develop the Framework for the Government of Quantum Technology and the features that are different between quantum computing and classical computing and affects to the business objective.

Table 4. Actions to be carried out in the s Objectives of Domain APO

Objective	Action	Features
APO01. Managed I&T Management Framework	Adapt	- Features of the computing paradigm.
APO02. Managed Strategy	Adapt	- External environment
APO03. Managed Enterprise Architecture	Adapt	- Business architecture
APO04. Managed Innovation	Maintain	
APO05. Managed Portfolio	Adapt	- Features of the computing paradigm.
APO06. Managed Budget and Costs	Maintain	
APO07. Managed Human Resources Focus Area	Adapt	- Knowledge and skills
APO08. Managed Relationships	Maintain	
APO09. Managed Service Agreements	Adapt	- Relationship with suppliers
APO10. Managed Vendors	Adapt	- Relationship with vendors
APO11. Managed Quality	Adapt	- Quality features
APO12. Managed Risk	Adapt	- Risks
APO13. Managed Security	Adapt	- Security features
APO14. Managed Data	Maintain	
APO15. Managed integration with Classical Computing	Include	- Coexistence between the classical and quantum paradigm in companies

3.5 Domain Monitor, Evaluate and Assess

The Domain Monitor, Evaluate and Assess (MEA) groups 4 Objectives.

The Table 7 shows the actions to be carried out on each of the objectives of domain Deliver, Service and Support to develop to develop the Framework for the Government of Quantum Technology and the features that are different between quantum computing and classical computing and affects to the business objective.

Table 5. Actions to be carried out in the Objectives of Domain BAI

Objective	Action	Features
BAI01. Managed Programs	Adapt	- Programs requirements
BAI02. Managed Requirements Definition	Adapt	- Stakeholders needs - Requirements definition
BAI03. Managed Solutions Identification and Build	Adapt	- Solution architecture - Development methodologies
BAI04. Managed Availability and Capacity	Adapt	- Capacity and availability features
BAI05. Managed Organizational Change	Maintain	
BAI06. Managed IT Changes	Adapt	- Changes requirements
BAI07. Managed IT Change Acceptance and Transitioning	Adapt	- Acceptance requirements - Transition requirements
BAI08. Managed Knowledge	Maintain	
BAI09. Managed Assets	Adapt	- Business requirements
BAI10. Managed Configuration	Adapt	- Assets Requirements
BAI11. Managed Projects	Adapt	- Projects requirements
BAI12. Coordinate the management of classical and quantum computing projects	Include	- Coexistence between the classical and quantum paradigm in companies.

Table 6. Actions to be carried out in the Business Objectives of Domain DSS

Objective	Action	Features
DSS01. Managed Operations	Adapt	- Operational requirements
DSS02. Managed Service Requests and Incidents	Adapt	- Services requirements
DSS03. Managed Problems	Maintain	
DSS04. Managed Continuity	Adapt	- Continuity requirements
DSS05. Managed Security Services	Adapt	- Security requirements
DSS06. Managed Business Process Controls	Adapt	- Security requirements
DSS07. Coordinate the management of deliver, service and control between the classical and quantum computing	Include	- Coexistence between the classical and quantum paradigm in companies

Table 7. Actions to be carried out in the Business Objectives of Domain MEA

Objective	Action	Features
MEA01. Managed Performance and Conformance Monitoring	Adapt	- Conformance requirements
MEA02. Managed System of Internal Control Focus	Adapt	- Security requirements
MEA03. Managed Compliance with External Requirements	Adapt	- External and compliance requirements
MEA04. Managed Assurance	Maintain	

4   Conclusions and Future Work

Quantum computing and technology is emerging as a computing paradigm, it will solve amount of problems more efficiently than nowadays is solved with the currently technology. Computing and quantum technology impact multiple industrial sectors and companies that invest in this technology have a great competitive advantage.

It is necessary to develop a quantum technology governance and management framework that helps organizations implement this technology and can take advantage of it. This article proposes the construction of this governance and management framework for technology and quantum computing, proposing modifications to COBIT as a governance and management framework for IT.

This is the first step in the development of this line of research that gives rise to the analysis, development and implementation of the changes to be made to COBIT in order to create a Governance and Management Framework for quantum computing and technology.

References

1. Mykhailova, M., Svore, K.M.: Teaching quantum computing through a practical software-driven approach. In: 51st ACM Technical Symposium on Computer Science Education (SIGCSE 2020), pp. 1019–1025. ACM, Portland (2020)
2. Humble, T.S., DeBenedictis, E.P.: Quantum realism. IEEE Comput. **52**(6), 13–17 (2019)
3. MIT Technology Review. https://www.technologyreview.com/s/610250/serious-quantum-computers-are-finally-here-what-are-we-going-to-do-with-them/. Accessed 14 June 2020
4. Maslov, D., Nam, Y., Kim, J.: An outlook for quantum computing. Proc. IEEE **107**(1), 5–10 (2019)
5. Allende Lopez, M.: Quantum technologies. Digital transformation, social impact and cross-sector disruption. Interamerican Development Bank (2019)
6. Smarter With Gartner. https://www.gartner.com/smarterwithgartner/the-cios-guide-to-quantum-computing/. Accessed 14 June 2020
7. Efe, A.: Anticipating the Disruptive and Incremental Innovations Brought by Quantum Computing. ISACA J. **1**, 26–32 (2020)
8. Boston Consulting Group: https://www.bcg.com/publications/2019/quantum-computers-create-value-when.aspx. Accessed 14 June 2020
9. ISACA®: COBIT 2019 Framework. ISACA (2019). https://www.isaca.org/resources/cobit

Quantum Agile Development Framework

Guillermo José Hernández González[✉] and Claudio Andrés Paradela

Aquantum, 28030 Madrid, Spain
Guillermo.hernandez@m2iformacion.com

Abstract. The interest in quantum computing has grown exponentially in recent years, with large technology companies engaging in the creation of computers and quantum technologies. The number of qubits skyrockets and makes the future practical implementation of mathematical algorithms and the creation of commercial systems increasingly viable. However, the growth of hardware is not being accompanied by programming and engineering methodologies adapted to this new paradigm, with new needs and risks. Associated with this, we are also in a world in which current development projects are carried out in multiple paradigms associated with different needs. In this paper, our findings and proposals are defined to anticipate the future needs of quantum software project management, taking into account the new roles, requirements and deficiencies of this new technology. Specifically, we focus on defining a classical-agile hybrid project management framework that can be adapted to the needs of these new programming paradigms, taking into account not only quantum programming, but projects that integrate classical-quantum hybrid developments.

Keywords: Project management · Agile · Quantum computing

1 Historical Context of Project Management and Development Frameworks

It could be said that in 1911 with the publication of "The principle of Scientific Management" by Frederic Taylor [1], the idea of the need for project management in various scientific areas was planted. This evolution only continues with the creation of the Gantt chart in 1917 [2].

Most of these foundations and many others, created by other people and organizations, such as the PMI project management institute, created in 1969. They lead to the creation of a series of development frameworks, which as a whole, we currently call cascade or traditional development frameworks. The original version for this type of framework was proposed and is consolidated by Winston W. Royce in 1970 [3] and later revised by Barry Boehm in 1980 [4] and Ian Sommerville in 1985 [5].

In 1986 Scrum was first named as a project management style, transforming it into the framework of reference for the other main strand of development frameworks: Agile development.

© Springer Nature Switzerland AG 2020
M. Shepperd et al. (Eds.): QUATIC 2020, CCIS 1266, pp. 284–291, 2020.
https://doi.org/10.1007/978-3-030-58793-2_23

2   Current Situation

Currently there are three main types of management of development projects:

- Cascade or classics: Frameworks or methodologies based on the philosophy of cascade development and fixed phases.
- Agile: Frameworks or methodologies based on the principles of the agile manifesto.
- Hybrids: Composed of mixed waterfall and classic methods. They typically use an early phase of requirements taking and classic design with agile-based development cycles.

3   Current Situation Current Evolution

Classic projects arise as a basis for the need for project management in different scientific areas and have provided a series of accumulated good practices that allow applying a series of tools and facilitating decision-making in specific situations.

Agile approaches appear as a response to uncertainty and incremental complexity that was occurring in expanded software projects due to the series of problems associated with said complexity, such as:

- Lack of knowledge and little experience in certain technical sectors.
- High level of risk.
- Reduced time to market.
- Business integration needs.
- Quick response to changes.

Since 1980 theories of the use of quantum computers begin to emerge; in 2012 IBM announces the creation of the first quantum chip; In 2011, the first sale of a quantum computer was made, the 128-qubit D-Wave One; in 2013 D-Wave systems launches the first quantum computer faster than a traditional computer and in 2019 IBM announces the first commercial quantum computer. Parallel to the creation of these quantum hardware systems, development tools begin to appear created by the manufacturers of these computers such as Qiskit from IBM in mid-2017 or other development tools not associated with any of the hardware manufacturers initially, such as Q# de Microsoft in December 2017.

We will call quantum software the software developed to use quantum computers or simulators of them. This software is currently developed and used largely for research or scientific use, but gradually some companies use it alongside adiabatic quantum machines or other more commercial implementations. According to multiple studies [6, 7], some of the fields in which quantum computing-based software could have imminent use are: transportation, logistics, telecommunications, aeronautics, health, wellness sciences, government, financial services, chemistry or logistics.

There is, therefore, a need to be able to adapt or create new frameworks or development methods that can be used for the development of quantum software. Today, it is difficult to find information on the management of these projects, since most are for research and are managed as such, so we must draw on our development experience with quantum software within Alhambra IT to talk about such projects.

4   Status of Quantum Software Development Projects

Quantum software development projects move in highly complex and experimental environments, due to the constant evolution of the underlying physical technology; although in a positive way, the existing development tools are being stable and having a positive evolution.

Despite the complexities mentioned, it is also true that specialized literature begins to appear in specialized literature in Quantum Software Engineering (QSE), of which Talavera Manifesto [8] is a good example and, in particular, the relationship of principle that promotes to contribute to the quality of quantum software. Based on this, we should try to standardize or lay the foundations of methods for managing the development of quantum software.

Quantum software development projects currently have numerous features that fit neatly into the agile paradigm, such as adding features evolutionarily or using trial-and-error algorithms. In any case, quantum software projects currently meet the highest requirement of agile management need: most of the time it is difficult to define an immutable end state.

A fundamental characteristic of quantum software development projects is that in many cases, due to the current situation, they will go hand in hand with classic software development projects, initially quantum software will be integrated with traditional software or will coexist as part of the same project; This is driven by the fact that organizations are not going to dispose of all their current software and systems, that quantum software is not necessary for every software solution and that the use of quantum machines, at least in the short and medium term, is highly expensive. So in most cases, in the same project, totally different roles will coexist from the usual ones in IT projects that must be taken into account, and with integration requirements between both worlds that cannot be ignored. For this reason, QSE adopts the coexistence of classical and quantum computing, and advocates the use of reengineering techniques to integrate new quantum algorithms with existing classical information systems [8].

5   Reference Framework

Although we think the idea of taking Scrum as the starting frame of reference is correct because of its diffusion and high percentage of use in companies.

However, we are aware that Scrum has its limitations because it is designed for a self-sufficient team of a relatively small volume of people with all the necessary and transversal knowledge throughout the project team. This in the case of quantum software we believe is highly difficult to perform and impractical.

In general, agile projects need some type of framework that allows scaling to multiple teams so that each can work on different elements of the same project, sometimes creating hybrid background frameworks, such as SAFe or Nexus, which focus on management. from multiple teams. In the case of quantum software development projects, this type of vertical scaling adds some complexities to those known in classic projects, due to the multi-professional integration of the teams (engineers, mathematicians, physicists,...), to which it will add, in the case of projects that integrate both classical and quantum software, which from now on we will call classical-quantum projects, the need to be able to coordinate multiple teams made up of different types of professionals with very different profiles than those professionals IT professionals are more used to, therefore scaling teams horizontally.

Quantum project managers should manage projects based on detailed knowledge of processes, organization, principles, policies and frameworks, information, culture, ethics and behavior, people, skills and competencies as well as services, infrastructure and applications associated with quantum software and provided by organizations [8].

6 Some of the Required Adaptations

In order to (re) define and adapt an agile framework it is necessary to take into account the different types of professionals involved, in general for a quantum project we could form teams of:

- Developers, product owner and Scrum Master.
- Non-computer specialists who are actively involved in projects (such as physicists, mathematicians, and statisticians specializing in quantum environments).

Both groups speak in very different languages, so it is interesting to have some additional coordination role, with a highly technical profile for these new specialists in subjects that, in traditional settings, are not very common.

Due to the characteristics of quantum projects, it is not possible to consider starting a construction phase without a minimum- or not so minimal- definition of objectives, and an underlying architecture that facilitates work in this type of project. For this reason, an initial phase of Inception (in some agile environments also called sprint 0, but which is not part of Scrum as such) is considered a mandatory feature in any project.

The relationship with external providers, which in the case of access to quantum computers is a necessity, is also an element that is not treated in Scrum as such and the best way to work together with them must be investigated. This profile is also critical given that as we have said previously, quantum hardware is the most volatile element and its characteristics constantly evolve.

It is necessary to redefine the scaling of multidisciplinary teams in quantum software development projects and it should be considered to be able to have a team of specialists shared in different projects in order to condense the knowledge into a highly specialized layer that facilitates access to the knowledge of physicists and mathematicians by multiple teams working on different projects.

The framework for quantum software development projects also has to take risk management into account, which Scrum again does not explicitly take into account and therefore an adaptive version for these projects should be proposed that falls within that framework. Intermediate profile. In the development of quantum software to the usual development risks, uncertainty is linked by the evolution of hardware, development tools, error management of quantum software and software and the coordination of very different profiles.

These adaptations are a first approximation, it is evolving and improving with the creation of practical knowledge associated with the realization to a greater extent and scale of quantum software development projects.

7 Agile

Initially, it is proposed to use an agile framework that takes Scrum as a reference for its extension and general knowledge, but with the necessary adaptations. At this point we begin to define a framework that has little to do with Scrum, so being purists is more like ScrumBut (Scrum.org, 2020), that is, the partial adoption of Scrum and modifying the benefits it brings. But we are talking about an entirely new paradigm and the conviction that quantum computing will redefine many concepts. Therefore, since we consider that it is more appropriate not to speak of Scrum for the management of quantum software development projects, we think that it would be more appropriate to speak of an agile approach, in a generic way, focused on:

- Decision making based on experience, that is, the empiricism with which Scrum advocates.
- Close cooperation between all parties involved.
- Stakeholders' commitment to collaboration and support for the project.
- Accepting change, as the only way to be aligned with the changing needs of stakeholders.
- Continuous improvement of processes and tools.
- Knowledge sharing between business, development team and other scientific profiles.

8 Classic-Quantum Projects

Due to the characteristics of quantum projects in which it will be necessary to use a quantum computer and specific tools typical of this environment, and on the other hand, the same equivalent elements but from the point of view of classical computing, that is, traditional computers, the current, and their corresponding tools such as programming languages that were not specifically designed for quantum use such as C# or Java. In these classic-quantum projects, where in addition to the technical complexity we find different approaches to their definition and management, we can also talk about the possible life cycles and how a life cycle based on hybrid management (combination of agile and waterfall) would be especially interesting to facilitate not only its development, but also its evolution.

9 Hybrid Lifecycles

In software projects and in general, different life cycles can be applied depending on the type and needs of the project we are undertaking (PMI (Project Management Institute, Inc.), 2017):

- Predictive or Traditional, it is the classic project in which the scope, time and cost of the project is planned and fixed during the initial phases of the project.
- Iterative, when we set the scope initially, but we vary the estimates of time in cost as we progress in the project.
- Incremental, when the deliverable is generated through a series of iterations, whose functionality is considered complete in the last iteration.
- Adaptive or Agile, when the scope is defined during the start of the iteration (sprint in the case of Scrum).
- Hybrid, when predictive and adaptive life cycles coexist simultaneously.

The use of all these life cycles during the execution of certain projects, and in particular quantum ones, can generate additional complexity, the decision to use hybrid life cycles where a more agile or traditional methodology is used in each phase/predictive depends on the needs or restrictions of each phase or technology.

For quantum development projects you propose a hybrid approach, in which we can use more robust requirements and design phases that require quantum software integration, but including agile cycle-based development, giving us flexibility for uncertainty and change.

We must keep in mind that in many cases you can even work with two independent teams, one focused on the traditional project part and another specialized team in quantum computing that will be in charge of giving that differential value to the proposed quantum solution. These teams should be managed and coordinated thanks to the new proposed coordination role, sharing the same product backlog and holding meetings similar to the Scrum of Scrums, as proposed by Scrum.

For all this, a hybrid solution, as we explain, can provide the solution to the complexity in which we embark for these projects, always placing special emphasis on the following points, which take the best of each approach:

- Coordination of various work teams, these being quantum or classic teams.
- Follow-up meetings to review progress by teams and between teams.
- Planning based on phases and milestones.
- Backlog based on phases instead of having a complete product backlog.

10 Inception Phases

In general, projects that apply Scrum as a framework do not define specific phases, limiting themselves to a generic construction phase, with no division between analysis or testing phases (Sutherland & Schwaber, 2017). Even this approach generates certain drawbacks in classic projects where the initial knowledge of the problem to be solved is limited by the development team, therefore in classical-quantum projects, where there is greater uncertainty due to the lack of maturity of the technology, considers it interesting to define at least an initial phase.

We believe that an initial inception phase integrated at the beginning of the classic phase of the traditional part design, will allow to share among all the participants in the project both the architecture, the team, an initial identification of the risks, the testing strategies, the vision of the project and the required technological needs.

This phase will be followed by a more classical design phase of the part that is ultimately assigned to quantum teams to minimize uncertainty. But this phase of agile inception will be critical to create a common product idea, lay the foundations for collaboration of the different quantum and classical teams, and in general lay a series of foundations for classical-quantum integration.

It will be during the construction phase where the development of the project will take place, including tests and deployments in both environments (classical and quantum). The evolution of quantum technology and therefore of your projects will determine whether the formal definition of a specific phase of deployment or transition (as it is called Disciplined Agile) will be necessary.

11 Risk Management

As the good practices for risk identification propose, the identification of risks and their categorization should be started as soon as possible, so that a series of measures that minimize the risk can be applied (DeMarco & Lister, 2003). This early identification should start in the Inception phase or better still during pre-project phases, such as in the creation of the Business Case, which justifies the start of the project.

The categories proposed for this type of project, based on the possible areas of greatest conflict or complexity are the following:

- Quantum hardware.
- Quantum software.
- Quantum algorithms.
- Stakeholders.

12 Roles

In these projects there will be various roles that will be specific to different types of projects depending on the sector to which the benefits of quantum computing are applied, such as:

- Simulation.
- Development of new materials.
- Development of new medicines.
- Cryptography.
- Machine Learning.

The specialists by sector will be the professionals who are directly associated with all these practical applications where knowledge and expertise of the business is fundamental and very specific to each industrial sector.

The procurement manager will be a purchasing expert, with the appropriate experience to understand the capabilities and limitations of the different providers of quantum computers and to enable them to reach the appropriate agreements for each type of project and sector, depending on the needs of each project and the algorithm to be applied, either by number of qubits, the error level of the response or by the type of computer required (AQC-Adiabatic Quantum Computation- or QA-quantum annealing-).

Mathematicians and physicists as specialists, applying their skills as such, are the great unknown in typical software projects, but in the case of projects that include quantum software development, they will provide the mathematical knowledge necessary for the definition of quantum algorithms when they are not available for solving specific problems associated with each project.

13 Final Conclusion

Due to the characteristics of quantum projects in which it will be necessary to use a quantum computer and specific tools typical of this environment, and on the other hand, the same equivalent elements but from the point of view of classical computing, that is, traditional computers, the current, and their corresponding tools such as programming languages that were not specifically designed for quantum use such as C# or Java. In these classic-quantum projects, where in addition to the technical complexity we find different approaches to their definition and management, we can also talk about the possible life cycles and how a life cycle based on hybrid management (combination of agile and waterfall) would be especially interesting to facilitate not only its development, but also its evolution.

References

1. Taylor, F.W.: The Principles of Scientific Management. Dover Publications, New York (2012)
2. Gantt, H.L.: Work, Wages and Profit. The Engineering Magazine, New York
3. Royce, W.W.: Managing the development of large software systems. In: Proceedings of IEEE WESCON, vol. 26, pp. 1–9
4. Boehm, B.: A spiral model of software development and enhancement. ACM SIGSOFT Softw. Eng. Notes 11(4), 14–24 (1986)
5. Sommerville, I.: Software Engineering. Addison Wesley, Boston (1985)
6. Accenture Labs: Innovating with Quantum Computing (2017)
7. Homeland Security Research Corp.: Quantum Computing Market & Technologies - 2018–2024, HSRC, January 2018
8. Piattini, M., et al.: The talavera manifesto for quantum software engineering and programming. In: Piattini, M., et al. (Ed.) QANSWER 2020. QuANtum SoftWare Engineering & pRogramming, pp. 1–5. CEUR-WS, Talavera de la Reina (2020)

On the Source Code Structure
of Quantum Code: Insights
from Q# and QDK

Miguel-Angel Sicilia[✉], Salvador Sánchez-Alonso, Marçal Mora-Cantallops,
and Elena García-Barriocanal

Computer Science Department, University of Alcalá, Polytechnic Building,
Ctra. Barcelona km. 33.6, 28871 Alcalá de Henares (Madrid), Spain
{msicilia,salvador.sanchez,marcal.mora,elena.garciab}@uah.es

Abstract. A considerable number of high-level quantum programming
languages have been proposed and implemented in the last years. This
fact opens the possibility to study the structure of the source code of
quantum software, using initially the same metrics typically used in classical software. Here we report a preliminary study in module structure
and use of quantum gates in the libraries of Microsoft's quantum development platform QDK (Quantum Developer Kit) that uses a specific
language, Q#. The structure of dependencies and the use of primitives
is analyzed across all the source code available in the Github repositories
related to the platform to date.

Keywords: Quantum programming languages · Software metrics ·
Dependency structures

1   Introduction

High-level programming languages for quantum computers have been proposed
and discussed since decades, even before there were actual quantum computers to
run the programs. Recently, a number of software platforms have emerged that
can be used with emulators; they include tools and libraries with both basic
and fundamental algorithms implemented, along with some specific libraries for
applications in chemistry, finance and other domains. Several general-purpose
gate-level quantum computing software platforms have appeared in the last years
[1]. Notable examples include Forest from Rigetti, Qiskit from IBM, ProjectQ
from ETH Zurich and the Quantum Development Kit (QDK) from Microsoft.

Understanding the software engineering aspects that are specific to high-
level quantum programming languages will be a key driver in an eventual future
context in which quantum computers gain widespread use. While it is still early
to reach conclusions due to the limited use of those languages, platforms as
those mentioned above present an opportunity for research, given that their open
source nature makes them candidates for the empirical study of coding practices.

© Springer Nature Switzerland AG 2020
M. Shepperd et al. (Eds.): QUATIC 2020, CCIS 1266, pp. 292–299, 2020.
https://doi.org/10.1007/978-3-030-58793-2_24

Here we focus on Microsoft's QDK to understand the structure of the libraries and code examples provided from the perspective of module dependencies and the use of specific quantum primitives (gates). As a preliminary study, we analyze code using the same constructs often used in classical software metrics, deferring the proposal of quantum-specific metrics to future work.

The rest of this paper is structured as follows. Section 2 provides background on the elements analyzed. Then, the results regarding dependency and subroutine structure are provided in Sect. 3. Finally, conclusions and outlook are provided in Sect. 4.

2 Background

Q# is a programming language initially released to the public by Microsoft as part of the QDK in 2017. The QDK includes a quantum computer simulator and the hardware stack that will eventually come together with Q# is expected to implement topological qubits. Q# programs consist of one or more operations that describe side effects quantum operations can have on quantum data and several functions with classical code. We depart from the assumption that there might be specific elements in quantum programming that deserve attention from an empirical software engineering standpoint, both at the level of source code and at the level of modular structure. In that regard, we will briefly consider previous work useful as a point of departure.

Source Code Metrics
Source code metrics for classical software based on lines of code (LOC) countings, object-oriented (OO) code structure or complexity metrics have been used in a number of past studies, but the specifics of the separation of concerns between quantum operations and regular code have not been addressed to date, which may be considered from outside as a kind of procedural programming, if the internals of the quantum operations are abstracted out. In a recent systematic review [2], cyclomatic complexity and traditional LOC are the most used in studies together with a number of other countings involving operators, operands or statements, to name a few. The review identified few new metrics proposed in recent years, and most of them related to the OO or aspect-oriented paradigms. Here we approached metrics by concentrating on the main quantum primitives, as they may reflect the complexity of Q# programs better than measures based on traditional control structures. The consideration of the aggregation of quality metrics is also important [3] in quantum programs, as it can be hypothesized that the differences in quantum programming and classical programming does not make existing reported empirical studies comparable to new studies focused on quantum code. Recent studies show thresholds for source code metrics and their significance as predictors of defects [4] but they can hardly be taken as baselines for quantum code as the scope, maturity and creators of the latter are likely to be completely different.

Class Dependency Graphs

Class dependency graphs are networks built from the relationships among the classes of software systems, where each node represents a unique class and links between them reflect their dependencies. Class dependency networks are constructed from the header information of the classes; as this information is often determined by a group of developers before actual software development takes place, it could be argued that is less influenced by the subjective effect of each particular developer. Previous work has shown how such graphs can be useful to, for instance, study the Java libraries [5]. Other authors have also used complex network analysis on dependency networks to capture structural characteristics and to enable a maintainability and reliability analysis [6] or to analyze the evolution of software systems [7], acknowledging how these techniques provide "a different dimension to our understanding of software evolution", becoming useful for the design and development of software systems while easing the process of identifying software components that violated common software design principles. This is also the principle behind Zimmermann and Nagappan's work [8], who evaluated Windows Server 2003 and found that, when using network metrics, their models improved by ten points and identified twice as many critical binaries. The complex network analysis approach, thus, provides additional tools and metrics to assess and potentially improve software quality, as "traditional software reliability evaluation approaches lack the analysis of inter-component interactions of component-based software systems" [9].

3   Results and Discussion

3.1   Primitive Usage

We have extracted all the source code appearances of primitives in the namespace `Microsoft.Quantum.Intrinsic`[1]. We acknowledge that this decision does not exhaust all the significant aspects of code complexity in the libraries, which seems obvious, but it was chosen as a first attempt to understand the codebase. For the purpose of the analysis, we have separated those primitives in a number of categories[2]:

- Assertions: `Assert, AsserProb`.
- Gates: `CCNOT, CNOT, H, I, S, SWAP, T, X, Y, Z`
- Rotations: `R, R1, R1Frac, RFrac, Rx, Ry, Rz`
- Transformations: `Exp, ExpFrac`
- Initializations: `Reset, ResetAll`

The `Random` operation was kept apart, as it performs a random index selection in an array based on array values, which is difficult to group in the categories

---

[1] https://docs.microsoft.com/en-us/qsharp/api/qsharp/microsoft.quantum.intrinsic.

[2] It should be noted that some operations as `MResetZ` that include various primitives in one sentence have not been included which may affect the results (thanks to anonymous reviewer for pointing this).

above. Concretely, the information extracted are tuples with information on each call according to the format (module, operation, primitive), but there is also information about the length of the modules in lines of code in the form (module, mLOC). Operations in Q# –as opposed to regular functions– can be called from classical .NET applications as well as by other operations within Q#. Each operation defined may then call any number of other operations, including the built-in intrinsic operations defined by the language. A total of 1,657 calls to intrinsic subroutines in 124 modules (files) was obtained. Around 60% of the calls (across all the source code) found are gates, and 14% initialization. Rotations amount to 3% only, measurements 4% and transforms 7%. It should be noted that the functions and operations were structured in 47 namespaces. A total of 412 subroutines were identified as having calls, of which only 7 are functions, and the rest operations. This appears consistent with the fact that functions in Q# are pure, thus not allowing many types of calls that are not deterministic inside them. Figure 1 shows the rough distribution of the size of modules considering number of calls to primitives and module LOC. As it is apparent, most modules have a small size and a reduced number of calls.

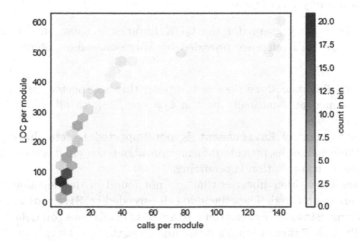

Fig. 1. Hexbin view of module LOC and number of calls to primitives

The distribution of calls per subroutine is highly skewed, with a maximum of 101, and a mean of 4, with 90% of the subroutines having at most eight calls. A closer examination of that number leads to the conclusion that the most "complex" subroutines (more calls to primitives) concentrate fundamentally in tests. The 11 subroutines two standard deviations away from the mean were inspected. Three containing modules were test bundles (SystemTest.qs, QeccTests.qs, Tests.qs, SystemTestJWOptimizedES.qs). These are not representatives of complexity, e.g. the longer operation ExpTest is a sequence of combinations of transformation primitives with different gates, surrounded by initialization and assertions per test. An operation that deserves attention is _LogicalANDMeasAndFix in Multiplexer.qs that implements a logical AND of multiple qubits. The algorithm (based on [10]) and is yet an optimization. Due to its general-purpose applicability, it can be considered a critical module. Near the two standard deviations threshold, we have ApplyOracleFromFunctionOnCleanTarget implementing an Oracle (a "black box" operation that is used as input to another algorithm.) for a given function. This is another example of a fundamental building block for other algorithms.

We attempted to find frequent patterns of co-occurrence of gates in subroutines using the algorithms APriori and FPMAX, with the only frequent pattern being that of gates H and X, however, these correspond to superposition and NOT, which are common operations, so we found no relevant interpretation for the pattern.

The detailed definitions of the Q# language can be found in the open source compiler, concretely, grammar is defined in the SyntaxProcessing module (in the Microsoft.Quantum.QsCompiler namespace), written in F#. We have developed a partial Q# language processor using the SLY Python library[3].

3.2   Dependency Structure

The class dependency graph for the QDK libraries is shown in Fig. 2. When compared to the API reference provided by Microsoft a few differences can be noticed:

- Microsoft.Quantum.Core does not appear; this is expected, as this namespace is opened automatically by the Q# compiler, so all its elements are always available.
- Microsoft.Quantum.Environment is not imported by any library in the QDK; these functions provide information about the environment in which the quantum computation is occurring.
- There are a few other libraries that are not found in the dependency graph as they are deprecated. These include (all preceded by Microsoft.Quantum): Extensions.Bitwise, Extensions.Diagnostics, Extensions.Math, Extensions.Oracle, Extensions.Testing and Primitive.
- Microsoft.Quantum.Extensions.Convert, although being deprecated (and replaced by Microsoft.Quantum.Convert) is still imported by one class.
- Microsoft.Quantum.Bitwise is not imported by any class, even though it replaces Microsoft.Quantum.Extensions.Bitwise.

Table 1 lists, for each library, the number of libraries that directly depend on it (DD), transitively depend on it (TD) and the reciprocity (R) as a percentage of the number of reciprocal dependencies.

Other interesting findings on dependencies are derived from the link analysis algorithm HITS (hubs and authorities). When applied to the directed graph formed by the class dependencies of the QDK libraries, HITS assigns two scores for each library: authority and hub value. According to the original formulation

---

[3] https://github.com/dabeaz/sly.

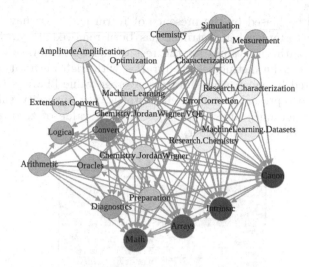

Fig. 2. Dependency graph (all libraries in "Microsoft.Quantum")

Table 1. DD: Direct Dependencies, TD: Transitive Dependencies, R: Reciprocity.

Q# library	DD	TD	R	Q# library	DD	TD	R
AmplitudeAmplification	1	22	0	Extensions.Diagnostics	0	0	0
Arithmetic	6	22	0.143	Extensions.Math	0	0	0
Arrays	16	22	0.364	Extensions.Testing	0	0	0
Bitwise	0	0	0	Intrinsic	18	22	0
Canon	19	22	0.621	Logical	6	22	0.222
Characterization	3	4	0	MachineLearning	1	1	0
Chemistry	3	3	0	MachineLearning.Datasets	0	0	0
Chemistry.JordanWigner	2	2	0	Math	16	22	0.286
Chemistry.JordanWigner.VQE	0	0	0	Measurement	5	22	0.25
Convert	11	22	0.286	Optimization	1	22	0
Core	NA	NA	NA	Oracles	6	22	0.286
Diagnostics	7	22	0.545	Preparation	4	22	0
Environment	0	0	0	Primitive	0	0	0
ErrorCorrection	0	0	0	Research.Characterization	0	0	0
Extensions.Bitwise	0	0	0	Research.Chemistry	0	0	0
Extensions.Convert	1	1	0	Simulation	5	22	0.154

in the context of web pages, the authority of a page estimates the value of the content of the page, while the hub value estimates the value of its links to other pages. When applied to our graph of dependencies, the authority value represents the relative importance of a given library in terms of the number of imports from other libraries. Because the library Intrinsic includes the primitives to operate the quantic processor, the calculation of the relative importance of the ODK

libraries would be biased by the presence of Intrinsic, so, we have produced a
new dependency graph where Intrinsic has been removed. Figure 3 shows the
distribution of authority values for the rest of the QDK libraries, where four
different levels can be distinguished: libraries with high authority value (over
0.3) are imported by most other libraries, average value libraries (between 0.1
and 0.21) which represent a middle class status, low authority value libraries
(below 0.1 but not null) and finally those with a value of zero, representing
libraries not imported by any other.

Library	Authority	Hub
Canon	0.473672	0.28887
Arrays	0.452327	0.204726
Math	0.445842	0.182797
Convert	0.349092	0.139942
Arithmetic	0.216633	0.279752
Diagnostics	0.213948	0.191135
Oracles	0.198933	0.058149
Logical	0.185118	0.112881
Measurement	0.158826	0.113677
Preparation	0.14848	0.266293
Simulation	0.13238	0.280508
Characterization	0.085725	0.32627
Chemistry	0.081065	0.129132
Chemistry.JordanWigner	0.046411	0.282289
Optimization	0.039336	0.112881
AmplitudeAmplification	0.032691	0.235686
Extensions.Convert	0.019031	0.0
Bitwise	0.0	0.0
Extensions.Math	0.0	0.0
Extensions.Oracles	0.0	0.0
MachineLearning	0.0	0.320429
Chemistry.JordanWigner.VQE	0.0	0.155021
MachineLearning.Datasets	0.0	0.0

Fig. 3. HITS authority: the importance of each library in terms of being imported

4   Conclusions and Outlook

The empirical study of source code metrics and its eventual relation to software
defects has not been addressed to date. We have reported herein a first study
on source code analysis of the quantum code in Microsoft's Github repositories
using the Q# language. Insights from the use of primitive operations in source
code are that unsurprisingly it is in its majority made up of gate calls and reset
operations. Most modules have a limited number of calls, and only a few show a
high density of calls relative to LOC. Subroutines with a high density of calls are
mostly tests, except a few fundamental general-purpose algorithms that deserve
attention as critical building blocks. The study of the network of dependencies, from both the perspective of transitive dependency and HITS authority,
shows a core of libraries that are imported by many of the others, a far from
optimal situation which seems prone to error propagation. Future work should
include other circuit-based quantum programming languages [1] and additional
libraries eventually available. Further, dependencies and primitive usage should

be complemented with the analysis of the interfaces (operation signatures) and code structure (e.g. cyclomatic complexity or functional composition) to come up with a better understanding of programming patterns, and also account for the number of qbits used in operations and other potential drivers of complexity. Finally, the preliminary data presented here is just an initial step towards an understanding of patterns and pitfalls in high-level quantum programming, and they should eventually be combined with knowledge about the internals of quantum languages and compilers [11], and also with higher level usage across applications or domains.

References

1. LaRose, R.: Overview and comparison of gate level quantum software platforms. Quantum **3**, 130 (2019)
2. Nuñez-Varela, A.S., Pérez-Gonzalez, H.G., Martínez-Perez, F.E., Soubervielle-Montalvo, C.: Source code metrics: a systematic mapping study. J. Syst. Softw. **128**, 164–197 (2017)
3. Mordal, K., Anquetil, N., Laval, J., Serebrenik, A., Vasilescu, B., Ducasse, S.: Software quality metrics aggregation in industry. J. Softw. Evol. Process **25**(10), 1117–1135 (2013)
4. Yamashita, K., et al.: Thresholds for size and complexity metrics: a case study from the perspective of defect density. In: 2016 IEEE International Conference on Software Quality, Reliability and Security (QRS), Vienna, Austria, 1–3 August, pp. 191–201 (2016)
5. Šubelj, L., Bajec, M.: Community structure of complex software systems: analysis and applications. Phys. A Stat. Mech. Appl. **390**(16), 2968–2975 (2011)
6. Chong, C.Y., Lee, S.P.: Analyzing maintainability and reliability of object-oriented software using weighted complex network. J. Syst. Softw. **110**, 28–53 (2015)
7. Pan, W., Li, B., Ma, Y., Liu, J.: Multi-granularity evolution analysis of software using complex network theory. J. Syst. Sci. Complex. **24**(6), 1068–1082 (2011)
8. Zimmermann, T., Nagappan, N.: Predicting defects using network analysis on dependency graphs. In: Schafer, W., Dwyer, M.B., Gruhn, V. (eds.) Proceedings of the 30th International Conference on Software Engineering, Leipzig, pp. 531–540 (2018)
9. Li, K., Yu, M., Liu, L., Zhai, J., Liu, W.: A novel reliability analysis approach for component-based software based on the complex network theory. Softw. Test. Verif. Reliab. **28**(6), e1674 (2018)
10. Gidney, C.: Halving the cost of quantum addition. Quantum **2**, 74 (2018)
11. JavadiAbhari, A., et al.: ScaffCC: scalable compilation and analysis of quantum programs. Parallel Comput. **45**, 2–17 (2015)

Safety, Security and Privacy

Towards a Framework for Improving Experiments on DoS Attacks

Marta Catillo(✉), Antonio Pecchia, and Umberto Villano

Dipartimento di Ingegneria, Università degli Studi del Sannio, Benevento, Italy
{marta.catillo,antonio.pecchia,villano}@unisannio.it

Abstract. In recent years, a number of solutions have been proposed for the detection of Denial of Service (DoS) attacks. Most of them have been tuned and tested by means of publicly available labelled datasets, which can be conveniently used to overcome the scarceness of real-life data gathered under incidents and attacks from production environments. Notwithstanding the high detection rates of existing algorithms, there is little concern about the representativeness of public traffic data and the impact on continuity of operation of the victim services.

This paper presents a starting step towards a framework for replaying and assessing DoS attacks. The framework aims to improve experiments on DoS attacks by allowing to replay previously-recorded attack network traffic. It features a number of components, such as a victim and a load generator, that allow to conduct experiments in a controlled and configurable environment. Overall, this makes it possible to assess DoS traffic itself and contextualize the effect on the service under assessment and potential countermeasures. The framework is tested by means of direct DoS emulation and traffic replay.

Keywords: DoS · Traffic replay · Network capture dataset

1 Introduction

Nowadays Denial of Service (DoS) attacks pose a significant threat to the availability of network services [11]. During a DoS attack a malicious user floods the victim server with many service requests with the aim of clogging it or even interrupting its activity [13]. As such, the server may fail to provide services to legitimate users. In this context, early attack detection and prevention are crucial in order to guarantee the continuity of service to the end user.

In the last years, DoS attacks evolved into a *second generation*, i.e., the so-called Slow DoS attacks [17]. These use low-bandwidth approaches that exploit application-layer vulnerabilities. Thanks to the plethora of ready-to-use and easy-to-find attack tools available on the net, performing both flooding and slow DoS attacks is extremely simple and does not require any coding expertise. However, if these tools have made extremely easy the task of attackers, on the other hand have led to the collection of datasets of network traffic under attack that can be used for intrusion detection research.

© Springer Nature Switzerland AG 2020
M. Shepperd et al. (Eds.): QUATIC 2020, CCIS 1266, pp. 303–316, 2020.
https://doi.org/10.1007/978-3-030-58793-2_25

A number of countermeasures have been taken over the years to mitigate DoS attacks [18]. Some conventional approaches are based on the monitoring of the connection request rate. A requesting client whose connection request rate is higher than a pre-established threshold is marked as an attacker. Of course, this is mostly uneffective for Slow DoS attacks. Moreover, in some cases even a legitimate requesting user could have a short-term burst of connection requests without leading an attack. Moreover, they are mostly uneffective for Slow DoS attacks. In recent years, with the rapid diffusion of deep learning techniques, many machine learning-based DoS detectors have spread in the literature [10]. All these solutions achieve encouraging results in terms of detection rate, which in some cases can even reach values close to 100%. In most cases, the experimentation and evaluation of a new detector takes place on public-domain datasets, which are used as a sort of benchmark to assess the validity of a given proposal. These data are typically made available in the form of pcap data files and correspond to several different attacks emulated in a test environment. Popular public-domain intrusion detection datasets are CICIDS2017 [14], UNSW-NB15 [12], ISCX 2012 [15]. Unfortunately, most of the times these datasets are used blindly, thus overlooking the representativeness of the traffic data therein. As a matter of fact, in the relevant literature it is possible to observe the tendency to pay more attention to the tuning of the detection algorithm than to the data on which these algorithms are evaluated. As this would invalidate the effectiveness of detection under real-world traffic conditions, it is necessary to ensure that research datasets conform to representative operating conditions.

This paper represents a starting step towards a framework for replaying and assessing DoS attacks. We aim to improve experiments on DoS attacks by allowing to replay previously-recorded attack traffic –available in packets data files– within a controlled and configurable environment. In particular, our tool leverages pcap trace files, which are typically generated by network utility programs such as tcpdump. Our framework has been designed to meet several open challenges in current DoS research:

- Public research datasets might not conform to representative operating conditions. Our replay tool could be a key component for assessing the impact of traffic data, with a consequent construction of more rigorous intrusion detection datasets. Noteworthy, many existing intrusion detection datasets come with pcap trace files that can be replayed within our framework;
- Many machine learning-based algorithms are currently spreading for the detection of network intrusions and, in particular, DoS attacks. Most of them are tested and evaluated with public domain datasets that contain DoS attacks launched in a simulated environment. Our framework can support the tuning of detection algorithms by reliving the attacks within controllable and configurable victim services and load conditions;
- Finding the suitable "defense threshold" of the system under assessment is always a complex operation. Since our replay tool allows an effective evaluation of the impact of a DoS attack, it could be used to understand whether to strengthen or loosen the defenses as appropriate.

Although in the literature there are some traffic replay tools for network analysis purposes, there are no frameworks that allow to carry out traffic assessments in a structured way, with the aim of conducting comprehensive security experiments. Our ultimate goal is to create a framework that collects a series of "best practices" –traffic replay is one of them– to conduct rigorous security experiments. The framework features a number of components, such as a victim server and a load generator, that allow to replay attack traffic data in a controlled environment and to configure desired workload conditions. The framework is tested by means of direct DoS emulation and traffic replay with CICIDS2017, i.e., a recent dataset that is gaining massive attention by the community. Results indicate that our tool can reproduce the impact of a previously-recorded DoS and conveniently replay third-party data from an existing dataset.

This paper is organized as follows. Section 2 deals with related work. Section 3 describes our replay approach. The paper illustrates the framework in Sect. 4 and describes the experiments that aim to provide practical insights into its usage in Sect. 5. Finally, the conclusions are drawn and our future work outlined.

2   Related Work

There are many solutions in the literature that propose detection algorithms tuned and tested by means of public domain intrusion detection datasets (trace-based). A machine learning-based DoS detection system is presented in [9]. The approach used by the Authors is based on inference and the detection rate achieved is 96%. In [8], instead, it is described a feature reduction method in order to detect DoS in a reduced feature space with the PART classifier. At best, the Authors hit a 99.98% recall for DoS Hulk. In [2] the Authors describe a hierarchical intrusion detection system that provides for the combination of several classifiers. The system uses three classifiers placed on different levels of the training phase. They reach an overall detection rate of 94.475% and a false alarm rate of 1.145%. Finally, in [4] the Authors propose a DoS anomaly detector that uses a deep autoencoder as core component of the infrastructure. The Authors highlight the potential of the proposal for 0-day attacks.

In this context of network security experiments, the use of appropriate tools for generating controllable, reproducible, and realistic network traffic is of extraordinary importance. Therefore, with the aim of testing environments for security products, over time several network traffic replay tools have spread. In general, replay tools can be either *stateless* or *stateful*. Those that follow a *stateless* approach replay packets according to their timestamps, and the content of replayed network packets is exactly the same as that stored in the original network traces. On the other hand, *stateful* replay tools are much more sophisticated. They manage the state of connections during replay, and therefore the content of replayed network packets may need to be altered in order to fit the "new" network configuration. As for the *payload* generation methods, instead, there are replay tools that do not alter the payload of the original packets, while others are able to replay packets with a new, "re-generated" payload.

Table 1. Replay tools - summary of comparison.

Tool	Is stateful?	Payload	Approach	Main feature
tcpreplay [1]	No	Original payload	Trace-based	Replays traces at a specified rate
tcpliveplay [16]	Yes	Original payload	Trace-based	Replays traces using new TCP connections
TCPOpera [7]	Yes	Original payload	Statistical-based	TCP state emulation
Our tool	Yes	Original payload	Trace-based	TCP replay for security experiments

Another possible difference is between tools that follow a *trace-based* replay and others that perform a *statistical* replay. The former provide that the traffic sent over the network during replay is identical to the traffic contained in the capture file. The latter, instead, analyze the original captured traffic in order to collect statistical information (overall packet frequency, timing between packets, etc.) and generate new traffic traces that are similar to the original capture.

One of the most famous replay tools is surely tcpreplay [1]. In fact, it is a suite of tools containing a series of open-source UNIX utilities. In particular, tcpreplay it is a command-line tool designed to work with standard network cards. It simply replays previously captured traffic traces at a specified rate and does not actively modify the information of the transport layer header and the payload of a packet. However, tcpreplay is completely stateless and is unable to handle the update of TCP sequence and acknowledgement numbers. As such, although it replays traffic to a server, it does not actually communicate with the server. In order to overcome this limitation, the same suite provides tcpliveplay [16], a tool that replays packet captures statefully by keeping track and updating TCP sequence numbers.

Finally, a tool that performs a statistical replay is TCPOpera [7]. It is designed for a stateful emulation of TCP connections. TCPOPera does not provide trace-based replay of the captured data. It first develops analytics from a packet trace, then creates a statistical model of the identified events, and finally generates synthetic traffic flows from the model.

The tool on which hinges the framework proposed in this paper uses a stateful replay approach, starting from the captured DoS traces in pcap format and preserving the original payload of packets. Unlike the aforementioned tools, designed essentially for network analysis or diagnostic activities, it is conceived as a lightweight, ready-to-use solution for replaying and assessing DoS attacks that typically appear in pcap format in most intrusion detection datasets. It is, therefore, a key tool for conducting a robust experimentation and validation of the detection techniques commonly tested and tuned on public DoS network traffic data for cybersecurity research. Table 1 summarizes the characteristics of the above cited replay tools with respect to our proposal.

3 Preliminary Replay Tool

3.1 Background and Approach

As briefly mentioned in the introduction, our framework hinges on a tool that allows to replay previously-recorded network traffic under realistic conditions, so as to measure the impact of attacks on a suitably-configured web server and load conditions. One of the hallmarks of our replay tool is surely simplicity, both in terms of design and use. As a matter of fact, given an input `pcap` file, it can be used as a common command line tool. In particular, the input `pcap` trace file contains the network capture we want to replay (that in our case includes a DoS attack to a web server). PCAP (Packet CAPtures) files are commonly used for storing traffic network traces. Currently there are multiple widely accepted `pcap` formats, but one of the most popular is `LibPCAP` [6]. The name derives from the library of the same name, where it is formally defined. `LibPCAP` is the oldest `pcap` format, but it is the most popular, mainly because is the default format used by widely used network applications such as `tcpdump`. In addition, most intrusion detection datasets provide DoS traces in `LibPCAP` format. The typical structure of a `LibPCAP` file is shown in Fig. 1. In particular, the first element is a *Global Header (GH)* with general traffic information, such as the correction to UTC time or the specific endianness (big/little). There then follow packets characterized by *Packet Header (PH)* (including timestamps and data sizes) and *Packet Data (PD)*.

As previously mentioned our replay tool follows a *trace-based* replay approach. In particular, its ultimate goal is to relive previously-recorded traffic towards arbitrary IP addresses and over brand-new sockets and connections, without altering the payload of the original packets. Therefore, since the tool supports replaying data exchanges to/from a server, it can be considered fully *stateful*. This feature is not trivial, as most existing replay tools are not able to replay traces using new TCP connections. It is worth pointing out that the proposal closest to our work, in that offers a similar replay service, is `tcpliveplay` [16]. Unfortunately, the use of `tcpliveplay` for our purposes has not produced the expected result. The weaknesses of `tcpliveplay` are also confirmed by the intense ongoing bug fixing activity carried out by the community[1].

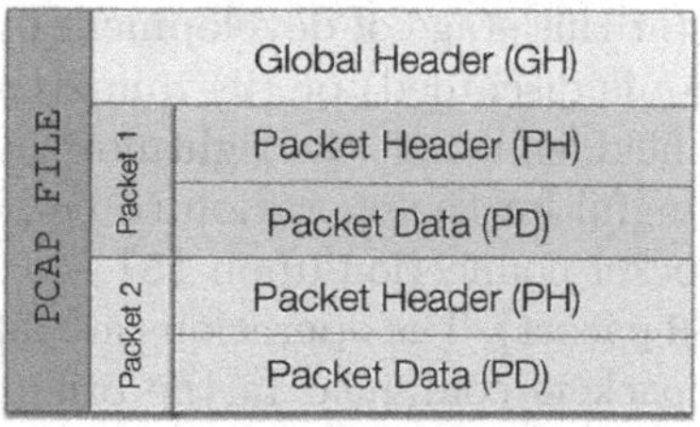

PCAP FILE	Packet 1	Global Header (GH)
		Packet Header (PH)
		Packet Data (PD)
	Packet 2	Packet Header (PH)
		Packet Data (PD)

Fig. 1. LibPCAP file structure.

---

[1] https://github.com/appneta/tcpreplay/issues/540.

```
09:07:05.766440 IP 192.168.56.102.39842 > 192.168.56.101.http:
 Flags [S], seq 2633020550, win 64240, options [mss 1460,sackOK,
 TS val 2720361938 ecr 0,nop,wscale 7], length 0
09:07:05.766674 IP 192.168.56.102.39842 > 192.168.56.101.http:
 Flags [.], ack 1353780858, win 502, options [nop,nop,TS val
 2720361938 ecr 153334785], length 0
09:07:05.766728 IP 192.168.56.102.39842 > 192.168.56.101.http:
 Flags [P.], seq 0:19, ack 1, win 502, options [nop,nop,TS val
 2720361939 ecr 153334785], length 19: HTTP: GET /?12 HTTP/1.1
```

Fig. 2. Human-readable `tcpdump` -r of three example packets.

3.2 Implementation

The tool has been implemented in `python`, exploiting `dkpt3`[2], i.e., a module for fast packet creation and parsing with definitions for the basic TCP/IP protocols. Unlike other available software, our tool replays traffic *at the same rate* it was originally recorded in the `pcap` file. This functionality is extremely important to reproduce effectively the original traffic conditions.

The whole replay process, which starts from the acquisition of a DoS `pcap` file and leads to the replay of the original trace, is described below. From the input `pcap`, containing a previously-recorded DoS attack, we extract the packets sent by a given source address to a given destination. More specifically, source and destination identify the attacker and the victim, respectively. A visual and simplified representation of the `pcap` content is shown in Fig. 2. It shows a human-readable `tcpdump` -r of three example packets (one packet spans three lines) sent by IP 192.168.56.102 to IP 192.168.56.101. These addresses match the IP of the attacking and the victim node used in our testbed, presented in the next section. It is important to note that the figure shows just a small window of the input `pcap` file, which typically consists of millions packets.

Given the input packets, since we want to replay a two-way communication with data exchanges to/from a server, the destination address is *rewritten* with the address of the server node towards which the traffic is intended to be sent for replay purposes.

Then the adjusted file is scanned sequentially. For each packet in the file, the tool either (i) discards it (at this stage of development our focus is only on TCP traffic, and everything else is discarded) or (ii) mimics socket operations based on the value of the *Flags* field, shown at the rightmost part of the lines in Fig. 3. The *Flags* letter is meaningful for the operation to be performed. For example, the tool initiates a new socket connection upon [S] (i.e., a SYN packet) or sends data upon [P] (i.e., a PUSH packet). The operations are differentiated on the basis of the timestamp of the packets contained in the original capture. This allows to intercept and replay the actual timing of the recorded packets. Moreover, at any time the tool maintains a suitable number of active concurrent connections

---

[2] https://dpkt.readthedocs.io/en/latest/.

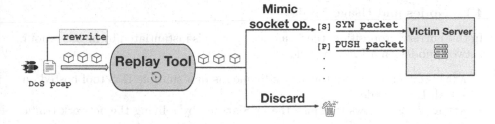

Fig. 3. Replay process.

towards the destination address, based on the actual number of socket opening and closing operations encountered across the input packets. The whole replay process is depicted in Fig. 3.

It is worth noting that the current implementation of the replay tool is not "tuned" to manage some isolated cases. For example, in the original `pcap` trace there may be packets corresponding to `GET` URL requests valid on the "original" victim node, but invalid for the server on which the replay experiment is being performed. Furthermore, the tool might accidentally attempt to replay SSH traffic with consequent and unavoidable authentication issues. Although we have not yet addressed these issues, the current implementation allows to successfully replay a significant class of DoS attacks. In particular, we are able to replay both flooding and slow DoS. The two DoS categories exploit distinct attack strategies, and therefore they leave different "fingerprints" inside the trace files. The behavior of the replay tool is always aligned to the specific type of attack to be replayed (more on this later).

4   Proposed Framework

We are striving for a comprehensive framework consisting of a number of components that allow to conduct controlled and configurable DoS experiments. Whilst our replay tool is a key addition towards addressing several open challenges in DoS research stated in the Introduction, a typical security experiment includes further steps, such as attack emulation, traffic data collection and evaluation of performance metrics. As such, our "core" traffic replay tool is meant to be instantiated in a controlled network testbed featuring a *victim sever*, i.e., the target of the assessment, a *load generator*, i.e., the component supplying a configurable workload to exercise the victim, and a supplementary *attacker node*, which allows to conduct controlled attack emulations aimed at complementing the findings obtained by means of replay. Although not covered at this starting stage, in the future the framework will be enriched with additional facilities, such as network flows extractors and intrusion detectors, which will be accompanied by suitable data filtering algorithms [5]. Overall, the framework is conceived to follow a series of "best practices" in computer performance evaluation.

4.1   Nodes and Usage Modes

In this current proposition, the framework above is instantiated by means of four network nodes on a LAN, as follows:

- Attacker_1: emulates the attack by means of a suitable DoS tool hosted on a Kali Linux node.
- Attacker_2: allows to replay the DoS attack by reliving the network traffic gathered from a DoS previous capture stored in a pcap file.
- Victim: Apache 2.2 web server node.
- Load generator: triggers, through httperf[3], HTTP requests that serve as benign background load to exercise and to check the status of the web server during the experiments.

Further information about the nodes is reported in Table 2. Noteworthy, the framework we set up allows us to make experiments that involve both direct emulation and replay of previously-recorded attacks. As such, it supports two distinct usage modes:

1. *attack emulation mode:* consists in emulating real attacks by means of a given DoS tool;
2. *attack replay mode:* consists in replaying a DoS attack by reliving the network traffic from a previous capture.

Attacker nodes are used as follows. Attacker_1 allows emulating real attacks by means of various DoS tools hosted by the Kali Linux node: it is unused in *replay* mode. Attacker_2, instead, allows to replay an attack by reliving the network traffic from a previous capture stored in a pcap file: it is unused in *emulation* mode. Therefore, during the experimentation phase, the two attackers are never simultaneously active. It is worth noting that in both operating modes the web server is exercised concurrently with both DoS traffic (either emulated or replayed in the two modes, respectively) and benign background HTTP load generated by httperf. We selected the Apache web server as a significant case

Table 2. Nodes description.

IP address (role)	Operating System	Application
192.168.56.101 (Victim)	Ubuntu LTS 12.04	Apache 2.2 web server
192.168.56.103 (Load Generator)	Ubuntu LTS 12.04	httperf
192.168.56.102 (Attacker_1)	Kali GNU/Linux Roling 2019.4	DoS tool
192.168.56.1 (Attacker_2)	macOS Sierra 101.2.6	Proposed replay tool

---

[3] https://github.com/httperf/httperf.

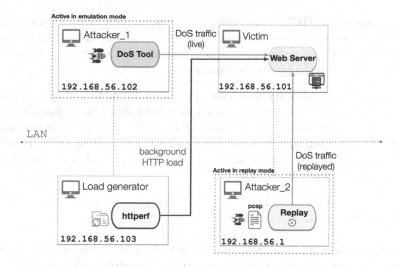

Fig. 4. Proposed assessment framework.

study, given its widespread use. In Fig. 4 we show a complete representation of our framework and its components.

4.2 Configurations and Evaluation Metrics

In order to emulate a realistic experiment, we adjusted the web server default parameters (that can be found at **/etc/apache2/apache2.conf** in a typical Linux-based system) because they may not be representative of real-life production server. In the adjusted configuration we set `MaxKeeplAliveRequests`, i.e., number of requests over the same connection, to 0 (unlimited), `ThreadLimit` to 1024, `ThreadPerChild` to 256 and `MaxClients` to 20148. These are crucial parameters for making realistic assessments on production servers.

Our current focus is on DoS attacks. This type of attack often involves the opening of a substantial number of concurrent connections to the target. By default, Unix-like machines often have a ceiling to the allowed number of simultaneously open files (1024 by default) and hence to the maximum number of currently opened sockets available to a process. We set this number to 200,000 with `ulimit -n` before launching the attack. This number is large enough to avoid any interference or saturation effect by the operating system. Evaluation metrics selected for our experiments are:

- **Load (L):** the desired level of load to stress the web server during a testing timeframe. We set this value by exploiting parameters supported by `httperf`, such as *total connections*, *HTTP requests per connection* and *connection rate*. The load submitted to the server is measured in HTTP requests per second (*req/s* in the following).

- **Response Time (RT):** the time taken to serve a request measured in milliseconds (ms). It is useful for evaluating server performance. For completed HTTP requests, the response time is a fundamental index as it impacts the QoS perceived by the application users.

We conducted a **capacity analysis** of the web server before performing any experiment, in order to discover the maximum load that can be handled by the server in attack-free conditions. The details of the capacity analysis are omitted here due to space limitations; however, we found out that in normal DoS-free conditions the RT of the server in our testbed is 0.2 ms, without exceeding its maximum load capacity.

5   Experimental Results

Experiments aim to provide practical insights into the usage of the proposed framework to replay DoS attacks. Evaluation is **twofold**: (i) replay of a fully "controlled" DoS attack generated within our framework, and (ii) replay of a DoS taken from a state-of-the-art public research dataset. The former is intended to demonstrate the ability of our framework at reproducing the impact of a DoS; the latter entails a potential use case of the framework in assessing the resiliency of a victim service by leveraging existing third-party malicious traffic. The experiments presented here focus on **Slowloris**, which is a DoS attack that aims to saturate the victim server, opening connections, but never completing the HTTP requests. It is a well-known *application-level* attack, often effective: as such, it is strongly relevant in the context of our work.

5.1   Replay of a Controlled DoS

We mimic a real Slowloris DoS, beforehand. Emulation is done in our controlled network by attacking the victim server, i.e., `192.168.56.101`, with a well-consolidated Slowloris GitHub tool[4] hosted by the Kali Linux node, i.e., `Attacker_1`. This will be referred to as the "original" attack throughout this Section. Moreover, during the progression of the attack the victim undergoes a concurrent, benign, load of 1,000 reqs/s generated by `httperf`, whose response time is monitored in order to assess the impact of the DoS. It should be noted that at this stage we also record the attack traffic in a `pcap` packet data file, so that it can be replayed later on, which is the purpose of our framework.

Figure 5 (•-*marked* series) shows how RT varies during the progression of the original attack. In the plot, the x-axis represents the time since the beginning of the experiment; the y-axis is given in log scale to better appreciate fluctuations around low RT values. The duration of the experiment is large enough to collect a large sample, i.e., more than 30 observations, in order to make statistical claims. It can be noted that the attack impacts service operations, whose RT = 0.2 ms in attack-free conditions, and –occasionally– it causes up to RT = 10 ms, which

---

[4] https://github.com/gkbrk/slowloris.

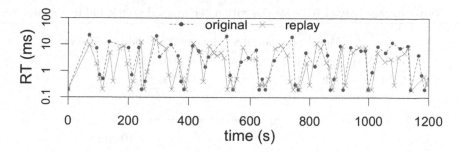

Fig. 5. RT during the original attack and its replay (y-axis is in log scale).

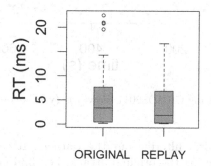

Fig. 6. Boxplot of the response time.

is a significant degradation. Noteworthy, 10 ms is seen as a typical maximum *tolerable* delay for a response of a web server in order to be usefully deployed in multilayer workflows [3].

The second part of the experiment consists in replaying the traffic recorded during the "original" attack: our aim is to verify whether we can reproduce similar effects on the server. As in the previous experiment, the victim server is exercised with a load $L = 1,000$ reqs/s during the progression of the replay; however, the attacker is now represented by the **replay node** (which is fed with the `pcap` file recorded) rather than Kali Linux. RT measured during the replay is shown in Fig. 5 (×-*marked* series) and superimposed to the original attack for better comparison. Interestingly, the "appearance" of the time series is similar: replay seems to reasonably well mimic the original attack.

Beside the *visual test*, we conduct further statistical analysis. Figure 6 shows the paired boxplots of the response time of the original attack and its replay. The leftmost boxplot highlights few sporadic outliers (depicted by o-*marked* points) in case of the original attack. Most notably, IQRs[5] (Inter Quartile Ranges), which catch the dispersion of the RT around the median value, strongly overlap. Table 3 shows sample mean, standard deviation and 95% confidence interval of

---

[5] The Inter Quartile Range (IQR) of a boxplot is the difference between the *third* and *first* quartile.

Table 3. Summary of RT statistics within the original attack and its replay.

	Mean	Standard deviation	95% Confidence interval
ORIGINAL	3.97	4.02	(2.96, 4.99)
REPLAY	3.40	3.77	(2.59, 4.22)

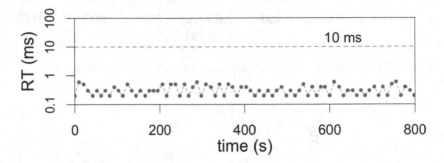

Fig. 7. RT during CICIDS2017 Slowloris (y-axis is in log scale).

the RT observations after filtering out the outliers. It can be noted that the sample mean of RT during the original attack, i.e., 3.97 ms is within the CI of the replay and viceversa: as such, it can be reasonably claimed that the impact of the original attack and its replay are not statistically different. For the data in hand, the proposed replay framework produces an attack that is *statistically* the same as the original in terms of the effects on the server.

5.2   Replay of a Third-Party DoS

We present here a replay experiment done with the Slowloris attack traffic of CICIDS2017. It is worth noting that CICIDS2017 is a recent dataset that gained massive attention by the community: the experiment is done to show the potential of our framework at handling *unseen* third-party traffic. Given the `pcap` packet data file available at the dataset's webpage[6] we (i) extract all the packets sent by `172.16.0.1` to `192.168.10.50` (i.e., attacker and victim in CICIDS2017, respectively) within the timeframe of the Slowloris attack emulated by the Authors and (ii) rewrite the destination as `192.168.56.101`, which is the address of the victim server in our testbed. The `pcap` obtained is fed to the replay framework and run against our victim web server. Such as the previous experiments, the victim undergoes a concurrent, benign, load of 1,000 reqs/s, which is monitored to measure RT.

Figure 7 shows how RT varies during the replay of CICIDS2017 Slowloris; again, the y-axis is in log scale. Surprisingly, it can be noted that the attack causes only marginal fluctuations above the normative response time of the

---

[6] https://www.unb.ca/cic/datasets/ids-2017.html.

server, which is 0.2 ms in attack-free conditions. Another interesting outcome is that RT under attack is always significantly lower than 10 ms (again, the indication of the maximum tolerable delay for a response in many practical settings), which is a further remark of the scarse effectiveness of the attack. This is quite surprising given the large body of literature on anomaly detection that capitalizes on CICIDS2017. A closer look into CICIDS2017 Slowloris traffic revealed that –although somewhat relevant due to the abusive consumption of network resources– the attack was not disruptive enough against a well "tuned-up" server resembling a real-life configuration, such as the one of our testbed.

Although beyond the scope of this paper, this finding has major practical implications when it comes to the representativeness of public datasets for cybersecurity research and it will be investigated in the future. Noteworthy, it provides some initial insights into the above-mentioned challenges in DoS research, which pertains to the potential limitations of existing datasets in conform to representative operating conditions. This is particularly relevant in the context of machine-learning-based research on attack detection, which appears to be among the major use cases of public datasets so far.

6 Conclusions

The goal of our work is to meet several open challenges in DoS cybersecurity experiments, with a focus on the quality of network capture datasets. The paper is a step towards the design of a framework for replaying DoS attacks and the implementation of a tool that allows to relive previously-recorded network traffic.

Our work is driven by the observation that research datasets might not conform to representative operating conditions. We show the validity of our proposal by evaluating the replay of both a fully controlled attack and a DoS taken from a state-of-the-art public research dataset. Results show that the proposed framework replays a DoS attack while obtaining –from the statistical standpoint– the same effects on the server as the original attack. The use of the framework with state-of-the-art datasets will give valuable insights on their actual representativeness for cybersecurity research. This analysis will be conducted in the future in order to provide concrete guidelines for the construction of rigorous datasets.

Our long term objective is to develop an integrated set of tools that enable traffic assessments in a structured way, with the aim of creating complete security experiments. In particular, we aim to create a *ready-to-use* framework for both researchers and practitioners that enables security experiments starting with the deep analysis of the data and ending with the tuning of the detection algorithm. In the future we will extend our replay tool to support additional attack scenarios. We will extend the analysis to further datasets, such as those designed to evaluate DoS attacks, other attacks and victim platforms.

References

1. Aaron, T., Bing, M.: Tcpreplay tool (2012). https://tcpreplay.appneta.com
2. Ahmim, A., Maglaras, L.A., Ferrag, M.A., Derdour, M., Janicke, H.: A novel hierarchical intrusion detection system based on decision tree and rules-based models. In: International Conference on Distributed Computing in Sensor Systems, pp. 228–233. IEEE (2019)
3. Alizadeh, M., et al.: Data center TCP (DCTCP). ACM SIGCOMM Comput. Commun. Rev. **40**(4), 63–74 (2010)
4. Catillo, M., Rak, M., Villano, U.: Discovery of DoS attacks by the ZED-IDS anomaly detector. J. High Speed Netw. **25**, 349–365 (2019)
5. Cotroneo, D., Paudice, A., Pecchia, A.: Empirical analysis and validation of security alerts filtering techniques. IEEE Trans. Dependable Secure Comput. **16**(5), 856–870 (2019)
6. Harris, G.: Development/libpcapfileformat, March 2011. https://wiki.wireshark.org/Development/LibpcapFileFormat/
7. Hong, S.-S., Wu, S.F.: On interactive internet traffic replay. In: Valdes, A., Zamboni, D. (eds.) RAID 2005. LNCS, vol. 3858, pp. 247–264. Springer, Heidelberg (2006). https://doi.org/10.1007/11663812_13
8. Kshirsagar, D., Kumar, S.: Identifying reduced features based on IG-Threshold for DoS attack detection using PART. In: Hung, D.V., D'Souza, M. (eds.) ICDCIT 2020. LNCS, vol. 11969, pp. 411–419. Springer, Cham (2020). https://doi.org/10.1007/978-3-030-36987-3_27
9. de Lima Filho, F.S., Silveira, F.A.F., de Medeiros Brito Júnior, A., Vargas-Solar, G., Silveira, L.F.: Smart detection: an online approach for DoS/DDoS attack detection using machine learning. Secur. Comm. Netw. **2019**, 1–15 (2019)
10. Liu, H., Lang, B.: Machine learning and deep learning methods for intrusion detection systems: a survey. Appl. Sci. **9**(20), 4396 (2019)
11. Mantas, G., Stakhanova, N., Gonzalez, H., Jazi, H., Ghorbani, A.: Application-layer denial of service attacks: taxonomy and survey. Int. J. Inf. Comput. Secur. **7**(2), 216–239 (2015)
12. Moustafa, N., Slay, J.: UNSW-NB15: a comprehensive data set for network intrusion detection systems (UNSW-NB15 network data set). In: Military Communications and Information Systems Conference, pp. 1–6. IEEE (2015)
13. Purwanto, Y., Kuspriyanto, H., Rahardjo, B.: Traffic anomaly detection in DDos flooding attack. In: International Conference on Telecommunication Systems Services and Applications, pp. 1–6 (2014)
14. Sharafaldin, I., Lashkari, A.H., Ghorbani., A.A.: Toward generating a new intrusion detection dataset and intrusion traffic characterization. In: International Conference on Information Systems Security and Privacy, pp. 108–116. SciTePress (2018)
15. Shiravi, A., Shiravi, H., Tavallaee, M., Ghorbani, A.: Toward developing a systematic approach to generate benchmark datasets for intrusion detection. Comput. Secur. **31**(3), 357–374 (2012)
16. Siam, Y.: Tcpreplay tool (2013). https://tcpreplay.appneta.com/wiki/tcpliveplay-man.html
17. Sikora, M., Gerlich, T., Malina, L.: On detection and mitigation of slow rate denial of service attacks. In: 11th International Congress on Ultra Modern Telecommunications and Control Systems and Workshops, pp. 1–5 (2019)
18. Zargar, S.T., Joshi, J., Tipper, D.: A survey of defense mechanisms against distributed denial of service (DDoS) flooding attacks. IEEE Commun. Surv. Tutor. **15**(4), 2046–2069 (2013)

A Cloud SecDevOps Methodology: From Design to Testing

Valentina Casola[1], Alessandra De Benedictis[1], Massimiliano Rak[2],
and Giovanni Salzillo[2]([⊠])

[1] University of Napoli Federico II, Naples, Italy
{valentina.casola,alessandra.debenedictis}@unina.it
[2] University of Campania Luigi Vanvitelli, Aversa, CE, Italy
{massimiliano.rak,giovanni.salzillo}@unicampania.it

Abstract. DevOps is becoming one of the most popular software development methodologies, especially for cloud-based applications. In spite of its popularity, it is still difficult to integrate non-functional requirements, such as security, in the full application development life-cycle. In some recent works, security DevOps (or SecDevOps) has been introduced, in order to enable the adoption of Security-by-Design principles in DevOps processes. In [4], a novel SecDevOps methodology was proposed to exploit such integration, but the security assessment and testing were performed with a static approach. In this paper, we propose to extend the SecDevOps methodology with the adoption of a novel security testing technique in order to dynamically test security properties in the operational phase, too. In order to validate the proposed approach, a cloud application case study involving the WordPress software module is presented and analyzed.

Keywords: Secure development methodologies · Secure cloud applications · Security testing

1 Introduction

DevOps methodologies are becoming very popular, especially in the development of cloud-based applications but, in spite of their wide adoption, they are hardly integrated with security design methodologies. The term SecDevOps, or Security DevOps, has recently appeared in the researchers and developers communities, but the management of security in a DevOps life cycle is still hard due to the lack of automatic tools to evaluate and assess security in both the design and the operation phases.

In [4], authors introduced a novel Security-by-Design development methodology for cloud applications providing automated mechanisms to support developers in the security-related analysis, design and assessment phases of the development process. *Secure by design*, in software engineering, means that "the software has been designed from the foundation to be secure. At this aim, the alternate

© Springer Nature Switzerland AG 2020
M. Shepperd et al. (Eds.): QUATIC 2020, CCIS 1266, pp. 317–331, 2020.
https://doi.org/10.1007/978-3-030-58793-2_26

security tactics and patterns are first thought and, among them, the best are selected and enforced by the application designer, and then used as guiding principles for developers" [16]. The approach proposed in [4] used models and quantitative metrics to enable the Security-by-Design approach and help developers take secure-informed choices. Moreover, authors showed that it was easy to be adopted by DevOps teams (mainly developers and tester, not security experts) and that it could be easily integrated within common agile methodologies (e.g. SCRUM).

Despite its potential, however, that methodology presents some limitation: in fact, it is meant to support developers during the design and deployment phases of a secure application, enabling to perform only a *preliminary* security assessment, which does not take into account possible security issues that may arise after deployment. In order to ensure that the designed security features are correctly enforced after deployment, in fact, the security assessment should include a dynamic security testing of the application when in operation.

To overcome this limitation, in this paper we propose an extension of the Secure DevOps methodology that entails the integration of a dynamic security assessment process at the operational phase, provided with the adoption of innovative and semi-automated security penetration techniques. To demonstrate the extended methodology, we applied it to a case study application, showing how it is possible to launch guided security tests and detect possible flaws in the design and implementation phase that would be otherwise difficult to identify with just a static security assessment.

The reminder of the paper is structured as follows. In Sect. 2, we present the extended Secure DevOps methodology. In Sect. 3, we discuss the security testing phase and the methodology proposed to enable the semi-automation of penetration tests. In Sect. 4, we illustrate the application of the testing methodology to a case study cloud application. In Sect. 5, we report some relevant work in existing state of the art and discuss limitations of current approaches. Finally, in Sect. 6 we draw our conclusions and discuss the future work.

2 An Innovative Security DevOps Methodology

As anticipated in the Introduction, authors of [4] proposed a Security-by-Design methodology for the development of secure (cloud) applications, relying upon a guided risk analysis process and a completely automated security assessment phase. The methodology was meant to support application developers through the execution of three fundamental steps of the security-aware development process:

1. the *identification of the existing security threats* based on the application architecture and implementation (i.e., based on the type of involved software components, on their internal behavior and on the components interconnections),
2. the *identification of the needed* countermeasures to mitigate existing threats, in terms of standard *security controls*, and

3. the *assessment of the* actual *security controls* enforced by the application, depending not only on whether and how such controls have been integrated into the application implementation, but also on the enforcement of the controls at a lower level, i.e., at the level of the software and hardware resources used for the application deployment.

The whole methodology leverages on Security Service Level Agreements (SLA) to model both the application security requirements identified after the risk analysis process, and the security guarantees that the application is able to provide based on the assessment results. Security SLAs are built in compliance with the reference model introduced in [2], which enables to express the security features requested or granted by a generic service in terms of standard security controls, belonging to a standard security control framework. In this paper in particular, we will refer to the NIST Security Control Framework [13], which collects more than 900 different technical and organizational security controls belonging to 18 different families.

The above steps are carried out in a semi-automated way (requiring only a very limited intervention from the developer team), starting from a model of the application under development and by suitably exploiting a complex knowledge base (the Threat Catalogue [4]) that collects several well-known threats in different domains.

In particular, with regard to application modeling, authors adopted the *MACM* formalism, originally proposed in [14] to model multi-cloud applications. The MACM formalism enables to easily describe the high-level architecture of a complex application in terms of a graph, whose nodes represent the main components building the application and whose edges represent the components interconnections. As shown in Table 1, which reports the component types currently supported by the MACM formalism, MACM nodes not only model the logic components which, together, help realize the application behavior, but they also allow for the representation of the resources that enable the application deployment and execution, and of the possible third-party providers of such resources.

With regard to supported node interconnections, the MACM formalism distinguishes among a few different relationships: *provides* identifies the services (either IaaS or SaaS) offered by a given CSP, *hosts* identifies the SaaS services deployed on an infrastructure resource, and *uses* identifies a dependency among services.

Finally, it is worth mentioning that the MACM formalism enables also to model the security features of a component through SLAs, represented in compliance with the reference model presented in [2].

As mentioned, the whole methodology relies upon a Threat Catalogue, which suitably maps together different concepts related to assets (i.e., component types), well-known threats affecting specific assets, and security controls that mitigate such threats. Thanks to this catalogue, it is possible to elicit the security requirements of an application based on its behavior and internal structure, by performing a guided *risk analysis* aimed at identifying existing threats and

Table 1. MACM node types

Node type	Description
CSP	Service Providers that offers generic cloud-based services
IaaS:Service	Cloud-based infrastructure resource (Virtual Machines)
SaaS:Service	Software service, either developed ad-hoc or offered directly by an external CSP, which needs an infrastructure resource for deployment and execution

at quantifying related risks. Moreover, by leveraging the information included in the catalogue, it is possible to verify whether the elicited requirements are met by the application implementation even when considering the impact of the selected deployment configuration. The *security assessment* procedure is carried out by means of a composition process discussed in detail in [14] and [4], which leverages a set of pre-defined composition rules that are suitably identified and invoked based on the security controls to assess and on the application model in input. The output of this process is an *assessed SLA*, representing the set of security-related guarantees that the application is (nominally) able to provide.

The data model supporting the methodology is shown in Fig. 1, it allows to link together different concepts, including vulnerabilities, threats, attacks and controls that will be used in the novel testing techniques.

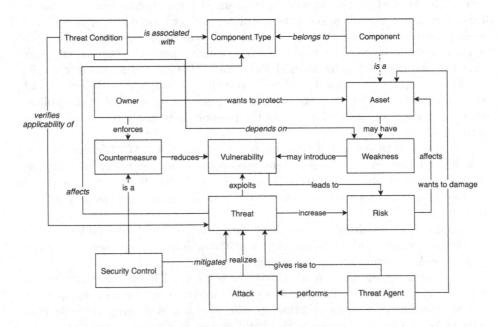

Fig. 1. Security model

Despite its great potential, the above summarized methodology has some limitations. In fact, the supported security assessment process is *static*, in the sense that it does not consider the actual application behavior at runtime, but it only performs a "forecast" based on static information, collected a-priori before deployment and execution. Adding support for a dynamic assessment in terms of security testing at runtime would sensibly improve the effectiveness and utility of the whole methodology, especially in order to make it better suited for a complete SecDevOps process. For this reason, we came up with an enhancement of the methodology presented in [4], which is sketched in Fig. 2.

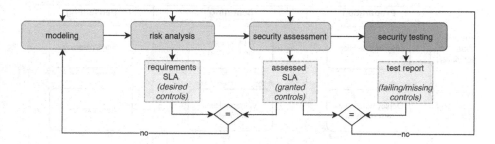

Fig. 2. The extended Security DevOps Methodology

As shown in the figure, we included a further step after the security assessment phase, devoted to *security testing*. In this step, the application is tested by launching a penetration testing campaign, conducted on the basis, again, of the information included in the Threat Catalogue and of the model of the application. In case of a cloud application the tests are conducted in a private cloud environment. The core idea is to link detected security violations, as reported in the test results, to failing or missing security controls. As shown in Fig. 2, the comparative analysis of the test reports and of the assessed SLA built at the end of the assessment phase provides a feedback to the previous phases: if any control belonging to the assessed SLA is detected as failing by the test reports, it means that there is probably a flaw somewhere in the implementation of a component or in the security assessment phase (which relies on a catalogue that may be not complete). If the reports identify a violation of a control that was not included in the assessed SLA, it means that the control was not considered by the risk analysis and, therefore, this phase must be repeated by adding new requirements.

In [3], authors presented a preliminary technique to enable the automated penetration testing of cloud applications, by sketching the main needed steps and by identifying the information to collect to automate, as much as possible, the tests. In this paper, we refine and extend this technique and integrated it in the methodology, as presented in more details in the next section.

3   Automating the Security Testing Phase

The security testing phase of the SecDevOps methodology relies upon the automation of penetration testing techniques by leveraging the security SLA and the security models, used to represent the application architecture with the identified Security Controls, and its security properties in terms of applicable threats, vulnerabilities and weaknesses, and by executing specific tasks enabling the actual penetration testing activities.

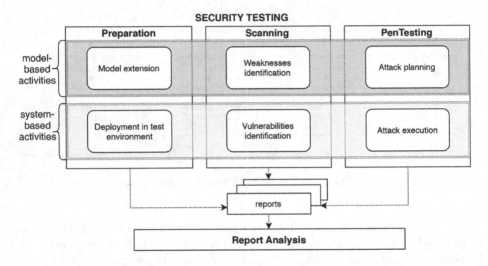

Fig. 3. Security testing phases

As shown in Fig. 3, the security testing consists of three phases, namely *Preparation*, *Scanning* and *PenTesting*, which include both *model-based* activities and *system-based* activities. The model-based activities are driven by the SLA, the application model formalized according to the MACM and by the security model behind the Threat Catalogue. System-based activities, instead, are carried out by launching publicly-available tools that are suitably selected and configured based on the information derived from the models. The security testing starts after the security assessment phase, and takes as inputs the application model (MACM), the threat model and the risk evaluation resulting from the risk analysis phase, and the SLA produced at the end of the assessment phase (the interested reader can find details on these in [4]). In the *Preparation* phase, the system-based activities include the deployment of the cloud application in a testing environment, as much as possible similar to the target production environment. Note that, due to security policies or legal laws, the direct execution of penetration testing activities may be impossible (or illegal) on the target production CSPs. The model-based activities performed during the preparation phase consist in the enrichment of the application model with the details related to the deployment configuration, needed for the correct planning of penetration tests. This information is collected by launching, in a semi-automated way, publicly available scanning tools able to identify running services, open ports and protocols etc.

The *Scanning* phase aims at identifying the weaknesses and vulnerabilities affecting the application under test, in order to verify whether existing threats can actually be exploited on the target system. Model-based activities focus on weaknesses identification, which is still a work in progress at current state. System-based activities focus on the detection of existing vulnerabilities and leverage well-known tools, as seen for the previous phase. Finally, during the *Pen-Testing* phase, weaknesses and vulnerabilities are effectively exploited through adequate attacks, in order to evaluate the actual security level of the application. As shown in Fig. 3, each of the above described phases is based on a continuous reporting process, which allows to log all the executed steps and to generate reports.

The final security report includes succeeded and failed attacks, as well as exploited vulnerabilities and threats for each tested asset. According to the model illustrated in Fig. 1, a successful attack exploits a specific threat and is linked to one or more vulnerabilities, and a threat can be mitigated by suitably enforcing a set of controls. This means that, from a successful attack, it is possible to derive the set of broken or missing controls.

In particular, a successful attack shows up as a broken application SLA, which in turn can be accounted backwards to three root causes: (i) the control is not enforced at all and an additional component should be added to the application design to enforce its implementation, (ii) the control has not been correctly identified in the risk analysis phase, (iii) the control has not been implemented correctly as stated during the assessment.

Often, especially in the early stages of development, developers may be totally unaware of particular security problems (or classes of them), which results in missing the proper countermeasures in the design, namely in missing the implementation/integration of dedicated security components. Since the risk analysis phase is an iterative process and must be tuned to several factors, even a slight modification or a wrong value in the considered risk parameters can strongly alter the risk rate of particular threats, lowering the level of risk. As a consequence, some security controls could not be considered at all. In this case, it is necessary to reconsider the threat through a new risk analysis process and implement the proper security controls to lower the affected level of risk. Lastly, the security testing processes can point out mistakenly implemented security controls, that can be promptly fixed accordingly, outlining an error done in the security assessment.

4   A Case Study

We designed a simple multi-tier cloud application based on WordPress[1] to demonstrate the advantages of the penetration testing process introduced in the SecDevOps flow. WordPress is one of the most widely used open-source Content Management Systems (CMS), usually adopted for blog, show-case site or e-commerce platforms. It runs on top of PHP and supports the two common Apache and NGNIX webservers, while it uses a MySQL database to store web application data.

Wordpress has several features, including a well structured plugin architecture and a flexible template system, which enables developers to integrate it to virtually every existing back-end system.

Figure 4 shows the MACM representation of the case study web application that we built during the modeling stage.

The deployment configuration consists of four virtual machines (red nodes) provided by an IaaS cloud service provider (violet node): two VMs host two WordPress instances, based on Apache and NGINX (*WP1, WP2 nodes*) respectively, one VM hosts the MySQL DBMS (*db node*) and, finally, the last VM hosts a load balancer (based on HAProxy, *lb node*) that we deployed to equally distribute the incoming requests across the two web-server instances. The services are all depicted with blu nodes. Note that, in this configuration, only the load balancer is exposed to the Internet, while the other VMs are hosted inside a virtual private LAN provided by the CSP.

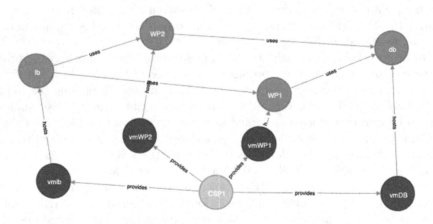

Fig. 4. Testing application - MACM model (Color figure online)

According to the methodology, we first performed a guided risk analysis, which produced a threat list and a requirement SLA (expressed as a list of security controls to enforce) for each of the assets (red and blue nodes in the

---

[1] https://wordpress.org.

Table 2. Threats for the Load Balancer Component

Threat	Description	ID
Security Misconfiguration	An attacker may exploit unpatched flaws or access default accounts, unused pages, unprotected files and directories etc to gain unauthorized access or knowledge of the system	T99
Using Components with Known Vulnerabilities	An attacker may exploit the vulnerabilities of the components used by an application to perform some malicious action	T102
Broken Authentication	An attacker may steal users access credentials or forge session data to gain unauthorized access to websites	T95
XML External Entities (XXE)	An attacker may exploit vulnerable XML processors to extract data, execute a remote request from the server, scan internal systems, perform a denial of service attack, as well as execute other attacks	T97
Insecure Deserialization	Applications and APIs may be vulnerable if they deserialize hostile or tampered objects supplied by an attacker	T101
Sensitive Data Exposure	An attacker may steal sensitive data, both in transit and at rest	T96
Insufficient Logging and Monitoring	Attackers may rely on the lack of monitoring and timely response to achieve their goals without being detected	T103
Broken Access Control	An attacker may exploit access control to disclose, modify or disrupt all data, or to perform a business function outside of his/her limits	T98
Cross Site Scripting (XSS)	An attacker may inject client-side scripts into web pages viewed by other users. A cross-site scripting vulnerability may be used by attackers to bypass access controls	T100
Injection	An attacker may send hostile data to an interpreter to steal sensitive data or execute malicious commands. Some of the more common injections are SQL, NoSQL, OS command, Object Relational Mapping (ORM), LDAP, and Expression Language (EL) or Object Graph Navigation Library (OGNL) injection	T94

MACM representation). Table 2 summarizes the threats identified for the Load Balancer component (lb node), while Table 3 reports a subset of the security controls recommended for the load balancer component.

Table 3. Security Controls recommended for the of the Load Balancer Component

Control ID	Control name
AC-1	ACCESS CONTROL POLICY AND PROCEDURES
AC-10	CONCURRENT SESSION CONTROL
AC-11	SESSION LOCK
AC-12	SESSION TERMINATION
AC-17	REMOTE ACCESS
...	...
SI-10(1)	INFORMATION INPUT VALIDATION — MANUAL OVERRIDE CAPABILITY
SI-10(2)	INFORMATION INPUT VALIDATION — REVIEW/RESOLUTION OF ERRORS
SI-10(3)	INFORMATION INPUT VALIDATION — PREDICTABLE BEHAVIOR
SI-10(4)	INFORMATION INPUT VALIDATION — REVIEW/TIMING INTERACTIONS
SI-10(5)	INFORMATION INPUT VALIDATION — RESTRICT INPUTS TO TRUSTED SOURCES AND APPROVED FORMATS
SI-15	INFORMATION OUTPUT FILTERING

The threats have been automatically identified, based on the involved assets, by suitably querying the Threat Catalogue, while the security controls of interest have been automatically selected based on these threats and on the results of a guided risk assessment process, which helped to find the proper countermeasures to enforce based on the current level of risk. After the risk analysis process, we executed the static security assessment step, which enabled us to take into account the specific security features of involved deployment resources and the interconnections among components to build the final assessed SLA of the whole application.

After these steps, we finally launched the security testing phase, aimed at testing the correct implementation of the recommended security controls. Note that, at current state, the penetration testing phase adopts a grey-box approach: we are aware of the components and of the network topology, but initially we do not have much more details than the ones originally described in the MACM model of the application. Moreover, we conducted the security analysis from the outside of the private cloud virtual network, in particular against the services exposed by the load balancer. Basically, we emulated the attacks performed by an external threat agent, altough we intend to consider additional threat agents in future and execute more automated tests.

The *Preparation* step involves the deployment of the cloud application in a testing environment and the enrichment of the MACM model with extra information deduced from the deployed system. This additional information can be obtained by (semi-)automatically chaining the execution of publicly available scanning tools. In particular, at state of art, our automation scripts relies on `nmap` and `nikto`. At the end of this step, we obtained a detailed description of the system: we were able to identify, for instance, the existence of the Word-Press application and the services exposed by the load balancer node, expressed in terms of open ports and service versions, besides other few information.

The enriched MACM model is an input to the *Scanning* step, where existing weaknesses and vulnerabilities of the target system are identified. While the weakness identification from the model is still a work in progress, vulnerabilities are recovered through another set of well-known tools, whose activation and configuration is guided by the extended MACM model. We used in particular `vulscan` (an nmap plugin), `nikto` and `WPscan` (a WordPress specific scanning tool).

By using the above tools, we discovered the following vulnerabilities:

- **CVE-2019-9978.** The social-warfare plugin before 3.5.3 for WordPress has stored XSS, as exploited in the wild in March 2019. This affects Social Warfare and Social Warfare Pro.
- **WPVULNDB ID 9259.** Unauthenticated remote code execution has been discovered in functionality that handles settings import.

Both these vulnerabilities are based on the same improper sanity checking validation against a parameter directly passed to a *eval()* php function in a Word-Press plugin (Social Warfare), which is installed automatically by the adopted template.

After that, we started the *PenTesting* step and produced the actual testing plans to verify the exploitability of the identified vulnerabilities, not reported here for brevity reasons. For example, the exploitability of the XSS vulnerability can be verified by forging a text file containing the JavaScript code to be automatically executed on the plugin's admin page.

This file must be uploaded to a web server accessible by the target word-press application in order to be able to perform a remote file inclusion attack on the plugin extension. By visiting the following address http://[URL to wp frontend]/wp-admin/admin-post.php?swp_debug=load_options&swp_url=[URL to evil js text file] the javascript file specified into the last part of the URL would be included and stored remotely into the wordpress plugin's admin page.

The second vulnerability also makes use of the same remote vulnerable endpoint, though the file specified in the URL must contain the actual system commands to be executed on the remote machine. The test plan for the XSS vulnerability led us to display an alert ('message') in every back-end page referred by the affected plugin, whereas the second test plan enabled us to execute commands on the remote host operating system and take the control by opening a reverse shell to the penetration tester's machine. As direct consequences, the application database asset is immediately compromised, since the credentials are stored in clear in a WordPress configuration file. At this point, other attacks can be attempted on the other virtual machines.

The discovered vulnerabilities are linked to the XSS and injection threats (ID T94 and T100), previously identified during the risk analysis phase, and associated to the security controls SI-10 and SI-15 selected for their mitigation (which respectively address the information input validation and the information output filtering).

It is worth to outline that these controls had been identified during the risk analysis to cover security requirements, then they were erroneously included in the assessed security SLA, since the assessment involved only the WordPress core and not the (automatically) installed plugin (Social Warfare), but they were instead found faulty during the testing phase. To conclude, the testing phase enabled us to find a security flaw in the implementation of controls SI-10 and SI-15 which otherwise would have been very hard to discover. In general, the possibility to launch semi-automated security tests during the SecDevOps process enabled to easily and quickly identify the main existing security flaws and support the developer teams in taking proper remediation actions without involving highly-skilled security personnel.

5   Related Work

Security engineering practices [1] aim at building systems that are acceptably robust against possible disruptions, threats and hazards. These practices typically suggest the adoption of processes that must be applied systematically to a target system and carried out during its entire life cycle [15], even if they are historically focused on the post-development testing activities, aimed to validate the effectiveness of already enforced security controls or to identify existing weaknesses and guide future security efforts and investments [6,17].

However, Security-by-Design approach [5] suggests the adoption of proactive measures against existing security threats and the implementation of the secure-by-default paradigm in the configuration of both software components and access policies. Based on this principle, several Secure Development Life Cycles (SDL) have recently been defined. The most common ones are Microsoft SDL, OWASP OpenSAMM and Cisco SDL. All these life-cycles include threat modeling at the beginning of the development process, and continuous security testing and assessment over all the phases of the software product development. The main limitation of such approaches is the cost they typically imply. In fact, while a few solutions exist aimed at partially automating the testing and assessment processes in several domains (including IoT [7,18]), the assessment phase typically assumes the involvement of an "expensive" team of security experts over the whole development life cycle and/or of security-skilled developers. The interested reader is referred for additional information to the surveys [8,10].

In such methodologies the last step is always the security testing, which is an expert-guided activity: despite the needs, as outlined in [12], at state of art, does not exist any standard devoted to describe penetration testing activities. In the following, we briefly summarize the most known penetration testing methodologies and security assurance techniques.

It is worth noticing that our methodology fully exploits the potentiality of DevOps approach and Cloud paradigm, which are recently being more and more affirmed, enabling a continuous deployment in testing environment enabling a mostly automated penetration testing, that reduces the costs and enable the adoption of agile practices (which are one of the main goals of the proposed methodology [4]).

It should be noted that few stable methodologies exists for penetration testing, as an example the ones proposed in **NIST SP-800-115**'s special publication [11] or the Penetration Testing Execution Standard (**PTES**) and the Open Source Security Testing Methodology Manual (**OSSTMM**) [9]. However all such methodologies are time and cost expensive and all of them focuses on discovering technical vulnerabilities, instead of relating possible attacks to high-level threats understandable to the end user. The approach we propose, on the contrary, starts from the end-user perception of the risks and clearly offers a feedback to the system designers and developers in order to correct and improve system countermeasures.

6   Conclusions and Future Work

Security testing of cloud application is one of the most critical steps in existing secure development methodologies: it is performed at the end of the development life cycle, its results may affect the overall design and it is mostly manual, so the quality of results depends on the tester experience.

In this paper we addressed such challenges by integrating into an existing Security-by-Design methodology a technique that aims at automating the penetration testing phase. The result is a methodology that is compatible with agile and DevOps paradigms, enabling a semi-automated penetration testing in a dedicated environment.

We tested our approach against a simple cloud application: a WordPress deployment which integrates a load balancer, a DB and multiple front-ends. As a main result we were not only able to identify and exploit vulnerabilities, but even to indicate which are the security controls that were declared and incorrectly or incompletely assessed, offering a clear feedback to the developers enabling a fast identification and resolution of the security issue. Furthermore, thanks to the adoption of proper security models and security SLAs, the developed application will be able to guarantee that the security featurers specified are correctly assessed and implemented as stipulated in the agreement.

The proposed solution is a new step in the direction of fully automated penetration testing, that offers the advantage of assessing security controls in a concrete way, but it still needs improvements. The testing plans, that we build in an iterative way, need additional formalization, in order to enable full automation. The scanning phase is limited to vulnerability scanning, while we aim at extending the methodology in order to identify possible design weaknesses using existing knowledge bases like MITRE CWE, and correlating them with our models. All these challenges will be addressed in future work.

References

1. Anderson, R.: Security Engineering: A Guide to Building Dependable Distributed Systems, 2nd edn (2008). http://www.cl.cam.ac.uk/~rja14/book.html
2. Casola, V., De Benedictis, A., Erascu, M., Modic, J., Rak, M.: Automatically enforcing security SLAs in the cloud. IEEE Trans. Serv. Comput. **10**(5), 741–755 (2017)
3. Casola, V., De Benedictis, A., Rak, M., Villano, U.: A methodology for automated penetration testing of cloud applications. Int. J. Grid Util. Comput. **11**(2), 267–277 (2020)
4. Casola, V., De Benedictis, A., Rak, M., Villano, U.: A novel security-by-design methodology: modeling and assessing security by SLAs with a quantitative approach. J. Syst. Softw. **163**, 110537 (2020)
5. Cavoukian, A., Chanliau, M.: Privacy and security by design: an enterprise architecture approach (2013). https://www.ipc.on.ca/wp-content/uploads/Resources/pbd-privacy-and-security-by-design-oracle.pdf
6. Common Criteria: CCMB-2017-04-001: Common Criteria for Information Technology Security Evaluation v3.1 rev5 (2017). https://www.commoncriteriaportal.org/files/ccfiles/CCPART1V3.1R5.pdf
7. Dejon, N., Caputo, D., Verderame, L., Armando, A., Merlo, A.: Automated security analysis of IoT software updates. In: Laurent, M., Giannetsos, T. (eds.) WISTP 2019. LNCS, vol. 12024, pp. 223–239. Springer, Cham (2020). https://doi.org/10.1007/978-3-030-41702-4_14
8. Geer, D.: Are companies actually using secure development life cycles? Computer **43**(6), 12–16 (2010)
9. Herzog, P.: OSSTMM 3: the open source security testing methodology manual-contemporary security testing and analysis (2010). http://www.isecom.org/
10. Jayaram, K., Mathur, A.P.: Software engineering for secure software-state of the art: a survey. Purdue University (2005)
11. Scarfone, K., Souppaya, M., Cody, A., Orebaugh, A.: Technical guide to information security testing and assessment. NIST Special Publication 800–115 (2008)
12. Knowles, W., Baron, A., McGarr, T.: The simulated security assessment ecosystem: does penetration testing need standardisation? Comput. Secur. **62**, 296–316 (2016). https://doi.org/10.1016/j.cose.2016.08.002
13. National Institute of Standards and Technology: SP 800-53 Rev 4: Recommended Security and Privacy Controls for Federal Information Systems and Organizations. Technical report (2013). http://nvlpubs.nist.gov/nistpubs/SpecialPublications/NIST.SP.800-53r4.pdf
14. Rak, M.: Security assurance of (multi-)cloud application with security SLA composition. In: Au, M.H.A., Castiglione, A., Choo, K.-K.R., Palmieri, F., Li, K.-C. (eds.) GPC 2017. LNCS, vol. 10232, pp. 786–799. Springer, Cham (2017). https://doi.org/10.1007/978-3-319-57186-7_57
15. Ross, R., McEvilley, M., Oren, J.C.: NIST SP 800–160: systems security engineering: considerations for a multidisciplinary approach in the engineering of trustworthy secure systems (2016). https://nvlpubs.nist.gov/nistpubs/SpecialPublications/NIST.SP.800-160v1.pdf
16. Santos, J.C.S., Tarrit, K., Mirakhorli, M.: A catalog of security architecture weaknesses. In: 2017 IEEE International Conference on Software Architecture Workshops (ICSAW), pp. 220–223 (2017)

17. The Software Assurance Forum for Excellence in Code (SAFECode): Fundamental Practices for Secure Software Development Essential Elements of a Secure Development Lifecycle Program - Third Edition (2018)
18. Verderame, L., Caputo, D., Migliardi, M., Merlo, A.: AppIoTTE: an architecture for the security assessment of mobile-IoT ecosystems. In: Barolli, L., Amato, F., Moscato, F., Enokido, T., Takizawa, M. (eds.) WAINA 2020. AISC, vol. 1150, pp. 867–876. Springer, Cham (2020). https://doi.org/10.1007/978-3-030-44038-1_79

Accountability in the A Posteriori Access Control: A Requirement and a Mechanism

Farah Dernaika[1,2](✉), Nora Cuppens-Boulahia[3](✉), Frédéric Cuppens[3](✉), and Olivier Raynaud[2](✉)

[1] IMT Atlantique, Rennes, France
farah.dernaika@imt-atlantique.fr
[2] Be-ys Research, Geneva, Switzerland
oraynaud.ext@almerys.com
[3] Polytechnique Montreal, Montreal, Canada
{nora.boulahia-cuppens,frederic.cuppens}@polymtl.ca

Abstract. The a posteriori access control is a flexible type of access control in which policy violations are deterred by applying accountability. However, the definition of the accountability process is frequently underestimated, as the auditors usually pay more attention to detecting violations. In this paper, we define accountability as a requirement and as a mechanism to serve the a posteriori access control.

Keywords: Accountability · A posteriori access control · Sanctions

1 Introduction

Setting the right access control is essential for organizations to ensure confidentiality, integrity, and availability in their information systems. It can be implemented in various ways depending on the environment.

Traditional access control models verify users' privileges before granting them access to information resources to avoid misuse. However, it is a prerequisite to take into account the organization's uses and practices, so that the deployed security solution is not perceived as a constraint for users with a significant risk of rejection. Therefore, the preventive access control can be inadequate in environments where exceptions may occur and can impose undesirably high computational costs. In this regard, the use of a more flexile access control appeared to be convenient.

The a posteriori access control is relatively open where a *break-glass* mechanism is deployed, and in which the user can override the access restrictions with or without the intervention of the administrator. To be effective, the a posteriori access control must be based on efficient monitoring mechanisms to detect potential violations of the security policy. It must also be combined with a dissuasive sanction and reparation policy so that users are not tempted to violate

© Springer Nature Switzerland AG 2020
M. Shepperd et al. (Eds.): QUATIC 2020, CCIS 1266, pp. 332–342, 2020.
https://doi.org/10.1007/978-3-030-58793-2_27

the security policy. That being said, the a posteriori access control works on deterring access violation rather than preventing it. But how?

In the literature, the a posteriori access control was defined as composed of three critical components that are logging, auditing, and accountability. Logging ensures that users' actions are being logged and traced in the system to serve as evidence in case of a future suspicious violation. Next, auditing is a process in which the logs are solicited and analyzed to check their consistency and compliance with the defined security policy. As for accountability, several definitions were given to it since it is used broadly in a variety of fields. For instance, [17] gave the following definition for accountability: "Accountability is the ability to hold an entity, such as a person or organization, responsible for its actions". [12] considered that accountability is about punishing policy violators. Thus, regardless if the sanctions will be actually applied or not, we can all agree that "accountability is a way to deter the user from committing violations", as it constitutes a threat of punishment that pressures the user psychologically.

A good number of researches treated the a posteriori access control by focusing mainly on its first two components that are concerned in detecting violations, but unfortunately they underestimated the importance of developing an accountability mechanism. In this paper, we define a framework for accountability to decide whether the user should be held responsible or not once a violation is detected. The rest of this paper is organized as follows: Sect. 2 presents our accountability framework, Sect. 3 discusses related work, and Sect. 4 concludes.

2   Accountability in the A Posteriori Access Control

As mentioned earlier, in the a posteriori access control, users' actions are monitored to assure their compliance with the security policy. We consider that the security policy of an information system corresponds to a set of rules defining access control requirements (permissions, prohibitions) as well as usage control requirements (obligations) relating to the actions that a user carries out in this information system. This policy can be modeled according to different access control models such as RBAC [13], ABAC [15], OrBAC [9], etc. Thus, when a user performs an action that is not conform with the rules defined in the security policy, the action is considered a violation. However, the flexibility that offers the a posteriori access control allows having certain exceptions for which the actions of users become permitted, or the user becomes blameless. In the rest of this paper, we consider a violation as an event, that is an action op done by a subject u on an object o at a specific time, that abuses the security policy without taking in consideration the exceptions. In this connection, security analysts can derive different conclusions when analyzing access logs: 1) the concerned subject did not violate the security policy, in this case the problem would arise either from errors in system functions or from external malice, 2) the subject has violated the security policy but there are legitimate reasons which justify this behaviour and which invalidates this violation but does not exclude the responsibility of the subject without sanctioning him, or 3) the subject has violated the security policy but no mitigating circumstances could be determined, he is then responsible and punishable for his unauthorized action.

Even if in an a posteriori environment the user is trusted, there is always a motivating reason that convinces him to breach the law to serve his self-interest and access data. Therefore, it is evident that leaving the access open to users exposes the system to different security threats that can be internal/external, malicious/non malicious, intentional/accidental [16], and that can cause severe consequences such as fraud, disclosure or destruction of information, etc. Since the a posteriori access control is based on a trustworthy environment in which users are knowledgeable of their rights (in reality, users are usually notified of their responsibilities and validate them by signing a confidentiality charter), we consider that the detected access policy violations are internal and intentional. Thus, the first possibility of the violation being caused externally is eliminated. Now that access policy violations are presumed, decisions should be made to determine whether the violator should be punishable or not.

In contrast, the accountability framework can be seen in two different angles: 1) it can be considered a set of requirements (a theory) that should be employed in the system to enforce the deterrence of policy violations, and 2) it can be thought of as a mechanism to define and apply sanctions when violations are committed. Moreover, it has been argued about whether increasing the probability of punishment is more effectively deterrent than an increase in the severity of punishment [14]. It all depends on whether the person who is tempted to violate the policy is a risk lover or not. In the following we discuss the requirements that should be adopted to deter policy violations and we propose an accountability mechanism *in case of the a posteriori access control.*

2.1   Accountability as Requirement

Deploying measures that increase the users' perception of accountability in the information system will likely make the users experience systematic processing and awareness which will increase conformance with the policy. In [20], the authors presented an accountability theory to reduce access policy violations through system artifacts and showed how this theory could increase accountability perception. We thus recall the three discussed system dimensions that heighten accountability perception that are *identifiability, evaluation, and social presence. Identifiability* ensures that user's actions can be linked to him/her while *evaluation* assesses his actions according to some normative ground rules and with some implied consequences. As for *social presence*, it assumes that user's performances can be seen by others.

Indeed, these three criteria are assured in the a posteriori access control. First, logging makes sure that all accesses can be traced; hence, their subjects can be identified. In addition, the monitoring and auditing that is done by analyzing logs evaluate the conformity of these accesses with the security policy. Finally, although it is not always the case where one can see an other's actions especially in environments in which sensitive data is involved, the administrator or the auditor can always have a peek regardless if he is performing monitoring or not.

Having these three requirements in the information system will decrease the user's intent to commit access policy violations. However, unexpected circumstances could happen which will force the user to perform an unauthorized action or have an exceptional access. To take into consideration these latter, we consider a fourth requirement that is the *justification obligation*.

The *justification obligation* is an *obligation* that states that in case of exception (e.g., emergency) that pushes the user to perform an action that is outside his sphere of access, the user must declare his access with a *justification*. A *justification* is the reason (purpose) for which the user has performed an unauthorized access. Each access event can only have one justification. Thus, we denote a *justification j* as $j = (u, op, o, r, t)$, where r is the reason for which the user u performed an unauthorized action op on the object o, and which is logged at time t. It is also worth mentioning that most of the times, in case of a sudden emergency, the user does not have the time to justify his action before doing it. Therefore, we consider that this obligation should be done *a posteriori* during a certain period of time after the access. This time period is usually defined by the organization. Moreover, we consider that once the justification is logged, it can not be modified later on.

At this point some might be wondering how this requirement will enforce the deterrence of policy violations. In fact, not respecting this obligation is a violation by itself; hence, the probability of applying punishments will increase and risk-taking will decrease. Now that we enforced the deterrence of the a posteriori policy violation, we should integrate this requirement in the a posteriori access control.

2.2   Accountability as a Mechanism

After what has been discussed in the previous sections, a user is held accountable in the a posteriori access control once he/she violates the security policy; hence, he/she is *responsible* for his/her actions and their consequences. However, the concept of *responsibility* can have different meanings [6]. As accountability regards the responsibility and liability of accesses performed by a user in an information system, we consider a user is *liable* when he should be blamed and sanctioned for his undesirable actions. It is evident that every *liable* user is also *responsible*, however this latter is not necessarily sanctioned. Since we assumed that the accountability process starts once violations are detected, the user is always responsible. Nevertheless, we distinguish, in the following, the cases in which the user is liable; hence, should be punished.

The Case of a Static Policy. In this section, we treat the case of a static security policy in which its expression is defined once and for all.

A user is *liable* if he violated the security policy and did not justify his violation as follows:

$$violation(u, op, o) \wedge \neg \exists j [justification((u, op, o), j)] \rightarrow is\text{-}liable(u, op, o) \quad (1)$$

While it is certain that the user is liable in case of non-existence of justification since the *justification obligation* is violated, it is not the case when a justification exists. As a matter of fact, other factors should be taken into account: 1) the reason of access provided in the justification should be categorized as an "allowed exception", and 2) the justification should be "honest". In contrast, in traditional RBAC or ABAC access control models that are not leveraged to dynamically adapt to fringe cases [1,10], exceptions are not encoded. Therefore, we consider a particular setting, where an exception policy, that specifies how the rights of users to access resources are affected in various exceptional situations, complements the security policy. It is generally a less constraining version of the security policy. For example, in a hospital, an access control policy specifies that each doctor has access to the medical records of his/her own patients. However, if a patient has a heart attack, then any doctor in the ward can have access to that patient's medical record during this emergency. Figure 1 shows our a posteriori access control setting.

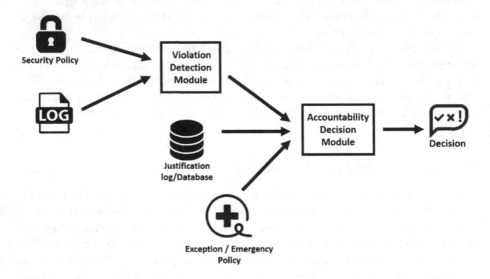

Fig. 1. A posteriori access control

In this respect, a justification is considered to be valid if the reason provided in it is relevant to the permissions defined the exception policy. We refer to [1,5] for inferring the relevance between an access permission and a purpose. Therefore, the user is also liable if he provided an invalid justification:

$$violation(u, op, o) \land is\text{-}invalid(justification((u, op, o), j)) \\ \rightarrow is\text{-}liable(u, op, o) \tag{2}$$

Moving on to deciding if the justification is honest or not, the problem becomes more difficult. It must be pointed out that the honesty of a justification is investigated only if this latter is valid. As previously mentioned, the user will have a limited time period after his/her exceptional access to justify it. Moreover, it has been shown in [18] that users tend to lie when they are pressured in time and are more likely to be honest when they have enough time to answer when they are being interrogated. In consequence, the time period chosen by the organization should have a reasonable length but should not either be so long so that the user will not have the time to plan a lie. Nevertheless, the user might sometimes justify his exceptional access after the defined time period because he/she had successive emergencies or simply because he/she forgot to do so. Therefore, we distinguish between *onTimeJustification*, that is a justification that is logged during the required time period, and *lateJustification*, that is a justification that is given after the time period. That being said, we consider that when a user logs an *onTimeJustification*, he/she is being honest. This assumption was made since the user provided a valid justification in the right time; hence, he/she is respecting the security rules. On the other hand, qualifying a *lateJustification* can be confusing as it can be the object of a malicious (dishonest) user and a non-malicious (honest) one. To solve this problem, we examine the *impact* or the *damage* (e.g., data destruction) that results following an exceptional access in the information system. Thus, a *lateJustification* is considered to be dishonest if there is an impact on the system. Besides, when a *lateJustification* is provided with no impact, the concerned user will be given a *warning* while always being responsible for his action:

$$
\begin{aligned}
&violation(u, op, o) \land \exists j[is\text{-}valid(lateJustification((u, op, o), j)] \land \\
&\neg \exists i[impact((u, op, o), i)] \rightarrow is\text{-}responsible(u, op, o) \land warning(u, w)
\end{aligned}
\tag{3}
$$

Furthermore, if a user receives more than n warnings, then he is classified as malicious; in other words, his $(n+1)^{th}$ late justification is dishonest (even if it is honest, he did not respect the *justification obligation* several times). n is also defined by the organization. This condition was put to not oppress the user in case he is being honest even though he violated in a way the *justification obligation*. The *warning* will give him the chance to adapt his behavior in the future; hence, will serve as a reminder to respect the obligation. Nevertheless, n should not take a great value so that the probability of being sanctioned remains high (ideally should be equal to 1 or 2). The steps over which the accountability decision model reasons is depicted in Fig. 2.

As a consequence, we define the profile of a *sanctionable* user as a user who did not provide a justification, or provided an invalid justification, or provided a valid *lateJustification* and his unauthorized access had an impact on the system, or got *n + 1 warnings*:

$$
\begin{aligned}
&is\text{-}sanctionable(u) \equiv \\
&\quad \neg \exists[justification((u, op, o), j)] \lor \\
&\quad is\text{-}invalid(justification((u, op, o), j)) \lor \\
&\quad \exists j[is\text{-}valid(lateJustification((u, op, o), j))] \land \exists i[impact((u, op, o), i)] \lor \\
&\quad totalWarnings(u, n + 1)
\end{aligned}
\tag{4}
$$

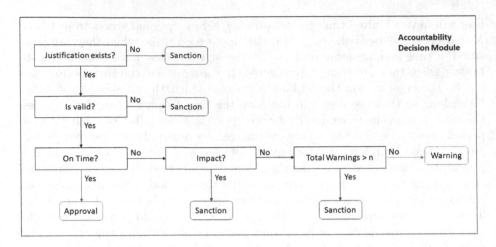

Fig. 2. Accountability decision module

As a result, the user will be liable, if he provoked a violation and he is sanctionable:

$$violation(u, op, o) \land is\text{-}sanctionable(u) \rightarrow is\text{-}liable(u, op, o) \qquad (5)$$

We can notice that (1) and (2) can be derived from (5).

Once the decision has been made about the user's accountability, sanctions and remedies should be applied. When thinking of sanctions, we first imagine an amount of money. Therefore, we consider a *sanction S* as a *penalty* that is calculated based on whether the user is sanctionable or not. The value of the penalty is chosen by the organization (for example, it can be equal to the salary of the employee). However, it must be noted that different types of sanctions can be considered such as getting fired, prison, etc. We define γ as a boolean variable that indicates if the user is sanctionable or not. Thus, $\gamma = 1$ ($\bar{\gamma} = 0$) if the user is sanctionable and 0 otherwise. In consequence, the sanction value can be calculated as follows:

$$S = penalty \times (1 + \gamma - \bar{\gamma}). \qquad (6)$$

In addition, other remedies can be put in place such as taking away the right of "breaking the glass", that is the ability to perform prohibited actions when necessary. This remedy will be adopted when the organization looses the confidence she had in the user, after this latter had caused several violations and been given multiple sanctions.

The Case of an Administrative Policy. When security rules are controlled by an administrative policy, administrators can also be held accountable following their actions. Normally, they are responsible of creating the security rules that permit or prohibit regular users from performing an access. Moreover, in order to do a *break-glass* action, the user might ask the administrator to create him/her a specific rule to perform the action. The administrator can also create/remove rules on his/her own without prior demand from the user. Whatever the reason for the rule's creation/removal is, the rules should be appropriate, and the administrator should not abuse his/her rights. We thus, consider the same setting represented in Fig. 1, but this time the security policy can be changed over time by administrators. Nevertheless, the expression of the exception policy remains static. That being said, a security auditor s can blame the administrator, with respect to a *justification*, without exempting the user of his/her responsibilities. It is worth noting that the security auditor must be different than the concerned administrator so that the accountability decision will not be biased. That being said, the user remains responsible since even if it was the administrator's fault, he is the one who performed the unauthorized action; hence, participated in the violation. In this case, the user will be given a warning, and the administrator is held responsible too:

$$
\begin{aligned}
& violation(u, op, o) \wedge \exists j[justification((u, op, o), j)] \wedge blame(s, (a, op, r)) \\
& \rightarrow is\text{-}responsible(u, op, o) \wedge warning(u, w) \wedge is\text{-}responsible(a, op, r)
\end{aligned} \tag{7}
$$

In contrast, a new regulation came into force in May 2018, that is the General Data Protection Regulation (GDPR) [21]. GDPR requires the collected data to be used only for *specific purposes*. Therefore, [4] proposed a framework to design access control policies in reference to the legal environment of the GDPR. In consequence, we suppose that when an administrator has the right to create/remove/modify a specific rule, his/her action leads to a GDPR compliant access control policy (ACP), enforcing the principle of data protection by design and by default. In consequence, when an administrator is blamed for his/her actions or when he simply commits a violation, the first thing to check if the resulted ACP from performing the action is GDPR compliant. If it is not the case, the administrator is liable and should be sanctioned. On the other hand, if the resulting ACP is GDPR compliant, the process returns to the normal liability check. In this connection, the *justification obligation* is also imposed on the administrators. Thus, the same conditions are applied to have a sanctionable administrator (*c.f.* (5)). As a result, an administrator is liable for performing an operation on a security rule, if the resulting ACP is not GDPR Compliant or if he is sanctionable as follows:

$$
\begin{aligned}
& violation(a, op, r) \wedge [\neg GDPRCompliant(a, op, r) \vee is\text{-}sanctionable(a)] \\
& \rightarrow is\text{-}liable(a, op, r)
\end{aligned} \tag{8}
$$

The functioning of this new version of the accountability decision module is shown is Fig. 3.

Moving on to calculating the sanction's value, it is the same as in Eq. (6). Nevertheless, when the ACP is not GDPR compliant, the sanctions will be set according to the GDPR, that is 4% of the total global annual turnover or 20 million euros, whichever is the higher. The GDPR's fine is normally imposed by authorities on the company. However, the organization can also charge the administrator, as he is the one representing it, and the value of the sanction is normally made precise in a previously established agreement.

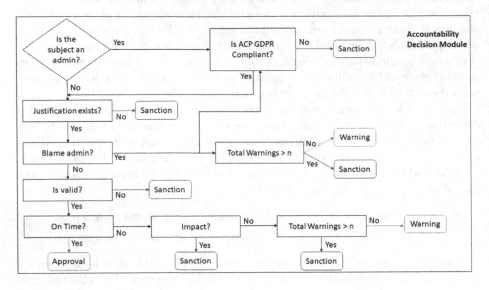

Fig. 3. Accountability decision module in case of an evolutive policy

3   Related Work

One of the first works to address the problematic of the a posteriori access control was [7], where the authors proposed a language that allows agents to distribute data with usage policies in a decentralized architecture. They designed a logic that allows audited agents to prove their actions and authorization to possess particular data. Moreover, they showed how this logic allows different kinds of accountability (agent accountability and data accountability), and demonstrated the soundness of this logic. Their vision of accountability is different than ours, as for them an agent passes the accountability test if he provides proofs that rely on a usage policy that is attached to the data and that specifies which actions can be done to this data. In our proposal, we impose an obligation to the user to justify his exceptional actions *a posteriori*, and the evaluation of accountability is based on this justification.

Another work on the a posteriori access control was [11], where a logical framework for a posteriori policy enforcement that combines trust management and elements of audit logic was provided. Moreover, the a posteriori access control had a wide success in the healthcare domain. For instance, [8] outlined the needed architecture to apply audit-based access control in electronic health record systems. Other efforts in the medical domain were [2] and [3]. However, none of these works proposed a solution for accountability.

4   Conclusion and Future Work

In this paper, we proposed a framework for accountability in the a posteriori access control. We showed how accountability can be seen as a requirement and a mechanism, and how integrating the *justification obligation* in the process can increase the probability and the severity of sanctions.

This current work highlights many insights that should be treated in the future. First, our accountability framework considers that the violations are already detected. As the investigations are usually done by analyzing multiple logs and correlating them, it might be hard sometimes to detect violations especially when we cannot find all the needed attributes that are defined in the security policy. Thus, it is interesting to provide an accountability solution when the violation is indecisive. Moreover, in our accountability framework, we considered both cases in which the expression of the security policy can be static or subject to changes using an administrative model. Nevertheless, we did not take into consideration the evolution of the exception policy that can also change depending on the context. For instance, in case of a crisis, access permissions are updated assuring the validity of a higher number of justifications [19]. In fact, finding valid justifications when treating the violations a posteriori would allow us to enrich and contextualize the exception policy. Therefore, we would like to treat the changes of this policy along this contextualization process that will influence the applicability of sanctions.

Acknowledgments. This research is funded by *Be-ys Research*, Meyrin 123, c/o BDO SA, 1219 Châtelaine, GENEVE, a mark of the group *be-ys* dedicated to research and innovation.

References

1. Alves, S., Fernández, M.: A framework for the analysis of access control policies with emergency management. Electron. Notes Theor. Comput. Sci. **312**, 89–105 (2015)
2. Azkia, H., Cuppens-Boulahia, N., Cuppens, F., Coatrieux, G.: Reconciling IHE-ATNA profile with a posteriori contextual access and usage control policy in healthcare environment. In: 2010 Sixth International Conference on Information Assurance and Security, pp. 197–203. IEEE (2010)
3. Azkia, H., Cuppens-Boulahia, N., Cuppens, F., Coatrieux, G.: Ontology based log content extraction engine for a posteriori security control. Stud. Health Technol. Inform. **180**, 746–750 (2012)
4. Bartolini, C., Daoudagh, S., Lenzini, G., Marchetti, E.: Towards a lawful authorized access: a preliminary GDPR-based authorized access. In: 14th International Conference on Software Technologies (ICSOFT 2019), Prague, Czech Republic, pp. 26–28 (2019)
5. Byun, J.W., Li, N.: Purpose based access control for privacy protection in relational database systems. VLDB J. **17**(4), 603–619 (2008)
6. Cholvy, L., Cuppens, F., Saurel, C.: Towards a logical formalization of responsibility. In: Proceedings of the 6th International Conference on Artificial Intelligence and Law, pp. 233–242 (1997)

7. Corin, R., Etalle, S., den Hartog, J., Lenzini, G., Staicu, I.: A logic for auditing accountability in decentralized systems. In: Dimitrakos, T., Martinelli, F. (eds.) Formal Aspects in Security and Trust. IIFIP, vol. 173, pp. 187–201. Springer, Boston, MA (2005). https://doi.org/10.1007/0-387-24098-5_14

8. Dekker, M.A.C., Etalle, S.: Audit-based access control for electronic health records. Electron. Notes Theor. Comput. Sci. **168**, 221–236 (2007)

9. El Kalam, A.A., et al.: Or-bac: un modèle de contrôle d'accès basé sur les organisations. Cahiers francophones de la recherche en sécurité de l'information **1**, 30–43 (2003)

10. Essaouini, N., Cuppens, F., Cuppens-Boulahia, N., El Kalam, A.A.: Specifying and enforcing constraints in dynamic access control policies. In: 2014 Twelfth Annual International Conference on Privacy, Security and Trust, pp. 290–297. IEEE (2014)

11. Etalle, S., Winsborough, W.H.: A posteriori compliance control categories and subject descriptors, pp. 11–20 (2007)

12. Feigenbaum, J.: Accountability as a driver of innovative privacy solutions. In: Privacy and Innovation Symposium (2010)

13. Ferraiolo, D., Cugini, J., Kuhn, D.R.: Role-based access control (RBAC): features and motivations. In: Proceedings of 11th Annual Computer Security Application Conference, pp. 241–48 (1995)

14. Friesen, L.: Certainty of punishment versus severity of punishment: an experimental investigation. South. Econ. J. **79**(2), 399–421 (2012)

15. Hu, V.C., et al.: Guide to attribute based access control (ABAC) definition and considerations (draft). NIST special publication 800-162 (2013)

16. Jouini, M., Rabai, L.B.A., Aissa, A.B.: Classification of security threats in information systems. ANT/SEIT **32**, 489–496 (2014)

17. Lampson, B.: Accountability and freedom. In: Cambridge Computer Seminar, Cambridge, UK, pp. 1–26 (2005)

18. Shalvi, S., Eldar, O., Bereby-Meyer, Y.: Honesty requires time (and lack of justifications). Psychol. Sci. **23**(10), 1264–1270 (2012)

19. Smari, W.W., Clemente, P., Lalande, J.F.: An extended attribute based access control model with trust and privacy: application to a collaborative crisis management system. Future Gener. Comput. Syst. **31**, 147–168 (2014)

20. Vance, A., Lowry, P.B., Eggett, D.: Using accountability to reduce access policy violations in information systems. J. Manag. Inf. Syst. **29**(4), 263–290 (2013)

21. Voigt, P., Von dem Bussche, A.: The EU General Data Protection Regulation (GDPR). A Practical Guide. Springer, Cham (2017). https://doi.org/10.1007/978-3-319-57959-7

Secure Agile Software Development: Policies and Practices for Agile Teams

Carlos Magnum M. Bezerra[1,2] (ID), Suzana C. B. Sampaio[2](✉) (ID),
and Marcelo L. M. Marinho[2] (ID)

[1] Tempest Security Intelligence, Recife, Brazil
`carlos.bezerra@tempest.com.br`
[2] Department of Computer Science (DC),
Federal Rural University of Pernambuco (UFRPE), Recife, PE, Brazil
{`suzana.sampaio,marcelo.marinho`}`@ufrpe.br`

Abstract. In recent years there has been a significant shift from traditional development towards agile. Agile adoption has been reported to
result in more efficient and productive projects. Information security is
becoming an important entity for most organizations. Cyber security has
been a major concern in the digital world. However, despite its importance, agile methodologies hardly address the security requirements. In
result, many security problems have been exposed in recent years, often
leading to financial and social losses. As software is one of the computational assets most exposed to security threats, it is imperative that
its development process includes special attention to security requirements. In this scenario, the need arises to include safety practices in the
daily life of agile teams. In this paper, we highlight a security policies
that presents practices suitable for agile teams. In order to do that this
study (a) synthesizes the extant literature in this domain; (b) prioritizes
the agile security practices; (c) groups these practices in policies based
on the results of a workshop in a cyber security company (d) evaluates
the policies based on security and agile specialist assessment; and (e)
considering the feedback, presents the final security policies for software
development agile teams.

Keywords: Software security · Security · Secure software
development · Agile · Secure software development policies · Agile
methodologies

1 Introduction

Nowadays, organizations are looking for methods that meet their needs to adapt
to complex environments and successive changes [37]. In order to deliver software
products more efficiently and with greater value to the customer, many Software
Development (SD) companies have migrated to Agile Methodologies (AM), such
as: Scrum and XP. Therefore, the AM became the most noticeable change in
SD world and are the most used methodologies among the Software Projects

© Springer Nature Switzerland AG 2020
M. Shepperd et al. (Eds.): QUATIC 2020, CCIS 1266, pp. 343–357, 2020.
https://doi.org/10.1007/978-3-030-58793-2_28

worldwide [1]. However, the use of these methodologies imposes some limitations in the inclusion of security activities [5,6,29,39,40].

Several security flaws are due to the lack of security activities during the SD process [22]. Cybernetic attacks aims on obtaining confidential data, hiding valuable information in some way, retaliating against government or private initiative actions or, in some cases, on the simple pleasure of fulfilling overcoming a challenge of invading computer systems. Whatever are the intentions, these attacks always generate financial or other damages, therefore, currently, the search for computational security is growing [12]. Several initiatives can demonstrate the growth of these concerns, Google *Project Zero* [33], *The Open Web Application Security Project* (OWASP) [31] and the data protection laws, such LGPD [26] from Brazil and GPDR [21] from European Union.

Developing software with security attributes, as a way to prevent attacks, is essential [19]. The growing need for software security and the adoption of AM as a way to develop software efficiently, raise questions regarding the integration of these two concepts. Reconciling these two worlds in the development process is a research problem for several studies [2,5,7,11,19,29,30,35,39].

In this context, it is possible to establish the need to research ways to include security activities in agile processes and teams. Bansal and Jolly [40] highlights the lack of security requirements integrated view in agile practices. Authors, such as [7] and [14] depict the importance of integrating security practices into SD process, but not just as an isolated action. From these perspectives, it is urgent to look for ways to integrate the agile development model and the security practices and policies. Therefore, this study aims to address this gap on agile security practices and policies. This study contributes to the current literature in three ways: (i) by presenting a synthesis of identified security practices for agile SD; (ii) providing security policies with practical practices and security attributes for agile teams; (iii) by providing assistance to agile teams looking to enhance their security practices.

The rest of the paper is organized as follows: Sect. 2 presents the theoretical background. Section 3 provides an overview of the methodological approach. Section 4 describes our proposal, detailing the policies and its practices. Section 5 evaluates such proposal and discusses the findings. At last, Sect. 6 reports final considerations, limitations and future works.

2   Theoretical Background

2.1   Agile Methodologies

Due to the complex corporate environments, agility has become a necessary condition for obtaining a competitive market advantage in the market [37], and the number of software development companies adopting these methods continues to grow [16,37]. Several frameworks were created based on this concept such as Scrum [38] and XP [9]. Elements from these methodologies are covered during this research such as *Product Backlog* (List of all known requirements of the projects [38]), *Pair Programming* (methods that allows two developers to implement, in a collaborative manner, a project activity [3]), *Planning Poker* (estimation *"game"* in which the team reaches a consensus over a complexity value to *User Stories* [3]), among others.

2.2   Secure Software Development

Cyber security is a collection of tools, policies, concepts, guidelines, risk management, actions, training, practices, and technologies that can be used to protect users' environments, organization and assets [41]. Security is intended to guarantee maintenance of the organization's computational properties and user assets against relevant risks, present on the internet. For this, it is necessary to guarantee three main attributes: confidentiality, integrity and availability [41]. Confidentiality is a property that guarantees the absence of unwanted information disclosure [7]. The integrity attribute ensures that there will be no unauthorized changes [7]. And availability is associated with the service and information readiness and punctuality provided by the system [7].

Security must be considered a critical non-functional requirement, which needs to be fully incorporated by the development methodologies [40]. Lack of security requirements [40], technical implementation failures, lack of security validation [19] and lack of experience and care with security [14], are a few aspects problems in a mindset that does not include security requirements.

The secure development process is the main means, for implementing security practices [30]. The secure SD cycle includes the training, requirements, planning, implementation, verification, delivery and response processes [36]. Each of these processes must contain its security-related practices. Among those known security process presented by organizations in the market are: *Microsoft Security Development Lifecycle* (MSDL) [27], the *Comprehensive, Lightweight Application Security Process* (CLASP) of *The Open Web Application Security Project* (OWASP) [18]. Although not all processes practices are suitable for agile teams. Despite all the counterpoints, adapting security practices to the agile world is an important task. Next section analyses related studies conducted in this area.

2.3   Related Works

Many studies [2,5,30] point to a lack of support for security activities in the agile development. Some are quantitative studies [5,6], to evaluate security practices for SD in agile environments and propose a new agile process for secure development [5]. Other to assess compatibility of security practices with agile characteristics [6]. A few studies focus only in one process, such as [35], that demonstrates how to integrate security requirements in agile processes, and [40] that presents a systematic analysis of approaches to add security to the requirements process, within agile methodologies.

[7] presents practices that contribute to improving the agile SD process from the security point of view. For each practice, a description and its benefits were presented. Our study differentiates from theirs for adding the opinion and voice

from specialist not only to prioritise the practices but to group them into policies to support the secure and agile SD.

An integration analysis of agile development process and security-related activities, based on quantitative metrics to conclude which security activities are better to integrate in AD, is presented by [23] and [34]. Unlike those papers, our work, presents the qualitative point of view of the presented practices.

[11] seeks to demonstrate if security practices inclusion in software projects are compatible with AM. The author focus only in security practices from the traditional world and mindset and the practices are not presented or discussed. At last, [29] conducts six interviews in organizations that use agile methodologies. As a result, the authors present an extension to agile methods, including security activities. Our study goes further and enrich the possibilities by adding security specialist and security-agile specialist's point of view.

As seen, several studies address the inclusion of security activities in agile methodologies. Many of these, argue that much still needs to be studied in order to find a balance between safety and agility. Moreover, many focus only on the agile point of view. Aiming on filling this gap, this work explores the practices from these studies, to compose policies able to demonstrate how, when and who should apply them considering the life cycle of an agile project.

3   Methodological Approach

This Section explains the research approach presented in Fig. 1.

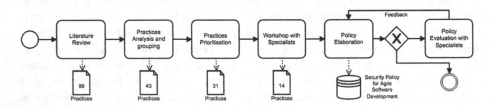

Fig. 1. Research approach

3.1   Literature Review

This study applied an exploratory approach [25] to obtain an understanding of the problem. Although exploratory, steps from Kitchenham and Charters' guidelines on a systematic literature review, as explained by [24] was used to allow the replication of the study. The review aimed on assessing security practices to be included in agile software projects. Therefore, the research question addressed by this review was *"What are the security practices used by agile teams?"*.

The inclusion criteria included: (i) The publication year must be equal or higher to 2010; (ii) The paper must be written in English; (iii) Must be published in journals and peer-reviewed conferences; and (iv) Must be directly related to the research questions. This process used five search engines: IEEE Xplore Digital Library, Springer Link, Science Direct and Google Scholar. In addition, the search process were performed using the following search string: ("Security" AND "Development" AND "Agile" AND ("Lifecycle" OR "Process") AND ("Practices" OR "Policies" OR "Challenges" OR "Factors")).

First all title and abstracts of all articles were read, in a second moment, for the remaining set of papers introduction and conclusion. At last, the remaining papers that answered the research question were read. After evaluating these articles, all practices were mapped, resulting in a total of 99 practices. Although, there was duplication, similarities and practices with the same goal. Therefore, the repetition were removed and similar practices were grouped, reducing to 43 (forty-three) practices discussed briefly in the next section.

3.2   Practices Prioritisation and Workshop with Specialists

In order to focus on the most relevant ones, practices with less than 3 citations were excluded. Twelve practices were excluded, among them *Identify Vulnerabilities, Verify and Validate the security* and *Define and use cryptography standards*. After that, thirty-one practices were analysed using workshops with specialists.

The workshop section was conducted with an agile SD team from a company specialized in cyber security, based in Recife-Brazil. This process sought to answer: (Q1) Can these practices be related to agile methodologies?; (Q2) Is it possible to group one or more of these practices? (Q3) How important is the application of the practice for secure software development? and (Q4) At what development stage should these practices be incorporated?

Based on the workshop's feedback, fourteen practices were prioritized. Fifteen practices were excluded for not offering enough benefit for agile teams, among them: *Countermeasure Graphs, Define and Monitor Metrics, Incident Plan, Define and use cryptography standards* and *Threat Modelling*. The practice *Prioritizing Security Risk* was grouped with *Protection Poker* and *Risk Analysis*, and *Security Master* was considered a role, not a practice.

At last, the practices were grouped by software development phase and five policies for secure and agile software development were created.

3.3   Policy Evaluation

The last evaluation aims on presenting policies and its practices to users in order to confirm their effectiveness, regarding security gains for agile teams. Ten interviews were conducted with security experts, agile team developers with security experience and experts in agile methods. Each policy was presented in order to answer the following questions: (i) Do you think it is possible to apply this policy to agile teams? If so, how?, (ii) Do the aggregated practices make sense in relation to the description and objectives of the policy? (iii) Which challenges and restrictions do you see regarding the policy's use?, and (iv) Would you include any other practices in this policy? Why?.

Finally, based on the feedback, the policies were adjusted and concluded.

4 Security Policies for Agile Teams

This section presents a short version of the five policies for secure SD in agile teams. The policies considered literature review and feedback from both agile and security specialists. For each policy, its description, practices and how to implement them and a few supporting references are given.

4.1 Security Readiness Policy

The main goal of this policy is to raise agile team awareness about the relevant characteristics of information security, to empower them, to share skills and spread security knowledge among the teams members.

Provide Security Training aims to prepare and educate agile team members on the importance of safety. During training, it is essential to address topics such as privacy policy, major attacks, defense strategies and threat modeling.

How to apply it: There are several ways to apply this training, such as online training platforms and to hire specialists to promote these training within the project environment. The best time to introduce the training is at the beginning of the project and update periodically to contribute to excellence and technical awareness [7]. In addition, new team members must conduct basic safety training. *Related works:* [6, 8, 18, 22, 29, 30, 32, 34, 36, 40].

Incentive Security Research establish and promote practices to encourage research related to security. Many new vulnerabilities are discovered over time, so the team need to be up to date on new forms of attack and protection measures.

How to apply it: Research can happen in several ways, such as: searches on specialized portals, such as those at OWASP and Microsoft Technical Blog; channels for updating languages, tools, operating systems and others (Microsoft Security Response Center, Golang Blog); social security discussion forums; database of vulnerabilities CVE Details, Exploits Database. There is no specific time to develop security research. It is possible to determine periods in which individuals carry out research work or to include activity in the project cycle to meet specific demands. *Related works:* [7, 20, 30, 40, 43].

4.2 Security Requirements Policy

Defining security requirements, in a clear, objective and consistent way is very important to develop a secure software. Mapping project security needs reduces the possibility to disregarding them. Adopting practices like *Security Backlog* and *Evil User Stories* support agile team to map security activities. Moreover, it will be possible to state, which security mechanisms have been implemented.

Define Security Requirements aims to identify security-related features, expressed explicitly, within a software project [5, 17]. It is necessary to ensure that these requirements are not put aside, due to the focus on functional requirements, so that they are included in the effort necessary to develop the application [14,18,22,35].

How to apply it: In order to apply, the team should help the client understand and define security requirements for the project. Known vulnerabilities can help in this task, such requirements that the client may not be aware of existence or importance [43]. These requirements should be updated and revised every cycle to reflect changes that occur naturally in the agile project cycle and also to consider changes in threat scenarios [14,27,35]. *Related works:* [6–8,13,20,22, 28,29,32,34,36,39,40].

Security Backlog should contain the list of activities related to the security items pointed out [7,29], and should have all security. This *Backlog* does not necessarily have to be separate from the *Product Backlog*.

How to apply it: It should follow the same operating modes as *Product Backlog*, which is already widespread in agile teams. Whether or not to separate security activities should be a decision of *Product Owner* and the team, according to the needs of the project. It should be raised and updated with each project requirements definition cycle. However, there is nothing to prevent new items from being added, discussed, and prioritized in other moments, to implemented in the following cycles. *Related works:* [4,40].

Evil User Stories describe security threats scenarios, demonstrating how the system can be affected by attackers [5]. The main objective is to based on the *Security Backlog*, stress the possibilities of threat scenarios in order to detect possible system vulnerabilities and weaknesses that can be exploited [5,7].

How to apply it: The *Evil User Stories* should be documented, much like *User Stories* [7]. But, it is necessary that those who write them have a good knowledge of security to get as close as possible to real attack scenarios. These artifacts must be defined in parallel with the items in the *Product Backlog* and *Security Backlog*, during the iterative cycles of the project. *Related works:* [8,13–15,28,29,35,40,44].

4.3 Security Design and Planning Policy

Often security problems are inserted into the project due to design and planning errors, such as not evaluating risks associated with functional requirements. During the planning and design phases, special care with architecture, risk analysis and monitoring of the project, is necessary in order to avoid security flaws. *Challenges:* The main challenge mentioned for agile teams is the time and cost restrictions imposed by some of the practices. In addition, conducting training with the entire team, in order to raise the level of expertise to a sufficient parameter for the application of this policy, can also be seen as a challenge.

Protection Poker is based on *Planning Poker* and it is intended to help prioritize development activities according to the security risk associated with them. In *Protection Poker* the higher the value given, the greater the associated security risk [7]. This practice is a collaborative way to guide the prioritization of project security requirements [44].

How to apply it: As in the *Planning Poker*, the activity to be voted is explained to everyone present. Then, a round of discussion precedes the scores. Next, everyone scores the activity, and this steps must be repeated a few times. The final score is defined based on the consensus among all, is the risk associated with that activity [44]. It should be conducted during the planning sessions for the next development cycle, including activities selected for implementation. *Related works:* [14,40].

In **Perform Risk Analysis**, the agile team analyzes the security risks based on the requirements. This is captured in the Risk Assessment Document, which is refined in subsequent iterations [5]. It can also be added to a canvas, or digital board available for the team.

How to apply it: During development iterations, there must be micro iterations of risk assessment, treatment and acceptance. However, in the initial phase of the project, the team will demand more accuracy in this analysis. Its outputs must update security requirements [20]. *Related works:* [17,29,39].

Establish Security Design Requirements deals with designing regarding security. Thus, includes activities to help requirements implementation in a safe manner. In many cases, the security features selection has proved so complicated that the design or implementation choices have likely resulted in vulnerabilities. Therefore, it is important that they are applied consistently and with a consistent understanding of the protection they provide [27].

How to apply it: In the first iterations an initial architecture must be defined. The architect goes through the list of initial product requirements and tries to discover the necessary architectural security features. It is important that the chosen architecture does not impose restrictions on possible security features that may be needed later. In addition to a general architecture decision, during the first iterations, whenever requirements for *software* are raised, the team will have to talk about these decisions, especially those that involve greater risk, as assessed [29]. *Related works:* [5,13,32,36].

4.4   Security Implementation Policy

Many developers are not aware of the correct way to implement certain features in order to avoid security breaches [22]. In order to add mechanisms that avoid problems of this type, this policy proposes practices that help developers to avoid, identify and correct these flaws, even in the implementation phase.

Security Coding Rules must be established in order to avoid the most common mistakes in this process, focusing on good practices related to software security. These rules should specify some important aspects, such as handling user input, avoiding the use of obsolete functions, using cryptography standards and care when using third party software and libraries [5,27,29].

How to apply it: Many rules can be listed through training and research, as noted in the Readiness Policy. Besides, programming guides and other practices cited in the literature can also help to define standards such as the definition and use of encryption standards and approved tools [5,27,36]. These rules must be followed throughout the implementation process, in particular, for items associated with high risks. *Related works:* [6, 8, 13, 18, 28, 32].

Security Code Review allows the team members to observe possible security problems during code review. Including safety precautions in this process, it will be possible to prevent known failures from being perpetuated during the implementation phase [10]. The review also help to distribute security skills, since you give and receive feedback.

How to apply it: Tools help to make the developed code available for review and allow to indicate the desired reviewers. Reviewers who have experience in security contributes to a better result. After the review, the person responsible for the code turns to the comments and solves the problems pointed out. This practice should be applied throughout the implementation phase of software. *Related works:* [5, 15, 30, 32, 39, 40].

Pair Programming it is an agile concept that defines the situation where developers code in pairs, solving and revising problems together, while the code is written [5]. This practice can encourage team members with more security experience to pass on their knowledge. Besides, this practice can shape the professional's mentality, so that he/she seeks more and more for security practices.

How to apply it: Two team members implement one activity in a cooperative way throughout the sprint or development cycle. It is useful not only for stories with high risk associate but to empower a new team member, it is useful for all evil stories. *Related works:* [14, 32].

4.5   Security Testing Policy

Well-performed specialized tests can expose not sufficiently secure code. Written automated tests, in theory, prove that safety items have been considered and implemented. The use of static code analysis tools can unveil common programming errors and possible problems, even during development [29].

Security Automated Testing takes advantage of automatic tests implementation and include validation of security-related features. By having security-related checks, it is possible to state that code developed to provide security will not be distorted in future changes and corrections made should not happen again and fixed vulnerabilities should not happen again [29].

How to apply it: Most, if not all, programming languages have their own automated test modules, in addition, there are several libraries for this purpose. When writing automated tests for security, you should ensure that you implement as many scenarios as possible and that they are as close as possible to real world scenarios. During the sprint, in parallel to code development, the related test code should be implemented [29]. *Related works:* [8, 20, 28, 34].

Security Code Analysis ensures that the code is analyzed by tools, looking for security holes in order to validate the implemented software security [5]. This practice basically consists on three verification methodologies: *Static Code Analysis, Dynamic Code Analysis* and *Fuzzy Testing*.

How to apply it: There are tools to perform the verification of each of the methodologies cited above, they just need to be configured correctly. OWASP maintains a list of tools for this purpose, [42]. The configuration of the code verification tools must be performed in the first iterations of the project [15]. Once they are configured, the team must find the best time to execute them. *Related works:* [6, 7, 12, 13, 18, 20, 22, 28–30, 32, 34, 36].

Security Specialized Testing Apply tests performed by security experts, will ensure that most of existing security flaws will be raised [29]. Their expertise and attacker's mindset, allow them to find flaws ignored or inserted during the development process [22].

How to apply it: Specialized tests usually requires security experts availability. Therefore, one of the ways to apply this approach is to hire a company or independent professionals that offer this service. In more critical scenarios, an team of these professionals can be hired to carry out this task. However, it might be a non available configuration. So, using those tests only during an application launch, or before each major release, which includes several new features [15] could be an option. *Related works:* [5, 6, 18, 20, 30, 32, 34].

5   Evaluation and Discussion

This section discusses the feedback from 10 (ten) practitioners. Table 1 depicts interviewees' profile, current role and experience in SD, agile and cyber security.

Table 1. Interviewee profile

ID	Current role	Exp.	Agile exp.	Cyber security exp.
E1	Sw Developer	Over 16	Over 10	Over 3
E2	Security Consultant	9	1	7
E3	Software Engineer	14	9	2
E4	Software Engineer	21	12	2
E5	Software Engineer	8	8	8
E6	Cyber Security Analyst	21	0	9
E7	Cyber Security Analyst	5	0	5
E8	Team Leader	12	12	7
E9	Software Engineer	Over 15	6	10
E10	Software Engineer	9	9	6

The lack of experience is one of the main factors that influences the lack of secure SD projects. Dealing with security aspects is vital for the secure SD (E7). The *Security readiness policy* was considered essential to enable the change in the team security mentality (E4, E5), leading to an effective decrease in security breaches (E2). This policy does not take a lot of time, and educates agile teams members to deal with security aspects (E8).

Regarding *Research practice*, some reservations were raised. The team may not be prepared to perform this activity even after training. Research can consume project time, if it is not well directed, and can become a flawed investment. According to E7, "It must have a very specific focus, such as new defense ways, tools" in order to bring the expected result. However, it has been demonstrated that there are associated benefits and keeping the team up to date is one of them. Interviewee E10 stated that consuming material on safety in the team's daily life can help to engage professionals in this practice.

Security requirements mapping gives visibility, both to the team and the client (E8). Although, there is a time restriction (E1, E10) and performing these activities within teams with little security experience is a challenge (E1). The *Security Backlog* can be a good way to keep developers aware of what security stories will be implemented (E3). The use of *Evil User Stories* will be a challenge, since an attacker mentality is necessary to write them, a characteristic that is hardly present in developers. "The team could struggle to write *Evil User Stories*" (E2, E6), "there is a lack of attack knowledge" (E4), or "lack of attack mindset generating fewer and insufficient scenarios" (E10). The expert advice or a security role on the team could mitigate this problem.

The applicability of *Security Design and Planning Policy* is threaten by complex and time consuming characteristics of *security and risk analysis* practice. According to E10, "Establishing security design at the beginning of the project is essential, since they are the foundation for SD to remain secure and to fasten security requirements integration". Furthermore, no definitive impediment for the agile world was raised, although it will demand adaptation. Further more, there was no doubts on its relevance and benefits.

Security Implementation showed the biggest acceptance. All interviewee agree that it brings great value for a secure and agile SD. It is easy to adopt within agile teams, mainly because there is already ceremonies to deal with it. Among the practices, *Pair Programming* is seen as having an extra advantage of perpetuating knowledge within the team (E6), in addition to helping in the development of more complex security requirements (E2, E10). And in some way, "They are already practiced, in most agile teams" (E2, E9).

Finally, *Security Test* was the most cherished policy. "Specialized tests are essential to find more complex threat scenarios, however, it demands time and resources for project development" (E6). Although there are free tools, it is also a consensus that *Security Code Analysis* and *Security Specialized Testing* will face restrictions due to lack of financial resources to either acquire a tool, or specif training or consultant to train the team. Moreover, the benefit for agile teams during SD projects are obvious and overcomes the constraints.

The results obtained shows that *Security Readiness Policy*, *Security Implementation Policy* are more coherent, ready and suitable for agile teams. Within the *Security Test Policy* aside from the *Security Specialized Testing* that demands a great cost and time, is a mandatory policy, ready to be used by agile teams. These three policies were better accepted by all specialists. All opinions converge to confirm that despite some reservations, it is plausible to incorporate these policies in the agile development process.

6   Final Considerations

The need to integrate agile methodologies and security requirements is still an open problem. This being mainly caused due to the fact that security activities were mostly conceived from the traditional model of software development. This leads to several challenges, which are mainly linked to the differences between these models. This research contributes to partially fill this gap, presenting policies that allow secure development within the agile world.

This work proposes 5 (five) security policies for agile teams: (I) *Security Readiness Policy*, (II) *Security Requirements Policy*, (III) *Security Design and Planning Policy*, (IV) *Security Implementation Policy* and (V) *Security Test Policy*. Each of them, adds a subset of practices brought from the literature review, and prioritised through a preliminary assessment with a group of experts. At last, specialists that were also users of many of these practices, contribute to evaluate the effectiveness regarding security gains for agile teams.

Furthermore, it was possible to observe two crucial needs for secure agile software development: to meet the team's training needs and to make available project time, space in the process for security-related activities. Another issue that arose from the interviews was that the developer's mindset is focused on how to protect the product, this can cause many attack scenarios to go unnoticed. Moreover, in order to use these policies there is a need to at least one specialist in security to spread the knowledge. Besides, lessons learned and known attacks could help the creation of security requirements and test scenarios. In the design context, there are other practices that could be added in this process, however, they would cause overload, reducing agility. In addition, as mentioned by E5, "totally safe, it is virtually impossible to reach". However, preparing the team is the best way to start dealing with security.

Even though some steps from systematic review was followed, some important articles may have gone unnoticed, this may lead to the incompleteness set of the practices. The interviewees profile diversity and number may have not been sufficient to make a complete analysis of the proposed policies. In order to fill the need of a secure development in the global world and to address the cyber security issues within the increasing number of agile teams. We propose the following future work: to conduct a multinational work on security practices in agile teams; elaborate a survey to analyse a quantitative study; to carry out an analysis of *Threat Modeling* practice and its application in the agile world; to conduct a empirical case study to analyse cost, effort, and return of investment when adopting these security policies within agile teams; at last to further analyse security scenarios in agile teams and evaluate time restrictions for the inclusion of security practices in agile projects.

References

1. 13th annual state of agile development survey. https://explore.versionone.com/state-of-agile/13th-annual-state-of-agile-report. Accessed 01 Dec 2019
2. Adelyar, S.H., Norta, A.: Towards a secure agile software development process. In: 10th International Conference on the Quality of Information and Communications Technology (QUATIC), pp. 101–106. IEEE (2016)
3. Agile Alliance (2019). https://www.agilealliance.org/. Accessed 28 Nov 2019
4. Azham, Z., Ghani, I., Ithnin, N.: Security backlog in scrum security practices. In: Malaysian Conference in Software Engineering, pp. 414–417. IEEE (2011)
5. Baca, D., Carlsson, B.: Agile development with security engineering activities. In: International Conference on Software and Systems Process, pp. 149–158. ACM (2011)
6. Bansal, S.K., Jolly, A.: An encyclopedic approach for realization of security activities with agile methodologies. In: 5th International Conference - Confluence The Next Generation Information Technology Summit (Confluence), pp. 767–772. IEEE (2014)
7. Barbosa, D.A., Sampaio, S.: Guide to the support for the enhancement of security measures in agile projects. In: 2015 6th Brazilian Workshop on Agile Methods (WBMA), pp. 25–31. IEEE (2015)
8. Bartsch, S.: Practitioners' perspectives on security in agile development. In: 6th International Conference on Availability, Reliability and Security, pp. 479–484. IEEE (2011)
9. Beck, K.: Extreme Programming Explained: Embrace Change. Addison-Wesley Professional, Boston (2000)
10. Bernhart, M., Mauczka, A., Grechenig, T.: Adopting code reviews for agile software development. In: Agile Conference, pp. 44–47. IEEE (2010)
11. Beznosov, K., Kruchten, P.: Towards agile security assurance. In: Workshop on New Security paradigms, pp. 47–54. ACM (2004)
12. Bodden, E.: State of the systems security. In: 40th International Conference on Software Engineering: Companion Proceedings, pp. 550–551. ACM (2018)
13. Boström, G., Wäyrynen, J., Bodén, M., Beznosov, K., Kruchten, P.: Extending XP practices to support security requirements engineering. In: International Workshop on Software Engineering for Secure Systems, pp. 11–18. ACM (2006)
14. Bowen, J.P., Hinchey, M., Janicke, H., Ward, M., Zedan, H.: Formality, agility, security, and evolution in software development. Computer 47(10), 86–89 (2014)
15. Chóliz, J., Vilas, J., Moreira, J.: Independent security testing on agile software development: a case study in a software company. In: 10th International Conference on Availability, Reliability and Security, pp. 522–531. IEEE (2015)
16. Choudhary, B., Rakesh, S.K.: An approach using agile method for software development. In: International Conference on Innovation and Challenges in Cyber Security (ICICCS-INBUSH), pp. 155–158. IEEE (2016)
17. Common Criteria (2019). https://www.commoncriteriaportal.org/. Accessed 19 Nov 2019
18. Comprehensive Lightweight Application Security Process (CLASP) (2019). https://www.owasp.org/index.php/CLASP_Concepts. Accessed 19 Nov 2019
19. Essafi, M., Labed, L., Ghezala, H.B.: Towards a comprehensive view of secure software engineering. In: The International Conference on Emerging Security Information, Systems, and Technologies, pp. 181–186. IEEE (2007)

20. Franqueira, V.N., Bakalova, Z., Tun, T.T., Daneva, M.: Towards agile security risk management in re and beyond. In: Workshop on Empirical Requirements Engineering (EmpiRE 2011), pp. 33–36. IEEE (2011)
21. General Data Protection Regulation (GDPR) (2018). https://gdpr-info.eu/. Accessed 23 Nov 2019
22. Kanniah, S.L., Mahrin, M.N.: A review on factors influencing implementation of secure software development practices. Int. J. Comput. Syst. Eng. **10**(8), 3032–3039 (2016)
23. Keramati, H., Mirian-Hosseinabadi, S.H.: Integrating software development security activities with agile methodologies. In: International Conference on Computer Systems and Applications, pp. 749–754. IEEE/ACS (2008)
24. Kitchenham, B., Charters, S.: Guidelines for performing systematic literature reviews in software engineering. Technical report, EBSE Technical Report EBSE-2007-01 (2007)
25. Kothari, C.R.: Research Methodology: Methods and Techniques. New Age International (2004)
26. Lei geral de proteção a dados (LGPD) (2019). http://www.planal-to.gov.br/ccivil_03/_ato2015-2018/2018/lei/L13709.htm. Accessed 23 Nov 2019
27. Microsoft Secure Development Lifecycle (2019). https://www.microsoft.com/en-us/securityengineering/sdl/practices. Accessed 19 Nov 2019
28. Munetoh, S., Yoshioka, N.: RAILROADMAP: an agile security testing framework for web-application development. In: 6th International Conference on Software Testing, Verification and Validation, pp. 491–492. IEEE (2013)
29. Nicolaysen, T., Sasson, R., Line, M.B., Jaatun, M.G.: Agile software development: the straight and narrow path to secure software? Int. J. Secure Softw. Eng. (IJSSE) **1**(3), 71–85 (2010)
30. Oueslati, H., Rahman, M.M., ben Othmane, L.: Literature review of the challenges of developing secure software using the agile approach. In: 10th International Conference on Availability, Reliability and Security, pp. 540–547. IEEE (2015)
31. Open Web Application Security Project OWASP (2019). https://www.owasp.org/index.php/Main_Page. Accessed 23 Nov 2019
32. Oyetoyan, T.D., Cruzes, D.S., Jaatun, M.G.: An empirical study on the relationship between software security skills, usage and training needs in agile settings. In: 11th International Conference on Availability, Reliability and Security, pp. 548–555. IEEE (2016)
33. Project zero (2019). https://googleprojectzero.blogspot.com/. Accessed 23 Nov 2019
34. Singhal, A.: Integration analysis of security activities from the perspective of agility. In: Agile India, pp. 40–47. IEEE (2012)
35. Siponen, M., Baskerville, R., Kuivalainen, T.: Integrating security into agile development methods. In: 38th Annual Hawaii International Conference on System Sciences, pp. 185a–185a. IEEE (2005)
36. Sodanil, M., Quirchmayr, G., Porrawatpreyakorn, N., Tjoa, A.M.: A knowledge transfer framework for secure coding practices. In: 12th International Joint Conference on Computer Science and Software Engineering (JCSSE), pp. 120–125. IEEE (2015)
37. Stoica, M., Mircea, M., Ghilic-Micu, B.: Software development: agile vs. traditional. Informatica Economica **17**(4) (2013)
38. Sutherland, J., Schwaber, K.: The definitive guide to scrum: the rules of the game. Scrum.org 268 (2013)

39. Terpstra, E., Daneva, M., Wang, C.: Agile practitioners' understanding of security requirements: insights from a grounded theory analysis. In: 25th International Requirements Engineering Conference Workshops (REW), pp. 439–442. IEEE (2017)
40. Villamizar, H., Kalinowski, M., Viana, M., Fernández, D.: A systematic mapping study on security in agile requirements engineering. In: 44th Euromicro Conference on Software Engineering and Advanced Applications (SEAA), pp. 454–461. IEEE (2018)
41. Von Solms, R., Van Niekerk, J.: From information security to cyber security. Comput. Secur. **38**, 97–102 (2013)
42. Vulnerability Scanning Tools (2001). https://www.owasp.org/index.php/Category: Vulnerability_Scanning_Tools. Accessed 23 Nov 2019
43. Wang, W., Gupta, A., Niu, N.: Mining security requirements from common vulnerabilities and exposures for agile projects. In: 1st International Workshop on Quality Requirements in Agile Projects (QuaRAP), pp. 6–9. IEEE (2018)
44. Williams, L., Meneely, A., Shipley, G.: Protection poker: the new software security game. IEEE Secur. Priv. **8**(3), 14–20 (2010)

A Privacy-By-Design Architecture for Indoor Localization Systems

Paolo Barsocchi[1] , Antonello Calabrò[1] , Antonino Crivello[1] ,
Said Daoudagh[1,2]([⊠]) , Francesco Furfari[1] , Michele Girolami[1] ,
and Eda Marchetti[1]

[1] CNR-ISTI, Pisa, Italy
{paolo.barsocchi,antonello.calabro,antonino.crivello,said.daoudagh,
francesco.furfari,michele.girolami,eda.marchetti}@isti.cnr.it
[2] University of Pisa, Pisa, Italy

Abstract. The availability of mobile devices has led to an arising development of indoor location services collecting a large amount of sensitive information. However, without accurate and verified management, such information could become severe back-doors for security and privacy issues. We propose in this paper a novel Location-Based Service (LBS) architecture in line with the GDPR's provisions. For feasibility purposes and considering a representative use-case, a reference implementation, based on the popular Telegram app, is also presented.

Keywords: Access control systems · GDPR · Indoor Localization Systems · Location-Based Services · Privacy-by-design

1 Introduction

The wide availability of mobile devices has led to an arising development of (indoor/outdoor) Location-Based Services (LBSs) for improving users' daily life and works. More specifically, a high number of stakeholders are exploiting such systems for providing commercial solutions, selling products, tracking facilities, social apps, and services. Most of the previously cited systems are supposed to acquire and store personal data such as IP address, the user's localization and the history of locations visited as well as a timestamp of such visits. As a result, the final users disseminate kinds of *digital crumbs* that might potentially disclose sensitive information without being aware of the actual risk.

Beyond Snowden [9] and the recent adoption in May 2018 of the General Data Protection Regulation (GDPR) [7], people sensitiveness about personal privacy, fortunately, has been increasing. However, in the context of Indoor Localization Systems (ILSs), there is still the missing of a standardized reference architecture that takes care of the security and privacy enforcement.

In this paper, we describe a novel LBS architecture in line with the GDPR provisions, i.e., able to strengthen the rights of individuals over their personal data and to make organizations more accountable regarding the regulation. The

© Springer Nature Switzerland AG 2020
M. Shepperd et al. (Eds.): QUATIC 2020, CCIS 1266, pp. 358–366, 2020.
https://doi.org/10.1007/978-3-030-58793-2_29

provided solution relies on the innovative idea of integrating a GDPR-based Access Control (AC) system inside the localization architecture. We argue that the AC represents a promising technique for developing adequate and fine-grained mechanisms taking into account legal requirements, such as the data usage purpose, the management of the user's consents as well as enforcing the data retention period [4,17,18]. Thus, the main contribution of this paper is to schematize an Indoor Localization System (ILS) reference architecture. We define the purposes of the data management, the management of the user's consents, and the rights related to privacy and data protection correctly enforced so as to guarantee the privacy-by-design GDPR compliance.

To the best of our knowledge, our solution is the first proposal that integrates three key-aspects: i) the design of smart and easy-to-use ILS architecture, ii) the use of access control systems for resource and data management inside localization environment and, iii) the enforcement of the GDPR's provisions inside the localization systems.

This article is structured as follows: in the next section, an overview of background and related work is presented. Then, in Sect. 3 we describe the proposed privacy-by-design solution, while in Sect. 4, we present an application example. Finally, Sect. 5 concludes the paper.

2   Background and Related Work

In this section, we briefly describe the indoor localization, the GDPR, and the AC basic knowledge and their related works.

Considering the ILSs, their main peculiarities are the positioning and localization functionalities. Several proposals have been presented in the last decade for ILSs, each one showing differences, in terms of methods and data sources. Main ready to the market solutions are: IndoorAtlas[1], Indoor Google Maps and Anyplace [10]. Even if ILSs are a generally accepted cross-domain solution, they still lack of a generic standard architecture and, more importantly, they are agnostic about the privacy principles and exposed to the risk of location privacy violation [14].

The GDPR [7] defines *Personal Data* as any information relating to an identified or identifiable natural person called *Data Subject*. That means that a data subject is a Natural Person (a living human being), whose data are managed by a *Controller*. The GDPR is applied to the processing of personal data, whether it is automated (even partially) or not. It defines, among others, the following principles and demands: *Purposes*, i.e., data should only be collected for determined, explicit and legitimate purposes, and should not be processed later for other purposes; *Accuracy*, i.e., the processed data must be accurate and up-to-date regularly; *Retention*, i.e., data must be deleted after a limited period; *Subject explicit consent*, i.e., data may be collected and processed only if the data subject has given his explicit consent.

---

[1] https://www.indooratlas.com/.

Concerning the design of the AC, it is usually implemented through *Access Control Mechanism (ACM)*, which is the system providing a decision to an authorization request, typically based on predefined *Access Control Policy (ACP)*. The eXtensible Access Control Markup Language (XACML) [15] is one of the most widely used AC languages, and it provides the reference architecture in the AC environment. An XACML policy is a specific statement of what is and is not allowed, on the basis of a set of rules. Rules are defined in terms of conditions on attributes of subjects, resources, actions, and environment, and by combining algorithms for establishing the order among the existing rules.

Notwithstanding the importance of the role of AC systems, their integration with a localization system architecture is still an emerging topic [12]. Most of the results achieved so far have been focused either on: (1) using access control mechanisms for (physical) protection within virtual perimeters [11]; (2) using location information for automatically authenticate customer [13]; (3) on specific security attributes that do not fully cover the GDPR requirements [1,5]. This paper enhances the current research by proposing, for the first time, a reference architecture that includes a location and topology-aware access control system to guarantee compliance with the GDPR's provisions.

3   A Privacy-By-Design Solution

In this section, we schematize the possible reference architecture for the indoor localization system which includes a GDPR-based AC system. The proposal extends and integrates our previous solutions presented in [3,6,8]. Figure 1 shows the main components of the proposed reference architecture that are:

User Agent (UA): the UA cooperates, on behalf of the user, with the indoor infrastructure to estimate the user's location. It is typically deployed in a smart device (e.g., smartphone, tablet or smartwatch). As shown in Fig. 1, the UA is in charge of managing the user interaction for: automatically detecting the existence of an ILS (through the Discovery Service), enabling the localization of the device (through the Positioning Service); rendering the device position on a map (through the Mapping Service); managing the user's consents and sending/receiving access requests/responses (through the device GUI);

Localization Infrastructure (LI): the Localization Infrastructure (LI) is an indoor distributed infrastructure in charge of determining the user's location. It relies on WiFi signals collected through the UA and it provides three main components: ① *Map Manager*, that manages the updating and storage of the internal maps; ② *Discovery Server*, that is in charge of sending the URL of the available ILSs to the different UA; ③; *Enhanced Indoor Localization System (E-ILS)*, that is the core component of LI and it relies on two databases for collecting the required information and personal data.

More specifically, the E-ILS is characterized by three main components: i) the *Communication and Interaction Orchestrator*, which is in charge of managing the communication to and from the E-ILS; ii) the *GDPR-Based Access Control System*, which rules the resources and data access; iii) the *ILS Engine*, which is in

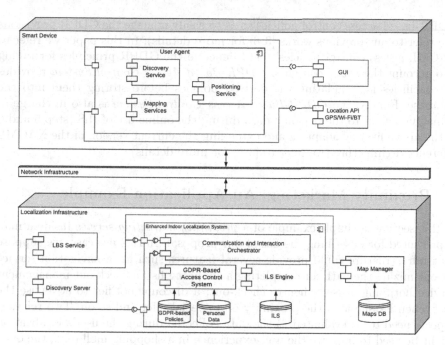

Fig. 1. The reference architecture: the UA implements the interaction between the users and the LI throughout a network infrastructure.

charge of estimating the User Agent's location. In turn, the *ILS Engine* returns back to the UA the timestamped coordinates, according to the map reference system (e.g., WGS84 reference system) [16].

The *ILS Engine* and the *GDPR-Based Access Control System* are designed to cooperate, since different people (e.g., the data owner, administrators or supervisors) and different services (e.g., booking services, advertisement services and navigation services) may ask the data access at different moments. More specifically, this last component is in charge of evaluating each single data access request and allowing or denying the access according to the collected consent, the data validity period, the specific users/service rights and the access control policies established inside the overall Localization Infrastructure. By extending the our previous solution described in [2], the *GDPR-Based Access Control System* provides facilities for: 1. Gather privacy requirements from collected consents; 2. Identify privacy attributes; 3. Author the GDPR-based policies; 4. Test GDPR-based policies; 5. Deploy GDPR-based policies on the E-ILS; 6. Manage the data access. Through the interaction with the UA component, the *GDPR-Based Access Control System* provides facilities to perform steps from 1 to 4. Specifically, *GDPR-Based Access Control System* is in charge of preparing the consents to be subscribed by the users, extracting useful personal data from the signed consents, and storing them into a secure and protect database. It also translates the consents first into processable structures, and then into enforceable

GDPR-based access control policies so as to easily manage the GDPR provisions (we refer to our previous works [3,6] for more details). In this paper we refer to XACML access control policies able to encode the GDPR principles for taking into account the users' consents. *GDPR-Based Access Control System* provides also facilities for validating the derived policies before storing them into the database. Finally, the *GDPR-Based Access Control System* is also in charge of managing access to the personal data during the online use of ILS (step 5 and 6 of the above list) by adapting and extending the current version of the XACML reference architecture (we refer to [3,6] for more details).

4   Proximity Marketing: An Application Example

In this section, a simple example of a *proximity marketing service* inside a mall is presented for describing the use of our proposal. In this use case, we suppose that infrastructure could provide several features such as: a navigation service for optimizing the path for completing a shopping list; a check-out management service notifying a user when to check-out; a discount notifier to advertise the user when he/she is in the proximity of a special offer and so on. Two relevant aspects need to be evaluated: i) the data collected during the user's localization might be used to improve the user-experience in a shopping mall (e.g., the optimal placement of products); ii) the appealing facilities of the indoor positioning can make available a set of personal data that can be misused and exploited in a way different than the users' expectations.

As an example of possible implementation, UA in Fig. 1 has been developed by extending the Telegram app [8]. In this case, the user starts the localization process by looking for the services available in the mall through the Telegram menu. Consequently, the UA retrieves information about the available localization infrastructures through a discovery service. This service performs a periodic Bluetooth/WiFi scan to retrieve information encoded in the payload of advertising messages of such technologies. In the current implementation, we encoded an URL on the payload of EddyStone beacons. In turn, the URL is used by the UA to retrieve the meta information of the ILS.

In the example of this section, the ILS engine implements the localization algorithm and the Map Server provides maps of the indoor environment. The localization algorithm leverages the WiFi signals received by the UA: it periodically scans the WiFi probes emitted by the WiFi Access Points (AP) in the nearby, and it analyzes the received signal strength (RSS) of the messages. The RSS collected from all the available WiFi APs are then transferred to the ILS, which analyzes them to estimate the device position. In turn, the ILS returns back the UA the timestamped coordinates so that to show on the map its current position. In our implementation, the user also receives through the UA GUI, a specific (textual) consent associated to the selected service, in which there is detailed information about the usage of personal data and their purpose such as (i) who is the data owner; (ii) how the data will be processed, and for which purposes; (iii) the time of detention, and so on. In our proposal, according to the GDPR demands, the user's personal data, the device position, the timestamp as well as the ACPs area all kept on an exclusive database ruled by the *GDPR-Based Access Control System* (Fig. 1). Moreover, the collected data are stored only for the time needed to provide the user with the required services.

Table 1. Example of attribute classification.

Identified attribute	Attribute category	GDPR category	AC category
Alice	Customer	Data Subject	Subject
Marketing Service	Service Provider	Controller	Subject
Read	Processing	Access	Action
Notification	Processing	Send	Action
Smart device ID	Indirect ID	Personal Data	Resource
GPS data	Location Data	Personal Data	Resource
Wi-Fi signal data	Location Data	Personal Data	Resource
On-board Sensors data	Location Data	Personal Data	Resource
Current Position	Location data	Personal Data	Resource
Advertising	Purpose	Specific Purpose	Resource

As described in Sect. 3, the data extracted from *proximity marketing service* accepted consent are used for: automatically mapping the personal data into access control attributes, instantiating a rule for each structured representation and combining them into GDPR-based ACPs (we refer to [3,6] for more details). As an example, considering the Art. 15.1 of the GDPR[2], Table 1 reports the mapping of the attributes for the following scenario: *Alice (Customer, i.e., Data Subject) provides the ID of her smart device, the GPS data, the WiFi signal data, and on-board sensors data. Such information are sent to the proximity marketing service (Controller) for advertising notifications when she is in proximity of a shop. Alice, at any time, can exercise her right of access pursuant the Art. 15.1.*

More precisely, column *Identified Attribute* of Table 1 contains the identified attributes; column *Attribute Category* shows their classification into a specific category; column *GDPR Category* maps attributes into regulation concepts; and finally, column *Access Control Category* maps to the access control entities. In Fig. 2 the derived GDPR-based Access control policy written in XACML-like language is provided. Specifically, the policy is applicable to the subject *Alice* and contains two rules: (1) the first rule, with RuleId equal to *readRule*, represents the AC rule associated with Art. 15.1 and guarantees that Alice can read her provided personal information; (2) the second rule, called *defaultRule*, denies all which is not allowed explicitly.

---

[2] Art. 15.1 of the GDPR: 1. The data subject shall have the right to obtain [...] the following information: (a) the purposes of the processing; (b) the categories of personal data concerned; [...] (Right of access by the data subject).

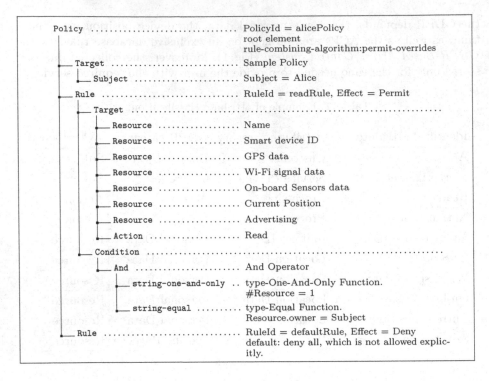

Fig. 2. Example of an XACML-like Policy.

5   Conclusions and Future Work

We present in this paper the architecture of an indoor localization able to guarantee the GDPR compliance through the integration of a specialized GDPR-based access control system. Our architecture replies to the users' need to be protected against unauthorized or unconscious privacy data collection and analysis. Indeed, according to the GDRP regulation, our privacy-preserving architecture can delegate to end-users the control of the provided personal data. We show the feasibility of our proposal by considering a proximity marketing service inside a mall. Even if very simple, the use case evidenced how the architecture could increase the privacy consciousness of end-users while they are using indoor environment services. By following this research line, we plan to extend our work with a real-world data collection campaign to evaluate the scalability of the platform at realistic conditions.

Acknowledgments. Partially Supported by CyberSec4Europe Grant Agreement ID 830929.

References

1. Barsocchi, P., Calabrò, A., Ferro, E., Gennaro, C., Marchetti, E., Vairo, C.: Boosting a low-cost smart home environment with usage and access control rules. Sensors **18**(6), 1886 (2018)
2. Bartolini, C., Daoudagh, S., Lenzini, G., Marchetti, E.: GDPR-based user stories in the access control perspective. In: Piattini, M., Rupino da Cunha, P., García Rodríguez de Guzmán, I., Pérez-Castillo, R. (eds.) QUATIC 2019. CCIS, vol. 1010, pp. 3–17. Springer, Cham (2019). https://doi.org/10.1007/978-3-030-29238-6_1
3. Bartolini, C., Daoudagh, S., Lenzini, G., Marchetti, E.: Towards a lawful authorized access: a preliminary GDPR-based authorized access. In: Proceedings of ICSOFT 2019, Prague, Czech Republic, 26–28 July 2019, pp. 331–338 (2019)
4. Basin, D., Debois, S., Hildebrandt, T.: On purpose and by necessity: compliance under the GDPR. In: Meiklejohn, S., Sako, K. (eds.) FC 2018. LNCS, vol. 10957, pp. 20–37. Springer, Heidelberg (2018). https://doi.org/10.1007/978-3-662-58387-6_2
5. Calabrò, A., Marchetti, E., Moroni, D., Pieri, G.: A dynamic and scalable solution for improving daily life safety. In: Proceedings of APPIS 2019, pp. 1–6 (2019)
6. Daoudagh, S., Marchetti, E.: A life cycle for authorization systems development in the GDPR perspective. In: Proceedings of the Fourth Italian Conference on Cyber Security (ITASEC), Ancona, Italy, 4–7 February 2020, pp. 128–140 (2020)
7. Regulation (EU) 2016/679 of the European Parliament and of the Council of 27 April 2016 (General Data Protection Regulation). Official Journal of the European Union L119, 1–88, May 2016
8. Furfari, F., Crivello, A., Barsocchi, P., Palumbo, F., Potortì, F.: What is next for indoor localisation? Taxonomy, protocols, and patterns for advanced location based services. In: Proceedings of IPIN 2019, pp. 1–8. IEEE (2019)
9. Gellman, B., Gribbons, J.M.: Edward snowden says motive behind leaks was to expose surveillance state (2013)
10. Georgiou, K., Constambeys, T., Laoudias, C., Petrou, L., Chatzimilioudis, G., Zeinalipour-Yazti, D.: Anyplace: a crowdsourced indoor information service. In: Proceedings of CMDM 2015, vol. 1, pp. 291–294. IEEE (2015)
11. Greaves, B., Coetzee, M., Leung, W.S.: Access control requirements for physical spaces protected by virtual perimeters. In: Furnell, S., Mouratidis, H., Pernul, G. (eds.) TrustBus 2018. LNCS, vol. 11033, pp. 182–197. Springer, Cham (2018). https://doi.org/10.1007/978-3-319-98385-1_13
12. Greaves, B., Coetzee, M., Leung, W.S.: A comparison of indoor positioning systems for access control using virtual perimeters. In: Yang, X.-S., Sherratt, S., Dey, N., Joshi, A. (eds.) Fourth International Congress on Information and Communication Technology. AISC, vol. 1041, pp. 293–302. Springer, Singapore (2020). https://doi.org/10.1007/978-981-15-0637-6_24
13. Haofeng, J., Xiaorui, G.: Wi-Fi secure access control system based on geo-fence. In: Proceedings of ISCC 2019, pp. 1–6 (2019)
14. Konstantinidis, A., Chatzimilioudis, G., Zeinalipour-Yazti, D., Mpeis, P., Pelekis, N., Theodoridis, Y.: Privacy-preserving indoor localization on smartphones. IEEE Trans. Knowl. Data Eng. **27**(11), 3042–3055 (2015)
15. OASIS: eXtensible Access Control Markup Language (XACML) Version 3.0, January 2013. http://docs.oasis-open.org/xacml/3.0/xacml-3.0-core-spec-os-en.html
16. Potortì, F., Crivello, A., Girolami, M., Barsocchi, P., Traficante, E.: Localising crowds through Wi-Fi probes. Ad Hoc Netw. **75**, 87–97 (2018)

17. Ramadan, Q., Salnitriy, M., Strüber, D., Jürjens, J., Giorgini, P.: From secure business process modeling to design-level security verification. In: Proceedings of MODELS 2017, pp. 123–133. IEEE, September 2017

18. Ranise, S., Siswantoro, H.: Automated legal compliance checking by security policy analysis. In: Tonetta, S., Schoitsch, E., Bitsch, F. (eds.) SAFECOMP 2017. LNCS, vol. 10489, pp. 361–372. Springer, Cham (2017). https://doi.org/10.1007/978-3-319-66284-8_30

ICT Verification and Validation

Reverse Engineering of Android Applications: REiMPAcT

Marco Gonçalves[1] and Ana C. R. Paiva[1,2]($\boxtimes$) (iD)

[1] Faculty of Engineering, University of Porto,
Rua Dr. Roberto Frias, s/n, 4200-465 Porto, Portugal
`{up201708897,apaiva}@fe.up.pt`
[2] INESC TEC, Rua Dr. Roberto Frias, s/n, 4200-465 Porto, Portugal

Abstract. Reverse engineering may be helpful for extracting information from existing apps to understand them better and ease their maintenance. Reverse engineering may be performed by a static analysis of the
apps' code but, when the code is not available, a dynamic approach may
be useful. This paper presents a tool that allows extracting dynamically,
in a complete black-box approach, the explored activities of Android
applications. It is an extension of iMPAcT testing tool that combines
reverse engineering, dynamic exploration, and testing. The extracted
information is later used to construct an HFSM (Hierarchical Finite State
Machine) with three distinct levels of abstraction. The top-level shows
the interactions needed to traverse the activities of the mobile application. The middle level shows the screens traversed while in a specific
activity. The bottom level shows all screens traversed during exploration.
This information helps to understand better the application which facilitates its maintenance and errors fixing. This paper provides a complete
description of the tool, its architecture and the results of some case studies conducted on mobile apps publicly available on the Google Store.

Keywords: Reverse engineering · Android crawler · Software testing ·
Android testing · Mobile testing

1 Introduction

According to IEEE, reverse engineering is "the process of analyzing a subject
system to identify the system's components and their interrelationships and to
create representations of the system in another form or at a higher level of
abstraction".

Reverse engineering may be useful to know more about the software system being analyzed which may contribute to improve the system and help its
maintenance, especially when such system lacks of up-to-date and adequate documentation.

There are some research works that apply reverse engineering to extract
information from mobile apps. The type of reverse engineering performed and

© Springer Nature Switzerland AG 2020
M. Shepperd et al. (Eds.): QUATIC 2020, CCIS 1266, pp. 369–382, 2020.
https://doi.org/10.1007/978-3-030-58793-2_30

the kind of information extracted varies. Reverse engineering may be static (look into the code without executing it), dynamic (where the software is executed) or historical (when looking into the changes performed in order to gain information about the evolution of the system) [1].

Given that mobile applications are Event-Based, a static approach is not the best approach. On the other hand, dynamic and hybrid approaches are the most suitable and used for mobile applications [12].

When developing Android apps it is possible to "combine multiple fragments in a single activity to build a multi-pane UI and reuse a fragment in multiple activities"[1]. So, relating the captured activities with their inner screens may the helpful to understand better how the app is structured.

As far as we know, there is no dynamic approach able to extract the activities and related screens of Android apps based on a complete black-box approach, i.e., without access to the code of the app in any phase of the reverse engineering process.

This paper presents a reverse engineering approach (REiMPAcT) that extends iMPAcT Tool (a testing tool for Android mobile applications). REiM-PAcT approach is able to extract an HFSM (Hierarchical Finite State Machine) from a dynamic black-box exploration of an Android app. It is able to extract the activities, their inner screens traversed, the user events available in each screen and navigation paths performed along the exploration. The generated HFSM is composed of three distinct levels of abstraction. The top level presents the activities traversed, the middle level presents the screens traversed for each activity explored, while the bottom level presents all the screens traversed during the exploration.

This paper presents some related work regarding reverse engineering of mobile applications in Sect. 2. Section 3 presents the motivational example. The REiMPAcT approach is described in Sect. 4, and the specifications of the approach and its architecture are presented in Sect. 5. Section 6 describes a case study and Sect. 7 discusses threats to validity. Finally, the conclusions are in Sect. 8.

2   State of the Art

Over the last few years, there has been a lot of research work on Software Reverse Engineering and many approaches have been developed for extracting models from Desktop [5,7,14] and Web applications [2,8,18].

However, although in less quantity, there are also some reverse engineering works performed over mobile applications. The goal is still to analyze and simulate the user interaction to obtain a descriptive model [12].

TrimDroid [9] performs a static analysis of the Android apps code in order to extract a Finite State Machine were states are the activities of the app.

The dynamic reverse engineering technique presented in [6] exercises the UI (user interface) of iOS mobile applications to extract information regarding run time behavior and for generating/extracting a user interface state model of the

---

[1] https://developer.android.com/guide/components/fragments.

application behavior. Despite being dynamic, this approach needs to access code because it combines reflection and code injection to track method calls.

An example of Hybrid approach is presented in [19]. The approach consists of an initial static phase that identifies possible events to be fired and a second dynamic phase that explores the application by automatically firing the events identified before and analyzing the effects on the application. The goal is to extract a FSM where states are different screens (named *visual observable states*).

Another reverse engineering approach is presented by [4]. The goal is to reverse-engineer application lifecycles of mobile platforms by testing.

Although there are several approaches in the area of mobile reverse engineering, none of them extracts information about the activities of an application using a black-box dynamic exploration technique and do not relate the activities with their inner different screens.

3   Motivational Example

There are currently 2.6 million apps available on the Google Play Store[2]. In such crowded market applications that do not have the necessary quality or that do not behave as desired are quickly replaced by other identical applications.

To ensure that the applications have quality and work as expected, it is necessary to intensively test the applications. Sometimes developers or even testers encounter problems in the application during those tests, and in several situations it is difficult to associate those problems with a specific activity. Because of that it may be more difficult to locate the source of the failure inside the code.

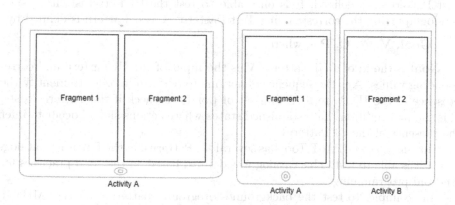

Fig. 1. App with one activity with 2 fragments (left); two activities with one fragment each (right).

[2] https://www.statista.com/statistics/266210/number-of-available-applications-in-the-google-play-store/.

The behaviour of a User Interface may be represented by fragments. A fragment belongs to an activity and may be reused in different activities. Also different fragments may be combined in a single activity. For example, Fig. 1 shows an Activity A with two fragments (on the left) and the same fragments belonging to two different activities (on the right).

Therefore, knowing the activity to which the fragment belongs can be helpful and interesting to reduce the amount of code to search for a defect that is the source of a failure.

4   iMPAcT Tool

iMPAcT tool [10,11,13] uses Reverse Engineering techniques and dynamic black-box testing techniques to automate the testing of recurring behavior (UI patterns) presented on Android apps.

Like other tools in the market, this tool was developed based on two Google APIs, it uses the API UI Automator[3] to interact with the device and the API UiAutomation[4] to read and extract information from the screen of the device.

The iMPAcT Tool can be decomposed into three different components: the Explorer; the UI Patterns Finder (reverse engineering); and the Tester. All these components work in iterative phases. While the Explorer component is crawling the application, the Finder component tries to identify the presence of UI Patterns. When a UI Pattern is identified the Tester component applies the associated Test Pattern (i.e., the test strategy to check if the UI pattern is well implemented).

This tool works based on a catalog where the UI patterns and corresponding Test Patterns are defined. It is only able to test the UI Patterns within such catalog applying the corresponding Test Pattern. A Test Pattern is defined by:

<Goal, V, A, C, P>, where:

Goal is the id of a UI Pattern. **V** is the input of the UI Pattern and corresponding values. **A** is the sequence of actions to perform in order to identify the presence of the UI Pattern. **C** is a set of points to check if the Pattern exists. **P** is the precondition that established states where actions should occur to infer the presence of the UI Pattern.

Currently, the iMPAcT Tool has several UI Patterns, in the Patterns Catalog, which it is able to test. This catalog was defined based on the good practices for Android programming[5].

For example, to test the background-foreground pattern [16], the iMPAcT Tool captures the information of the screen and sends the application under test (AUT) to the background by clicking on the home button. After that, the iMPAcT Tool brings the application to the foreground again by selecting it in the application manager. It then captures the information on the screen again

---

[3] https://developer.android.com/training/testing/ui-automator.

[4] https://developer.android.com/reference/android/app/UiAutomation.

[5] https://developer.android.com/distribute/best-practices/.

and compares it with the information previously captured. If the information captured before and after is different, the test fails.

Another example is the Call Test Pattern [15]. To test the Call Test Pattern two Emulators are needed: the Emulator A calls the Emulator B while the iMPAcT Tool is exploring the Emulator B. The iMPAcT Tool saves the screen state before receiving the call, then it disconnects the incoming call and saves the screen state again. If the screens' state are different before and after receiving the call, the test fails.

The counterpart of the iMPAcT Tool is the fact that it is only able of testing the UI Patterns that are in the Catalog.

The exploration and testing ends when the user presses the home button or when there is no more behaviour to explore/test.

The output/result is a key factor in all testing tools because it helps understanding and fixing the problems detected. The iMPAcT Tool has two distinct outputs: a Log File and a Finite State Machine (FSM). In the Log File, it saves information about the UI Patterns identified during exploration and lists the ones that passed the tests (correctly implemented) and the ones that failed the tests (wrongly implemented). The FSM has nodes and arrows between nodes. The nodes are screenshots of the AUT and the arrows describe the actions taken to navigate from screen to screen.

The iMPAcT Tool is able to identify the presence of UI patterns and compare two screens but it is not able of identifying the activities of the application under test traversed during the exploration. The extension presented in this paper (REiMPAcT) improves the reverse engineering component allowing to extract information about the activities and their inner screens and presenting an HFSM structured in three levels of abstraction to understand better the app under analysis.

5   Reverse Engineering Tool: REiMPAcT

The approach presented in this paper extends the iMPAcT Tool with additional reverse engineering capabilities. The REiMPAcT component is able to extract information about the activities and the states traversed by a dynamic exploration of an Android application.

This approach may be useful to:

- Create a navigation map of the explored application.
- Check if the navigation flow of an application is the one expected.
- Provide information about the activities and inner screens of the applications.

In addition, it should be noticed that this approach allows to extract dynamically the activities of the apps in a complete black-box approach without any access to the code neither APK of the application under analysis.

So, besides being useful to comprehend better the application under analysis, this approach may help in a software testing context where failures are found. This is a typical problem found in random testing tools. They are able to detect crashes of the applications but then, since they do not provide any kind of help, it is difficult to find the source of the problem within the code. With this tool, the tester may add information about the activity in which the failure was detected and so, help the developer to find out the source of the failure within the code.

The architecture of this approach can be seen in the Fig. 2.

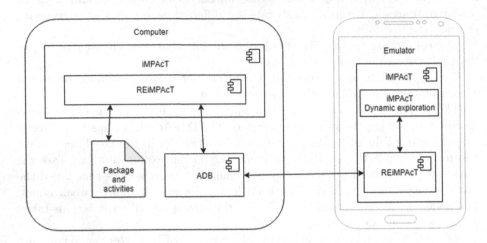

Fig. 2. The architecture of the reverse engineering approach (REiMPAcT)

The output (Fig. 3) of the REiMPAcT is an HFSM (Hierarchical Finite State Machine) composed by three distinct levels of abstraction (similar to the structure used in [17] for Desktop applications).

At the highest level of abstraction (First level), we can find a representation of the activities traversed by the dynamic exploration algorithm of the iMPAcT Tool. At this level, it is only necessary to know which activities are explored, and the order of exploration, i.e., the sequence of activities explored.

The navigation through activities is represented by arrows with numbers. An arrow between two activities describes user actions that allow navigating from the origin activity to the destination activity, i.e., actions that departure from a state/screen of the source activity and reaches a state/screen of target distinct activity. The numbers are useful to sequence those actions.

At the middle level of abstraction (Second level), it is possible to visualize, for each activity, which screens were traversed and the actions that allow such navigation flow. At this level, it is necessary to know which activity each screen belongs to and which actions traverse screens that belong to that same activity. This level of the HFSM shows the inner navigation for each activity of the explored application.

At the bottom level of abstraction (Third level), it is possible to visualize all screens traversed during the exploration. This third level is built using an already existing feature of the iMPAcT Tool that allows building the final state machine (FSM) of the application under test. At this level, it is necessary to have access to the print screens and the sequence of actions that traverse screens to build the FSM. This level of the HFSM shows the general navigation between screens.

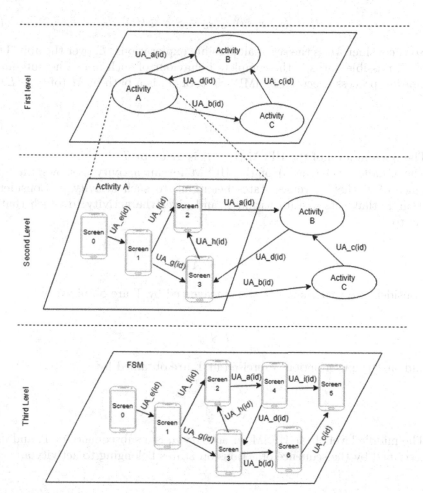

Fig. 3. Hierarchical Finite State Machine (HFSM) with 2nd level detailed for Activity A

Consider an app with a set of different activities,

$$A = \{a_1, ..., a_{|A|}\} \tag{1}$$

a set of different screens

$$S = \{s_1, ..., s_{|S|}\} \tag{2}$$

and the set of possible user actions over that app

$$UA = \{ua_1, ..., ua_{|UA|}\} \tag{3}$$

An exploration, E, of the app is a sequence of user actions traversing screens/states of the app.

$$E = [(s_o, x, s_d) | s_o, s_d \in S, x \in UA] \tag{4}$$

Now, consider M as the set of all possible explorations, E, over the app. This set of all possible paths is the complete behaviour of such app. The automatic exploration process executed by iMPAcT tool, T, is a path in M (of type E).

$$T \in M \tag{5}$$

The bottom level of the HFSM (Fig. 3) is given by T.

The middle level (Fig. 3) of the HFSM for an activity a shows the subsequence of T that traverses states belonging to such activity a. Consider a function F that gets a state within T and gives the activity to which that S belong to.

$$F(S) = A \tag{6}$$

Consider also that the set of states traversed by T are obtained by

$$T.S \tag{7}$$

and that the user actions exercised in T are obtained by

$$T.UA \tag{8}$$

The middle level of the HFSM for activity a, is a subsequence of T, and may be described by the sequence of actions on states belonging to activity a.

$$[(s1, ua, s2) | s1, s2 \in T.S \wedge ua \in T.UA \wedge F(s1) = F(s2) = a] \tag{9}$$

The top level of the HFSM shows the activities exercised by T.

$$[(F(so), ua, F(sd)) | so, sd \in T.S \wedge ua \in T.UA \wedge F(so)! = F(sd)] \tag{10}$$

The extraction of information regarding the activities traversed is conducted in parallel with the normal flow of execution of the iMPAcT Tool, i.e., in parallel with the exploration algorithm that exercises the application under analysis.

The REiMPAcT component runs a process on the iMPAcT Tool present in the computer (Fig. 2), that checks which is the current activity of the application every second. This time interval may be customized.

```
C:\Users_____>adb shell
shell@angler:/ $ dumpsys window windows | grep -E 'mCurrentFocus'
  mCurrentFocus=Window{c838a23 u0 com.android.vending/com.google.android.finsky.activities.MainActivity}
shell@angler:/ $
                          This is appPackage                    This is appActivity
```

Fig. 4. ADB Shell command output

To do this, REiMAPcT uses the ADB (Android Debug Bridge) command line tool that allows to communicate with a device. This command outputs the package name and the name of the current activity of the application under analysis in that moment, as it can be seen in the Fig. 4.

```
adb shell
dumpsys window windows | grep -E "mCurrentFocus"
```

All the information collected along the execution of the REiMPAcT is stored in a text file (including the name of the activity and the exact time in which this information was collected). Besides information about the traversed activities, the tool also gathers screenshots of the explored screens and the time in which such screenshots were taken; fired actions that change from one screen to another; and other metrics. Based on the information collected about time, activities, actions and screens, it is possible to determine which are the screens within each activity and construct the HFSM (which is displayed using the Java library called mxGraph).

6   Case Study

In order to validate the approach developed we performed an experiment over 20 apps available on Google Play store. The process followed was:

1. Select the Android mobile apps to analyze.
2. Execute the REiMPAcT tool over the apps selected.
3. Record the percentage of activities detected in a limited period of time.
4. Obtain the screens for each activity (2nd level of the HFSM)

6.1   Selection of the Android Mobile Applications

This study was performed on Android mobile applications that can be found in the Google Play Store. The final set of 20 Android mobile applications was selected randomly from the set of apps that met the following criteria:

- Its rating should be higher than 3.5 to ensure minimum quality
- It must been downloaded at least 5000 times
- It must use Gradle to build the application
- It must have GUI in order to be tested by the iMPAcT Tool
- It must be in English or Portuguese

The 20 Android apps selected belong to 9 different categories.

6.2   REiMPAcT Tool Execution over Apps Selected

We run the *REiMPAcT Tool* over the list of previously chosen Android mobile applications. The example presented below is the *REiMPAcT Tool* output for a 5-minute test performed on the *ametro.org* Android application.

The Fig. 5 presents the first level of the HFSM, the Fig. 6 presents the second level (for the activity *CityList* of the application) and Fig. 7 presents the third level of the HFSM.

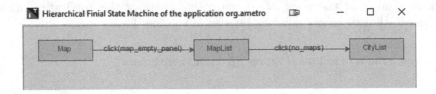

Fig. 5. The first level of the HFSM for the application org.ametro

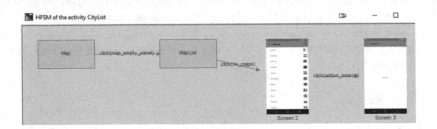

Fig. 6. Hierarchical Finite State Machine (HFSM) with 2nd level detailed for Activity CityList

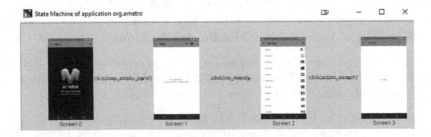

Fig. 7. The third level of the HFSM for the application org.ametro

Analysing the figures presented above it is possible to verify that:

1. During the dynamic exploration, it was possible to extract three distinct activities (*Map*, *MapList* and *CityList*).
2. The *CityList* activity is composed of Screen_2 and Screen_3 which are traversed after a click event on a screen element from the *MapList* activity.
3. The exploration captured four different screen shots.

We did not find any bugs during the exploration of these apps.

6.3   Percentage of Activities Explored

In order to calculate the percentage of activities explored, it is necessary to know the total number of activities that exist in the application and the number of activities explored. Using the REiMPAcT approach, it is possible to obtain the number of activities explored, but it is not possible to obtain the total number of activities of the application (it is a black-box approach). For that, it was necessary to perform static analysis over the source code, or the APK. Given that most of the chosen applications are not open-source it was necessary to parse the APK.

There are several platforms that allow downloading the APKs through the package name, and it is also possible to get the package name in the own Google Play Store. Once we get the APK for each application, it is possible to use the Analyze APK functionality of Android Studio to analyze the app and get *AndroidManifest.xml*.

Through the analysis of the *AndroidManifest.xml* it is possible to know how many activities there are in the application and, so, calculate the percentage of activities explored.

The exploration algorithm may influence the results achieved by REiMPAcT. If the explorer is not able to exercise the complete behavior of the application under analysis, the reverse engineering component will not be able to detect/extract the complete HFSM of the application. Discussing and comparing different crawlers is not the goal of this work, however, the description of a new crawler developed for iMPAcT tool may be found in [3].

The results from the 20 apps tested in a limited time period of 15 min can be found in Table 1.

From the 20 apps tested, only the exploration of the application *Wlingua* was able to get 100% of the activities. The worst results belong to the NBA application that only explored 10% of the activities. The total average number of activities explored in whole apps is approximately 40%.

It should be noticed that REiMPAcT tool is fully black-box and does not need to get access to *AndroidManifest.xml*. We only accessed the *AndroidManifest.xml* file to perform this experiment and assess the percentage of explored activities.

Table 1. Percentage of activities extracted

	App name	% of activities (15 min)
1	aMetro	67
2	Paris Metro	18
3	EasyBus Porto	67
4	ProCiv Madeira	50
5	Forest Fires	67
6	Portugal Newspaper	33
7	Sapo Newspaper	28
8	Google News	18
9	Wlingua	100
10	GeoChallenge	75
11	Math tricks	30
12	MyResults	33
13	NBA	10
14	Wallet	75
15	Expense manager	30
16	HomeWorkout	13
17	Pedometer	17
18	Medication Alarm	22
19	Moodpath	17
20	eBoox	33
	Average	40

7   Threats to Validity

It is important to remember that there are some threats to validity associated with the results presented.

This study was performed over 20 apps. The set size could be bigger, however, to mitigate this threat, we selected reliable apps of different categories to diversify the subjects used in this case of study.

The current approach uses time units to synchronize/relate the information regarding the screens and their activities, which is susceptible to error. Also, there are activities declared in *AndroidManifest.xml* that are not related to screens of the app. These activities will not be detected by REiMPAcT because it only gets the activities that has focus on the device. So, if we exclude those activities (not related to screens) the percentage of activities detected would be higher.

To mitigate all these threats we tested each app two times, so we got 2 executions per app. After testing each app two times we end up spending 30 min testing each app. So, we spend about 2 days with this experiment.

8 Conclusions

This paper presented a reverse engineering tool, *REiMPAcT*, able to extract a HFSM from a black-box dynamic exploration of Android applications.

The HFSM is structured in three levels: the top one shows the navigation among activities; the middle layer shows the navigation through different states of the Android application for each activity; and the bottom layer shows the screens traversed during the exploration. The HFSM is formalized and illustrated in real examples.

The main difference of *REiMAPcT* tool in relation to others is its complete black-box nature. It does not need to have any access to the code and it does not instrument the code. The architecture of the tool is presented in detail.

A case study was performed over real apps from Google Play Store. The goal was to check if it was possible to apply the approach in real scenarios and gather metrics about which percentage of activities it was possible to detect by this dynamic exploration process. As we did not find any errors in the experiment, we intend to carry out additional case studies, injecting errors into the applications and checking if the REiMPAcT tool can help to detect them more easily. Also, we aim to perform experiments in industrial environments, to access the applicability, utility and ease of use in this context.

References

1. Canfora, G., Di Penta, M., Cerulo, L.: Achievements and challenges in software reverse engineering. Commun. ACM **54**(4), 142–151 (2011). https://doi.org/10.1145/1924421.1924451
2. Di Francescomarino, C., Marchetto, A., Tonella, P.: Reverse engineering of business processes exposed as web applications. In: Proceedings of the 2009 European Conference on Software Maintenance and Reengineering, CSMR 2009, pp. 139–148. IEEE Computer Society, Washington, DC (2009). https://doi.org/10.1109/CSMR.2009.26
3. Ferreira, J., Paiva, A.C.R.: Android testing crawler. In: Piattini, M., Rupino da Cunha, P., García Rodríguez de Guzmán, I., Pérez-Castillo, R. (eds.) QUATIC 2019. CCIS, vol. 1010, pp. 313–326. Springer, Cham (2019). https://doi.org/10.1007/978-3-030-29238-6_23
4. Franke, D., Elsemann, C., Kowalewski, S., Weise, C.: Reverse engineering of mobile application lifecycles. In: 2011 18th Working Conference on Reverse Engineering, pp. 283–292, October 2011. https://doi.org/10.1109/WCRE.2011.42
5. Hackner, D., Memon, A.M.: Test case generator for GUITAR. In: Research Demonstration Track: International Conference on Software Engineering, ICSE 2008. IEEE Computer Society, Washington, DC (2008)
6. Joorabchi, M.E., Mesbah, A.: Reverse engineering iOS mobile applications. In: 2012 19th Working Conference on Reverse Engineering, pp. 177–186, October 2012. https://doi.org/10.1109/WCRE.2012.27
7. Memon, A.: GUI ripping: reverse engineering of graphical user interfaces for testing. In: Proceedings of the 10th Working Conference on Reverse Engineering, pp. 260–269 (2003)

8. Mesbah, A., van Deursen, A., Lenselink, S.: Crawling Ajax-based web applications through dynamic analysis of user interface state changes. ACM Trans. Web **6**(1), 3:1–3:30 (2012). https://doi.org/10.1145/2109205.2109208

9. Mirzaei, N., Garcia, J., Bagheri, H., Sadeghi, A., Malek, S.: Reducing combinatorics in GUI testing of Android applications. In: Proceedings of the 38th International Conference on Software Engineering, ICSE 2016, pp. 559–570. ACM, New York (2016). https://doi.org/10.1145/2884781.2884853

10. Morgado, I.C., Paiva, A.C.R.: The iMPAcT tool: testing UI patterns on mobile applications. In: 2015 30th IEEE/ACM International Conference on Automated Software Engineering (ASE), pp. 876–881, November 2015. https://doi.org/10.1109/ASE.2015.96

11. Morgado, I.C., Paiva, A.C.: The iMPAcT tool for Android testing. Proc. ACM Hum. Comput. Interact. **3**(EICS), 4:1–4:23 (2019). https://doi.org/10.1145/3300963

12. Morgado, I.C., Paiva, A.C.R.: Testing approach for mobile applications through reverse engineering of UI patterns. In: 30th IEEE/ACM International Conference on Automated Software Engineering Workshops, ASE Workshops 2015, Lincoln, NE, USA, 9–13 November 2015, pp. 42–49 (2015). https://doi.org/10.1109/ASEW.2015.11

13. Morgado, I.C., Paiva, A.C.R.: Mobile GUI testing. Softw. Qual. J. **26**(4), 1553–1570 (2017). https://doi.org/10.1007/s11219-017-9387-1

14. Morgado, I.C., Paiva, A.C.R., Faria, J.P.: Dynamic reverse engineering of graphical user interfaces. Int. J. Adv. Softw. **5**, 224–236 (2012)

15. Paiva, A.C.R., Gonçalves, M.A., Barros, A.R.: Testing Android incoming calls. In: 12th IEEE Conference on Software Testing, Validation and Verification, ICST 2019, Xi'an, China, 22–27 April 2019, pp. 441–448 (2019). https://doi.org/10.1109/ICST.2019.00053

16. Paiva, A.C.R., Gouveia, J.M.E.P., Elizabeth, J., Delamaro, M.E.: Testing when mobile apps go to background and come back to foreground. In: 2019 IEEE International Conference on Software Testing, Verification and Validation Workshops, ICST Workshops 2019, Xi'an, China, 22–23 April 2019, pp. 102–111 (2019). https://doi.org/10.1109/ICSTW.2019.00038

17. Paiva, A.C.R., Tillmann, N., Faria, J.C.P., Vidal, R.F.A.M.: Modeling and testing hierarchical GUIs. In: Proceedings of the 12th International Workshop on Abstract State Machines, ASM 2005, Paris, France, 8–11 March 2005, pp. 329–344 (2005)

18. Sacramento, C., Paiva, A.C.R.: Web application model generation through reverse engineering and UI pattern inferring. In: 2014 9th International Conference on the Quality of Information and Communications Technology, pp. 105–115, September 2014. https://doi.org/10.1109/QUATIC.2014.20

19. Yang, W., Prasad, M.R., Xie, T.: A grey-box approach for automated GUI-model generation of mobile applications. In: Cortellessa, V., Varró, D. (eds.) FASE 2013. LNCS, vol. 7793, pp. 250–265. Springer, Heidelberg (2013). https://doi.org/10.1007/978-3-642-37057-1_19

An Approach and a Prototype Tool for Generating Executable IoT System Test Cases

Dario Olianas(✉)[ID], Maurizio Leotta[ID], and Filippo Ricca[ID]

Dipartimento di Informatica, Bioingegneria, Robotica e Ingegneria dei Sistemi (DIBRIS), Università di Genova, Genova, Italy
dario.olianas@dibris.unige.it, {maurizio.leotta,filippo.ricca}@unige.it

Abstract. Internet of Things (IoT) systems are becoming ubiquitous and assuring their quality is of paramount importance, especially in safety-critical contexts. Unfortunately, few quality assurance proposals are present in the literature.

In this paper, we propose an approach for semi-automated model-based generation of executable test cases, oriented to system-level acceptance testing of IoT systems. Our approach is supported by a prototype tool taking in input a UML model of the system under test and some additional artifacts, and produces in output a test suite that checks if the behavior of the system is compliant with such a model.

The empirical evaluation of the approach executed on a mobile health IoT system for diabetic patients – involving sensors, actuators, a smartphone, and a remote cloud system – shows that the test suite generated with our tool has been able to kill between 87% and 98% of the mutants (i.e., artificial bugged versions of the system under test).

Keywords: IoT testing · Model-based test generation · Empirical study

1 Introduction

Internet of Things (IoT) systems are composed of interconnected physical devices that share data and often include a central remote control server on the cloud. The spread of such systems has had a significant impact on all aspects of the society, and in a few years has changed the life of billions of people.

Ensuring that IoT systems are secure, reliable, and compliant with the requirements is a fundamental task since they are often safety-critical. However, testing these kinds of systems can be difficult due to: a) the wide set of disparate technologies used to build them (hardware and software), b) the lacking of consolidated testing approaches and, c) the added complexity that comes with big data (the three 'V', huge volume, high velocity, and wide variety).

In this paper, we propose and evaluate a tool-supported approach for semi-automated acceptance testing of IoT systems. *Acceptance testing* is a type of

© Springer Nature Switzerland AG 2020
M. Shepperd et al. (Eds.): QUATIC 2020, CCIS 1266, pp. 383–398, 2020.
https://doi.org/10.1007/978-3-030-58793-2_31

black-box testing based on test scenarios, i.e., sequences of actions performed by the users, sensors, or the system. Acceptance testing has been chosen for our proposal since, according to many organizations [1], assembling an IoT system and testing it as a whole is the most simple and effective way to ensure its quality.

Our proposal can be classified as a *model-based* approach, since test cases are derived from the model of the system, represented as a UML State Machine and a Class diagrams in our case. The goal of the automated test generation tool implementing the approach is generating a test suite composed by executable test cases (i.e., test scripts) that: (Req_1) is complete "enough" to exercise all the use scenarios of the system under test (corresponding to paths on the state machine), and (Req_2) is correct with respect to the semantics of the provided model. To satisfy the *first requirement*, our prototype tool relies on a graph exploration algorithm that generates a set of paths starting from the target model (UML State Machine + Class diagrams). Such an algorithm guarantees that every transition of the state machine is traversed at least once considering all the generated paths. To satisfy the *second requirement*, the proposed approach relies on search-based algorithms to transform the previously generated test paths in feasible paths. *Search-based software engineering* [7] is a branch of software engineering that applies meta-heuristic search techniques to software engineering problems.

The proposed approach has been empirically evaluated to determine the effectiveness of the generated test suites in detecting bugs. A well established automated validation framework based on Mutation testing has been used to support the empirical evaluation. *Mutation testing* [12] is a technique that consists in exercising the test suite against slight variations (i.e., mutants) of the original code, simulating the errors a developer could introduce during development and maintenance activities.

Automatic test case generation from state machines is a well-known problem, with many existing techniques and tools. Existing works cover different aspects of the test generation problem, like criteria for state machine coverage in test generation and algorithms used to implement them [4], prioritization of relevant test cases (the ones that most likely will find bugs) [5,13], minimality of generated test suites (i.e., generating the minimum number of test cases able to satisfy the desired coverage criteria) [3], and transformation of abstract test cases in executable code [15]. However, to the best of our knowledge, no scientific work addresses explicitly the problem of generating test scripts from a model of an IoT system and proposes a prototype tool as in our proposal.

This paper is organized as follows: Sect. 2 describes the DiaMH case study. Section 3, 4, and 5 describe the proposed approach. Section 6 reports on the empirical evaluation of the approach, while Sect. 7 concludes the paper.

2   Case Study: Diabetes Mobile Health IoT System

DiaMH is a simplified Diabetes Mobile Health system that: (1) monitors a patient glucose level; (2) sends alarms to the patient smartphone when a dangerous glucose trend is detected; and (3) regulates insulin dose consequently. DiaMH has already been used as a case study in other works concerning testing of IoT systems [11] where, however, a manual approach to derive test cases from a model of the behavior of the system has been proposed in contrast to the automated generation proposed in this work. As shown in Fig. 1 the DiaMH system is composed by:

- a *glucose sensor* and an *insulin pump* both attached to the patient;
- the patient *smartphone*, wirelessly connected to both the sensor and the pump, and used to receive an alarm in case of dangerous glucose values;
- the analysis and control system, *DiaMH Core*, running on the cloud, that receives the glucose readings, analyzes their patterns and commands the proper actions.

DiaMH Required Behavior. The glucose sensor measures the glucose level of the patient at given timed intervals (e.g., every 30 min), and sends them to the smartphone. The mobile app displays the value and forwards it to the remote DiaMH Core. The core component of the system stores the last 20 glucose readings received from the patient's smartphone and, depending on how many readings exceed a given threshold, it will command an insulin injection, and if necessary, send an alarm to the patient. After receiving a value, the analysis and control system decides the state assigned to the user:

- *Normal:* between 0–3 values among the last 20 exceeded the threshold. No action required;
- *More insulin required:* between 4–15 values among the last 20 exceeded the threshold. An insulin injection is performed;
- *Problematic:* between 16–20 values among the last 20 exceeded the threshold. An insulin injection is performed and an alarm is displayed on the smartphone.

To prevent performing too many injections, and to allow insulin to make effect, every time an insulin injection is performed the following 5 glucose readings are ignored (e.g., 2.5 h). When an injection is required, the patient should confirm it: then the app will require the pump to inject the insulin dose. To prevent missing injections because of pump failures, the pump sends a feedback to the smartphone only if the injection is performed successfully: after receiving this feedback, the app shows the total number of injections performed in the current session.

Testing Execution Environment. In this work, we focus on testing at a level of *acceptance* using a partially emulated/virtualized version of DiaMH, where the sensor and the pump are virtualized by Node-RED flows, while the mobile app is running on Android emulator (note that the code of the mobile app is the same used in the real DiaMH system). The architecture of DiaMH and the corresponding testing environment and interactions are shown in Fig. 1.

Node-RED (https://nodered.org/) is a visual flow-based programming tool built on the Javascript server-side runtime environment Node.js, which allows developing applications as a flow of interconnected nodes. The developer uses a web-based flow editor to place different types of nodes in the flow and deploy it. The execution model is based on *nodes* and *messages*: a node is a functional unit of the flow delegated to a specific task. A message is a JSON object exchanged between nodes, that will perform some actions over its properties. It can be received from the network or generated by a node.

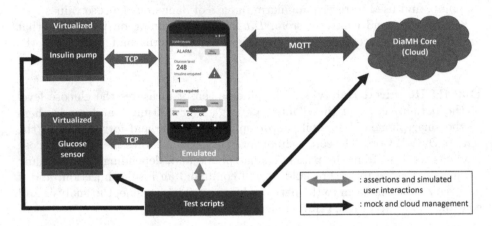

Fig. 1. DiaMH components, testing execution environment, and relations with test scripts

3 Overview of the Approach

Before starting to describe the approach, let's give some definitions. According to the definition of the IEEE/ISO/IEC Systems and software engineering vocabulary [2] with *test case* we mean a set of inputs, execution conditions and expected results developed for a particular objective, such as to exercise a particular program path or to verify compliance with a specific requirement. With *test path*, we mean an ordered sequence of state machine transitions, starting from an initial state, that represents a test case. We call *executable test path* a feasible path, i.e. a path that if traversed on the state machine, never meets a false guard. With *test script*, we mean the executable code that implements a test path.

Approach Steps. Our approach is composed by five steps. To automatically produce the test scripts the Test engineer has to:

1) *Design* a model of the IoT system;
2) *Implement* wrapper and mock classes following the model;

3) *Define* or *generate* some configuration files;
4) *Execute* our test generation prototype tool;
5) *Run* the generated test scripts against the IoT system.

The workflow, along with the involved artifacts and the relations among them, is shown in Fig. 2. In the next sections, we provide details about the various steps, even if, for space reasons, we cannot provide a full step-by-step guide to the application of our approach and usage of our tool. For the interested reader, further details about both the approach and the tool, its source code, and the complete model and artifacts of the DiaMH case study are available at: https://github.com/Quatic2020IoTTestGeneration/IoTExecutableTestCaseGeneration.

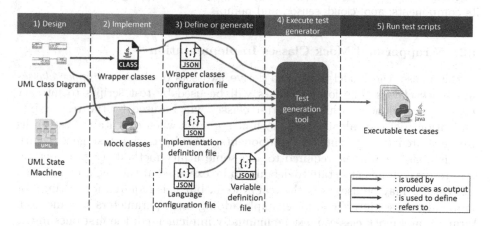

Fig. 2. Approach workflow

4 Input Data Preparation

In this section, we describe the first three steps of our approach dealing with the preparation of the various artifacts required by the test scripts generator.

4.1 Model Design of the System Under Test

Starting from existing artifacts describing the system's components and behavior, the test engineer has to *design* a testing model for the system composed by a UML Class and a UML State Machine diagram. Note that for serious industrial IoT systems, we can reasonably assume that an accurate description of the system components and required behavior exists and that it can be used as a starting point for a test engineer.

To follow our approach, the test engineer has to create a *class diagram* containing a class for each component of the IoT system, and each class can expose three kinds of members: (a) method operations that perform some action and may return a value, (b) operations generating call events, that will be used as events in the state machine (those latter operations should not return a value), and (c) fields, that store some value that is used by the system.

Then, the UML *state machine* describing the required behavior of the IoT system has to be modeled. Each transition can be labeled with a *triggering event*, a *guard* and an *action*. We call *enabled transition* a transition that has a true guard. The *execution* of the state machine happens in a context, where objects, i.e., instance of classes in class diagram, are declared. The execution flow of the state machine always starts from the initial pseudo-state (black circle). Figure 3 reports the state machine designed for DiaMH: there are three states representing a generic patient's condition: Normal, MoreInsulin, and Problematic together with all the details describing the required behavior of DiaMH and of its components: app, cloud, sensor, and pump.

4.2 Wrapper and Mock Classes Implementation

In this phase, the model is used to derive two sets of classes: *wrapper classes* and *mock classes*. The former classes will be used by test scripts to interact with IoT components while the latter classes will be used by the test scripts generation tool to evaluate state machine's guards when executable test paths are generated (i.e., to simulate components behavior during test generation). In this phase, it may be required to add some utility methods (e.g., a method that resets component's state to default, to be executed at the beginning of each test case: it may be useless in the real system, but it is required for testing), or to modify classes interfaces, for example adding some parameters to a method. Wrapper and mock classes must be manually implemented: the first ones in the language chosen for implementing the test scripts, the latter in Python, since they have to be executed by our tool implemented in Python. To reduce the effort required to the developer, for wrapper classes we may provide a framework offering some common use functionalities in IoT testing, like for example sending and receiving messages over different communication protocols. Mock classes, since they must emulate the behavior of the SUT, require to be carefully designed by the developer to make sure their behavior is compliant with the SUT's one. However, model-based code generation techniques can be employed to generate them from the model. As an example, we report a sketch of a wrapper class for DiaMH (for the InsulinPump component) and its methods and fields.

InsulinPump

- erogatedInjections: store the number of injections done in the current session;
- reset(): restore pump's internal variables to default values.

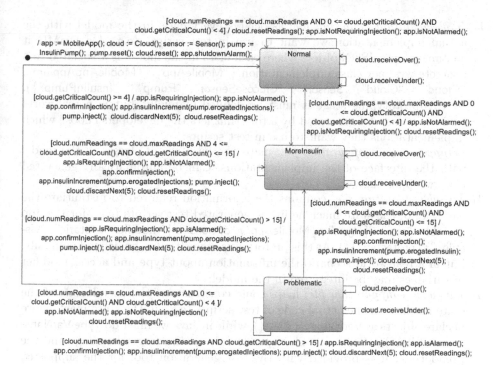

Fig. 3. DiaMH state machine diagram

In the following, a portion of the Python code of the Cloud mock class is provided:

```
class Cloud:
  def getCriticalCount(self):
    res = 0
    for x in self.glucoseReadings:
      if(x > self.threshold):
        res += 1
    return res
...
```

getCriticalCount(...) returns the number of glucose readings exceeding the threshold received by the cloud so far. It will be invoked every time the test generation tool traverses a transition which, in its guard, checks the number of values over the threshold.

4.3 Configuration Files Definition/Generation

Interfaces of wrapper and mock classes, although derived from the model, can significantly differ from the original components of the actual system under test. To fill the gap between model and implementation, some *configuration files* have to be *defined*. In our approach, there are four configuration files to make implementation details explicit:

1) *Implementation definition file*: associates every class in the model with the actual implementation we want to use in test scripts (e.g., for DiaMH it contains only a JSON object where each class in the model is associated to a concrete wrapper class implementation { "MobileApp" : "MobileAppAppium", "Cloud" : "Cloud", "Sensor" : "GlucoseSensor", "Pump" : "InsulinPump" }). At this prototyping stage it must be defined manually, but in a real-world scenario it may be generated by a tool that lets the developers choose which implementations they want to use in test scripts;

2) *Wrapper class configuration file*: maps the interface of classes in the model with the interface of the implementations. Can be automatically generated from wrapper classes;

3) *Variable definition file*: contains the information required to instantiate the variables of the state machine in the generated test scripts (e.g., for the app variable: "app" : { "type" : "MobileApp", "options" : { "modifier" : "static", "visibility": "protected" }}). At this prototyping stage it must be defined manually, but in a real-world scenario the information about type and access modifier of variables may be integrated in the model;

4) *Language configuration file*: maps some constructs of the pseudocode of the state machine in the actual code of test scripts (e.g., in the state machine we declare objects as VarName := Class(), while in Java we must do Type VarName = new Class();). Since this file depends only on the target language and the pseudocode, it is provided with the test generation tool for the supported target languages (Java and Python).

We chose to use four files instead of saving all this information in one to allow changing them independently when generating test scripts. For example, if we want to use a different implementation, we need to change only the implementation definition file.

The wrapper class configuration file can be compiled manually, or can be generated automatically if our wrapper classes are written in Java (and properly annotated). We defined two annotations: @ModelName, which specifies the model name of the class or method it annotates, and @Omitted, used to annotate parameters of wrapper classes that are not reported in the model.

5   Test Scripts Generation

At this point, all the inputs required by the test generation tool are ready. Now the tester is just required to run the tool providing them as input. The execution flow of the tool is summarized in Fig. 4 and described in detail in the following of the section. As the first step, the configuration builder (Step ①) inspects the wrapper classes using reflection and creates the Wrapper class configuration file. Then the tool analyzes the state machine (Step ②) and generates a set of paths that traverse it, starting from the initial state (Step ③). These paths, thanks to the code written in state machine's labels and implementation details stored in configuration files, are transformed by the tool in executable test scripts (Step ④ and ⑤) in a given target language (our implementation currently supports Java and Python).

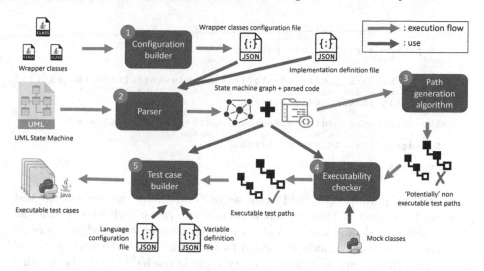

Fig. 4. Tool architecture and execution flow

5.1   Test Paths Building

After the generation of Wrapper class configuration files (Step ①), the tool reads the state machine, parses its code (Step ②) and finds an initial set of test paths using an algorithm that guarantees transition coverage (Step ③). Every transition of the state machine is traversed at least once considering all the generated paths.

The proposed algorithm (Step ③) is designed as follows: it takes in input a directed multigraph G (a directed graph which is permitted to have multiple edges, i.e., edges with the same source and target nodes) represented as a set of vertices V (the states of the diagram) and a set of edges E (the transitions of the diagram), and an initial state s. We assume that every state in V is reachable from s. Each element of E contains the edge itself and a boolean to mark if the edge has been visited yet. Each element of V contains the state itself and a path to reach it, saved the first time we visit the state. Each vertex v and edge e offers the following methods:

- v.hasOutEdges(): returns true if the vertex has outgoing edges, false otherwise;
- v.unvisitedOutEdges(): returns the list of outgoing edges from v not yet visited;
- e.getTarget(): returns the destination vertex of e;
- e.getSource(): returns the source vertex of e;

Pseudocode of the initial paths generation algorithm:

```
list findPathsForEdgeCoverage(V,E,s) {
  Queue edgeToVisit; List finalPaths;
  edgeToVisit.push(s.unvisitedOutEdges());
  while (TRUE) {
    e = edgeToVisit.pop();  vertex v = e.getTarget();
    e.visited = TRUE;
    if (v.path is empty) { // first time we visit the node
```

```
    /* the path to reach v is created by concatenating the current
            edge to the path bringing to its source state */
    v.path = e.getSource().path+e;
    /* if the current state has outgoing edges they are added to
        the unvisited queue */
    if (v.hasOutEdges()) edgeToVisit.push(v.unvisitedOutEdges());
    //if there are no outgoing edges the path is finalized
    else finalPaths.add(v.path);
    }
    else finalPaths.add(e.getSource().path+e); /* we already visited
            this node, so we finalize the path */
    if (edgeToVisit is empty) break;
  }
  return finalPaths;
}
```

The algorithm produces (i.e., add to the set of "Potentially" non-executable test path, see the output of Step ③) a new path in two cases: each time it visits an already visited node and when it visits a node without outgoing edges. Since all the unvisited edges of a node are added to the queue when the node is visited for the first time, if we assume that every node is reachable from the starting node s, every edge will appear in at least one produces path. Moreover, since the final path is always taken from the edgeToVisit queue, and since there are no duplicate edges in the queue (edges are added only when a node is visited for the first time), the algorithm also guarantees that every produced path ends with a different transition.

5.2 Paths' Executability Handling

Test paths generated in the previous step are built looking only at the graph structure of the state machine, without checking if transitions' guards are enabled. Therefore, they cannot be transformed immediately in executable test scripts. In case the state machine has been properly designed (and in particular, if all the used variables have been declared in the transitions outgoing from the initial state), we can analyze the paths using symbolic execution [9] to check if there are non-executable transitions, and add a *loop* (i.e., a sequence of transitions starting and ending in the state where the transition to enable starts) before them to enable them (Step ④).

A test path is an ordered sequence of transitions: to execute it means executing, starting from the first transition, all the code included in transition labels (events, guards, and actions) and entry actions (if any) of the target state. The code in the state machine refers to classes declared in the class diagram, and that is why we need the aforementioned mock classes: without them, we would not be able to execute test paths in this phase.

To choose which transitions traverse to make the predicate true, we must introduce the notion of *branch distance*. Described for the first time by Korel [10], branch distance is a metric that can be computed on boolean predicates, and tells us how close we are to make the given predicate true. The original version of Korel handled only relational predicates (equalities and inequalities), but it has been extended by Tracey et al. [14] to support negation, AND and OR. Usually, in input data generation for search-based test generation techniques, branch distance is used as fitness function (or as a component of the fitness function) for meta-heuristic search algorithms like hill-climbing, simulated annealing or genetic algorithm. In these scenarios, there is a big, potentially infinite search space, in which to find the input values that maximize (or minimize) a fitness function. In our case, the input we want to find is a *loop*, with a fixed maximum length, that enables a specific transition: the actions contained in the transitions composing the *loop* will enable the transition of interest (see the following example). But at each step, our search space is limited to the enabled outgoing transitions of the current state, so our search algorithm will be quite straightforward.

Let's make an example on the DiaMH state machine (see Fig. 3). At a given moment, we need to enable transition from the Normal to the MoreInsuline state. The context is: we already received 10 readings of which 2 above the threshold (i.e., critical). So we have to enable the transition guard [cloud.getCriticalCount()>=4]. Tracey et al. [14] report that the branch distance for a boolean predicate of kind E1>=E2 is 0 if E1>=E2 otherwise E2–E1. Thus the current distance d is 4–2=2. The algorithm needs to analyze the effect (on the branch distance of the guard of interest) of executing the other transitions. cloud.receiveOver(); increments of 1 the value of criticalCount, cloud.receiveUnder(); does not modify the value of criticalCount, while the remaining self-transition of the state Normal cannot be executed since maxReadings is equal to 20 and we have obtained only 10 readings so far. So to reduce the distance d to our goal (i.e., enabling the transition from Normal to MoreInsuline), the algorithm chooses to cycle twice on the self-transition labeled with cloud.receiveOver();. Indeed, in this way, d changes from 2 to 1 (after the first cycle), and then to 0 (after the second cycle). At this point, criticalCount becomes equal to 4 and the transition to MoreInsuline will be executed.

5.3   Test Scripts Building

At this point, almost all the information required to build executable test scripts is contained in the executable test paths (see the input to Step ⑤). We only need some additional implementation details that are language-dependent and can be stored in configuration files. More in detail, the language configuration file is used to translate from the pseudocode used in the state machine to the programming language used in actual test scripts; the variable definition file is used to correctly instantiate variables. A simple loop traverses each path and prints in a file the code found in traversed transitions and states, relying on the aforementioned language configuration file to generate test scripts with a correct syntax (e.g., if we are generating Java test scripts for the JUnit framework it should generate test methods annotated with the @Test annotation and using public void modifiers).

Test Scripts for DiaMH. Our prototype tool generated 12 test scripts for DiaMH, composed of 889 lines of code (LOCs). The longest test script is composed of 136 LOCs, the shortest of 9, with an average of 70 LOCs and a standard deviation of 48 LOCs. The high standard deviation is due to the business logic of DiaMH: to enable some transitions, we must send from 15 to 20 glucose values to the cloud, and each submission requires at least two lines of code. From the state machine's point of view, we can see that every state and transition is traversed at least once, considering all the generated test paths.

Test Input Generation. Here we provide some details on how test input data are managed. Our approach does not support arbitrary input coming from a user or from the environment: each input value must be either fixed or computed during the execution of the test generation tool. With *arbitrary input* we mean an input whose value does not depend on the system, but on something external like a user, the environment, or another system. Since usually systems do accept this kind of input (and DiaMH makes no exception: values coming from sensors are an example of arbitrary input), a solution must be found. We relied on *Equivalence partitioning*, a software testing technique that divides the input data of a program into partitions of values that produce an equivalent behavior (e.g., in DiaMH, below and above the threshold). Note that this strategy can be adopted when the input does not have too many partitions: otherwise would be impractical to add too much transition to represent the input completely.

6   Empirical Study

The goal of the empirical evaluation is to *determine the effectiveness of the proposed approach/prototype*. Thus, the only research question we investigated is the following:

RQ: Are the generated test suites able to detect bugs/faults in the IoT system under test?
To answer our research question, we must be able to quantify the bug-detection capability of generated test suites.

Mutation Testing. A possible solution to validate the effectiveness of a test suite is to apply *mutation testing* [12], a technique that consists in exercising the test suite against slight variations of the original code, simulating the errors a developer could introduce during development and maintenance activities. These variations, named *mutants*, are used to identify the weaknesses in the test artifacts by determining the parts of software that are poorly or never tested. For each mutant, the test scripts are run: if at least one test script fails, the mutant has been detected (killed) and this proves the effectiveness of the test suite in detecting the kind of fault introduced by the mutant. If no test fails, the mutant is not detected (i.e., it survives) and this proves the test suite weakness in detecting the kind of fault introduced by the mutant. Thus, our goal was to build a generator able to build test suites killing the highest number of generated mutants; a metric to evaluate the overall test suite quality is given by the percentage of mutants killed out of the total (i.e., the higher, the better).

6.1   Validation Framework

To the best of our knowledge, no test suite validation framework, based on mutation testing, for IoT systems exists. Thus we decided to implement a supporting tool meant to generate the mutants of DiaMH and, for each mutant, run the generated test suite and collect the results. More in detail, its execution flow is presented in Fig. 5. The starting point are the sources of the IoT system under test. The tool ① extracts code from function nodes of the system flows and saves them to file, then ② generates mutants of the extracted code, and ③ for each mutant M of a node N, generates a copy of the Node-RED flows with M in place of N. The Javascript Mutator subcomponent relies on *Stryker* (https://stryker-mutator.io/), a mutation tool for Javascript that supports various mutation operators for unary, binary, logical and updates instructions, boolean substitutions, conditional removals, arrays declarations, and block statements removals. Then, the Mutant manager and Test runner component ④ communicate with the Node-RED server and for each generated mutant Node-RED flow: (a) starts the Node-RED server executing the mutated flow; (b) runs the generated test suite on the SUT; (c) saves results; and (d) stops the server.

6.2   Results

For DiaMH a total of 185 mutants have been generated, precisely 20 for the sensor flow, 116 for the cloud flow, and 49 for the pump flow (note that we

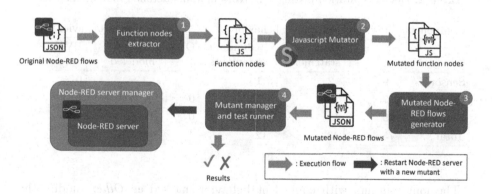

Fig. 5. Execution flow of the validation framework

Table 1. DiaMH mutation testing: preliminary results considering all generated mutants

Component	Mutants	Survived	Killed
Sensor	20	9 (45%)	11 (55%)
Cloud	116	37 (32%)	79 (68%)
Pump	49	29 (59%)	20 (41%)
Total	185	75 (41%)	110 (59%)

did not mutate the mobile app implementation). Table 1 shows the number of killed/survived mutants after the execution of the generated test suite. The first column indicates which *Component* has been mutated, *Mutants* indicates the number of generated mutants for that component, the *Survived* column indicates how many mutants were not detected by the generated test suite, the *Killed* how many were detected. From Table 1, it is evident that the generated test suite has been able to kill/detect the 59% of the mutants overall (110 out of 185). For mutants localized in the Cloud component (116 out of 185), the detection rate is even higher, reaching the 68%.

We have analyzed in detail why some mutants have not been discovered. Table 2 reports the results of our analysis. Of the 75 surviving mutants, 59 (43 + 12 + 4, 78%) are undetectable since they manifest exactly the same expected behavior of the original DiaMH (equivalent mutants), and therefore they cannot be detected with any black-box testing technique [6,8]. Of these equivalent mutants, the greatest majority (43 mutants, 57% of the survivors) affected only log print statements on the Node-RED server console.

Others mutants are equivalent because of redundant statements (12 mutants, 16% of the survivors): some instructions performed in a function node (usually loading a global variable and assigning its value to an attribute of the message) are performed identically in a subsequent node before any use, so modifying this assignment does not affect execution results.

Table 2. DiaMH mutation testing: survivors mutants detailed manual analysis

Component	Survived	Equivalent behavior			Different behavior	
		Print statements	Redundant statements	Other	Not modeled	BVA required
Sensor	9	2	1	4	2	0
Cloud	37	28	6	0	1	2
Pump	29	13	5	0	11	0
Total	75	43	12	4	14	2

The four mutants with equivalent behavior marked as *Other* modify the expressions that generate glucose readings. In the sensor flow, two expressions generate values, respectively under or over the threshold. These mutants change an operator in the expressions, but the modified expression still generates values in the right range.

Other survivors (14 mutants, 19%) change the behavior of DiaMH but on minor aspects that were not documented in the requirements and thus in the model (*Not modeled*). Thus, they differ from the original system in ways that are not checked by the generated test scripts. For example, in the insulin pump, some mutants prevent the pump from replying to pings coming from the smartphone. If the mobile app, when started, does not receive a response to the ping, a red

FAIL message will appear in the pump status info on the mobile app. But our test scripts do not check these status info, since in the designed state machine no assertion method checks them, and so the generated tests cannot detect these mutants (that is why the majority of *Not detected* are in the pump).

Finally, we have two mutants in the 'BVA required' column. This kind of mutants needs a specific input to be detected. BVA (Boundary Value Analysis)is a testing technique that focuses on values around boundaries of decision points. The two mutants in this category changed a '>' in '≥' in two nodes that check how many readings over the threshold are stored in the cloud's memory. To appreciate a difference with the original system, we should have sent input sequences that contain the precise threshold value.

Summary: the generated test scripts were able to detect the 59% of the mutants overall (110 out of 185). However, by analyzing in detail the surviving mutants, we discovered that several of them (59) cannot change the external behavior of the DiaMH system, because equivalent. This increases the real capability of our approach (87%, 110 out of 126). Finally, 14 additional mutants survived since they changed the behavior of DiaMH in minor not documented aspects. Excluding also these mutants – since this a limit more of the input model than of the approach – the mutants detection rate of our approach arrives to 98% (110 out of 112).

7   Conclusions and Future Work

In this paper, we have presented an approach for (semi-automated) model-based test generation, oriented to acceptance testing of IoT systems. The approach is supported by a prototype tool that automatically generates test scripts from an input model representing the behavior of the system. The approach has been empirically evaluated using mutation testing. The test suite generated with our approach was able to detect between 87% and 98% of the considered mutants.

The majority of the mutants modifying the behavior of DiaMH were not detected due to the incompleteness of the model. However, representing the complete behavior of an IoT system on a single state machine is a quite hard task. As a possible solution, we intend to use different state machines to describe the behavior of the system under test: every state machine will focus on only one specific aspect of the system behavior (e.g., main functionalities, reliability, connectivity).

Clearly, our approach does not pay-off for small IoT systems like DiaMH since its application is too complex. However, we believe it becomes cost-effective for complex IoT systems, when tens or hundreds of test scripts must be generated by our tool. To better understand this aspect, we are extending our experimental part with a complex, IoT system inspired by the Smart Santander (http://www.smartsantander.eu/) public parking management system, where each parking lot is monitored by a sensor, that allows users to ask for free parking in their surroundings, through a smartphone. Finally, we are preparing a guide able to teach how to follow the various steps required by our approach and learn how to use our tool.

References

1. End-to-end testing for IoT integrity. Technical report. https://alm.parasoft.com/end-to-end-testing-for-iot-integrity
2. ISO/IEC/IEEE 24765:2010(E) International Standard - Systems and Software Engineering - Vocabulary, pp. 1–418 (2010). https://doi.org/10.1109/IEEESTD.2010.5733835
3. Ammann, P., Offutt, J.: Introduction to Software Testing. Cambridge University Press, Cambridge (2016)
4. Friedman, G., Hartman, A., Nagin, K., Shiran, T.: Projected state machine coverage for software testing. SIGSOFT Softw. Eng. Notes **27**(4), 134–143 (2002). https://doi.org/10.1145/566171.566192
5. Gantait, A.: Test case generation and prioritization from UML models. In: Proceedings of 2nd International Conference on Emerging Applications of Information Technology, EAIT 2011, pp. 345–350. IEEE (2011)
6. Grün, B.J.M., Schuler, D., Zeller, A.: The impact of equivalent mutants. In: Proceedings of 2nd International Conference on Software Testing, Verification, and Validation Workshops, ICSTW 2009, pp. 192–199 (2009). https://doi.org/10.1109/ICSTW.2009.37
7. Harman, M., Mansouri, S.A., Zhang, Y.: Search-based software engineering: trends, techniques and applications. ACM Comput. Surv. **45**(1), 11:1–11:61 (2012). https://doi.org/10.1145/2379776.2379787
8. Jia, Y., Harman, M.: An analysis and survey of the development of mutation testing. IEEE Trans. Softw. Eng. **37**(5), 649–678 (2011). https://doi.org/10.1109/TSE.2010.62
9. King, J.C.: Symbolic execution and program testing. Commun. ACM **19**(7), 385–394 (1976). https://doi.org/10.1145/360248.360252
10. Korel, B.: Automated software test data generation. IEEE Trans. Softw. Eng. **16**(8), 870–879 (1990). https://doi.org/10.1109/32.57624
11. Leotta, M., et al.: An acceptance testing approach for Internet of Things systems. IET Softw. **12**, 430–436 (2018). https://doi.org/10.1049/iet-sen.2017.0344
12. Offutt, A.J., Untch, R.H.: Mutation 2000: uniting the orthogonal. In: Wong, W.E. (ed.) Mutation Testing for the New Century. ADBS, vol. 24, pp. 34–44. Springer, Boston (2001). https://doi.org/10.1007/978-1-4757-5939-6_7
13. Stallbaum, H., Metzger, A., Pohl, K.: An automated technique for risk-based test case generation and prioritization. In: Proceedings of 3rd International Workshop on Automation of Software Test, AST 2008, pp. 67–70 (2008)
14. Tracey, N., Clark, J., Mander, K., McDermid, J.: An automated framework for structural test-data generation. In: Proceedings of the 13th IEEE International Conference on Automated Software Engineering, ASE 1998, p. 285. IEEE (1998)
15. Utting, M., Legeard, B.: Practical Model-Based Testing: A Tools Approach. Morgan Kaufmann Publishers Inc. (2007)

Applied Statistical Model Checking
for a Sensor Behavior Analysis

Salim Chehida$^{(\boxtimes)}$ ⓘ, Abdelhakim Baouya ⓘ, Saddek Bensalem ⓘ,
and Marius Bozga ⓘ

University Grenoble Alpes, CNRS, VERIMAG, 38000 Grenoble, France
{salim.chehida,abdelhakim.baouya,saddek.bensalem,
marius.bozga}@univ-grenoble-alpes.fr

Abstract. The analysis of sensors' behavior becomes one of the essential
challenges due to the growing use of these sensors for making a decision in
IoT systems. The paper proposes an approach for a formal specification
and analysis of such behavior starting from existing sensor traces. A
model that embodies the sensor measurements over the time in the form
of stochastic automata is built, then temporal properties are feed to
Statistical Model Checker to simulate the learned model and to perform
analysis. LTL properties are employed to predict sensors' readings in
time and to check the conformity of sensed data with the sensor traces
in order to detect any abnormal behavior.

Keywords: IoT · Sensor · Stochastic automata · Statistical model
checking · LTL · BIP

1 Introduction

Internet of Things (IoT) has become one of recent technology mostly used in
various domains such as health and environmental monitoring [26], construction
and energy management [22], smart vehicles [2], and buildings [7]. It consists
of a collection of entities that interacts with users to fulfill a common goal.
The sensor is a critical device in the IoT ecosystem that allows to measure the
state information over time and monitor physical components. Data gathered
from different sensors are used to make a decision and promote automation in
IoT systems by providing efficient and intelligent services, whereas, corrupted
data during transmission or malfunction of sensors, due to natural events or
other causes can influence the correct operation of the entire system. Indeed,
the massive increase of these issues with the growing number of deployed sensors
push towards the sensors' behavior analysis by checking their sensed data.

The analysis of sensors' behavior and detecting the erroneous readings have
attracted great attention. Many approaches have been proposed based on several methods such as statistical methods [30], probabilistic methods [14,28],
clustering-based methods [12] and prediction-based methods [25]. Governed by

© Springer Nature Switzerland AG 2020
M. Shepperd et al. (Eds.): QUATIC 2020, CCIS 1266, pp. 399–411, 2020.
https://doi.org/10.1007/978-3-030-58793-2_32

the standard learning requirements, the approaches rely on the metadata and structure of the sensed data.

In this paper, we propose a model-based approach involving formal verification for sensor behavior analysis. Our approach aims to make the analysis process of sensed data rigorous, automatic, scalable, and meaningful. Figure 1 shows the steps of our approach. First, we start by collecting sensor traces and data preprocessing required to build an approximate model of the sensor behavior, then we apply formal verification techniques to analyze this model and then check if new measurements are compliant with the learned model.

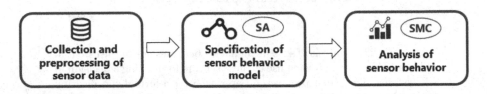

Fig. 1. Generic approach for sensor behavior analysis

Model checkers allow checking the conformity of a system model expressed in formal notation to a set of properties expressed in a logical language. In this study, we apply a type of model checkers called Statistical Model Checkers (SMC) to verify whether a sensor model expressed in Stochastic Automata (SA) satisfies a given logical property up to some probability, based on model simulations. We use quantitative properties expressed by Linear-time Temporal Logic (LTL) to predict the sensor readings in time and qualitative LTL properties to check the quality of sensed data and their compliance with the provided traces. Several SMC tools have been proposed such as PRISM-SMC [15], UPPAAL-SMC [8]. The BIP language [4] and $\mathcal{S}$BIP [17] are used in this paper for behavior modeling and SMC analysis. We apply our approach to the industrial case study of the Cecebre dam in Spain, which is equipped with wireless sensors that measure the water contributions to the dam.

This paper is organized as follows: we build the sensor behavior model in Sect. 2. The analysis results of the sensor model will be presented in Sect. 3. Finally, we present related works in Sect. 4 and draw our conclusions in Sect. 5.

2 Sensor Behavior Model

In this work, we use BIP[1] (Behavior, Interaction, Priority), a component-based language for rigorous design of systems. In BIP, components are finite-state automata having transitions labeled with ports and states that denote control locations (see Fig. 4). We first start by data preprocessing and extraction of some statistical information needed to build the behavior models of sensors.

---

[1] https://www-verimag.imag.fr/TOOLS/DCS/bip/doc/latest/html/index.html.

2.1 Data Preprocessing

In our case study, we consider three sensors deployed in the dam of *Cecebre* in the city of *la Coruna* in Spain. These sensors are used to measure the Water Height (WH), the Rain Precipitation (RP), and the Water output Flow (WF). As shown in Fig. 2, the data collected from sensors are used to control the opening of the spillgate in order to ensure that the water does not reach a maximum level in the dam. The anomalous behavior of these sensors can influence the correct operation of the dam system. Our objective is to build formal models that specify the normal behavior of the sensors. These models will be used to control the sensors' readings and to detect any failure or anomaly.

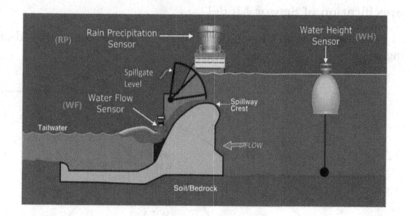

Fig. 2. Dam infrastructure

A trace of time series data recorded by each sensor per day since 1989 to 2016 has been collected. We reorganized the original trace by creating a separate CSV file per sensor. The new file contains the sensor readings per day for 28 years. As shown in Fig. 3, the data preprocessing is done in three steps:

1. Data cleaning: we use a filter to remove faulty sensors data. The filter deletes NaN data and data that not make sense, such as negative and inconsistent data.
2. Data discretization: we convert continuous (or quantitative) data into discrete (or qualitative) ones. The paper [27] presents the several methods proposed for time series data discretization. In this study, we use the EWD (Equal Width Discretization) method [9] because of its simplicity. It consists of mapping numerical values into predefined fixed intervals that have an equal-width. Each bin or level is associated with a distinct discrete value. In this work, we relied on data visualization using histograms to determine the number of levels. For the water height sensor, we use five levels for data discretization.
3. Generation of distribution: Once data was discretized, we extract some statistical information. We generate a sensor distribution file by counting the occurrence of each level of water height (WH_L) each day.

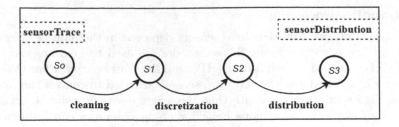

Fig. 3. Preprocessing of sensors data

2.2   Specification of Sensor Model

Figure 4 presents a behavior model for the water height sensor expressed in the BIP language.

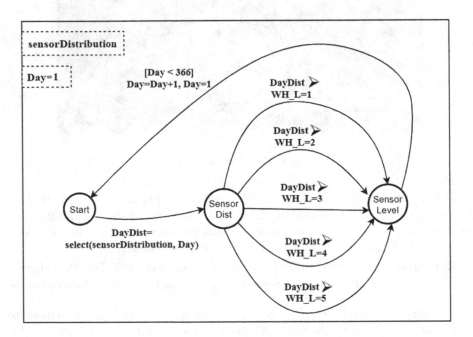

Fig. 4. Behavior model of water height sensor

BIP supports several formal modeling formalisms based on Discrete and Continuous Time Markov Chains (DTMC and CTMC) and Generalized Semi-Markov Process (GSMP). In this work, we use Stochastic Automata (SA) to express a behavior model of the sensors. The stochastic semantics is defined by variables based on the probability distributions. In the model of Fig. 4, we select the day distribution based on **sensorDistribution** file generated in the previous section. According to this distribution, the water high level (1, 2, 3, 4 or 5) is defined.

The models that specify the behaviors of the other sensors (RP and WF) are defined using the same pattern as WH sensor model. Only the number of levels can change depending on the sensor data. Using these models, we can simulate and analyze the behavior of the different sensors for any period of the year.

3   Analysis of Sensor Behavior

SBIP framework[2] has a graphical user-interface permitting to edit, compile and simulate models, and automates the different statistical analysis. As shown in Fig. 5, the input of the tool is a system model S expressed in BIP language like that of Fig. 4 and a property ϕ expressed in Linear-time Temporal Logic (LTL)[23] and/or Metric Temporal Logic (MTL) [3]. Using SBIP, we can perform two types of analysis:

1. Quantitative: we estimate the probability that the system S satisfies a given property ϕ.
2. Qualitative: we test whether the probability of a given property ϕ being satisfied by the system S is greater or equal to a certain threshold θ.

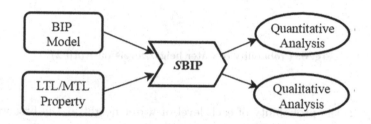

Fig. 5. SBIP statistical model checker

To decide whether S satisfies ϕ (written S $\models \phi$), SBIP refers to simulation based techniques: Probability Estimation (PE) [13] for quantitative properties and Hypothesis Testing (HT) [29] for qualitative properties.

3.1   Quantitative Analysis

In this work, we use a stochastic bounded variant of LTL to express properties. In LTL, path formulas are defined using four bounded temporal operators namely, Next ($N\psi_1$), Until ($\psi_1 \cup^k \psi_2$), Eventually ($F^k\psi_1$), and Always ($G^k\psi_1$), where k is an integer value that specifies the length of the considered system execution

---

[2] http://www-verimag.imag.fr/BIP-SMC-A-Statistical-Model-Checking.html?lang=en.

trace and ψ_1, ψ_2 are called state formulas, which is a Boolean predicate evaluated on the system states.

SBIP allows to check parametric property $\phi(\mathbf{x})$, where $\mathbf{x}$ is a parameter ranging over a finite instantiation domain. It also provides a summary of analysis results and generates specific curves and/or plots of results. We present four examples of quantitative properties:

Property 1: the probability of water height levels on April 27.
In LTL: $P_{=?}[F^{1000}\ (WH\_L = L\ \&\&\ Day = 117)];\quad L = 1:5:1;$

The results are given in Fig. 6. We find that level 5 is the most likely and levels 4 and 3 are less likely. However, levels 1 and 2 are never observed on this day. These predictions concerning water height sensor and estimations from other sensors can help the managers of dam infrastructure to adjust the spillgate level.

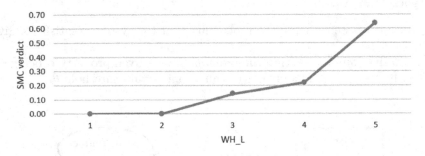

Fig. 6. Probability of water height levels on April 27

Property 2: the probability of each level of water height at the first weeks of January and May.
In LTL:

$$\begin{cases} P_{=?}[F^{1000}\ (WH\_L = L\ \&\&\ Day = T)];\quad T = 1:7:1; T = 121:127:1; \\ L = \{1,2,3,4,5\} \end{cases}$$

Figure 7 shows the SMC verdict of property 2. We see that level 5 is rarely observed in the first week of January, however, this level is most likely in the first week of May. The opposite for levels 1 and 2, which are more possible in the first week of January and rare in the first week of May. With LTL properties, we can predict the evolution of water height level at any period of the year.

Property 3: the probability that the water height level stays on the same level the last week of May.

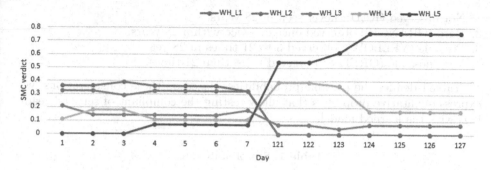

Fig. 7. Probability of water height levels at first weeks of January and May

In LTL:

$$\begin{cases} P_{=?}[G^{1000} \ (WH\_L = L \ \&\& \ Day = 145) \cup^{1000} \ (WH\_L = L \ \&\& \ Day = T)]; \\ T = 146:151:1; \quad L = \{1,2,3,4,5\} \end{cases}$$

As shown in Fig. 8, there is a high possibility that the water height level will remain at levels 4 or 5 in the last week of May.

Property 4: the probability that the water height changes from first level on January 16th to other levels on the next day.
In LTL:

$$\begin{cases} P_{=?}[\ (WH\_L = 1 \ \&\& \ Day = 16) \cup^{1000} \ (WH\_L = L \ \&\& \ Day = 17) \ ]; \\ L = \{2,3,4,5\} \end{cases}$$

Figure 9 shows that change to levels 2 and 3 is most likely while there is little chance of change to levels 4 and 5.

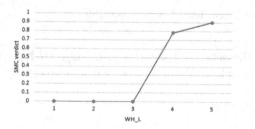
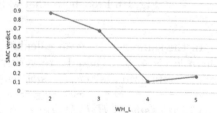

Fig. 8. Results of property 3   **Fig. 9.** Results of property 4

3.2 Qualitative Analysis

For qualitative analysis of sensor behavior, we rate sensors' readings based on their probabilities as following:

1. Not observed (RED): never seen in 28 years.
2. Rare (ORANGE): observed once or twice within 28 years.
3. Possible (YELLOW): observed 3 to 21 times in 28 years.
4. Very possible (GREEN): observed more than 21 times.

Table 1 defines the possible probabilities. Based on these considerations, we express qualitative properties that allow testing the compliant of sensors' readings with the learned model.

Table 1. Sensor state rate

State	Not observed	Rare	Possible	Very Possible
Probability	0	]0, 0.09]	]0.09, 0.75]	]0.75, 1]

Property 5: Check whether the probability that water height reaches level 5 is higher than 0.75.

In LTL: $P_{>0.75}[F^{1000} (WH\_L = 5 \text{ \&\& } Day = T)];$ $T = 1 : 365 : 1;$

Figure 10 shows the results provided by SBIP. This property allows calculating the set $DL5_{vp} = \{124, .., 202\}$ of days where the level 5 of water height is very possible.

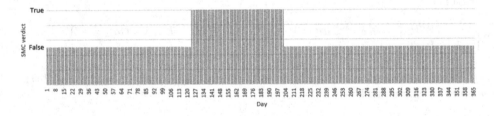

Fig. 10. Probability that water height level 5 is very possible

In the same way, we can calculate the sets $DL4_{vp}$, $DL3_{vp}$, $DL2_{vp}$, $DL1_{vp}$ where levels 4, 3, 2, and 1 are very possible. Based on these calculations, we define the function $isVeryPossibe$ as:

$isVeryPossibe(WH\_L, Day) \leftarrow$
$(WH\_L = 5 \text{ \&\& } Day \in DL5_{vp} \;||\; WH\_L = 4 \text{ \&\& } Day \in DL4_{vp}||$
$WH\_L = 3 \text{ \&\& } Day \in DL3_{vp} \;||\; WH\_L = 2 \text{ \&\& } Day \in DL2_{vp} \;||$
$WH\_L = 1 \text{ \&\& } Day \in DL1_{vp})$

We have also defined the functions $isPossible$, $isRare$, and $isNotObserved$ which allow respectively to check if the data collected by the sensors are possible, rarely observed, or never observed.

The defined functions are used to build the model of Fig. 11 that allows evaluating the conformity of any water height sensor reading regarding the provided trace. The model can help to distinguish between anomalous and correct sensor readings.

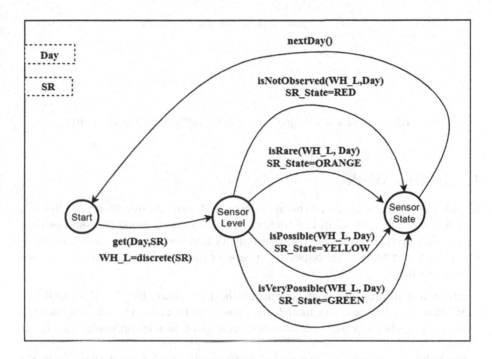

Fig. 11. Sensor state model

The sensor state model can be used to check the quality of sensed data from the existing trace. In Fig. 12, we discover very possible readings (Green points), possible readings (Yellow points), and rare readings (Orange points) in the months April and May of 2016. As shown in the Figure, some rare readings are detected at the beginning of April and May.

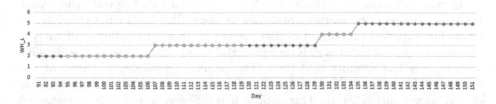

Fig. 12. Score of water height sensor data for April and May of 2016 (Color figure online)

The sensor state model also allows for checking new observations. Figure 13 presents the test results for April and May of 2017. We see that no unusual observation is found and that the observations of Avril are possible and the observations of May are highly possible.

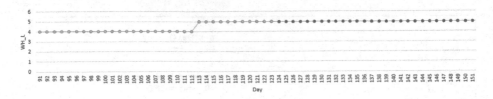

Fig. 13. Score of water height sensor data for April and May of 2017

4   Related Work

Time series analysis is one of the active areas of research due to its application in different fields, such as in the context of IoT-based systems. For sensors time series data, predicting the next measurements and detecting erroneous readings are the relevant tasks. The paper [11] presents the several approaches proposed for this purpose:

- Statistical approaches such as the method proposed by [30] that builds a window-based forecasting model from past observations, then it classifies the sensors' readings as anomalous based on a given prediction confidence interval.
- Probabilistic approaches use probabilistic models such as Bayesian Networks (BNs) [14] to measure the probability of sensors' readings. However, these approaches do not scale well.
- Proximity-based or clustering-based approaches such as [6,12] use distances between the sensed data to detect the erroneous readings. For high dimensional data, these approaches do not work well.
- Prediction-based approaches such as [16,25] use machine learning methods to predict the sensors' readings based on a model trained from past observations. However, training is time-intensive.

In our approach, we generate stochastic automata that specify the sensor behavior from past observations, and then we apply SMC to simulate the learned model and express LTL properties that predict the sensors' readings and analyze the sensor behavior in time. SMC is a powerful technique that handles scalability and requires less memory and time. The paper [1] provides a survey of the existing SMC tools. *S*BIP tool used in this work was applied for the analysis of various systems [5,20,21]. Our approach is different from all the approaches presented above. It allows to build a behavioral automata-based model from data and analyze this model using formal verification techniques. Among the works in this direction:

- The authors in [24] use Extended Finite Automata and residuals techniques to detect deviations of the behavior of the inhabitant in a smart home from a log of binary sensor events.
- The paper [18] models logs from SCADA systems using timed automata and applies the UPPAAL model checker to express a set of logic properties for detecting attacks targeting these systems.
- [19] uses Markov Decision Process for modeling the behavior of elastic cloud applications based on past log and then introduces probabilistic model checking to perform cloud elasticity decision using PCTL properties.
- [10] specifies a stochastic model in Deterministic-Time Markov Chain from the architecture description of the managed system considering different metrics related to cloud-infrastructure execution traces. Then, the PRISM model checker is used to optimize the self-adaptation decisions.

5 Conclusion

We presented an approach for a formal analysis of sensors' behavior. A formal model expressed as stochastic automata has been derived from sensor time series data then quantitative LTL properties expressed on this model are used to predict sensor readings. Also, qualitative LTL properties are used for defining a second automata-based model that allows checking if the new measurements are compliant with past observations. We have applied our approach to analyzing the behavior of three sensors from a dam infrastructure at different times. Our approach provides several advantages, including:

- We use BIP formalisms that allow the rigorous specification and analysis of sensor behavior.
- We use a component-based approach supported by BIP that facilitates portraying sensors behavior with reusability, and maintainability features.
- We developed a prototype that automatically generates sensor behavior and sensor state models from any existing traces.
- We use statistical model checkers that consume less memory and can check models with large state spaces.

In the future, we are planning to enhance the proposed approach by analyzing the consistency between the behaviors of a set of sensors and expressing inter-sensors properties.

Acknowledgments. The research leading to these results has been supported by the European Union through the BRAIN-IoT project H2020-EU.2.1.1. Grant agreement ID: 780089. The authors would like to thank EMALCSA Company for the data collected from the dam infrastructure.

References

1. Agha, G., Palmskog, K.: A survey of statistical model checking. ACM Trans. Modeling Comput. Simul. **28**(1), 1–39 (2018). https://doi.org/10.1145/3158668
2. Al-Turjman, F., Malekloo, A.: Smart parking in IoT-enabled cities: a survey. Sustain. Cities Soc. **49**, 101608 (2019)
3. Alur, R., Henzinger, T.: Real-time logics: complexity and expressiveness. Inf. Comput. **104**(1), 35–77 (1993). https://doi.org/10.1006/inco.1993.1025
4. Basu, A., et al.: Rigorous component-based system design using the BIP framework. IEEE Softw. **28**(3), 41–48 (2011)
5. Beaulaton, D., Said, N.B., Cristescu, I., Sadou, S.: Security analysis of IoT systems using attack trees. In: Albanese, M., Horne, R., Probst, C.W. (eds.) GraMSec 2019. LNCS, vol. 11720, pp. 68–94. Springer, Cham (2019). https://doi.org/10.1007/978-3-030-36537-0_5
6. Breunig, M.M., Kriegel, H.P., Ng, R.T., Sander, J.: LOF: identifying density-based local outliers. ACM SIGMOD Rec. **29**(2), 93–104 (2000). https://doi.org/10.1145/335191.335388
7. Daissaoui, A., Boulmakoul, A., Karim, L., Lbath, A.: IoT and big data analytics for smart buildings: a survey. Procedia Comput. Sci. **170**, 161–168 (2020). https://doi.org/10.1016/j.procs.2020.03.021
8. David, A., Larsen, K.G., Legay, A., Mikučionis, M., Poulsen, D.B.: Uppaal SMC tutorial. Int. J. Softw. Tools Technol. Transf. **17**(4), 397–415 (2015)
9. Dougherty, J., Kohavi, R., Sahami, M.: Supervised and unsupervised discretization of continuous features. In: Prieditis, A., Russell, S. (eds.) Machine Learning Proceedings 1995, pp. 194–202. Morgan Kaufmann, San Francisco (1995). https://doi.org/10.1016/B978-1-55860-377-6.50032-3
10. Franco, J.M., Correia, F., Barbosa, R., Zenha-Rela, M., Schmerl, B., Garlan, D.: Improving self-adaptation planning through software architecture-based stochastic modeling. J. Syst. Softw. **115**, 42–60 (2016). https://doi.org/10.1016/j.jss.2016.01.026
11. Giannoni, F., Mancini, M., Marinelli, F.: Anomaly Detection Models for IoT Time Series Data. ArXiv abs/1812.00890 (2018)
12. He, Z., Xu, X., Deng, S.: Discovering cluster-based local outliers. Pattern Recogn. Lett. **24**(9–10), 1641–1650 (2003). https://doi.org/10.1016/S0167-8655(03)00003-5
13. Hérault, T., Lassaigne, R., Magniette, F., Peyronnet, S.: Approximate probabilistic model checking. In: Steffen, B., Levi, G. (eds.) VMCAI 2004. LNCS, vol. 2937, pp. 73–84. Springer, Heidelberg (2004). https://doi.org/10.1007/978-3-540-24622-0_8
14. Hill, D.J., Minsker, B.S., Amir, E.: Real-time Bayesian anomaly detection in streaming environmental data: REAL-TIME BAYESIAN ANOMALY DETECTION. Water Resources Res. **45**(4) (2009). https://doi.org/10.1029/2008WR006956
15. Kwiatkowska, M., Norman, G., Parker, D.: Prism 4.0: verification of probabilistic real-time systems. In: Gopalakrishnan, G., Qadeer, S. (eds.) Computer Aided Verification, pp. 585–591. Springer, Heidelberg (2011). https://doi.org/10.1007/978-3-642-22110-1_47
16. Malhotra, P., Vig, L., Shroff, G., Agarwal, P.: Long short term memory networks for anomaly detection in time series. In: ESANN (2015)

17. Mediouni, B.L., Nouri, A., Bozga, M., Dellabani, M., Legay, A., Bensalem, S.: $\mathcal{S}$BIP 2.0: statistical model checking stochastic real-time systems. In: Lahiri, S.K., Wang, C. (eds.) ATVA 2018. LNCS, vol. 11138, pp. 536–542. Springer, Cham (2018). https://doi.org/10.1007/978-3-030-01090-4_33
18. Mercaldo, F., Martinelli, F., Santone, A.: Real-Time SCADA attack detection by means of formal methods. In: 2019 IEEE 28th International Conference on Enabling Technologies: Infrastructure for Collaborative Enterprises (WETICE), pp. 231–236. IEEE, Napoli, Italy, June 2019. https://doi.org/10.1109/WETICE.2019.00057
19. Naskos, A., Gounaris, A., Mouratidis, H., Katsaros, P.: Online analysis of security risks in elastic cloud applications. IEEE Cloud Comput. **3**(5), 26–33 (2016). https://doi.org/10.1109/MCC.2016.108
20. Nouri, A., Bensalem, S., Bozga, M., Delahaye, B., Jegourel, C., Legay, A.: Statistical model checking QoS properties of systems with SBIP. Int. J. Softw. Tools Technol. Transf. **17**(2), 171–185 (2014). https://doi.org/10.1007/s10009-014-0313-6
21. Nouri, A., Mediouni, B.L., Bozga, M., Combaz, J., Bensalem, S., Legay, A.: Performance evaluation of stochastic real-time systems with the SBIP framework. Int. J. Critical Comput.-Based Syst. **8**(3/4), 340 (2018)
22. Park, C., Kim, Y., Jeong, M.: Influencing factors on risk perception of IoT-based home energy management services. Telematics Inform. **35**(8), 2355–2365 (2018)
23. Pnueli, A.: The temporal logic of programs. In: 18th Annual Symposium on Foundations of Computer Science, pp. 46–57. IEEE Computer Society, USA, October 1977. https://doi.org/10.1109/SFCS.1977.32
24. Saives, J., Pianon, C., Faraut, G.: Activity discovery and detection of behavioral deviations of an inhabitant from binary sensors. IEEE Trans. Autom. Sci. Eng. **12**(4), 1211–1224 (2015). https://doi.org/10.1109/TASE.2015.2471842
25. Shahid, N., Naqvi, I.H., Qaisar, S.B.: One-class support vector machines: analysis of outlier detection for wireless sensor networks in harsh environments. Artif. Intell. Rev. **43**(4), 515–563 (2013). https://doi.org/10.1007/s10462-013-9395-x
26. Tao, Z.: Advanced Wavelet Sampling algorithm for IoT based environmental monitoring and management. Comput. Commun. **150**, 547–555 (2020). https://doi.org/10.1016/j.comcom.2019.12.006
27. Yang, Y., Webb, G.I., Wu, X.: Discretization methods. In: Maimon, O., Rokach, L. (eds.) Data Mining and Knowledge Discovery Handbook, pp. 101–116. Springer, Boston (2009). https://doi.org/10.1007/978-0-387-09823-4_6
28. Xie, Y., Shun-Zheng, Y.: A large-scale hidden semi-Markov model for anomaly detection on user browsing behaviors. IEEE/ACM Trans. Network. **17**(1), 54–65 (2009). https://doi.org/10.1109/TNET.2008.923716
29. Younes, H.L.S., Simmons, R.G.: Probabilistic verification of discrete event systems using acceptance sampling. In: Brinksma, E., Larsen, K.G. (eds.) CAV 2002. LNCS, vol. 2404, pp. 223–235. Springer, Heidelberg (2002). https://doi.org/10.1007/3-540-45657-0_17
30. Yu, Y., Zhu, Y., Li, S., Wan, D.: Time series outlier detection based on sliding window prediction. Math. Probl. Eng. **2014**, 1–14 (2014). https://doi.org/10.1155/2014/879736

Preliminary Experiences
in Requirements-Based Security Testing

João Miranda[1] , Ana C. R. Paiva[1,2]([⊠]) , and Alberto Rodrigues da Silva[3,4]

[1] Faculty of Engineering, University of Porto, Porto, Portugal
{up201802166,apaiva}@fe.up.pt
[2] INESC TEC, Porto, Portugal
[3] INESC-ID, Lisbon, Portugal
[4] Instituto Superior Técnico, Universidade de Lisboa, Lisbon, Portugal
alberto.silva@tecnico.ulisboa.pt

Abstract. Software requirements engineers and testers generally define technical documents in natural languages, but this practice can lead to inconsistencies between the documentation and the consequent system implementation. Previous research has shown that writing requirements and tests in a structured way, with controlled natural languages like RSL, can help mitigate these problems. This study goes further, discussing new experiments carried out to validate that RSL (with its complementary tools, called "ITLingo Studio") can be applied in different systems and technologies, namely the possibility of applying the approach to integrate test automation capabilities in security testing. The preliminary conclusion indicates that, by combining tools such as ITLingo Studio and the Robot Framework, it is possible to integrate requirements and test specifications with test automation, and that would bring benefits in the testing process' productivity.

Keywords: Tests automation · Security testing · Test case generation · Requirements engineering · RSL

1 Introduction

The vast majority of requirement specifications are written in natural languages. However, the use of natural language may lead to problems, such as ambiguity, incompleteness, inconsistency, and incorrectness [3] in the documentation, which, in turn, can lead to implementation errors. In addition, to define acceptance tests, testers rely on reading these documents. If the documents are not clear and complete, the test cases will also experience the same problems and the final system will be different from what is intended.

One of the approaches to mitigate these issues is by using controlled natural languages, like the ITLingo RSL (Requirements Specification Language) [14,16], which provides a structured way of writing requirements and test cases [16]. RSL provides the capability to specify use cases, use case tests, and many other constructs in a common language.

M. Shepperd et al. (Eds.): QUATIC 2020, CCIS 1266, pp. 412–425, 2020.
https://doi.org/10.1007/978-3-030-58793-2_33

Recently, Maciel et al. discussed an approach [6,10] that aims to integrate and combine requirements and test cases specification with test automation tools, to improve the process of defining and executing acceptance tests. In particular, they discussed how to integrate ITLingo Studio (i.e., a Eclipse-based IDE that supports RSL and other languages) with the Robot Framework [14]. However, the software application and the examples they used to illustrate the approach were very simple. Thus, the goal of this work is to assess the applicability of the approach in different settings. First, we aim to assess the applicability on web applications developed using other technologies, namely based on the SPA (i.e., single page application) architecture. Second, we aim to preliminary check if it is possible to extend the approach to perform security testing.

This paper is structured in 5 sections. Section 2 presents the proposed testing process. Section 3 describes the experiments performed and discusses the results achieved. Section 4 refers and discusses the related work. Finally, Sect. 5 presents final conclusion and open issues.

2   Proposed Testing Process

The proposed testing process intends to combine (1) both requirement and test specifications, defined in a tool like ITLingo Studio, with (2) test automation, supported by a tool like Robot Framework. This section briefly introduces the tools considered in this research, and overviews the proposed process.

2.1   Suported Tools: ITLingo Studio and Robot Framework

ITLingo-Studio is an Eclipse-based tool (i.e. a desktop IDE) for authoring IT technical documentation, such as requirements and tests (with the RSL language), project management plans (with the PSL language), or platform-independent application specifications (with the ASL). In the scope of this paper, we only consider the ITLingo RSL (or just RSL for brevity). RSL is a controlled natural language that helps the production of requirements and tests specifications in a systematic, rigorous and consistent way [3,14,16,17]. RSL includes a rich set of constructs like use cases, goals, user stories, but also use case tests, data entities, actors, stakeholders, and many others (further details in [10,15]. The ITLingo languages have been implemented with the Xtext framework (https://eclipse.org/Xtext/), so its specifications are rigorous and can be automatically validated and transformed into other representations and formats. Figure 1 depicts the ITLingo Studio with a test case specified in both RSL and Robot Framework languages.

Robot Framework (RF for short) is a generic open source automation framework that can be used for test automation and robotic process automation [11]. RF has an open and extensible architecture and can be integrated with other tools to create flexible automation solutions. Robot Framework provides a textual language with a keyword-based easy syntax, both machine and human-readable. Its capabilities can be extended by libraries implemented with Python or Java.

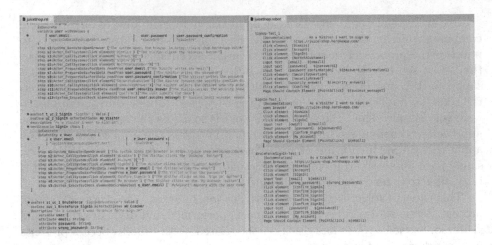

Fig. 1. RSL specification and test script in Robot.

In the scope of our research, the test cases defined in RSL [15] are generated to RF test scripts, and then these test scripts are executed by the RF's engine [12]. A key advantage of RF is its high modularity and extensibility, as it is platform-agnostic and thanks to its driver plugin architecture, the core framework does not require any previous knowledge of the system under test [13].

2.2 The Process

Figure 2 shows the approach originally proposed in [6], which considers an "end-to-end integration of requirements, test cases, and test scripts", namely by combining tools like the ITLingo Studio (with RSL specifications) and Robot Framework (with keyword-based test scripts).

This approach consists in a sequence of tasks, that varies from the specification of requirements until the execution of tests, as follows.

Requirements Specification. In the task "(1) Specify Requirements (manual)" the requirements are elicited and documented by requirement engineers using the RSL language. This may also involve other stakeholders (like testers or domain experts) for validation purposes. This task favors with a systematic specification of requirements and can be done manually with the ITLingo Studio (that is an Eclipse IDE for authoring RSL specs) or an Excel template.

Test Cases Specification and Validation. Task "(2) Specify Test Cases (semi-auto)" uses the requirements defined in the previous step to generate test cases, namely considering the mappings between use case and use case test, as defined in [16]. Task "(3) Refine Test Cases (manual)" allows the tests engineers to refine and complete the (previously generated) test cases with all the relevant test scenarios, steps, etc. Also, the tests generated from the previous task may be subject to manual validation and this could result in new test cases which are then added to the final specification. This test case validation is also a human-intensive and time-consuming task.

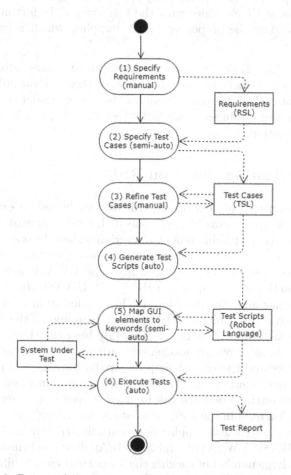

Fig. 2. Proposed testing approach, as originally defined in [6].

Test Scripts Generation. Once the specification and validation of test cases are completed, the task "(4) Generate Test Scripts (auto)" consists in the generation of test scripts, which can be then executed by a test automation tool, like the Robot Framework. This generation is based on the mappings established between the RSL specification and the concrete syntax of the Robot Framework [6].

Map the UI Elements. The user interface (UI) of a web application involves several UI elements [6]. To properly support the test automation based on the acceptance tests, these generic UI elements have to be mapped to concrete UI variables defined in the test scripts so as to act over related UI elements during test case execution. The establishment of this map is the purpose of task

"(5) Map GUI elements to keywords (semi-auto)". However, using a web scrapper browser extension, as the Selenium WebDriver (https://www.selenium.dev/projects/), it is possible to automatically capture and generate scripts that successfully map these UI elements with the test scripts. Unfortunately, most of these cases depend on the proper keywords mapping, which is hard to be fully automated.

Execute Test Scripts. Task "(6) Execute tests (auto)" takes into consideration the test scripts (previously generated, and with their UI variables mapped to concrete UI elements) and execute them on the system under test (SUT). This test automation task produces an artifact "Test Report", which includes the log details of its execution.

3   Security Testing Based on RSL

This section describes two sets of experiments conducted to explore different objectives. The first one aims to apply the RSL testing approach, as it is, but with a web application with different characteristics than the one considered originally in [6]. There are differences in technologies used to develop the Automation Practice website (used in the previous study) and OWASP Juice Shop. While Automation Practice is developed in PHP [6,13], OWASP Juice Shop is developed using Angular and Angular-Material library for styling [8]. The usage of Angular, in many cases, prevented the correct mapping of the UI elements to their respective keywords. This happens mainly because: there are unspecified element identifiers, elements are too generic, are not standard, or have overlays. These issues prevented the correct map of inputs, buttons and dropdown buttons, which are not found at all. The second set of experiments aims to evaluate if the RSL-based testing approach can be used as well to test security aspects.

The application used in these experiments is the Juice Shop web application, which is an open-source web application, entirely written in JavaScript, and listed in the OWASP VWA (Vulnerable Web Applications) directory [8]. Juice Shop includes a large number of hacking challenges and vulnerabilities that a user is supposed to exploit. As suggested in Fig. 3, Juice Shop mimics an e-commerce website that sells juices and vegetables, and so, it is a good application example for acceptance and security testing.

3.1   First Experiments

The first set of experiments aims to check the applicability of the RSL testing approach. The first step of these experiments was to define the requirements specification. For that we defined the data entities (e.g. user, product, and others), actors (e.g., visitor and cracker), use cases (e.g., sign-up, sign-in), and respective test cases.

The second step was to define test cases to check the behavior of the application related to the authentication functionality, namely: (1) Sign up; (2) Sign

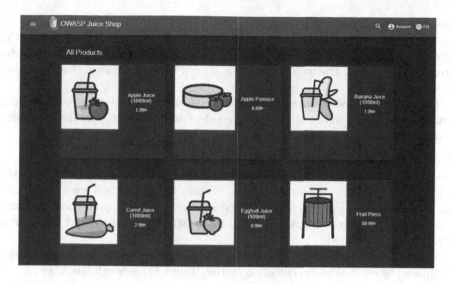

Fig. 3. Screenshot of the juice shop application.

in (Spec. 1.1); and (3) Sign in attempt by simulating a brute force attack (Spec. 1.3).

The test cases consist of a user trying to sign-up and then to sign-in. Afterwards, the goal is a brute force attempt by deliberately sending wrong passwords and, in the last time, submitting the correct password.

After the specification of these test cases, the RSL engine generates automatically the respective test scripts defined as Robot Framework (".robot") files.

Then, to support establishing the mapping between keywords and UI elements of the GUI, we used two tools: the one developed in previous work [6] and web scraper techniques to select elements to be used by the Robot Framework.

Web scraping can be achieved by mapping specific elements of a web page through their XML path (X-Path) or CSS selectors, generally speaking, X-Path is more trustworthy as it is possible to achieve certain elements selection more precisely [5,19]. The X-Path of a given element can be constructed by its XML absolute path or through additional selectors, that allow to "take shortcuts" on a document's structure in order to reach some element [5,19].

The solution we adopted to overcome this technical problem was to resort to X-Path mapping instead of CSS mapping. However, a X-Path based approach has also some issues, namely: most of the web-scrapping tools that support X-Path are not free; the free web-scrapping extension that supported X-Path was not accurate leading to unnecessary rework, the free web-scrapping extension that was used by default tries to find the X-Path using special selectors which may include CSS, classes, and relative selectors, thus we opted to use always the absolute X-Paths.

Sign-Up Test Case

The idea of the "Sign-Up" is to try to test an user registration by informing the correct parameters and check if the user is successfully created. This test can be extended to verify if the web application allows the same user to be registered twice, etc.

The test results were successful although some mapping issues with custom elements of angular material such as the select or the input were detected and fixed by the usage of X-Path.

Sign-In Test Case

The idea of the "Sign-In" test is to check if a previously registered user can sign in according to the documentation by providing the e-mail and their respective password. The result of this test is a success even though it presented the same issues as the previous test. A successful login attempt is made and the user is correctly authenticated.

Spec. 1.1 shows the Sign-In test case specified in the RSL language. Spec. 1.2 shows the equivalent specification in the Robot Framework language.

```
UseCaseTest t_uc_2_SignIn "Sign-In test case"  : Valid [
    useCase  uc_2_SignIn  actorInitiates  aU_Visitor
    description "As a Visitor I want to sign in"
    testScenario SignIn :Main [
        isConcrete
        dataEntity e_User   withValues (
        | e_User.email      | e_User.password   +|
        | "user001@awdrt.net" | "q1w2e3r4"       +|
        )
        step s1:System_Execute:OpenBrowser ["The system opens the browser in
            https://juice-shop.herokuapp.com/#/"]
        step s2:Actor_CallSystem:
            Click element('dismiss')
            ["The Visitor clicks the 'Dismiss' button"]
        step s3:Actor_CallSystem:
            Click element('Account')[""]
        step s4:Actor_CallSystem:
            Click element('SignIn')
            ["The Visitor clicks on the 'SignIn' button"]
        step s5:Actor_PrepareData:
            PostData readFrom e_User.email
            ["The Visitor writes the email"]
        step s6:Actor_PrepareData:
            PostData readFrom e_User.password
            ["The Visitor writes the password"]
        step s7:Actor_CallSystem:
            Click element('Confirm_SignIn')
            ["The Visitor clicks on the 'Sign In' button"]
        step s8:Actor_CallSystem:
            Click element('My_Account')
            ["The Visitor clicks on the 'My Account' button"]
        step s9:System_Execute:
            Check elementOnScreen(text e_User.firstName)
            ["'MyAccount' appears with the user name"]
    ]
]
```

Spec. 1.1. User Sign In test case (RSL spec).

```
*** Settings ***
Documentation                This is a basic test
Library                      Selenium2Library
*** Variables ***

${email1}    wypizsbdbmiazqybiz@awdrt.net
${password1}    q1w2e3r4

*** Test Cases ***

SignIn-Test_1
    [Documentation] As a Visitor I want to sign in
    open browser   https://juice-shop.herokuapp.com/
    Click element
```

```
//button[contains(@class,'mat-focus-indicator mat-raised-button')]
/following-sibling::button[1]
Click element
(//mat-toolbar-row[@class='mat-toolbar-row']//button)[3]
Click element
navbarLoginButton
input text
(//input[contains(@class,'mat-input-element mat-form-field-autofill-control')])[2]
${email1}
Input password
(//input[contains(@class,'mat-input-element mat-form-field-autofill-control')])[3]
${password1}
Click element
(//div[@id='login-form']//button)[2]
Click element
(//button[contains(@class,'mat-focus-indicator mat-menu-trigger')])[1]
Page Should Contain Element
(//simple-snack-bar[@class='mat-simple-snackbar ng-star-inserted']//span)[1]
${email1}
```

Spec. 1.2. User Sign In test (Robot Framework spec).

Multiple Invalid Login Attempts Test Case

This test aims to try and check, by repetition, if there is any kind of protection against multiple incorrect login attempts such as IP blocking, account locking, etc. This attempt tries emulate the incorrect submission of a username/password combination before attempting to login with the correct password to check if the user/account was blocked or not. The repeated submission of requests to a determined application could be also identified as a potential Denial of Service attack and an application that has protection against such attacks could also block a malicious user attempt after a number of login attempts.

The main point of this test is to check if after 3 to 5 attempts of requests with invalid passwords the system will present any kind of lock or captcha to block malicious attempts to sign-in. This test results showed that the web application has no countermeasures against brute force attacks as after 5 attempts it was possible to keep retrying until the password was correct.

```
UseCaseTest st_uc_1_BruteForce "SignInBruteForce": Valid [
  useCase suc_1_BruteForce_SignIn actorInitiates aU_Cracker
  description "As a Cracker I want to brute force sign in"
      variable user [
      attribute email: String
      attribute password: String
      attribute wrong_password: String   ]
  testScenario BruteForceSignIn : Main [
    isConcrete
    variable user   withValues (
      | user.email       | user.wrong_password   | user.password      +|
      | "user001@awdrt.net"| "q1w2e3r4t5"         | "q1w2e3r4"         +|
    )
    step s1:System_Execute:
        OpenBrowser ["The system opens the browser
        in https://juice-shop.herokuapp.com/#/"]
    step s2:Actor_CallSystem:
        Click element('Dismiss')
        ["The Visitor clicks the 'Dismiss' button"]
    step s3:Actor_CallSystem:
        Click element('Account')[""]
    step s4:Actor_CallSystem:
        Click element('SignIn')
        ["The Visitor clicks on the 'SignIn' button"]
    step s5:Actor_PrepareData:
        PostData readFrom user.reg_email
        ["The Visitor writes the email"]
    step s6:Actor_PrepareData:
        PostData readFrom user.reg_wrong_password
        ["The Visitor writes the wrong password"]
    step s7:Actor_CallSystem:
        Click element('Confirm_SignIn')
        ["The Visitor clicks on the 'Sign In' button"]
    step s8:Actor_CallSystem:
        Click element('Confirm_SignIn')
        ["The Visitor clicks on the 'Sign In' button"]
    step s9:Actor_CallSystem:
```

```
        Click element('Confirm_SignIn')
        ["The Visitor clicks on the 'Sign In' button"]
  step s10 : Actor_CallSystem :
        Click element('Confirm_SignIn')
        ["The Visitor clicks on the 'Sign In' button"]
  step s11 : Actor_CallSystem :
        Click element('Confirm_SignIn')
        ["The Visitor clicks on the 'Sign In' button"]
  step s12 : Actor_PrepareData :
        PostData readFrom user.reg_password
        ["The Visitor writes the correct password"]
  step s13 : Actor_CallSystem :
        Click element('Confirm_SignIn')
        ["The Visitor clicks on the 'Sign In' button"]
  step s14 : Actor_CallSystem : Click element('My_Account')
        ["The Visitor clicks on the 'My Account' button"]
step s15 : System_Execute : Check elementOnScreen(text e_User.firstName)
     [" 'MyAccount' appears with the user name"]
     ]
]
```

Spec. 1.3. Multiple invalid login attempts test case (RSL spec).

The result of this first set of tests showed that, although it is possible to perform such validations using RSL and ITLingo Studio, this may be a very repetitive and time consuming task, as the language currently does not support iteration operators, thus requiring manual implementation of each invalid sign in attempt. In the case of the Juice Shop application, after 5 attempts with wrong passwords, the test login with a correct password and was successfully authenticated, and thus, this shows that the Juice Shop application is not protected against brute force sign-in attacks.

3.2 Second Experiments

The goal of the second set of experiments is to check if it is possible to apply the proposed approach in security testing.

We analyzed the documentation of OWASP Juice Shop [8] to identify and understand the involved exploits. Most of its exploits referred to the following vulnerabilities: SQL Injection; XSS; Vulnerable Components; Sensitive Data Exposure; Broken Authentication; Broken Access Control.

Many of these exploits require tools that have to be combined with ITLingo Studio, namely to include features such as: use browser developer mode, use external programs to inspect requests, and penetration testing tools. In this preliminary study, we just explored the following vulnerabilities: SQL Injections and XSS based on UI inputs.

SQL Injection attack - Abuse Login as Administrator

The goal of this test is to check if it is possible to execute an SQL injection attack on the system. This requires some previous knowledge of the system architecture, but in general, this knowledge is available.

Spec. 1.4 shows an RSL specification of the "Abuse Login as Administrator" test case. This test is a simple example of an SQL injection attack. The goal of this test is to break the login query by sending a special sequence of characters (i.e., the string "OR 1=1-") that returns true, and that allows to login with the first user of the application's database: that happens to be the "administrator" user! With this test, it was possible to detect an important system vulnerability, since it is possible to incorrectly login as an administrator and, thus, login with higher privileges accessing information that should not be supposed to.

This test resulted in a successful login as administrator, which in a real scenario would allow an attacker to execute actions that normally should not be available to regular users.

```
UseCaseTest st_uc_1_SQLInject ""  :  Invalid [
  useCase suc_2_SQLi_Admin_User actorInitiates aU_Cracker
  description "As a Cracker I want to login as
    Administrator using SQLi"
  variable query [
    attribute login: String
    attribute password: String
  ]
  testScenario SQLinjectionAdministratorSignIn : Main [
    isConcrete
    variable query withValues (
    |query.login        |query.password+|
    |"' OR 1=1--"        |""            +|
)

      step s1:System_Execute:OpenBrowser
        ["The system opens the browser in
        https://juice-shop.herokuapp.com/#/"]
    step s2:Actor_CallSystem:
      Click element('Dismiss')
      ["The Visitor clicks the 'Dismiss' button"]
    step s3:Actor_CallSystem:
      Click element('Account')[""]
    step s4:Actor_CallSystem:
      Click element('SignIn')
      ["The Visitor clicks on the 'SignIn' button"]
    step s5:Actor_PrepareData:
      PostData readFrom query.login
      ["The Cracker writes the query"]
    step s6:Actor_PrepareData:
      PostData readFrom query.password
      ["The Cracker writes random data"]
    step s7:Actor_CallSystem:
      Click element('Confirm_SignIn')
      ["The Visitor clicks on the 'Sign In' button"]
    step s8:Actor_CallSystem:
      Click element('My_Account')
      ["The Visitor clicks on the 'My Account' button"]
    step s9:System_Execute:
      Check elementOnScreen(text query.login)
      ["'MyAccount' appears with the user name"]
  ]
```

Spec. 1.4. RSL Test Steps for SQL injection.

Embed IFrame Which Calls Another Website on Screen
This test consists in creating an address that would return a specific set of characters, then by inputting an IFrame that references that address and submit the search query to test if the system renders the input data as HTML.

This test aims to check if it is possible to fill in an input field with an IFrame redirecting to a new location that does not belong to the application under test. Indeed, it was possible to confirm this vulnerability since after the search input form, the system redirected to the new location. However, this test required the local execution of the OWASP Juice Shop as it is needed to access a local API.

With this preliminary study it is possible to conclude that the proposed approach (with tools like ITLingo Studio and Robot Framework) can be adopted to test security vulnerabilities. Nevertheless, it need to be extended and combined with additional functionalities and other cyber-security specific tools.

4   Related Work

The greatest problem of using natural language for documenting requirements is that it usually leads to well-known problems, such as ambiguity, incompleteness, inconsistency, and incorrectness [3]. Ambiguity is a particularly serious problem, as it allows for multiple interpretations of the same requirement [3]. This issue can make the automation of some subsequent activities of the software development process more difficult or even unfeasible. One way to overcome the ambiguity problem is to use structured languages and/or models.

4.1   Test Cases Generation

One of the less treated phases during a software development project is the testing and validation phase [4]. Therefore, a good way to combat this trend would be to increase the automation of testing activities, with the aim of improving the final quality of a software development project.

One test activity that is a candidate for automation is the generation of test cases. It is common to find research works that generate test cases from models of the system under development. The models adopted and data used by different approaches may vary significantly [2,7,18]. Besides this, it is also possible to find some works that try to generate test cases from requirements specified in natural languages [1].

Requirements specification in natural language are common. However, generating automatically test cases from them is challenging because they are often written in a non-standardized way.

The work presented in [1] uses Natural Language processing tools to generate automatically test cases from functional requirements written in natural language. The process followed is based on three steps, namely: (1) Functional Requirements specification; (2) Applying Natural Language Processing technique to analyze requirements and extract the data necessary for the construction of test cases; and (3) Generate the test cases from the extracted data.

To enable the generation of test cases, the requirements' document must be written according to a certain level of standardization, otherwise no results are produced.

An approach based on models is presented in [4] where test cases are generated from a *Round-Strip Strategy* and *Extended Use Cases*. In this work, the functional requirement may be treated as a graph or state machine which allows to apply path-finding algorithms. Each path can be used as a test case. In complement, the authors use a Category-Partition method on Use Cases to identify subsets of the domain for executing concrete pieces of the behavior.

In [9], the authors generate test cases from user execution traces, i.e., all user interactions with the web application are saved so as to work as regression test cases when the application suffers updates in the context of its maintenance. The original traces are extended by applying mutation operators that were designed to generate different sequences of interaction and ultimately exercise more behavior of the web application under test.

One of the challenges that these approaches have to deal with is to identify the User Interface (UI) elements to act upon when executing the final generated test scripts over the application under test. Sometimes this mapping between concepts of the specification level (either model elements or textual keywords) and UI elements is established manually which may require some effort. Although the keyword mapping is still done manually in ITLingo Studio, it does not require language processing capabilities since the specification is structured and it is simple to get all keywords that must be mapped to UI elements for test script execution.

5   Conclusion

At the moment, RSL and ITLingo Studio have some dependencies and work well in some specific scenarios. In the future, this approach should be extended and improved to provide a more simplified user experience.

One aspect that should be considered for improvement is to allow working with more types of applications based on different technologies. In addition, changing from the exclusive CSS mapping to the generic X-Path mapping will allow the use of CSS and X-Path mapping in the selection of UI elements. This change combined with a browser extension capable of inferring the absolute X-Path and, if necessary, in a second step, offering CSS alternatives, may allow a more direct way of mapping the elements of the user interface to the desired keywords.

Regarding the language, we noticed that the entire approach would benefit from some RSL extensions. In particular, it should be considered extending the RSL language with the ability to make direct references to entities. This may be useful for defining test scenarios. Another aspect is to extend RSL with a mechanism supporting iterations inside test scenarios. This problem was noticed when defining the "brute force" test case in Spec 1.3.

Regarding the overall approach, we think that it would benefit from adding a test data generation technique. This would ease the definition of the test cases. In addition, ITLingo's usability would improve if the components were integrated in a single environment. As it is now, it requires the use of different technologies and different IDEs to successfully run all necessary scripts.

Finally, and related to security tests, the tool has some limitations to perform this type of tests. However, some of the mentioned problems may be overcome if implemented in the scripting engine.

References

1. Ansari, A., Shagufta, M.B., Sadaf Fatima, A., Tehreem, S.: Constructing test cases using natural language processing. In: Proceedings of the 3rd IEEE International Conference on Advances in Electrical and Electronics, Information, Communication and Bio-Informatics, AEEICB (2017). https://doi.org/10.1109/AEEICB.2017.7972390
2. Barbosa, A., Paiva, A.C.R., Campos, J.C.: Test case generation from mutated task models. In: Proceedings of the 3rd ACM SIGCHI Symposium on Engineering Interactive Computing System, EICS 2011. ACM (2011). https://doi.org/10.1145/1996461.1996516

3. de Almeida Ferreira, D., da Silva, A.R.: RSLingo: an information extraction approach toward formal requirements specifications. In: 2nd IEEE International Workshop on Model-Driven Requirements Engineering, MoDRE (2012). https://doi.org/10.1109/MoDRE.2012.6360073

4. Gutiérrez, J., Aragón, G., Mejías, M., Domínguez Mayo, F.J., Ruiz Cutilla, C.M.: Automatic test case generation from functional requirements in NDT. In: Grossniklaus, M., Wimmer, M. (eds.) ICWE 2012. LNCS, vol. 7703, pp. 176–185. Springer, Heidelberg (2012). https://doi.org/10.1007/978-3-642-35623-0_18

5. Jr, V.S.: An Introduction to XPath: How to Get Started (2016). https://blog.scrapinghub.com/2016/10/27/an-introduction-to-xpath-with-examples

6. Maciel, D., Paiva, A.C., Da Silva, A.R.: From requirements to automated acceptance tests of interactive apps: an integrated model-based testing approach. In: ENASE 2019 - Proceedings of the 14th International Conference on Evaluation of Novel Approaches to Software Engineering (2019). https://doi.org/10.5220/0007679202650272

7. Moreira, R.M.L.M., Paiva, A.C.R., Nabuco, M., Memon, A.: Pattern-based GUI testing: bridging the gap between design and quality assurance. Softw. Test. Verification Reliab. $27(3)$ (2017). https://doi.org/10.1002/stvr.1629

8. OWASP: OWASP Juice Shop - demo and testing instance. https://juice-shop.herokuapp.com

9. Paiva, A.C.R., Restivo, A., Almeida, S.: Test case generation based on mutations over user execution traces. Softw. Qual. J. 1–14 (2020). https://doi.org/10.1007/s11219-020-09503-4

10. Paiva, A.C.R., Maciel, D., da Silva, A.R.: From requirements to automated acceptance tests with the RSL language. In: Damiani, E., Spanoudakis, G., Maciaszek, L.A. (eds.) ENASE 2019. CCIS, vol. 1172, pp. 39–57. Springer, Cham (2020). https://doi.org/10.1007/978-3-030-40223-5_3

11. Robot-Framework-Foundation: Robot Framework. https://robotframework.org/

12. Rwemalika, R., Kintis, M., Papadakis, M., Le Traon, Y., Lorrach, P.: On the evolution of keyword-driven test suites. In: Proceedings - 2019 IEEE 12th International Conference on Software Testing, Verification and Validation, ICST (2019). https://doi.org/10.1109/ICST.2019.00040

13. Selenium: Automation Practice. http://automationpractice.com/index.php?id_cms=4&controller=cms

14. da Silva, A.R.: Linguistic patterns and linguistic styles for requirements specification (i): an application case with the rigorous RSL/business-level language. In: Proceedings of the 22nd European Conference on Pattern Languages of Programs (2017)

15. da Silva, A.R.: Rigorous specification of use cases with the RSL language. In: 28th International Conference on Information Systems Development - IDS (2019)

16. da Silva, A.R., Paiva, A.C.R., da Silva, V.E.R.: A test specification language for information systems based on data entities, use cases and state machines. In: Hammoudi, S., Pires, L.F., Selic, B. (eds.) MODELSWARD 2018. CCIS, vol. 991, pp. 455–474. Springer, Cham (2019). https://doi.org/10.1007/978-3-030-11030-7_20

17. da Silva, A.R., Paiva, A.C.R., da Silva, V.E.R.: Towards a test specification language for information systems: focus on data entity and state machine tests. In: Proceedings of the 6th International Conference on Model-Driven Engineering and Software Development - MODELSWARD. INSTICC, SciTePress (2018). https://doi.org/10.5220/0006608002130224

18. Silva, P., Paiva, A.C.R., Restivo, A., Garcia, J.E.: Automatic test case generation from usage information. In: 11th International Conference on the Quality of Information and Communications Technology, QUATIC. IEEE Computer Society (2018). https://doi.org/10.1109/QUATIC.2018.00047
19. W3School: XML and XPath. https://www.w3schools.com/xml/xml_xpath.asp

Testing Chatbots with CHARM

Sergio Bravo-Santos, Esther Guerra, and Juan de Lara(✉)

Modelling and Software Engineering Research Group, Computer Science Department,
Universidad Autónoma de Madrid, Madrid, Spain
{sergio.bravos,esther.guerra,juan.delara}@uam.es
http://miso.es

Abstract. Chatbots are software programs with a conversational user interface, typically embedded in webs or messaging systems like Slack, Facebook Messenger or Telegram. Many companies are investing in chatbots to improve their customer support. This has led to a proliferation of chatbot creation platforms (e.g., Dialogflow, Lex, Watson). However, there is currently little support for testing chatbots, which may impact in their final quality.

To alleviate this problem, we propose a methodology that automates the generation of *coherence*, *sturdiness* and *precision* tests for chatbots, and exploits the test results to improve the chatbot precision. The methodology is supported by a tool called CHARM, which uses BOTIUM as the backend for automated test execution. Moreover, we report on experiments aimed at improving Dialogflow chatbots built by third parties.

Keywords: Chatbots · Testing · BOTIUM · Dialogflow

1 Introduction

Chatbots – also called conversational agents – are software programs that interact with users via conversation in natural language (NL) [9]. Many companies are developing chatbots to provide access to their services or automate customer support, and they are increasingly being used to automate software engineering tasks [4,6]. Their use is booming as they do not require installing dedicated apps but can be embedded in social networks – like Slack, Telegram or Twitter – for their use in mobile devices, as if talking with a colleague.

Because of this growing interest in chatbots, many tools for their development have appeared, such as Google's Dialogflow[1], IBM's Watson Assistant[2], Microsoft's bot framework[3] or Amazon's Lex[4]. Some of them are cloud-based low-code development environments that greatly facilitate the main chatbot construction steps, from the application of NL processing (NLP) for identifying the

---

[1] https://dialogflow.com/.
[2] https://www.ibm.com/cloud/watson-assistant/.
[3] https://dev.botframework.com/.
[4] https://aws.amazon.com/en/lex/.

© Springer Nature Switzerland AG 2020
M. Shepperd et al. (Eds.): QUATIC 2020, CCIS 1266, pp. 426–438, 2020.
https://doi.org/10.1007/978-3-030-58793-2_34

user intents, to the chatbot deployment in social networks. However, these tools barely provide support for testing chatbots, even if testing is essential to ensure the chatbot quality. At most, they offer a console where developers can manually test if the chatbot reacts properly to the NL inputs. While this helps during the development, a proper software process requires systematic, automatable testing mechanisms.

To address this need, a few chatbot testing tools are starting to emerge, most notably BOTIUM[5]. This tool successfully automates the chatbot testing process. Moreover, it permits synthesizing an initial set of test cases derived from the training phrases of the chatbot. However, the generated test cases only consider basic conversation flows, and need to be extended by hand. Our aim is to automate this manual process as much as possible.

In this paper, we propose a methodology for chatbot testing that extends the test case synthesizer of BOTIUM to cover more complex cases, such as context-dependent conversations. The generated test cases have two aims: testing the robustness of the NLP engine, and the precision of the chatbot to identify the user intents. For this purpose, our tests include variations of the chatbot training phrases, constructed via *fuzzing*/mutation functions [12]. Moreover, the test results can be used to improve the chatbot precision. The method is supported by a tool called CHARM, and has been evaluated through some experiments on chatbots developed by third parties.

In the remainder of the paper, Sect. 2 provides background on chatbots and their testing with BOTIUM; Sect. 3 presents our approach for test synthesis; Sect. 4 describes our methodology and its tool support; Sect. 5 reports on an initial evaluation; Sect. 6 compares with related work; and Sect. 7 presents the conclusions and lines of future work.

2 Background on Chatbots and Their Testing

This section overviews the working scheme of chatbots (Sect. 2.1) and how they can be tested with BOTIUM (Sect. 2.2).

2.1 What's in a Chatbot

Chatbots are programs with a conversational user interface. As Fig. 1 illustrates, the interaction starts when the user writes a sentence or *utterance* (label 1). Then, the chatbot tries to match the utterance to the most appropriate *intent* among a predefined set (label 2). For example, upon the receipt of the user utterance *"what types of pizza do you have?"*, a chatbot for food delivery would recognize that the user intent is obtaining information about the availability of some kind of food, and would reply with a list of pizza types. To identify the intent that corresponds to an utterance, intent definitions include sample phrases (i.e., different ways to express the intent) which are used for training the chatbot.

---

[5] https://www.botium.ai/.

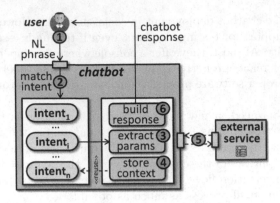

Fig. 1. Chatbot working scheme.

Upon matching an intent, the chatbot may need to extract information from the utterance (label 3). In the previous example, it may need to know the query target, which is *"types of pizza"*. Each piece of information is called *parameter*, and is typed by an *entity* which can be either predefined (e.g., date) or chatbot-specific (e.g., food type). Entities define a list of possible values (e.g., pizza, noodles) and synonyms, and some platforms like Dialogflow allow *fuzzy matching* to overcome misspellings and mistakes. If a parameter is mandatory but the utterance does not include it, the chatbot may ask for it in a follow-up intent. Moreover, chatbots sometimes need to store information about a conversation (e.g., desired type of pizza) to reuse it in subsequent intents. In Dialogflow, the conversation state is stored in *contexts* (label 4).

Finally, the chatbot may need to invoke an external service (e.g., the information system of a food delivery shop) to handle the user intent (label 5), and ultimately responds to the user (label 6) with a text, media elements, or widgets specific of the deployment platform (e.g., buttons in Telegram).

2.2   Testing Chatbots with BOTIUM

BOTIUM is a suite of open-source components for automated chatbot testing. It communicates with the chatbot under test via connectors. These are available for many chatbot platforms (like Dialogflow, Watson or Lex), and new ones can be added. BOTIUM executes all test cases found in a given folder against the chatbot. It follows a behaviour-driven development approach [10] similar to Cucumber[6], in which test cases consist of *convo* files that hold the global structure of the test conversation, and *utterance* files that contain the phrases used in the conversation.

As an example, Listing 1 shows a convo where the user (#me) provides any utterance in order_drink_utterance (i.e., any phrase in Listing 2), and the chatbot (#bot) is expected to match the intent order.drink. Overall, the convo would be

---

[6] https://cucumber.io/.

executed three times (once per utterance). As a result, BOTIUM reports the number of passed and failed tests, the reason for failure, and a confusion matrix with the percentage of tests that matched the expected intent. The latter matrix allows detecting loosely defined intents.

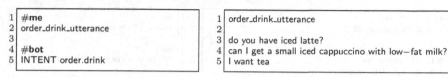

```
1  #me
2  order_drink_utterance
3
4  #bot
5  INTENT order.drink
```

Listing 1. Convo file.

```
1  order_drink_utterance
2
3  do you have iced latte?
4  can I get a small iced cappuccino with low−fat milk?
5  I want tea
```

Listing 2. Utterance file.

While test cases can be created by hand, BOTIUM also supports their automated generation from the chatbot specification. Specifically, it generates one convo and one utterance file per intent, the latter containing the intent training phrases. The generated tests are simple, e.g., they do not consider conversations with context or chatbot responses. Hence, the developer needs to create additional tests to tackle those scenarios. In the next section, we propose an extension of these test synthesis capabilities.

3   Test Synthesis

CHARM extends the set of test cases generated by BOTIUM in two ways. First, it produces further convos to test behaviour uncovered in the synthesized test set. This process is explained in Sect. 3.1. Second, CHARM augments the utterance files by means of mutation. This technique is introduced in Sect. 3.2.

3.1   Convo Generation

CHARM produces convos to test the following aspects:

– **Chatbot response:** BOTIUM produces convos that specify the intent that should be matched (see, for example, line 5 in Listing 1). CHARM extends these convos to include and assess the expected chatbot response as well.
– **Required parameters:** Intents may have required parameters, and the chatbot response may depend on their value (or lack of value). Hence, CHARM extends the base convos to tackle different parameter values.
– **Context:** CHARM generates new convos for testing the use of contexts (i.e., previously stored information). To this aim, for every intent that uses context variables, it creates all possible convo combinations that fill those variables and lead to the intent.

Example. Listing 3 shows a convo generated by CHARM for an intent with context and two required parameters: type of drink and delivery method. The convo emulates an interaction where the user utterance omits the delivery method (line 2). This triggers a follow-up question of the chatbot asking for it (line 6), to which the user replies delivery (line 9). Then, the chatbot recaps the order details and asks for confirmation (line 13), which requires retrieving the ordered drink and delivery method from the previous context. Thus, to generate this convo, CHARM needs to statically build a conversation flow that feeds the context with the necessary information, as done in lines 1–9.

```
 1  #me
 2  order_drink_nodeliv_utt
 3
 4  #bot
 5  INTENT order.drink
 6  order_drink_nodeliv_response
 7
 8  #me
 9  delivery
10
11  #bot
12  INTENT order.drink
13  order_drink_confirmation
14
15  #me
16  order_drink_nodeliv_yes_utt
17
18  #bot
19  INTENT order.drink.yes
20  order_drink_confirmation_yes
```

```
 1  me:
 2  Two medium cappuccinos
 3
 4  bot:
 5  Would you like delivery or pickup?
 6
 7
 8  me:
 9  delivery
10
11  bot:
12  You want two medium cappuccinos
13      for delivery, is that right?
14
15  me:
16  Yes
17
18  bot:
19  Have a nice day!
20
```

Listing 3. Convo for testing intent with context.   **Listing 4.** Conversation.

As an example, Listing 4 shows an instance of the execution of the convo with concrete utterances. We use the same line numbers as in Listing 3 to facilitate traceability.

3.2 Utterance Generation

Starting from the utterance set generated by BOTIUM, CHARM creates new utterance variants by applying the mutation operators shown in Table 1. We distinguish the following four kinds of mutation operators, which are applied with a customizable probability:

- **Character** operators emulate typing errors according to a given probability. Specifically, swap-char swaps a character with another one, swap-char-close swaps one character to another one which is close in the keyboard, and delete-char deletes one character.
- **Language** operators translate an utterance between a list of user-defined or random languages, and the result is translated back to the initial language. The goal is creating utterances with equivalent meaning but different form.
- **Word** operators change a word (adjectives, nouns or adverbs) by synonyms or antonyms. The aim is creating utterances accepted by the same intents as the original utterance.
- **Number** operators substitute numbers by equivalent words and vice versa.

Table 1. Mutation operators for utterances.

Mutation	Description	Example
Character		
swap-char	swaps a character to any other character	hello → hkllo
swap-char-close	swaps a character to another one close in the keyboard	hello → hwllo
delete-char	deletes a character	hello → hllo
Language		
translation-chain	translates between a list of languages	hello → hola → hi
Word		
word-to-synonym	changes an adjective, adverb or noun to a synonym	2 pants → 2 trousers
word-to-antonym	changes an adjective or adverb to an antonym	hot tea → cold tea
Number		
number-to-word	changes a number into an equivalent word	2 pants → two pants
word-to-number	changes a word to a number	two pants → 2 pants

4 Testing Methodology and Tool Support

In this section, we first introduce our proposed methodology for testing chatbots (Sect. 4.1), and then we overview our supporting tool CHARM (Sect. 4.2).

4.1 Testing Process

Figure 2 shows the chatbot testing process in our tool CHARM. It supports three kinds of tests: coherence, sturdiness and precision.

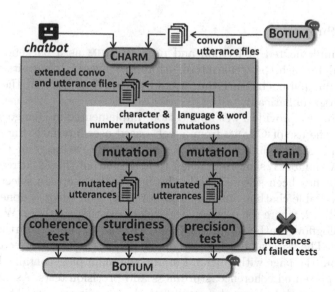

Fig. 2. CHARM's testing process.

First, CHARM invokes BOTIUM to create the base convo and utterance files, and extends the convo files as explained in Sect. 3.1. Then, depending on the kind of test, CHARM creates new utterances by applying a subset of the mutation operators detailed in Sect. 3.2. This stage may require the intervention of the tester to confirm that the new utterances preserve the original utterance semantics. Finally, the test cases are executed atop BOTIUM, and the results are interpreted according to the test kind:

- **Coherence test:** This is the simplest test. It executes the extended convo files but does not perform any utterance mutation. This test is typically performed first, to detect coarse-grained defects like duplicated training phrases in different intents, or too similar intents and entities.
- **Sturdiness test:** This test assesses how good the chatbot is at dealing with typing mistakes or different writing styles. For this purpose, CHARM applies the *character* mutations to emulate typing mistakes, and the *number* mutations to have a same utterance written in different ways (numbers vs words). This type of test actually evaluates the robustness of the NLP engine of the underlying chatbot platform. If the results are deemed bad, some platforms allow fine-tuning the intent matching process, e.g., by enabling *fuzzy matching*.
- **Precision test:** The precision test evaluates the ability of the chatbot to predict the correct intent when utterances have a different formulation from the intent training phrases. To do so, CHARM produces new utterances using the *language* and *word* mutations. If a test with a mutated utterance fails, then the utterance can be used as a training phrase to improve the chatbot precision. This testing-improvement cycle can be repeated until the chatbot precision is deemed adequate.

4.2 Tool Support

CHARM is implemented in Python and uses BOTIUM as a backend. The tool is freely available at https://charmtool.github.io/Charm/. It permits generating convo files and parameterizing the distribution probabilities of the mutation operators programmatically.

In addition, we provide a web application, implemented in Django and React, that enables the use of CHARM from a web-based user interface. Figure 3 shows this web application, which can be accessed from the webpage of CHARM. Its main page, with label 1, shows on the left top the chatbot that is currently active. If no chatbot has been selected, as in the figure, the user can select one from the list of available chatbots, or upload a new one. The latter is done using the page with label 2, where the user can also delete existing chatbots. We currently support Dialogflow chatbot definitions, but we plan to support further formats in the future. The user can upload hand-made convos, and generate convos using BOTIUM, from the page with label 3. Finally, the main page contains buttons to execute the presented coherence, sturdiness and precision tests. As an example, the page with label 4 shows the results of the sturdiness test. The displayed report is generated by BOTIUM.

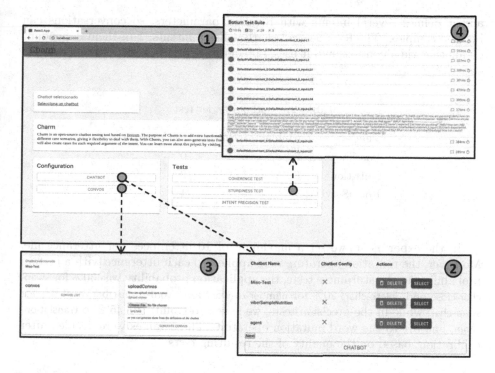

Fig. 3. Web-based user interface of CHARM: (1) Main window. (2) Chatbot management page. (3) Page for uploading and generating convos. (4) Results of sturdiness test (report obtained from BOTIUM).

5   Evaluation

In this section, we report on the results of an experiment aimed at answering the following two research questions (RQs):

RQ1 *Can* CHARM *uncover problems in chatbots that the default test cases generated by* BOTIUM *do not detect?*

RQ2 *Can the iterative testing process of* CHARM *improve the chatbot quality?*

5.1   Experiment Set-Up

The experiment considers the three Dialogflow chatbots shown in Table 2. The first one was built by us, and the other two are third-party chatbots found on github. The Baseline[7] chatbot has neither contexts nor entities, and so, the chatbot responses do not depend on parameter values or previous conversation states. The Nutrition[8] chatbot has 7 entities, some of them with more than 100 entries,

---

[7] https://github.com/CharmTool/Charm/blob/master/chatbots/Miso-Test.zip.

[8] https://github.com/Viber/apiai-nutrition-sample.

and it defines several intents with required parameters, so conversations can become complex. The RoomService[9] chatbot has 5 intents, 1 of them dependant on another via a context, and it uses 4 predefined entities and 1 chatbot-specific entity.

Table 2. Chatbots under test.

Chatbot	#Intents	#Entities	#Contexts
Baseline	4	0	0
Nutrition	4	7	0
RoomService	5	5	1

In the experiment, we set a maximum of 10 utterances per utterance file. Moreover, the mutation operators were applied to each utterance with a certain probability: in the sturdiness tests, the application probability was 30% for swap-char-close and delete-char, 20% for number-to-word and word-to-number, and 0% for swap-char; while in the precision tests, we gave probability 30–45% to translation-chain, and 5% to the word mutation operators. These values were decided after calibration, based on the quality of the resulting tests.

5.2 Experiment Execution

We run each type of test on every chatbot, and next, we extended the chatbot training set with the utterances of the failing cases of the precision tests, performing two improvement cycles. Table 3 summarizes the results. All chatbots obtained perfect score in the coherence test (2nd column). This means that the chatbots have no evident errors in their specification, and the default BOTIUM tests detect no faults.

Table 3. Results of the experiment.

	Coherence, 1st cycle		Sturdiness, 1st cycle		Sturdiness, fuzzy matching		Precision, 1st cycle		Precision, 1st cycle		Precision, 2nd cycle new training		Precision, 2nd cycle new training	
	Pass	Fail	Pass	Fail	Pass	Fail	Pass	Fail	Pass	Fail	Pass	Fail	Pass	Fail
Baseline	32	0	31	1	31	1	29	1	30	0	30	1	31	0
Nutrition	48	0	43	5	46	2	45	2	47	0	48	1	49	0
RoomService	32	0	29	3	28	4	29	2	31	0	33	2	35	0

To test sturdiness, the character and number mutation operators produced 32, 48 and 32 additional test utterances. All chatbots failed some test case (3rd column). If we activate *fuzzy matching* on the problematic entities (4th column),

---

[9] https://github.com/dialogflow/dialogflow-java-client-v2.

then the results of Baseline do not change because it has no entities, the results of Nutrition improve, but RoomService worsens. The latter is because the chatbot defines an entity "room name" with entries A, B and C, and CHARM generated an utterance with a different room name, which the chatbot (incorrectly) took as valid. This shows that *fuzzy matching* is not appropriate for this intent.

The precision tests produced the same number of utterances as the sturdiness tests, though using the language and word operators. Moreover, we manually filtered 4 of the generated test utterances out, as they were meaningless. From the remaining test cases, all chatbots failed some (5th column), so we trained the chatbots with the utterances of the failed cases, after which all tests succeeded (6th column). Next, we applied the precision test with new mutated utterances, obtaining fewer errors than in the first cycle (7th and 8th columns).

5.3   Discussion

Overall, we can answer RQ1 and RQ2 positively: CHARM produced tests that revealed faults, and also helped in improving the quality of the chatbots. However, we need to perform further experiments with more complex chatbots to strengthen this assessment. We observed that CHARM synthesized convo files to test the context in chatbot RoomService. While CHARM can generate tests that detect chatbot defects, there is still a manual step to filter meaningless utterances in precision tests. For instance, in our experiment, we had to remove around 3% of the automatically generated utterances.

To get an intuition of the synthesized tests, Table 4 shows some of the utterances generated by CHARM, together with the mutation operator that produced them. The last column of the table indicates whether the generated utterance was manually discarded or not. For example, we removed the last utterance

Table 4. Sample of generated utterances.

Chatbot	Utterance	Mutated utterance	Operator	Discarded?
Baseline	Just going to say hi	Just come to say hello	Translation-chain	No
Baseline	When are the meetings?	When is the meetings?	Translation-chain	No
Baseline	Good luck	good muck	Swap-char-close	No
Nutrition	Nutrition analysis	Food analysis	Word-to-synonym	No
Nutrition	Calories in 4 oz of steak	Calories in four oz of steak	Number-to-word	No
Nutrition	How many calories in one big mac	How many calories in 1 big mac	Word-to-number	No
Nutrition	Does a kiwi contain vitamin A	Not one kiwi fruit contains vitamin a	Translation-chain	Yes
RoomService	Is there any room free tomorrow?	Any rooms free	Translation-chain	No
RoomService	Do you have rooms for this monday?	Do you have rooms for thismonday?	Delete-char	No

shown for chatbot Nutrition, as the translation chain produced a sentence with almost opposite meaning to the original.

6   Related Work

While there are many tools for chatbot development, their support for testing is scarce. Most development platforms (like Dialogflow, Lex or Watson) provide a web chat console that permits informal, manual testing of the chatbots. Approaches based on programming languages – like Rasa[10], which is built atop Python – can rely on the debugging and testing support offered by the programming language itself. Only a few platforms, like Dialogflow, offer debugging facilities to inspect the matched intent and related information. In addition, Dialogflow includes checks of the chatbot quality, like detecting intents with similar training phrases.

Some companies have developed their own chatbot testing tools. For example, haptik.ai provides a testing tool[11] that automates the interaction with the chatbot via simple scripts, and can be integrated with automation servers such as Jenkins. BOTIUM can also be integrated in testing flows using Jenkins. However, these tools require manual building or extension of the test suites, which our work aims to automate.

Regarding academic proposals, in [1], the authors use AI planning techniques to generate tests traversing the conversation flow. More similar to us, the metamorphic chatbot testing approach in [3] applies mutation operators (e.g., replacing a word by a synonym, or a number by another one) to a set of utterances to produce follow-up test cases, which should match the same intent. In a similar vein, BoTest [8] creates divergent inputs (word order errors, incorrect verb tense, synonyms) from an initial utterance set. We also rely on mutation, but in addition, we classify our mutation operators to obtain different types of tests (to test either the robustness of the NLP engine or the precision of the intent definitions), provide automation on top of BOTIUM, and a methodology for chatbot improvement.

To reduce the human cost of chatbot testing, *Bottester* [11] simulates users who interact with chatbots, and collects some interaction metrics like the answer frequency, the response time or the precision of the intent recognition. While *Bottester* targets chatbots created with in-house technology, CHARM is based on BOTIUM and so can test chatbots for the major chatbot creation platforms. Moreover, our testing process covers different chatbot aspects and provides a cycle of chatbot improvement.

CHARM is focused on testing the NL aspect of the chatbot, but other (non-functional) aspects need to be tested as well, like the communication with external services or the chatbot security [2]. For example, *Alma*[12] is a chatbot that

---

[10] https://rasa.com/.
[11] https://haptik.ai/tech/automating-bot-testing/.
[12] http://chatbottest.com.

helps in evaluating Messenger and Telegram bots across seven categories: personality, onboarding, understanding, navigation, error management, intelligence and response time. While *Alma* is based on questions to the chatbot users, we support automated testing. One of the decisive aspects for chatbot acceptance is their usability. Some heuristics for bot usability have been proposed[13], but more actionable usability patterns – possibly integrated within chatbot development tools – and automated means for usability evaluation are needed [7].

7   Conclusions and Future Work

The increasing use of chatbots for varying activities makes necessary techniques to ensure their quality. This paper contributes to solve this need by proposing a set of techniques for automated chatbot test synthesis, a methodology supporting three different types of tests, and a supporting tool that uses BOTIUM for test automation.

In the future, we would like to extend our set of mutation operators (for example, to enable adversarial text generation [5]), support new types of tests, improve the functionality of the CHARM service, and enable the integration of CHARM with continuous testing and integration workflows.

Acknowledgments. We would like to thank the anonymous reviewers for their comments. This work has been partially funded by the Spanish Ministry of Science (project MASSIVE, RTI2018-095255-B-I00) and the R&D programme of Madrid (project FORTE, P2018/TCS-4314).

References

1. Bozic, J., Tazl, O.A., Wotawa, F.: Chatbot testing using AI planning. In: AITest, pp. 37–44. IEEE (2019)
2. Bozic, J., Wotawa, F.: Security testing for chatbots. In: Medina-Bulo, I., Merayo, M.G., Hierons, R. (eds.) ICTSS 2018. LNCS, vol. 11146, pp. 33–38. Springer, Cham (2018). https://doi.org/10.1007/978-3-319-99927-2_3
3. Bozic, J., Wotawa, F.: Testing chatbots using metamorphic relations. In: Gaston, C., Kosmatov, N., Le Gall, P. (eds.) ICTSS 2019. LNCS, vol. 11812, pp. 41–55. Springer, Cham (2019). https://doi.org/10.1007/978-3-030-31280-0_3
4. Erlenhov, L., de Oliveira Neto, F.G., Scandariato, R., Leitner, P.: Current and future bots in software development. In: Proceedings of the 1st International Workshop on Bots in Software Engineering BotSE@ICSE, pp. 7–11. IEEE / ACM (2019)
5. Jin, D., Jin, Z., Zhou, J.T., Szolovits, P.: Is BERT really robust? a strong baseline for natural language attack on text classification and entailment. In: AAAI (2020)
6. Pérez-Soler, S., Guerra, E., de Lara, J.: Collaborative modeling and group decision making using chatbots in social networks. IEEE Softw. **35**(6), 48–54 (2018)
7. Ren, R., Castro, J.W., Acuña, S.T., de Lara, J.: Evaluation techniques for chatbot usability: a systematic mapping study. Int. J. Softw. Eng. Knowl. Eng. **29**(11&12), 1673–1702 (2019)

---

[13] https://haptik.ai/blog/usability-heuristics-chatbots/.

8. Ruane, E., Faure, T., Smith, R., Bean, D., Carson-Berndsen, J., Ventresque, A.: Botest: a framework to test the quality of conversational agents using divergent input examples. In: IUI Companion. ACM (2018)
9. Shevat, A.: Designing Bots: Creating Conversational Experiences. O'Reilly, Sebastopol (2017)
10. Solís, C., Wang, X.: A study of the characteristics of behaviour driven development. In: 37th EUROMICRO Conference on Software Engineering and Advanced Applications SEAA, pp. 383–387. IEEE Computer Society (2011)
11. Vasconcelos, M., Candello, H., Pinhanez, C., dos Santos, T.: Bottester: testing conversational systems with simulated users. In: IHC, pp. 73:1–73:4. ACM (2017)
12. Zeller, A., Gopinath, R., Böhme, M., Fraser, G., Holler, C.: Mutation-based fuzzing. In: The Fuzzing Book. Saarland University (2019). https://www.fuzzingbook.org/html/MutationFuzzer.html. Accessed June 2020

A Dataset of Regressions in Web Applications Detected by End-to-End Tests

Óscar Soto-Sánchez, Michel Maes-Bermejo[(✉)], Micael Gallego, and Francisco Gortázar

Universidad Rey Juan Carlos, 28933 Móstoles, Spain
{oscar.soto,michel.maes,micael.gallego,francisco.gortazar}@urjc.es

Abstract. End-to-end (e2e) tests present many challenges in the industry, however, academics are not addressing them and there is little work on this kind of tests. Running e2e tests is hard and time consuming, therefore we believe that the availability of a dataset containing regression bugs, e2e tests, documentation and logs might help in easing the path towards researching them. This paper presents a dataset for e2e tests and regression bugs in 3 web applications using Spring Framework in Java, with 6 well-documented synthetic regression bugs. The dataset also includes all the tools needed to reproduce the errors.

Keywords: Dataset · Testing · End-to-end tests

1 Introduction

Empirical studies in software testing research require projects that are the subject of that study. There are frameworks [13], infrastructures [6] and repositories [3,22] in which different researchers have collected (or added manually) and documented existing bugs in different projects being available to researchers, allowing studies to be compared using the same bug dataset as a reference. The projects considered are usually open source projects, which are more easily available, and they're usually libraries rather than applications. Some of the research datasets include the tests that reveal the different bugs. However, these tests are mostly unitary, which in many investigations can be a limitation, due to the specific characteristics that non-unitary tests (integration, end-to-end or performance tests) have.

These studies are limited because they do not have access to more complex tests, like integration, performance or end-to-end tests. Thus, researching these is difficult. Usually, libraries only have unitary tests. Non-unitary tests are usually available as part of more complex projects (usually complete applications) that expose a front-end to interact with the user, a back-end to handle requests and a database where the information persisted, as an example. These applications tend to have end-to-end test (e2e), which allow revealing failures introduced

© Springer Nature Switzerland AG 2020
M. Shepperd et al. (Eds.): QUATIC 2020, CCIS 1266, pp. 439–448, 2020.
https://doi.org/10.1007/978-3-030-58793-2_35

when simulating the interaction of a user with the application. These tests allow studies to be carried out with a broader scope by including real applications. Some of the problems faced by the industry are based on the non-scalability of Continuous Integration systems in terms of dealing with an ever-increasing code base and tests, as Memon et al. [15] report in Google, where every day 800,000 builds and 150 million test runs are performed in more than 13,000 projects. Most of the computational efforts are due to functional tests (integration and end-to-end) that require from minutes to hours to execute and much more computational resources (memory and cpu) than unitary tests.

This paper presents a dataset of regression bugs which are revealed by e2e test to support software testing research. A regression bug is defined by Nir et al. [18] as *a bug which causes a feature that worked correctly to stop working after a certain event (system upgrade, system patching, daylight saving time switch, etc)*. The contributions of this paper are as follows:

- A repository comprised of 3 complex applications with multiple components. Each project consists of a git repository with different branches that allow you to explore the different changes the project has undergone as well as the buggy versions that have a documented regression bug.
- Tools to build the projects and run the tests, using Docker[1] and Docker Compose. These tools allow researchers to reproduce any version of the code in a simple way to check the applications and their outputs (both in versions that work correctly and in those that contain an error).
- Extensive documentation of each regression bug accompanied by all resources that help to identify it; logs of the cases where the tests pass and fail, a visual diff-comparative of logs and videos of the e2e tests.

The paper is structured as follows: Previous work is presented in Sect. 2. The characteristics of the regression bugs is presented in Sect. 3 and this dataset is detailed in Sect. 4. Finally, Sect. 5 concludes the paper.

2   Related Work

There have several attempts at building a dataset of bugs and regression tests for them. As early as in 1994, Siemens Corporate Research conducted an experimental study that led to building a dataset containing a set of 130 errors [12], introduced manually by the researchers in 7 projects written in C.

The first attempt we found that proposes a dataset of real bugs for use in software research is proposed by H. Do et al., *Subject-Artifact Infrastructure Repository* [6], an infrastructure of 24 projects with documentation on 662 bugs (only 35 of them are real, the rest have been introduced by hand). In most projects, all the bugs are introduced by a single commit, being complicated to treat them individually. It is a dataset oriented to studies where the execution of the code is not a priority, oriented to make a static analysis of the code like in

---

[1] https://www.docker.com/.

Test Case Prioritization (TCP) when using approaches based on the similarity of the test cases.

Spacco et al. [22] collect the bugs produced by students in a tool (Marmoset) where you can upload your code and it is checked on a server automatically. It includes 8 different projects, carried out individually by 73 students, resulting in a total of 569 projects. They include not only the errors in the test, but also build errors of the project.

Bugs.jar [21] is a large-scale dataset for research in automated debugging, patching, and testing of Java programs. It contains a total of 1,158 bugs and patches from 8 large open source Java projects.

The iBugs [3] project provides a repository of real bugs in Java projects. It contains 364 bugs, of which there is only one test that reveals the bug. It includes mechanisms to get the corrected version of the bug, as well as its previous version for comparison. It also allows the execution of the tests in both versions.

Defects4J [13] is a extensible framework which provides real bugs to enable reproducible studies. This framework contains 357 real bugs from 5 real-world open source projects written in Java. Each bug included in their dataset contains information about the commit where the bug is fixed (which includes at least one test that reveals the bug), plus a failed commit to compare them. All bugs have their origin in the source code, are reproducible (both their failed and fixed versions) and the fix-commit does not include changes unrelated to the fix.

BugsJS [10] is the first large benchmark of 453 real manually selected and validated JavaScript bugs from 10 popular server-side programs. Like Defects4J, it facilitates the reproducibility of the execution of the tests, specifically reproducing the environment from a Docker image.

3 Generation of the Regression Bugs

The main difference between our dataset and the ones mentioned in Sect. 2 is the use of more complete programs with e2e test (in comparison to the unit tests used by these datasets). To the best of our knowledge there are no other datasets including e2e tests. This section describes the methodology used to generate the bugs as well as the characteristics of those bugs. The main objective is to make the process as close as possible to how actual projects introduce new regression bugs.

3.1 Methodology

The approach is to generate a new branch in git that includes multiple commits, simulating the changes that would occur in a real project, introducing a regression in one of them. We will call this commit that introduces the regression the commit of the regression ($C_{regression}$). The introduced regression must be detected with a test that must pass in a satisfactory way in the commit previous to the creation of the branch (C_{branch}). In the context of continuous integration (CI) it is common that these tests are not executed in each commit, so the regression is not detected until, for example, we try to merge again this branch with the master branch. We will call this commit, where the error is detected, the error commit (C_{error}). After verifying that C_{error} fails the test, we will proceed to introduce a fix commit (C_{fix}), which fixes the regression so that the test passes again and we can merge it with master. An example of this structure can be seen in Fig. 1.

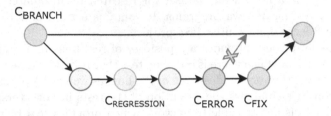

Fig. 1. A simplified example of a commit history

3.2   Characteristics

We carefully designed the regression bugs so that they have the following characteristics:

- **The bug is reproducible.** Any regression bug must be able to be reproduced, i.e., the execution of the tests always generates the same output.
- **The bug is related to source code.** The bug cannot be related to the build system, the configuration or the test files. Instead, the root cause of the bug must be related to a change in the source code of the application.
- **The change is realistic.** The commit in which the bug is introduced must contain more changes than the bug itself. The branch where this bug is placed must contain more commits with different changes in the application. This is to imitate the natural changes that occur in the application and in which a regression usually appears.
- **The tests are end-to-end.** The tests that detect the regression check a functionality as the user would do it.

4   Dataset of Regression Bugs

4.1   Subject Applications

For the realization of our dataset we have selected applications from the students of the subject *Development of Web Applications*, these projects simulate a real applications.

- **Webapp-1.** This application consists of a back-end developed in Java with Spring, and a front-end developed in Angular with TypeScript. This application is a social network of films, series and books.
- **Webapp-2.** This application consists of a back-end developed in Java with Spring, and a front-end developed in Angular with TypeScript. This application is a platform for online courses.
- **Webapp-3.** This application consists of a back-end developed in Java with Spring and a front-end developed with Moustache using Spring. This application is the web page of a library.

Both Webbapp-1 and Webapp-2 are *Single Page Applications* (SPA), whereas Webapp-3 is a MVC application. The three applications are complex ones composed of several parts which is why we decided to use them for the creation of our dataset.

Just to give an idea of the kind of regression bugs introduced, one of the bugs, introduced in Webapp-1, is related to the correct visualization of some parts of the webpage. When the bug is introduced, a part of the application that allowed to create lists stops rendering in the page. There is an e2e test that checks that lists can be created. Other bug types that we introduced are related to security, erroneous information displayed and components not shown.

All in all the dataset thus created contains three projects, and a total of 6 regression bugs, as it is shown in Table 1. Figure 2 shows the commit history of Webapp-1, containing two branches and two regression bugs. Each branch exposes a different regression bug.

Table 1. Applications and number of regression bugs available in our dataset

Application	# of regressions
Webapp-1	2
Webapp-2	3
Webapp-3	1

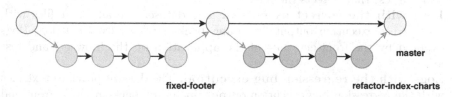

Fig. 2. In this figure we can see the webapp-1 git history graph, this application present two regression bugs.

4.2   Dataset Contents

The dataset is composed of a set of 3 applications. For each one of the applications there are a series of bugs or regressions properly documented. Logs, videos and detailed information of the commit where the regression is introduced, as well as the commit where the bug is fixed, are included. It is interesting that any researcher is able to obtain the same logs when running the tests on the different highlighted commits. For this purpose, a Docker image is provided to allow the deployment and execution of the tests in an simple way. A conceptual model of the dataset can be observed in the Fig. 3.

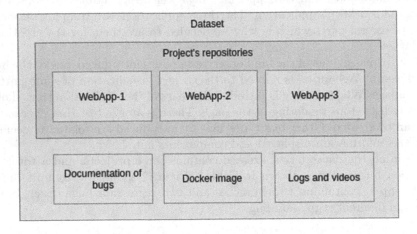

Fig. 3. Conceptual model of e2e dataset

Each of the artifacts in the dataset is detailed below:

- **Source code.** The dataset provides a git code repository with the source code of the three applications used for the creation of the regression bugs.
- **Document with bugs.** A document is provided describing the regression bugs, explaining how they works, where the regression bug was introduced and the test that detects the bug.
- **Logs with the correct execution.** The dataset contains text files with the correct execution output, including back-end logs, front-end logs (logs exposed by the front-end part of the application on the browser) and test logs.
- **Logs with the regression bug execution.** The dataset provides text files with the regression bug execution output, including back-end logs, front-end logs and test logs.
- **Logs comparison.** The dataset provides a comparison between the correct execution and regression bug execution. For this comparison we use the library diff-math-patch[2], which makes use of the Myer's algorithm [16].

---

[2] https://github.com/google/diff-match-patch.

- **Videos.** The dataset contains two videos of the test, the first video corresponds to a correct execution of the application and the second video corresponds to the regression bug execution.
- **Docker image.** The dataset provides a docker image with the projects and all dependencies that are needed in order to run the application, along with a script to build the image for any commit in history.

In order to be able to collect all the information related to the application execution, we have used the ElasTest tool [1,8,9] which allowed the authors to execute tests, capture the logs and the videos, and produce the log comparisons.

The dataset is public and available on a GitHub repository:

https://github.com/e2e-tests-dataset/e2e-tests-dataset

4.3 Applications for End-to-End Bugs in Software Research

We strongly believe that e2e tests should be subject of study, and practitioners are continuously expressing their frustration due to the several problems that this kind of tests have in their CI environments. In this section we will present in which cases the bugs included in our dataset may be useful for researching different problems.

This dataset could be used to compare the different proposals of *Test Case Prioritization (TCP)*, a subject studied extensively in the literature [2,11,24]. These proposals usually use as subjects simple programs/applications, prioritizing unit tests, with low execution times (less than 1 s). Since time is not a metric to work with, it was ignored in literature, despite being the main reason why tests are prioritized (to execute first the tests that tend to fail). Adjusting these proposals with a dataset with more realistic tests of more complex applications (e2e) would extend their applicability to industrial projects, where running a test before another could save minutes, even hours.

Automatic Repair is another subject dealt with in literature [5,7,14,20,23] that requires a collection of documented bugs in order to build different proposals. Researchers in this field often use simple program examples. Our dataset provides repairable bugs that present a challenge, since the error can be obtained in another component. From this dataset more complex proposals would be generated and applicable to the applications that we find in the real world.

Bug localization is another research field that can be explored through the glasses of e2e tests using this dataset. It could be used to measure the effect of having more or less information in the search of bugs [4,25].

Bug classification is a possible research that can be done with our dataset, using all the data sources it offers [17,19].

4.4 Limitations and Threats to Validity

Authors see mainly two threats to validity for the dataset described in the paper. One threat we face is related to external validity, specifically to the representativeness of the selected subjects. These projects arise from the academic field, they are not real applications. We tried to implement the functionalities of the applications they pretend to imitate without being under the property of any company, making them perfect candidates to investigate. The number of regression bugs is limited due to the time it takes to develop them (in the context of other changes in the project) and document them properly, but the efforts made to introduce them are similar to real industrial projects.

The other threat comes from the limitation in the number of projects and bugs. Authors aim is to increase the number of projects and bugs, both manually and automatically, so that a dataset of significant size can be provided.

Another threat contemplated but which does not apply to our dataset (but has to be taken into account when creating such a dataset or expanding it) is that in e2e testing, many smaller bugs may be hidden behind a revealed (inadvertent) bug.

5   Conclusions and Future Work

This paper presents a dataset of Java application bugs, which are detected by e2e test. The dataset includes not only the source code of the applications and the tests, but also extensive documentation of each of the bugs, logs for the different pieces composing the applications, their comparison and video recordings of the execution of the tests. This work intends to be a starting point to create a more sophisticated dataset that allows researchers to work with a type of bugs (e2e) not usually considered, but that are part of the development of numerous software projects. We plan to expand the dataset with new projects and errors, starting from the methodology presented in this paper.

Acknowledgments. This work has been supported by the Government of Spain through project "BugBirth" (RTI2018-101963-B-100), the Regional Government of Madrid (CM) through project Cloud4BigData (S2013/ICE-2894) cofunded by FSE & FEDER and the European Commission through European Project H2020 822717: MICADO.

References

1. Bertolino, A., Calabró, A., De Angelis, G., Gallego, M., García, B., Gortázar, F.: When the testing gets tough, the tough get ElasTest. In: Proceedings of the 40th International Conference on Software Engineering: Companion Proceeedings, pp. 17–20. ACM (2018)
2. Catal, C., Mishra, D.: Test case prioritization: a systematic mapping study. Softw. Qual. J. **21**(3), 445–478 (2013)
3. Dallmeier, V., Zimmermann, T.: Extraction of bug localization benchmarks from history. In: Proceedings of the Twenty-second IEEE/ACM International Conference on Automated Software Engineering ASE 2007, pp. 433–436. ACM, New York (2007). https://doi.org/10.1145/1321631.1321702. http://doi.acm.org/10.1145/1321631.1321702

4. Dao, T., Zhang, L., Meng, N.: How does execution information help with information-retrieval based bug localization? In: 2017 IEEE/ACM 25th International Conference on Program Comprehension (ICPC), pp. 241–250, May 2017. https://doi.org/10.1109/ICPC.2017.29
5. DeMarco, F., Xuan, J., Le Berre, D., Monperrus, M.: Automatic repair of buggy if conditions and missing preconditions with SMT. In: Proceedings of the 6th International Workshop on Constraints in Software Testing, Verification, and Analysis, pp. 30–39. ACM (2014)
6. Do, H., Elbaum, S., Rothermel, G.: Supporting controlled experimentation with testing techniques: an infrastructure and its potential impact. Empirical Softw. Eng. **10**(4), 405–435 (2005)
7. Durieux, T., Martinez, M., Monperrus, M., Sommerard, R., Xuan, J.: Automatic repair of real bugs: an experience report on the defects4J dataset (2015)
8. Gortázar, F., et al.: The elastest platform: supporting automation of end-to-end testing of large complex applications (2018)
9. Gortazár, F., Gallego, M., García, B., Carella, G.A., Pauls, M., Gheorghe-Pop, I.D.: Elastest-an open source project for testing distributed applications with failure injection. In: 2017 IEEE Conference on Network Function Virtualization and Software Defined Networks (NFV-SDN), pp. 1–2. IEEE (2017)
10. Gyimesi, P., et al.: BugsJS: a benchmark of Javascript bugs. In: Proceedings of 12th IEEE International Conference on Software Testing, Verification and Validation (ICST) (2019)
11. Hao, D., Zhang, L., Mei, H.: Test-case prioritization: achievements and challenges. Front. Comput. Sci. **10**(5), 769–777 (2016). https://doi.org/10.1007/s11704-016-6112-3
12. Hutchins, M., Foster, H., Goradia, T., Ostrand, T.: Experiments on the effectiveness of dataflow-and control-flow-based test adequacy criteria. In: Proceedings of 16th International Conference on Software Engineering, pp. 191–200. IEEE (1994)
13. Just, R., Jalali, D., Ernst, M.D.: Defects4J: a database of existing faults to enable controlled testing studies for Java programs. In: Proceedings of the 2014 International Symposium on Software Testing and Analysis ISSTA 2014, pp. 437–440. ACM, New York (2014). https://doi.org/10.1145/2610384.2628055. http://doi.acm.org/10.1145/2610384.2628055
14. Le Goues, C., Nguyen, T., Forrest, S., Weimer, W.: GenProg: a generic method for automatic software repair. IEEE Trans. Softw. Eng. **38**(1), 54–72 (2012)
15. Memon, A., et al.: Taming google-scale continuous testing. In: Proceedings of the 39th International Conference on Software Engineering: Software Engineering in Practice TrackICSE-SEIP 2017, pp. 233–242. IEEE Press, Piscataway (2017). https://doi.org/10.1109/ICSE-SEIP.2017.16
16. Myers, E.W.: Ano (ND) difference algorithm and its variations. Algorithmica **1**(1–4), 251–266 (1986)
17. Neelofar, Javed, M.Y., Mohsin, H.: An automated approach for software bug classification. In: 2012 Sixth International Conference on Complex, Intelligent, and Software Intensive Systems, pp. 414–419, July 2012. https://doi.org/10.1109/CISIS.2012.132
18. Nir, D., Tyszberowicz, S., Yehudai, A.: Locating regression bugs. In: Yorav, K. (ed.) HVC 2007. LNCS, vol. 4899, pp. 218–234. Springer, Heidelberg (2008). https://doi.org/10.1007/978-3-540-77966-7_18

19. Pingclasai, N., Hata, H., Matsumoto, K.: Classifying bug reports to bugs and other requests using topic modeling. In: 2013 20th Asia-Pacific Software Engineering Conference (APSEC), vol. 2, pp. 13–18, December 2013. https://doi.org/10.1109/APSEC.2013.105

20. Qi, Z., Long, F., Achour, S., Rinard, M.: An analysis of patch plausibility and correctness for generate-and-validate patch generation systems. In: Proceedings of the 2015 International Symposium on Software Testing and Analysis, pp. 24–36. ACM (2015)

21. Saha, R., Lyu, Y., Lam, W., Yoshida, H., Prasad, M.: Bugs. jar: a large-scale, diverse dataset of real-world java bugs. In: 2018 IEEE/ACM 15th International Conference on Mining Software Repositories (MSR), pp. 10–13. IEEE (2018)

22. Spacco, J., Strecker, J., Hovemeyer, D., Pugh, W.: Software repository mining with marmoset: an automated programming project snapshot and testing system. In: ACM SIGSOFT Software Engineering Notes, vol. 30, pp. 1–5. ACM (2005)

23. Xuan, J., et al.: Nopol: Automatic repair of conditional statement bugs in large-scale object-oriented programs. IEEE Trans. Softw. Eng. (2015, Underreview)

24. Yoo, S., Harman, M.: Regression testing minimization, selection and prioritization: a survey. Softw. Testing Verification Reliabil. **22**(2), 67–120 (2012)

25. Zhou, J., Zhang, H., Lo, D.: Where should the bugs be fixed? more accurate information retrieval-based bug localization based on bug reports. In: 2012 34th International Conference on Software Engineering (ICSE), pp. 14–24, June 2012. https://doi.org/10.1109/ICSE.2012.6227210

Towards Failure Prediction in Scientific Workflows Using Stochastic Petri Nets and Dynamic Logic

Bruno Lopes(✉)🔟 and Daniel de Oliveira🔟

Instituto de Computação, Universidade Federal Fluminense, Niterói, Brazil
{bruno,danielcmo}@ic.uff.br

Abstract. Scientific workflows are models composed of activities, parameters, data, and dependencies, whose goal is to implement a complex computer simulation. Scientific workflows are commonly managed by Workflow Management Systems (WfMS). Several existing workflows demand many computing resources since they process a massive volume of data. This way, High-Performance Computing (HPC) environments allied to parallelization techniques have to be applied to support the execution of such workflows. Although HPC environments offer several advantages, failures are a reality rather than a possibility due to the high number of compute nodes involved in the execution. Thus, WfMS should be able to calculate the probability of a failure occurs in order to spare resources. In this paper, we propose the usage of $\mathcal{DS}_3$, a dynamic logic tailored to reason about stochastic Petri nets, to verify and predict failures in scientific workflows.

Keywords: Scientific workflow · Stochastic Petri nets · Logic

1 Introduction

Scientific workflows (henceforth names only as workflows) may be defined as a formal specification of a scientific process, which represents the steps to be executed within an *in silico* scientific experiment [2,13]. Such steps (*i.e.*, activities) are commonly associated to program and/or services invocations that perform a series of transformations over scientific data, *i.e.*, data selection, data aggregation, filtering and summarization, *etc.* A workflow can be formally defined as a directed acyclic graph $Wf(A, Dep)$ where nodes $A = \{a_1, a_2, ..., a_n\}$ are the activities and the edges Dep represent the data dependencies among activities in A. Thus, given $a_i \mid (1 \leq i \leq n)$, the set $P = \{p_1, p_2, ..., p_m\}$ represents the possible input parameters (*e.g.*, values, file pointers, *etc*) for activity a_i that define the behavior of a_i.

Let us also define *activation* [9] as the smallest unit of work that can be processed in parallel and consumes a specific data chunk [7] and consider

This work was partially sponsored by CAPES, CNPq and FAPERJ.

$Ac = \{ac_1, ac_2, ..., ac_k\}$ as the set of activations of the workflow Wf. Each ac_i is associated with a specific activity a_j that is represented as $act(ac_i) = a_j$. Activations also present data dependencies, thus $input(ac_i) \in I$ and $output(ac_i) \in O$ and the dependency between two activations ac_i and ac_j can be represented as $dep(ac_i, ac_j) \leftrightarrow \exists r \in input(ac_j) | r \in output(ac_i) \wedge dep(act(ac_i), act(ac_j))$. Let us also define $PV_i = \{pv_{1i}, pv_{2i}, .., pv_{mi}\}$ as the parameter values (*e.g.*, values consumed by an activation ac_i during execution). Workflows are commonly modeled, enacted and monitored by complex engines called Workflow Management Systems (WfMS) that support the specification of the workflow in terms of executable artifacts (programs or services). Well-known WfMSs are Pegasus [3] and Swift/T [16], among others. The majority of these WfMS, in addition to the execution of activities and activations, capture historical data of the workflow, called provenance data [4].

Scientists commonly vary input parameters and data to evaluate a hypothesis. This parameter exploration is commonly data and compute-intensive and requires a parallel execution using high-performance computing (HPC) environments to produce results in a timely manner. In these environments, failures are a reality rather than a possibility due to the high number of processors and machines. Thus, it is far from trivial to identify possible failures in a workflow execution, especially when the workflow is composed of several activations executed in parallel in a HPC environment. Provenance data can play an important role in this failure prediction task since it can provide historical information that can be used to identify common failure patterns or to calculate the probability of a failure to occur. However, it is still an arduous task to identify such patterns that can be used by existing WfMS to predict failures and inform the scientist that a given activation ac_i consuming certain set of parameter values PV_i is likely to generate execution errors or produce undesired results.

In this paper, we propose the usage of $\mathcal{DS}_3$ [8], a dynamic logic tailored to reason about Stochastic Petri nets (SPN), to check and predict failures in workflows based on provenance data collected by WfMSs. It is well known that workflows benefit from Petri nets to check workflow executions that lead to the desired result, regardless of how it may execute, according to Aalst *et al.* [14]. The advantage of using $\mathcal{DS}_3$ in comparison with traditional Petri net approaches for predicting failures in workflows is that the expressive power is increased by combining Petri nets with logic models and it takes advantage of an stochastic approach specially when dealing with cases of high computational costs. We evaluate our approach using the astronomy Montage workflow running on a virtual cluster deployed on Amazon AWS.

2   The $\mathcal{DS}_3$ Logic

The logic $\mathcal{DS}_3$ [8] is a dynamic logic in which each program is a Stochastic Petri net. Among its advantages, we have that $\mathcal{DS}_3$ is proved to be sound, complete and decidable and has some deductive systems. We recover the definitions originally presented in Lopes *et al.* [8] that are required in this paper. The $\mathcal{DS}_3$ language consists of:

Propositional symbols: p, q..., where Φ is the set of all propositional symbols
Place names: *e.g.:* $a, b, c, d \ldots$
Transition types: $\mathbf{T_1}$:at_1b, $\mathbf{T_2}$:abt_2c and $\mathbf{T_3}$:at_3bc, each transition has a unique type
Petri net Composition symbol: $\odot$
Sequence of names: $S = \{\epsilon, s_1, \ldots\}$, where ϵ is the empty sequence. We use the notation $s \prec s'$ to denote that all names occurring in s also occur in s'.

A $\mathcal{DS}_3$ program is a pair (Π, Λ) where Π is a composition of transitions. A firing relation $f : S \times \pi_b \to S$ receives as input a sequence and a SPN and return a sequence that corresponds to the result of a firing in the net.

Definition 1. $\mathcal{DS}_3$ *Frame*
A frame for $\mathcal{DS}_3$ is a tuple $\mathcal{F}_3 = \langle W, R_\pi, M, (\Pi, \Lambda), \delta \rangle$ where

- *W is a non-empty set of states*
- *$M : W \to S$*
- *(Π, Λ) is a stochastic Petri*
- *$\delta(w, \pi) = \langle d_1, d_2, \ldots, d_n \rangle$ is the sequence of firing delays of the program $\pi \in \Pi$ in the world $w \in W$ respectively for each program $\pi_1 \odot \pi_2 \odot \cdots \odot \pi_n = \pi$*
- *we inductively define a binary relation R_η, for each Petri net program $\eta = \eta_1 \odot \eta_2 \odot \cdots \odot \eta_n$, as $R_\eta = \{(w, v) \mid \exists \eta_i, \exists u$ such that $s_i \prec M(u)$ and $wR_{\eta_i}u$ and $\delta(w, \eta_i) = \min(\delta(w, \Pi))$ and $uR_\eta v\}$ where $s_i = f(s, \eta_i)$, for all $1 \leq i \leq n$.*

Definition 2. $\mathcal{DS}_3$ *Model*
A model for $\mathcal{DS}_3$ is a pair $\mathcal{M} = \langle \mathcal{F}_3, \mathbf{V} \rangle$, where $\mathcal{F}_3$ is an $\mathcal{DS}_3$ frame and $\mathbf{V}$ is a valuation function $\mathbf{V} : \Phi \to 2^W$.

The probability of $\mathcal{M}_3, w \Vdash \langle s, \pi_b \rangle \varphi$ is (let $s = M(w)$)

$$\Pr(\mathcal{M}_3, w \Vdash \langle s, \pi_b \rangle \varphi \mid \delta(w, \Pi)) = \frac{\delta(w, \pi_b)}{\displaystyle\sum_{\pi_b \in \Pi : f(s, \pi_b) \neq \epsilon} \delta(w, \pi_b)}$$

So if we say that $\mathcal{M}_3, w \Vdash \langle s, \eta \rangle \varphi$ then it means that the program η beginning with the markup s has probability of running greater than one (i.e. the probability of a firing happens is greater than zero) and that when it stops φ holds in the current state.

3   System Design

In this section, we present how we couple the $\mathcal{DS}_3$ logic and the SPN framework with an existing WfMS. The $\mathcal{DS}_3$ is implemented within a component named

FoWL (Failure prediction in Workflow based on Logic). The architecture is composed of 4 main components: ETL Component (extractor), FoWL component, the WfMS and the provenance database.

The first component to be invoked is the *ETL* (Extract, Transform, and Load) component that extracts information from the provenance database and the workflow specification to be sent to *FoWL* component. It is worth noticing that the *ETL* component should be customized for each different type of provenance database (*e.g.,* relational, RDF, *etc*). In its current version, we implemented a python script that extracts information from the provenance database and represents it in XML. Once the ETL component converts the information, it invokes the FoWL component, which is a program that reads the produced XML and uses DS_3 logic to reason about stochastic Petri nets, to verify and predict activation failures in the input workflows. Once the failures are identified (with an associated probability), FoWL informs the WfMS in order to avoid (or stop) the execution of such activations. In this paper, we extended SciCumulus SWfMS [10] to load the list of activations that present high probability of failure. Since SciCumulus is a database-oriented WfMS (all data is stored in a relational database), it is simple to inform the WfMS what are the activations that present high failure probability using a SQL UPDATE command in the *eactivation* table, *i.e.,* each activation is represented in a tuple in the *eactivation* table and there is a field that informs the failure probability provided by FoWL. For more information about SciCumulus provenance schema, please refer to Oliveira *et al.* [10].

4   Experimental Evaluation

We modeled the Montage workflow in SciCumulus using Montage astronomy toolkit for assembling astronomical images into custom mosaics using a suitable format for large scale data processing of the sky. This toolkit comprises a set of components that provides astronomy image mosaic services to build mosaics in the Flexible Image Transport System (FITS) file format. FITS format respects the common astronomy coordinate system, arbitrary image sizes and rotations, and all World Coordinate System (WCS) map projections. The Montage workflow uses different astronomical images to blend them into custom mosaics, considering the necessary geometric transformations.

The Montage workflow is composed of nine activities. We have added an extra activity in the original Montage workflow that extracts the FITS images to be processed (this activity is not considered in the Petri net since it is a simple activation that only lists the files to be processed). This way, the first activity (List FITS) extracts several FITS files from a compressed file (obtained from an external astronomy repository - 2MASS[1]). Each input FITS file has several attributes, which are defined as attributes in the relations in the workflow algebra used in SciCumulus [9]. The second activity (Projection) computes the projection of these astronomy-positioning references into a specific plane (extraction of

---

[1] https://www.ipac.caltech.edu/2mass/releases/allsky/.

2 attributes and propagation of 19 previous attributes). Then, the following 3 activities join FITS projection files that are associated to the same mosaic (extraction of 2 attributes). Create Uncorrected Mosaic activity creates a mosaic without overlap interferences and color corrections and, as a result, it creates a JPG image. The other activities from the Montage workflow are defined to consider overlap interferences and color corrections in order to create a corrected custom mosaic. For more details about Montage, please refer to Jacob *et al.* [5].

4.1 The Montage Workflow as a Stochastic Petri Net

Figure 1(a) presents the translation from Montage workflow specification to a stochastic Petri net. The translation from Montage workflow specification to a SPN considers each node as a place and defines a transition for each dependence in the workflow. Using a $\mathcal{DS}_3$ model one can verify all the standard desired properties as the absence of deadlocks, liveness, *etc.* It is possible to improve the model for failure handling.

In Fig. 1(b) we also extend the basic translation to include failure prediction. Using provenance information of past failures we may model the presence of failures in the several activations of the workflow. Exponentially distributed random variables are widely used into the literature to model failures. We use the provenance data to identify activation failures and define transitions that represent the reaction, *i.e.* the actions that have to be performed when a failure occurs (*e.g.* e_1 and e_2); after that we estimate the parameter which by maximum likelihood is

$$\hat{\lambda} = \frac{n}{\sum_1^n x_i}. \tag{1}$$

Hence, it is possible to predict activation failures not only by simulation (as in ordinary Petri net models) but also using a $\mathcal{DS}_3$ model $\mathcal{M}_3 = \langle W, R_\pi, M, (\Pi, \Lambda), \mathbf{V} \rangle$. Let $\pi \in \Pi$ the correspondent SPN program and $e \in \Phi$ a propositional symbol that means that a failure occurred when $s61$ was being processed. To verify if it is possible that a failure may occur in $s61$ we only have to check if the transition e_1 is enabled. Supposing yes, to verify the probability of this failure occurring in a state w, we may compute

$$\Pr(\mathcal{M}_3, w \Vdash \langle s, s61e_1p \rangle e | \delta(w, \Pi)) = \frac{\delta(w, s61e_1p)}{\sum_{s61e_1p \in \Pi : f(s, s61e_1p) \neq \epsilon} \delta(w, s61e_1p)} \tag{2}$$

4.2 Results and Discussion

In this first experiment we considered 100 executions of Montage_50 instance as presented in the Workflow Generator site[2]. In these executions we have artificially inserted failures in 10 executions in order to have activations failures for $\mathcal{DS}_3$ to detect, *i.e.*, the executions failure rate is of 20%.

---

[2] https://confluence.pegasus.isi.edu/display/pegasus/workflowgenerator.

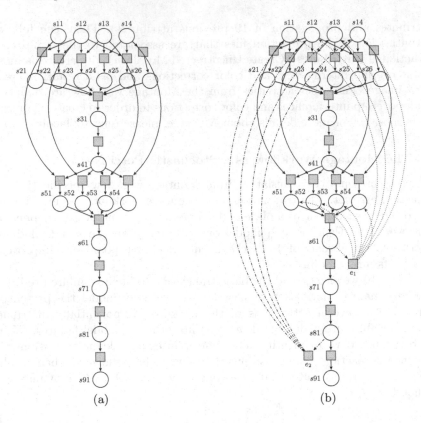

(a)   (b)

Fig. 1. (a) The Montage workflow as a Petri net and (b) The Montage work flow as a Petri net with failure handling

We artificially inserted failures in activations ID00003 (in 7 executions) and ID00002 (in 3 executions). Activations ID00011, ID00019, ID00023, ID00025, ID00029, ID00033, ID00041 and ID00046 have failed due to data dependencies to activation ID00003. On the other hand, activations ID00015, ID00018, ID00019, ID00032 and ID00040 have failed due to data dependencies to activation ID00002. Using Eq. 1 it is possible to estimate the parameters of the random variables to the Petri net and define the firing rates.

To verify if any two activations may execute in parallel (*e.g.* from $s41$ to $s51$ and $s52$), we only have to verify the results of the firing function. To verify for the probability of successfully processing $s31$ (let π the whole Petri net), we compute Compute $\Pr(\mathcal{M}, w \Vdash \langle M(w), s31t_1s41 \rangle \top \mid \delta(w, \pi))$, which results in computing $\dfrac{\delta(w, s31t_1s41)}{\sum\limits_{\pi_b \in \pi : f(M(w), \pi_b) \neq \epsilon} \delta(w, \pi_b)}$. In this experiment we achieved value 0.95.

We also can logically prove that entire workflow may fail (*e.g.* $\mathcal{M} \Vdash \neg[M(w), s31t_1s41]\top$) using model checking techniques (the implementation of such tools are considered in future work section as an ongoing work). For any other action in the workflow the aforementioned equation holds. What is interesting is the possibility of formally proving, when required, but it is also possible to have a probabilistic result when it is not possible (due to high computational efforts required) to use logical methods.

The Petri net will have two "failure handling" transitions. This idea is that the WfMS can perform modifications in the workflow specification or scheduling in order to redo necessary computations in case of failure to achieve the desired results.

5 Related Work

The relation between scientific workflows and Petri nets has been widely discussed [11]. Petri nets may be used as a design language for complex workflows [14] with a wide framework to the analysis correctness verification [12,14]. Their usage leads to the possibility of verify conceptual properties as the absence of deadlocks, liveness, *etc.* Zhao *et al.* [15] propose a modeling method based on CCS to describe behaviors between activities in workflows. They add constraints of dependency and parameters into activations expressions. They also provide a specification language to establish a formal model. Their approach is evaluated in a case study using a developed prototype.

Relating scientific workflows with logic is also already present into the literature [1]. Logical frameworks are very powerful but the computational complexity of satisfiability and theorem proving may lead to impracticable scenarios (the SAT problem complexity of CTL [1] is known to be EXPTime-Complete). Liang and Zhao [6] propose a verification method for scientific workflows that is based on propositional logic. This logic-based workflow verification approach presents some advantages such as logical formalism and its ability to handle generic activity-based process models. They showed that this approach is capable of detecting process anomalies in workflow models, but they do not consider probabilities.

The $\mathcal{DS}_3$ logic [8] is a system tailored to reason about stochastic Petri nets. Despite its high complexity of SAT-problem, $\mathcal{DS}_3$ has stochastic components that make it possible to use stochastic reasoning when logical approaches may be impracticable.

6 Conclusions and Future Work

This paper presents an initial effort on combining logic, a formal method and probability to model and reason about failures in large-scale scientific workflows. We show how to model scientific workflows as Petri nets and how to use $\mathcal{DS}_3$ logic to reason about activation failures.

Using the Montage workflow we defined an experiment from which we calculated the parameters of the SPN and presented how to compute some desired properties, focusing on failure prediction, *i.e.*, we are able to discover the probability of an activation failure based on provenance data.

Future work includes more sophisticated experiments with more instances of Montage and new workflows, and the integration with some tools that automatize the reasoning (an ongoing work). This is a step towards workflow systems to be able to certify and/or predict failures automatically.

References

1. Curcin, V., Ghanem, M.M., Guo, Y.: Analysing scientific workflows with Computational Tree Logic. Cluster Comput. **12**(4), 399–418 (2009)
2. Deelman, E., Gannon, D., Shields, M., Taylor, I.: Workflows and e-science: an overview of workflow system features and capabilities. FGCS **25**(5), 528–540 (2009)
3. Deelman, E., Mehta, G., Singh, G., Su, M.-H., Vahi, K.: Pegasus: mapping large-scale workflows to distributed resources. In: Taylor, I.J., Deelman, E., Gannon, D.B., Shields, M. (eds.) Workflows for e-Science, pp. 376–394. Springer, Heidelberg (2007). https://doi.org/10.1007/978-1-84628-757-2_23
4. Freire, J., Koop, D., Santos, E., Silva, C.T.: Provenance for computational tasks: a survey. In: CSE, pp. 20–30 (2008)
5. Jacob, J.C., et al.: Montage: an astronomical image mosaicking toolkit. **1**, 10036 (2010)
6. Liang, Q.A., Zhao, J.L.: Verification of unstructured workflows via propositional logic. ICIS **2008**, 247–252 (2008)
7. Liu, J., Pacitti, E., Valduriez, P., Mattoso, M.: A survey of data-intensive scientific workflow management. JoGC **13**(4), 457–493 (2015)
8. Lopes, B., Benevides, M., Haeusler, E.H.: Extending propositional dynamic logic for petri nets. Elec. Notes Theoret. Comput. Sci. **305**(11), 67–83 (2014)
9. Ogasawara, E., De Oliveira, D., Valduriez, P., Dias, J., Porto, F., Mattoso, M.: An algebraic approach for data-centric scientific workflows. Proc. VLDB Endow. **4**(12), 1328–1339 (2011)
10. Oliveira, D., Ogasawara, E., Ocaña, K., Baião, F., Mattoso, M.: An adaptive parallel execution strategy for cloud-based scientific workflows. CCPE **24**(13), 1531–1550 (2012)
11. Salimifard, K., Wright, M.: Petri net-based modelling of workflow systems: an overview. EJOR **134**(3), 664–676 (2001)
12. ter Hofstede, A.H.M., Orlowska, M.E., Rajapakse, J.: Verification problems in conceptual workflow specifications. Data Knowl. Eng. **24**(3), 239–256 (1998)
13. Travassos, G.H., Barros, M.O.: Contributions of in virtuo and in silico experiments for the future of empirical studies in software engineering. In 2nd Workshop on Empirical Software Engineering the Future of Empirical Studies in Software Engineering, pp. 117–130 (2003)
14. van der Aalst, W.M.P.: The application of Petri nets to workflow management. J. Circ. Syst. Comput. **8**(1), 21–66 (1998)
15. Zhao, L., Li, Q., Liu, X., Du, N.: A modeling method based on CCS for workflow. In: ICUIMC 2009, pp. 376–384 (2009)
16. Zhao, Y., et al.: Swift: fast, reliable, loosely coupled parallel computation. In: 2007 IEEE Congress on Services, pp. 199–206. IEEE (2007)

RE, MDD and Agile

From Rigorous Requirements and User Interfaces Specifications into Software Business Applications

Ivo Gamito[✉] and Alberto Rodrigues da Silva[ORCID]

INESC-ID, Instituto Superior Técnico, Universidade de Lisboa, Lisbon, Portugal
{ivo.gamito,alberto.silva}@tecnico.ulisboa.pt

Abstract. Software applications have been developed with multiple programming languages (specific software libraries and frameworks) and deployed on various software and hardware infrastructures. This paper introduces and discusses the ASL language (short for "Application Specification Language") that combines constructs from two previous languages: ITLingo RSL and IFML. ASL specifications are strict and rigorous sentences that allow us to define both requirements and user interfaces aspects of software applications in a consistent and integrated way. Alike RSL, and differently from IFML, ASL is a controlled natural language with a textual concrete syntax. Furthermore, the proposed approach includes model-to-model and model-to-code transformations that may considerably improve the quality and productivity of both the requirements specification and the development of software applications.

Keywords: Requirements engineering · Model-driven engineering · Web engineering · ITLingo RSL · IFML · ITLingo ASL

1 Introduction

Currently, developers use expressive programming languages, software libraries and frameworks that help them develop a multitude of software applications. However, developers have to master details of these tools and technologies which [1] are complex, require long learning curves, and raise challenges like the need to create appealing and cross-platform user interfaces, and the need to deal with cross-cutting concerns like scalability, performance, security and others [2].

In this scope, the importance of requirements engineering (RE) has been crucial to the development and management of software, and to reduce software errors at the early stages of the development process. RE has had a crucial role in different stages of software engineering and has provided a variety of approaches [3]. RE practices have been essential to give a broad understanding of the problem-domain before starting any sort of effort toward the design, development and deployment of a given solution, as well as to prevent rework costs [4, 5]. Also, RE has also been crucial for the success of a project and it has dealt with socio-technical challenges like the adoption of elicitation techniques, communication difficulties, and or with conflicting and ambiguous requirements [6].

© Springer Nature Switzerland AG 2020
M. Shepperd et al. (Eds.): QUATIC 2020, CCIS 1266, pp. 459–473, 2020.
https://doi.org/10.1007/978-3-030-58793-2_37

System requirements are the description of what services and features the system shall provide, as well as its quality attributes and other constraints [5]. These requirements reflect the needs of different stakeholders, like customers, end-users, but also software engineers. System requirements are often broadly classified as functional (FRs), non-functional requirements (NFRs) and constraints. They are statements of features and services the system shall provide and may define how the system responds to its users' inputs, what outputs to generate. FRs may be defined in multiple NFRs, like use cases or scenarios. On the other hand, non-functional requirements define the cross-cutting quality attributes of the system, such as availability, performance, usability, or security. Finally, constraints are requirements that can affect the product itself or the involved development process, and can be defined as a technology, legal or process constraints.

We propose in this paper an approach to improve the RE process by mitigating some of its problems, namely in what concerns the specification and validation of requirements. This is also a model-driven approach. i.e., an approach that considers models not just documentation artifacts, but also central artifacts in the software engineering area, allowing automatic creation of software applications starting from those models. Model-driven engineering (MDE) involves the adoption of languages and transformation engines to address the diversity and complexity of software platforms and frameworks [7]. In the scope of MDE, we consider a model as an abstraction of a system often used to replace the system under study [8]. MDE aims to raise the abstraction level of software specifications and increase automation in software development. Using executable model transformations, a model can be transformed into another (lower level) model until it can be transformed or generated into (programing language) artifacts, or it can be directly executed by some interpretation engine [8].In this context, we introduce and discuss the ASL specification language ("Application Specification Language") that combines constructs from two languages (further details in the next section): ITLingo RSL [4, 9, 20, 23] and IFML [10]. Like with ITLingo RSL, the ASL specifications (or ASL models) are strict and rigorous sentences. However, ASL is comprehensive enough to specify user interface (UI) aspects, based on the concepts found in modeling languages like IFML. ASL gathers characteristics and advantages from both RSL and IFML. Likewise RSL, and differently from IFML (and that is a visual modeling language), ASL is a controlled natural language with a textual concrete syntax (that is the reason we named it as a "specification language" instead of a "modeling language"). Also, to the rigorous and systematic specification of software applications, we show that it is possible to take advantage of these specifications to semi-automatically generate software applications following an MDE approach: this means that with appropriate tools, an ASL user can create web applications, which can be generated through automatic transformations techniques, from ASL rigorous specifications.

2 Background

This section briefly introduces ITLingo RSL and IFML languages, in which the ASL is based on.

2.1 RSL

ITLingo RSL (or just RSL for brevity) is a specification language created to mitigate problems that arise when writing requirements. RSL is a controlled natural language that helps writing requirements and test specifications in a systematic, rigorous and consistent way. RSL includes a rich set of constructs logically arranged in views according to concerns that exist at different abstraction levels, such as stakeholders, actors, data entities, use cases, goals, use case tests [9, 20, 23, 24].

RSL constructs are logically classified according to two cross-cutting dimensions: abstraction levels and RE specific concerns. According to the abstraction level, the constructs can be used to define businesses, applications, software or even hardware systems. According to the RE concerns dimension, the constructs are classified in the following aspects: active structure, behavior, passive structure, requirements, tests, relations and sets, and others [9, 23]. Spec. 1 illustrates a simple example of an RSL specification that defines the actor "Blogger", whom participates in the use-case "Manage Blog Posts", which involves the management of the data entity "Blog's Post".

```
Actor aU_Blogger "Blogger": User

DataEntity e_Post "Blog Post": Document [
    attribute Id "Post ID" : Integer [isNotNull isUnique]
    attribute State "Post State" : DataEnumeration enum_PostState
    attribute Title "Post Title" : String(30) [isNotNull]
    attribute Body "Post Body" : Text
    [...] ]

UseCase uc_1_ManagePost "Manage Blog Posts": EntitiesManage [
    actorInitiates aU_Blogger
    dataEntity e_Post
    actions Create, Read, Update, Delete]
```

Spec 1. Simple example of a RSL specification.

2.2 IFML

Interaction Flow Modeling Language (IFML) is a standard modeling language in the field of software engineering. IFML allows us to define platform independent models of graphical user interfaces (GUIs) of software applications. IFML describes the structure and the behavior of the applications as perceived by end-users [10].

IFML brings benefits to the development process of application front-ends, namely [11]: supports the specification of application front-ends with different perspectives (the connection with the business logic, the data model, and the graphical presentation layer); isolates the front-end specification from implementation-specific details; (iii) separates the concerns between roles in the interaction design; and enables the communication of UI design to non-technical stakeholders.

IFML was developed by WebRatio and inspired by the previous WebML notation [22], as well as by other experiences in the Web modeling field [10]. IFML intends to solve a problem mentioned above in the introduction: the variety of hardware devices and software platforms and, consequently, the complexity of designing and developing software applications. IFML supports the specification of the following perspectives [10]: UI structure, UI content specification, events, events transition specification and parameter binding. The UI structure specification consists of the UI containers, while the UI content specification focus on the data contained. The events specification consists of the definition of events that may affect the UI while the specification of events transition defines the changes to apply after those events occur. Finally, specifications of parameter binding consist of the definition of the input-output dependencies between view components and between view components and actions. Figure 4 (left) shows a simple example of an IFML model.

3   ASL Language

The ASL language combines the main aspects of the RSL and the IFML languages to support the specification of software applications systematically and rigorously. These applications can also be classified as "business applications, in which data is a core asset, and support several business activities, like planning, forecasting, control, coordination, decision making and operational activities [17]. Popular classes of software business applications are e-commerce, ERP (enterprise resource planning), CRM (customer relationship management), SCM (supply chain management).

This section introduces the ASL architecture. This discussion is supported by a simple running example named "MyTinyBlog" application, described as follows: «*MyTinyBlog is a simple web application that allows a blogger to setup and manage his own blog. The blogger may add categories and posts to the blog. Each blog post has a title, a body, the creation date and authors. Also, a post can be classified by a given category, and can be in one of the following states: "Draft" or "Published". Only published posts are visible to the blog's audience (readers). Readers can add and read comments of a published post but can only edit or delete their own comments»*.

Figures 1 and 2 illustrate some models of the MyTinyBlog application: the domain model and the use-cases model. The main feature of this application involves managing blog posts through typical create, read, update and delete (CRUD) operations.

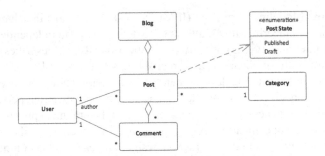

Fig. 1. MyTinyBlog data model (UML class diagram)

3.1   Data Entities

ASL adopts and extends the definition of the DataEntity construct as defined initially in RSL [9, 20]. DataEntity is the construct used to define domain concepts or information

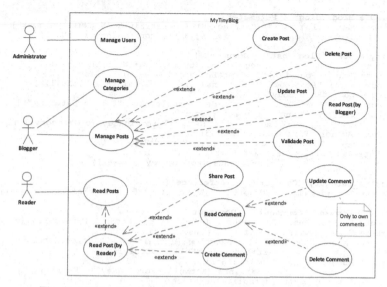

Fig. 2. MyTinyBlog use cases model (UML use cases diagram)

entities such as goods, people, or business transactions. A DataEntity denotes an individual structural entity that might include the specification of attributes, foreign keys and other data constraints [9]. A DataEntity can be classified by type and subtype. The types are the following: (1) Parameter, which can include data that is specific to an industry or business; (2) Reference, simple reference data, which is required to operate a business process; (3) Master, data assets of the business, usually reflects more complex data (e.g., customers, vendors, projects); (4) Document, worksheet data that might be converted into transactions later (e.g., invoices); and (5) Transaction, the operational transaction data of the business (e.g., paid invoices).

In the MyTinyBlog example, we define the following data entities, as also suggested in Fig. 1: Blog, Blog Post, Category, Comment and User (see Spec. 2).

```
DataEntity e_Blog "Blog" : Parameter [
    attribute Name "Blog Name" : String(30) [ constraints (NotNull Unique) ]
    attribute Slogan "Blog Slogan" : String(80) [ constraints (NotNull) ]

DataEntity e_Post "Blog Post" : Document [
    attribute Id "Post ID" : Integer [ constraints (NotNull Unique) ]
    attribute State "Post State" : DataEnumeration enum_PostState
    attribute Title "Post Title" : String(30) [ constraints ( NotNull) ]
    attribute Body "Post Body" : Text
    attribute Date "Post Date" : Datetime [defaultValue "CurrentDateTime" ]
    attribute Category "Post Category" : String
                        [ constraints (NotNull ForeignKey (e_Category)) ]
    attribute Author "Post Author" : String
                    [ constraints ( NotNull  ForeignKey   e_User) ]
    attribute LastEditAuthor "Last Edit Author" : String
                    [ constraints (ForeignKey (e_User)) ] ]

DataEntity e_Category "Category" :  Reference [
    attribute CategoryName "Category Name" : String(30) [constraints (Unique)] ]

DataEntity e_Comment "Comments" : Document [
    attribute PostID "Post ID": Integer [constraints (NotNull ForeignKey (e_Post))]
    attribute Text "Comment" : String [ constraints  NotNull) ]
    attribute Date "Comment Date" : Datetime [defaultValue "CurrentDateTime"
                        constraints (NotNull ReadOnly)]
    attribute Author "Post Author" : String
                        [constraints (NotNull  ForeignKey (e_User))]
    attribute Like: Boolean [defaultValue "True"]]

DataEntity e_User "Blog User" : Master [
  attribute UserName: String [ constraints (NotNull Unique) ]
  attribute RegistrationDate : Datetime [defaultValue "CurrentDateTime"]
  tag (name "User" value "User") ]
```

Spec 2. Specification of MyTinyBlog's data entities (in ASL)

After defining the data entities, DataEntityClusters can be defined. A DataEntity-Cluster construct denotes a cluster of structural entities that present logical arrangements among them and are commonly used in the context of use cases.

In this example, we define three data clusters with specific roles to their involved data entities. The "main" role represents the primary data entity involved, while the "child" role represents a "part of" (or "child") data entity, and the "uses" role represents other logical dependencies between entities [9]. Furthermore, the tag "Inline" with value "Stacked", in the ec_PostComment cluster, is used as an extended property to influence model-to-model or model-to-code transformations (in what respect the UI definition of the application).

```
DataEntityCluster ec_Blog "Blog" : Parameter [main e_Blog]
DataEntityCluster ec_Users "Users" : Parameter [main e_Users]
DataEntityCluster ec_Post "Posts" : Document
    [main e_Post uses e_Category uses e_User ]
DataEntityCluster ec_Category "Categories" : Reference [main e_Category]
DataEntityCluster ec_PostComment  : Document [master e_Post child e_Comment
    uses e_Category tag (name "Inline" value "Stacked") ]
```

Spec 3. Specification of data entity clusters (in ASL)

3.2 Use Cases

A use case is defined as a sequence of interactions between an actor(s) and the system under consideration, which gives some value to the actor [9]. Use cases is a popular technique of modelling user tasks, that can be complemented with informal storyboards and free-form scenarios [9]. Likewise with the RSL, ASL includes the UseCase construct that allows to define several properties such as: the involved DataEntityCluster; the actor that initiates the use-case and other participating actors or the actions that may be performed in the use case scope, e.g. CRUD actions.

In the MyTinyBlog example (see Spec. 4), we define the ContextActor "Blogger" that creates and manages blog posts. The use case "Manage Blog Posts" is initiated by the "Blogger" that involves the management of data cluster "Blog Posts" (ec_Post) with CRUD actions and a validation action.

```
ContextActor aU_Admin "Administrator": User
ContextActor aU_Blogger "Blogger": User
ContextActor aU_Reader " Reader": User
UseCase uc_1_ManageUsers "Manage Users": EntitiesManage [
    actorInitiates aU_Administrator
    dataEntity ec_Users
    actions aCreate, aRead, aDelete, aUpdate ]
UseCase uc_2_ManagePosts "Manage Blog Posts": EntitiesManage [
    actorInitiates aU_Blogger
    dataEntity ec_Post
    actions aCreate, aRead, aDelete, aUpdate, aValidate ]

UseCase uc_3_ManageCategories "Manage Posts Categories": EntitiesManage [
    actorInitiates aU_Blogger
    dataEntity ec_Category
    actions aCreate, aRead, aDelete, aUpdate ]

UseCase uc_4_ReadPosts "Read Blog Posts": EntitiesBrowse [
    actorInitiates aU_Reader
    dataEntity ec_Post
    actions aRead, aShare, aAddComment ]

UseCase uc_5_CreateComment "Manage Comment on Post": EntitiesManage [
    actorInitiates aU_Reader
    dataEntity ec_PostComment
    actions aCreate, aRead, aDelete ]
```
Spec 4. Specification of MyTinyBlog's actors and use cases (in ASL)

3.3 User Interface Elements

As seen above, using ASL we can define Data Entities, Data Entities Clusters, Use Cases, Context Actors and other constructs needed to specify the application. We may also define UI elements, namely (and following the IFML terminology): UI containers, UI components and UI parts. The rules to express such elements in ASL are aligned with the IFML definition. The UI components supported by ASL are of the following types: List, Details, Form, Dialog and Menu. These UI components can be further classified as different sub-types like List-MultiChoice, List-Tree, List-Table, etc. as suggested in Fig. 4 (Table 1).

Table 1. Supported types used for the UIViewComponent definition

Type	List	Detail	Form	Dialog	Menu
Sub-type	MultiChoice		Simple	Success	Main
	Tree		MasterDetail	Error	Contextual
	Table		Other	Warning	
	Nested			Info	
				Message	

4   The ASL-Based Approach

Figure 3 suggests the approach proposed to systematically and rigorously define software applications based on the ASL language. This approach includes the possibility of automatically generating the software application for a specific software platform.

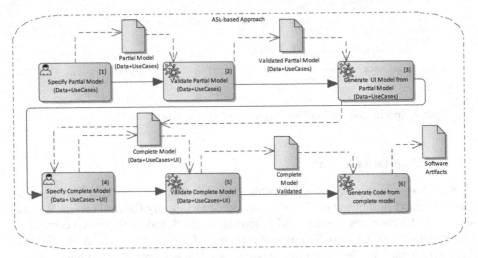

Fig. 3. ASL-based proposed approach

The proposed approach consists in 6 main tasks, represented in Fig. 3. Task 1 starts with a developer specifying the data and use cases models. Then, Task 2 automatically validates that partial model. If this model is valid, the ASL may run tool support may run model-to-model transformations to generate ASL UI specifications (Task 3) automatically. Then, in the Task 4, the developer can still add or change the generated model with their preferences and repeat the process (this is not illustrated in the figure for the sake of legibility). After this hybrid set of manual and automatic tasks, the complete model shall be validated (Task 5) before running model-to-code transformations (Task 6), and producing the source code artifacts for the target software infrastructure.

4.1 Model-to-Model Transformation

The proposed approach follows an idea initially introduced with the XIS approach [12]: the idea of smart and dummy modeling approaches. According to that approach, the designer has just to define the Domain, Business Entities, Actors and Use Cases views (based on the XIS terminology), and then the User Interfaces views are automatically generated based on model-to-model (M2M) transformations and a predefined set of UI patterns [12].

We integrate that "smart approach" to the ASL approach, which allows to generate UI specifications, as referred above in Task 3. These generated ASL files include UI specifications that depend on the data entities and use cases previously defined. For instance, considering the use-case defined in Spec. 4 (i.e., use case "Manage Blog Posts"(uc_1_ManagePost)), it generates UI elements to support CRUD actions of posts. The "databinding" mentions the e_Post entity. Features or actions like Listing, filtering and searching of e_Post can be then manually customized.

```
//Search
component uiCo_Search_e_Post: Details [
    dataBinding e_Post [searchAttributes e_Post.Title, e_Post.Id ]]
```
Spec 5. Generated specification for searching on MyTinyBlog (in ASL)

As suggested in Spec. 5 and Fig. 4, the specification of that UI list table can be subject of further customization, like the definition of data attributes can be considered for filter and search features, or we can even customize the properties of each data attribute.

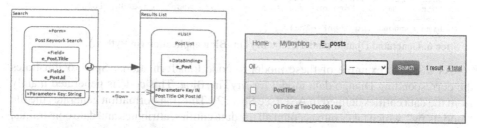

Fig. 4. Search posts: IFML model (left) and UI (right)

4.2 Model-to-Code Transformation

The transformation referred above as Task-3 generates ASL UI specifications, but the target software application (e.g., MyTinyBlog) is not yet developed and deployed. However, a complete specification of the application under consideration can be used to produce the target application into a different number of software frameworks. As a proof of concept, we have developed model-to-code transformations into the Django web framework. Django is an open-source high-level Python Web framework that encourages rapid development and clean, pragmatic design [13, 23].

```python
from django.db import models
from datetime import datetime
from django.contrib.auth.models import User

ENUM_POSTSTATE_CHOICES = (('published','Published'),('draft','Draft'),)

class e_User(models.Model):

    User = models.OneToOneField(User, on_delete=models.CASCADE)
    UserName = models.CharField(max_length=30)
    RegistrationDate = models.DateTimeField(default=datetime.now, blank=True)

class e_Post(models.Model):

    Id = models.IntegerField()
    State = models.CharField(max_length=15, choices=ENUM_POSTSTATE_CHOICES)
    Title = models.CharField(max_length=100)
    Body = models.TextField()
    Date = models.DateTimeField(default=datetime.now, blank=True)
    Category = models.ForeignKey(e_Category, on_delete=models.CASCADE, relat-
ed_name='PostCategory')
    Author = models.ForeignKey(e_User, on_delete=models.CASCADE, relat-
ed_name='PostAuthor')
    LastEditAuthor = models.ForeignKey(e_User, on_delete=models.CASCADE, relat-
ed_name='LastEditAuthor')

class e_Blog(models.Model):

    Name = models.CharField(max_length=100)
    Slogan = models.CharField(max_length=100)
    State = models.CharField(max_length=15, choices=ENUM_POSTSTATE_CHOICES)

class e_Comment(models.Model):

    PostID = models.ForeignKey(e_Post, on_delete=models.CASCADE, relat-
ed_name='PostID')
    Text = models.CharField(max_length=100)
    Date = models.DateTimeField(default=datetime.now, blank=True)
    Author = models.ForeignKey(e_User, on_delete=models.CASCADE, relat-
ed_name='CommentAuthor')
    Like = models.BooleanField()
```

Spec 6. Generated Django model of the MyTinyBlog application (in Python)

As a simple example of these model-to-code transformations, Spec. 6 illustrates the corresponding Django data model for MyTinyBlog. This code is generated mainly from the data entities defined in ASL (see Spec. 2). This transformation generates the file "models.py", which takes into account all the data entities, attributes and data constraints, including foreign keys constraints.

This generated Python file defines the domain model with the application's data structure and allows to create and update the respective database. Then, a developer can customize and refine that model and still add more information (by default, Django uses SQLite database to store the data [13]).

Users (who were given permissions) can create, read, update or delete the blog posts using the Django admin site [13]. This site reads metadata from the models and provides a simple model-centric interface.

To perform CRUD operations, we need to register those models in the "admin.py" file. This file is created by default when a Django project is started. However, we replace it with new settings; It shall contain the models to be registered, and other constraints generated from the ASL specifications files (spec. 5). These options are visible in the generated application, as suggested in Fig. 5.

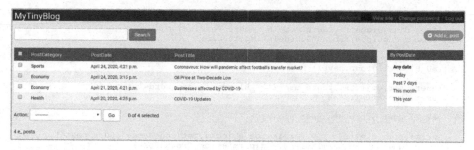

Fig. 5. MyTinyBlog posts list

4.3 Actors and Permissions

The implemented model-to-code transformations can also speed up the process of managing users and permissions (see Table 2 for some concepts mapping between ASL and Django). Python interpreter allows to create groups and assign permissions to users. However, Django Admin provides a built-in authentication system that allows the same features through a simple, intuitive interface [14].

Table 2. ASL to Django – Concepts mapping

ASL	Django
Context Actor	Group instance
Context Actor (name)	User
Use Case Actions	Permissions

In the MyTinyBlog application, the blog administrator oversees those tasks. In his turn, the blog editor should be able to create, read, update and delete posts. ASL tool generates a Python script to insert groups and users in the database. This script also assigns user groups different permissions. To quickly validate the authorization features, this script adds one user to each user group. All these settings can be later directly managed by a superuser using the Django admin site. (If logged in as a superuser, the user can create, edit, and delete any object; he can as well modify groups/permissions [14]).

```
from django.contrib.auth.models import Group
from django.contrib.auth.models import Permission
from django.contrib.auth.models import User

aU_Blogger_group = Group(name='aU_Blogger_group')
aU_Blogger_group.save()

user=User.objects.create_user('aU_Blogger', password='password')
user.is_staff=True
user.save()
aU_Blogger_group.user_set.add(user)

permission_CreatePost = Permission.objects.get(codename='add_e_post')
aU_Blogger_group.permissions.add(permission_CreatePost)
```

Spec 7. Example of generated Django roles script of the MyTinyBlog application (in Python).

5 Related Work

Some approaches and tools have either improved and accelerated how the community has produced software applications, either developed by the industry (e.g., Mendix, Outsystems, or WebRatio) or by research settings (e.g., EMF on Rails, ADM, XIS or ITLingo RSL).

Mendix is a commercial platform designed to enable different groups of people to create software that delivers business value. It was founded in the early 2000 s with the belief that software development could be improved with a paradigm shift [15]. Mendix builds a wide range of transactional, event-driven, and adjacent applications for all kinds of industries [15]. In Mendix perspective, it is becoming harder to keep up to date with the evolving number of programming tools and languages across the spectrum [15]. To reduce the development effort and to improve the feedback loop, Mendix follows a model-driven approach that includes tools like Mendix Studio and Mendix Studio Pro. These tools provide visual drag-and-drop features for UI, data, logic, and navigation using no-code or low-code development [15].

OutSystems is another commercial platform for low-code rapid application development with advanced capabilities for enterprise mobile and web apps [16]. Starting in 2001, OutSystems recognized that a vast majority of software projects were failing, due to multiple reasons. Therefore, OutSystems software is an integrated development environment that covers the entire development lifecycle, namely: development, quality assurance, deployment, monitoring and management [16].

Mendix and Outsystems platforms surpass ASL transformations by providing a user-friendly interface that allows development of applications with features and customization aspects. ASL provides a good start for many situations due to its flexibility and extensibility. Using a lower code-level, it can be challenging for people that do not usually work with programming languages and other IT tools. Still, it may simplify the communication of the software application's vision. From the generated application, we still have control over the necessary code to scale the web application.

EMF on Rails proposes an approach that combines MDE with automation frameworks for web development like Spring Roo [18]. It uses ATL, a rule-based declarative model transformation language, where "transformations are specified by mapping object

patterns from the source model into patterns of the target model". Like ASL, it acceler-
ates the generation of CRUD operations on data models [18]. A difference of our project
and EMF on Rails transformations is when their impact is more visible, as ASL promotes a better understanding of requirements at the start and final specifications through
interfaces and use-cases specifications.

ADM (Ariadne Development Method) is another approach with the primary goal
of accelerating the development of web systems [21]. Like ASL, it offers constructs to
specify these systems making use of Labyrinth++. This tool allows the specification of
all the components for web systems and includes a pattern language. Those patterns are
organized according to the nature of the problem they solve and make the development
of solution easier for less-experienced web developers [21].

WebML (Web Modeling Language) is a domain-specific language for designing
complex, distributed, multi-actor, and adaptive applications deployed on the Web and
Service-Oriented Architectures using Web Services [3]. WebML provides graphical, yet
formal, specifications, embodied in a complete design process, which can be assisted by
visual design tools. It was extended to cover a broader spectrum of front-end interfaces,
thus resulting in the Interaction Flow Modeling Language (IFML), adopted as a standard
by the OMG. Formerly known as the WebML, it is now IFML because it is no longer
limited to web development but also used for mobile apps [11].

XIS is a research project that has developed and evaluated mechanisms and tools
to produce business applications more efficiently and productively than it was done
[12]. XIS intends to reduce costs and improve the fulfillment of the requirements in
software production. XIS approach defends that the most significant effort in a project
shall not be in the implementation phase; these activities shall be performed almost
automatically, based on high-level and platform-independent specifications. Defining
the right specifications shall be the main effort of the developers. XIS also defends
a model-driven approach for designing interactive systems at a platform-independent
level, considering its modeling languages (i.e., the XIS* languages) that are defined
as UML profiles [25–27]. The approach discussed in this paper gathers the benefits
from the tools and approaches mentioned above. For example, like the IFML, it supports a platform-independent description of graphical user interfaces. Like RSL, but on
the contrary of IFML, the concrete syntax of ASL specs are textual and consequently
more natural to be rigorously defined and validated. ASL adapts the XIS smart approach, where UI models can be generated from high-level models. Unlike XIS, ASL
can allow to specify and to automatize the process of creating different types of users,
assigning distinct roles and respective permissions. Due to its platform-independent and
human-friendly text-based syntax, ASL specifications are more open and easier to be
manipulated and interoperated comparing with the options referred above, namely the
commercial solutions. One relevant work to explore in the future is to verify if ASL
could be suitable to support interoperability between the models developed with these
low-code or no-code platforms.

6 Conclusion

This paper discusses a new approach that combines the disciplines of requirements
engineering and web engineering. This approach intends to address the followings issues:

How to better specify requirements and business applications' (user interfaces) in an integrated way and how to increase the productivity of developers by automatizing the production of artifacts like technical documentation and software code.

We discuss some existing solutions, namely those mostly related to the RSL and IFML languages, in which the ASL language design is based. ASL allows to rigorously specify requirements (namely use cases with their relationships with actors and data entities), but also to specify user interface elements of the applications. We show that this language can be combined with tools that support both model-to-model and model-to-code transformations, and thus can considerably improve the quality and productivity of both the requirements definition and the development of these applications. We support the discussion with a simple but effective example, considering a popular class of web applications (i.e., a Blog application) on top of a popular Python-based framework (the Django framework).

Future research shall consider improving the customization of either the specification and generation of the business applications and shall specify and develop multiple cases studies. The integration with other popular software (e.g., NodeJS, JavaScript frameworks, .NET) and low-code frameworks (e.g., Mendix, OutSystems or Genio [19]) can also be considered as they can bring more flexibility to this solution. This research shall discuss how to consider how to deal with cross-cutting quality attributes such as availability, performance, usability or security.

Acknowledgments. Work supported by funds under FCT UID/CEC/50021/2019 and 02/SAICT/2017/29360.

References

1. Ousterhout, J.K.: A Philosophy of Software Design. Yaknyam Press, Palo Alto (2018)
2. Martin, R.C.: Clean Architecture: A Craftsman's Guide to Software Structure and Design, 1st edn. Prentice Hall, Upper Saddle River (2017)
3. Al-Fedaghi, S.: Developing web applications. Int. J. Softw. Eng. Appl. **5**(2), 57–68 (2011)
4. Ferreira, D., Silva, A.R.: RSLingo: an information extraction approach toward formal requirements specifications. In: 2nd IEEE International Workshop on Model-Driven Requirements Engineering. IEEE Computer Society (2012)
5. Sommerville, I.: Software Engineering, 9th edn. Pearson, Boston (2011)
6. Shah, T., Patel, S.: A review of requirement engineering issues and challenges in various software development methods. Int. J. Comput. Appl. **99**(15), 36–45 (2014)
7. Schmidt, D.: Model-driven engineering. IEEE Comput. **39**, 41–47 (2006)
8. Silva, A.R.: Model-driven engineering: a survey supported by a unified conceptual model. Comput. Lang. Syst. Struct. **43**, 139–155 (2015)
9. Silva, A.R.: Rigorous specification of use cases with the RSL language. In: Proceedings of the Information Systems Development (ISD 2019) Conference. AIS (2019)
10. OMG: Interaction Flow Modeling Language Specification Version 1.0. https://www.omg.org/spec/IFML/1.0/. Accessed 25 Apr 2020
11. Brambilla, M., Fraternali, P.: Interaction flow modeling language: model-driven UI engineering of web and mobile apps with IFML (2014)
12. Silva, A.R., Saraiva, J., Silva, R., Martins, C.: XIS – UML profile for eXtreme modeling interactive systems. In: Proceedings of the MOMPES 2007. IEEE Computer Society (2007)

13. Pinkham, A.: Django Unleashed, 1st edn. Pearson, Indiana (2016)
14. Rubio, D.: Beginning Django: Web Application Development and Deployment with Python, 1st edn. Apress, California (2017)
15. Mendix Evaluation Guide. https://www.mendix.com/evaluation-guide. Accessed 26 Apr 2020
16. OutSystems Evaluation Guide, 16. https://www.outsystems.com/evaluation-guide. Accessed 26 Apr 2020
17. Stair, R., Reynolds, G.: Fundamentals of Information Systems, 9th edn., Cengage Learning (2017)
18. López-Landa, R., Noguez, J., Guerra E., Lara, J.: EMF on rails. In: ICSOFT 2012 - Proceedings of the 7th International Conference on Software Paradigm Trends, pp. 273–278 (2012)
19. Genio Plataforma. https://genio.quidgest.com/plataforma/. Accessed 26 Jun 2020
20. Silva, A.R.: Linguistic patterns and linguistic styles for requirements specification (I): an application case with the rigorous RSL/business-level language. In: Proceedings of EuroPLOP 2017. ACM (2017)
21. Montero, S., Díaz, P., Aedo, I.: From requirements to implementations: a model-driven approach for web development. EJIS **16**, 407–419 (2007). https://doi.org/10.1057/palgrave.ejis.3000689
22. Stefano, C., Fraternali, P., Bongio, A.: Web modeling language (WebML): a modeling language for designing web sites. Comput. Netw. **33**, 137–157 (2000). https://doi.org/10.1016/S1389-1286(00)00040-2
23. da Silva, A.R., Paiva, Ana C.R., da Silva, Valter E.R.: A test specification language for information systems based on data entities, use cases and state machines. In: Hammoudi, S., Pires, L.F., Selic, B. (eds.) MODELSWARD 2018. CCIS, vol. 991, pp. 455–474. Springer, Cham (2019). https://doi.org/10.1007/978-3-030-11030-7_20
24. Paiva, A.C.R., Maciel, D., da Silva, A.R.: From requirements to automated acceptance tests with the RSL language. In: Damiani, E., Spanoudakis, G., Maciaszek, L.A. (eds.) ENASE 2019. CCIS, vol. 1172, pp. 39–57. Springer, Cham (2020). https://doi.org/10.1007/978-3-030-40223-5_3
25. Ribeiro, A., Silva, A.R.: XIS-mobile: a DSL for mobile applications. In: Proceedings of the 29th Annual ACM Symposium on Applied Computing (2014)
26. Ribeiro, A., Silva, A.R.: Evaluation of XIS-mobile, a domain specific language for mobile application development. J. Softw. Eng. Appl. **7**(11), 906–919 (2014)
27. Seixas, J., Ribeiro, A., Silva, A.R.: A model-driven approach for developing responsive web apps. In: Proceedings of ENASE 2019. SCITEPRESS (2019)
28. Django. https://www.djangoproject.com/. Accessed 25 Jun 2020

The Human Factors of the Agile Software Tester

Lucas Paruch[ID], Viktoria Stray[✉][ID], and Raluca Florea[ID]

Department of Informatics, University of Oslo, Oslo, Norway
{lucasp,stray,ralucamf}@ifi.uio.no

Abstract. Although there has been extensive research on the technological aspects of the software testers, little investigation has been conducted within human factors determinant for the software testing role. The current paper explores the human factors of the software testers working in agile projects, through a qualitative study focusing on the perception of these factors, in a software service company. We interviewed 13 agile team members; 6 testers, 5 developers, and 2 designers. Additionally, we observed 11 meetings and observed the teams at work. Our results show that the following six traits are pivotal for the software testing role, seen by working agile software professionals: able to see the whole picture, having good communication skills, being detailed-oriented, structured, creative, and adaptable. Based on our results, we propose how organizations may think when recruiting agile software testers, how the traits may be used as a reference for those considering a software testing career.

Keywords: Human factors · Character traits · Soft skills · Human qualities · Software testing · Agile software development

1 Introduction

Currently, agile software development is a widely adopted practice of companies seeking to improve their industrial competitiveness [30]. As advantageous as it may be, working in an agile environment brings challenges such as parallel information flow, collaborative work, opportunistic use of technology, and lack of alignment among teams [10].

As such, the human factors play a vital role in agile projects, in all the development facets of the software products, from the requirements elicitation, stakeholder meetings, development, testing, and release. Personality traits of developers have been investigated (e.g., [1, 27]), some going as far back as 1980s [9]. For testers, there are a few recent studies. For example, one study found an abundance of soft skills shaping software testing role, with greater diversity in particular for the agile testers [15]. Kanij et al. [22] utilized the Big Five taxonomy from the psychology field to explore the personality traits of software testers. However, more studies on human factors in software testing and the testers' mindset are needed [17].

© Springer Nature Switzerland AG 2020
M. Shepperd et al. (Eds.): QUATIC 2020, CCIS 1266, pp. 474–487, 2020.
https://doi.org/10.1007/978-3-030-58793-2_38

To explore human factors of the agile software tester, we conducted a qualitative study in a software service company. We aimed at answering the following research question: *Which human factors do the software professionals, working in agile projects, perceive as significant for the software testing role?*

2 Background

2.1 The Agile Software Tester

One of the seven ISTQB testing principles states that quality assurance activities should be started as early as possible in the life-cycle to avoid additional cost and time [4]. In agile, a noticeable divergence from traditional development methods entails involving testers from the beginning of each development increment. The early involvement allows testers to identify different test environments and scenarios early on - thus increasing the overall productivity and test validity. In agile, it is expected that developers perform unit-tests on their own. Additionally, developers may also do other testing tasks, such as reviewing user stories and creating test conditions. Therefore, dedicated testers may be able to implement a myriad of test techniques, such as exploratory testing, usability testing, and improving test coverage with the developers [3,26]. In such work environments, knowledge transfer also happens more frequently and naturally amongst developers and testers, as both testing and development happen concurrently during each iteration. While new team members may benefit from the active feedback, agile testers can also focus even more on eliminating misunderstandings or confusion during development. The tight coupling between testers and the rest of the team enables fast learning and understanding.

While the software designers and programmers' roles are intrinsically constructive, in the sense that they create products, a tester's job is most often of a destructive nature - involving many repeated attempts to break the software constructed [21,22]. Kanji et al. argue that the effectiveness of a tester role is somehow related to their personality. Their findings suggest that testers have a significantly higher level of conscientiousness than other software engineering roles [22]. Conscientiousness is closely related to being disciplined, hard-working, and dedicated. Although highly conscientious individuals are important in any profession, Kanji et al. suggest that these qualities might be particularly crucial for testers. Following the destructive nature of the testers' job, automation testing is seen as a 'safety-net' for testers to reduce confrontation because they can refer to the automatic tests failing. Florea et al. [13] found that automation testing is rising in demand and that there is a definite shift of the tester towards being a more technical profession than before.

Itkonen et al. [20] investigated what knowledge types testers utilized during exploratory software testing, and came up with three knowledge types: domain knowledge, system knowledge (the act of knowing the system's mechanisms, logic, interactions), and generic software engineering knowledge (knowledge of usability of the system and the ability to interpret error messages).

Livonen et al. [24] investigated the characteristics of *high performing* testers (characterized by either having a high defect detection rate or possessing characteristics seen as important by managers and testers). They found four themes that were important: experience, ability to reflect, motivation, and personality. The most important personal characteristics of high performing testers were thoroughness, carefulness, patience, and conscientiousness [24].

Two studies focused purely on what soft skills are required for software testers. Matturro [25] investigated what soft skills software companies in Uruguay required. The author analyzed 43 advertisements to investigate the frequency of soft skills within software testing. The majority of the advertisements asked for skills like teamwork, initiative, and analytical problem-solving skills. Similarly, Florea and Stray [12] analyzed 400 advertisements specifically for software testers across 33 countries. The most popular traits asked were communication skills, analytical problem-solving skills, team-player, and independent-working skills. Both articles suggest that there is a more definite need for teamwork and communication skills, analytical problem-solving skills, and pro-activeness. These traits have also, to some degree, been confirmed by other studies [8,24].

3   Research Method

The study of the software professionals' perception of the human factors characteristic for the agile testers was conducted with the support and collaboration of a software service company for the finance and banking sector, employing over 500 IT specialists across Europe. The company's motivation for participating in the research was to understand better how to support their employees in the software testing roles and better understand the traits they should focus on when hiring new software testers. Besides, the company aimed at giving its software testing professionals autonomy to think differently, be creative, and further improve their testing skills.

We conducted semi-structured interviews of 13 software professionals: six testers, five developers, and two interaction designers see Table 1. All the interviewees were located in Oslo, Norway. In addition to the interviews, we observed many of the participants working, and attended eight daily stand-up meetings, two test status meetings, and one domain expert workshop. We also had access to all the participants' on Slack[1], as well as access to a common channel for the testers. The observation notes and Slack logs were mostly used to affirm our findings from the interviews.

All the respondents consented to the recording of the dialogue and the publication of the results. Where it was necessary, we furthered the understanding of our participants' responses with follow-up questions and confirmed that we captured their responses entirely and unambiguously. We steered the interviews' direction by having a clear understanding of the objectives we pursued, asking

---

[1] Slack is an electronic communication tool, a trademark of Slack Technologies.

Table 1. Overview of the interviews

Interviewee software field	Work experience	Interview length
Software testing	7 months	53 min
Software testing	1 year	1h 3 min
Software testing	4 years	51 min
Software testing	6 years	1h 6 min
Software testing	3 years	41 min
Software testing	11 years	30 min
Software development	1 year	23 min
Software development	1 year	24 min
Software development	2.5 years	20 min
Software development	2 years	26 min
Software development	10 years	38 min
Interaction design	1.5 years	37 min
Interaction design	4 years	41 min

targeted questions, and giving appropriate feedback to the respondents: encouraging them to talk, reflecting on their remarks, and probing on their remarks. At the same time, the interviews were, to a great extent, protected from interruptions from the outside, from competing distractions, and by not asking inhibiting questions. The atmosphere of the interview was relaxed and invited communication. Furthermore, we took notes of other relevant information and captured our impression after each of the interviews we carried out. The interviews ranged approximately from 45 min to 1 h and were held solely with employees from the service provider company.

We employed semi-structured individual interviews, as they allowed us to gain insight into the participant's views on the software-testing human factors, based on their work experience. Some of the questions we asked were as follows:

- Can you tell me about your role, and what are typical tasks and assignments?
- What attributes do you think a software tester should have?
- Do we need dedicated testers?
- To what degree do you feel 'connected/associated' to the team?
- How much time do you spend on interaction with others to complete a task?
- How do team members and teams coordinate?
- Assume that you have found a bug during testing, how would you present it to the team? What do you do if someone says it is not a bug?
- Have there been cases where bugs have slipped through testing onto the production? How did it happen?
- Have there been challenges working with others in the team?
- How much knowledge do you have about the other team members' fields?
- Could you imagine to switch to something other than your current role?

- Have there been cases where you had to re-prioritize a task or do something unplanned in your workday?
- What keeps you going during work?

We analyzed the data using thematic analysis [5]. We coded the collected data, and grouped the codes into themes, see Fig. 1. For this purpose, we used NVivo, as it enabled us to organize the codes and explore the relationships between them easily. During our analysis, a total of 95 different codes emerged - these were grouped into different traits. Our analysis suggested that six traits were vital for agile software testers, as seen from both testers themselves and the other team members. We also found one other trait that seemed important but did not emerge as any of the top six traits. Eagerness-to-learn was a trait that seemed inherent to all of the interviewed testers but was not mentioned by any of the other roles. All traits we included were stated as important by all of the three roles (testers, developers, and designers).

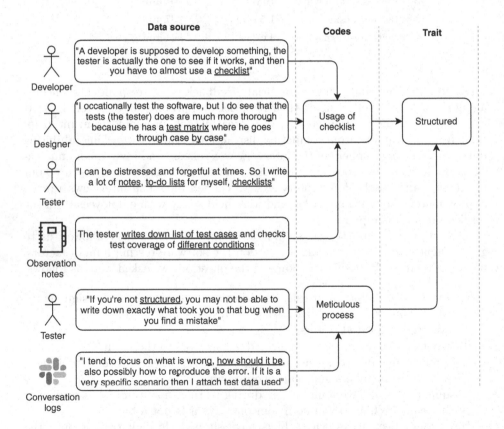

Fig. 1. Example of the thematic coding of the collected data

The interviewed professionals used agile methods and mainly Kanban development, combined with Scrum ceremonies. They used Product Backlog Items

(PBI) extensively - usually in the form of a user story. Some of the intervie-wees had no time-boxed sprints, working rather with a continuous stream of tasks, as they appeared in the backlog. They were involved in the prioritization of tasks and maintenance of the PBI. The professionals within the testing also participated in the test automation process, thus enhancing agile development by automation-as-they-go.

Table 2. Number of interviewees stating importance of the trait

Trait	Testers (6)	Developers (5)	Designers (2)
Able to see the whole picture	6	5	2
Detail-oriented	6	5	2
Good communication skills	6	5	2
Structured	6	3	2
Creative	6	2	2
Adaptable	4	5	2

The professionals had daily stand-up meetings, which were held every day at 09:00. The purpose of these meetings was to update team members on each other's progression and to bring up problems with regards to specific fields. On average, the meetings lasted from five to ten minutes and rarely reached the 15 min mark. The meetings were conducted online using Microsoft Teams and video-chat, to include the team members overseas.

Additional to the daily stand-up meetings, the interviewees with a test-ing role attended test-status meetings held on a bi-weekly basis. The pur-pose of these meetings was to establish coordination through communication between projects. Each tester reported their current test status in their projects and discussed any issues currently facing. Additionally, the testers could ask other testers for help. Exemplified by the common test-environment used by all projects - due to them being partly dependent on each other - each project needs to make sure that data are correct and not manipulated by others under testing.

4   Results

Our analysis of the data material revealed six essential characteristic traits of the agile software tester, as presented in Table 2, displaying the human factors seen by software professionals as pivotal traits of the agile software tester. We will now present each of the traits.

4.1   Able to See the Whole Picture

The participants stated that being able to understand the project as a whole was essential for a tester. The ability to have an overview of the project objec-tives, customer requirements, quality demands, and both domain-knowledge and technical knowledge was voiced as vital testers' traits by those we interviewed. Similarly, the interviewees holding a tester role stated that having such a perspective often helped them to find unusual bugs and see things from a different perspective than others.

One tester mentioned the need to understand the critical parts of the system: *"It's not about finding most bugs or fewest bugs or run most test-cases. A tester who completed one test-case but has found that the system works how it is supposed to, is often more effective than a tester who ran a hundred test-cases and have not found anything. So it's about being able to see the total picture"*.

One interaction designer recalled that the testers they worked with were impressive in terms of possessing both domain and technical skills and a good balance between the two: *"...he is the only one in the team who has a good overview of how things are connected, helicopter-perspective, how insurance works, the scope of different insurance types, how things are connected back-end"*.

As well, the developers brought-up that the software testers needed to have the ability to understand the big picture. One participant stated *"Often as a developer, you receive a task and you do it. They are not very involved in the entire process. I think it's more exciting to be involved in both the functional and technical aspects, not just super-technical"*.

4.2 Detail-Oriented

We found that agile software testers needed to be attentive to a multitude of details. The interviewees mentioned that having this attribute as a software tester was focal. One tester stated that he had to manage a considerable amount of small details on things he's worked on. The non-tester interview participants experienced that testers were very attentive and used the trait to further improve the product. We found two common kinds of attentiveness: user experience-related and technical-related.

Both the interaction designers that we interviewed mentioned that the testers they worked with helped them spot user-experience faults that the respectively overlooked. One designer mentioned: *"I remember he went through an old application, he began to carefully read the text that was there. I thought we were pretty attentive on death insurances - the fact that someone needed to report it when a person dies. He tested the whole process and made me aware of the text; it wasn't pleasant in a highly sensitive situation. So yeah, he is very aware of details"*.

Similarly to the designers, the developers stated that software testers needed to have attention to details. One developer stated: *"...this is why I love working with them, because of exactly that- they pick up things that we don't see, and things we haven't even thought of. They inform us that 'this is wrong' and 'this wouldn't work because of this method and this module,' very logical individuals..."*. Another developer mentioned: *"If it's a complex, tangible product, then it is nice to have a tester next to you. It gives me safety in the form of 'okay, he confirms that everything I do is correct. Then it's more likely that what I'm doing is correct"*.

4.3   Good Communication Skills

In addition to their core tasks of their role, it emerged from the interviews that the agile software testers were often needed to provide support for their fellow team members, by clarifying requirements or providing additional bug-related information. However, some testers frequently communicated with various stakeholders of the project in order to conduct rigorous testing - hence internal and external communication, respectively.

Testers needed to be friendly and provide constructive feedback regarding the issues they discovered though their testing to mitigate potential negative team dynamics. For example, one software tester mentioned that *"I was on a project a few years back where I sat next to the developers. When I've found a bug, I stood up and walked towards them with a friendly smile"*. Another mentioned that *"Whenever I find a bug, I go to the developer in mind and ask him if it's suppose to be like that. I try not to point any fingers because that's never pleasant for anyone, and it's not appreciated"*. Part of the interviewees mentioned that testers had to be good at asking for additional information from external stakeholders. A tester recalled *"...if the specification is too vague and we find that there can be many different ways to interpret it, then often I'm the one who has to go ask the ones who wrote the specification and find out what exactly do they mean, because I'm the one who specifies concrete requirements to the developers"*. This aspect was also brought up by a second tester *"...it could be that the developers have interpreted correctly, or that I have interpreted it correctly, we don't know. That's why I often have to go to the (customers') desk and ask"*. A developer asserted that it was important for testers to ask about commodities and try to find out how things work; *"They are very active in meetings with product-owners and ask questions about functionalities and what they need to find out about in order to set up test-scenarios"*. Furthermore, the team members appreciated to communicate on Slack, and we observed that they often discussed test automation with distributed team members. The testers would also often conduct an ad-hoc video meeting on Slack to give developers a thorough explanation of discovered bugs.

4.4   Structured

During the interviews, the software testers disclosed that they were structured, and not only at work. The majority of testers disclosed that they usually noted everything down in checklists, notes, or in their calendars. One tester voiced her usual course-of-action when it comes to planning and being systematic; *"Every Friday, I look at the calendar to see what's happening next week. Also, once a month, I look through the whole calendar for the next month so that I can plan and leave some room for unexpected meetings"*. Another tester stated that in order to succeed as a tester, one had to be structured; *"...Even if one performs exploratory testing - through just playing around - if you're not structured, then you might not be able to describe the steps you performed when you found a bug. If you're just exploring without being systematic, then I don't think you can retrace your steps. So, in my opinion, all testers must be structured"*. One developer recalled the results of the systematic work of the testers: *"...they worked really hard to systematically map, find out and clarify the requirement specifications for us - and even found out things that we overlooked. And as a result, also adjusted and improved our work processes"*.

4.5   Creative

The interviewees stated the importance of being creative in software testing, which allowed them to find abnormal bugs. One participant stated *"I've managed to find weird bugs by being creative, such as mid-way force shutdowns and performing unusual process-sequences. One has to test like that because the users are always creative"*. The interviewed designers mentioned that the testers they worked with were creative in solving issues, such as suggesting several alternative ways to resolve obstacles. Furthermore, they stated that a creative mind was what made testers valuable; *"...one finds strange things and loopholes by being creative. This is very much appreciated from a tester because we (non-testers) have 'tunneled' ways of testing, there are many guest-testers that test precisely how it's supposed to be used, meaning we'd only test the system's behavior when we do things right"*.

The tester interviewees voiced that creativity was necessary for the profession. However, one of the participants in a software testing role added that even though creativity could help find weird bugs, it could that the team could choose not to fix it; *"I daresay I use a lot of creativity to the point that I was told 'the bug you've reported, it is so specific that it only affects one specific customer during a leap year, so we're not going to fix it'.*

One of the testers also mentioned that they did not always get to be creative, mainly due to time pressure. The participant stated that some of the bugs found post-testing could have been found during the stage if only he would have time to think or toyed with it more; *"There isn't always enough time, so I have to focus on getting the most important pieces to work, and then deliver it to the business analysts to test"*.

The developers mentioned that creativity was more important for a tester to possess, mainly because of the difference in the role: *"As a developer, you receive a business requirement. Your job is to only fulfill those requirements. You can have a creative process where you construct the architecture, choose frameworks etc. But in the end, you're fulfilling a requirement. Testers are supposed to test a system that's going to work 100%, and there could be many anomalies. So a creative tester is most likely much more important to have in a team than a creative developer"*.

4.6   Adaptable

Three of the interviewees with a testing role mentioned that one has to adapt, by following the current situation quickly. One commented: *"Yes, it can sometimes be as early as after I looked over my tasks and feel ready to start, someone would pat me on the shoulder and say that I have to do something else"*, another said: *"We work with prioritization, when an item of high priority is incomplete from the developers' side, I'll start to work on something with medium (priority). However, often the developers finish before I get to complete the testing on that item, so I have to drop it and start testing on the other one (with high priority)".*

One tester with a junior position stated that since she was newly qualified, the constant context-switching proved to be quite challenging to keep up with the rest of the team. During our time of observation, she mentioned working extensively together with a more experienced tester had greatly improved her ability to context-switch.

5 Discussion

In the previous section, we described the human factors that emerged from the data analysis describing the software tester in agile teams. The first notable result is related to the overall perception of the role. In a previous study [7], it was found that testing was not a popular job due to that it was seen as'second-class' and unattractive career development. Currently, this perception has drastically changed, as our participants with a software testing role voiced the full recognition of the merits of their role. The testing and non-testing interviewees stated that testers were seen on the same line as other roles and that the teams had a flat structure. This incidentally improved their motivation in bettering their work - an exciting find, considering previous research such as Shah et al. [28], who reported testing as a stepping stone for the developer career.

Another notable result is the usage of digital communication tools in agile teams. We noted that Slack had a significant positive impact on testers and increased team transparency - supporting recent studies [6,29] stating that the use of Slack makes communication more transparent.

We now discuss our research question: *Which human factors do the software professionals, working in agile projects, perceive as significant for the software testing role?*. Our findings show that the views on the human factors shaping the role of the agile software tester crystallized in six distinct dimensions: the ability to see the whole picture, being detailed-oriented, having communication skills, being structured, being creative, and being adaptable.

Our results show that testers need to have, in addition to technical abilities, and even more complex overview than other roles in agile teams. This finding supports Florea et al. [14], with regards to the number and diversity of skills necessary for the software testers. The results also show a change in the perception of the role in the last decade, when Capretz et al. [7], and Shah et al. [28] found that people were choosing a software testing role when they were technically proficient. Our findings support Hernandez et al. [19], who pointed that software testers worked on a wide variety of topics, because it *"requires a complete view of the software"*, as well as the communication skill as a necessary trait to possess, to factor for effective collaboration with other departments.

Most of the participants to the interview voiced attention to detail as imperative for a tester to possess since it was useful in user-experience, technical solutions, and enhancing domain-knowledge and technical-knowledge, in line with the survey research conducted by Kanij et al. [21], in which most respondents agreed that this trait was something a good software tester should have. However, Capretz et al. [7] found a set of demotivated factors, in which the requirement of detail-oriented skill demotivated Cuban software testers.

We found that having good communication skills was seen as crucial for agile software testers, as was also found in earlier studies [8,12]. Ahmed et al. [2] described software testers as"the software development team's worst enemy" and, therefore, in need of good relational skills. A recent study showed that people were more careful in their communication if a conflict was thought to occur [18]. As the software testing role implies bringing unwanted news to the team, our findings confirm the need for good communication skills, in a way that does not provoke conflicts.

Most testers stated that writing check-lists and creating notes allowed them to free up their brains to focus on other things. Kanji et al. utilized the Big Five Taxonomy from psychology to highlight testers' personalities. Their findings show that testers generally have a higher level of conscientiousness than other roles - conscientiousness being orderliness, self-discipline, hard-working, and dedication [22]. Our results show that testers tend to be more organized, systematic, and structured - which all can be subsumed under conscientiousness.

Even though creativity is generally useful in software development, the degree of importance varies greatly amongst roles [23]. Regarding software testers, our study shows that creativity was perceived necessary in two courses of action: to conduct software testing by making up different user personas in different scenarios, and to come up with creative ways of testing the technicalities of the system. Our study confirms the results obtained by Itkonen et al. [20], who found that exploratory testing nurtured diverse and creative opportunities for testing.

Ekwoge et al. [11] mentioned that adaptability was needed for new tool usage and techniques of testing. Our results suggest that although adaptability does indeed benefit the technical proficiency, the trait is more holistic in the sense that adaptability also concerns domain-knowledge, and the ability to quickly switch between different context and different mindsets.

5.1 Implications for Practice

Given the effort that software companies invest in recruiting and retaining the best-suited individuals for the roles, the first implication for the practice of our study concerns the employers in the software development industry. This paper's findings could benefit the industry by providing the set of relevant traits that software testers should possess, useful as a checklist to those in charge of hiring new testing personnel. Additionally, our findings could benefit all those professionals, whether with a technical background or not, considering a software tester career by setting a frame of expectations for the role in soft factors. Garousi et al., recently reported that one of the top-ranked knowledge gaps from software engineers was software testing, and argue that it is vital to teach more testing [16]. The second implication of our findings relates to the ISTQB's syllabus for the agile tester: As it resulted from the self-description of the software testers, backed by the description of testers by the other roles in the team, the listed skills of the agile software tester should be updated with, for example, being able to see the whole picture and being creative.

5.2 Limitations

As our study was conducted at one specific company in one geographical location, the results could have been influenced by the cultural and organizational values specific to the company or particular to the interview location. We mitigated this influence by interviewing three roles within the software development team, asking them to describe the relevant human factors composing the software tester role. To avoid ambiguity, to allow time for reflection on the questions. We were open to all input and insight, and we kept in contact with our respondents until the finalization of the study. We routinely checked the data's consistency in the transcripts, the codes, and the themes we used.

6 Conclusion and Future Work

Through a qualitative study of 13 software professionals, in order to capture their view of the relevant traits composing the software testing role, we brought to light that the software testers in agile settings need to have a helicopter perspective of the project, encompassing technical and domain-specific abilities, in order to conduct testing effectively. Testers need to think creatively in two courses to test the software: from the consumer perspective by testing user personas, domain condition coverage, and unique scenarios. Nevertheless, they need also to test the system's technical perspective, such as system flow, memory leak, and SQL injections. Software testers need also be detail-oriented in terms of the user experience, such as refining the user-journey or the technical aspect where testers can suggest alternative solutions to developers. Testers need to be more structured than other roles in order to test and retrace steps systematically. They should finally be adaptable to changes and adept context-switchers.

The findings of the study can be used by the industry, in particular those in charge of the hiring of software testers, to check that the candidates for the role do possess these traits. Moreover, those considering a career in software testing should use our results to scrutinize and assess their fitness for a software testing role in an agile environment.

Findings show that the agile software testers had a self-image of the human factors of importance to their role following the perception of the other team members. Additionally, to the human factors listed in the ISTQB agile syllabus, we found the ability to see the whole picture and being creative. Future work should be conducted to investigate the manifestations of the constituent parts of these newly-revealed traits.

Acknowledgements. We want to thank all the participants for their generous and thoughtful collaboration on this study and for allowing us to observe and conduct interviews. A special thanks to the company supporting our research, for making the collaboration setup possible.

References

1. Acuña, S.T., Gómez, M., Juristo, N.: How do personality, team processes and task characteristics relate to job satisfaction and software quality? Inf. Softw. Technol. **51**(3), 627–639 (2009)
2. Ahmed, F., Capretz, L.F., Campbell, P.: Evaluating the demand for soft skills in software development. IT Prof. **14**(1), 44–49 (2012). https://doi.org/10.1109/MITP.2012.7
3. Bai, A., Mork, H.C., Stray, V.: A cost-benefit analysis of accessibility testing in agile software development: results from a multiple case study. Int. J. Adv. Softw. **10**(1&2), 96–107 (2017)
4. Black, R., van Veenendaal, E., Graham, D.: Foundations of Software Testing ISTQB Certification. Cengage Learning EMEA; 3rd edn. (2012)
5. Braun, V., Clarke, V., Hayfield, N., Terry, G.: Thematic analysis. In: Liamputtong, P. (ed.) Handbook of Research Methods in Health Social Sciences. Springer, Singapore (2019). https://doi.org/10.1007/978-981-10-5251-4_103
6. Calefato, F., Giove, Andrea, L.F., Losavio, M.: A case study on tool support for collaboration in agile development. In: IEEE/ACM International Conference on Global Software Engineering (ICGSE 2020), 5–6 October 2020, Seoul, Republic of Korea. ACM, New York (2020)
7. Capretz, L.F., Waychal, P., Jia, J., Varona, D., Lizama, Y.: Studies on the software testing profession. In: 2019 IEEE/ACM 41st International Conference on Software Engineering: Companion Proceedings (ICSE-Companion), pp. 262–263. https://doi.org/10.1109/ICSE-Companion.2019.00105
8. Deak, A.: What characterizes a good software tester? – a survey in four norwegian companies. In: Merayo, M.G., de Oca, E.M. (eds.) ICTSS 2014. LNCS, vol. 8763, pp. 161–172. Springer, Heidelberg (2014). https://doi.org/10.1007/978-3-662-44857-1_11
9. DeMarco, T., Lister, T.: Peopleware: Productive Projects and Teams. Dorset House Publishing Co. Inc, New York City (1987)
10. Dingsøyr, T., Falessi, D., Power, K.: Agile development at scale: the next frontier. IEEE Softw. **36**(2), 30–38 (2019)
11. Ekwoge, O.M., Fontão, A., Dias-Neto, A.C.: Tester experience: concept, issues and definition. In: 2017 IEEE 41st Annual Computer Software and Applications Conference. vol. 1, pp. 208–213. https://doi.org/10.1109/COMPSAC.2017.232
12. Florea, R., Stray, V.: Software tester, we want to hire you! an analysis of the demand for soft skills. In: Garbajosa, J., Wang, X., Aguiar, A. (eds.) XP 2018. LNBIP, vol. 314, pp. 54–67. Springer, Cham (2018). https://doi.org/10.1007/978-3-319-91602-6_4
13. Florea, R., Stray, V.: A global view on the hard skills and testing tools in software testing. In: Proceedings of the 14th International Conference on Global Software Engineering ICGSE 2019, pp. 133–141. IEEE Press (2019). https://doi.org/10.1109/ICGSE.2019.00036
14. Florea, R., Stray, V.: The skills that employers look for in software testers. Softw. Qual. J. **27**(4), 1449–1479 (2019). https://doi.org/10.1007/s11219-019-09462-5

15. Florea, R., Stray, V.: A qualitative study of the background, skill acquisition, and learning preferences of software testers. In: Proceedings of the Evaluation and Assessment in Software Engineering EASE 2020, pp. 299–305. Association for Computing Machinery, New York (2020). https://doi.org/10.1145/3383219.3383252
16. Garousi, V., Giray, G., Tuzun, E., Catal, C., Felderer, M.: Closing the gap between software engineering education and industrial needs. IEEE Softw. **37**, 68–77 (2019)
17. Garousi, V., Mäntylä, M.V.: A systematic literature review of literature reviews in software testing. Inf. Softw. Technol. **80**, 195–216 (2016)
18. Gren, L.: The links between agile practices, interpersonal conflict, and perceived productivity. In: Proceedings of the 21st International Conference on Evaluation and Assessment in Software Engineering, pp. 292–297 (2017)
19. Hernández, T.P.R.y., Marsden, N.: Understanding software testers in the automotive industry a mixed-method case study. In: 2014 9th International Conference on Software Engineering and Applications (ICSOFT-EA), pp. 305–314 (2014)
20. Itkonen, J., Mäntylä, M.V., Lassenius, C.: The role of the tester's knowledge in exploratory software testing. **39**(5), 707–724. https://doi.org/10.1109/TSE.2012.55
21. Kanij, T., Merkel, R., Grundy, J.: A preliminary survey of factors affecting software testers. In: 2014 23rd Australian Software Engineering Conference, pp. 180–189 (2014). https://doi.org/10.1109/ASWEC.2014.32
22. Kanij, T., Merkel, R., Grundy, J.: An empirical investigation of personality traits of software testers. In: 2015 IEEE/ACM 8th International Workshop on Cooperative and Human Aspects of Software Engineering, pp. 1–7 (2015). https://doi.org/10.1109/CHASE.2015.7
23. Li, P.L., Ko, A.J., Begel, A.: What distinguishes great software engineers? Empirical Softw. Eng. **25**, 322–352 (2019)
24. Livonen, J., Mantyla, M., Itkonen, J.: Characteristics of high performing testers: a case study. In: Proceedings of the International Symposium on Empirical Software Engineering and Measurement ESEM 2010
25. Matturro, G.: Soft skills in software engineering: a study of its demand by software companies in uruguay. In: 2013 6th International Workshop on Cooperative and Human Aspects of Software Engineering (CHASE), pp. 133–136. https://doi.org/10.1109/CHASE.2013.6614749
26. Santos, A.M.d., Karlsson, B.F., Cavalcante, A.M., Correia, I.B., Silva, E.: Testing in an agile product development environment: an industry experience report. In: 2011 12th Latin American Test Workshop (LATW), pp. 1–6 (2011). https://doi.org/10.1109/LATW.2011.5985897
27. Sfetsos, P., Stamelos, I., Angelis, L., Deligiannis, I.: An experimental investigation of personality types impact on pair effectiveness in pair programming. Empirical Softw. Eng. **14**(2), 187 (2009)
28. Shah, H., Harrold, M.J.: Studying human and social aspects of testing in a service-based software company: case study. In: Proceedings of the 2010 ICSE Workshop on Cooperative and Human Aspects of software Engineering, pp. 102–108 (2010)
29. Stray, V., Moe, N.B.: Understanding coordination in global software engineering: A mixed-methods study on the use of meetings and slack. J. Syst. Softw. 1–33. https://doi.org/10.1016/j.jss.2020.110717. (In press)
30. Yang, C., Liang, P., Avgeriou, P.: A systematic mapping study on the combination of software architecture and agile development. J. Syst. Softw. **111**, 157–184 (2016)

An Experience with the Application of Three NLP Tools for the Analysis of Natural Language Requirements

Monica Arrabito[1], Alessandro Fantechi[2,3(✉)], Stefania Gnesi[3], and Laura Semini[1,3]

[1] Dipartimento di Informatica, Università di Pisa, Pisa, Italy
monica.arrabito@hotmail.it, laura.semini@unipi.it
[2] Dipartimento di Ingegneria dell'Informazione, Università di Firenze, Florence, Italy
alessandro.fantechi@unifi.it
[3] Istituto di Scienza e Tecnologie dell'Informazione "A.Faedo" Consiglio Nazionale delle Ricerche, ISTI-CNR, Pisa, Italy
stefania.gnesi@isti.cnr.it

Abstract. We report on the experience made with three Natural Language Processing analysis tools, aimed to compare their performance in detecting ambiguity and under-specification in requirements documents, and to compare them with respect to other qualities like learnability, usability, and efficiency. Two industrial tools, Requirements Scout and QVscribe, and an academic one, QuARS, are compared.

Keywords: Natural Language Processing · Natural language requirements · Ambiguity

1 Introduction

Natural language (NL) is the most common way to express software requirements even though it is intrinsically ambiguous, and ambiguity is seen as a possible source of problems in the later interpretation of requirements. Ambiguity is one of the most difficult defects to avoid since natural language is ambiguous by nature and devoid of formal semantics. The lack of intrinsic formalism of the requirements document must therefore be compensated by a detailed analysis during the initial stages of the product life cycle in order to correctly extrapolate all the needed information. For this reason, part of the work carried out during the analysis phase is intended for disambiguation of the requirements.

Natural Language Processing (NLP) techniques have been used to analyse requirement documents to single out, among other issues, ambiguity and under-specification defects, analyzing the structure of sentences using grammatical and lexical analysis, dictionaries and parsers for natural language [1].

Work partially funded by MIUR project PRIN 2017FTXR7S *IT MaTTerS* (Methods and Tools for Trustworthy Smart Systems).

Recently, several tools have been developed for analyzing NL requirements in a systematic and automatic way by means of NLP techniques with a focus on ambiguity detection.

In this paper, we report on the experience made with thee NLP analysis tools, aimed to compare their performance in detecting ambiguity and under-specification, and to compare them with respect to other qualities like learnability, usability, efficiency. Two industrial tools, Requirements Scout and QVscribe, and an academic one, QuARS, are analysed.

2 The Scope of the Experience

The choice of the three mentioned tools can be traced back to their similarities:

- they perform an automatic detection of possible language defects that may determine interpretation problems and affect the following development stages;
- they highlight the word or construct that they reveal as defective;
- the detected defects may however be false positives, and a subsequent manual analysis is needed.

The limited scope of our experience on the one hand allows us to focus on similar tools to better highlight the differences, on the other hand it is a threat to the validity of our results. To broaden the investigation, other requirement analysis tools (see for instance Sect. 2.4) can be considered in a future work.

Notwithstanding its limited extension, we believe that this study can provide some useful insights on the current state of the art of automatic detection of ambiguity in natural language requirements.

In the following, we introduce the NLP tools we use for the comparison: QuARS, QVscribe, and Requirements Scout.

2.1 QuARS

QuARS - Quality Analyzer for Requirement Specifications - is a tool for analyzing NL requirements in a systematic and automatic way by means of NLP techniques with a focus on ambiguity detection [5].

QuARS performs an automatic linguistic analysis of a requirements document in plain text format, based on a given quality model. Its output indicates the defective requirements and highlights the words that reveal the defect.

Below, we present the indicators used by QuARS to detect defects of lexical and syntactic ambiguity in NL sentences.

Defect	Indicators
Vagueness	Dictionary: clear, easy, strong, good, bad, adequate...
Subjectivity	Dictionary: similar, have in mind, take into account, ...
Optionality	Dictionary: or, and/or, possibly, eventually, case, if possible, if appropriate...
Weakness	Dictionary: can, could, may, ...
Implicity	Demonstrative adjectives or pronouns
Under-specification	Wordings missing a qualification (e.g.: interface or information without a qualifier, such as user and price, respectively)
Multiplicity	Multiple syntactic constructs such as multiple verbs or multiple subjects

The defect identification process is divided into two, independent, parts. The first part, *lexical analysis*, detects candidate defective terms using a set of dictionaries. Lexical analysis permits to capture *optionality, subjectivity, vagueness, optionality, and weakness* defects. The second part is *syntactical analysis*, that captures *implicity, multiplicity and under-specification* defects.

Other features of QuARS are (i) metrics derivation for evaluating the quality of NL requirements; (ii) the capability to modify existing dictionaries, and to add new dictionaries for new indicators; (iii) view derivation, to identify and collect together those requirements belonging to given functional and non functional characteristics, by defining specific requirements.

2.2   QVscribe

QVscribe [6] is an industrial tool for requirements analysis for quality and consistency, developed by QRA (https://qracorp.com/). QVscribe analyzes the quality of the requirements, highlighting ambiguity, inconsistencies and possible similarities, providing scores to the single requirements and to the whole document. It generates a detailed report that can be used to increase the quality of requirements, reducing the review and rewriting work.

The analysis performed by QVscribe is based on part of the rules defined by the INCOSE Guide for Writing Requirements. The defects detected by the tool and the related indicators can be classified according to following table.

Defect	Indicators
Imperatives	Absence, negation, or multiple occurrence of imperatives
Optional escape clauses	Optional terms like: possibly, may, ...
Vague words	Vague nouns and verbs as: various, completed, ...
Cross-referencing pronouns	Both, everybody, anyone, it, ...
Non-specific temporal words	Early, years ago, before, ...
Continuances	Otherwise, in particular, below, following, ...
Superfluous infinitives	Since they can hide the subject, as in: shall permit
Passive voice	Since it can hide the subject, ex: based, found, shipped
Immeasurable quantification	Abundant, far, always, all, ...
Incomplete sentences	Missing critical details of who must do something or what must be done

2.3 Requirements Scout

Requirements Scout [3] is developed by Qualicen GmbH, to analyze requirements specifications (https://www.qualicen.de/en/). It is distributed as pluging of NL editors, including Microsoft Word, which makes is suitable for immediate feedback when writing requirements. Requirements Scout operates similarly to QuARS and QVscribe, using dictionaries and syntactic rules to specify the critical words that might denote a quality smell. We list below defects and indicators.

Defect	Indicators, if any, or motivation
Long&complicated sentences	Which are difficult to read and prone to ambiguities
Passive voice	Done, found, sent, ... since they can hide the subject
Multiple negations	Requirements must be expressed in positive terms
Universal quantifiers	All, always, every, any, nothing, ...
Imprecise phrases (vagueness)	Possibly, various, current, small, general, if possible, ...
Vague pronouns	That, which, their, it, nobody, ...
Comparatives & superlatives	Faster than, fastest, bigger than, ... they make a requirement not understandable in isolation
Exactly one shall or should	More than one occurrence of shall or should
Occurrence of will or may	Weak verbs such as will, may, ...
Wrong abstraction level	To exclude implementation details
Dangerous slash	"/", that can be interpreted both as an *and* and an *or*
UI details	Requirements should not contain details of the user interface.
Cloning	Since duplicates burden successive maintenance

Besides identifying the defects, it also permits to keep track of different versions of the requirements, creating a complete history of the detected defects: as soon as the requirements are updated, the tool re-analyzes the modified parts and shows whether the update has eliminated existing defects or has introduced new ones.

2.4   Other Tools

A recent industrial tool for assisting the analyst in the definition of NL requirements is ReqSuite, by OSSENO Software GmbH. Differently than the tools considered in this paper, which highlight defective words or constructs, ReqSuite
supports rigorous requirement definition by correcting the writer according to
some patterns and hence is out of the scope for our study.

Other candidate tools to experiment with are RAT (Requirements Authoring
Tool) from REUSE (https://www.reusecompany.com/) and IBM RQA (https://
www.ibm.com/products/requirements-quality-assistant), both able to detect
ambiguities, but those, for their commercial nature, were not immediately available for our study.

An alternative to the experimentation of off-the-shelf tools is the adoption
and customization of more general and flexible NLP tools, that allow to tune
the kind of detected ambiguities and other defects. GATE [2] is an example of
such tools: it collects several NLP modules and provides a means to define ad
hoc rules (JAPE rules), so to create advanced and customized NLP solutions.
As an example related to requirement analysis, in [4] GATE was used to tune
the proposed requirement analysis according to the requirement writing style
adopted by the involved company, achieving a significantly better quality of the
analysis.

3   Application of the Tools to a E-Shop Case Study

We report our observations when applying QuARS, QVscribe and Requirements
Scout to a running example, a simple E-shop (requirements in Table 1). The
tools are analysed first for their general qualities, then in their ability to support
ambiguities detection in requirements.

3.1   General Qualities Evaluation

We first address *documentation, learnability*, and *usability*. QuARS was simple
to learn and use without referring to any manual. QVscribe comes equipped
with good documentation and video tutorials and it was easy to be acquainted
with. Requirements Scout is the tool were most difficulties were encountered,
because of lack of documentation, a non intuitive interface, and a complex setup
of the user profile. To give a rough measure of learnability, we report the number
of hours of training in order to proficiently use them: 30 for QuARS, 36 for
QVscribe, 48 for Requirements Scout.

Table 1. Requirements of the E-shop case study

R1	The system shall enable the user to enter the search text on the screen
R2	The system shall display all the matching products based on the search
R3	The system possibly notifies with a pop-up the user when no matching product is found on the search
R4	The system shall allow a user to create his profile and set his credentials
R5	The system shall authenticate user credentials to enter the profile
R6	The system shall display the list of active and/or the list of completed orders in the customer profile
R7	The system shall maintain customer email information as a required part of customer profile
R8	The system shall send an order confirmation to the user through email
R9	The system shall allow an user to add and remove products in the shopping cart
R10	The system shall display various shipping methods
R11	The order shall be shipped to the client address or, if the "collect in-store" service is available, to an associated store
R12	The system shall enable the user to select the shipping method
R13	The system may display the current tracking information about the order
R14	The system shall display the available payment methods
R15	The system shall allow the user to select the payment method for order
R16	After delivery, the system may enable the users to enter their reviews or ratings
R17	In order to publish the feedback on the purchases, the system needs to collect both reviews and ratings
R18	The "collect in-store" service excludes the tracking information service

Efficiency was found to be an issue for Requirements Scout – to analyze documents of 20 and 50 requirements the tool takes 1 min and 2 min respectively – while it was not for QVscribe and QuARS: with both tools the analysis time for the considered documents was few seconds. The problem was probably due to the larger amount of checks performed by Requirements Scout, so it has to be considered as an issue related to the particular usage of the tool for ambiguity detection, rather than a generic low performance of the tool.

Extensibility is represented by the ability to add new quality indicators. QuARS has this feature and it also permits the user to select the indicators she wants to use for the analysis. In QVscribe, only the modification of the indicators already present in the tool is permitted, by adding or removing terms to be identified during the analysis. Requirements Scout implements indicators' selection too, but indicators are fixed.

Report generation is possible in QuARS and QVscribe. In QuARS the report contains, for each quality indicator, the list of requirements that present an ambiguity, together with the terms deemed incorrect. The report generated by QVscribe assigns to each requirement a score ranging from 1 to 5, depending on the gravity of the defects. Results can be filtered to focus on specific defects.

Other qualities are *interoperability* and *version control*. A particularly important positive aspect of QVscribe is the possibility of integrating the tool as a Word feature, so that the analysis of a document can be started by selecting QVscribe from the Word ribbon, and selecting the requirements to be analyzed.

A version control system is offered by Requirements Scout: the tool records the history containing the various versions of a document so that the comparison of two versions of the same document returns the list of defects added or removed. However the tool does not permit any editing of the document under analysis: the user has to edit the document externally and load the new version.

3.2 Evaluation of the Ability to Detect Defects in the Requirements

We now focus on analysing the three tools from the point of view of the ability of their indicators to detect ambiguities and under-specifications. We report in Table 2 the raw outcomes of the analysis of the E-shop example with the three tools, requirement by requirement: the "Indicator" column shows the words that have been considered by each tool to indicate a certain defect (reported in the last column). The detected defects results have then been manually analysed to distinguish real defects from false positives. The detailed results of this analysis are discussed in the following indicator by indicator. Table 3 cumulatively shows the number of *false positives* and *ambiguities*, as the result of the manual analysis of the tools' outcome of Table 2.

For *vagueness* QuARS detects a defect, QVscribe and Requirements Scout detect four defects each. The vagueness related to requirement **R10**, detected both by QuARS and Requirements Scout, can be indeed classified as a real defect (*various*). The same happens for the term *possibly* detected by Requirements Scout in **R3**. All the other defects are false positives.

We note that the term *possibly* in QuARS and QVscribe is an indicator of Optionality and is hence detected according to another indicator.

With respect to *optionality*, we refer to its meaning as in QuARS, and include the term *possibly*, classified as Optional Escape Clause by QVscribe. According to this indicator, there are four ambiguities detected by QuARS (**R3**, **R6**, **R11**, and **R16**) and one by QVscribe (**R3**). Optionality is not an indicator of Requirement Scout. The good number of defects detected by QuARS is due to fact that it is the only tool looking for occurrences of *or* and of *and/or*.

For *weakness* all the tools perform the same on E-shop. Weakness is referred to as *optional escape clause* in QVscribe and *occurrence of will or may* in Requirement Scout. When applying the tools to other documents, we have also observed that QuARS and QVscribe detect the weak verb *can* which is not detected by Requirements Scout.

The only two defecs related to *multiplicity* in QuARS are indeed disjunctions (**R11**, **R16**) that were already detected by *optionality* indicators.

Table 2. Results of the application of QuARS, QVscribe, and Requirements Scout to the e-shop case study. Requirements **R5**, **R8**, and **R14** contain no defect according to all tools.

Requirement	Tool	Indicator	Defect
R1 The system shall enable the user to enter the search text on the screen	QuARS	-	Multiplicity
	QVscribe	Enable	Vague words
	Req. Scout	Screen	UI details
R2 The system shall display all the matching products based on the search	QuARS		
	QVscribe	All	Universal quantifiers
		Based	Passive voice
	Req. Scout	All	Universal quantifiers
R3 The system possibly notifies with a pop-up the user when no matching product is found on the search.	QuARS	Possibly	Optionality
		-	Multiplicity
	QVscribe	Possibly	Optional escape clauses
		When	Immeasurable quantification
		No	Universal quantifiers
		Found	Passive voice
		-	No imperatives
	Req. Scout	Possibly	Vagueness
		Found	Passive voice
		-	Exactly one shall or should
R4 The system shall allow a user to create his profile and set his credentials	QuARS	-	Multiplicity
	QVscribe	Allow	Superfluous infinitives
		His	Cross-referencing pronouns
	Req. Scout	His	Vague pronouns
R6 The system shall display the list of active and/or the list of completed orders in the customer profile	QuARS	And/or	Optionality
	QVscribe		
	Req. Scout	Completed	Vagueness
		And/or	Dangerous slash
R7 The system shall maintain customer email information as a required part of customer profile	QuARS	-	Multiplicity
	QVscribe	Maintain	Superfluous infinitives
		As	Immeasurable quantification
	Req. Scout		
R9 The system shall allow an user to add and remove products in the shopping cart	QuARS	-	Multiplicity
	QVscribe	Allow	Superfluous infinitives
	Req. Scout	-	-
R10 The system shall display various shipping methods	QuARS	Various	Vagueness
	QVscribe	-	-
	Req. Scout	Various	Vagueness
R11 The order shall be shipped to the client address or, if the "collect in-store" service is available, to an associated store	QuARS	-	Multiplicity
		Or	Optionality
	QVscribe	Shipped	Passive voice
	Req. Scout	Shipped	Passive voice
R12 The system shall enable the user to select the shipping method	QuARS	-	Multiplicity
	QVscribe	Enable	Vague words
	Req. Scout	-	-

(*continued*)

Table 2. (*continued*)

Requirement	Tool	Indicator	Defect
R13 The system may display the current tracking information about the order	QuARS	May	Weakness
	QVscribe	May	Optional escape clauses
		About	Vague words
		-	No imperatives
	Req. Scout	Current	Vagueness
		May	Occurrence of will or may
		-	Exactly one shall or should
R15 The system shall allow the user to select the payment method for order	QuARS	-	-
	QVscribe	Allow	Superfluous infinitives
	Req. Scout	-	-
R16 After delivery, the system may enable the users to enter their reviews or ratings	QuARS	-	Multiplicity
		Or	Optionality
		May	Weakness
	QVscribe	After	Non-specific temporal words
		May	Optional escape clauses
		Enable	Vague words
		Their	Cross-referencing pronouns
	Req. Scout	-	No imperatives
		Their	Vague pronouns
		May	Occurrence of will or may
		-	Exactly one shall or should
R17 In order to publish the feedback on the purchases, the system needs to collect both reviews and ratings	QuARS	-	-
	QVscribe	Both	Cross-referencing pronouns
		-	No imperatives
	Req. Scout	-	Exactly one shall or should
R18 The "collect in-store" service excludes the tracking information service	QuARS	-	-
	QVscribe	-	No imperatives
	Req. Scout	-	Exactly one shall or should

Looking at Table 3, we notice that the absence of imperatives is a main ambiguity indicator. This is an indicator considered by QVScribe (*no imperatives*) and in Requirement Scout (*exactly one shall or should*), but not by QuARS. However, we can notice that the requirements lacking an imperative and being defective (**R3, R13, R16**) are those containing terms such as *if possible*, or weak verbs such as *may* or *can*. QuARS captures them with other indicators, namely *optionality, weakness* and *cross-tree constraints* indicators.

Table 3. Summary of ambiguity detection (n.a. means not applicable)

E-shop	QuARS		Qvscribe		Requirements Scout	
	F.Pos.	Amb.	F.Pos.	Amb.	F.Pos.	Amb.
Vagueness	-	1	4	-	2	2
Optionality	-	4	-	1	n.a.	
Weakness	-	2	-	2	-	2
Multiplicity	6	2	n.a.		n.a.	
Under-Specificaiton	-	-	n.a.		n.a.	
Imperatives	n.a.		2	3	2	3
Vague Pronouns	n.a.		1	2	-	2
Passive voices	n.a.		1	2	-	2
Immeasurable quantification	n.a.		2	2	1	-
Superflous infinitives	n.a.		4	-	n.a.	
Incomplete sentences	n.a.		-	-	n.a.	
Long/complicated sentences	n.a.		n.a.		-	-
Multiple negations	n.a.		n.a.		-	-
Comparatives, superlatives	n.a.		n.a.		-	-
Wrong abstraction level	n.a.		n.a.		-	-
Dangerous slash	n.a.		n.a.		-	1
UI details	n.a.		n.a.		1	-

4   Conclusions

The three tools examined have shown to be comparable in all the considered dimensions. They apparently use different indicators but in the end (e.g. weak verbs vs no imperatives) they find roughly the same defects. Best performances are obtained with best dictionaries, which means that there is room for lowering the false negative rate with better dictionaries: to this end the extensibility features of QuARS, permitting to add and modify dictionaries and of QVscribe that permits to modify the built-in dictionaries are suited and helpful.

There are some differences when considering other quality aspects, and the outcome of the comparison can help the vendors to refactor their tool and beat the competitors. However, in the end, they all share a similar defect detecting strategy, and from this respect younger tools (QVscribe and Requirements Scout) do not perform better than QuARS developed 20 years before.

References

1. Arora, C., Sabetzadeh, M., Briand, L., Zimmer, F.: Automated checking of conformance to requirements templates using natural language processing. IEEE Trans. on Softw. Eng. **41**(10), 944–968 (2015)

2. Cunningham, H.: Gate, a general architecture for text engineering. Comput. Humanit. **36**(2), 223–254 (2002)
3. Femmer, H.: Requirements quality defect detection with the Qualicen requirements Scout. In: Joint Proceedings of 23rd International Conference on Requirements Engineering: Foundation for Software Quality (REFSQ 2018). CEUR Workshop Proceedings, vol. 2075. CEUR-WS.org (2018)
4. Ferrari, A., Gori, G., Rosadini, B., Trotta, I., Bacherini, S., Fantechi, A., Gnesi, S.: Detecting requirements defects with NLP patterns: an industrial experience in the railway domain. Empirical Softw. Eng. **23**(6), 3684–3733 (2018). https://doi.org/10.1007/s10664-018-9596-7
5. Gnesi, S., Lami, G., Trentanni, G.: An automatic tool for the analysis of natural language requirements. Comput. Syst. Sci. Eng. **20**(1), 1–17 (2005)
6. Kenney, O., Cooper, M.: Automating requirement quality standards with QVscribe. In: Joint Proceedings of the 26th International Conference on Requirements Engineering: Foundation for Software Quality (REFSQ 2020). CEUR Workshop Proceedings, vol. 2584. CEUR-WS.org (2020)

Author Index

Printed in the United States
By Bookmasters